Readings on the
Development of Children

Readings on the Development of Children

Third Edition

Edited by

Mary Gauvain
University of California, Riverside

Michael Cole
University of California, San Diego

WORTH PUBLISHERS

Readings on the Development of Children, Third edition

Copyright © 2001 by Worth Publishers
Copyright © 1997 by W. H. Freeman and Company
Copyright © 1993 by Scientific American Books

Manufactured in the United States of America

ISBN: 0-7167-5135-6

Printing: 1 2 3 4 - 04 03 02 01

Sponsoring Editor: Jessica Bayne
Project Editor: Margaret Comaskey
Marketing Manager: Renée Ortbals
Art Director/Cover Design: Barbara Reingold
Cover Illustration: Marks Productions/Image Bank
Design: Paul Lacy
Production Manager: Barbara Anne Seixas
Composition: Progressive Information Technologies
Printing and Binding: Quebecor World Dubuque

Library of Congress Cataloging-in-Publication Data

Readings on the development of children / edited by Mary Gauvain, Michael Cole. — 3rd ed.
    p. cm.
  Includes bibliographical references and index.
   ISBN 0-7167-5135-6
   1. Developmental psychology. 2. Child psychology. 3. Child development. I. Gauvain,
Mary. II. Cole, Michael, 1938 –

BF713 .R43 2000
155.4 – dc21   00-020549

Worth Publishers
41 Madison Avenue
New York, NY 10010
http://www.worthpublishers.com

Contents

Preface

Human development is a process of change that occurs over the entire life span. It involves the interaction of biological, social, and cultural factors that together define the course of human growth. Developmental psychologists strive to explain this process of change by observing children, conducting experiments, and devising theories.

Students approach the subject of human development with a rich background based on their own experience of growing up as well as their observations of people of all ages. This background is a valuable resource when attempting to understand the scientific approaches to the study of human development encountered in textbooks. However, it has been our experience as instructors that textbooks alone, despite their great value as organized overviews of the field, often leave students puzzled about the process by which developmental psychologists construct their theories, collect their data, and draw conclusions. Textbooks, by their very nature, cannot devote sufficient space to the in-depth discussion of concepts or studies that form the basis of developmental theory.

The articles included in this book of readings have been selected with this issue in mind. Our intention has been to provide students with primary source material that introduces them to a broad range of scientific thinking about human development in all its diversity. We do not shy away from exposing students to classical contributions to the field simply because they do not carry an up-to-the-minute publication date; after all, physicists do not hesitate to teach about Newton's laws of motion although they were formulated several hundred years ago. On the other hand, human development is a rapidly growing discipline, so most of our selections—especially research reports—were first published in the past few years.

The inspiration for this reader came from *The Development of Children,* Fourth Edition, by Michael Cole and Sheila R. Cole. Although typical of introductory texts in many ways, *The Development of Children* is unusual in the balanced emphasis it places on the biological, social, and cultural factors that make up development. We have not, however, specifically keyed these readings to any one textbook. Instead we have selected articles that provide a representative sample of the wide range of approaches to the study of human development.

The theoretical articles provide students direct access to important and provocative statements by acknowledged leaders in the field. For example, selections by Jean Piaget and Lev Vygotsky are included. Each theoretical article was chosen for its power in capturing the essence of the theorist's ideas in a brief, but compelling, way. The articles focusing on research were selected to provoke thought and discussion about the ways researchers collect evidence on the process of development and how they interpret and draw conclusions from this evidence. We have taken special care to include articles about the development of children from many cultures in order to avoid the misrepresentation of middle-class European-Americans as the criterion against which the development of all children is measured.

All the articles were selected with the undergraduate reader in mind. Because most of our selections were originally written for a professional audience, the text sometimes contains concepts which at first may be difficult to grasp. To alleviate this problem, we have provided introductory notes that should help orient the reader to the article's main points. To help students understand the important issues in the selections, we pose questions at the end of each article. These questions are designed to help the student identify and summarize the key points of the articles, as well as provoke them to think critically about the issues that are raised. Over the years, this book has changed as the field has changed. Our efforts to select and update our readings have been aided by comments from colleagues and students. We express our appreciation to those of you who provided valuable feedback to us in the course of developing this reader.

M. G.
M. C.

Introduction

In the last two decades a revolution in the study of human development has taken place. This revolution has drawn on the research and thinking of earlier periods, in particular the ideas of the theorists Jean Piaget and Lev Vygotsky, and on the views of contemporary scholars. Most developmental theory and research today emphasizes the coordination of the biological, social, and cultural aspects of the human experience. At the heart of this research are assumptions about the nature of the human organism, specifically the idea that humans are social beings that strive to create meaning and understanding over the course of their daily lives. These efforts "to know and understand" are supported and constrained by the type of biological organism we are and the complex and highly structured social and cultural system in which we live.

This introductory section includes five articles that describe, in various ways, how human development occurs. Each places a somewhat different emphasis on the biological, the social, and the cultural contributions to growth. Two of the articles were written by the important developmental theorists Piaget and Vygotsky, whose thinking continues to influence developmental study. These articles are included because, in our view, it is not possible to understand contemporary studies of human development without some appreciation of their monumental contributions. Two other articles in this section, one by Bronfenbrenner and one by Rogoff and Morelli, characterize the ways in which current research and thinking include social and cultural factors in the study of human development. Considering social and cultural experience as influential in human development does not in any way suggest social determinism. Even though the social and cultural context of development plays a huge role in all aspects of human development, this role does not, in and of itself, define development. There are many other factors that contribute to growth. What these factors are exactly, and how they contribute to development, are the object of much research. This perspective has led, as you will see over the course of reading this book, to an increasingly complex approach to human development. This is because no single factor, not the biological, the social, or the cultural, explains development in its entirety.

The final article in this section is by Werner. It describes results from a classic study of child development on the island of Kauai in the Hawaiian Islands. This research stands as a reminder that development is not predetermined by any single factor. Despite what may seem like overwhelming odds, paths of resilience in development can be found.

Together, the five articles in this section introduce you to the ways in which contemporary theory and research deal with the complex biological, social, and cultural forces that guide human development.

1 Ecological Models of Human Development

URIE BRONFENBRENNER

According to Urie Bronfenbrenner, in order to understand human development it is important to consider the entire ecological system in which growth occurs. In this article, Bronfenbrenner describes this ecological system as having five socially organized contexts or subsystems that help support and guide human development. The contexts range from the microsystem, which is the immediate environment of children's everyday life, such as the school and family, to the macrosystem, which includes patterns of culture, such as the economy, customs, and bodies of knowledge.

Bronfenbrenner's conceptualization of these various layers of context provides developmental researchers with a way of thinking about different social and environmental influences on children's lives. In addition, it describes a way of examining the different layers of context simultaneously. This helps investigators study the challenges children face when the layers are in conflict with one another. For instance, for some children a family's values may be inconsistent with certain school practices. Perhaps a family emphasizes collaboration and assistance, while the school rewards individual performance. Although family and school are both unique aspects of the microsystem, they are linked in another layer called the mesosystem. In the mesosystem, communication between microsystems occurs. How two contexts, such as the family and the school, interact with and support each other has consequences for development.

Although this conceptual framework has yet to develop into a complete theory of development supported by research at all the levels of the ecological system, it nonetheless provides researchers with a way of characterizing the many experiential influences on human development. As a result it serves as a guide for formulating research questions, hypotheses, and designs.

Ecological models encompass an evolving body of theory and research concerned with the processes and conditions that govern the lifelong course of human development in the actual environments in which human beings live. Although most of the systematic theory-building in this domain has been done by Bronfenbrenner, his work is based on an analysis and integration of results from empirical investigations conducted over many decades by researchers from diverse disciplines, beginning with a study carried out in Berlin in 1870 on the effects of neighborhood on the development of children's concepts (Schwabe and Bartholomai 1870). This entry consists of an exposition of Bronfenbrenner's theoretical system, which is also used as a framework for illustrating representative research findings.

1. THE EVOLUTION OF ECOLOGICAL MODELS

Bronfenbrenner's ecological paradigm, first introduced in the 1970s (Bronfenbrenner 1974, 1976, 1977, 1979), represented a reaction to the restricted scope of most research then being conducted by developmental psychologists. The nature of both the restriction and the reaction is conveyed by this oft-quoted description of the state of developmental science at that time: "It can be said that much of developmental psychology is the science of the strange behavior of children in strange situations with strange adults for the briefest possible periods of time" (Bronfenbrenner 1977, p. 513).

In the same article, Bronfenbrenner presented a conceptual and operational framework (supported by

Reprinted with permission from the *International Encyclopedia of Education*, Vol. 3, 2nd ed., 1994, 1643–1647, Elsevier Sciences, Ltd., Oxford, England.

the comparatively small body of relevant research findings then available) that would usefully provide the basis and incentive for moving the field in the desired direction. During the same period, he also published two reports pointing to the challenging implications of an ecological approach for child and family policy (1974) and educational practice (1976).

Within a decade, investigations informed by an ecological perspective were no longer a rarity. By 1986, Bronfenbrenner was able to write:

> Studies of children and adults in real-life settings, with real-life implications, are now commonplace in the research literature on human development, both in the United States and, as this volume testifies, in Europe as well. This scientific development is taking place, I believe, not so much because of my writings, but rather because the notions I have been promulgating are ideas whose time has come. (1986b p. 287).

At the same time, Bronfenbrenner continued his work on the development of a theoretical paradigm. What follows is a synopsis of the general ecological model as delineated in its most recent reformulations (Bronfenbrenner 1989, 1990, Bronfenbrenner and Ceci 1993).

2. THE GENERAL ECOLOGICAL MODEL

Two propositions specifying the defining properties of the model are followed by research examples illustrating both.

Proposition 1 states that, especially in its early phases, and to a great extent throughout the life course, human development takes place through processes of progressively more complex reciprocal interaction between an active, evolving biopsychological human organism and the persons, objects, and symbols in its immediate environment. To be effective, the interaction must occur on a fairly regular basis over extended periods of time. Such enduring forms of interaction in the immediate environment are referred to as *proximal processes*. Examples of enduring patterns of proximal process are found in parent-child and child-child activities, group or solitary play, reading, learning new skills, studying, athletic activities, and performing complex tasks.

A second defining property identifies the threefold source of these dynamic forces. Proposition 2 states that the form, power, content, and direction of the proximal processes effecting development vary systematically as a joint function of the characteristics of the developing person; of the environment—both immediate and more remote—in which the processes are taking place; and the nature of the developmental outcomes under consideration.

Propositions 1 and 2 are theoretically interdependent and subject to empirical test. A research design that permits their simultaneous investigation is referred to as a process-person-context model. A first example illustrating the model is shown in Figure 1. The data are drawn from a classic longitudinal study by Drillien (1963) of factors affecting the development of children of low birth weight compared to those of normal weight. The figure depicts the impact of the quality of mother-infant interaction at age 4 on the number of observed problems at age 4 as a joint function of birth weight and social class. As can be seen, a proximal process, in this instance mother-infant interaction across time, emerges as the most powerful predictor of developmental outcome. In all instances, good maternal treatment appears to reduce substantially the degree of behavioral disturbance exhibited by the child. Furthermore, as stipulated in Proposition 2, the power of the process varies systematically as a function of the environmental context (in this instance, social class) and of the characteristics of the person (in this case, weight at birth). Note also that the proximal process has the general effect of reducing or buffering against environmental differences in developmental outcome; specifically, under high levels of mother-child interaction, social class differences in problem behavior become much smaller.

Unfortunately, from the perspective of an ecological model the greater developmental impact of proximal processes in poorer environments is to be expected only for indices of developmental dysfunction, primarily during childhood. For outcomes reflecting developmental competence (e.g., mental

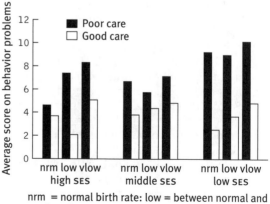

FIGURE 1

Problem behavior at age 4 (by birth weight, mother's care, and social class).

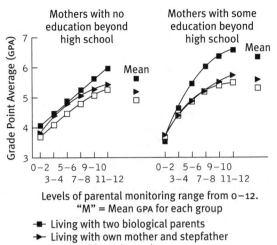

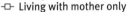

Levels of parental monitoring range from 0–12.
"M" = Mean GPA for each group

- ■- Living with two biological parents
- ►- Living with own mother and stepfather
- ▫- Living with mother only

GPA Scale: 2 = mostly D's or less. 3 = $\frac{1}{2}$ C's, $\frac{1}{2}$ D's. 4 = mostly C's.
5 = $\frac{1}{2}$ B's, $\frac{1}{2}$ C's. 6 = mostly B's. 7 = $\frac{1}{2}$ A's, $\frac{1}{2}$ B's. 8 = mostly A's.

FIGURE 2

Effect of parental monitoring on grades in high school by family structure and mother's level of education.

ability, academic achievement, social skills) proximal processes are posited as having greater impact in more advantaged and stable environments throughout the life course. An example of this contrasting pattern is shown in Figure 2, which depicts the differential effects of parental monitoring on school achievement for high school students living in the three most common family structures found in the total sample of over 4,000 cases. The sample is further stratified by two levels of mother's education, with completion of high school as the dividing point. Parental monitoring refers to the effort by parents to keep informed about, and set limits on, their children's activities outside the home. In the present analysis, it was assessed by a series of items in a questionnaire administered to adolescents in their school classes.

Once again, the results reveal that the effects of proximal processes are more powerful than those of the environmental contexts in which they occur. In this instance, however, the impact of the proximal process is greatest in what emerges as the most advantaged ecological niche, that is, families with two biological parents in which the mother has had some education beyond high school. The typically declining slope of the curve reflects the fact that higher levels of outcome are more difficult to achieve so that at each successive step, the same degree of active effort yields a somewhat smaller result.

3. ENVIRONMENTS AS CONTEXTS OF DEVELOPMENT

The foregoing example provides an appropriate introduction to another distinctive feature of the ecological model, its highly differentiated reconceptualization of the environment from the perspective of the developing person. Based on Lewin's theory of psychological fields (Bronfenbrenner 1977; Lewin 1917, 1931, 1935), the ecological environment is conceived as a set of nested structures, each inside the other like a set of Russian dolls. Moving from the innermost level to the outside, these structures are defined as described below.

3.1 MICROSYSTEMS

A microsystem is a pattern of activities, social roles, and interpersonal relations experienced by the developing person in a given face-to-face setting with particular physical, social, and symbolic features that invite, permit, or inhibit engagement in sustained, progressively more complex interaction with, and activity in, the immediate environment. Examples include such settings as family, school, peer group, and workplace.

It is within the immediate environment of the microsystem that proximal processes operate to produce and sustain development, but as the above definition indicates, their power to do so depends on the content and structure of the microsystem. Specific hypotheses regarding the nature of this content and structure, and the as yet limited research evidence on which they are based are documented in the work of Bronfenbrenner (1986a, 1986b, 1988, 1989, 1993). Most of the relevant studies of proximal processes have focused on the family, with all too few dealing with other key developmental settings, such as classrooms and schools. A notable exception in this regard is the work of Stevenson and his colleagues (Stevenson and Stigler 1992, see also Ceci 1990).

3.2 MESOSYSTEMS

The mesosystem comprises the linkages and processes taking place between two or more settings containing the developing person (e.g., the relations between home and school, school and workplace, etc.). In other words, a mesosystem is a system of microsystems.

An example in this domain is the work of Epstein (1983a, 1983b) on the developmental impact of two-way communication and participation in decision-making by parents and teachers. Elementary school pupils from classrooms in which such joint involvement was high not only exhibited greater initiative and independence after entering high school, but also received higher grades. The effects of family and school processes were greater than those attributable to socioeconomic status or race.

3.3 EXOSYSTEMS

The exosystem comprises the linkages and processes taking place between two or more settings, at least one of which does not contain the developing person, but in which events occur that indirectly influence processes within the immediate setting in which the developing person lives (e.g., for a child, the relation between the home and the parent's workplace; for a parent, the relation between the school and the neighborhood peer group).

Especially since the early 1980s, research has focused on three exosystems that are especially likely to affect the development of children and youth indirectly through their influence on the family, the school, and the peer group. These are the parents' workplace (e.g., Eckenrode and Gore 1990), family social networks (e.g., Cochran et al. 1990), and neighborhood-community contexts (e.g., Pence 1988).

3.4 MACROSYSTEMS

The macrosystem consists of the overarching pattern of micro-, meso-, and exosystems characteristic of a given culture or subculture, with particular reference to the belief systems, bodies of knowledge, material resources, customs, life-styles, opportunity structures, hazards, and life course options that are embedded in each of these broader systems. The macrosystem may be thought of as a societal blueprint for a particular culture or subculture.

This formulation points to the necessity of going beyond the simple labels of class and culture to identify more specific social and psychological features at the macrosystem level that ultimately affect the particular conditions and processes occurring in the microsystem (see Bronfenbrenner 1986a, 1986b, 1988, 1989, 1993).

3.5 CHRONOSYSTEMS

A final systems parameter extends the environment into a third dimension. Traditionally in the study of human development, the passage of time was treated as synonymous with chronological age. Since the early 1970s, however, an increasing number of investigators have employed research designs in which time appears not merely as an attribute of the growing human being, but also as a property of the surrounding environment not only over the life course, but across historical time (Baltes and Schaie 1973, Clausen 1986, Elder 1974, Elder et al. 1993).

A chronosystem encompasses change or consistency over time not only in the characteristics of the person but also of the environment in which that person lives (e.g., changes over the life course in family structure, socioeconomic status, employment, place of residence, or the degree of hecticness and ability in everyday life).

An excellent example of a chronosystem design is found in Elder's classic study *Children of the Great Depression* (1974). The investigation involved a comparison of two otherwise comparable groups of families differentiated on the basis of whether the loss of income as a result of the Great Depression of the 1930s exceeded or fell short of 35 percent. The availability of longitudinal data made it possible to assess developmental outcomes through childhood, adolescence, and adulthood. Also, the fact that children in one sample were born eight years earlier than those in the other permitted a comparison of the effects of the Depression on youngsters who were adolescents when their families became economically deprived with the effects of those who were still young children at the time.

The results for the two groups presented a dramatic contrast. Paradoxically, for youngsters who were teenagers during the Depression years, the families' economic deprivation appeared to have a salutary effect on their subsequent development, especially in the middle class. As compared with the nondeprived who were matched on pre-Depression socioeconomic status, deprived boys displayed a greater desire to achieve and a firmer sense of career goals. Boys and girls from deprived homes attained greater satisfaction in life, both by their own and by societal standards. Though more pronounced for adolescents from middle-class backgrounds, these favorable outcomes were evident among their lower-class counterparts as well. Analysis of interview and observation protocols enabled Elder to identify what he regarded as a critical factor in investigating this favorable developmental trajectory: the loss of economic security forced the family to mobilize its own human resources, including its teenagers, who had to take on new roles and responsibilities both within and outside the home and to work together toward the common goal of getting and keeping the family on its feet. This experience provided effective training in initiative, responsibility, and cooperation.

4. GENETIC INHERITANCE IN ECOLOGICAL PERSPECTIVE

The most recent extension of the ecological paradigm involves a reconceptualization of the role of genetics in human development (Bronfenbrenner and Ceci 1993). The new formulation calls into question and replaces some of the key assumptions underlying the established "percentage-of-variance" model employed in behavior genetics. Specifically, in addition to incorporating explicit measures of the environment conceptualized in systems terms, and allowing for nonadditive, synergistic effects in genetics-environment interaction, the proposed "bioecological" model posits proximal processes as the empirically assessable mechanisms through which genotypes are transformed into phenotypes. It is further argued, both on theoretical and empirical grounds, that heritability, defined by behavioral geneticists as "the proportion of the total phenotypic variance that is due to additive genetic variation" (Cavalli-Storza and Bodmer 1971 p. 536), is in fact highly influenced by events and conditions in the environment. Specifically, it is proposed that heritability can be shown to vary substantially as a direct function of the magnitude of proximal processes and the quality of the environments in which they occur, potentially yielding values of heritability that, at their extremes, are both appreciably higher and lower than those hitherto reported in the research literature.

If this bioecological model sustains empirical testing, this would imply that many human beings may possess genetic potentials for development significantly beyond those that they are presently manifesting, and that such unrealized potentials might be actualized through social policies and programs that enhance exposure to proximal processes in environmental settings providing the stability and resources that enable such processes to be maximally effective.

Certainly, thus far it has by no means been demonstrated that this latest extension of the ecological paradigm has any validity. Nor is the validation of hypotheses the principal goal that ecological models are designed to achieve. Indeed, their purpose may be better served if the hypotheses that they generate are found wanting, for the primary scientific aim of the ecological approach is not to claim answers, but to provide a theoretical framework that, through its application, will lead to further progress in discovering the processes and conditions that shape the course of human development.

However, beyond this scientific aim lies a broader human hope. That hope was expressed in the first systematic exposition of the ecological paradigm:

> Species *Homo sapiens* appears to be unique in its capacity to adapt to, tolerate, and especially to create the ecologies in which it lives and grows. Seen in different contexts, human nature, which I had once thought of as a singular noun, turns out to be plural and pluralistic; for different environments produce discernible differences, not only across but within societies, in talent, temperament, human relations, and particularly in the ways in which each culture and subculture

brings up the next generation. The process and product of making human beings human clearly varies by place and time. Viewed in historical as well as cross-cultural perspective, this diversity suggests the possibility of ecologies as yet untried that hold a potential for human natures yet unseen, perhaps possessed of a wiser blend of power and compassion than has thus far been manifested. (Bronfenbrenner 1979 p. xiii)

REFERENCES

Baltes, P. B., Schaie, W. 1973. *Life-span Developmental Psychology: Personality and Socialization*. Academic Press, New York.

Bronfenbrenner, U. 1974. Developmental research, public policy, and the ecology of childhood. *Child Dev.* 45(1): 1–5.

Bronfenbrenner, U. 1976. The experimental ecology of education. *Teach. Coll. Rec.* 78(2): 157–204.

Bronfenbrenner, U. 1977. Toward an experimental ecology of human development. *Am. Psychol.* 32: 515–31.

Bronfenbrenner, U. 1979. *The Ecology of Human Development: Experiments by Nature and Design*. Harvard University Press, Cambridge, Massachusetts.

Bronfenbrenner, U. 1986a. Ecology of the family as a context for human development: Research perspectives. *Dev. Psychol.* 22(6): 723–42.

Bronfenbrenner, U. 1986b. Recent advances in the ecology of human development. In: Silbereisen, R. K., Eyferth, K., Rudinger, G. (eds.) 1986 *Development as Action in Context: Problem Behavior and Normal Youth Development*. Springer-Verlag, Berlin.

Bronfenbrenner, U. 1988. Interacting systems in human development: Research paradigms, present and future. In: Bolger, N., Caspi, A., Downey, G., Moorehouse, M. (eds.) 1988 *Persons in Context: Developmental Processes*. Cambridge University Press, Cambridge.

Bronfenbrenner, U. 1989. Ecological systems theory. In: Vasta, R. (ed.) 1989 *Six Theories of Child Development: Revised Formulations and Current Issues*. Vol. 6. JAI Press, Greenwich, Connecticut.

Bronfenbrenner, U. 1990. The ecology of cognitive development. *Zeitschrift für Sozialisationsforschung und Erziehungssoziologie (ZSE)*. 10(2): 101–14.

Bronfenbrenner, U. 1993. The ecology of cognitive development: Research models and fugitive findings. In: Wozniak, R. H., Fischer, K. (eds.) 1993 *Thinking in Context*. Erlbaum, Hillsdale, New Jersey.

Bronfenbrenner, U., Ceci, S. J. 1993. Heredity, environment, and the question "how?": A new theoretical perspective for the 1990s. In: Plomin, R., McClearn, G. E. (eds.) 1993 *Nature, Nurture, and Psychology*. APA Books, Washington, DC.

Cavalli-Storza, L. L., Bodmer, W. F. 1971. *The Genetics of Human Populations*. W. H. Freeman, San Francisco, California.

Ceci, S. J. 1990. *On Intelligence . . . More or Less: A Bioecological Treatise on Intellectual Development*. Prentice-Hall, Englewood Cliffs, New Jersey.

Clausen, J. A. 1986. *The Life Course: A Sociological Perspective*. Prentice-Hall, Englewood Cliffs, New Jersey.

Cochran, M., Larner, M., Riley, D., Gunnarsson, L., Henderson, C. R., Jr. 1990. *Extending Families: The Social Networks of Parents and their Children*. Cambridge University Press, New York.

Drillien, C. M. 1963. *The Growth and Development of the Prematurely Born Infant*. E. and S. Livingston Ltd., Edinburgh.

Eckenrode, J., Gore, S. (eds.) 1990. *Stress between Work and Family*. Plenum Press, New York.

Elder, G. H., Jr. 1974. *Children of the Great Depression: Social Change in the Life Experience*. University of Chicago Press, Chicago, Illinois.

Elder, G. H., Jr., Modell, J., Parke, R. D. 1993. *Children in Time and Place: Individual, Historical and Developmental Insights*. Cambridge University Press, New York.

Epstein, J. L. 1983a. *Effects on Parents of Teacher Practices of Parent Involvement*. Center for the Social Organization of Schools, Johns Hopkins University, Baltimore, Maryland.

Epstein, J. L. 1983b. Longitudinal effects of family-school-person interactions on student outcomes. *Research in Sociology of Education and Socialization* 4: 101–27.

Lewin, K. 1917. Kriegslandschaft. *Zeitschrift für Angewandte Psychologie* 12: 440–47.

Lewin, K. 1931. Environmental forces in child behavior and development. In: Murchison, C. (ed.) 1931 *A Handbook of Child Psychology*. Clark University Press, Worcester, Massachusetts.

Lewin, K. 1935. *A Dynamic Theory of Personality*. McGraw-Hill, New York.

Pence, A. R. (ed.) 1988. *Ecological Research with Children and Families: From Concepts to Methodology*. Teachers College, Columbia University, New York.

Schwabe, H., Bartholomai, F. 1870. Der Vorstellungskreis der Berliner Kinder beim Eintritt in die Schule. In: *Berlin und seine Entwicklung: Städtisches Jahrbuch für Volkswirthschaft und Statistik Vierter Jahrgang*. Guttentag, Berlin.

Stevenson, H. W., Stigler, J. W. 1992. *The Learning Gap: Why Our Schools are Failing and What We Can Learn from Japanese and Chinese Education*. Summit Books, New York.

QUESTIONS

1. How do ecological models describe the process of child development?
2. What do you think Bronfenbrenner means by the statement that "developmental psychology is the science of the strange behavior of children in strange settings with strange adults for the briefest possible periods of time"?
3. What are the five subsystems of the ecological context that Bronfenbrenner describes? Think of a particular process of development, such as peer relations or language development, and try to describe it from the perspective of each of these subsystems.
4. Why does Bronfenbrenner include the chronosystem in his framework?
5. Why is Bronfenbrenner interested in recent views of genetic inheritance that suggest that the genotype is influenced by events and conditions in the environment?
6. In theory, the ecological systems approach is rich in the amount of new information it can provide about human development. But is it a practical approach to research?

2 Perspectives on Children's Development from Cultural Psychology

BARBARA ROGOFF · GILDA MORELLI

Over the last few decades, psychologists have come to recognize the important role that culture plays in children's development. In the following article Barbara Rogoff and Gilda Morelli discuss an approach to development that focuses on the complex interaction between children's development and the cultural context in which growth occurs. They stress two levels of culture, the institutional level and the interpersonal level, that play important roles in organizing and directing children's development in the cultural context.

One of the chief difficulties in understanding the relation between culture and human development is how to understand the role of the developing child in this process. In modern developmental theory children are conceptualized as active agents. At any given point in development, children use the capabilities they have available to them to seek knowledge and interact with the world. What Rogoff and Morelli describe is how much of what children learn and experience over the course of development is mediated by the many culturally based experiences that children have every day—experiences that range from interpersonal interactions with family and friends to participation in cultural institutions like schools and political systems.

Rogoff and Morelli describe a perspective that is often referred to as a sociocultural approach to human development. This is an increasingly influential view that is evident in all areas of developmental research.

This article summarizes how cultural research can inform mainstream psychology. It focuses on an organizing theme that has been explored in research in non-Western groups: the role of specific cultural practices in organizing human endeavors. This perspective has influenced the direction of mainstream research, encouraging the advancement of our ideas of the domain-specific nature of psychological processes, and their relation to sociocultural practices. The article provides a brief description of Vygotsky's theoretical approach, a perspective comfortable for many working within this tradition. Finally, a discussion of research on children in cultural groups in the United States suggests that the cultural perspective can be useful in advancing research on issues involving American children with different cultural backgrounds.

Attention to the cultural context of child development has yielded important insights into the opportunities and constraints provided by the society in which children mature. Research with children of different cultures provides a broader perspective on human development than is available when considering human behavior in a single cultural group.

The purpose of this article is to indicate how cultural research can inform mainstream psychology. We discuss one organizing theme that has been explored in research in non-Western groups, the role of specific cultural practices in organizing all human

Reprinted with permission from the authors and *American Psychologist, 44,* 1989, 343–348. Copyright 1989 by the American Psychological Association.
We thank Ana Estrada for her comments on this essay.

endeavors. This perspective has influenced the direction of mainstream research, encouraging the advancement of our ideas of the domain-specific nature of psychological processes, and their relation to sociocultural practices. We provide a brief description of Vygotsky's theoretical approach, a perspective comfortable for many working within this tradition. Finally, we suggest that the cultural perspective can be useful in advancing research on issues involving American children varying in cultural background.

LESSONS LEARNED FROM CROSS-CULTURAL STUDIES OF DEVELOPMENT

Investigations of the role of culture in development have taken advantage of the impressive variations in the human condition, which occur around the world, to advance understanding of human adaptation. Reviews and discussion of cross-cultural developmental research appear in Bornstein (1980); Dasen (1977); Field, Sostek, Vietze, and Leiderman (1981); Laboratory of Comparative Human Cognition (1979, 1983); Leiderman, Tulkin, and Rosenfeld (1977); LeVine (in press); Munroe and Munroe (1975); Munroe, Munroe, and Whiting (1981); Rogoff, Gauvain, and Ellis (1984); Rogoff and Mistry (1985); Schieffelin and Ochs (1986); Serpell (1976); Super and Harkness (1980); Triandis and Heron (1981); Wagner and Stevenson (1982); Werner (1979); and Whiting and Edwards (1988).

Cross-cultural studies have focused especially on children in nontechnological (non-Western) societies because these children contrast in important ways with children from the United States and other Western nations. This first section thus describes lessons learned from cross-cultural studies involving children around the world; psychological research on minorities in the United States has followed a somewhat different course, described later.

PERSPECTIVES OFFERED BY CROSS-CULTURAL RESEARCH

An important function of cross-cultural research has been to allow investigators to look closely at the impact of their own belief systems (folk psychology) on scientific theories and research paradigms. When subjects and researchers are from the same population, interpretations of development may be constrained by implicit cultural assumptions. With subjects sharing researchers' belief systems, psychologists are less aware of their own assumptions regarding the world of childhood, the involvement of others in child development, and the physical and institutional circumstances in which development is embedded. Working with people from a quite different background can make one aware of aspects of human activity that are not noticeable until they are missing or differently arranged, as with the fish who reputedly is unaware of water until removed from it. Viewing the contrasts in life's arrangements in different cultures has enabled psychologists to examine very basic assumptions regarding developmental goals, the skills that are learned, and the contexts of development.

Cross-cultural research also allows psychologists to use cultural variation as a natural laboratory to attempt to disentangle variables that are difficult to tease apart in the United States and to study conditions that are rare in the United States. For example, one can examine how gender differences manifest themselves in differing cultural circumstances (Whiting & Edwards, 1988). Cross-cultural studies have examined the extent to which advances in intellectual skills are related to schooling versus children's age, a comparison that cannot be made in a country with compulsory schooling (Laboratory of Comparative Human Cognition, 1979; Rogoff, 1981). Other research examines conditions that are seen as normal in other cultures but carry connotations of being problematic in the United States. For example, studies have been made of gender roles in polygynous societies in which fathers are absent from the household because they have several wives (Munroe & Munroe, 1975), and of child care and infant psychological development in societies in which nonmaternal care (care by other adults or by child nurses) is valued and expected (Fox, 1977; Tronick, Morelli, & Winn, 1987; Zaslow, 1980).

Another function of cross-cultural studies is to examine the generality of theories of development that have been based on Western children. Examples include investigations of the universality of the stages of development proposed by Piaget, the family role relations emphasized by Freud, and patterns of mother-infant interaction taken to index security of attachment (Bretherton & Waters, 1985; Dasen, 1977; Dasen & Heron, 1981; Greenfield, 1976; Malinowski, 1927; Price-Williams, 1980). In such research, modifications to the assumptions of generality have often been suggested by cross-cultural findings. For example, findings that the highest stage of Piaget's theory, formal operations, seldom can be seen in non-Western cultures prompted Piaget to modify his theory in 1972 to suggest that the formal operational stage may not be universal but rather a product of an individual's expertise in a specific domain.

Research in a variety of cultures has also provided evidence of impressive regularities across cultures in developmental phenomena. For instance, there is marked similarity across cultures in the sequence and timing of sensorimotor milestones in infant development, smiling, and separation distress (Gewirtz, 1965; Goldberg, 1972; Konner, 1972; Super, 1981; Werner, 1988) and in the order of stages in language acquisition (Bowerman, 1981; Slobin, 1973).

AN EMPHASIS ON UNDERSTANDING THE CONTEXT OF DEVELOPMENT

An important contribution resulting from cultural challenges to researchers' assumptions is the conceptual restructuring emphasizing that human functioning cannot be separated from the contexts of their activities. Although there are other sources of contextual theorizing in the field of psychology, an important impetus has been the consistent findings that behavior and development vary according to cultural context.

Developmental researchers who have worked in other cultures have become convinced that human functioning cannot be separated from the cultural and more immediate context in which children develop. They observed that skills and behavior that did not appear in laboratory situations appeared in the same individuals in everyday situations. A subject whose logical reasoning or memory in a laboratory task seemed rudimentary could skillfully persuade the researcher or remind the researcher of promises outside the laboratory, or might be very skilled in a complex everyday task such as navigation or weaving (Cole, 1975; Cole, Hood, & McDermott, 1978; Gladwin, 1970; Laboratory of Comparative Human Cognition, 1979; Rogoff, 1981; Scribner, 1976). Such informal observations called into question the widespread assumption that individuals' skills and behaviors have a generality extending across contexts.

Systematic studies noted the close relation between the skills or behavior exhibited by an individual and the contexts of elicitation and practice (Lave, 1977; Saxe, 1988). Children's nurturance and aggression varied as a function of the age and gender of the people with whom they interacted (Wenger, 1983; Whiting & Whiting, 1975). Perceptual modeling skills of Zambian and English children varied as a function of the cultural familiarity of the specific modeling activity (Serpell, 1979). Literacy provides practice with specific cognitive activities, leading to advances in particular skills rather than conferring general cognitive ability (Scribner & Cole, 1981). Such results point to the importance of considering the contexts in which people practice skills and behaviors, as well as those in which we as researchers observe them.

Many of the cognitive activities examined in developmental research, such as memory, perception, logical reasoning, and classification, have been found in cross-cultural studies to relate to children's experience of schooling (Lave, 1977; Rogoff, 1981; Sharp, Cole, & Lave, 1979). The extensive studies of the relation between school and cognitive skills call attention to a context of learning that is easily overlooked as an influence on cognitive development in the United States, where school is ubiquitous in the lives of children.

Remembering or classifying lists of unrelated objects may be unusual activities outside of literate or school-related activities (Goody, 1977; Rogoff & Waddell, 1982). The taxonomic categories seen as most appropriate in literate situations may not be valued in other circumstances, as is illustrated by Glick's (1975) report of Kpelle subjects' treatment of a classification problem. They sorted the 20 objects into functional groups (e.g., knife with orange, potato with hoe) rather than into categorical groups that the researcher considered more appropriate. When questioned, they often volunteered that that was the way a wise man would do things. "When an exasperated experimenter asked finally, 'How would a fool do it,' he was given back sorts of the type that were initially expected—four neat piles with food in one, tools in another, and so on" (p. 636).

People who have more schooling, such as older children and Western peoples, may excel on many kinds of cognitive tests because not only the skills but also the social situations of testing resemble the activities specifically practiced in school. In contrast with everyday life, where people classify and remember things in order to accomplish a functional goal, in schools and tests they perform in order to satisfy an adult's request to do so (Skeen, Rogoff, & Ellis, 1983; Super, Harkness, & Baldwin, 1977). Individuals with experience in school are likely to have more experience carrying out cognitive processes at the request of an adult without having a clear practical goal (Cazden & John, 1971; Rogoff & Mistry, in press).

Similar emphasis on contexts of development has come from other domains of cross-cultural research. In the area of infant sensorimotor development, Super (1981) and Kilbride (1980) have argued that the controversy over precocious development in African infants is best resolved by considering the practices of the cultural system in which the babies develop. African infants routinely surpass American infants in their rate of learning to sit and to walk, but not in learning to crawl or to climb stairs. African parents provide experiences for their babies that are apparently intended to teach sitting and walking—propping young infants in a sitting position supported by rolled blankets in a hole in the ground, exercising the newborn's walking reflex, and bouncing babies on their feet. But crawling is discouraged, and stair-climbing skills may be limited by the absence of access to stairs. Infant sensorimotor tests assess an aggregate of skills varying in rate of development according to the opportunity or encouragement to practice them.

Even infant sleep patterns vary as a function of culturally determined sleeping arrangements (Super, 1981). In the United States, the common developmental milestone of sleeping for eight uninterrupted hours by age four to five months is regarded as a sign of neurological maturity. In many other cultures, however, the infant sleeps with the mother and is allowed to nurse on demand with minimal distur-bance of adult sleep. In such an arrangement, there is less parental motivation to enforce "sleeping through the night," and Super reported that babies continue to wake about every four hours during the night to feed, which is about the frequency of feeding during the day. Thus, it appears that this developmental mile-stone, in addition to its biological basis, is a function of the context in which it develops.

Cross-cultural studies demonstrating that individ-uals' behavior and skills are closely tied to specific ac-tivities have contributed to examination of important questions regarding the generality of the develop-ment of skills and behaviors, the structure of the ecol-ogy of development, and how to conceptualize the sociocultural context of practice of skills and behav-ior. These issues have recently pervaded the study of developmental psychology, with some large measure of influence from research on culture.

CONCEPTUALIZING THE SOCIOCULTURAL CONTEXT

Many researchers in the field of culture and develop-ment have found themselves comfortable with Vygot-sky's theory, which focuses on the sociocultural con-text of development. Vygotsky's theory, developed in the 1930s in the Soviet Union, has gradually become more accessible to English-speaking researchers, with a rapid upsurge of interest following the publication of *Mind in Society* in 1978 (see also Laboratory of Comparative Human Cognition, 1983; Rogoff, 1982; Scribner & Cole, 1981; Wertsch, 1985a, 1985b). Al-though Vygotsky's theory focuses on cognitive devel-opment, it is gaining interest with researchers in emo-tional and social development as well, perhaps due to its integration of cognitive and social processes, as well as its emphasis on socialization (see, for example, Newson & Newson, 1975).

Vygotsky's theory offers a picture of human devel-opment that stresses how development is inseparable from human social and cultural activities. This con-trasts with the image of the solitary little scientist pro-vided by Piaget's theory. Vygotsky focused on how the development of higher mental processes such as voluntary memory and attention, classification, and reasoning involve learning to use inventions of soci-ety (such as language, mathematical systems, and memory devices) and how children are aided in devel-opment by guidance provided by people who are al-ready skilled in these tools. Central to Vygotsky's the-ory is a stress on both the institutional and the interpersonal levels of social context.

The Institutional Level Cultural history provides organizations and tools useful to cognitive activity (through institutions such as school and inventions such as the calculator or literacy) along with practices that facilitate socially appropriate solutions to prob-lems (e.g., norms for the arrangement of grocery shelves to aid shoppers in locating or remembering what they need; common mnemonic devices). Partic-ular forms of activity are practiced in societal institu-tions such as schools and political systems.

For example, Kohlberg's hierarchy of moral devel-opment can be tied to the political system of a society, with the bureaucratic systems' perspective (Stage Four) appropriate for people whose political frame of reference is a large industrialized society, but inappro-priate for people in small traditional tribal societies: "The two types of social systems are very different (though of course both are valid working types of sys-tems), and thus everyday social life in them calls forth different modes of moral problem solving whose ade-quacy must be judged relative to their particular con-texts" (Edwards, 1981, p. 274). The political institu-tions of a society may channel individual moral reasoning by providing standards for the resolution of moral problems.

The cultural institution of Western schooling pro-vides norms and strategies for performance that are considered advanced in cognitive tests. Goodnow (1976) has suggested that differences between cul-tural groups may be ascribed largely to the interpreta-tion of what problem is being solved in the task and to different values regarding "proper" methods of so-lution (e.g., speed, reaching a solution with a mini-mum of moves or redundancy, physically handling materials versus mental shuffling). The cultural tools and techniques used in school involve specific con-ventions and genres, such as conventions for repre-senting depth in two-dimensional pictures and story problem genres (similar to logical syllogisms) in which one must rely only on information given in the problem to reach the answer. Cross-cultural studies indicate that nonschooled subjects are unfamiliar with such conventions and genres. For example, they are uncomfortable having to answer questions for which they cannot verify the premises (Cole, Gay, Glick, & Sharp, 1971; Scribner, 1977).

The Interpersonal Level In Vygotsky's theory (1978), children develop skills in higher mental processes through the immediate social interactional context of activity, as social interaction helps struc-ture individual activity. Information regarding tools and practices is transmitted through children's inter-action with more experienced members of society during development, and patterns of interpersonal re-lations are organized by institutional conventions and the availability of cultural tools. For example, social aspects of experimental and observational situations relate to cultural practices. The relation between experimenter and subject may be rapidly grasped by

Western children familiar with testing in school, but it may be highly discrepant from familiar adult–child interactions for non-Western children and young Western children. In some cultural settings, it is unusual for an adult who already knows an answer to request information from a child who may only partially know the subject matter, and it may be inappropriate for children to show off knowledge (Cazden & John, 1971; Irvine, 1978; Rogoff, Gauvain, & Ellis, 1984).

Similarly, in observational situations such as mother–child interaction, culturally varying agendas for public behavior may influence what people do in the presence of an observer (Zaslow & Rogoff, 1981). "It seems likely that one influence of the observer on parents is to produce a heightened frequency of behavior that the participants judge to be more socially desirable and inhibit behavior considered socially undesirable" (Pedersen, 1980, p. 181). Graves and Glick (1978) found that exchanges between middle-class mothers and their toddlers varied as a function of whether mothers thought that they were being videotaped. Mothers spoke more, used indirect directives more often, and spent more time in joint interactive focus with their children when they thought they were being observed. Clearly, peoples' interpretation of the goals of a task and cultural rules guiding social behavior influence the display of public behavior. Values regarding interpersonal relations may be inseparable from the activities observed for research purposes.

In addition to the cultural structuring of social interaction that has importance for research into human development, social interaction provides an essential context for development itself. Vygotsky stressed that interpersonal situations are important for guiding children in their development of the skills and behaviors considered important in their culture. Working within the "zone of proximal development," adults guide children in carrying out activities that are beyond the children's individual skills, and this joint problem solving provides children with information appropriate to stretch their individual skills. Cole (1981) argues that the zone of proximal development is "where culture and cognition create each other." Thus Vygotsky's conceptualization of how individual efforts are embedded in the interpersonal and institutional contexts of culture is proving useful for understanding the relation between culture and the individual.

RESEARCH ON CULTURE INVOLVING MINORITIES IN THE UNITED STATES

Historically, research on minorities in the United States has followed a different course than the cross-cultural investigations discussed earlier. For many years, researchers were intent on comparing the behavior and skills of minority children with mainstream children without taking into consideration the cultural contexts in which minority and mainstream children develop. This approach involved "deficit model" assumptions that mainstream skills and upbringing are normal and that variations observed with minorities are aberrations that produce deficits; intervention programs were designed to provide minority children with experiences to make up for their assumed deficits (Cole & Bruner, 1971; Hilliard & Vaughn-Scott, 1982; Howard & Scott, 1981; Ogbu, 1982).

The deficit model previously used in research on minority children contrasts sharply with the assumptions of the cross-cultural approach, which attempts to avoid ethnocentric evaluation of one group's practices and beliefs as being superior without considering their origins and functions from the perspective of the reality of that cultural group. With research in their own country, however, researchers have had more difficulty avoiding the assumption that the majority practices are proper (Ogbu, 1982). Variations have been assumed to account for the generally lower social status of the minority group members. It is only recently, and largely through the efforts of researchers with minority backgrounds, that deficit assumptions have been questioned in research on minority children.

The working model that appears to predominate in current minority research is one in which the positive features of cultural variation are emphasized. Although this is a valuable shift, we feel that research on minorities must move beyond reiterating the value of cultural diversity and begin more seriously to examine the source and functioning of the diversity represented in the United States to increase our understanding of the processes underlying development in cultural context.

Not only is the diversity of cultural backgrounds in our nation a resource for the creativity and future of the nation, it is also a resource for scholars studying how children develop. To make good use of this information, cultural research with minorities needs to focus on examining the processes and functioning of the cultural context of development. This requires "unpackaging" culture or minority status (Whiting, 1976) so as to disentangle the workings of the social context of development. This has become a central effort of cross-cultural research on non-Western populations.

Pioneering researchers of minorities are also beginning to look at the contexts in which children from different cultures develop, and these efforts provide a basis for a greater understanding of how culture channels development. (Examples include Brown & Reeve, 1985; Cazden, John, & Hymes, 1975; Chisholm, 1983; Erickson & Mohatt, 1982; Laboratory of Comparative Human Cognition, 1986; Ogbu, 1982.) It is notable that some of the most interesting efforts involve combining approaches from anthropology and education with those of psychology (see also recent issues of *Anthropology and Education Quarterly).*

The potential from research on cultural groups around the world as well as down the street lies in its challenge to our systems of assumptions and in the creative efforts of scholars to synthesize knowledge from observations of differing contexts of human development. Such challenge and synthesis is fruitful in the efforts to achieve a deeper and broader understanding of human nature and nurture.

REFERENCES

Bornstein, M. H. (1980). Cross-cultural developmental psychology. In M. H. Bornstein (Ed.), *Comparative methods in psychology* (pp. 231–281). Hillsdale, NJ: Erlbaum.

Bowerman, M. (1981). Language development. In H. C. Triandis & A. Heron (Eds.), *Handbook of cross-cultural psychology* (Vol. 4, pp. 93–185). Boston: Allyn & Bacon.

Bretherton, I., & Waters E. (Eds.). (1985). Growing points of attachment theory and research. *Monographs of the Society for Research in Child Development, 50* (1–2, Serial No. 209).

Brown, A. L., & Reeve, R. A. (1985). *Bandwidths of competence: The role of supportive contexts in learning and development* (Tech. Rep. No. 336). Champaign: University of Illinois at Urbana-Champaign, Center for the Study of Reading.

Cazden, C. B., John, V. P., & Hymes, D. (Eds.). (1975). *Functions of language in the classroom.* New York: Teachers College Press.

Cazden, C. B., & John, V. P. (1971). Learning in American Indian children. In M. L. Wax, S. Diamond, & F. O. Gearing (Eds.), *Anthropological perspectives in education* (pp. 252–272). New York: Basic Books.

Chisholm, J. S. (1983). *Navajo infancy: An ethological study of child development.* Hawthorne, NY: Aldine.

Cole, M. (1975). An ethnographic psychology of cognition. In R. W. Brislin, S. Bochner, & W. J. Lonner (Eds.), *Cross-cultural perspectives on learning* (pp. 157–175). New York: Wiley.

Cole, M. (1981, September). *The zone of proximal development: Where culture and cognition create each other* (Report No. 106). San Diego: University of California, Center for Human Information Processing.

Cole, M., & Bruner, J. S. (1971). Cultural differences and inferences about psychological processes. *American Psychologist, 26,* 867–876.

Cole, M., Gay, J., Glick, J. A., & Sharp, D. W. (1971). *The cultural context of learning and thinking.* New York: Basic Books.

Cole, M., Hood, L., & McDermott, R. P. (1978). Concepts of ecological validity: Their differing implications for comparative cognitive research. *The Quarterly Newsletter of the Institute for Comparative Human Development, 2,* 34–37.

Dasen, P. R. (Ed.). (1977). *Piagetian psychology: Cross-cultural contributions.* New York: Gardner Press.

Dasen, P. R., & Heron, A. (1981). Cross-cultural tests of Piaget's theory. In H. C. Triandis & A. Heron (Eds.), *Handbook of cross-cultural psychology* (Vol. 4, pp. 295–341). Boston: Allyn & Bacon.

Edwards, C. P. (1981). The comparative study of the development of moral judgment and reasoning. In R. H. Munroe, R. L. Munroe, & B. B. Whiting (Eds.), *Handbook of cross-cultural human development* (pp. 501–528). New York: Garland.

Erickson, F., & Mohatt, G. (1982). Cultural organization of participation structures in two classrooms of Indian students. In G. Spindler (Ed.), *Doing the ethnography of schooling* (pp.132–174). New York: Holt, Rinehart & Winston.

Field, T. M., Sostek, A. M., Vietze, P., & Leiderman, P. H. (Eds.). (1981). *Culture and early interactions.* Hillsdale, NJ: Erlbaum.

Fox, N. A. (1977). Attachment of kibbutz infants to mother and metapelet. *Child Development, 48,* 1228–1239.

Gewirtz. J. L. (1965). The course of infant smiling in four child-rearing environments in Israel. In B. M. Foss (Ed.), *Determinants of infant behavior* (Vol. 3, pp. 205–248). London, England: Methuen.

Gladwin, T. (1970). *East is a big bird.* Cambridge, MA: Belknap Press.

Glick, J. (1975). Cognitive development in cross-cultural perspective. In F. Horowitz (Ed.), *Review of child development research* (Vol. 4, pp. 595–654). Chicago: University of Chicago Press.

Goldberg, S. (1972). Infant care and growth in urban Zambia. *Human Development, 15,* 77–89.

Goodnow, J. J. (1976). The nature of intelligent behavior. Questions raised by cross-cultural studies. In L. B. Resnick (Ed.), *The nature of intelligence* (pp. 169–188). Hillsdale, NJ: Erlbaum.

Goody, J. (1977). *The domestication of the savage mind.* Cambridge, England: Cambridge University Press.

Graves, Z. R., & Glick, J. (1978). The effect of context on mother–child interaction. *The Quarterly Newsletter of the Institute for Comparative Human Development, 2,* 41–46.

Greenfield, P. M. (1976). Cross-cultural research and Piagetian theory: Paradox and progress. In K. R Riegel & J. A. Meacham (Eds.), *The developing individual in a changing world* (Vol. 1, pp. 322–345). Chicago: Aldine.

Hilliard, A. G., III, & Vaughn-Scott, M. (1982). The quest for the "minority" child. In S. G. Moore & C. R. Cooper (Eds.), *The young child: Reviews of research* (Vol. 3, pp. 175–189). Washington, DC: National Association for the Education of Young Children.

Howard, A., & Scott, R. A. (1981). The study of minority groups in complex societies. In R. H. Munroe, R. L. Munroe, & B. B. Whiting (Eds.), *Handbook of cross-cultural human development* (pp. 113–152). New York: Garland.

Irvine, J. T (1978). Wolof "magical thinking": Culture and conservation revisited. *Journal of Cross-Cultural Psychology, 9,* 300–310.

Kilbride, P. L. (1980). Sensorimotor behavior of Baganda and Samia infants. *Journal of Cross-Cultural Psychology, 11,* 131–152.

Konner, M. (1972). Aspects of the developmental ethology of a foraging people. In N. Blurton-Jones (Ed.), *Ethological studies of child behavior* (pp. 285–328). Cambridge, England: Cambridge University Press.

Laboratory of Comparative Human Cognition. (1979). Cross-cultural psychology's challenges to our ideas of children and development. *American Psychologist, 34*, 827–833.

Laboratory of Comparative Human Cognition. (1983). Culture and cognitive development. In W. Kessen (Ed.), *Handbook of Child Psychology: Vol. 1. History, theory, and methods* (pp. 294–356). New York: Wiley.

Laboratory of Comparative Human Cognition. (1986). Contributions of cross-cultural research to educational practice. *American Psychologist, 41*, 1049–1058.

Lave, J. (1977). Tailor-made experiments and evaluating the intellectual consequences of apprenticeship training. *The Quarterly Newsletter of the Institute for Comparative Human Development, 1*, 1–3.

Leiderman, P. H., Tulkin, S. R., & Rosenfeld, A. (Eds.). (1977). *Culture and infancy*. New York: Academic Press.

LeVine, R. A. (in press). Environments in child development: An anthropological perspective. In W. Damon (Ed.), *Child development today and tomorrow*. San Francisco: Jossey-Bass.

Malinowski, B. (1927). *The father in primitive psychology*. New York: Norton.

Munroe, R. L., & Munroe, R. H. (1975). *Cross-cultural human development*. Monterey, CA: Brooks/Cole.

Munroe, R. H., Munroe, R. L., & Whiting, B. B. (Eds.). (1981). *Handbook of cross-cultural human development*. New York: Garland.

Newson, J., & Newson, E. (1975). Intersubjectivity and the transmission of culture: On the social origins of symbolic functioning. *Bulletin of the British Psychological Society, 28*, 437–446.

Ogbu, J. U. (1982). Socialization: A cultural ecological approach. In K. M. Borman (Ed.), *The social life of children in a changing society* (pp. 253–267). Hillsdale, NJ: Erlbaum.

Pedersen, R. A. (1980). *The father–infant relationship: Observational studies in the family setting*. New York: Praeger.

Piaget, J. (1972). Intellectual evolution from adolescence to adulthood. *Human Development, 15*, 1–12.

Price-Williams, D. R. (1980). Anthropological approaches to cognition and their relevance to psychology. In H. C. Triandis & W. Lonner (Eds.), *Handbook of cross-cultural psychology* (Vol. 3, pp. 155–184). Boston: Allyn & Bacon.

Rogoff, B. (1981). Schooling and the development of cognitive skills. In H. C. Triandis & A. Heron (Eds.), *Handbook of cross-cultural psychology* (Vol. 4, pp. 233–294). Boston: Allyn & Bacon.

Rogoff, B. (1982). Integrating context and cognitive development. In M. E. Lamb & A. L. Brown (Eds.), *Advances in developmental psychology* (Vol. 2, pp. 125–170). Hillsdale, NJ: Erlbaum.

Rogoff, B., Gauvain, M., & Ellis, S. (1984). Development viewed in its cultural context. In M. H. Bornstein & M. E. Lamb (Eds.), *Developmental Psychology* (pp. 533–571). Hillsdale, NJ: Erlbaum.

Rogoff, B., & Mistry, J. J. (1985). Memory development in cultural context. In M. Pressley & C. Brainerd (Eds.), *Progress in cognitive development* (pp. 117–142). New York: Springer-Verlag.

Rogoff, B., & Mistry, J. J. (in press). The social and motivational context of children's memory skills. In R. Fivish & J. Hudson (Eds.), *What young children remember and why*. Cambridge, England: Cambridge University Press.

Rogoff, B., & Waddell, K. J. (1982). Memory for information organized in a scene by children from two cultures. *Child Development, 53*, 1224–1228.

Saxe, G. B. (1988). *Mathematics in and out of school*. Unpublished manuscript, University of California at Los Angeles.

Schieffelin, B. B., & Ochs, E. (Eds.). (1986). *Language socialization across cultures*. Cambridge, England: Cambridge University Press.

Scribner, S. (1976). Situating the experiment in cross-cultural research. In K. F. Riegel & J. A. Meacham (Eds.), *The developing individual in a changing world* (Vol. 1, pp. 310–321). Chicago: Aldine.

Scribner, S. (1977). Modes of thinking and ways of speaking: Culture and logic reconsidered. In P. N. Johnson-Laird & P. C. Wason (Eds.), *Thinking* (pp. 483–500). Cambridge, England: Cambridge University Press.

Scribner, S., & Cole, M. (1981). *The psychology of literacy*. Cambridge, MA: Harvard University Press.

Serpell, R. (1976). *Culture's influence on behavior*. London, England: Methuen.

Serpell, R. (1979). How specific are perceptual skills? A cross-cultural study of pattern reproduction. *British Journal of Psychology, 70*, 365–380.

Sharp, D., Cole, M., & Lave, C. (1979). Education and cognitive development: The evidence from experimental research. *Monographs of the Society for Research in Child Development, 44*, (1–2, Serial No. 178).

Skeen, J., Rogoff, B., & Ellis, S. (1983). Categorization by children and adults in communication contexts. *International Journal of Behavioral Development, 6*, 213–220.

Slobin, D. I. (1973). Cognitive prerequisites for the development of grammar. In C. A. Ferguson & D. I. Slobin (Eds.), *Studies of child language development* (pp. 175–200). New York: Holt, Rinehart & Winston.

Super, C. M. (1981). Behavioral development in infancy. In R. H. Munroe, R. L. Munroe, & B. B. Whiting (Eds.), *Handbook of cross-cultural human development* (pp. 181–270). New York: Garland.

Super, C. M., & Harkness, S. (Eds.). (1980). *Anthropological perspectives on child development*. San Francisco: Jossey-Bass.

Super, C. M., Harkness, S., & Baldwin, L. M. (1977). Category behavior in natural ecologies and in cognitive tests. *The Quarterly Newsletter of the Institute for Comparative Human Development, 1*, 4–7.

Triandis, H. C., & Heron, A. (Eds.). (1981). *Handbook of cross-cultural psychology* (Vol. 4). Boston: Allyn & Bacon.

Tronick, E. Z., Morelli, G. A., & Winn, S. (1987). Multiple caretaking of Efe (pygmy) infants. *American Anthropologist, 89* (1), 96–106.

Vygotsky, L. S. (1978). *Mind in society*. Cambridge, MA: Harvard University Press.

Wagner, D. A., & Stevenson, H. W. (Eds.). (1982). *Cultural perspectives on child development*. San Francisco: Freeman.

Wenger, M. (1983). *Gender role socialization in East Africa: Social interactions between 2-to-3-year olds and older children, a social ecological perspective.* Unpublished doctoral dissertation, Harvard University, Cambridge, MA.

Werner, E. E. (1979). *Cross-Cultural child development.* Monterey, CA: Brooks/Cole.

Werner, E. E. (1988). A cross-cultural perspective on infancy. *Journal of Cross-Cultural Psychology, 19* (1), 96–113.

Wertsch, J. V. (Ed.). (1985a). *Culture, communication, and cognition: Vygotskian perspectives.* Cambridge, England: Cambridge University Press.

Wertsch, J. V. (1985b). *Vygotsky and the social formation of mind.* Cambridge, MA: Harvard University Press.

Whiting, B. B. (1976). The problem of the packaged variable. In K. F. Riegel & J. A. Meacham (Eds.), *The developing individual in a changing world.* Chicago: Aldine.

Whiting, B. B., & Edwards, C. P. (1988). *Children of different worlds.* Cambridge, MA: Harvard University Press.

Whiting, B. B., & Whiting, J. W. M. (1975). *Children of six cultures: A psycho-cultural analysis.* Cambridge, MA: Harvard University Press.

Zaslow, M. (1980). Relationships among peers in kibbutz toddler groups. *Child Psychiatry and Human Development, 10,* 178–189.

Zaslow, M., & Rogoff, B. (1981). The cross-cultural study of early interaction: Implications from research in culture and cognition. In T. Field, A. Sostek, P. Vietze, & H. Leiderman (Eds.), *Culture and early interactions* (pp. 237–256). Hillsdale, NJ: Erlbaum.

QUESTIONS

1. What are two of the ways in which cross-cultural research can increase understanding of human development?
2. Why is it so difficult to detect when cultural belief systems influence scientific theories and research questions?
3. What is one piece of evidence from cross-cultural research that illustrates how this research can contribute in unique ways to the study of human development?
4. What does research on infant motor development in Africa tell us about motor development more generally?
5. What is the interpersonal level of development? What is the institutional level? Why do you think Vygotsky included both of these levels in his theory of development?
6. Institutions of society, especially the availability and types of schools, play an important role in human development. What effect might inequalities in schooling within a society have on individual psychological development?

3 The Stages of the Intellectual Development of the Child*

JEAN PIAGET

Jean Piaget was one of the most influential thinkers in the twentieth century on the topic of child development. Although he was not trained as a developmental psychologist, his life's work was devoted to examining one important part of human development, the growth of intelligence. At the present time, Piaget's thinking remains influential in the field. A number of specific aspects of his thinking have been challenged, however; for example, the strict characterization of the stages of mental development that he proposed. Data have poured in over the last several decades that indicate much more unevenness in understanding at all points in development than Piaget's stage-based theory suggests. Despite these challenges, the fact remains that Piaget provided insights into intellectual development that are still pertinent to the field.

This article is the text of a lecture that Piaget gave in the United States in 1961. In addition to his description of the four stages of his theory, several things are worth noting. First, Piaget did not write like a psychologist, at least not like a modern psychologist. His intellectual influences were philosophy, mathematics, physics, and biology, and he tended to rely on certain forms of explanation in his writing, including "thought demonstrations" and case examples. Second, an important characteristic of Piaget's theory is his emphasis on interaction in development. For Piaget, interaction between the child and the world promotes intellectual growth, and he provides examples at each stage of development of this process.

Some of the concepts that Piaget discusses in this article you may find difficult. Be assured that many who read Piaget have difficulty understanding all his arguments. However, reading about his theory in his own words is worth the time and effort. Piaget's keen observational sense and creative examination of the developing mind are evident in his writings, and they convey why it is that he has remained so influential in the study of intellectual development.

A consideration of the stages of the development of intelligence should be preceded by asking the question, What is intelligence? Unfortunately, we find ourselves confronted by a great number of definitions. For Claparède, intelligence is an adaptation to new situations. When a situation is new, when there are no reflexes, when there are no habits to rely on, then the subject is obliged to search for something new. That is to say, Claparède defines intelligence as groping, as feeling one's way, trial-and-error behavior. We find this trial-and-error behavior in all levels of intelligence, even at the superior level, in the form of hypothesis testing. As far as I am concerned, this definition is too vague, be-cause trial and error occurs in the formation of habits, and also in the earliest established reflexes: when a newborn baby learns to suck.

Karl Bühler defines intelligence as an act of immediate comprehension; that is to say, an insight. Bühler's definition is also very precise, but it seems to me too narrow. I know that when a mathematician solves a problem, he ends by having an insight, but up to that moment he feels, or gropes for, his way; and to say that the trial-and-error behavior is not intelligent and that intelligence starts only when he finds the solution to the problem, seems a very narrow definition. I would, therefore, propose to define intelligence not

Reprinted with permission of Guilford Publications from *Bulletin of the Menninger Clinic*, 26 (1962), pp. 120–128.

*The three lectures by Doctor Piaget contained in this issue of the *Bulletin* were presented as a series to the Menninger School of Psychiatry March 6, 13, and 22, 1961.

by a static criterion, as in previous definitions, but by the direction that intelligence follows in its evolution, and then I would define intelligence as a form of equilibration, or forms of equilibration, toward which all cognitive functions lead.

But I must first define equilibration. Equilibration in my vocabulary is not an exact and automatic balance, as it would be in Gestalt theory; I define equilibration principally as a compensation for an external disturbance.

When there is an external disturbance, the subject succeeds in compensating for this by an activity. The maximum equilibration is thus the maximum of the activity, and not a state of rest. It is a mobile equilibration, and not an immobile one. So equilibration is defined as compensation; compensation is the annulling of a transformation by an inverse transformation. The compensation which intervenes in equilibration implies the fundamental idea of reversibility, and this reversibility is precisely what characterizes the operations of the intelligence. An operation is an internalized action, but it is also a reversible action. But an operation is never isolated; it is always subordinated to other operations; it is part of a more inclusive structure. Consequently, we define intelligence in terms of operations, coordination of operations.

Take, for example, an operation like addition: Addition is a material action, the action of reuniting. On the other hand, it is a reversible action, because addition may be compensated by subtraction. Yet addition leads to a structure of a whole. In the case of numbers, it will be the structure that the mathematicians call a "group." In the case of addition of classes which intervene in the logical structure it will be a more simple structure that we will call a grouping, and so on.

Consequently, the study of the stages of intelligence is first a study of the formation of operational structures. I shall define every stage by a structure of a whole, with the possibility of its integration into succeeding stages, just as it was prepared by preceding stages. Thus, I shall distinguish four great stages, or four great periods, in the development of intelligence: first, the sensori-motor period before the appearance of language; second, the period from about two to seven years of age, the preoperational period which precedes real operations; third, the period from seven to 12 years of age, a period of concrete operations (which refers to concrete objects); and finally after 12 years of age, the period of formal operations, or positional operations.

SENSORI-MOTOR STAGE

Before language develops, there is behavior that we can call intelligent. For example, when a baby of 12 months or more wants an object which is too far from him, but which rests on a carpet or blanket, and he pulls it to get to the object, this behavior is an act of intelligence. The child uses an intermediary, a means to get to his goal. Also, getting to an object by means of pulling a string when the object is tied to the string, or when the child uses a stick to get the object, are acts of intelligence. They demonstrate in the sensori-motor period a certain number of stages, which go from simple reflexes, from the formation of the first habits, up to the coordination of means and goals.

Remarkable in this sensori-motor stage of intelligence is that there are already structures. Sensori-motor intelligence rests mainly on actions, on movements and perceptions without language, but these actions are coordinated in a relatively stable way. They are coordinated under what we may call schemata of action. These schemata can be generalized in actions and are applicable to new situations. For example, pulling a carpet to bring an object within reach constitutes a schema which can be generalized to other situations when another object rests on a support. In other words, a schema supposes an incorporation of new situations into the previous schemata, a sort of continuous assimilation of new objects or new situations to the actions already schematized. For example, I presented to one of my children an object completely new to him—a box of cigarettes, which is not a usual toy for a baby. The child took the object, looked at it, put it in his mouth, shook it, then took it with one hand and hit it with the other hand, then rubbed it on the edge of the crib, then shook it again, and gave the impression of trying to see if there were noise. This behavior is a way of exploring the object, of trying to understand it by assimilating it to schemata already known. The child behaves in this situation as he will later in Binet's famous vocabulary test, when he defines by usage, saying, for instance, that a spoon is for eating, and so on.

But in the presence of a new object, even without knowing how to talk, the child knows how to assimilate, to incorporate this new object into each of his already developed schemata which function as practical concepts. Here is a structuring of intelligence. Most important in this structuring is the base, the point of departure of all subsequent operational constructions. At the sensori-motor level, the child constructs the schema of the permanent object.

The knowledge of the permanent object starts at this point. The child is not convinced at the beginning that when an object disappears from view, he can find it again. One can verify by tests that object permanence is not yet developed at this stage. But there is there the beginning of a subsequent fundamental idea which starts being constructed at the sensori-motor level. This is also true of the construction of the ideas of space, of time, of causality. What is being done at the sensori-motor level concerning all the foregoing ideas will constitute the substructure of the subsequent, fully achieved ideas of permanent objects, of space, of time, of causality.

In the formation of these substructures at the sensori-motor level, it is very interesting to note the beginning of a *reversibility*, not in thought, since there is not yet representation in thought, but in action itself. For example, the formation of the conception of space at the sensori-motor stage leads to an amazing decentration if one compares the conception of space at the first weeks of the development with that at one and one-half to two years of age. In the beginning there is not one space which contains all the objects, including the child's body itself; there is a multitude of spaces which are not coordinated: there are the buccal space, the tactilokinesthetic space, the visual and auditory spaces; each is separate and each is centered essentially on the body of the subject and on actions. After a few months, however, after a kind of Copernican evolution, there is a total reversal, a decentration such that space becomes homogenous, a one-and-only space that envelops the others. Then space becomes a container that envelops all objects, including the body itself; and after that, space is mainly coordinated in a structure, a coordination of positions and displacements, and these constitute what the geometricians call a "group"; that is to say, precisely a reversible system. One may move from A to B, and may come back from B to A; there is the possibility of returning, of reversibility. There is also the possibility of making detours and combinations which give a clue to what the subsequent operations will be when thought will supersede the action itself.

PRE-OPERATIONAL STAGE

From one and one-half to two years of age, a fundamental transformation in the evolution of intelligence takes place in the appearance of symbolic functions. Every action of intelligence consists in manipulating significations (or meanings) and whenever (or wherever) there is significations, there are on the one hand the "significants" and on the other the "significates." This is true in the sensori-motor level, but the only significants that intervene there are perceptual signs or signals (as in conditioning) which are undifferentiated in regard to the significate; for example, a perceptual cue, like distance, which will be a cue for the size of the distant object, or the apparent size of an object, which will be the cue for the distance of the object. There, perhaps, both indices are different aspects of the same reality, but they are not yet differentiated significants. At the age of one and one-half to two years a new class of significants arises, and these significants are differentiated in regard to their significates. These differentiations can

be called symbolic function. The appearance of symbols in a children's game is an example of the appearance of new significants. At the sensori-motor level the games are nothing but exercises; now they become symbolic play, a play of fiction; these games consist in representing something by means of something else. Another example is the beginning of delayed imitation, an imitation that takes place not in the presence of the original object but in its absence, and which consequently constitutes a kind of symbolization or mental image.

At the same time that symbols appear, the child acquires language; that is to say, there is the acquisition of another phase of differentiated significants, verbal signals, or collective signals. This symbolic function then brings great flexibility into the field of intelligence. Intelligence up to this point refers to the immediate space which surrounds the child and to the present perceptual situation; thanks to language, and to the symbolic functions, it becomes possible to invoke objects which are not present perceptually, to reconstruct the past, or to make projects, plans for the future, to think of objects not present but very distant in space—in short, to span spatio-temporal distances much greater than before.

But this new stage, the stage of representation of thought which is superimposed on the sensori-motor stage, is not a simple extension of what was referred to at the previous level. Before being able to prolong, one must in fact reconstruct, because behavior in words is a different thing from representing something in thought. When a child knows how to move around in his house or garden by following the different successive cues around him, it does not mean that he is capable of representing or reproducing the total configuration of his house or his garden. To be able to represent, to reproduce something, one must be capable of reconstructing this group of displacements, but at a new level, that of the representation of the thought.

I recently made an amusing test with Nel Szeminska. We took children of four to five years of age who went to school by themselves and came back home by themselves, and asked them if they could trace the way to school and back for us, not in design, which would be too difficult, but like a construction game, with concrete objects. We found that they were not capable of representation; there was a kind of motor-memory, but it was not yet a representation of a whole—the group of displacements had not yet been reconstructed on the plan of the representation of thought. In other words, the operations were not yet formed. There are representations which are internalized actions, but actions still centered on the body itself, on the activity itself. These representations do not allow the objective combinations, the decentrated combinations that the operations would. The actions are centered on the body. I used to call this egocentrism; but it is better thought of as lack of reversibility of action.

At this level, the most certain sign of the absence of operations which appear at the next stage is the absence of the knowledge of conservation. In fact, an operation refers to the transformation of reality. The transformation is not of the whole, however; something constant is always untransformed. If you pour a liquid from one glass to another there is transformation; the liquid changes form, but its liquid property stays constant. So at the pre-operational level, it is significant from the point of view of the operations of intelligence that the child has not yet a knowledge of conservation. For example, in the case of liquid, when the child pours it from one bottle to the other, he thinks that the quantity of the liquid has changed. When the level of the liquid changes, the child thinks the quantity has changed—there is more or less in the second glass than in the first. And if you ask the child where the larger quantity came from, he does not answer this question. What is important for the child is that perceptually it is not the same thing any more. We find this absence of conservation in all object properties, in the length, surface, quantity, and weight of things.

This absence of conservation indicates essentially that at this stage the child reasons from the configuration. Confronted with a transformation, he does not reason from the transformation itself; he starts from the initial configuration, then sees the final configuration, compares the two but forgets the transformation, because he does not know how to reason about it. At this stage the child is still reasoning on the basis of what he sees because there is no conservation. He is able to master this problem only when the operations are formed and these operations, which we have already sensed at the sensori-motor level, are not formed until around seven to eight years of age. At that age the elementary problems of conservation are solved, because the child reasons on the basis of the transformation per se, and this requires a manipulation of the operation. The ability to pass from one stage to the other and be able to come back to the point of departure, to manipulate the reversible operations, which appears around seven to eight years of age, is limited when compared with the operations of the superior level only in the sense that they are concrete. That is to say, the child can manipulate the operations only when he manipulates the object concretely.

STAGE OF CONCRETE OPERATIONS

The first operations of the manipulation of objects, the concrete operations, deal with logical classes and with logical relations, or the number. But these operations do not deal yet with propositions, or hypotheses, which do not appear until the last stage.

Let me exemplify these concrete operations: the simplest operation is concerned with classifying objects according to their similarity and their difference. This is accomplished by including the subclasses within larger and more general classes, a process that implies inclusion. This classification, which seems very simple at first, is not acquired until around seven to eight years of age. Before that, at the pre-operational level, we do not find logical inclusion. For example, if you show a child at the pre-operational level a bouquet of flowers of which one half is daisies and the other half other flowers and you ask him if in this bouquet there are more flowers or more daisies, you are confronted with this answer, which seems extraordinary until it is analyzed: The child cannot tell you whether there are more flowers than daisies; either he reasons on the basis of the whole or of the part. He cannot understand that the part is complementary to the rest, and he says there are more daisies than flowers, or as many daisies as flowers, without understanding this inclusion of the subclass, the daisies, in the class of flowers. It is only around seven to eight years of age that a child is capable of solving a problem of inclusion.

Another system of operation that appears around seven to eight years of age is the operation of serializing; that is, to arrange objects according to their size, or their progressive weight. It is also a structure of the whole, like the classification which rests on concrete operations, since it consists of manipulating concrete objects. At this level there is also the construction of numbers, which is, too, a synthesis of classification and seriation. In numbers, as in classes, we have inclusion, and also a serial order, as in serializing. These elementary operations constitute structures of wholes. There is no class without classification; there is no symmetric relation without serialization; there is not a number independent of the series of numbers. But the structures of these wholes are simple structures, groupings in the case of classes and relations, which are already groups in the case of numbers, but very elementary structures compared to subsequent structures.

STAGE OF FORMAL OPERATIONS

The last stage of development of intelligence is the stage of formal operations or propositional operations. At about eleven to twelve years of age we see great progress; the child becomes capable of reasoning not only on the basis of objects, but also on the basis of hypotheses, or of propositions.

An example which neatly shows the difference between reasoning on the basis of propositions and reasoning on the basis of concrete objects comes from Burt's tests. Burt asked children of different ages to compare the colors of the hair of three girls: Edith is fairer than Susan, Edith is darker than Lilly; who is the darkest of the three? In this question there is seriation, not of concrete objects, but of verbal statements which supposes a more complicated mental manipulation. This problem is rarely solved before the age of 12.

Here a new class of operations appears which is superimposed on the operations of logical class and number, and these operations are the propositional operations. Here, compared to the previous stage, are fundamental changes. It is not simply that these operations refer to language, and then to operations with concrete objects, but that these operations have much richer structures.

The first novelty is a combinative structure; like mathematical structures, it is a structure of a system which is superimposed on the structure of simple classifications or seriations which are not themselves systems, because they do not involve a combinative system. A combinative system permits the grouping in flexible combinations of each element of the system with any other element of that system. The logic of propositions supposes such a combinative system. If children of different ages are shown a number of colored disks and asked to combine each color with each other two by two, or three by three, we find these combinative operations are not accessible to the child at the stage of concrete operations. The child is capable of some combination, but not of all the possible combinations. After the age of 12, the child can find a method to make all the possible combinations. At the same time he acquires both the logic of mathematics and the logic of propositions, which also supposes a method of combining.

A second novelty in the operations of propositions is the appearance of a structure which constitutes a group of four transformations. Hitherto there were two reversibilities: reversibility by inversion, which consists of annulling, or canceling; and reversibility which we call reciprocity, leading not to cancellation, but to another combination. Reciprocity is what we find in the field of a relation. If A equals B, by reciprocity B equals A. If A is smaller than B, by reciprocity B is larger than A. At the level of propositional operations a new system envelops these two forms of reversibility. Here the structure combines inversion and reversibility in one single but larger and more complicated structure. It allows the acquisition of a series of fundamental operational schemata for the development of intelligence, which schemata are not possible before the constitution of this structure.

It is around the age of 12 that the child, for example, starts to understand in mathematics the knowledge of proportions, and becomes capable of reasoning by using two systems of reference at the same time. For example, if you advance the position of a board and a car moving in opposite directions, in order to understand the movement of the board in relation to the movement of the car and to other movement, you need a system of four transformations. The same is true in regard to proportions, to problems in mathematics or physics, or to other logical problems.

The four principal stages of the development of intelligence of the child progress from one stage to the other by the construction of new operational structures, and these structures constitute the fundamental instrument of the intelligence of the adult.

QUESTIONS

1. What, according to Piaget, is equilibration and what role does it play in intellectual development?
2. Why is Piaget called an interactionist? Give an example from one of the stages that illustrates his interactionist approach.
3. Why did Piaget consider the appearance of symbolic functions in the preoperational stage so important for intellectual development?
4. What is an operation? How can children manipulate operations in the concrete operational stage? Give an example of this from either a classification or a seriation task.
5. Reversibility plays a role in each of the four stages. What is reversibility and how does children's understanding of reversibility change from infancy to adolescence?
6. Suppose that you are a Piagetian scholar and you are asked to consult at an elementary school about children's understanding of scientific concepts like the conservation of weight and volume. Several second- and third-graders at this school are having difficulty with these concepts. What would you advise the teachers to do to help these children?

4 Interaction Between Learning and Development

Lev S. Vygotsky

In the early part of the twentieth century, a new form of psychology was developed in Russia. This psychology was different from that in the United States at the time because it emphasized (1) mental processes and (2) the social and cultural contributions to the development of mental processes. One of the main figures in this new theoretical approach was Lev S. Vygotsky. Although he lived a relatively short life (he died at the age of 37), he was extremely productive. The scope of his interests was broad and included the development of scientific reasoning, intellectual development in retarded children, and the role of language and culture in the development of thinking. He even studied how culture and social situations influence art and literature.

Underlying all these interests was a common question. How does the social and cultural experience of development become part of individual experience and psychology? For Vygotsky, intelligence is a social product, and he strived to describe its development from this vantage point. One of Vygotsky's main concerns was the mechanism or way by which the social and the cultural become part of a child's mental life. He hypothesized that this occurs in the everyday experiences that children have as they interact with more culturally experienced members in their community. For Vygotsky, these interactions create opportunities for cognitive development. The interactions are most likely to lead to development when the child and a more experienced partner interact in the child's *zone of proximal (or potential) development*. This process is described in this chapter, taken from one of Vygotsky's books, *Mind in Society*, which was published in the United States posthumously.

Vygotsky's theory, and theories related to and derived from it, such as sociocultural approaches to development, are very influential in the study of human development today. In large part, this is because this approach is the first in modern psychological study to formalize a view of human development that takes into account the cultural and social experiences of development, which scholars agree are critical components of human psychology.

The problems encountered in the psychological analysis of teaching cannot be correctly resolved or even formulated without addressing the relation between learning and development in school-age children. Yet it is the most unclear of all the basic issues on which the application of child development theories to educational processes depends. Needless to say, the lack of theoretical clarity does not mean that the issue is removed altogether from current research efforts into learning; not one study can avoid this central theoretical issue. But the relation between learning and development remains methodologically unclear because concrete research studies have embodied theoretically vague, critically unevaluated, and sometimes internally contradictory postulates, premises, and peculiar solutions to the problem of this fundamental relationship; and these, of course, result in a variety of errors.

Essentially, all current conceptions of the relation between development and learning in children can be reduced to three major theoretical positions.

The first centers on the assumption that processes of child development are independent of learning. Learning is considered a purely external process that is not actively involved in development. It merely utilizes the achievements of development rather than providing an impetus for modifying its course.

In experimental investigations of the development of thinking in school children, it has been

This article is reprinted with permission of Harvard University Press, from L. S. Vygotsky, 1978, *Mind in Society*. Cambridge, MA: Harvard University Press, 79–91.

assumed that processes such as deduction and understanding, evolution of notions about the world, interpretation of physical causality, and mastery of logical forms of thought and abstract logic all occur by themselves, without any influence from school learning. An example of such a theory is Piaget's extremely complex and interesting theoretical principles, which also shape the experimental methodology he employs. The questions Piaget uses in the course of his "clinical conversations" with children clearly illustrate his approach. When a five-year-old is asked "why doesn't the sun fall?" it is assumed that the child has neither a ready answer for such a question nor the general capabilities for generating one. The point of asking questions that are so far beyond the reach of the child's intellectual skills is to eliminate the influence of previous experience and knowledge. The experimenter seeks to obtain the tendencies of children's thinking in "pure" form entirely independent of learning.[1]

Similarly, the classics of psychological literature, such as the works by Binet and others, assume that development is always a prerequisite for learning and that if a child's mental functions (intellectual operations) have not matured to the extent that he is capable of learning a particular subject, then no instruction will prove useful. They especially feared premature instruction, the teaching of a subject before the child was ready for it. All effort was concentrated on finding the lower threshold of learning ability, the age at which a particular kind of learning first becomes possible.

Because this approach is based on the premise that learning trails behind development, that development always outruns learning, it precludes the notion that learning may play a role in the course of the development or maturation of those functions activated in the course of learning. Development or maturation is viewed as a precondition of learning but never the result of it. To summarize this position: learning forms a superstructure over development, leaving the latter essentially unaltered.

The second major theoretical position is that learning is development. This identity is the essence of a group of theories that are quite diverse in origin.

One such theory is based on the concept of reflex, an essentially old notion that has been extensively revived recently. Whether reading, writing, or arithmetic is being considered, development is viewed as the mastery of conditioned reflexes; that is, the process of learning is completely and inseparably blended with the process of development. This notion was elaborated by James, who reduced the learning process to habit formation and identified the learning process with development.

Reflex theories have at least one thing in common with theories such as Piaget's: in both, development is conceived of as the elaboration and substitution of innate responses. As James expressed it, "Education, in short, cannot be better described than by calling it the organization of acquired habits of conduct and tendencies to behavior."[2] Development itself is reduced primarily to the accumulation of all possible responses. Any acquired response is considered either a more complex form of or a substitute for the innate response.

But despite the similarity between the first and second theoretical positions, there is a major difference in their assumptions about the temporal relationship between learning and developmental processes. Theorists who hold the first view assert that developmental cycles precede learning cycles; maturation precedes learning and instruction must lag behind mental growth. For the second group of theorists, both processes occur simultaneously; learning and development coincide at all points in the same way that two identical geometrical figures coincide when superimposed.

The third theoretical position on the relation between learning and development attempts to overcome the extremes of the other two by simply combining them. A clear example of this approach is Koffka's theory, in which development is based on two inherently different but related processes, each of which influences the other.[3] On the one hand is maturation, which depends directly on the development of the nervous system; on the other hand is learning, which itself is also a developmental process.

Three aspects of this theory are new. First, as we already noted, is the combination of two seemingly opposite viewpoints, each of which has been encountered separately in the history of science. The very fact that these two viewpoints can be combined into one theory indicates that they are not opposing and mutually exclusive but have something essential in common. Also new is the idea that the two processes that make up development are mutually dependent and interactive. Of course, the nature of the interaction is left virtually unexplored in Koffka's work, which is limited solely to very general remarks regarding the relation between these two processes. It is clear that for Koffka the process of maturation prepares and makes possible a specific process of learning. The learning process then stimulates and pushes forward the maturation process. The third and most important new aspect of this theory is the expanded role it ascribes to learning in child development. This emphasis leads us directly to an old pedagogical problem, that of formal discipline and the problem of transfer.

Pedagogical movements that have emphasized formal discipline and urged the teaching of classical languages, ancient civilizations, and mathematics have assumed that regardless of the irrelevance of these particular subjects for daily living, they were of the greatest value for the pupil's mental development. A variety of studies have called into question the soundness of this idea. It has been shown that learning in one area has very little influence on overall development. For example, reflex theorists Woodworth and Thorndike found that adults who, after special exercises, had achieved considerable success in determining the length of short lines, had made virtually no progress in their ability to determine the length of long lines. These same adults were successfully trained to estimate the size of a given two-dimensional figure, but this training did not make them successful in estimating the size of a series of other two-dimensional figures of various sizes and shapes.

According to Thorndike, theoreticians in psychology and education believe that every particular response acquisition directly enhances overall ability in equal measure.[4] Teachers believed and acted on the basis of the theory that the mind is a complex of abilities—powers of observation, attention, memory, thinking, and so forth—and that any improvement in any specific ability results in a general improvement in all abilities. According to this theory, if the student increased the attention he paid to Latin grammar, he would increase his abilities to focus attention on any task. The words "accuracy," "quick-wittedness," "ability to reason," "memory," "power of observation," "attention," "concentration," and so forth are said to denote actual fundamental capabilities that vary in accordance with the material with which they operate; these basic abilities are substantially modified by studying particular subjects, and they retain these modifications when they turn to other areas. Therefore, if someone learns to do any single thing well, he will also be able to do other entirely unrelated things well as a result of some secret connection. It is assumed that mental capabilities function independently of the material with which they operate, and that the development of one ability entails the development of others.

Thorndike himself opposed this point of view. Through a variety of studies he showed that particular forms of activity, such as spelling, are dependent on the mastery of specific skills and material necessary for the performance of that particular task. The development of one particular capability seldom means the development of others. Thorndike argued that specialization of abilities is even greater than superficial observation may indicate. For example, if, out of a hundred individuals we choose ten who display the ability to detect spelling errors or to measure lengths, it is unlikely that these ten will display better abilities regarding, for example, the estimation of the weight of objects. In the same way, speed and accuracy in adding numbers are entirely unrelated to speed and accuracy in being able to think up antonyms.

This research shows that the mind is not a complex network of general capabilities such as observation, attention, memory, judgment, and so forth, but a set of specific capabilities, each of which is, to some extent, independent of the others and is developed independently. Learning is more than the acquisition of the ability to think; it is the acquisition of many specialized abilities for thinking about a variety of things. Learning does not alter our overall ability to focus attention but rather develops various abilities to focus attention on a variety of things. According to this view, special training affects overall development only when its elements, material, and processes are similar across specific domains; habit governs us. This leads to the conclusion that because each activity depends on the material with which it operates, the development of consciousness is the development of a set of particular, independent capabilities or of a set of particular habits. Improvement of one function of consciousness or one aspect of its activity can affect the development of another only to the extent that there are elements common to both functions or activities.

Developmental theorists such as Koffka and the Gestalt School—who hold to the third theoretical position outlined earlier—oppose Thorndike's point of view. They assert that the influence of learning is never specific. From their study of structural principles, they argue that the learning process can never be reduced simply to the formation of skills but embodies an intellectual order that makes it possible to transfer general principles discovered in solving one task to a variety of other tasks. From this point of view, the child, while learning a particular operation, acquires the ability to create structures of a certain type, regardless of the diverse materials with which she is working and regardless of the particular elements involved. Thus, Koffka does not conceive of learning as limited to a process of habit and skill acquisition. The relationship he posits between learning and development is not that of an identity but of a more complex relationship. According to Thorndike, learning and development coincide at all points, but for Koffka, development is always a larger set than learning. Schematically, the relationship between the two processes could be depicted by two concentric circles, the smaller symbolizing the learning process and the larger the developmental process evoked by learning.

Once a child has learned to perform an operation, he thus assimilates some structural principle whose sphere of application is other than just the operations of the type on whose basis the principle was assimilated. Consequently, in making one step in learning, a child makes two steps in development, that is, learning and development do not coincide. This concept is the essential aspect of the third group of theories we have discussed.

Zone of Proximal Development: A New Approach

Although we reject all three theoretical positions discussed above, analyzing them leads us to a more adequate view of the relation between learning and development. The question to be framed in arriving at a solution to this problem is complex. It consists of two separate issues: first, the general relation between learning and development; and second, the specific features of this relationship when children reach school age.

That children's learning begins long before they attend school is the starting point of this discussion. Any learning a child encounters in school always has a previous history. For example, children begin to study arithmetic in school, but long beforehand they have had some experience with quantity—they have had to deal with operations of division, addition, subtraction, and determination of size. Consequently, children have their own preschool arithmetic, which only myopic psychologists could ignore.

It goes without saying that learning as it occurs in the preschool years differs markedly from school learning, which is concerned with the assimilation of the fundamentals of scientific knowledge. But even when, in the period of her first questions, a child assimilates the names of objects in her environment, she is learning. Indeed, can it be doubted that children learn speech from adults; or that, through asking questions and giving answers, children acquire a variety of information; or that, through imitating adults and through being instructed about how to act, children develop an entire repository of skills? Learning and development are interrelated from the child's very first day of life.

Koffka, attempting to clarify the laws of child learning and their relation to mental development, concentrates his attention on the simplest learning processes, those that occur in the preschool years. His error is that, while seeing a similarity between preschool and school learning, he fails to discern the difference—he does not see the specifically new elements that school learning introduces. He and others assume that the difference between preschool and school learning consists of non-systematic learning in one case and systematic learning in the other. But "systematicness" is not the only issue; there is also the fact that school learning introduces something fundamentally new into the child's development. In order to elaborate the dimensions of school learning, we will describe a new and exceptionally important concept without which the issue cannot be resolved: the zone of proximal development.

A well known and empirically established fact is that learning should be matched in some manner with the child's developmental level. For example, it has been established that the teaching of reading, writing, and arithmetic should be initiated at a specific age level. Only recently, however, has attention been directed to the fact that we cannot limit ourselves merely to determining developmental levels if we wish to discover the actual relations of the developmental process to learning capabilities. We must determine at least two developmental levels.

The first level can be called the *actual developmental level*, that is, the level of development of a child's mental functions that has been established as a result of certain already completed developmental cycles. When we determine a child's mental age by using tests, we are almost always dealing with the actual developmental level. In studies of children's mental development it is generally assumed that only those things that children can do on their own are indicative of mental abilities. We give children a battery of tests or a variety of tasks of varying degrees of difficulty, and we judge the extent of their mental development on the basis of how they solve them and at what level of difficulty. On the other hand, if we offer leading questions or show how the problem is to be solved and the child then solves it, or if the teacher initiates the solution and the child completes it or solves it in collaboration with other children—in short, if the child barely misses an independent solution of the problem—the solution is not regarded as indicative of his mental development. This "truth" was familiar and reinforced by common sense. Over a decade even the profoundest thinkers never questioned the assumption; they never entertained the notion that what children can do with the assistance of others might be in some sense even more indicative of their mental development than what they can do alone.

Let us take a simple example. Suppose I investigate two children upon entrance into school, both of whom are ten years old chronologically and eight years old in terms of mental development. Can I say that they are the same age mentally? Of course. What does this mean? It means that they can independently deal with tasks up to the degree of difficulty that has been standardized for the eight-year-old level. If I stop at this point, people would imagine that the subsequent course of mental development and of school learning for these children will be the same, because it depends on their intellect. Of course, there may be other factors, for example, if one child was sick for half a year while the other was never absent from school; but generally speaking, the fate of these children should be the same. Now imagine that I do not terminate my study at this point, but only begin it. These children seem to be capable of handling problems up to an eight-year-old's level, but not beyond that. Suppose that I show them various ways of dealing with the problem. Different experimenters might employ different modes of demonstration in different cases: some might run through an entire demonstration and ask the children to repeat it, others might initiate the solution and ask the child to finish it, or offer leading questions. In short, in some way or another I propose that the children solve the problem with my assistance. Under these circumstances it turns out that the first child can deal with problems up to a twelve-year-old's level, the second up to a nine-year-old's. Now, are these children mentally the same?

When it was first shown that the capability of children with equal levels of mental development to learn under a teacher's guidance varied to a high degree, it became apparent that those children were not mentally the same age and that the subsequent course of their learning would obviously be different. This difference between twelve and eight, or between nine and eight, is what we call *the zone of proximal development. It is the distance between the actual developmental level as determined by independent problem solving and the level of potential development as determined through problem solving under adult guidance or in collaboration with more capable peers.*

If we naively ask what the actual developmental level is, or, to put it more simply, what more independent problem solving reveals, the most common answer would be that a child's actual developmental level defines functions that have already matured, that is, the end products of development. If a child can do such-and-such independently, it means that the functions for such-and-such have matured in her. What, then, is defined by the zone of proximal development, as determined through problems that children cannot solve independently but only with assistance? The zone of proximal development defines those functions that have not yet matured but are in the process of maturation, functions that will mature tomorrow but are currently in an embryonic state. These functions could be termed the "buds" or "flowers" of development rather than the "fruits" of development. The actual developmental level characterizes mental development retrospectively, while the zone of proximal development characterizes mental development prospectively.

The zone of proximal development furnishes psychologists and educators with a tool through which the internal course of development can be understood. By using this method we can take account of not only the cycles and maturation processes that have already been completed but also those processes that are currently in a state of formation, that are just beginning to mature and develop. Thus, the zone of proximal development permits us to delineate the child's immediate future and his dynamic develop-

mental state, allowing not only for what already has been achieved developmentally but also for what is in the course of maturing. The two children in our example displayed the same mental age from the viewpoint of developmental cycles already completed, but the developmental dynamics of the two were entirely different. The state of a child's mental development can be determined only by clarifying its two levels: the actual developmental level and the zone of proximal development.

I will discuss one study of preschool children to demonstrate that what is in the zone of proximal development today will be the actual developmental level tomorrow—that is, what a child can do with assistance today she will be able to do by herself tomorrow.

The American researcher Dorothea McCarthy showed that among children between the ages of three and five there are two groups of functions: those the children already possess, and those they can perform under guidance, in groups, and in collaboration with one another but which they have not mastered independently. McCarthy's study demonstrated that this second group of functions is at the actual developmental level of five-to-seven-year-olds. What her subjects could do only under guidance, in collaboration, and in groups at the age of three-to-five years they could do independently when they reached the age of five-to-seven years.[5] Thus, if we were to determine only mental age—that is, only functions that have matured—we would have but a summary of completed development while if we determine the maturing functions, we can predict what will happen to these children between five and seven, provided the same developmental conditions are maintained. The zone of proximal development can become a powerful concept in developmental research, one that can markedly enhance the effectiveness and utility of the application of diagnostics of mental development to educational problems.

A full understanding of the concept of the zone of proximal development must result in reevaluation of the role of imitation in learning. An unshakable tenet of classical psychology is that only the independent activity of children, not their imitative activity, indicates their level of mental development. This view is expressed in all current testing systems. In evaluating mental development, consideration is given to only those solutions to test problems which the child reaches without the assistance of others, without demonstrations, and without leading questions. Imitation and learning are thought of as purely mechanical processes. But recently psychologists have shown that a person can imitate only that which is within her developmental level. For example, if a child is having difficulty with a problem in arithmetic and the teacher solves it on the blackboard, the child may grasp the solution in an instant. But if the teacher were to solve a problem in higher mathematics, the child would not be able to understand the solution no matter how many times she imitated it.

Animal psychologists, and in particular Köhler, have dealt with this question of imitation quite well.[6] Köhler's experiments sought to determine whether primates are capable of graphic thought. The principal question was whether primates solved problems independently or whether they merely imitated solutions they had seen performed earlier, for example, watching other animals or humans use sticks and other tools and then imitating them. Köhler's special experiments, designed to determine what primates could imitate, reveal that primates can use imitation to solve only those problems that are of the same degree of difficulty as those they can solve alone. However, Köhler failed to take account of an important fact, namely, that primates cannot be taught (in the human sense of the word) through imitation, nor can their intellect be developed, because they have no zone of proximal development. A primate can learn a great deal through training by using its mechanical and mental skills, but it cannot be made more intelligent, that is, it cannot be taught to solve a variety of more advanced problems independently. For this reason animals are incapable of learning in the human sense of the term; *human learning presupposes a specific social nature and a process by which children grow into the intellectual life of those around them.*

Children can imitate a variety of actions that go well beyond the limits of their own capabilities. Using imitation, children are capable of doing much more in collective activity or under the guidance of adults. This fact, which seems to be of little significance in itself, is of fundamental importance in that it demands a radical alteration of the entire doctrine concerning the relation between learning and development in children. One direct consequence is a change in conclusions that may be drawn from diagnostic tests of development.

Formerly, it was believed that by using tests, we determine the mental development level with which education should reckon and whose limits it should not exceed. This procedure oriented learning toward yesterday's development, toward developmental stages already completed. The error of this view was discovered earlier in practice than in theory. It is demonstrated most clearly in the teaching of mentally retarded children. Studies have established that mentally retarded children are not very capable of abstract thinking. From this the pedagogy of the special school drew the seemingly correct conclusion that all teaching of such children should be based on the use of concrete, look-and-do methods. And yet a considerable amount of experience with this method resulted

in profound disillusionment. It turned out that a teaching system based solely on concreteness—one that eliminated from teaching everything associated with abstract thinking—not only failed to help retarded children overcome their innate handicaps but also reinforced their handicaps by accustoming children exclusively to concrete thinking and thus suppressing the rudiments of any abstract thought that such children still have. Precisely because retarded children, when left to themselves, will never achieve well-elaborated forms of abstract thought, the school should make every effort to push them in that direction and to develop in them what is intrinsically lacking in their own development. In the current practices of special schools for retarded children, we can observe a beneficial shift away from this concept of concreteness, one that restores look-and-do methods to their proper role. Concreteness is now seen as necessary and unavoidable only as a stepping stone for developing abstract thinking—as a means, not as an end in itself.

Similarly, in normal children, learning which is oriented toward developmental levels that have already been reached is ineffective from the viewpoint of a child's overall development. It does not aim for a new stage of the developmental process but rather lags behind this process. Thus, the notion of a zone of proximal development enables us to propound a new formula, namely that the only "good learning" is that which is in advance of development.

The acquisition of language can provide a paradigm for the entire problem of the relation between learning and development. Language arises initially as a means of communication between the child and the people in his environment. Only subsequently, upon conversion to internal speech, does it come to organize the child's thought, that is, become an internal mental function. Piaget and others have shown that reasoning occurs in a children's group as an argument intended to prove one's own point of view before it occurs as an internal activity whose distinctive feature is that the child begins to perceive and check the basis of his thoughts. Such observations prompted Piaget to conclude that communication produces the need for checking and confirming thoughts, a process that is characteristic of adult thought.[7] In the same way that internal speech and reflective thought arise from the interactions between the child and persons in her environment, these interactions provide the source of development of a child's voluntary behavior. Piaget has shown that cooperation provides the basis for the development of a child's moral judgment. Earlier research established that a child first becomes able to subordinate her behavior to rules in group play and only later does voluntary self-regulation of behavior arise as an internal function.

These individual examples illustrate a general developmental law for the higher mental functions that we feel can be applied in its entirety to children's learning processes. We propose that an essential feature of learning is that it creates the zone of proximal development; that is, learning awakens a variety of internal developmental processes that are able to operate only when the child is interacting with people in his environment and in cooperation with his peers. Once these processes are internalized, they become part of the child's independent developmental achievement.

From this point of view, learning is not development; however, properly organized learning results in mental development and sets in motion a variety of developmental processes that would be impossible apart from learning. Thus, learning is a necessary and universal aspect of the process of developing culturally organized, specifically human, psychological functions.

To summarize, the most essential feature of our hypothesis is the notion that developmental processes do not coincide with learning processes. Rather, the developmental process lags behind the learning process; this sequence then results in zones of proximal development. Our analysis alters the traditional view that at the moment a child assimilates the meaning of a word, or masters an operation such as addition or written language, her developmental processes are basically completed. In fact, they have only just begun at that moment. The major consequence of analyzing the educational process in this manner is to show that the initial mastery of, for example, the four arithmetic operations provides the basis for the subsequent development of a variety of highly complex internal processes in children's thinking.

Our hypothesis establishes the unity but not the identity of learning processes and internal developmental processes. It presupposes that the one is converted into the other. Therefore, it becomes an important concern of psychological research to show how external knowledge and abilities in children become internalized.

Any investigation explores some sphere of reality. An aim of the psychological analysis of development is to describe the internal relations of the intellectual processes awakened by school learning. In this respect, such analysis will be directed inward and is analogous to the use of x-rays. If successful, it should reveal to the teacher how developmental processes stimulated by the course of school learning are carried through inside the head of each individual child. The revelation of this internal, subterranean developmental network of school subjects is a task of primary importance for psychological and educational analysis.

A second essential feature of our hypothesis is the notion that, although learning is directly related to the course of child development, the two are never accomplished in equal measure or in parallel. Development in children never follows school learning the way a shadow follows the object that casts it. In actuality, there are highly complex dynamic relations between developmental and learning processes that cannot be encompassed by an unchanging hypothetical formulation.

Each school subject has its own specific relation to the course of child development, a relation that varies as the child goes from one stage to another. This leads us directly to a reexamination of the problem of formal discipline, that is, to the significance of each particular subject from the viewpoint of overall mental development. Clearly, the problem cannot be solved by using any one formula; extensive and highly diverse concrete research based on the concept of the zone of proximal development is necessary to resolve the issue.

NOTES

1. J. Piaget, *The Language and Thought of the Child* (New York: Meridian Books, 1955).
2. William James, *Talks to Teachers* (New York: Norton, 1958), pp. 36–37.
3. Koffka, *The Growth of the Mind* (London: Routledge and Kegan Paul, 1924).
4. E. L. Thorndike, *The Psychology of Learning* (New York: Teachers College Press, 1914).
5. Dorothea McCarthy, *The Language Development of the Pre-school Child* (Minneapolis: University of Minnesota Press, 1930).
6. W. Köhler, *The Mentality of Apes* (New York: Harcourt, Brace, 1925).
7. Piaget, *Language and Thought*.

QUESTIONS

1. For Vygotsky, are learning and development the same thing? How are they alike? How are they different?
2. Why was Vygotsky dissatisfied with Piaget's view of development?
3. What is the zone of proximal development? What role does it play in learning and what role does it play in cognitive development?

4. According to Vygotsky, can children imitate any actions they observe or are they limited in what they can imitate? Why was this of interest to Vygotsky?

5. If you were to design a new IQ test based on Vygotsky's idea of the zone of proximal development, what would it be like? How might a child's score on this test be useful in designing his lessons at school?

6. How does social and cultural experience become part of each individual's mental life?

5 Children of the Garden Island

Emmy E. Werner

Does exposure to problematic and stressful experiences in early life lead to the development of an unhealthy personality? Are some individuals more resilient than others to developmental difficulties such as birth complications or poverty?

The best technique available in developmental psychology for answering these questions is the longitudinal research design in which the same individuals are observed over time to determine if and how their early experiences relate to later development. A classic longitudinal study of the long term effects of early developmental difficulties was conducted on the Hawaiian island of Kauai by Emmy Werner and her colleagues. This study took place over a 30-year period and involved a group of approximately 700 individuals. Werner found that a number of children who had experiential barriers to healthy development were nevertheless resistant to these barriers and developed into healthy adults. Resilient children such as these challenge the traditional assumption that there is a simple and direct link between early experiences and later development.

Although this study was completed over 15 years ago (and therefore the children described here are well into middle age), it is regarded as one of the most important longitudinal studies in the field. It is a model of how to conduct research that truly studies the process of development. It also provides an explanation of development that stresses the role that the social context plays in development, as well as the flexibility of the human organism to these circumstances of growth.

In 1955, 698 infants on the Hawaiian island of Kauai became participants in a 30-year study that has shown how some individuals triumph over physical disadvantages and deprived childhoods.

Kauai, the Garden Island, lies at the northwest end of the Hawaiian chain, 100 miles and a half-hour flight from Honolulu. Its 555 square miles encompass mountains, cliffs, canyons, rain forests and sandy beaches washed by pounding surf. The first Polynesians who crossed the Pacific to settle there in the eighth century were charmed by its beauty, as were the generations of sojourners who visited there after Captain James Cook "discovered" the island in 1778.

The 45,000 inhabitants of Kauai are for the most part descendants of immigrants from Southeast Asia and Europe who came to the island to work on the sugar plantations with the hope of finding a better life for their children. Thanks to the islanders' unique spirit of cooperation, my colleagues Jessie M. Bierman and Fern E. French of the University of California at Berkeley, Ruth S. Smith, a clinical psychologist on Kauai, and I have been able to carry out a longitudinal study on Kauai that has lasted for more than three decades. The study has had two principal goals: to assess the long-term consequences of prenatal and perinatal stress and to document the effects of adverse early rearing conditions on children's physical, cognitive and psychosocial development.

The Kauai Longitudinal Study began at a time when the systematic examination of the development of children exposed to biological and psychosocial risk factors was still a bit of a rarity. Investigators attempted to reconstruct the events that led to physical or psychological problems by studying the history of individuals in whom such problems had already surfaced. This retrospective approach can create the impression that the outcome is inevitable, since it takes into account only the "casualties," not the "survivors."

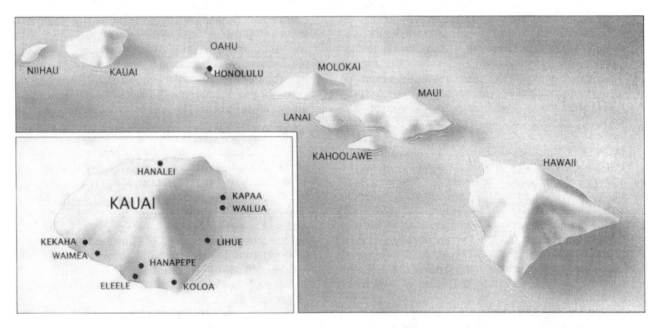

FIGURE 1

Kauai, the Garden Island, lies at the northwest end of the Hawaiian archipelago. The towns that participated in the Kauai Longitudinal Study are shown in the inset. Lihue is the county seat; it is about 100 miles from Honolulu, the capital of Hawaii.

We hoped to avoid that impression by monitoring the development of all the children born in a given period in an entire community.

We began our study in 1954 with an assessment of the reproductive histories of all the women in the community. Altogether 2,203 pregnancies were reported by the women of Kauai in 1954, 1955 and 1956; there were 240 fetal deaths and 1,963 live births. We chose to study the cohort of 698 infants born on Kauai in 1955, and we followed the development of these individuals at one, two, 10, 18 and 31 or 32 years of age. The majority of the individuals in the birth cohort—422 in all—were born without complications, following uneventful pregnancies, and grew up in supportive environments.

But as our study progressed we began to take a special interest in certain "high risk" children who, in spite of exposure to reproductive stress, discordant and impoverished home lives and uneducated, alcoholic or mentally disturbed parents, went on to develop healthy personalities, stable careers and strong interpersonal relations. We decided to try to identify the protective factors that contributed to the resilience of these children.

Finding a community that is willing or able to cooperate in such an effort is not an easy task. We chose Kauai for a number of reasons, not the least of which was the receptivity of the island population to our endeavors. Coverage by medical, public-health, educational and social services on the island was comparable to what one would find in communities of similar size on the U.S. mainland at that time. Furthermore, our study would take into account a variety of cultural influences on childbearing and child rearing, since the population of Kauai includes individuals of Japanese, Philipino, Portuguese, Chinese, Korean and northern European as well as of Hawaiian descent.

We also thought the population's low mobility would make it easier to keep track of the study's participants and their families. The promise of a stable sample proved to be justified. At the time of the two-year follow-up, 96 percent of the living children were still on Kauai and available for study. We were able to find 90 percent of the children who were still alive for the 10-year follow-up, and for the 18-year follow-up we found 88 percent of the cohort.

In order to elicit the cooperation of the island's residents, we needed to get to know them and to introduce our study as well. In doing so we relied on the skills of a number of dedicated professionals from the University of California's Berkeley and Davis campuses, from the University of Hawaii and from the island of Kauai itself. At the beginning of the study five nurses and one social worker, all residents of Kauai, took a census of all households on the island, listing the occupants of each dwelling and recording demographic information, including a reproductive history of all women 12 years old or older. The interviewers asked the women if they were pregnant; if a woman was not, a card with a postage-free envelope was left with the request that she mail it to the Kauai Department of Health as soon as she thought she was pregnant.

Local physicians were asked to submit a monthly list of the women who were coming to them for prenatal care. Community organizers spoke to women's groups, church gatherings, the county medical society and community leaders. The visits by the census takers were backed up with letters, and milk cartons were delivered with a printed message urging mothers to cooperate. We advertised in newspapers, organized radio talks, gave slide shows and distributed posters.

Public-health nurses interviewed the pregnant women who joined our study in each trimester of pregnancy, noting any exposure to physical or emotional trauma. Physicians monitored any complications during the prenatal period, labor, delivery and the neonatal period. Nurses and social workers interviewed the mothers in the postpartum period and when the children were one and 10 years old; the interactions between parents and offspring in the home were also observed. Pediatricians and psychologists independently examined the children at two and 10 years of age, assessing their physical, intellectual and social development and noting any handicaps or behavior problems. Teachers evaluated the children's academic progress and their behavior in the classroom.

From the outset of the study we recorded information about the material, intellectual and emotional aspects of the family environment, including stressful life events that resulted in discord or disruption of the family unit. With the parents' permission we also were given access to the records of public-health, educational and social-service agencies and to the files of the local police and the family court. My collaborators and I also administered a wide range of aptitude, achievement and personality tests in the elementary grades and in high school. Last but not least, we gained the perspectives of the young people themselves by interviewing them at the age of 18 and then again when they were in their early 30's.

Of the 698 children in the 1955 cohort, 69 were exposed to moderate prenatal or perinatal stress, that is, complications during pregnancy, labor or delivery. About 3 percent of the cohort—23 individuals in all—suffered severe prenatal or perinatal stress; only 14 infants in this group lived to the age of two. Indeed, nine of the 12 children in our study who died before reaching two years of age had suffered severe perinatal complications.

Some of the surviving children became "casualties" of a kind in the next two decades of life. One out of every six children (116 children in all) had physical or intellectual handicaps of perinatal or neonatal origin that were diagnosed between birth and the age of two and that required long-term specialized medical, educational or custodial care. About one out of every five children (142 in all) developed serious learning or behavior problems in the first decade of life that required more than six months of remedial work. By the time the children were 10 years old, twice as many children needed some form of mental-health service or remedial education (usually for problems associated with reading) as were in need of medical care.

By the age of 18, 15 percent of the young people had delinquency records and 10 percent had mental health problems requiring either in- or outpatient care. There was some overlap among these groups. By the time they were 10, all 25 of the children with long-term mental-health problems had learning problems as well. Of the 70 children who had mental health problems at 18, 15 also had a record of repeated delinquencies.

As we followed these children from birth to the age of 18 we noted two trends: the impact of reproductive stress diminished with time, and the developmental outcome of virtually every biological risk condition was dependent on the quality of the rearing environment. We did find some correlation between moderate to severe degrees of perinatal trauma and major physical handicaps of the central nervous system and of the musculo-skeletal and sensory systems; perinatal trauma was also correlated with mental retardation, serious learning disabilities and chronic mental-health problems such as schizophrenia that arose in late adolescence and young adulthood.

But overall rearing conditions were more powerful determinants of outcome than perinatal trauma. The better the quality of the home environment was, the more competence the children displayed. This could already be seen when the children were just two years old: toddlers who had experienced severe perinatal stress but lived in middle-class homes or in stable family settings did nearly as well on developmental tests of sensory-motor and verbal skills as toddlers who had experienced no such stress.

Prenatal and perinatal complications were consistently related to impairment of physical and psychological development at the ages of 10 and 18 only when they were combined with chronic poverty, family discord, parental mental illness or other persistently poor rearing conditions. Children who were raised in middle-class homes, in a stable family environment and by a mother who had finished high school showed few if any lasting effects of reproductive stress later in their lives.

How many children could count on such a favorable environment? A sizable minority could not. We designated 201 individuals—30 percent of the surviving

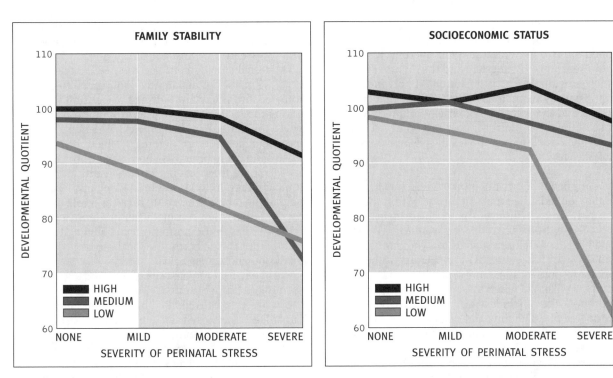

FIGURE 2

Influence of environmental factors such as family stability (left) or socioeconomic status (right) appears in infancy. The "developmental quotients" derived from tests given at 20 months show that the rearing environment can buffer or worsen the stress of perinatal complications. Children who had suffered severe perinatal stress but lived in stable, middle-class families scored as well as or better than children in poor, unstable households who had not experienced such stress.

children in this study population—as being high-risk children because they had experienced moderate to severe perinatal stress, grew up in chronic poverty, were reared by parents with no more than eight grades of formal education or lived in a family environment troubled by discord, divorce, parental alcoholism or mental illness. We termed the children "vulnerable" if they encountered four or more such risk factors before their second birthday. And indeed, two-thirds of these children (129 in all) did develop serious learning or behavior problems by the age of 10 or had delinquency records, mental-health problems or pregnancies by the time they were 18.

Yet one out of three of these high-risk children— 72 individuals altogether—grew into competent young adults who loved well, worked well and played well. None developed serious learning or behavior problems in childhood or adolescence. As far as we could tell from interviews and from their record in the community, they succeeded in school, managed home and social life well and set realistic educational and vocational goals and expectations for themselves when they finished high school. By the end of their second decade of life they had developed into competent, confident and caring people who expressed a

strong desire to take advantage of whatever opportunity came their way to improve themselves.

They were children such as Michael, a boy for whom the odds on paper did not seem very promising. The son of teen-age parents, Michael was born prematurely, weighing four pounds five ounces. He spent his first three weeks of life in a hospital, separated from his mother. Immediately after his birth his father was sent with the U.S. Army to Southeast Asia, where he remained for two years. By the time Michael was eight years old he had three siblings and his parents were divorced. His mother had deserted the family and had no further contact with her children. His father raised Michael and his siblings with the help of their aging grandparents.

Then there was Mary, born after 20 hours of labor to an overweight mother who had experienced several miscarriages before that pregnancy. Her father was an unskilled farm laborer with four years of formal education. Between Mary's fifth and 10th birthdays her mother was hospitalized several times for repeated bouts of mental illness, after having inflicted both physical and emotional abuse on her daughter.

Surprisingly, by the age of 18 both Michael and Mary were individuals with high self-esteem and sound values who cared about others and were liked by their peers. They were successful in school and looked forward to the future. We looked back at the lives of these two youngsters and the 70 other resilient individuals who had triumphed over their circumstances and compared their behavioral characteristics and the features of their environment with those of the other high-risk youths who developed serious and persistent problems in childhood and adolescence.

We identified a number of protective factors in the families, outside the family circle and within the resilient children themselves that enabled them to resist stress. Some sources of resilience seem to be constitutional: resilient children such as Mary and Michael tend to have characteristics of temperament that elicit positive responses from family members and strangers alike. We noted these same qualities in adulthood. They include a fairly high activity level, a low degree of excitability and distress and a high degree of sociability. Even as infants the resilient individuals were described by their parents as "active," "affectionate," "cuddly," "easygoing" and "even tempered." They had no eating or sleeping habits that were distressing to those who took care of them.

The pediatricians and psychologists who examined the resilient children at 20 months noted their alertness and responsiveness, their vigorous play and their tendency to seek out novel experiences and to ask for help when they needed it. When they entered elementary school, their classroom teachers observed their ability to concentrate on their assignments and noted their problem-solving and reading skills. Although they were not particularly gifted, these children used whatever talents they had effectively. Usually they had a special hobby they could share with a friend. These interests were not narrowly sex-typed; we found that girls and boys alike excelled at such activities as fishing, swimming, horseback riding and hula dancing.

We could also identify environmental factors that contributed to these children's ability to withstand stress. The resilient youngsters tended to come from families having four or fewer children, with a space of two years or more between themselves and the next sibling. In spite of poverty, family discord or parental mental illness, they had the opportunity to establish a close bond with at least one caretaker from whom they received positive attention during the first years of life.

The nurturing might come from substitute parents within the family (such as grandparents, older siblings, aunts or uncles) or from the ranks of regular baby-sitters. As the resilient children grew older they seemed to be particularly adept at recruiting such surrogate parents when a biological parent was unavailable (as in the case of an absent father) or incapacitated (as in the case of a mentally ill mother who was frequently hospitalized).

Maternal employment and the need to take care of younger siblings apparently contributed to the pronounced autonomy and sense of responsibility noted among the resilient girls, particularly in households where the father had died or was permanently absent because of desertion or divorce. Resilient boys, on the other hand, were often first-born sons who did not have to share their parents' attention with many additional children in the household. They also had some male in the family who could serve as a role model (if not the father, then a grandfather or an uncle). Structure and rules in the household and assigned chores were part of the daily routine for these boys during childhood and adolescence.

Resilient children also seemed to find a great deal of emotional support outside their immediate family. They tended to be well liked by their classmates and had at least one close friend, and usually several. They relied on an informal network of neighbors, peers and elders for counsel and support in times of crisis and transition. They seem to have made school a home away from home, a refuge from a disordered household. When we interviewed them at 18, many resilient youths mentioned a favorite teacher who had become a role model, friend and confidant and was particularly supportive at times when their own family was beset by discord or threatened with dissolution.

For others, emotional support came from a church group, a youth leader in the YMCA or YWCA or a favorite minister. Participation in extracurricular activities—such as 4-H, the school band or a cheerleading team which allowed them to be part of a cooperative enterprise—was also an important source of emotional support for those children who succeeded against the odds.

With the help of these support networks, the resilient children developed a sense of meaning in their lives and a belief that they could control their fate. Their experience in effectively coping with and mastering stressful life events built an attitude of hopefulness that contrasted starkly with the feelings of helplessness and futility that were expressed by their troubled peers.

In 1985, 12 years after the 1955 birth cohort had finished high school, we embarked on a search for the members of our study group. We managed to find 545 individuals—80 percent of the cohort—through parents or other relatives, friends, former classmates, local telephone books, city directories and circuit-court, voter-registration and motor-vehicle registration records and marriage certificates filed with the State Department of Health in Honolulu. Most of the young men and women still lived on Kauai, but 10 percent had moved to other islands and 10 percent lived on the mainland; 2 percent had gone abroad.

We found 62 of the 72 young people we had characterized as "resilient" at the age of 18. They had finished high school at the height of the energy crisis and joined the work force during the worst U.S. recession since the Great Depression. Yet these 30-year-old men and women seemed to be handling the demands of adulthood well. Three out of four (46 individuals) had received some college education and were satisfied with their performance in school. All but four worked full time, and three out of four said they were satisfied with their jobs.

Indeed, compared with their low-risk peers from the same cohort, a significantly higher proportion of high-risk resilient individuals described themselves as being happy with their current life circumstances (44 percent versus 10 percent). The resilient men and women did, however, report a significantly higher number of health problems than their peers in low-risk comparison groups (46 percent versus 15 percent). The men's problems seemed to be brought on by stress: back problems, dizziness and fainting spells, weight gain and ulcers. Women's health problems were largely related to pregnancy and childbirth. And although 82 percent of the women were married, only 48 percent of the men were. Those who were married had strong commitments to intimacy and sharing with their partners and children. Personal competence and determination, support from a spouse or mate, and a strong religious faith were the shared qualities that we found characterized resilient children as adults.

We were also pleasantly surprised to find that many high-risk children who had problems in their teens were able to rebound in their twenties and early thirties. We were able to contact 26 (90 percent) of the teen-age mothers, 56 (80 percent) of the individuals with mental-health problems and 74 (75 percent) of the former delinquents who were still alive at the age of 30.

Almost all the teen-age mothers we interviewed were better off in their early thirties than they had been at 18. About 60 percent (16 individuals) had gone on to additional schooling and about 90 percent (24 individuals) were employed. Of the delinquent youths, three-fourths (56 individuals) managed to avoid arrest on reaching adulthood. Only a minority (12 individuals) of the troubled youths were still in need of mental-health services in their early thirties. Among the critical turning points in the lives of these individuals were entry into military service, marriage, parenthood and active participation in a church group. In adulthood, as in their youth, most of these individuals relied on informal rather than formal sources of support: kith and kin rather than mental-health professionals and social-service agencies.

Our findings appear to provide a more hopeful perspective than can be had from reading the extensive literature on "problem" children that come to the attention of therapists, special educators and social-service agencies. Risk factors and stressful environments do not inevitably lead to poor adaptation. It seems clear that, at each stage in an individual's development from birth to maturity, there is a shifting balance between stressful events that heighten vulnerability and protective factors that enhance resilience.

As long as the balance between stressful life events and protective factors is favorable, successful adaptation is possible. When stressful events outweigh the protective factors, however, even the most resilient child can have problems. It may be possible to shift the balance from vulnerability to resilience through intervention, either by decreasing exposure to risk factors or stressful events or by increasing the number of protective factors and sources of support that are available.

It seems clear from our identification of risk and protective factors that some of the most critical determinants of outcome are present when a child is very young. And it is obvious that there are large individual differences among high-risk children in their responses to both negative and positive circumstances in their caregiving environment. The very fact of individual variation among children who live in adverse conditions suggests the need for greater assistance to some than to others.

If early intervention cannot be extended to every child at risk, priorities must be established for choosing who should receive help. Early-intervention programs need to focus on infants and young children who appear most vulnerable because they lack—permanently or temporarily—some of the essential social bonds that appear to buffer stress. Such children may be survivors of neonatal intensive care, hospitalized children who are separated from their families for extended periods of time, the young offspring of addicted or mentally ill parents, infants and toddlers whose mothers work full time and do not have access to stable child care, the babies of single or teen-age parents who have no other adult in the household and migrant and refugee children without permanent roots in a community.

Assessment and diagnosis, the initial steps in any early intervention, need to focus not only on the risk factors in the lives of the children but also on the protective factors. These include competencies and informal sources of support that already exist and that can be utilized to enlarge a young child's communication and problem-solving skills and to enhance his or her self-esteem. Our research on resilient children has shown that other people in a child's life—grandparents, older siblings, day-care providers or teachers—can play a supportive role if a parent is incapacitated or unavailable. In many situations it might make better sense and be less costly as well to strengthen such available informal ties to kin and community than it would to introduce additional layers of bureaucracy into delivery of services.

Finally, in order for any intervention program to be effective, a young child needs enough consistent nurturing to trust in its availability. The resilient children in our study had at least one person in their lives who accepted them unconditionally, regardless of temperamental idiosyncracies or physical or mental handicaps. All children can be helped to become more resilient if adults in their lives encourage their independence, teach them appropriate communication and self-help skills and model as well as reward acts of helpfulness and caring.

Thanks to the efforts of many people, several community-action and educational programs for high-risk children have been established on Kauai since our study began. Partly as a result of our findings, the legislature of the State of Hawaii has funded special mental-health teams to provide services for troubled children and youths. In addition the State Health Department established the Kauai Children's Services, a coordinated effort to provide services related to child development, disabilities, mental retardation and rehabilitation in a single facility.

The evaluation of such intervention programs can in turn illuminate the process by which a chain of protective factors is forged that affords vulnerable children an escape from adversity. The life stories of the resilient individuals on the Garden Island have taught us that competence, confidence and caring can flourish even under adverse circumstances if young children encounter people in their lives who provide them with a secure basis for the development of trust, autonomy and initiative.

FURTHER READING

Kauai's Children Come of Age. Emmy E. Werner and Ruth S. Smith. The University of Hawaii Press, 1977.

Vulnerable But Invincible: A Longitudinal Study of Resilient Children and Youth. Emmy E. Werner and Ruth S. Smith. McGraw-Hill Book Company, 1982.

Longitudinal Studies in Child Psychology and Psychiatry: Practical Lessons from Research Experience. Edited by A. R. Nichol. John Wiley & Sons, Inc., 1985.

High Risk Children in Young Adulthood: A Longitudinal Study from Birth to 32 Years. Emmy E. Werner in *American Journal of Orthopsychiatry*, Vol. 59, No. 1, pages 72–81; January, 1989.

QUESTIONS

1. What does it mean to say that children are at risk for healthy development?
2. Why is longitudinal research important for studying resilience in children?
3. What types of protective factors contribute to a favorable environment for child development?
4. In this research, did all the high-risk children who had problems in their teens end up with difficulties in adulthood? Why or why not?
5. What do these findings suggest about the long-term prognosis for children or adolescents who are identified as high risk?
6. Do you think that intervention programs in the schools or the community for children or adolescents who are at risk are worthwhile? Based on this study, what ingredients should they have?

PART I

In the Beginning

The introductory section emphasized the social and cultural contributions to development. In Part I, the biological contributions are highlighted. Just as the last decade has witnessed a revolution in the understanding of the role of social and cultural experience in human development, it has also seen a dramatic change in the ways in which biological contributions are understood. Much of this change has been based on progress in two areas of research, neuroscience and behavioral genetics.

One of the most important contributions to developmental study that has emerged from neuroscience is a better understanding of neural plasticity, discussed in the article by Nelson. Behavioral genetics has redefined understanding of human development by reexamining in sophisticated and measurable ways the classic question of nature versus nurture. This field has been aided by advances in the biological study of genetics, as well as by unique family arrangements resulting from fertility procedures and adoption, which are discussed in the article by Segal.

In addition to progress in these two areas of research, there has also been significant progress in understanding the competencies and character of newborns and infants. The article by DeCasper and Fifer illustrates how competent newborns are in the sensory domain, and the articles by Brazelton, Koslowski, and Tronick and by Kagan discuss the organization and role of temperament in early life.

Together, these articles describe the rich biological template that is instrumental to the course of human development.

6 Neural Plasticity and Human Development

CHARLES A. NELSON[1]

The human brain is an incredible organ. It works all the time, controlling or directing both conscious thought and automatic systems, and it keeps working even while we sleep. Because the brain is so complex and because it is designed to adapt to circumstances, it takes time to develop. A relatively new field of psychology, developmental neuroscience, has introduced an important dimension to the way in which we understand brain development.

Neuroscience is the study of brain anatomy and physiology at the neural level, and developmental neuroscience studies how the neural system changes. Developmental psychologists are especially interested in neuroscience research that examines brain plasticity. Plasticity, which is a characteristic of the mammalian brain, is the ability to be shaped by the environment. Thus, as the brain interacts with the world, changes occur. However, these changes are not willy-nilly; they are defined by the structure and the properties of the brain itself. The relation between the intrinsic properties of the brain and the extrinsic experiences that humans have is dynamic. That is, these forces, the internal and the external, inform one another, and in so doing, the course of development is defined.

Brain plasticity is an important part of the larger picture of human development as a process nested in and shaped by social and cultural experiences. Plasticity allows brain functions to be organized in a variety of ways, depending on the experiences that individuals have over the course of development. The human brain can develop along a variety of paths, especially early in development. This suggests that variability is a feature of the normal developmental process. This article by Charles A. Nelson describes how neural plasticity is part of human brain development. As you will see, this research raises new questions about what is meant when something is described as "innate" or "genetic."

In this article, I argue that experience-induced changes in the brain may be a useful way of viewing the course of human development. Work from the neurosciences supports the claim that most of the behavioral phenomena of interest to psychologists (e.g., cognition, perception, language, emotion) are instantiated by the process of neural plasticity. When development is viewed in this manner, the fallaciousness of the long-standing and often contentious debate over nature versus nurture becomes apparent. Moreover, by utilizing the neuroscientific tools used to examine the effects of experience on brain and behavioral development (e.g., functional neuroimaging), we may improve how we conceptualize our notions of intervention, competence, and resilience.

Neural plasticity can best be thought of as the subtle but orchestrated dance that occurs between the brain and the environment; specifically, it is the ability of the brain to be shaped by experience and, in turn, for this newly remolded brain to facilitate the embrace of new experiences, which leads to further neural changes, *ad infinitum*. As a rule, there are three mechanisms by which experience induces changes in

Reprinted with permission of Blackwell Publishers from *Current Directions in Psychological Science*, vol. 8, pp. 42–45.

Institute of Child Development and Department of Pediatrics, University of Minnesota, Minneapolis, Minnesota.
Acknowledgments The writing of this essay was made possible by a grant to the author from the John D. and Catherine T. MacArthur Foundation and the J. S. McDonnell Foundation, through their support of their research network on Early Experience and Brain Development. The author wishes to thank Floyd Bloom, John Bruer, and Richard Weinberg for their helpful comments on an earlier draft of this article.

the brain. An *anatomical* change might be the ability of existing synapses (i.e., connections between nerve cells) to modify their activity by sprouting new axons or by expanding the dendritic surface. A *neurochemical* change might be reflected in the ability of an existing synapse to modify its activity by increasing synthesis and release of chemicals that transmit nerve impulses (i.e., neurotransmitters). Finally, an example of a *metabolic* change might be the fluctuations in metabolic activity (e.g., use of glucose or oxygen) in the brain in response to experience.

All of these changes can occur at virtually any point in the life cycle, although to varying degrees of success. For example, some domains of behavior can be acquired only during a sensitive or critical period. Examples include song learning in the Zebra finch, social imprinting[2] in some mammals, and the development of binocular vision (for discussion, see Knudsen, 1999). Other behaviors, such as learning and memory, depend less on experience occurring at a particular point in development, and thus occur throughout the life span (see Nelson, in press). Regardless of whether there is or is not a critical period, experience is responsible for the changes that occur in the brain, which in turn determines the behavioral profile and development of the organism. Alas, this malleability is a two-edged sword, in that such changes can be both adaptive and maladaptive for the organism.

MALADAPTIVE CHANGES

Let us begin with the bad news, which is that the wrong experiences can have deleterious effects on the brain. Perhaps the clearest example concerns the effects of stress on the developing and developed brain. Rats exposed to stress pre- or postnatally show a wide range of changes in the brain's serotonin, catecholamine, and opiate systems.[3] Similarly, rats raised in social isolation make more learning errors than socially raised rats. Finally, brief maternal deprivation in the rat pup can alter the sensitivity of the hypothalamic pituitary adrenal (HPA) axis (see Black, Jones, Nelson, & Greenough, 1998, for review), thereby potentially altering the animal's ability to regulate and mount a behavioral response to threat.

Similarly, pregnant Rhesus monkeys exposed to different stressors at different points in time give birth to offspring that show seemingly permanent neurobehavioral changes. For example, at the cognitive level, the achievement of object permanence (the concept that objects out of sight continue to exist) can be delayed, and performance on tests of explicit memory[4] can be impaired. At the behavioral level, these animals display long-lasting changes in their ability to control their emotional state (see Schneider, in press).

The effects of prenatal exposure to stress are not limited to the rat or monkey. For example, Lou et al. (1994) reported that stress during pregnancy affected the head circumference of human newborns. (Head circumference is a coarse measure of brain growth.) In addition, prenatal stress was related to less than optimal outcome in the newborn period. As researchers have hypothesized for the rat and monkey, Lou et al. speculated that the effects of maternal stress on fetal brain development might be mediated by stress hormones (glucocorticoids) circulating in the bloodstream. A similar mechanism has been proposed to account for the observation that adults who have survived abuse as children show reduced volume of the hippocampus (a brain structure important for explicit memory) and, correspondingly, impairments on memory tasks. In this case, glucocorticoids act toxically on the hippocampus, which is well endowed with glucocorticoid receptors (see McEwen & Sapolsky, 1995).

Overall, there is clear evidence that early or late exposure to stress can deleteriously affect a range of brain systems, and thus a range of behaviors. In this context, one may view stress as something akin to a psychological lesion that exerts its effects to varying degrees depending on what system is targeted, the age of the organism when the stress occurred, and whether there are protective or exacerbating factors that can moderate the effects.

ADAPTIVE CHANGES

Having begun with the bad news, let us now turn to the good news, which is that being exposed to the "right" experiences can have beneficial effects on brain and behavior. Greenough and his colleagues have demonstrated that rats raised in complex environments (e.g., those filled with lots of toys and other rats) perform better than rats reared in normal laboratory cages on a variety of cognitive tasks (see Greenough & Black, 1992, for review). Correspondingly, the brains of these rats show improved synaptic contacts, and a greater number of dendritic spines. Even more impressive changes are observed in perceptual-motor tasks. For example, Black and Greenough (see Black et al., 1998) required rats to learn complex motor coordination tasks and found the rats developed more synapses within the cerebellum, a brain structure important for performance of such tasks. Kleim, Vij, Ballard, and Greenough (1997) demonstrated that these changes can be long lasting.

Reorganization of the brain based on selective experience is not limited to the rat. For example, Mühlnickel, Elbert, Taub, and Flor (1998) have reported that adults suffering from tinnitus (ringing in the ears) show a dramatic reorganization of the region of the cortex that deals with hearing. This same group (Elbert, Pantev, Wienbruch, Rockstroh, & Taub, 1995) has also shown that in musicians who play string instruments, the region of the somatosensory cortex (the region of the brain that subserves the sense of touch) that represents the fingers of the left hand (the hand requiring greater fine-motor learning) is larger than the area that represents the right hand (which is used to bow), and larger than the left-hand area in nonmusicians. Finally, Ramachandran, Rogers-Ramachandran, and Stewart (1992) have observed similar findings in patients who have experienced limb amputation. The region of the somatosensory cortex that sits adjacent to the region previously representing the missing limb encroaches on this area. This, in turn, may account for why patients experience sensation in the missing limb (e.g., the forearm) when this new area (e.g., that representing the cheek) is stimulated (Ramachandran et al., 1992). Collectively, this work suggests that the adult human cortex can be reorganized based on experiences that occur relatively late in life.

What of plasticity during childhood? Tallal and Merzenich (Merzenich et al., 1996; Tallal et al., 1996) have speculated that in some children, difficulty in parsing ongoing speech into sound segments leads to difficulty discriminating speech sounds. These authors have reported improvements in both speech discrimination and language comprehension when such children are given intensive training in speech processing. Although the brains of these children were not examined, presumably changes at the level of the auditory-thalamo-cortical pathway were modified by this experience.

These are but a few examples of how the brain is modified by experience; many others, in various domains of functioning, and at various points in development, could be provided. This is not to say, however, that experience-induced changes are possible in all domains of behavior at all points in time. For example, there is evidence from studies of deprivation that children not exposed to normal caretaking environments during their first few years of life may suffer long-lasting changes in their socioemotional functioning (although some individuals show sparing or recovery of function that is quite remarkable). Similarly, we have known for many years that being able to see with only one eye in the first few years of life yields intractable deficits in binocular depth perception, and that prolonged linguistic deprivation yields similarly intractable long-term deficits in language, speech perception, or both. Even these cases, however, speak to the importance of experience, as without normative experiences normal development goes awry.

IMPLICATIONS OF WORK ON NEURAL PLASTICITY FOR BEHAVIORAL DEVELOPMENT

The foregoing observations suggest that the "innate"-versus-"learned" debate is fallacious. An example from the literature on face perception illustrates this point (some aspects of language development may be another example). Some investigators have argued that face recognition is innate, by which they (presumably) mean that it develops without benefit of experience. However, we know that infants come into contact with faces as soon as they are born. Thus, it seems just as reasonable to argue that experience drives the development of the neural tissue (perhaps selected by evolutionary pressures, given the importance of face recognition in survival) that takes on this function and that this tissue becomes specialized rather quickly. (The brain structures responsible for face recognition in the adult are in the right temporal cortex and include the fusiform gyrus.) This process would allow the ability to recognize faces to appear early in development, but this is not the same thing as saying this ability is innate *qua* innate. Conversely, to argue that face recognition is "learned" does not do justice to the fact that such learning by default necessitates changes in the brain, which in turn alter which genes are expressed (i.e., activated). Even if one argues that an ability is "genetic" (although proving such a case would seem insurmountable without benefit of being able to specify the genes), gene expression is influenced by experience, and once experience occurs, the brain is altered, which in turn alters gene expression, and so on and so forth.

What are the practical implications of the approach I am advocating? Two come to mind. The first pertains to intervention. By understanding precisely how the brain is modified by experience, we can better identify the experiences needed to bring children back on a normal developmental trajectory, or prevent them from moving off this trajectory. In addition, we can target our interventions more judiciously, rather than targeting the whole child. Finally, using the tools of the neuroscientist, we may be able to examine the brain before and after an intervention, and in so doing better determine where in the nervous system change occurred. For example, if damage to the auditory-thalamo-cortical pathway appears to be responsible for some language-learning disorders, might noninvasive procedures such as event-related potentials (electrical activity generated by the brain in response to discretely presented events) or functional magnetic resonance imaging be used to (a) confirm or disconfirm this hypothesis and (b) evaluate the effectiveness (or lack thereof) of a given intervention and its effects on brain structure and function (see Nelson & Bloom, 1997)?

A second implication of the perspective advocated in this essay pertains to our understanding of competence and resilience. As work by Masten and Garmezy (Masten et al., in press) has shown, not all children reared in suboptimal conditions (including those at significant risk for psychopathology) move off a normal trajectory. Similarly, not all children who suffer frank brain damage experience disastrous outcomes. And, in both cases, many of those who do fall off a normal trajectory show some recovery—even considerable recovery in some instances. Might we view those children who are otherwise at risk but do not show any deleterious effects as an example of neural sparing, and those who show some deficits followed by a return to a normal trajectory as an example of recovery of function? If so, can we identify how the brains of these children incorporated experience differently than the brains of children who show no sparing or recovery of function? And can we evaluate these changes using the latest tools from the neurosciences?

CONCLUSIONS

It is indisputable that some aspects of pre- and postnatal human development have their origin in the expression of genetic scripts conserved through evolution and expressed at key points in development. One example may be the prenatal expression of the genes that regulate the formation of body parts (i.e., homeotic genes); another may be the postnatal expression of genes (not yet identified) that lead to the cascade of hormonal changes that usher in puberty. Even in these cases, of course, experience may influence the outcome; for example, the presence of teratogens may corrupt the influence of the homeotic genes (e.g., thalidomide can cause limb deformities), and culture or other experiences can influence pubertal timing. These examples notwithstanding, the changes in behavior that occur over time and that are of most interest to behavioral scientists (e.g., changes in perception, cognition, social-emotional behavior) are likely mediated by experientially induced changes in the nervous system. Thus, it may serve us well to rethink how the brain develops and changes across the life span by considering the important role of experience in sculpting neural systems. In so doing, we may be able to shed some of the contentious history that has plagued our discipline for years (e.g., nature vs. nurture; innate vs. learned), and embrace new theoretical and empirical approaches to human development and brain function.

RECOMMENDED READING

Black, J. E., Jones, T. A., Nelson, C. A., & Greenough, W. T. (1998). (See References)

Greenough, W. T., & Black, J. E. (1992). (See References)

Kolb, B., Forgie, M., Gibb, R., Gorny, G., & Rowntree, S. (1998). Age, experience, and the changing brain. *Neuroscience and Biobehavioral Reviews, 22,* 143–159.

Nelson, C. A. (in press). The neurobiological bases of early intervention. In J. P. Shonkoff & S. J. Meisels (Eds.), *Handbook of early childhood intervention* (2nd ed.). New York: Cambridge University Press.

Nelson, C. A., & Bloom, F. E. (1997). (See References)

NOTES

1. Address correspondence to Charles A. Nelson, Institute of Child Development, University of Minnesota, 51 East River Rd., Minneapolis, MN 55455; e-mail: canelson@ tc.umn.edu
2. Social imprinting is the process by which an animal forms a relationship of some kind to another animal, such as the famous case of the ducklings that followed Konrad Lorenz around.
3. Serotonin and catecholamines are neurotransmitters that play a role in social and emotional behavior. The natural opiates produced by the body can induce feelings of euphoria or well-being.
4. Explicit memory is a form of memory that can be stated explicitly or declared, that can be brought to mind as an image or proposition in the absence of ongoing perceptual support, or of which one is consciously aware.

REFERENCES

Black, J. E., Jones, T. A., Nelson, C. A., & Greenough, W. T. (1998). Neuronal plasticity and the developing brain. In N. E. Alessi, J. T. Coyle, S. I. Harrison, & S. Eth. (Eds.), *Handbook of child and adolescent psychiatry: Vol. 6. Basic psychiatric science and treatment* (pp. 31–53). New York: John Wiley & Sons.

Elbert, T., Pantev, C., Wienbruch, C., Rockstroh, B., & Taub, E. (1995). Increased cortical representation of the fingers of the left hand in string players. *Science, 270,* 305–307.

Greenough, W. T., & Black, J. E. (1992). Induction of brain structure by experience: Substrates for cognitive development. In M. R. Gunnar & C. A. Nelson (Eds.), *Developmental behavioral neuroscience* (Minnesota Symposia on Child Psychology, Vol. 24, pp. 155–200). Hillsdale, NJ: Erlbaum.

Kleim, J. A., Vij, K., Ballard, D. H., & Greenough, W. T. (1997). Learning-dependent synaptic modifications in the cerebellar cortex of the adult rat persist for at least four weeks. *Journal of Neuroscience, 17,* 717–721.

Knudsen, E. I. (1999). Early experience and critical periods. In M. J. Zigmond, F. E. Bloom, S. C. Landis, J. L. Roberts, & L. R. Squire (Eds.), *Fundamental neuroscience* (pp. 637–654). New York: Academic Press.

Lou, H. C., Hansen, D., Nordentoft, M., Pryds, O., Jensen, F., Nim, J., & Hemmingsen, R. (1994). Prenatal stressors of human life affect fetal brain development. *Developmental Medicine and Child Neurology, 36,* 826–832.

Masten, A. S., Hubbard, J. J., Gest, S. D., Tellegen, A., Garmezy, N., & Ramirez, M. (in press). Adaptation in the context of adversity: Pathways to resilience and maladaption from childhood to late adolescence. *Development and Psychopathology.*

McEwen, B. S., & Sapolsky, R. M. (1995). Stress and cognitive function. *Current Opinion in Neurobiology, 5,* 205–216.

Merzenich, M. M., Jenkins, W. M., Johnston, P., Schreiner, C., Miller, S. L., & Tallal, P. (1996). Temporal processing deficits of language-learning impaired children ameliorated by training. *Science, 271,* 77–81.

Mühlnickel, W., Elbert, T., Taub, E., & Flor, H. (1998). Reorganization of auditory cortex in tinnitus. *Proceedings of the National Academy of Sciences, USA, 95,* 10340–10343.

Nelson, C. A. (in press). Neural plasticity and human development: The role of early experience in sculpting memory systems. *Developmental Science.*

Nelson, C. A., & Bloom, F. E. (1997). Child development and neuroscience. *Child Development, 68,* 970–987.

Ramachandran, V. S., Rogers-Ramachandran, D., & Stewart, M. (1992). Perceptual correlates of massive cortical reorganization. *Science, 258,* 1159–1160.

Schneider, M. L. (in press). Effect of prenatal stress on development: A nonhuman primate model. In C. A. Nelson (Ed.), *The effects of early adversity on neurobehavioral development* (Minnesota Symposia on Child Psychology, Vol. 31). Mahwah, NJ: Erlbaum.

Tallal, P., Miller, S. L., Bedi, G., Byma, G., Wang, X., Nagarajan, S. S., Schreiner, C., Jenkins, W. M., & Merzenich, M. M. (1996). Language comprehension in language-learning impaired children improved with acoustically modified speech. *Science, 271,* 81–84.

QUESTIONS

1. What are the three mechanisms by which experience can induce change in the brain?
2. What does research on the effect of stress on brain development conclude?
3. How do enriched environments affect brain development?
4. Why is Nelson critical of the word "innate" when describing infant face perception?
5. Developmental neuroscientists argue that there is no aspect of development that can be said to be strictly genetic, that is, that a behavior is solely a product of information contained in a gene. How do findings in neural plasticity lend support to this claim?
6. In what ways does brain plasticity shed light on the issue of resilience in children to deleterious experiences?

7 Behavioral Aspects of Intergenerational Cloning: What Twins Tell Us

NANCY L. SEGAL*

In 1996 an adult sheep named Dolly was cloned. Scientific reaction to this was mostly positive. A long-anticipated accomplishment had finally occurred. The public reaction was mixed, however. Many people worried about what this might mean for the cloning of human beings. In response to these concerns, a report by the National Bioethics Advisory Commission was published in 1997. This report raised many questions similar to those that developmental psychologists raise about the relative contributions of nature and nurture to human development.

In the following article, Nancy L. Segal, a developmental psychologist who studies twins, addresses many of the concerns raised in the report. She describes research involving twins and other forms of sibling relationships that have resulted from innovative fertility techniques and adoption procedures. Her response to the report raises important questions about what cloning human beings actually means. It also explains several of the ways in which research with twins has given us a better sense of how genes and the environment interact to shape development.

While reading this article, you are very likely to come across arrangements of twinning and families that you have never heard of before. These new family settings provide developmental psychologists with natural laboratories for studying one of the oldest and most difficult questions in the field: How do nature and nurture work together to produce human development?

The 1996 cloning of an adult sheep transformed the prospect of adult human cloning from vague uncertainty to real possibility.[1] This landmark event forces a hard look at scientific, religious, ethical, and legal questions that would inevitably arise should this procedure prove viable at the human level. Members of the National Bioethics Advisory Commission (NBAC or Commission) have provided an invaluable service in bringing these issues to the fore, with full realization that anticipating the details and nuances of each and every issue is an impossibility.[2]

Discussion of behavioral aspects of intergenerational cloning would benefit substantially from reference to the rich psychological literature on experiential aspects of twinning. Researchers representing diverse theoretical and methodological approaches have undertaken analyses of the unique social features of monozygotic (MZ or identical) twins, and experiential differences between MZ and dizygotic (DZ or fraternal) twins.[3] Discussion of human cloning would also benefit from reference to the wealth of twin, family, and adoption studies of human behav-

---

*Nancy L. Segal is Professor of Psychology and Director of the Twin Studies Center at California State University, Fullerton. A fellow of the American Psychological Association and American Psychological Society, she has written extensively on psychological and legal issues involving twins and multiple birth families. Direct correspondence to Nancy L. Segal, Psychology Department, 800 N. State College Boulevard, Fullerton, CA 92834, 714-278-2142.

1. *See* Ian Wilmut et al., *Viable Offspring Derived from Fetal and Adult Mammalian Cells*, 385 Nature 810 (1997).
2. *See* Cloning Human Beings: Report and Recommendations of the National Bioethics Advisory Commission (1997) [hereinafter NBAC Report].
3. John C. Loehlin & Robert C. Nichols, Heredity, Environment, and Personality: A Study of 850 Sets of Twins (1976); Mari Siemon, *The Separation-Individuation Process in Adult Twins*, 34 Am J. Psychotherapy 387 (1980): Charles B. Crawford &

ioral variation. These investigations of genetic and environmental influences on individual differences in intellectual abilities, personality traits, and physical measures offer insights into average expected resemblance between relatives.

Closer inspection of twin research findings does not provide the last word on the human cloning debate. However, this body of work can sharpen our thinking on behavioral issues, which Commission members currently regard as speculative, and clarify some statements in the NBAC report.

I. WHO IS A TWIN?

I have avoided using the term "'*delayed' genetic twin*," the label chosen by the Commission to refer to individuals resulting from cloning procedures.[4] I prefer to substitute the term *intergenerational clone* (IGC) because of its greater accuracy as a referent to these individuals. Surprisingly, the Commission's report omitted the term *twin* from the glossary.[5] Understanding the concept of twinning is requisite to an informed discussion of behavioral features associated with IGCs, especially because some arguments the Commission presented against IGCs rested on suppositions concerning human identical twins.[6]

Identical twins are clones, but clones are not identical twins. A clone, as defined in the glossary of the Report, is "a precise copy of a molecule, cell, or individual plant or animal."[7] Identical human twins fit this definition, having split from a single fertilized egg, or zygote, within the first 14 days following conception.[8] Barring rare errors in early cell division, identical twins are genetically the same, so any physical or behavioral differences between them, such as in fetal size, in childhood IQ, or in adult personality are nongenetic in origin. However, clones are not identical twins for several reasons: (1) identical twins originate at the same time; (2) identical twins share intrauterine environments;[9] (3) identical twins are born at the

same time, thereby sharing familial and cultural events. Of course, there are variations on these features of twinship, such as prenatal death of one twin or separate rearing of twins from early infancy. However, these events do not interfere with the multiple birth status of the individuals in question because these events follow natural twinning processes. IGCs are not characterized by any of the three features listed above and so while they do generate a novel "twin-like" relationship, they are not strictly classifiable as twins. The hypothetical situation of cloning a child to serve as a blood marrow donor for a terminally ill child would *not* create "identical twins of different ages,"[10] but would create individuals who are genetically the same, i.e., IGCs.

Multiple birth families, especially families who have both twin and non-twin children, are uniquely sensitive to subtle and more apparent defining features of twinship. The nature of parents' responses to a groundbreaking medical event (as communicated to me personally) bear significantly upon conceptions of twinning. In 1988, the world witnessed the first successful birth of three infants born 21 months apart at the AMI South Bay Hospital in Redondo Beach, California.[11] A couple underwent fertility treatment involving retrieval and fertilization of ten eggs, four of which were implanted in the mother's uterus, yielding one successful birth. The remaining embryos were frozen and later implanted, resulting in the birth of twin daughters. The three infants were described as *triplets* because of their common date of origin, but members of a mothers of twins organization took considerable exception to this classification. They based their negative response on the infants' different intrauterine environments and the infants' different chronological ages, despite their simultaneous conception. Of course, the elder sibling and younger twins share the same genetic relationship as fraternal twins and full siblings (half their genes on average, by descent), but their prenatal and postnatal circumstances are at odds with those of twins. Given their

---

Judith L. Anderson. *Sociobiology: An Environmentalist Discipline?*, 44 Am. Psychologist 1449 (1989); Nancy L. Segal, *Twin, Sibling, and Adoption Methods: Tests of Evolutionary Hypotheses*, 48 Am. Psychologist 943 (1993); Nancy L. Segal, *Twin Research Perspective on Human Development, in* Uniting Psychology and Biology: Integrative Perspectives on Human Development 145 (N.L. Segal et al. eds., 1997) [hereinafter Segal, *Twin Research Perspective on Human Development*].

4. *See, e.g.,* NBAC Report, *supra* note 2, at i.

5. *See id.* at App.

6. *See, e.g., id.* at 67–68.

7. *Id.* at App.

8. Elizabeth M. Bryan, The Nature and Nurture of Twins 15 (1983).

9. Identical twins' common intrauterine environments can differ greatly, due to unequal blood circulation, fetal crowding, or other factors. It is a common misconception that prenatal factors contribute to identical twins' similarity in physical and behavioral traits. In fact, given the differing prenatal circumstances of some identical twins it is remarkable that they are as alike as they are, a finding most likely associated with their shared genes.

10. NBAC Report, *supra* note 2, at 80.

11. Rowland Company (Media), Nation's First Triplets Born 21 Months Apart Announces AMI South Bay Hospital In Vitro Fertilization Center, 88285MA, Dec. 19, 1988 (also appearing at *Triplets Have Nearly 2-Year Age Difference*, S.F. Chron., Dec. 23, 1988, at A24).

21-month difference, it is unlikely that the singleton and twins would actually be treated as part of a common birth, but to label them as triplets may establish unfair expectations of similarity or social compatibility. (Individual fraternal twins may, however, vary in degree of similarity or compatibility.) I believe it would be prudent to engage families of identical twins in future dialogues concerning human cloning because parents and other relatives closely witness the benefits and liabilities of growing up as an identical twin.

II. EXPERIENTIAL ASPECTS OF TWINSHIP

Most psychological twin studies demonstrate greater social closeness and affiliation between MZ twins than between DZ twins.[12] This finding characterizes male and female twins, twin children and adults, and twins reared together and apart. However, social closeness does not imply loss of individuality, and most identical twins enjoy their relationship and the emotional support, trust, and understanding it uniquely affords. Interestingly, some reunited MZ twins confessed concern about loss of individuality prior to meeting their genetically identical twin, but admitted this concern proved groundless after reunion. Parents of young twins are sometimes frustrated at routine placement of identical twins in separate school classes because of educators' unsubstantiated concerns over diminished autonomy, suggesting instead that educators make such decisions on a case-by-case basis.[13] A study of high school-age twins found that MZ and DZ twins did not differ in overall level of satisfaction with being a twin.[14] However, within pairs, identical twins showed greater agreement in how they viewed the twinship experience, suggesting more coordinated perception and communication.

Individuation can be problematic for some identical twins, especially at adolescence, when individuals typically confront issues of identity and selfhood.[15]

Separation from the twin, possibly in the form of acquisition of different experiences and friends, may occur, but most identical twins weather these "storms" with equanimity. Unfortunately, the relative minority of identical twins whose struggles with personal identity are severe and enduring are those likely to attract professional and public attention. This can provide the false impression that identical twins necessarily suffer individuation problems and are overrepresented in clinical populations. Pathological blurring of identical twins' personal boundaries is also a familiar theme in books and movies, a situation that unfortunately fuels this misconception.[16]

The developmental situations of identical twins may differ from those of non-twins, especially in language development, in which twins show an average delay relative to non-twins. This deficit has been associated with reduced opportunities for verbal interaction with parents, due to their caring for two same-age children at the same time, a situation that would not apply to IGCs. Regardless, social development proceeds normally for most twins,[17] and most investigators have failed to find an excess of twins among individuals with mental disorders or other behavioral difficulties.[18]

It is instructive to return to the psychological situation of reunited identical twins. These twins are unanimous in their satisfaction at finding one another and in obtaining answers to the origins of current medical conditions or predispositions. For example, a pair of identical twin males who independently developed mixed headache syndrome at age 18 learned that a genetic tendency, in addition to stress, was probably responsible. The majority of reunited twins establish close social relations with one another, without apparent damage to their sense of selfhood. The fear of diminished autonomy raised in the NBAC's Report could be interpreted to suggest that reared apart twins might be better off never meeting, or (even more extreme) that identical twins should routinely be reared apart. However, empirical observation reveals this is *not* the case. There are many recog-

12. Nancy L. Segal, *Cooperation, Competition, and Altruism in Human Twinships: A Sociobiological Approach, in* Sociobiological Perspectives on Human Development 168, 175–76 (Kevin B. MacDonald ed., 1988); Segal, *Twin Research Perspective on Human Development, supra* note 3.

13. Nancy L. Segal & Jean M. Russell, *Twins in the Classroom: School Policy Issues and Recommendations*, 3 J. Educ. & Psychol. Consultation 69 (1992).

14. Loehlin & Nichols, *supra* note 3, at 70.

15. Elizabeth M. Bryan, Twins, Triplets and More: Their Nature, Development and Care (1992).

16. *See, e.g.,* Dead Ringers, a David Cronenberg film.

17. Bryan, *supra* note 15.

18. *See* Michael Rutter & Jane Redshaw, *Annotation: Growing Up as a Twin: Twin-Singleton Differences in Psychological Development*, 32 J. Child Psych. & Psychiatry & Allied Disciplines 885 (1991). Studies by Emily Simonoff. *A Comparison of Twins and Singletons with Child Psychiatric Disorders: An Item Sheet Study*, 33 J. Child Psych. & Psychiatry & Allied Disciplines 1319 (1992), and Ulla Klaning et al., *Increased Occurrence of Schizophrenia and Other Psychiatric Illnesses Among Twins*, 168 Brit. J. Psychiatry 688 (1996), suggest an excess of twins with conduct disorder and schizophrenia, relative to singletons. However, these exceptional findings warrant further analysis and replication.

nized benefits associated with identical twinship, such as life-long companionship, sharing, and assistance. The experiences of identical twins, both reared apart and together, offer a stringent test of the concern that identical genes might imply loss of self. This simply does not occur in identical twins born in the same generation, where it might be *more* likely to occur than between IGCs born in different generations.

In summary, findings from studies of identical twins reared together and apart do not support the concern that genetically identical people are not individuals in their own right. This realization does not justify human cloning, but it challenges reasons given for preventing it.

III. NOVEL KINSHIPS

The quality of relationships that would evolve between IGCs are unknown, because this particular human kinship has never existed. The definition of parental and grandparental roles is uncertain, but this has also been the case in families conceiving children through assisted reproductive technology (ART), as the Report notes.[19] Complex novel kinships have also been created by marriages between men and women with children from former unions, especially if they go on to have children of their own, giving rise to "blended" or "reconstituted" families. Preliminary comparison of parenting roles and child adjustment in families with adopted children, families with artificially conceived children, and families with birth children have been undertaken. Adoptive parents and parents conceiving children through ART expressed greater warmth and emotional involvement with children, as well as greater satisfaction with parenting roles, relative to birth parents. Children conceived by ART did not differ from naturally conceived children in emotions, behavior, or quality of family relations.[20] These findings may reflect these parents' greater investment in and commitment to raising children, given the efforts and expense involved in having them. However, sample sizes were small and parental group differences might possibly fade as the young

children in the study age. In contrast, blended families often require children to adapt to new rules and regulations and to altered relationships with parents and siblings, situations that can prove stressful.[21] However, these children's outcomes also depend on the general quality of family functioning, as well as on their age and sex. Difficulties associated with this living arrangement come largely from changes in caretakers and caretaking routines, a situation that would not characterize IGCs.

A new twin-like sibship has also been created by adoption of same-age children, or of a child near in age to a birth child. (I call these UST-SAs: unrelated same-age siblings reared together of the same age.)[22] The implications of what adoption agencies call "artificial twinning" for the individuality and family place of unrelated same-age siblings has been a matter of some debate.[23] However, parents' comments generally convey enthusiasm for the companionship each child offers to the other. Early evaluation of a small sample of these children showed a lower frequency of behavioral problems relative to clinical and nonclinical comparison populations, although a possible excess of attentional difficulties relative to some twin samples was suggested.[24] However, symptoms of inattention and hyperactivity in adopted children may be associated with inherited difficulties in impulse control from birth mothers,[25] rather than with specific features of the near-in-age sibships. Continued analysis of the advantages and disadvantages of this unusual sibling arrangement is expected.

The nature and quality of social relations between IGCs, and between IGCs and other family members, are currently speculative. Changing social mores and advanced medical technology have generated many new family arrangements and kinships that perhaps we can learn from. Many of these relationships remain untested, although evidence of positive outcomes is accumulating. Rejecting human cloning because of the uncertainty of social outcomes does not seem defensible, even though positive social outcomes and other unusual kinships may not alone offer sufficient justification for implementing cloning procedures.

---

19. *See* NBAC Report, *supra* note 2, at 70.
20. Susan Golombok et al., *Families Created by the New Reproductive Technologies: Quality of Parenting and Social and Emotional Development of the Children*, 66 Child Dev. 285, 295 (1995); *cf.* Frank van Balen, *Child-Rearing Following In Vitro Fertilization*, 37 J. Child Psychol. & Psychiatry & Allied Disciplines 687, 692 (1996).
21. *See* Laura E. Berk, Child Development 563 (4th ed. 1997).
22. Nancy L. Segal, *Same-Age Unrelated Siblings: A Unique Test of Within-Family Environmental Influences on IQ Similarity*, 89 J. Educ. Psychol. 381 (1997).
23. Patricia Irwin Johnston, *Artificial Twinning: An Instant Family at What Price?*, Adoptive Families, May–June 1997, at 20.
24. Patrick J. Giordani & Nancy L. Segal, An Analysis of Problem Behaviors in Unrelated Siblings Reared Together from Infancy of the Same Age (UST-SA), as Measured by the CBCL, paper presented to Behavior Genetics Association, Toronto, Canada, July 10–13, 1997.
25. *See* Berk, *supra* note 21.

IV. Twin Studies of Human Behavior and Development

The following statements excerpted from the NBAC Report warrant consideration in light of twin research findings. These statements also seem somewhat contradictory to the general thrust of arguments presented against human cloning.

> Even identical twins . . . have different likes and dislikes, and can have very different talents.[26]

> Common experience demonstrates how distinctly different [identical] twins are, both in personality and in personhood. At the same time, observers cannot help but imbue identical bodies with some expectation that identical persons occupy those bodies since body and personality remain intertwined in human intuition.[27]

Identical twins are clearly less behaviorally alike than most people think. Identical twin correlations for physical characteristics, intellectual abilities, personality traits, vocational interests, and social attitudes are all less than 1.0, meaning that prenatal, perinatal, and postnatal environments affect virtually every measured human trait.[28] At the same time, *identical twins are more alike than any other pair of relatives*. The greater similarity of *identical twins reared apart* as compared to *fraternal twins reared together* is compelling evidence that common genes do influence personality similarity.[29] Of course, some identical pairs are more (or less) alike than others. However, while identical twins *can* have different dislikes and talents, identical twins as a group are more similar, relative to fraternal twins and siblings.

One of the most surprising and dramatic findings emerging from the behavioral-genetic literature in the last decade is that shared environments *do not* contribute to personality similarity between relatives living together.[30] This conclusion, based on an extensive review of twin and adoption studies of personality, psychopathology, and cognition, is also supported by similar personality correlations (about .50

for most personality traits) for identical twins reared together and reared apart.[31] Although somewhat counterintuitive, this finding reveals that common genes are responsible for personality similarity between relatives, and that environmental influences affecting personality development are those that individuals uniquely experience apart from their families.

The statement that identical twins are "distinctly different" requires qualification. Although identical twins show personality similarity as indicated by the average .50 correlation, some individual identical pairs are more alike than others. So, distinguishing between identical co-twins can be difficult, especially upon initial meetings. Interestingly, psychologists studying infant twins observed that "[i]n each of these [four identical] pairs the personalities merged into a single picture. . . . This merger could not be ascribed to similar appearance, for there was no difficulty in recording other identical looking pairs who exhibited some clear-cut differences."[32] In addition, there is no evidence that personality similarity implies absence of individuality.

The statement that "observers cannot help but imbue identical bodies with some expectation that identical persons occupy those bodies, since body and personality remain intertwined in human intuition" also deserves careful appraisal.[33] Research shows that parents' treatment of identical twins does not create behavioral similarities; rather, parental treatment is a response or reaction to twins' similar behaviors. Interestingly, investigators showed that parents of most similar looking identical twins rated them *least alike* in behavior, relative to parents of other twins.[34] This suggests that parents may be especially sensitive to subtle differences in twins' behaviors that are not apparent to strangers, and shows there is no necessary connection between similarity in physical attributes and similarity in behavioral traits. If more "look-alike" identical twins receive more similar treatment than less "look-alike" identical twins, this treatment should not lead to more similar behavior because it does not affect biological functions underlying

---

26. NBAC Report, *supra* note 2, at 33.

27. *Id.* at 67.

28. *See* Thomas J. Bouchard, Jr. et al., *Sources of Human Psychological Differences: The Minnesota Study of Twins Reared Apart*, 250 Science 223, 226 (1990). This formulation of the nature-nurture controversy captures the idea of active-gene environment correlation.

29. *See* Auke Tellegen et al., *Personality Similarity in Twins Reared Apart and Together*, 54 J. Personality & Soc. Psychol. 1031, 1035 (1988).

30. *See* Robert Plomin & Denise Daniels, *Why Are Children in the Same Family so Different from One Another?*, 10 Behavioral & Brain Sci. 1 (1987).

31. Tellegen et al., *supra* note 29, at 1035.

32. Daniel G. Freedman & Barbara Keller, *Inheritance of Behavior in Infants*, 140 Science 196, 197–98 (1963).

33. NBAC Report, *supra* note 2, at 67.

34. Adam P. Matheny et al., *Relations Between Twins' Similarity of Appearance and Behavioral Similarity: Testing an Assumption*, 6 Behav. Genetics 343, 349 (1976).

personality.[35] Furthermore, even when parents misjudge twin type, their personality ratings of twins are consistent with true twin type. In other words, identical twins perceived to be fraternal are generally perceived to be as alike in personality as identical twins are in general. Therefore, identical twins can be behaviorally similar despite some perceived developmental differences.[36]

It has long been accepted that interactions between genes and environments are too complex to predict individual behavior with certainty.[37] Nevertheless, scientists can estimate lifetime risks for some medical conditions. For example, the risk for schizophrenia is one percent for the general population, but rises to 15–17 percent for twins of affected fraternals and to 40–48 percent for twins of affected identicals.[38] Identical twins' similarity in medical life histories is not perfect, but some conditions (e.g., bipolar disorder and diabetes) are more highly influenced by genetic factors than others (e.g., anorexia nervosa and breast cancer). Identical twins inherit the same disease predispositions, but exposure to differing prenatal or postnatal environmental influences can differentially trigger or suppress expression. Knowledge and understanding of disease risk allows unaffected identical twins with affected co-twins to purposefully avoid known environmental triggers of disease. The same principle applies to IGCs, although advances in medical treatment or changing environmental factors might reduce the likelihood of disease in the younger individual.

The greater average personality similarity of identical twins, relative to other individuals, suggests that the personalities of some pairs of IGCs would also be alike, although perfect correspondence would not be expected. It seems to me that the key question is not whether the personalities of IGCs would be alike, but whether those who are alike might experience undue emotional or psychological distress because of it. There is no compelling evidence that identical twins who are more alike in personality than others are especially distressed—in fact, every year thousands of identical twins gather at national and international conventions to celebrate their twinship and their likenesses. These findings may dispel some concerns raised over human cloning, but again do not necessarily justify the procedure.[39]

V. Nature via Nurture or Nurture via Nature?

The statement that "the extent to which human beings are shapers and creators of their personal and collective futures continues to be important and contested"[40] should be addressed in light of what twin studies reveal about human behavioral development. Behavioral-geneticists refer to *active-gene environment correlation*, the concept that individuals seek out certain people, places, and events congenial with their genetically based intellectual abilities, personality traits, and recreational interests. This process may explain the behavioral parallels observed between identical twins reared in separate environments—the idea that twins select certain elements of their environment from among the array of available elements. No one endorses the idea of a "gene for rock climbing" or a "gene for divorce," but both of these behaviors may be associated with genetically influenced risk-taking tendencies or aggressive personality styles. People *choose* to engage in rock-climbing and *decide* to end marriages—their genes do not "tell" them to do this—but their genes may predispose them toward these behaviors so long as their environments support these opportunities. In other words, people cannot go rock-climbing if terrain is unsuitable and people cannot divorce if laws do not allow it.

What propels people to act as they do is a complex mix of genetic and environmental factors whose relative proportions can be estimated at the population level, but not at the individual level. The old *nature vs. nurture* debate was refashioned as the *nature-nurture* debate in the 1950s and 60s, emphasizing that both

---

35. David C. Rowe, The Limits of Family Influence: Genes, Experience, and Behavior 45–48 (1994).

36. *See* Sandra Scarr, *Environmental Bias in Twin Studies, in* Behavioral-Genetics: Method and Research 597, 604 (Martin Manosevitz et al. eds., 1969).

37. *See* NBAC Report, *supra* note 2, at 32–33.

38. Irving I. Gottesman, Schizophrenia Genesis: The Origins of Madness 110 (1991); E. Fuller Torrey et al., Schizophrenia and Manic-Depressive Disorder: The Biological Roots of Mental Illness as Revealed by the Landmark Study of Identical Twins 10–12 (1994). Risk figures for schizophrenia in identical and fraternal twins presented in the text are based on probandwise concordance in which a pair of concordant twins is counted twice if each was ascertained independently during subject recruitment. These figures can be compared with risk figures for other relatives. An alternate measure, pairwise concordance, is calculated as the number of concordant pairs divided by the total number of concordant and discordant pairs in the study. Risk figures based on pairwise concordance are 28% for identical twins and 6% for fraternal twins.

39. Repeated references to behavioral differences between identical twins were somewhat perplexing—if identical twins are assumed to be different then concern over cloning should be less intense. It is possible that inattention to findings supporting genetic influence on behavior reflects the legacy of environmentalist perspectives prevalent since the turn of the century. Behavioral-genetic research did not join the mainstream of psychology until the early 1980s.

40. NBAC Report, *supra* note 2, at 48.

sources of influence are involved. Bouchard and others later refined this concept as *nature via nurture* to convey the idea that genetic factors are expressed "by influencing the character, selection, and impact of experiences during development."[41] Most recently, Bouchard asserted that children's characteristics appear to drive their parents' rearing practices, recommending *nurture via nature* as another appropriate term for the melding of genes and experience in behavioral development.[42] This more recent formulation captures the notion of *reactive gene-environment correlation*, the idea that parental treatment is largely guided by children's genetically influenced temperaments and talents.

The foregoing does not suggest that genetic influence on behavior denies or diminishes the free will of the individual who chooses to act or not to act. For example, individuals with genetic predispositions to cardiac conditions can decide to exercise or not, or to follow a healthy diet or an unhealthy one. IGCs enter different generations with different standards, values, and opportunities, so differences in behavioral expression are expected. (As stated earlier, IGCs may also differ in behavior due to errors in cell replication, despite their identical genes.) Identical twins reared apart, while part of the same generation, find themselves in different environments (sometimes in different cultures), yet they often end up being very similar in behavior. It may be that IGCs will also show behavioral similarities, freely chosen and compatible with genetically influenced tendencies. Concern that human cloning reduces free will does not seem to follow from what is known about identical twins. However, eliminating this concern does not necessarily admit human cloning into the arena of acceptable or favorable practices in the future.

VI. COMMENT

The real possibility of adult human cloning raises many multi-faceted questions for which simple solutions are lacking. More informed discussion of behavioral issues can proceed once relevant data have been assembled. One plan would be to systematically gather information on identical twins' own perceptions of their similarity *and* their views on how similarities affect their happiness, well-being, life choices, and other measures. Data are currently available on the nature of identical twins' relationship and their satisfaction with their relationship relative to fraternal twins, but less is known about how their perceptions of similarity (or dissimilarity) affect satisfaction with their relationship. A second plan would be to focus on naturally occurring human models that mimic essential aspects of IGCs. For example, it should be possible to study similarity and social relations between same-sex siblings,[43] and between parents and children[44] who look or behave very much alike, but who naturally differ in age.

It is currently impossible to evaluate, or to imagine, the many scenarios in which human cloning might prove either justifiable or unacceptable, although the Commission's Report presented compelling examples of both. No doubt, dialogue and discussion will continue and it is my hope that behavioral issues will move beyond speculation to increased reliance on empirical evidence.

QUESTIONS

1. How are identical twins and intergenerational clones alike? How are they different?
2. Do you think that the three infants born to a mother in California that were formed from a single fertilization procedure, but born 21 months apart, are triplets? Why or why not?
3. Do identical twins enjoy being identical twins? Use evidence from research to support your answer.
4. What is "artificial twinning" and what consequences do you think it might have for the children's development?
5. Why do twins who look more alike end up being the least alike behaviorally? What does this suggest about the effect of experience (or nurture) on the development of twins?
6. What do you think: Should humans be cloned? Why or why not?

---

41. Bouchard et al., *supra* note 28, at 228. This formulation of the nature-nurture controversy captures the idea of active-gene environment correlation.

42. Thomas J. Bouchard, Jr., *The Genetics of Personality, in* Handbook of Psychiatric Genetics 273, 290 (Kenneth Blum & Ernest P. Noble eds., 1997).

43. It is theoretically possible for fraternal twins and full siblings to share 100% of their genes, although a realistic range is 25–75%. *See* Andrew Pakstis et al., *Genetic Contributions to Morphological and Behavioral Similarities Among Sibs and Dizygotic Twins: Linkages and Allelic Differences.* 19 Soc. Biology 185 (1972).

44. The remarkable resemblance between Isabella Rossellini and her late mother, actress Ingrid Bergman, in both appearance and in voice is well-known.

8 Of Human Bonding: Newborns Prefer Their Mothers' Voices

ANTHONY J. DeCASPER · WILLIAM P. FIFER

Over the past two decades there has been a huge increase in developmental research describing infant capabilities such as perception, emotional regulation, and social behavior. This increase is due in part to technical innovations that allow researchers to study infant behavior during the early days and months of life. But it also reflects a shift in psychologists' conception of infancy. Whereas infants were once seen as having few inherent capabilities, they are now considered to be quite capable.

The following article describes one of these early capabilities: the neonate's ability to discriminate the sounds of particular human voices. The adaptive benefits of this ability are immense and its presence in newborns attests to the complex biological preparedness of the human infant—a preparedness that helps even very young babies play an active role in their own development.

This research, along with many of the other studies that show the amazing capabilities of newborns, has redefined the study of human development. No longer are infants seen as helpless, reactive beings, but as active, information-seeking organisms ready to learn about and interact with the world. This research also indicates that infants demonstrate preferences for certain information. Whether preference for the mother's voice early in life is a result of familiarity from the womb or due to some other complex process, like emotional arousal, is unknown. But it is certain that a preference toward significant others helps infants become integrated with a critical element of their surroundings—the social world in which they live.

By sucking on a nonnutritive nipple in different ways, a newborn human could produce either its mother's voice or the voice of another female. Infants learned how to produce the mother's voice and produced it more often than the other voice. The neonate's preference for the maternal voice suggests that the period shortly after birth may be important for initiating infant bonding to the mother.

Human responsiveness to sound begins in the third trimester of life and by birth reaches sophisticated levels (*1*), especially with respect to speech (*2*). Early auditory competency probably subserves a variety of developmental functions such as language acquisition (*1, 3*) and mother-infant bonding (*4, 5*). Mother-infant bonding would best be served by (and may even require) the ability of a newborn to discriminate its mother's voice from that of other females. However, evidence for differential sensitivity to or discrimination of the maternal voice is available only for older infants for whom the bonding process is well advanced (*6*). Therefore, the role of maternal voice discrimination in formation of the mother-infant bond is unclear. If the newborn's sensitivities to speech subserves bonding, discrimination of and preference for the maternal voice should be evident near birth. We now report that a newborn infant younger than 3 days of age can not only discriminate its mother's voice but also will work to produce her voice in preference to the voice of another female.

The subjects were ten Caucasian neonates (five male and five female) (*7*). Shortly after delivery we tape-recorded the voices of mothers of infants selected for testing as they read Dr. Seuss's *To Think That I Saw It On Mulberry Street.* Recordings were edited to provide 25 minutes of uninterrupted prose, and testing of whether infants would differentially

Reprinted with permission from the authors and *Science, 208*, 1980, 1174–1176. Copyright 1980 by the American Association for the Advancement of Science.

produce their mothers' voices began within 24 hours of recording. Sessions began by coaxing the infant to a state of quiet alertness (*8*). The infant was then placed supine in its basinette, earphones were secured over its ears, and a nonnutritive nipple was placed in its mouth. An assistant held the nipple loosely in place; she was unaware of the experimental condition of the individual infant and could neither hear the tapes nor be seen by the infant. The nipple was connected, by way of a pressure transducer, to the solid-state programming and recording equipment. The infants were then allowed 2 minutes to adjust to the situation. Sucking activity was recorded during the next 5 minutes, but voices were never presented. This baseline period was used to determine the median interburst interval (IBI) or time elapsing between the end of one burst of sucking and the beginning of the next (*9*). A burst was defined as a series of individual sucks separated from one another by less than 2 seconds. Testing with the voices began after the baseline had been established.

For five randomly selected infants, sucking burst terminating IBI's equal to or greater than the baseline median (t) produced only his or her mother's voice (IBI $\geq t$), and bursts terminating intervals less than the median produced only the voice of another infant's mother (*10*). Thus, only one of the voices was presented, stereophonically, with the first suck of a burst and remained on until the burst ended, that is, until 2 seconds elapsed without a suck. For the other five infants, the conditions were reversed. Testing lasted 20 minutes.

A preference for the maternal voice was indicated if the infant produced it more often than the nonmaternal voice. However, unequal frequencies not indicative of preference for the maternal voice per se could result either because short (or long) IBI's were easier to produce or because the acoustic qualities of a particular voice, such as pitch or intensity, rendered it a more effective form of feedback. The effects of response requirements and voice characteristics were controlled (i) by requiring half the infants to respond after short IBI's to produce the mother's voice and half to respond after long ones and (ii) by having each maternal voice also serve as the nonmaternal voice for another infant.

Preference for the mother's voice was shown by the increase in the proportion of IBI's capable of producing her voice; the median IBI's shifted from their baseline values in a direction that produced the maternal voice more than half the time. Eight of the ten medians were shifted in a direction of the maternal voice (mean = 1.90 seconds, a 34 percent increase) (sign test, $P = .02$), one shifted in the direction that produced the nonmaternal voice more often, and one median did not change from its baseline value (Figure 1).

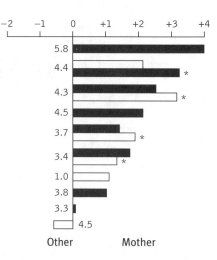

FIGURE 1

For each subject, signed difference scores between the median IBI's without vocal feedback (baseline) and with differential vocal feedback (session1). Differences of the four reversal sessions (*) are based on medians with differential feedback in sessions 1 and 2. Positive values indicate a preference for the maternal voice and negative values a preference for the nonmaternal voice. Filled bars indicate that the mother's voice followed IBI's of less than the baseline median; open bars indicate that her voice followed intervals equal to or greater than the median. Median IBI's of the baseline (in seconds) are shown opposite the bars.

If these infants were working to gain access to their mother's voice, reversing the response requirements should result in a reversal of their IBI's. Four infants, two from each condition, who produced their mother's voice more often in session 1 were able to complete a second session 24 hours later, in which the response requirements were reversed (*11*). Differential feedback in session 2 began immediately after the 2-minute adjustment period. The criterion time remained equal to the baseline median of the first session. For all four infants, the median IBI's shifted toward the new criterion values and away from those which previously produced the maternal voice. The average magnitude of the difference between the medians of the first and reversal sessions was 1.95 seconds.

Apparently the infant learned to gain access to the mother's voice. Since specific temporal properties of sucking were required to produce the maternal voice, we sought evidence for the acquisition of temporally differentiated responding. Temporal discrimination within each condition was ascertained by constructing the function for IBI per opportunity: IBI's were collected into classes equal to one-fifth the baseline

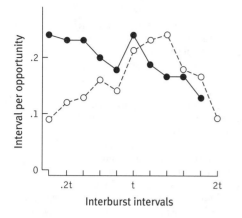

FIGURE 2

Interburst interval per opportunity when the maternal voice followed intervals less than the baseline median (solid line) and intervals equal to or greater than the median (dashed line). The IBI's are represented on the abscissa by the lower bound of interval classes equal to one-fifth the baseline median (t).

TABLE 1   Mean X and Standard Deviation (S.D.) of the Relative Frequency of Sucking During a Stimulus Associated with the Maternal Voice Divided by the Relative Frequency of Sucking During a Stimulus Associated with the Nonmaternal Voice

Stimulus associated with maternal voice	First third		Last third	
	$\overline{X}$	S.D.	$\overline{X}$	S.D.
Tone	0.97	.33	1.26	.33
No tone	1.04	.31	1.22	.19
Last: Combined	1.00[a]	.32	1.24	.27

[a] A ratio of 1.0 indicates no preference.

median, and the frequency of each class was divided by the total frequency of classes having equal and larger values (*12*). When IBI's less than the baseline median were required, the likelihood of terminating interburst intervals was highest for classes less than the median (Figure 2), whereas when longer intervals were required, the probability of terminating an IBI was maximal for intervals slightly longer than the median. Feedback from the maternal voice effectively differentiated the temporal character of responding that produced it: the probability of terminating IBI's was highest when termination resulted in the maternal voice.

Repeating the experiment with 16 female neonates and a different discrimination procedure confirmed their preference for the maternal voice (*13*). The discriminative stimuli were a 400-Hz tone of 4 seconds duration (tone) and a 4-second period of silence (no tone). Each IBI contained an alternating sequence of tone-no-tone periods, and each stimulus was equally likely to begin a sequence. For eight infants, a sucking burst initiated during a tone period turned off the tone and produced the Dr. Seuss story read by the infant's mother, whereas sucking bursts during a no-tone period produced the nonmaternal voice. The elicited voice remained until the sucking burst ended, at which time the tone-no-tone alternation began anew. The discriminative stimuli were reversed for the other eight neonates. Testing with the voices began immediately after the 2-minute adjustment period and lasted 20 minutes. Each maternal voice also served as a nonmaternal voice.

During the first third of the testing session, the infants were as likely to suck during a stimulus period correlated with the maternal voice as during one correlated with the nonmaternal voice (Table 1). However, in the last third of the session the infants sucked during stimulus periods associated with their mother's voice approximately 24 percent more often than during those associated with the nonmaternal voice, a significant increase [$F(1, 14) = 8.97, P < .01$]. Thus, at the beginning of testing there was no indication of stimulus discrimination or voice preference. By the end of the 20-minute session, feedback from the maternal voice produced clear evidence of an auditory discrimination; the probability of sucking during tone and no-tone periods was greater when sucking produced the maternal voice.

The infants in these studies lived in a group nursery; their general care and night feedings were handled by a number of female nursery personnel. They were fed in their mothers' rooms by their mothers at 9:30 A.M. and at 1:30, 5:00, and 8:30 P.M. At most, they had 12 hours of postnatal contact with their mothers before testing. Similarly reared infants prefer the human voice to other acoustically complex stimuli (*14*). But, as our data show, newborns reared in group nurseries that allow minimal maternal contact can also discriminate between their mothers and other speakers and, moreover, will work to produce their mothers' voices in preference to those of other females. Thus, within the first 3 days of postnatal development, newborns prefer the human voice, discriminate between speakers, and demonstrate a preference for their mothers' voices with only limited maternal exposure.

The neonate's capacity to rapidly acquire a stimulus discrimination that controls behavior (*15*) could provide the means by which limited postnatal experience with the mother results in preference for her voice. The early preference demonstrated here is possible because newborns have auditory competencies adequate for discriminating individual speakers: they are sensitive to rhythmicity (*16*), intonation (*17*), frequency variation (*1, 13*), and phonetic components of speech (*18*). Their general sensory competency may enable other maternal cues, such as her odor (*19*) and the manner in which she handles her infant (*20*), to serve as supporting bases for discrimination and vocal preference. Prenatal (intrauterine) auditory experience may also be a factor. Although the significance and nature of intrauterine auditory experience in humans is not known, perceptual preferences and proximity-seeking responses of some infrahuman infants are profoundly affected by auditory experience before birth (*21*).

REFERENCES AND NOTES

1. R. B. Eisenberg, *Auditory Competence in Early Life: The Roots of Communicative Behavior* (University Park Press, Baltimore, 1976.)

2. P. D. Eimas, in *Infant Perception: From Sensation to Cognition*, L. B. Cohen and P. Salapatek, Eds. (Academic Press, New York, 1975), vol. 2., p. 193.

3. B. Friedlander, *Merrill-Palmer Q., 16*, 7 (1970).

4. R. Bell, in *The Effect of the Infant on Its Caregiver*, M. Lewis and L. A. Rosenblum, Eds. (Wiley, New York, 1974), p. 1; T. B. Brazelton, E. Tronick, L. Abramson, H. Als, S. Wise, *Ciba Found. Symp., 33*, 137 (1975).

5. M. H. Klaus and J. H. Kennel, *Maternal Infant Bonding* (Mosby, St. Louis, 1976); P. DeChateau, *Birth Family J., 41*, 10 (1977).

6. M. Miles and E. Melvish, *Nature (London) 252*, 123 (1974); J. Mehler, J. Bertoncini, M. Baurière, D. Jassik-Gershenfeld, *Perception, 7*, 491 (1978).

7. The infants were randomly selected from those meeting the following criteria: (i) gestation, full term; (ii) delivery, uncomplicated; (iii) birth weight, between 2500 and 3850 grams; and (iv) APGAR score, at least eight at 1 and 5 minutes after birth. If circumsized, males were not observed until at least 12 hours afterward. Informed written consent was obtained from the mother, and she was invited to observe the testing procedure. Testing sessions began between 2.5 and 3.5 hours after the 6 A.M. or 12 P.M. feeding. All infants were bottle-fed.

8. P. H. Wolff, *Psychol. Issues, 5*, 1 (1966). The infants were held in front of the experimenter's face, spoken to, and then presented with the nonnutritive nipple. Infants failing to fixate visually on the experimenter's face or to suck on the nipple were returned to the nursery. Once begun, a session was terminated only if the infant cried or stopped sucking for two consecutive minutes. The initial sessions of two infants were terminated because they cried for 2 minutes. Their data are not reported. Thus, the results are based on 10 of 12 infants meeting the behavioral criteria for entering and remaining in the study.

9. With quiet and alert newborns, nonnutritive sucking typically occurs as bursts of individual sucks, each separated by a second or so, while the bursts themselves are separated by several seconds or more. Interburst intervals tend to be unimodally distributed with modal values differing among infants. [K. Kaye, in *Studies in Mother-Infant Interaction*, H. R. Schaffer, Ed. (Academic Press, New York, 1977)]. A suck was said to occur when the negative pressure exerted on the nipple reached 20 mm-Hg. This value is almost always exceeded during nonnutritive sucking by healthy infants, but is virtually never produced by nonsucking mouth movement.

10. The tape reels revolved continuously, and one or the other of the voices was electronically switched to the earphones when the response threshold was met. Because the thresholds were detected electronically, voice onset occurred at the moment the negative pressure reached 20 mm-Hg.

11. Two infants were not tested a second time, because we could not gain access to the testing room, which served as an auxiliary nursery and as an isolation room. The sessions of two infants who cried were terminated. Two other infants were tested a second time, but in their first session one had shown no preference and the other had shown only a slight preference for the nonmaternal voice. Their performance may have been affected by inconsistent feedback. Because their peak sucking pressures were near the threshold of the apparatus, very similar sucks would sometimes produce feedback and sometimes not, and sometimes feedback would be terminated in the midst of a sucking burst. Consequently, second session performances of these two infants, which were much like their initial performances, were uninterpretable.

12. D. Anger, *J. Exp. Psychol., 52*, 145 (1956).

13. Three other infants began testing with the voices, but their sessions were terminated because they cried. Their data are not included. This study is part of a doctoral thesis submitted by W.P.F.

14. E. Butterfield and G. Siperstein, in *Oral Sensation and Perception: The Mouth of the Infant*, J. Bosma, Ed. (Thomas, Springfield, Ill., 1972).

15. E. R. Siqueland and L. P. Lipsitt, *J. Exp. Child. Psychol. 3*, 356 (1966); R. E. Kron, in *Recent Advances in Biological Psychiatry*, J. Wortis, Ed. (Plenum, New York, 1967), p. 295.

16. W. S. Condon and L. W. Sander, *Science, 183*, 99 (1974).

17. R. B. Eisenberg, D. B. Cousins, N. Rupp, *J. Aud. Res., 7*, 245 (1966); P. A. Morse, *J. Exp. Child. Psychol., 14*, 477 (1972).

18. E. C. Butterfield and G. F. Cairns, in *Language Perspectives: Acquisition, Retardation and Intervention*, R. L. Schiefelbusch and L. L. Lloyd, Eds. (University Park Press, Baltimore, 1974), p. 75; A. J. DeCasper, E. C. Butterfield, G. F. Cairns, paper presented at the fourth biennial conference on Human Development, Nashville. April 1976.

19. A. MacFarlane, *Ciba Found. Symp., 33*, 103 (1975).

20. P. Burns, L. W. Sander, G. Stechler, H. Julia. *J. Am. Acad. Child Psychiatry, 11*, 427 (1972), E. B. Thoman, A. F. Korner, L. Bearon-Williams, *Child Dev., 48*, 563 (1977).

21. G. Gottlieb, *Development of Species Identification in Birds: An Inquiry into the Prenatal Determinants of*

Perception (Univ. of Chicago Press, Chicago, 1971); E. H. Hess. *Imprinting* (Van Nostrand-Reinhold, New York, 1973).

22. Supported by Research Council grant 920. We thank the infants, their mothers, and the staff of Moses Cane Hospital, where this work was performed, and A. Carstens for helping conduct the research.

QUESTIONS

1. Describe the method that DeCasper and Fifer used to test an infant's preference for the mother's voice. Are you surprised that infants are capable of doing this task? Why?
2. Why was it that for half of the infants their sucking rate needed to increase in order to hear the mother's voice and for half of the infants their sucking rate needed to decrease in order to hear the mother's voice?
3. Do you think that prenatal exposure to the mother's voice may play a role in the preferences exhibited in this study?
4. What purpose does such early auditory discrimination serve for infants?
5. What types of perceptual information about mothers do you think deaf infants might focus on?
6. What other early sensory capabilities help prepare infants to interact socially?

9 Neonatal Behavior Among Urban Zambians and Americans

T. BERRY BRAZELTON · BARBARA KOSLOWSKI · EDWARD TRONICK

One way in which psychologists study the contributions of biological and experiential factors in human development is by comparing behaviors and abilities across individuals reared in very different cultural settings. This research often takes psychologists into the field, both at home and abroad, where behavioral observation becomes the main method of data collection.

In the research described in this article, T. Berry Brazelton, Barbara Koslowski, and Edward Tronick observed newborns in Zambia and the United States. They were interested in the infants' ability to regulate their emotional states and in how infants react to the environment over the first 10 days of life. They expected differences in the two communities because of the different child-rearing practices in the groups. Their results revealed differences in the rates at which these skills develop in these two populations. However, even more interesting than the identification of these differences so early in life is the answer to the question of how such differences come about.

In answer to this, Brazelton and colleagues offer a thought-provoking discussion about the ways in which genetic and nongenetic inheritance are coordinated with child-rearing practices to produce particular patterns of human growth. This study illustrates the utility of a cross-cultural approach for understanding how cultural practices contribute, even very early in life, to the adaptive organization of social behavior and development.

Geber's classic report of infant development in Africa (Geber and Dean, 1959) suggested that African babies are developmentally more advanced in their first year than are their Western European counterparts. Her tests reported precocity in motor development between the two groups, but did not document sensory or cognitive differences.

Studies of other cultures (Ainsworth, 1967; Brazelton et al., 1969; Freedman and Freedman, 1969; Goldberg, 1971; Schaffer, 1960) have supported Geber's finding that developmental differences can be found early in a child's life—indeed, as early as the neonatal period. Several of these studies also suggested that infants in different cultural groups showed differences in behavior at birth that might influence the outcome of their subsequent development.

We wondered whether these observations might be relevant to observed Zambian-American differences in early childhood. Would these groups of infants differ during the neonatal period? Would these differences lie in interactive and perceptual abilities as well as in motor development?

PROCEDURE

Ten Zambian and 10 American infants were seen on days 1, 5, and 10 after birth. All mothers were reported to have had normal pregnancies terminated at 40 weeks, and no bleeding or infection was noted.

The U.S. babies were delivered via "natural childbirth": no anesthesia was administered to the mothers, and no more than one injection of Nisentil (a mild

Reprinted with permission from *Journal of Child Psychiatry*, 15, 1976, 97–107. Copyright 1976 by Pergamon Press Ltd. This research was supported in part by a grant from the National Early Childhood Research Council, Inc. (Edcom), Princeton, N.J., and was presented at the Biennial Meeting of the Society for Research in Child Development, Minneapolis, Minn., in 1971.

Reprints may be requested from Dr. Brazelton, 23 Hawthorn Street, Cambridge, Mass. 02138.

muscle relaxant, 30 mgm.) was given during the period of labor 6 hours prior to delivery. No other medication was administered. All the infants were firstborn and came from middle-class families. They were normal at birth. Apgars were above 8-9-9 at 1, 5, and 15 minutes (Apgar, 1953). Neurological and pediatric examinations were consistently normal. We evaluated all babies for neurological adequacy on the scale taught one of us (ET) by Prechtl (Prechtl and Beintema, 1964). In addition, we evaluated each baby with the Brazelton (1973) Neonatal Behavioral Assessment at 1, 5, and 10 days.

This Neonatal Behavioral Assessment Scale is a psychological scale for the newborn human infant. It assesses his reflexive and motor behavior, as well as his general physical state as he recovers from labor and delivery. It allows for an assessment of the infant's capabilities along dimensions that we think are relevant to his developing social relationships. It reconceptualizes Prechtl's use of state[1] in such an assessment. State is no longer regarded as a static error variable, but serves to set a dynamic pattern which reflects the wholeness of the infant. Specifically, the examination tracks the pattern of state change over the course of the examination, its lability, and its directionality in response to external and internal stimuli. Thus, the variability of state becomes a dimension of assessment, pointing to the infant's initial abilities for self-organization.

An assessment of the infant's ability for self-organization is contained in the items which measure his capacity for self-quieting after exposure to aversive stimuli. This is contrasted to the infant's use of external stimuli to help him quiet after such stimulation. The latter item contains a graded series of examiner-administered procedures—talking to him, placing one's hand on his belly, rocking and holding him—maneuvers which are designed to calm the infant. The assessment results in an evaluation of how control is achieved by the infant. The infant's responsiveness to animate stimulation (voice and face, holding and cuddling, etc.) as well as to inanimate stimulation (rattle, bell, red ball, pinprick, temperature change, etc.) are quantified. Other items assess neuroreflexive adequacy and the vigor and attentional excitement exhibited by the infant throughout the exam. In all of this test, there is an attempt to elicit the infant's *best* performance in response to different kinds of stimulation.

The Zambian mothers were given no medication before or during delivery. These mothers had had several pregnancies in rapid succession at about 12- to 13-month intervals, among these several spontaneous abortions. But they all had more than three children living at home. There was historical evidence of low protein intake both before and during pregnancy, coupled with a high incidence of gastrointestinal infection in the mother during pregnancy. The resulting intrauterine conditions of a depleted uterus, low protein, and increased infections were a reflection of the conditions of recent urbanization as well as of a breakdown in traditional practices (Goldberg, 1970).

The Zambian mothers we saw had recently moved to the urbanized slums of Lusaka because of the disruption of the economy in the country under an economic plan that stressed industrialization. In the country, the maternal grandmother dictated her daughter's diet and saw to it that protein was a daily requirement. In the urbanized group, the husband took over this prerogative. He set up a series of myths which we heard from our subjects: "If you eat fish, your baby will drown. If you eat meat, your baby will bleed to death. If you eat eggs, your baby will be born bald." The breakdown in dietary protection of pregnant women occurs in the city, where jobs and money are scarce and protein is expensive, and the family cannot afford to spend the little money they have on high-protein foods which might not satisfy hunger. The other powerful change in the urbanized groups around Lusaka had to do with birth control practices centered around pregnancy. In the country, a family is made up of several women and one man. A sexual relationship is maintained with a wife who is not pregnant and not nursing. This practice fosters a kind of birth control and recovery of the uterus in the postnatal period before subsequent pregnancy. In Lusaka, given the economic conditions, this pattern is impossible. A family is made up of a male and one female, and she suffers from the effects of rapidly repeated pregnancies.

All of the infants of the group examined lived in the semirural urbanized slum area which surrounds the city of Lusaka. Dwellings ranged from huts to small brick cottages. All families were reported to be recently (one generation) urbanized, and few had the advantage of extended families nearby (Goldberg, 1970, 1971).

Our study consisted of three examinations on days 1, 5, and 10 after birth for each infant. We all shared

---

1. "State" or "state of consciousness" is one of the most important variables in any observation period of neonatal behavior. Reactions to stimuli must be interpreted within the context of the present state of consciousness. We used a schema of six states (two sleep, three awake, and one intermediate state). State depends on physiological variables such as hunger, degree of hydration, time within the sleep-wake cycle. But each observable reaction is governed by the state within which it is perceived. The infant's state patterns and his use of state to govern his physiological and psychological reactions may be uniquely individual and may be the most important framework for observing all of his reactions.

TABLE 1 BEHAVIORAL MEASURES IN NEONATAL SCALE

Vigor	General tonus
Lability of states	Self-quieting activity
Tremulousness	Habituation to light
Amount of startling	in eyes
Amount of mouthing	Motor maturity
Hand to mouth activity	Pulled-to-sit response
Motor activity	Passive movements
Rapidity of buildup	Following with eyes
Defensive movements	Cuddliness
to cloth on face	Alertness
Tempo of activity at peak	Social interest in *E*
Irritability	Reactions to sound
Consolability	Reactivity to
	stimulation

the examinations of the Zambians, although one (ET) was responsible for most of the examinations of U.S. controls. Interscorer reliability on the Brazelton scale had been tested in the United States and was retested in Africa, for we feared that we were becoming biased by our experience there. Repeated reliability tests were .85 or more on all items and between each pair of observers. The infants were scored on the 24 items listed in Table 1 as well as on 18 neurological items adapted from Prechtl and Beintema's (1964) neurological exam.

The first examination of the American infants was done in the hospital nurseries of the Boston Hospital for Women and Cambridge City Hospital, and on the Zambian infants in the University Hospital of Lusaka. On the first day the examination was administered two hours after feeding. The examinations on days 5 and 10 were carried out in the homes. An attempt was made to control conditions, e.g., to have the baby fed and comfortable; to include the mother, but exclude the other members of the family; and to standardize light, temperature, and noise as much as possible. This was difficult in the home examinations.

An estimate of the infants' pediatric, neurological, and nutritional status[2] was made in each case, and two infants were excluded because of possibly abnormal reactions. None of the babies in either group was found to be abnormal on any examination, including neurological evaluations. All babies in each group were being breastfed.

RESULTS

In the Zambian group, observations in the neonatal nursery on day 1 demonstrated pediatric evidence of intrauterine depletion in each of these infants. The average birth weight was 6 pounds, and the length was an average of 19 1/2 inches. The infants' skin was dry and scaly; their faces were wrinkled. The stumps of their umbilical cords were somewhat dried and yellow at birth. In short, the infants demonstrated the signs of dysmaturity which indicate recent depletion of nutrients in utero (Clifford, 1954). Their weight and size suggested placental dysfunction, and suggested that the infants had been affected by their mothers' inadequate protein diet and their stressed uteri with placentae inadequate to feed them—especially in the period just prior to birth. On this first examination, the Zambian infants' muscle tone was very poor. Little resistance was evidenced to passive extension or flexion of their limbs. Head control on being pulled to sit was extremely poor. And, lastly, when held, the Zambian infants made no active attempt to mold or adjust themselves to being held. They were essentially limp and unresponsive in the motor sphere.

The American infants were not depleted. They averaged 7.6 pounds, 20 1/4 inches in length, and showed no clinical evidence of dysmaturity or prematurity. They were active and responsive on the first day in all spheres of behavior.

On days 5 and 10 the Zambian infants were no longer clinically dehydrated. Because the mothers were multiparous and had nursed infants before, their milk came in rapidly, and nursing was uniformly successful. By day 5, the Zambian infants were filled out, dry skin was peeling away, and their eyes and mouths were moist. Their skin and subcutaneous tissue were normal again. Their energy level had considerably increased, as was reflected in their performance (see Table 2).

The performance of the two groups of infants on the Brazelton scale was compared item by item for each day of the examination with the Mann-Whitney U Test. The most striking differences were found on the 1st-day (6 items) and 10th-day (8 items) examinations, with only 2 items differentiating the two groups on the 5th-day examination.

Before describing these differences, we wish to note a certain stability and lack of change discernible in the United States babies. The scores of the American infants in this sample stayed within an average range on all three days. This is in contrast to results obtained in other groups of American infants who typically score below the average on day 1 and who

---

2. Pediatric and nutritional assessments for evidences of prematurity and dysmaturity according to Dubowitz et al. (1970) and Clifford (1954).

TABLE 2   MEAN SCORES FOR ZAMBIANS AND FOR AMERICANS ON DAY 1, 5, AND 10 FOR ALL MEASURES THAT DISTINGUISHED BETWEEN GROUPS ON AT LEAST ONE DAY[a]

Measures	Day 1		Day 5		Day 10	
	Zamb.	Amer.	Zamb.	Amer.	Zamb.	Amer.
Motor activity	*3.00*	*4.90*	5.89	5.50	*4.60*	*5.90*
Tempo at height	*3.20*	*5.77*	5.90	5.50	*4.40*	*6.44*
Rapidity of buildup	*3.22*	*4.80*	*5.62*	*4.50*	*3.50*	*5.50*
Irritability	*2.50*	*4.40*	4.40	4.70	3.80	5.00
Consolability	6.60	5.56	5.00	4.63	*6.12*	*4.75*
Social interest	4.20	4.29	6.20	5.22	*6.70*	*4.33*
Alertness	3.40	4.20	*6.30*	*5.11*	*7.40*	*4.80*
Follow with eyes	*2.40*	*4.16*	4.60	4.70	4.67	5.11
Reactivity to stimulation	3.35	4.38	5.30	4.71	*6.14*	*4.67*
Defensive movements	3.20	4.38	5.11	5.50	*4.90*	*6.11*
Cuddliness	*3.30*	*4.40*	5.22	5.60	6.30	5.12

[a]Scores in italics indicate that the difference between them was significant.

recover by day 5 (Brazelton, 1970). These latter groups were obtained from mothers who were medicated during delivery and whose infants demonstrated a resulting depression in all behavior. Note that the infants in the present sample were delivered with a minimal use of drugs, and by "natural" childbirth.

On the day 1 examination, there were 6 items on which the two groups of infants were significantly different. The Zambian infants scored lower on following with eyes ($p < .05$), motor activity ($p < .02$), tempo at height ($p < .10$), irritability ($p < .05$), rapidity of buildup ($p < .10$), and cuddliness ($p < .10$). On the day 5 examination, only 2 items differentiated the groups, with Americans scoring lower on rapidity of buildup ($p < .10$) and on alertness ($p < .10$).

The 10th-day examination comparisons found 8 items which distinguished the two groups. The Zambian infants scored lower on reactivity to stimulation ($p < .07$), defensive movements ($p < .05$), motor activity ($p < .05$), rapidity of buildup ($p < .05$), and tempo at height ($p < .02$). The Zambians scored higher on consolability ($p < .06$), social interest ($p < .02$), and alertness ($p < .02$). By day 10, also, muscle tone was better than average, in contrast to day 1. No longer were the Zambians limp. Their head control was good; passive resistance of limbs to flexion and extension normal; and they actively responded upon being held (scores on cuddliness were above average). Reference to Table 2 emphasizes again that it is the Zambian group which is changing, not the American group.

To summarize: the Americans remained approximately within the average range on all three days. On day 1, the Zambians scored lower than the Americans on items that seemed to reflect reactivity. By day 10, however, although (or maybe, because) the Zambians were still scoring low on items which measured motor reactivity, they were scoring higher on items which measured social attentiveness.

DISCUSSION

One of the questions we had been interested in was whether behavioral differences existed between cultural groups during the neonatal period. This question was certainly answered in the affirmative.

The most striking feature of the results is the difference in the pattern of increase in the scores of the Zambian and American infants. On the day 1 examination the Zambian infants scored low relative to the American infants and to their own later performance on behaviors related to activity and to alertness. They were not very irritable and did not invest much energy in being upset (as indicated by their scores on irritability, tempo, and rapidity of buildup). They also lacked energy for relating to the social and inanimate environment (as demonstrated by poor responses to being cuddled and to visual stimulation).

By the 10th day, there had been a dramatic change. They were alert, controlled in motor activities, and oriented toward their social environment. Their high scores on alertness and social interest were coupled with a high degree of consolability and low scores on overreactiveness—motor activity, rapidity of buildup, and tempo at height of disturbance. Their scores in defensive reactions and reactivity to inanimate stimulation seemed to indicate that their energy was directed toward and invested in the social environment. In contrast, the American infants' scores remained stable throughout the first 10 days.

Interesting though these differences may be, the real question is: what accounts for them?

We suggest that these differences are compatible with a view of some so-called "cultural" differences as resulting from a combination of the effects of genetic and nongenetic inheritance, operating in conjunction with certain child-rearing practices.

We start with the nongenetic inherited factors. We know that nongenetic inheritance certainly plays a role in determining the characteristics of children under some circumstances. The effects of changes in nongenetic inheritance are exemplified in a number of situations: Down's syndrome (which results from chromosomal changes that are highly correlated with mother's age); changes in the infant that result either from drugs ingested by the mother in early pregnancy or from hormonal imbalance during pregnancy (Baker, 1960; Brazelton, 1970; Money et al., 1968). Additionally, there are the nongenetic but inherited effects of protein malnutrition (Schaffer, 1960; Zamenhof et al., 1968); of infections suffered by the mother during pregnancy (Klein et al., 1971); and of depletion of the uterus, a depletion that results from a series of pregnancies following so closely upon one another that there is no opportunity for the uterus to recover. We know that the last three factors affect the infant's gain in body weight and growth in length in the uterus. Might they not also be responsible for behavioral differences between the neonates of different cultures?

The differences between Zambians and Americans on day 1 were differences in behavior that are usually associated with sheer physical energy. That the lack of energy was, in fact, the primary cause of the Zambian infants' low scores is made more credible by what we know of these infants' physical state. We could see that they were dehydrated. We also knew that their mothers had had low protein intake during pregnancy as well as a series of closely spaced pregnancies. These facts made it clear that the day 1 differences could easily reflect the effects of a stressed intrauterine environment. This environment was inherited, but nongenetic, and its effects were dramatic. Once their mothers began to nurse them, thereby both rehydrating them and providing them with needed nutrients, the Zambian infants became much more reactive.

An additional and complementary argument is also possible. Behavioral differences after birth are rapidly affected by factors other than inheritance. They are quickly molded by social factors, especially by such divergent child-rearing practices as these two groups were exposed to.

The change in behavior that was evident by day 10 was of a different quality from the changes that took place between days 1 and 5. First, the change involved more than simple recovery from a poor physiological environment. The behaviors that improved from day 1 to day 5 were behaviors that seemed to require a certain level of physical energy: the behaviors that changed from day 5 to day 10 were those commonly seen as requiring a certain level of social interest.

The changes from day 1 to day 5 seemed to be primarily attributable to the rehydration and nutrition that resulted from nutrients. We thought that the changes from day 5 to day 10 resulted primarily from certain child-rearing practices, and that these were of the sort that facilitate the development of muscle tone, alertness, and social responsivity.

The kind of motoric stimulation that the infants received seemed to put a premium on developing muscle tone. When asked to rouse their babies, the Zambian mothers picked them up under the arms and tossed them up and down in the air. All cries were first responded to with nursing. However, if this did not quiet the infant, the mother resorted to vigorous activity and bouncing. Goldberg (1971) has noted that from as early as 24 hours after delivery, the Zambian mother secures her infant to her body with a *dashica*, a long piece of cloth, in such a way that the infant essentially rides on the mother's hip. In this position, the infant's body has no support from the armpits up. Since his head is not supported, the infant must maintain a strong shoulder girdle response to keep his head steady. The mother places the infant in her *dashica* either by holding him by the arm or by holding his trunk under the arm and then swinging him over her shoulder. In short, this active handling of the infant seems to encourage the development of muscle tone.

But in addition to favoring the development of muscle tone, carrying the infant in a *dashica* seems to encourage alertness as well (Korner, 1970). In this position, an infant is able to see more than he would in other positions. Long periods of being carried also provide more opportunities for the infant to be tactually stimulated. This tactile stimulation by another person encourages social responsiveness on the part of the infant, but other practices also seem to facilitate social responsivity. Breast feeding is frequent and in response to any indication from the infant that he is either hungry or fussy. There is little attempt to make him wait (Goldberg, 1970, 1971).

When the infants are not being carried about, they are left uncovered on a bed in a family room where everyone, including siblings and visitors, can admire, play with, and hold the tiny infant. At night, the infant is swaddled loosely next to his mother in the same bed.

Since at birth the Zambian infants were very limp and quite unresponsive, one might wonder at their mothers's willingness to provide the infants with vigorous, stimulating experiences. We concluded that the mothers' practices were based on their expectancies of how their infants would develop. Assuming that the infants in our sample were not atypical of the population, one can infer that the Zambian mothers in our sample had seen other Zambian infants recover shortly after birth. One can also infer that these mothers thus had reason to expect that their infants, too, would recover in the same way. Individually, each mother's expectations were probably also reinforced by the dramatic change in muscle tone and responsivity that took place in her infant from day 1 to day 5, which she could easily have interpreted as evidence that her infant would continue to show improvement.

These expectations were based both on the Zambian mother's observation of her own and other infants' recovery from their state on day 1. The infants' ability to recover must reflect genetic capacities to respond to these practices. Such rapid recovery seems to point to inherited potential which is not incapacitated by conditions of intrauterine deprivation.

Contrast the Zambian caretaker practices with those of our American mothers. The American infants' behavior reflected very different inherited (genetic and nongenetic) potential at birth. In addition, they remained in the hospital environment for a minimum of 4 days. Five of the babies roomed in with their mothers after 48 hours, and it is presumed that their cries were responded to with nursing or handling by their mothers. The 5 infants who were kept in the nursery were fed every 4 hours, day and night, on hospital schedules. The rooming-in mothers were urged to feed the babies on a similar schedule, and because of their inexperience and the delay in getting breast milk (4 to 5 days in a primiparous mother), it is obvious that there was less feeding and handling than there was among Zambian mothers. When these American mothers went home, they followed the cultural emphasis in the United States on quieting the infant and protecting him from external stimulation. There is no care practice that even approximates the Zambian mother's almost constant contact with her infant. From our observation of them in their homes, it was quite obvious that these American mothers provided a very different early environment for their infants. The unchanging behavior over the 10 days reflects a different inheritance as well as the relatively nonstimulating environment to which the babies were exposed in this period.

SUMMARY

The abilities of an infant and the changes in those abilities reflect inherited factors—both genetic and nongenetic—cultural practices and expectations. An understanding of the recovery of the Zambian infants and the pattern of performance of the American infants reflects all three. The Zambian infants recovered rapidly from an intrauterine (inherited) environment which had been physiologically inadequate. Their rapid recovery reflected the infants' genetic abilities as well as the supportive child-rearing practices and the cultural expectations for early precocious development. The American infants reflected an adequate intrauterine environment with their more unchanging behavioral patterns. The protective, relatively nonstimulating child-rearing practices were suited to genetic capabilities as well as to cultural expectations of a "prolonged" and protected infancy.

REFERENCES

Ainsworth, M. D. S. (1967), *Infancy in Uganda: Infant Care and the Growth of Love.* Baltimore: Johns Hopkins Press.

Apgar, V. (1953), A proposal for a new method of evaluation of the newborn infant. *Curr. Res. Anesth. Analges.,* 32:260–283.

Baker, J. B. E. (1960), The effects of drugs on the fetus. *Pharmacol. Rev.,* 12:37–90.

Brazelton, T. B. (1970), Effect of prenatal drugs on the behavior of the neonate. *Amer. J. Psychiat.* 126:1261–1266.

_____ (1973), *Neonatal Behavioral Assessment Scale.* London: Heinemann.

_____, Koslowski, B., & Main, M. (1973), Origins of reciprocity: mother and infant interaction. In: *Origins of Behavior,* Vol. I, ed. M. Lewis & L. Rosenblum. New York: Wiley, pp. 49–76.

_____, Robey, J. S., & Collier, G. A. (1969), Infant development in the Zinacanteco Indians of Southern Mexico. *Pediatrics,* 44:274–290.

Clifford, S. H. (1954), Postmaturity with placental dysfunction: clinical syndrome and pathologic findings. *J. Pediat.,* 44:1–13.

Dubowitz, L. M. S., Dubowitz, V., & Goldberg, C. (1970), Clinical assessment of gestational age in the newborn infant. *J. Pediat.,* 77:1–10.

Freedman, D. G. & Freedman, N. (1969), Behavioral differences between Chinese-American and American newborns. *Nature,* 224:1227.

Gerber, M. & Dean, R. F. A. (1959), The state of development of newborn African children. *Lancet,* 1: 1216.

Goldberg, S. A. (1970), Infant care in Zambia: Measuring maternal behavior. HDRU Reports No. 13, Lusaka, Zambia.

_____ (1971), Infant care and growth in urban Zambia. Presented at the meetings of the Society for Research in Child Development, Minneapolis, Minn., April 4.

Klein, R. E., Habicht, J. P., & Yarbrough, C. (1971), Effect of protein-calorie malnutrition on mental development. Incap (Institute of Nutrition of Central America, Panama) publication no. I-571, Guatemala, CA.

Korner, A. (1970), Visual alertness in neonates: individual differences and their correlates. *Percept. Mot. Skills*, 31:499–509.

Money, J., Ehrhardt, A. A., & Masica, D. N. (1968), Fetal feminization induced by androgen insensitivity in the Testicular Feminizing Syndrome. *Johns Hopkins Med. J.*, 123:105–114.

Prechtl, H. & Beintema, O. (1964), *The Neurological Examination of the Full Term Newborn Infant.* London: Heinemann.

Schaffer, A. J. (1960), *Diseases of the Newborn.* Philadelphia: Saunders, p. 628.

Zamenhof, S., Van Marthens, E., & Margolis, F. L. (1968), DNA and protein in neonatal brain: alteration by maternal dietary restriction. *Science*, 160:322–323.

QUESTIONS

1. What is the Neonatal Behavioral Assessment Scale and what newborn abilities does it assess?
2. What infant ability is measured when an infant is talked to, rocked, and a hand is placed on the baby's belly?
3. What group differences between Zambian and American babies were found on day 10 of the assessment?
4. What specific child-rearing practices in these two communities may have led to the differences in infant behavior that were observed?
5. Do you agree with Brazelton and his colleagues about the importance of culture in organizing the infant's emotional states in the first few days of life? Why or why not?
6. In this study, Zambian babies appear to be raised in a way that prepares them for the social expectations of their community. What do the child-rearing practices of the American mothers prepare their babies for?

10 Temperament and the Reactions to Unfamiliarity

JEROME KAGAN

Temperament is defined as the way in which an individual behaves. It includes stylistic aspects of behavior, such as emotional vigor, tempo, and regularity of responsiveness to experience. Temperament is interesting because it emerges early in life, it is evident across a wide range of situations, and it appears to be relatively stable over time. There is also evidence that some aspects of temperament may be inherited. Characteristics such as emotionality, activity, and sociability are more similar in identical than in fraternal twins. For these reasons, many psychologists consider temperament the seed of what becomes an individual's unique personality.

One way in which temperament is measured in infancy is by seeing how children react to unfamiliar events. Some babies react in a heightened fashion with much movement and distress. Others remain relaxed and calm. In this article, Jerome Kagan, a leading researcher in the area of infant temperament, discusses research that examines how children with these different styles reacted to unfamiliar events when they were infants and when they were 5 years old. The data Kagan describes suggest some stability in these styles of reaction over this time period. However, some aspects of temperament changed.

These data illustrate an important point about development. Even when characteristics are developmentally stable, they typically assume different forms at different developmental periods. Furthermore, maturation of the system can sometimes modify extreme behaviors.

The behavioral reactions to unfamiliar events are basic phenomena in all vertebrates. Four-month-old infants who show a low threshold to become distressed and motorically aroused to unfamiliar stimuli are more likely than others to become fearful and subdued during early childhood, whereas infants who show a high arousal threshold are more likely to become bold and sociable. After presenting some developmental correlates and trajectories of these 2 temperamental biases, I consider their implications for psychopathology and the relation between propositions containing psychological and biological concepts.

INTRODUCTION

A readiness to react to events that differ from those encountered in the recent or distant past is one of the distinguishing characteristics of all mammalian species. Thus, the events with the greatest power to produce both an initial orienting and sustained attention in infants older than 3 to 4 months are variations on what is familiar, often called discrepant events (Fagan, 1981; Kagan, Kearsley, & Zelazo, 1980). By 8 months of age, discrepant events can produce a vigilant posture of quiet staring and, occasionally, a wary face and a cry of distress if the event cannot be assimilated easily (Bronson, 1970). That is why Hebb (1946) made discrepancy a major basis for fear reactions in animals, why a fear reaction to strangers occurs in the middle of the first year in children growing up in a variety of cultural settings, and, perhaps, why variation in the initial behavioral reaction to novelty exists in almost every vertebrate species studied (Wilson, Coleman, Clark, & Biederman, 1993).

Recent discoveries by neuroscientists enrich these psychological facts. The hippocampus plays an impor-

Reprinted with permission of the Society for Research in Child Development from *Child Development,* 68 (1997), pp. 139–143.

Address and affiliation: Corresponding author: Jerome Kagan, Harvard University, Department of Psychology, Cambridge, MA 02138; e-mail: JK@WJH.HARVARD.EDU

tant role in the detection of discrepant events (Squire & Knowlton, 1995). Projections from the hippocampus provoke activity in the amygdala and lead to changes in autonomic function and posture and, in older children, to reflection and anticipation (Shimamura, 1995). Because these neural structures and their projections are influenced by a large number of neurotransmitters and neuromodulators, it is reasonable to expect inherited differences in the neurochemistry of these structures and circuits and, therefore, in their excitability. Variation in the levels of, or receptors for, corticotropin releasing hormone, norepinephrine, cortisol, dopamine, glutamate, GABA, opioids, acetylcholine, and other molecules might be accompanied by differences in the intensity and form of responsivity to unfamiliarity (Cooper, Bloom, & Roth, 1991). This speculation is supported by research with infants and children (Kagan, 1994). This article summarizes what has been learned about two temperamental types of children who react in different ways to unfamiliarity, considers the implications of these two temperamental categories for psychopathology, and comments briefly on the relation between psychological and biological constructs.

INFANT REACTIVITY AND FEARFUL BEHAVIOR

About 20% of a large sample of 462 healthy, Caucasian, middle-class, 16-week-old infants became both motorically active and distressed to presentations of brightly colored toys moved back and forth in front of their faces, tape recordings of voices speaking brief sentences, and cotton swabs dipped in dilute butyl alcohol applied to the nose. These infants are called high reactive. By contrast, about 40% of infants with the same family and ethnic background remained motorically relaxed and did not fret or cry to the same set of unfamiliar events. These infants are called low reactive. The differences between high and low reactives can be interpreted as reflecting variation in the excitability of the amygdala and its projections to the ventral striatum, hypothalamus, cingulate, central gray, and medulla (Amaral, Price, Pitkanen, & Carmichael, 1992; Davis, 1992).

When these high and low reactive infants were observed in a variety of unfamiliar laboratory situations at 14 and 21 months, about one-third of the 73 high reactives were highly fearful (4 or more fears), and only 3% showed minimal fear (0 or 1 fear) at both ages. By contrast, one-third of the 147 low reactives were minimally fearful at both ages (0 or 1 fear), and only 4% displayed high levels of fear (Kagan, 1994).

The profiles of high and low fear to unfamiliar events, called inhibited and uninhibited, are heritable,

to a modest degree, in 1- to 2-year-old middle-class children (DiLalla, Kagan, & Reznick, 1994; Robinson, Kagan, Reznick, & Corley, 1992). Further, high reactives show greater sympathetic reactivity in the cardiovascular system than low reactives during the first 2 years (Kagan, 1994; Snidman, Kagan, Riordan, & Shannon, 1995).

As children approach the fourth and fifth years, they gain control of crying to and reflex retreat from unfamiliar events and will only show these responses to very dangerous events or to situations that are not easily or ethically created in the laboratory. Hence, it is important to ask how high and low reactive infants might respond to unfamiliar laboratory situations when they are 4–5 years old. Each species has a biologically preferred reaction to novelty. Rabbits freeze, monkeys display a distinct facial grimace, and cats arch their backs. In humans, restraint on speech seems to be an analogue of the immobility that animals display in novel situations (Panksepp, Sacks, Crepeau, & Abbott, 1991), for children often become quiet as an initial reaction to unfamiliar situations (Asendorpf, 1990; Kagan, Reznick, & Gibbons, 1989; Kagan, Reznick, & Snidman, 1988; Murray, 1971). It is also reasonable to expect that the activity in limbic sites provoked by an unfamiliar social situation might interfere with the brain states that mediate the relaxed emotional state that is indexed by smiling and laughter (Adamec, 1991; Amaral et al., 1992).

When the children who had been classified as high and low reactive were interviewed at $4\frac{1}{2}$ years of age by an unfamiliar female examiner who was blind to their prior behavior, the 62 high reactives talked and smiled significantly less often (means of 41 comments and 17 smiles) than did the 94 low reactives (means of 57 comments and 28 smiles) during a 1 hour test battery: $F(1, 152) = 4.51$, $p < .05$ for spontaneous comments; $F(1, 152) = 15.01$, $p < .01$ for spontaneous smiles. Although spontaneous comments and smiles were positively correlated ($r = 0.4$), the low reactives displayed significantly more smiles than would have been predicted from a regression of number of smiles on number of spontaneous comments. The high reactives displayed significantly fewer smiles than expected. Every one of the nine children who smiled more than 50 times had been a low reactive infant.

However, only a modest proportion of children maintained an extreme form of their theoretically expected profile over the period from 4 months to $4\frac{1}{2}$ years, presumably because of the influence of intervening family experiences (Arcus, 1991). Only 19% of the high reactives displayed a high level of fear at both 14 and 21 months (> 4 fears), together with low values (below the mean) for both spontaneous comments and smiles at $4\frac{1}{2}$ years. But not one low reactive infant actualized such a consistently fearful and emotionally subdued profile. By contrast, 18% of low reactive infants showed the opposite profile of low fear (0 or 1 fear) at both 14 and 21 months together with high values for both spontaneous smiles and spontaneous comments at $4\frac{1}{2}$ years. Only one high reactive infant actualized that prototypic, uninhibited profile. Thus, it is uncommon for either temperamental type to develop and to maintain the seminal features of the other type, but quite common for each type to develop a profile that is characteristic of the less extreme child who is neither very timid nor very bold.

The $4\frac{1}{2}$-year-old boys who had been high reactive infants had significantly higher resting heart rates than did low reactives, but the differences between high and low reactive girls at this older age took a different form. The high reactive girls did not show the expected high negative correlation (-0.6 to -0.8) between heart rate and heart rate variability. It is possible that the greater sympathetic reactivity of high reactive girls interfered with the usual, vagally induced inverse relation between heart rate and heart rate variability (Porges, Arnold, & Forbes, 1973; Richards, 1985).

Honest disagreement surrounds the conceptualization of infant reactivity as a continuum of arousal or as two distinct categories. The raw motor activity score at 4 months formed a continuum, but the distribution of distress cries did not. Some infants never fretted or cried; others cried a great deal. A more important defense of the decision to treat high and low reactivity as two distinct categories is the fact that within each of the two categories variation in motor activity and crying was unrelated to later fearfulness or sympathetic reactivity. If reactivity were a continuous trait, then a low reactive infant with extremely low motor and distress scores should be less fearful than one who showed slightly more arousal. But that prediction was not affirmed. Second, infants who showed high motor arousal but no crying or minimal motor arousal with frequent crying showed developmental profiles that were different from those who were categorized as low or high reactive. Finally, high and low reactives differed in physical and physiological features that imply qualitatively different genetic constitutions. For example, high reactives have narrower faces than low reactives in the second year of life (Arcus & Kagan, 1995). Unpublished data from our laboratory reveal that the prevalence of atopic allergies among both children and their parents is significantly greater among high than low reactive infants. Studies of monozygotic and dizygotic same-sex twin pairs reveal significant heritability for inhibited and uninhibited behavior in the second year of life (Robinson et al., 1992). These facts imply that the two temperamental groups represent qualitatively different types and do not lie on a continuum of arousal or reactivity to stimulation.

The decision to regard individuals with very different values on a construct as members of the discrete categories or as falling on a continuum will depend on the scientists' purpose. Scientists who are interested in the relation, across families and genera, between brain size and body mass treat the two measurements as continuous. However, biologists interested in the maternal behavior of mice and chimpanzees regard these two mammals as members of qualitatively different groups. Similarly, if psychologists are interested in the physiological foundations of high and low reactives, it will be more useful to regard the two groups as categories. But those who are giving advice to mothers who complain about the ease of arousal and irritability of their infants may treat the arousal as a continuum.

IMPLICATIONS

The differences between high reactive–inhibited and low reactive–uninhibited children provoke speculation on many issues; I deal briefly with implications for psychopathology and the relation between psychological and biological propositions.

ANXIETY DISORDER

The high reactive infants who became very inhibited 4-year-olds—about 20% of all high reactives—have a low threshold for developing a state of fear to unfamiliar events, situations, and people. It is reasonable to expect that these children will be at a higher risk than most for developing one of the anxiety disorders when they become adolescents or adults. The childhood data do not provide a clue as to which particular anxiety profile will be most prevalent. However, an extensive clinical interview with early adolescents (13–14 years old), who had been classified 11 years earlier (at 21 or 31 months) as inhibited or uninhibited (Kagan et al., 1988), revealed that social phobia was more frequent among inhibited than among uninhibited adolescents, whereas specific phobias, separation anxiety, or compulsive symptoms did not differentiate the two groups (Schwartz, personal communication). This intriguing result, which requires replication, has interesting theoretical ramifications.

Research with animals, usually rats, suggests that acquisition of a fear reaction (e.g., freezing or potentiated startle) to a conditioned stimulus (light or tone) that had been paired with electric shock is mediated by a circuitry that is different from the one that mediates the conditioned response to the context in which the conditioning had occurred (LeDoux, 1995).

Davis (personal communication) has found that a potentiated startle reaction in the rat to the context in which light had been paired with shock involves a circuit from the amygdala to the bed nucleus of the stria terminalis and the septum. The potentiated startle reaction to the conditioned stimulus does not require that circuit. A phobia of spiders or bridges resembles an animal's reaction of freezing to a conditioned stimulus, but a quiet, avoidant posture at a party resembles a fearful reaction to a context. That is, the person who is extremely shy at a party of strangers is not afraid of any particular person or of the setting. Rather, the source of the uncertainty is a situation in which the shy person had experienced anxiety with other strangers. Thus, social phobia may rest on a neurophysiology that is different from that of specific phobia.

Conduct Disorder

The correlation between social class and the prevalence of conduct disorder or delinquency is so high it is likely that the vast majority of children with these profiles acquired their risk status as a result of life conditions, without the mediation of a particular temperamental vulnerability. However, a small proportion—probably no more than 10%—who began their delinquent careers before age 10, and who often committed violent crimes as adolescents, might inherit a physiology that raises their threshold for the conscious experience of anticipatory anxiety and/or guilt over violating community standards for civil behavior (Tremblay, Pihl, Vitaro, & Dubkin, 1994). Damasio (1994) and Mountcastle (1995) have suggested that the surface of the ventromedial prefrontal cortex receives sensory information (from the amygdala) that originates in the peripheral targets, like heart, skin, gut, and muscles. Most children and adults who think about committing a crime experience a subtle feeling that accompanies anticipation of the consequences of an antisocial act. That feeling, which might be called anticipatory anxiety, shame, or guilt, provides an effective restraint on the action. However, if a small proportion of children possessed a less excitable amygdala, or a ventromedial surface that was less responsive, they would be deprived of the typical intensity of this feeling and, as a result, might be less restrained than the majority (Kochanska, Murray, Jacques, Koenig, & Vandegeest, 1996; Zahn-Waxler, Cole, Welsh, & Fox, 1995). If these children are reared in homes and play in neighborhoods in which antisocial behavior is socialized, they are unlikely to become delinquents; perhaps they will become group leaders. However, if these children live in families that do not socialize aggression consistently and play in neighborhoods that provide temptations for antisocial behavior, they might be candidates for a delinquent career.

Biology and Psychology

The renewed interest in temperament has brought some psychologists in closer intellectual contact with neuroscientists. Although this interaction will be beneficial to both disciplines, there is a tension between traditional social scientists who describe and explain behavioral and emotional events using only psychological terms and a smaller group who believe that an acknowledgment of biological events is theoretically helpful. The recent, dramatic advances in the neurosciences have led some scholars to go further and to imply that, in the future, robust generalizations about psychological processes might not be possible without study of the underlying biology (LeDoux, 1995).

Although some neuroscientists recognize that the psychological phenomena of thought, planning, and emotion are emergent—as a blizzard is emergent from the physics of air masses—the media suggest, on occasion, that the biological descriptions are sufficient to explain the psychological events. This publicity creates a misperception that the biological and psychological are competing explanations when, of course, they are not. Vernon Mountcastle notes that although "every mental process is a brain process, . . . not every mentalistic sentence is identical to some neurophysiological sentence. Mind and brain are not identical, no more than lung and respiration are identical" (Mountcastle, 1995, p. 294).

Some neuroscientists, sensing correctly the community resistance to a strong form of biological determinism, are emphasizing the malleability of the neuron's genome to environmental events. A few neurobiologists have come close to declaring that the human genome, like Locke's image of the child's mind, is a tabula rasa that is subject to continual change. This position tempts citizens unfamiliar with neuroscience to conclude that there may be a linear cascade that links external events (e.g., loss of a loved one) directly to changes in genes, physiology, and, finally, behavior, with the psychological layer (e.g., a mood of sadness) between brain physiology and apathetic behavior being relatively unimportant. This error is as serious as the one made by the behaviorists 60 years ago when they assumed a direct connection between a stimulus and an overt response and ignored what was happening in the brain. Both corpora of evidence are necessary if we are to understand the emergence of psychological qualities and their inevitable variation. "The phenomena of human existence and experience are always simultaneously biological and social, and an adequate explanation must involve both" (Rose, 1995, p. 380).

ACKNOWLEDGMENTS

This paper represents portions of the G. Stanley Hall Lecture delivered at the annual meeting of the American Psychological Association, New York City, August 1995. Preparation of this paper was supported, in part, by grants from the John D. and Catherine T. MacArthur Foundation, William T. Grant Foundation, and NIMH grant 47077. The author thanks Nancy Snidman and Doreen Arcus for their collaboration in the research summarized.

REFERENCES

Adamec, R. E. (1991). Anxious personality and the cat. In B. J. Carroll & J. E. Barett (Eds.), *Psychopathology in the brain* (pp. 153–168). New York: Raven.

Amaral, D. J., Price, L., Pitkanen, A., & Carmichael, S. T. (1992). Anatomical organization of the primate amygdaloid complex. In J. P. Aggleton (Ed.), *The amygdala* (pp. 1–66). New York: Wiley.

Arcus, D. M., (1991). *Experiential modification of temperamental bias in inhibited and uninhibited children*. Unpublished doctoral dissertation, Harvard University.

Arcus, D. M., & Kagan, J. (1995). Temperament and craniofacial variation in the first two years. *Child Development, 66,* 1529–1540.

Asendorpf, J. B. (1990). Development of inhibition during childhood. *Developmental Psychology, 26,* 721–730.

Bronson, G. W. (1970). Fear of visual novelty. *Developmental Psychology, 2,* 33–40.

Cooper, J. R., Bloom, F. E., & Roth, R. H. (1991). *Biochemical basis of neuropharmacology*. New York: Oxford University Press.

Damasio, A. (1994). *Descartes' error*. New York: Putnam.

Davis, M. (1992). The role of the amygdala in conditioned fear. In J. P. Aggleton (Ed.), *The amygdala* (pp. 256–305). New York: Wiley.

DiLalla, L. F., Kagan, J., & Reznick, J. S. (1994). Genetic etiology of behavioral inhibition among two year olds. *Infant Behavior and Development, 17,* 401–408.

Fagan, J. F. (1981). Infant intelligence. *Intelligence, 5,* 239–243.

Hebb, D. O. (1946). The nature of fear. *Psychological Review, 53,* 259–276.

Kagan, J. (1994). *Galen's prophecy*. New York: Basic.

Kagan, J., Kearsley, R. B., & Zelazo, P. R. (1980). *Infancy*. Cambridge, MA: Harvard University Press.

Kagan, J., Reznick, J. S., & Gibbons, J. (1989). Inhibited and uninhibited types of children. *Child Development, 60,* 838–845.

Kagan, J., Reznick, J. S., & Snidman, N. (1988). Biological bases of childhood shyness. *Science, 240,* 167–171.

Kochanska, G., Murray, K., Jacques, T. Y., Koenig, A. L., & Vandegeest, K. A. (1996). Inhibitory control in young children and its role in emerging internalization. *Child Development, 67,* 490–507.

LeDoux, J. E. (1995). In search of an emotional system in the brain. In M. S. Gazzinaga (Ed.), *The cognitive neurosciences* (pp. 1049–1062). Cambridge, MA: MIT Press.

Mountcastle, V. (1995). The evolution of ideas concerning the function of the neocortex. *Cerebral Cortex, 5,* 289–295.

Murray, D. C. (1971). Talk, silence, and anxiety. *Psychological Bulletin, 75,* 244–260.

Panksepp, J., Sacks, D. S., Crepeau, L. J., & Abbott, B. B. (1991). The psycho and neurobiology of fear systems in the brain. In M. R. Denny (Ed.), *Fear, avoidance, and phobias* (pp. 17–59). Hillsdale, NJ: Erlbaum.

Porges, S. W., Arnold, W. R., & Forbes, E. J. (1973). Heart rate variability: An index of attention responsivity in human newborns. *Developmental Psychology, 8,* 85–92.

Richards, J. E. (1985). Respiratory sinus arrhythmia predicts heart rate and visual responses during visual attention in 14 to 20 week old infants. *Psychophysiology, 22,* 101–109.

Robinson, J. L., Kagan, J., Reznick, J. S., & Corley, R. (1992). The heritability of inhibited and uninhibited behavior: A twin study. *Developmental Psychology, 28,* 1030–1037.

Rose, R. J. 1995. Genes and human behavior. In J. T. Spence, J. M. Darley, & D. P. Foss (Eds.), *Annual review of psychology* (pp. 625–654). Palo Alto, CA: Annual Reviews.

Shimamura, A. P. (1995). Memory and frontal lobe function. In M. S. Gazzinaga (Ed.), *The cognitive neurosciences* (pp. 803–814). Cambridge, MA: MIT Press.

Snidman, N., Kagan, J., Riordan, L., & Shannon, D., (1995.) Cardiac function and behavioral reactivity in infancy. *Psychophysiology, 31,* 199–207.

Squire, L. R., & Knowlton, B. J. (1995). Memory, hippocampus, and brain systems. In M. S. Gazzinaga (Ed.), *The cognitive neurosciences* (pp. 825–838). Cambridge, MA: MIT Press.

Tremblay, R. E., Pihl, R. O., Vitaro, F., & Dubkin, P. L. (1994). Predicting early onset of male antisocial behavior from preschool behavior. *Archives of General Psychiatry, 51,* 732–739.

Wilson, D. S., Coleman, K., Clark, A. B., & Biederman, L. (1993). Shy-bold continuum in pumpkinseed sunfish (*Lepomis gibbosus*): An ecological study of a psychological trait. *Journal of Comparative Psychology, 107,* 250–260.

Zahn-Waxler, C., Cole, P., Welsh, J. D., & Fox, N. A. (1995). Psychophysiological correlates of empathy and prosocial behavior in preschool children with behavioral problems. *Development and Psychopathology, 7,* 27–48.

Questions

1. Why are reactions to unfamiliar events used to assess infant temperament?
2. What are the behavioral characteristics of inhibited and uninhibited children?
3. How did high-reactive children respond to the interview when they were 5 years of age? How did low-reactive children respond?
4. What do the longitudinal findings indicate about the stability of reactivity over the first 5 years of life?
5. Are shy children more likely to be high- or low-reactive children? Why?
6. Does temperamental inhibition play a role in antisocial behavior in adolescence? If so, what proportion of antisocial behavior might it explain and why?

PART **II**
Infancy

The period of infancy is a remarkable time of growth. In fact, the rapid pace of change in the first two years of life is the fastest period of change that humans experience after birth. Changes during infancy occur across the entire spectrum of human behavior and include physical growth, perceptual and cognitive skills, language, and social and emotional competence. Most research on infants concentrates on development in one of these areas. This is because the design and conduct of infant research is very difficult. Infants have only brief periods every day during which their behavioral state is suited to research observation. Although the length of these periods increases with development over the first two years, there are still other challenges in studying infants. Their social and language skills are just emerging, so many of the usual data–gathering techniques that involve conversation or interaction are problematic.

Despite these challenges, two important points stand out in the research included in this section. First, infants are extremely competent in a number of ways. The following articles demonstrate this capability in the areas of memory (Rovee-Collier), emotion (Campos, Bertenthal, and Kermoian), language (Werker), social coordination (Bruner and Sherwood), and emotional adjustment (Radke-Yarrow, Cummings, Kuczynski, and Chapman). Considered together, these competencies paint a portrait of the infant as an extremely complex organism that is on a rapid and directed course of growth. Second, researchers have devised a number of creative techniques to observe infants, which have allowed us to begin to understand infants "on their terms." That is, these procedures build on the competencies and interests of infants and use them in ways to distinguish competing explanations of what is developing early in life.

It is important to remember as you read these articles that they not only describe important qualities of infant experience and development, they also describe the nature of the human organism itself. What is clear in all these studies is that the infant is an organism that has powerful cognitive and perceptual skills that connect the child in multiple ways to the social and cultural world in which development occurs. This context not only supports development during this period, it guides the course of growth. Different cultural communities respond to this period of development in different ways.

For instance, in the United States today and in many Western nations, there is increasing use of nonfamily-based care in the early years, which is the topic of the article by Scarr, Phillips, and McCartney. Despite their differences, each culture establishes ways of supporting development that are coordinated with the needs of the infant and the goals of the family and the society. This is the type of coordination across institutional levels that Bronfenbrenner discusses in his ecological model of development.

11 Early Rule Structure: The Case of "Peekaboo"

JEROME S. BRUNER · V. SHERWOOD

Humans are social animals and we create and participate in many social activities that are governed by rules. From the beginning of life, infants participate in some social activities that are structured by adults. For these activities to be successful, they must be coordinated with the emerging skills and capabilities of the infants involved. A common activity involving adults and young children is the game peekaboo. This game draws on the infant's emerging skills of responsiveness, anticipation, and object knowledge. The adult helps coordinate the infant's skills with the rule structure of the game.

In the following article, Bruner and Sherwood describe the social synchronization that occurs in infant–mother play and suggest that development occurs through participation in such activities. What is especially interesting about this research is that the same mother–child dyads were observed playing this game over a 10-month period beginning when the child was 7 months of age. The partners maintained interest in this game over this time. However, in many ways the nature of the game changed. In particular, as the children developed, their participation changed. They assumed more responsibility for the game and showed increased awareness of the conventions or rules of play. By the end of the observational period, children not only played the game, they began inventing new ways to play it. However, as you will see, not all dyads were successful at this. Bruner and Sherwood demonstrate that the very flow of ordinary interaction forms the substrate of individual development in a number of ways.

They also show that this flow is not a foregone conclusion. Variation exists, and different forms have different consequences for development.

Peekaboo surely must rank as one of the most universal forms of play between adults and infants. It is rich indeed in the mechanisms it exhibits. For in point of fact, the game depends upon the infant's capacity to integrate a surprisingly wide range of phenomena. For one, the very playing of the game depends upon the child having some degree of mastery of object permanence, the capacity to recognize the continued existence of an object when it is out of sight (e.g. Piaget, 1954). Charlesworth (1966) has shown, moreover, that the successful playing of the game is dependent in some measure on the child being able to keep track of the location in which a face has disappeared, the child showing more persistent effects when the reappearance of a face varied unexpectedly with respect to its prior position. Greenfield (1970) has also indicated that the initial effect of the game depends upon the presence not only of the reappearing face, but also of an accompanying vocalization by the mother, although with repetition the role of vocalization declined. She also found that the voice was increasingly important the less familiar the setting in which the game was played. It is quite plain, then, that complex expectancies are built up in the infant in the course of playing the game, and that these expectancies are characterized by considerable spatio-temporal structuring.

Another way of saying the same thing is to note that the child very soon becomes sensitive to the 'rules of the game' as he plays it. That is to say, he expects disappearance and reappearance to be in a certain place, at a certain time, accompanied by certain vocalizations, in certain general settings. The bulk of the studies reported in the literature suggest that these 'conventions', though they may rest upon certain preadapted readinesses to respond to disappearance and reappearance, are soon converted into rules for defining the pattern of play. If this were the case, one would expect that not only would the child have learned procedures, but would have learned them in a way that is characteristic of rule learning— i.e. in a general form, with assignable roles, with permissible substitutions of moves, etc.

The present study is concerned specifically with the conversion of peekaboo procedures into rule structures and, without intending to minimize the importance of preadapted patterns of response in making the game possible, we shall concentrate upon this aspect of the matter.

The study is based upon an intensive investigation of six infants over a period of 10 months, from seven to 17 months of age. The infants and their mothers were seen once a fortnight at our laboratory for an hour, and among the instructions given to the mothers was one asking them to show us the games that they and their infants most enjoyed playing. Our observations of peekaboo are all based upon behaviour spontaneously produced by the mothers in play, all but one of them including peekaboo in the play they exhibited. All sessions were videotaped and analysis was carried out on the video records. Partly for convenience of reporting and partly because each pair developed somewhat different procedures, we shall concentrate on a single mother-infant dyad over the 10-month period. The corpus of such play for this dyad consisted of 22 episodes of peekaboo, the first at 10 months, the last at 15 months. Peekaboo starts earlier than our initial age and goes on later, but the sample of games over the five-month period suffices to illustrate the points we wish to make. Though the other infant-mother dyads show some differences from the one we are reporting, they are in no sense different in pattern.

OBSERVATIONS

The first thing to be noted in the one mother–daughter (Diane) dyad on which we shall concentrate is that all instances of the game are quite notably constrained with respect to their limits. That is to say, the game always starts after the two players have made an explicit contact. This is the opening move, but it should be noted immediately that here, as in other features of the game, variation prevails. In most instances, initial contact is by face-to-face mutual looking. Where this does not occur, the mother may use either vocalization to contact the child or make the hiding 'instrument' conspicuous. The following table gives the frequencies of opening moves.

Face-to-face contact	16 (of 21 episodes in which orientation could be ascertained)
Vocalization	9 (of 22)
Highlighting of instrument	3 (of 22)

Typically, vocalization and face-to-face contact go together, with seven out of nine episodes of vocalization being accompanied by face-to-face contact. Interestingly enough, the mother will sometimes use a chance event as a 'starter' as when, inadvertently, her smock hides the child's face and the mother uses this as a start for a round of peekaboo. Also, there is what might best be called the 'opportunistic start', in which the mother when drying the child's hair after a bath 'lightens' the occasion by turning the drying with towel into an episode of peekaboo—a pattern also used by mothers to divert a fretting baby.

As Garvey (in press) has put it, social games can be described in terms of (a) the nature of the format, (b) the turns of each player and (c) the rounds in which the turns are sequenced. In the peekaboo situation, the initial round is a mutual attention-focusing episode that seems invariant although its form, as we have seen, may vary from one instance of the peekaboo format to the next.

The second round of peekaboo is the actual act of hiding and its accompaniments. Note first that there are four alternatives possible: mother can be hidden, or child, and the act of hiding can be initiated by the mother or the infant. The four alternatives and their frequencies are as follows.

M initiated, M hidden	8
C initiated, C hidden	2
M initiated, C hidden	11
C initiated, M hidden	0
[Ambiguous	1]

We may note that whilst there are at most three instances of the child initiating the hiding act, and all of these came at 15 months, they indicate that the child is by no means always a passive participant. We shall have more to say of this later in discussing role reversal. One of the striking features of what is hidden is that it is about equally distributed between the mother's face being masked and the child's—one of the forms of variation that the mother uses in order to keep uncertainty operative within the game. The child seems readily to accept this variation in the format and, indeed, seems to take a certain delight in it.

What is very notable is that there is virtually complete openness with regard to the instrument and mode used for hiding. The game when first observed was carried out exclusively with a nappy and hiding was controlled by the mother, and this occurred six times, hiding herself four times and the child twice. Thereafter, the distribution of the remaining episodes was five times nappy, five times clothing, three times a towel, two times a chair, and once with the child averting her head. In short, the nature of the hiding instrument and the masking act might almost be called optional in constrast to certain obligatory features, such as the requirement of initial contact.

During the period of hiding, and we shall discuss the limits on its length below, there is a further ancillary feature of the game—a mode of sustaining contact during hiding. This occurs both on the mother's side and on the child's. In 16 of the 22 episodes, mother uses either the rising intonation pattern of the typical Where question ('Where's Diane?' or 'Where's baby?' or 'Where's mummy?') or employs an extended 'Ahhhh', sometimes with a rising intonation pattern. In one sense, this act on the part of the mother can be thought of as helping the child sustain attention and bridging any uncertainty concerning the mother's 'conservation' behind the hiding instrument. The child's responses during hiding seem, on the other hand, to be expressions of excitement or anticipation, though they help the mother control her own output of bridging vocalizations to keep the child at an appropriate activation level. There are 13 in 19 episodes involving a hiding cloth where the child actively seeks to remove the hiding mask from the mother's or her own face. It is to these initiatives that the mother often responds with vocalization as if to control the child's activation. This part of the game is characteristically 'non-rule bound' and seems to be an instance, rather, of the mother providing a scaffold for the child.

We come now to a crucial round in the game: uncovering and reappearance. Note first a point already made—hiding time is very constrained: 19 of the 22 episodes range between two and seven seconds, with only one being above seven (at 10 months) and two at one second. It is only at 15 months, when the child consistently controls reappearance, that there is a fairly homogeneous and rapid hiding time: five episodes in a row ranging from one to two seconds. But note that at this age the child has virtually given up 'static' peekaboo for an ambulatory version, so that variation is now in format rather than in timing. The five uniformly fast episodes were all with a nappy—an old and familiar game that is much less exciting for the child than the ambulatory game we shall describe below. One of these episodes, a one-second instance, was completely controlled by the child, and between

two was an instance where the child demanded the game vocatively after she had failed to cover her own face successfully. We believe that the constraint on time of hiding is a reflection of the appreciation of the child's limited attention span by both members of the pair—the mother reacting to signs of the child's impatience, the child responding directly to his own.

The actual act of uncovering is open to considerable variation. We find instances where it is controlled by the child, others where the mother controls uncovering. Occasionally, the mother, by drawing near and vocalizing, provokes the child into removing the mask from her face, as if to stimulate more control from the infant. Indeed, one even encounters partial, 'tempting' uncovering by the mother to provoke the child into completion, where the mother exposes a corner of her eye. In terms of control of unmasking, we note that before 12 months, nine of 12 of the episodes of unmasking are controlled by the mother. From 12 on, none are, and six in 10 are controlled by the child alone—a phenomenon seen only once before this age.

Following uncovering, there is again a rather standard ritual: remaking contact. In the 19 episodes where we were able to determine it 14 uncoverings were accompanied by face-to-face contact immediately or shortly after. In all instances of uncovering but one, mother sought to establish such conduct, though in four she failed to do so. Moreover, in 16 of 22 episodes, mother vocalized upon uncovering, usually with a 'Boo' or a 'Hello' or an 'Ahhh'. Obviously, there is considerable release of tension at this point, since laughter accompanies the above 15 times for the child (and indeed 12 for the mother, always in accompaniment with the child).

At 15 months, the child invents and controls a new variation of the game, as already noted. It consists of her moving behind a chair, out of sight of her mother, then reappearing and saying 'Boo'. She has now become the agent in the play, mother being recipient of her action. The format has been revised by the child and the prior role of agent and recipient reversed. This variation in agency has, of course, appeared before in the more static form of the game involving a hiding instrument. But it is important to note that the child has now extended the rules under her own control to a new, but formally identical format—again involving initial face-to-face contact, hiding and reappearing by self-initiated movement, and reestablishing contact. From there on out, peekaboo is a game embedded in self-directed movement by the child that produces disappearance and reappearance. The child has not only learned to conform to the rules of the static game as initiated by mother and by child, but also to use the rules for the initiation of a variant of the old format. At this point, the range of possible games incorporating the basic rules of peekaboo becomes almost limitless, and what provides unity is the agreement of mother and infant to maintain a skeleton rule structure with new instruments for hiding and new settings in which to play. We can say that at this point the child is no longer performance-bound, but rather has achieved a proper 'competence' for generating new versions of an old game.

But we must turn now to the question of what brought the child to a full realization of the 'syntax' of the game of peekaboo so that he can henceforth be fully 'generative' in his disappearance-reappearance play. Before we do so, however, we must examine briefly three of the other children on whom we have sufficient data for analysis.

In the case of Lynn and her mother, the pattern is much the same as described, save for the fact that she begins to take over the active role of initiator of the game and controller of the mask as early as 10 months. She too, at 10 months, begins to use a stationary object, a chair, as a hiding mask behind which she moves, looking through the legs to effect reappearance. But she is still quite confused about it, and when mother says 'Boo' to herald her reappearance hides again rather than remaking contact. But she is on the way towards mastering the ambulatory variant.

Where Nan is concerned, the game is rather more sophisticated in an important respect. She and her mother share control. For example, at 11 months Nan lifts her petticoat over her face and leaves it in place until her mother says 'Boo' and then lowers it. This joint feature is a very consistent aspect of their games, but it must be regarded as a variant, for instances occur without joint control as well. Their turn-taking is also much more precisely segmented. For example, Nan raises her petticoat over her face, then lowers it after a few seconds, and waits for mother to say 'Boo' before showing any reaction herself—then usually responding to the mother's vocalizations with laughter. There is, in this instance, a separation between unmasking and vocalization, with a further timing element between the two.

Sandy and his mother are instances of a failure to develop workable rules because of excessive variation and some misreading by the mother. But the failure is instructive. Too often, the mother starts the game without having enlisted Sandy's attention. In other instances, when Sandy is having difficulty in hiding his own face behind a cloth, the mother takes the cloth (and the initiative) away from him and tries to do the masking herself. Interestingly, the game does not develop, and in its place there emerges a game in which Sandy crawls away from mother, she in pursuit, with excitement being exhibited by both when she catches him. He never serves as agent in this game. They are an instructive failure, and the disappearance of the game is reminiscent of the failures reported by Nelson (1973) that occur when mother attempts to correct the child's linguistic usage or insists upon an interpretation of the child's utterance that does not accord

with his own. Under the circumstances, the lexical items in question disappear from the child's lexicon, just as peekaboo disappears from the game repertory of this pair.

DISCUSSION

When peekaboo first appears, our mothers often report, it is an extension or variation of a looming game in which the mother approaches the child from a distance of a meter or so, looms towards him almost to face-to-face contact, accompanying the close approach with a 'Boo' or a rising intonation. We know from the work of Bower (1971), Ball and Tronick (1971) and White (1963) that such looming produces considerable excitement and, indeed, when the loom is directly towards the face, a real or incipient avoidance response. The play may start by substituting disappearance of the face at a close point at which excitement has already been aroused. But this is not necessary. The only point one would wish to make is that, at the start, peekaboo involves an arousal of responses that are either innate or fairly close to innate. For even without the link to the looming game, disappearance and reappearance are 'manipulations' of object permanence, which is itself either innate or maturing through very early experience along the lines indicated by Piaget (1954). At least one can say unambiguously that, at the outset, peekaboo is not a game in the sense of it being governed by rules and conventions that are, in any respect, arbitrary. It is, rather, an exploitation by the mother of very strong, preadapted response tendencies in the infant, an exploitation that is rewarded by the child's responsiveness and pleasure.

William James (1890) comments in the *Principles* that an instinct is a response that only occurs once, thereafter being modified by experience. And surely one could say the same for the interaction involved in peekaboo. For once it has occurred, there rapidly develops a set of reciprocal anticipations in mother and child that begin to modify it and, more importantly, to conventionalize it. At the outset, this conventionalization is fostered by a quite standard or routine set of capers on the part of the mother—as we have noted, the early version involves a very limited range of hiding instruments, masking acts, vocalizations and time variations. At the outset, it is also very important for mother to keep the child's activation level at an appropriate intensity, and one is struck by the skill of mothers in knowing how to keep the child in an anticipatory mood, neither too sure of outcome nor too upset by a wide range of possibilities.

But what is most striking thereafter is precisely the systematic introduction of variations constrained by set rules. The basic rules are:

Initial contact

Disappearance

Reappearance

Reestablished contact

Within this rule context, there can be variations in degree and kind of vocalization for initial contact, in kind of mask, in who controls the mask, in whose face is masked, in who uncovers, in the form of vocalization upon uncovering, in the relation between uncovering and vocalization, and in the timing of the constituent elements (though this last is strikingly constrained by a capacity variable). What the child appears to be learning is not only the basic rules of the game, but the range of variation that is possible within the rule set. It is this emphasis upon patterned variation within a constraining rule set that seems crucial to the mastery of competence and generativeness. The process appears much as in concept attainment, in which the child learns the regularity of a concept by learning the variants in terms of which it expresses itself. What is different in peekaboo is that the child is not only learning such variants, but obviously getting great pleasure from the process and seeking it out.

It is hard to imagine any function for peekaboo aside from practice in the learning of rules in converting 'gut play' into play with conventions. But there may be one additional function. As Garvey (in press) has noted, one of the objectives of play in general is to give the child opportunity to explore the boundary between the 'real' and the 'make-believe'. We have never in our sample of peekaboo games seen a child exhibit the sort of separation pattern noted by Ainsworth (1964) when mother *really* leaves the scene. Mothers often report, moreover, that they frequently start their career of playing peekaboo by hiding their own faces rather than the infant's for fear of his being upset. Eight of the nine mothers asked about this point reported behaving in this way (Scaife, 1974). This suggests a sensitivity on the part of mothers to where the line may be between

'real' and 'make-believe' for the child. This function doubtless dwindles in time. Yet the game continues in its formal pattern, sustained in its attractiveness by being incorporated into new formats involving newly emergent behaviours (such as crawling or walking). An old pattern seems, then, to provide a framework for the pleasurable expression of new behaviour and allows the new behaviour to be quickly incorporated into a highly skilled, rule-governed pattern.

REFERENCES

Ainsworth, M. D. S. (1964). Patterns of attachment behaviour shown by the infant in interaction with his mother. *Merrill-Palmer Quarterly, 10*, 51.

Ball, W., and Tronick, E. (1971). 'Infant responses to impending collision: optical and real', *Science, 171*, 818.

Bower, T. G. R. (1971). 'The object in the world of the infant', *Scientific American, 225*, 30.

Charlesworth, W. R. (1966). 'Persistence of orienting, and attending behaviour in infants as a function of stimulus-locus uncertainty', *Child Development, 37*, 473.

Garvey, C. (In press). 'Some properties of social play', *Merrill-Palmer Quarterly*.

Greenfield, P. M. (1970). 'Playing peekaboo with a four-month-old: a study of the role of speech and nonspeech sounds in the formation of a visual schema', Unpublished manuscript.

James, W. (1890). *The Principles of Psychology*, New York, Henry Holt.

Nelson, K. (1973). 'Structure and strategy in learning to talk', *Monographs of The Society for Research in Child Development, 38*, 1.

Piaget, J. (1954). *The Construction of Reality in the Child*, New York, Basic Books.

Scaife, M. (1974). Personal communication, Department of Experimental Psychology, Oxford University, Oxford.

White, B. L. (1963). 'Plasticity in perceptual development during the first six months of life', Paper presented to the American Association for the Advancement of Science, Cleveland, Ohio, 30 December.

QUESTIONS

1. What skills does an infant need in order to begin to play peekaboo?
2. What behaviors need to be coordinated in order for the infant and mother to be successful at peekaboo?
3. What does playing games like peekaboo have to do with the development of a more general understanding of rule structures? What evidence do Bruner and Sherwood use to support this claim?
4. How did the way in which the mother and infant play peekaboo change over the 10-month observation period?
5. What roles do emotional arousal and emotional regulation play in the infants' ability to sustain their part in this game?
6. What type of learning do you think results from interactions, like those of Sandy and his mother, that are unsuccessful in following the rules of the game?

12 The Development of Infant Memory

CAROLYN ROVEE-COLLIER

Ten years ago, the idea of infant memory was restricted to basic forms of recognition memory, like visual or auditory responses. Since then, researchers like Carolyn Rovee-Collier have discovered that infants remember far more than was previously assumed. Furthermore, this research has shown that very early memories can be somewhat long lasting. One interesting part of this story is that, in many ways, infant memory is similar to that of adults. As with adults, if a memory is not reactivated in an infant's mind, it fades.

This article by Rovee-Collier summarizes some of the main findings from recent research conducted in her laboratory on infant memory. It indicates that there is much more developmental continuity in memory processing than was formerly assumed. However, it also suggests some fascinating discontinuities in the development of this important cognitive function. Take special note of the laboratory techniques Rovee-Collier has devised to study early memory. These ingenious tasks allow infants to display their memorial competence with behaviors that are developmentally accessible and of interest to them.

These findings provide insight into a number of questions about early memory: What is infantile amnesia and how does it come about? Are early memories retained even if we are not consciously aware of them? And what role does language play in making and maintaining memory?

Over the first year and a half of life, the duration of memory becomes progressively longer, the specificity of the cues required for recognition progressively decreases after short test delays, and the latency of priming progressively decreases to the adult level. The memory dissociations of very young infants on recognition and priming tasks, which presumably tap different memory systems, are also identical to those of adults. These parallels suggest that both memory systems are present very early in development instead of emerging hierarchically over the 1st year, as previously thought. Finally, even young infants can remember an event over the entire "infantile amnesia" period if they are periodically exposed to appropriate nonverbal reminders. In short, the same fundamental mechanisms appear to underlie memory processing in infants and adults.

All people have a natural curiosity about their own memory. This curiosity was tweaked several years ago by reports in the popular press of recovered memories from early childhood. These reports also renewed a long-standing debate about whether infants can actually remember for any length of time. Some researchers argue that infants possess only a primitive memory system that cannot encode specific events (Mandler, 1998), that early development is characterized by "infantile amnesia" (the absence of enduring memories; Pillemer & White, 1989), that children cannot remember events until they can rehearse them by talking about them (Nelson, 1990), and that children younger than 18 months are incapable of representation (Piaget, 1952); others argue that the behavior of older infants and children is shaped by their earlier experiences (Watson, 1930) and that adult personality is shaped by memories of events that occurred in infancy (Freud, 1935). Surprisingly, this debate has been waged in the absence of data from infants themselves.

This article reviews new evidence that infants' memory processing does not fundamentally differ

Reprinted with permission of Blackwell Publishers from *Current Directions in Psychological Science*, vol. 8, pp. 80–85.
Acknowledgments This research was supported by Grants R37-MH32307 and K05-MH00902 from the National Institute of Mental Health.
Note Address correspondence to Carolyn Rovee-Collier, Department of Psychology, Rutgers University, 152 Frelinghuysen Rd., Piscataway, NJ 08854-8020; e-mail: rovee@rci.rutgers.edu.

from that of older children and adults. Not only can older children remember an event that occurred before they could talk, but even very young infants can remember an event over the entire infantile-amnesia period if they are periodically reminded.

DEVELOPMENTAL CHANGES IN RECOGNITION

Before now, the major impediment to research on infants' memory development was methodological: Tasks commonly used with older infants were inappropriate for younger ones. This problem is not surprising when one considers the considerable physical and behavioral changes that infants undergo over the first 18 months of life. Unfortunately, even when the same task was used, researchers often changed stimuli and task parameters nonsystematically; failed to equate age differences in motivation, stimulus salience, task demands, or original learning; or used identical instructions or prompts with infants who differed in verbal competence. Such practices made cross-age comparisons precarious at best.

To sidestep these problems, my colleagues and I have used two nonverbal tasks to study infants' memory development—a mobile task with 2- to 6-month-olds and a train task with 6- to 18-month-olds. All task parameters are standardized and age-calibrated. Because the memory performance of 6-month-olds is identical on these two tasks, comparisons between the memory performance of older and younger infants is not confounded by the shift in task.

In the mobile task, infants learn to move a crib mobile by kicking via a ribbon strung between the mobile hook and one ankle. The rate at which they initially kick before the ankle ribbon is connected to the mobile serves as a baseline for comparison with their kick rate during the subsequent recognition test, when infants are again placed under the mobile while the ankle ribbon is disconnected. If they recognize the mobile, they kick above their baseline rate; otherwise, they do not. In the train task, infants learn to move a miniature train around a circular track by depressing a lever. Again, baseline is measured, and retention is tested when the lever is deactivated; infants who recognize the train respond above their baseline rate.

Infants ages 2 to 18 months have been identically trained for 2 successive days in the mobile or train task and tested after a series of different delays. They exhibit equivalent retention after short delays, but their duration of retention increases linearly with age (see Fig. 1)—a result not attributable to age differences in activity or speed of learning. At any given age, however, memory performance can be altered simply by changing the parameters of training. If given three 6-min training sessions instead of two 9-min sessions,

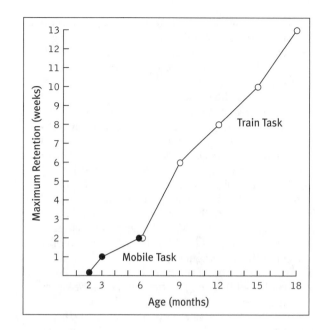

FIGURE 1

Maximum duration of retention over the first 18 months of life. Filled circles show retention on the mobile task, and open circles show retention on the train task; 6-month-olds were trained and tested in both tasks.

for example, 8-week-olds remember for 2 weeks (as long as 6-month-olds given two 6-min sessions), instead of 1 or 2 days only.

Age differences in retention that have been obtained with other paradigms similarly reflect differences in task parameters and not in the underlying memory processes. In the deferred-imitation paradigm, for example, infants watch an adult manipulate an object and are asked to imitate those actions later. At 6 months (the youngest age at which this paradigm can be used), infants who watch for 30 s in a single session successfully imitate if tested immediately afterward, but not if tested 24 hr later; if they watch for 60 s, however, they can imitate successfully 24 hr later (Barr, Dowden, & Hayne, 1996). Similarly, 18-month-olds exhibit deferred imitation for 4 weeks after one session but for 10 weeks after two sessions.

DEVELOPMENTAL CHANGES IN MEMORY SPECIFICITY

Because only cues that are highly similar to what is in a memory can retrieve it, the informational content of infants' memories can be determined by probing the memories with different retrieval cues and seeing which ones are effective. We followed this strategy with infants from 2 to 12 months of age by testing them after a series of delays either with a new mobile or train or in a context different from where they were trained. Because infants remember increasingly longer as they get older (see Fig. 1), we compared their memory performance after equivalent delays—the shortest, middle, and longest points on the forgetting function of each age.

For infants between 2 and 6 months of age, only the original mobile (or train) is an effective retrieval cue when testing occurs 1 day after training; a novel one is not. For infants between 9 and 12 months of age, however, a novel train can cue retrieval when testing occurs within 2 weeks of training, but not after longer delays (from 3 to 8 weeks), when only the original train can cue retrieval. A similar pattern is seen in deferred-imitation tests, although the duration of retention in this paradigm is shorter overall. Six-month-olds will not imitate if the test object is novel. Twelve-month-olds will—but only after delays on the order of minutes; after longer delays, they will imitate only if the test object is the one they saw originally (Hayne, MacDonald, & Barr, 1997). The fact that novel objects can cue retrieval only after delays when they can be clearly differentiated from the original training objects indicates that older infants actively disregard the difference. This emerging strategy enables older infants to "test the waters" and determine whether or not new objects that they encounter in the same context are functionally equivalent to the old ones.

When the training and testing contexts differ, infants exhibit a different pattern. At 3, 9, and 12 months of age, infants recognize the training object in a different context after all but the very longest test delays. Apparently, when the memory is weak, information about the context facilitates its retrieval. Between 12 and 24 months of age, infants will also imitate an action that they saw in one context (e.g., the day-care center) when tested with the same object in a different context (e.g., the laboratory) a few days later. Taken together, these findings reveal that infants can remember what they learn in one place if tested in another except after relatively long delays. Parents, educators, and public policy experts will be comforted to know that infants can transfer what they learn at the day-care center or in nursery school to home if given an opportunity to do so before too much time has passed.

DEVELOPMENTAL CHANGES IN PRIMING LATENCY

Even if infants cannot recognize a stimulus, like adults, they can still respond to it if they are exposed to a memory prime (or prompt) before the retention test. The prime, an isolated component of the original training situation, such as the original mobile or con-

text, initiates a perceptual identification process that facilitates retrieval of the latent memory by increasing its accessibility. In a recent series of studies, Hildreth and I primed memories that infants had forgotten (i.e., their performance on the long-term retention test was at baseline) and then assessed how long it took for the memories to be recovered (i.e., for infants to exhibit significant retention on the ensuing test; Hildreth & Rovee-Collier, 1999). Infants from 3 to 12 months of age were trained in the mobile or train task and were primed—only briefly and only once—with the original mobile or train 1 week after they no longer recognized it. Even though the time it took infants to forget the training event increased linearly with age (see Fig. 1), the latency of priming decreased over this same period until, at 12 months of age, infants responded instantaneously to the prime (see Fig. 2).

This result reveals that the speed of memory processing increases over the 1st year of life. Even at 3 months of age, however, infants respond instantaneously if a prime is presented if the memory was recently acquired. Infants who were trained with a

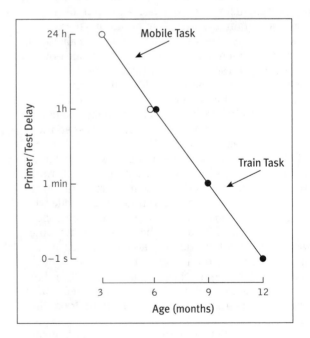

FIGURE 2

Decrease in priming latency (graphed in log seconds) over the 1st year of life. Open circles show results on the mobile task, and filled circles show results on the train task; 6-month-olds were trained, primed, and tested in both tasks. Each data point indicates how long it took infants of a given age to exhibit retention after being exposed to a 2-min prime.

three-mobile serial list, for example, recognized only the first mobile on the list 24 hr later—a classic primacy effect. If primed with the first mobile immediately before the 24-hr test, however, they also recognized the second mobile; and if successively primed with the first two mobiles on the study list, they recognized the third mobile (Gulya, Rovee-Collier, Galluccio, & Wilk, 1998).

DEVELOPMENT OF MULTIPLE MEMORY SYSTEMS

The notion that memory processing is mediated by two functionally different and independent memory systems originated more than a quarter-century ago with clinical observations that amnesics are impaired relative to normal adults on recognition but not on priming tests. Amnesics, for example, performed poorly when asked to recognize which of four words was on a list they had studied just minutes earlier, but they performed as well as normal adults when given a word fragment (the prime) and asked to complete it with the first word that came to mind. Typically, they completed the word fragments with words from the previous study list, even though they could not recognize them. This dissociation suggested that recognition and priming tests tap different underlying memory systems—one that is impaired in amnesia (explicit or declarative memory) and one that is not (implicit or nondeclarative memory). Since then, more than a dozen independent variables have been found to differentially affect adults' memory performance on recognition and priming tests, and memory dissociations have become a diagnostic for the existence of two memory systems.

For years, these memory systems were thought to develop hierarchically, with infants possessing only the primitive, perceptual-priming system until late in their 1st year. This assumption was based on the Jacksonian "first in, last out" principle of the development and dissolution of function (i.e., the function that appears earliest in development disappears last when the organism is undergoing demise), but empirical support for it in the domain of memory came only from studies of aging amnesics (McKee & Squire, 1993)—not infants. Now, new evidence has shown that all of the same independent variables that produce dissociations on recognition and priming tests with adults produce dissociations on recognition and priming tests with infants as well (Rovee-Collier, 1997). For example, priming produces the same degree of retention after all training-test delays, but the degree of retention on recognition tests decreases as the training-test delay becomes longer for both adults (Tulving, Schacter, & Stark, 1982) and infants. This evidence demonstrates that the Jacksonian principle does not apply to the development of memory systems; rather, both systems are present and functional from early infancy.

MAINTAINING MEMORIES WITH REMINDERS

Two recent studies from our laboratory have demonstrated that periodic nonverbal reminders can maintain the memory of an event from early infancy (2 and 6 months of age) through $1\frac{1}{2}$ to 2 years of age—the entire span of the developmental period thought to be characterized by infantile amnesia. In the first study (Rovee-Collier, Hartshorn, & DiRubbo, in press), 8-week-olds learned the mobile task. Every 3 weeks thereafter until infants were 26 weeks of age, they received a preliminary retention test followed by a 3-min visual reminder—either a reactivation (priming) treatment in which they merely observed a mobile moving (a nonmoving mobile is not an effective reminder) or a reinstatement treatment in which they moved it themselves by kicking. Their final retention test occurred at 29 weeks of age, when the experiment had to be terminated because the infants outgrew the task. Although 8-week-olds forget after 1 to 2 days (see Fig. 1), after exposure to periodic reminders, they still exhibited significant retention $4\frac{1}{2}$ months later, and most still remembered $5\frac{1}{4}$ months later. Control infants who were not trained originally but saw the same reminders as their experimental counterparts exhibited no retention after any delay.

The impact of periodic reminders is illustrated in Figure 3, which shows the retention data of individual 8-week-olds superimposed on the retention function from Figure 1. When the experiment ended, four 8-week-olds had remembered as long as expected of $2\frac{1}{4}$-year-olds, one had remembered as long as expected of 2-year-olds, and the infant with the "poorest" memory had remembered for as long as children almost $1\frac{1}{2}$ years old. Had we been able to continue the study, some infants undoubtedly would have remembered even longer.

In the second study (Hartshorn, 1998), 6-month-olds learned the train task, were briefly reminded at 7, 8, 9, and 12 months of age, and were tested at 18 months of age. Although 6-month-olds typically forget after 2 weeks, after being periodically reminded, they still exhibited significant retention 1 year later, at 18 months of age. In addition, 5 of 6 infants who were reminded immediately after the 18-month test still remembered when retested at 24 months of age, $1\frac{1}{2}$ years after the original event. These infants had encountered only one reminder (at 18 months) in the preceding year!

Unfortunately, the mobile task is inappropriate for infants older than 6 months, and the train task is

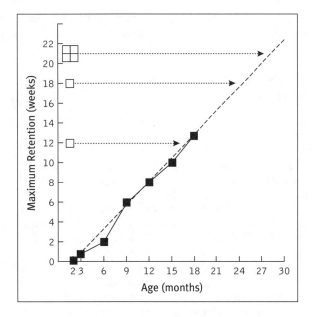

FIGURE 3

Maximum duration of retention of individual 2-month-olds who were reminded every 3 weeks through 26 weeks of age (open squares) relative to the maximum duration of retention of unreminded infants (solid line, from Fig. 1). The dashed line, fitted by eye, extrapolates the original retention function through 30 months of age. By following each arrow to a point on the function and reading down to the x-axis, one can determine the age equivalent for the duration of retention of each reminded 2-month-old.

inappropriate for infants younger than 6 months. However, because periodic nonverbal reminders maintained memories of these two comparable events over an overlapping period between 2 months and 2 years of age, it seems highly likely that periodic nonverbal reminders could also maintain the memory of a single event from 2 months through 2 years of age, if not longer.

WHENCEFORTH INFANTILE AMNESIA?

The preceding evidence raises serious doubts about the generality of infantile amnesia, as well as the accounts that have been put forth to explain it. Clearly, neither the immaturity of their brain nor their inability to talk limits how long young infants can remember an event. As long as they periodically encounter appropriate nonverbal reminders, their memory of an event can be maintained—perhaps forever. Because a match between the encoding and retrieval contexts is critical for retrieval after very long delays, however, a

shift from nonverbal to verbal retrieval cues or any other contextual change—either natural or perceived—would lessen the probability that a memory encoded in infancy would be retrieved later in life. In addition, because contextual information disappears from memories that have been reactivated once or twice, older children and adults may actually remember a number of early-life events but not know where or when they occurred. In short, even if an appropriate retrieval cue were to recover an early memory later in life, a person would probably be unable to identify it as such.

RECOMMENDED READING

Campbell, B.A., & Jaynes, J. (1966). Reinstatement. *Psychological Review, 73*, 478–480.

Gulya, M., Rovee-Collier, C., Galluccio, L., & Wilk, A. (1998). (See References)

Hartshorn, K., Rovee-Collier, C., Gerhardstein, P., Bhatt, R.S., Wondoloski, T.L., Klein, P., Gilch, J., Wurtzel, N., & Campos-de-Carvalho, M. (1998). The ontogeny of long-term memory over the first year-and-a-half of life. *Developmental Psychobiology, 32*, 1–31.

Hayne, H., MacDonald, S., & Barr, R. (1997). (See References)

Rovee-Collier, C. (1997). (See References)

REFERENCES

Barr, R., Dowden, A., & Hayne, H. (1996). Developmental changes in deferred imitation by 6- to 24-month-old infants. *Infant Behavior and Development, 19*, 159–170.

Freud, S. (1935). *A general introduction to psychoanalysis.* New York: Clarion Books.

Gulya, M., Rovee-Collier, C., Galluccio, L., & Wilk, A. (1998). Memory processing of a serial list by very young infants. *Psychological Science, 9*, 303–307.

Hartshorn, K. (1998). *The effect of reinstatement on infant long-term retention.* Unpublished doctoral dissertation, Rutgers University, New Brunswick, NJ.

Hayne, H., MacDonald, S., & Barr, R. (1997). Developmental changes in the specificity of memory over the second year of life. *Infant Behavior and Development, 20*, 233–245.

Hildreth, K., & Rovee-Collier, C. (1999). *Decreases in the latency of priming over the first year of life.* Manuscript submitted for publication.

Mandler, J.M. (1998). Representation. In W. Damon (Ed.), *Handbook of child psychology: Vol. 2. Cognition, perception, and language* (pp. 255–308). New York: Wiley.

McKee, R.D., & Squire, L.R. (1993). On the development of declarative memory. *Journal of Experimental Psychology: Learning, Memory, and Cognition, 19*, 397–404.

Nelson, K. (1990). Remembering, forgetting, and childhood amnesia. In R. Fivush & J.A. Hudson (Eds.), *Knowing and remembering in young children* (pp. 301–316). Cambridge, England: Cambridge University Press.

Piaget, J. (1952). *Origins of intelligence in children* (M. Cook, Trans.). New York: International Universities Press.

Pillemer, D.B., & White, S.H. (1989). Childhood events recalled by children and adults. In H.W. Reese (Ed.), *Advances in child development and behavior* (Vol. 21, pp. 297–340). New York: Academic Press.

Rovee-Collier, C. (1997). Dissociations in infant memory: Rethinking the development of implicit and explicit memory. *Psychological Review, 104*, 467–498.

Rovee-Collier, C., Hartshorn, K., & DiRubbo, M. (in press). Long-term maintenance of infant memory. *Developmental Psychobiology*.

Tulving, E., Schacter, D.L., & Stark, H.A. (1982). Priming effects in word-fragment completion are independent of recognition memory. *Journal of Experimental Psychology: Learning, Memory, and Cognition, 8*, 336–342.

Watson, J.B. (1930). *Behaviorism.* Chicago: University of Chicago Press.

QUESTIONS

1. What are some of the explanations that have been used to characterize infant memory as qualitatively different from the memory capabilities of individuals beyond the years of infancy?
2. In the mobile task, why was the baby's ankle tied by a ribbon to the mobile?
3. What is deferred imitation and how does it change in the mobile memory task from 6 months to 18 months of age?
4. Early memory is affected by whether the retrieval cue is identical to the item the infant originally saw and by similarity of the context in which the item appeared. As children get older, these factors are less important. What do you think this tells us about how memory changes in the first year of life?
5. Why do reminders help memories last longer?
6. Based on her data, how does Rovee-Collier explain infantile amnesia?

13 Becoming a Native Listener

JANET F. WERKER

The development of language is, for many researchers, our most impressive accomplishment as human beings. In fact, for some researchers, language is the distinguishing characteristic of the human species. But when does language development begin? A quick reply would most likely be "when someone begins to speak." However, this is not so. Long before children utter their first word at about 12 months of age, much has happened to mark the development of language.

One important skill that develops before children produce speech is the ability to distinguish speech sounds produced by others. Across the species, human speech is composed of a vast range of sounds. However, only a subset of these sounds are used in any single language. This means that learning to discriminate the sounds of a child's own language needs to occur before the child can begin to speak. This enables learners to attend to the sounds they will eventually learn to produce.

This article by Janet F. Werker describes the development of this ability. It is important research, not only because of what it describes about language development. It also demonstrates the capability of even very young members of the species to develop skills uniquely adapted to the circumstances in which growth occurs.

The syllables, words, and sentences used in all human languages are formed from a set of speech sounds called phones. Only a subset of the phones is used in any particular language. Adults can easily perceive the differences among the phones used to contrast meaning in their own language, but young infants go much farther: they are able to discriminate nearly every phonetic contrast on which they have been tested, including those they have never before heard. Our research has shown that this broad-based sensitivity declines by the time a baby is one year old. This phenomenon provides a way to describe basic abilities in the young infant and explore the effects of experience on human speech perception.

To put infants' abilities in perspective, adult speech perception must be understood. The phones that distinguish meaning in a particular language are called phonemes. There is considerable acoustic variability in the way each individual phoneme is realized in speech. For example, the phoneme /b/ is very different before the vowel /ee/ in "beet" from the way it is before the vowel /oo/ in "boot." How do adults handle this variability? As first demonstrated in a classic study by Liberman and his colleagues (1967), they treat these acoustically distinct instances of a single phoneme as equivalent. This equivalency is demonstrated in the laboratory by presenting listeners with a series of pairs of computer-synthesized speech stimuli that differ by only one acoustic step along a physical continuum and asking them first to label and then to try to discriminate between the stimuli. Adult listeners are able to discriminate reliably only stimuli that

---

Reprinted with permission of Sigma Xi Scientific Research Society from *American Scientist*, 77(1989), pp. 54–59.
Janet F. Werker is an assistant professor of developmental psychology at the University of British Columbia. She received a B.A. from Harvard University and a Ph.D. in psychology from the University of British Columbia in 1982. She was an assistant professor of psychology at Dalhousie University from 1982 to 1986, and joined the faculty at the University of British Columbia in 1986. The research reported here was supported by the Natural Sciences and Engineering Research Council of Canada and the Social Science and Humanities Research Council. In addition, portions of this work were made possible by an NICHD grant to Haskins Laboratories. Address: Department of Psychology, University of British Columbia, Vancouver, British Columbia, V6T 1Y7, Canada.

they have labeled as different—that is, they cannot easily discriminate between two acoustically different stimuli that they labeled /pa/, but they can discriminate between two similar stimuli if one is from their /ba/ category and one from their /pa/ category.

The phenomenon by which labeling limits discrimination is referred to as categorical perception. This has obvious advantages for language processing. It allows a listener to segment the words he hears immediately according to the phonemic categories of his language and to ignore unessential variations within a category.

Given that adults perceive speech categorically, when do such perceptual capabilities appear? To find out, Eimas and his colleagues (1971) adapted the so-called high-amplitude sucking procedure for use in a speech discrimination task. This procedure involves teaching infants to suck on a pacifier attached to a pressure transducer in order to receive a visual or auditory stimulus. After repeated presentations of the same sight or sound, the sucking rate declines, indicating that the infants are becoming bored. The infants are then presented with a new stimulus. Presumably, if they can discriminate the new sight or sound from the old, they will increase their sucking rate.

In Eimas's experiment, infants one and four months old heard speech sounds that varied in equal steps from /ba/ to /pa/. Like adults, they discriminated between differences in the vicinity of the /ba/-/pa/ boundary but were unable to discriminate equal acoustic changes from within the /ba/ category. Rather than having to learn about phonemic categories, then, infants seem capable of grouping speech stimuli soon after birth.

Experiments in the 17 years since Eimas's original study have shown that infants can discriminate nearly every phonetic contrast on which they are tested but are generally unable to discriminate differences within a single phonemic category (for a review, see Kuhl 1987). That is, like adults, infants perceive acoustically distinct instances of a single phoneme as equivalent but easily discriminate speech sounds from two different categories that are not more acoustically distinct.

Of special interest are demonstrations that young infants are even able to discriminate phonetic contrasts not used in their native language. In an early study, Streeter (1976) used the high-amplitude sucking procedure to test Kikuyu infants on their ability to discriminate the English /ba/-/pa/ distinction, which is not used in Kikuyu. She found that the infants could discriminate these two syllable types. Similar results have been obtained from a variety of laboratories using other nonnative phonetic contrasts (Lasky et al. 1975; Trehub 1976; Aslin et al. 1981; Eilers et al. 1982). This pattern of results indicates that

the ability to discriminate phones from the universal phonetic inventory may be present at birth.

DEVELOPMENTAL CHANGES

Given these broad-based infant abilities, one might expect that adults would also be able to discriminate nearly all phonetic contrasts. However, research suggests that adults often have difficulty discriminating phones that do not contrast meaning in their own language. An English-speaking adult, for example, has difficulty perceiving the difference between the two /p/ phones that are used in Thai (Lisker and Abramson 1970). So too, a Japanese-speaking adult initially cannot distinguish between the English /ra/ and /la/, because Japanese uses a single phoneme intermediate between the two English phonemes (Miyawaki et al. 1975; MacKain et al. 1981). This pattern of extensive infant capabilities and more limited capabilities in the adult led to the suggestion that infants may have a biological predisposition to perceive all possible phonetic contrasts and that there is a decline in this universal phonetic sensitivity by adulthood as a function of acquiring a particular language (Eimas 1975; Trehub 1976).

My work has been designed to explore this intriguing possibility. In particular, I wanted to trace how speech perception changes during development. Are infants actually able to discriminate some pairs of speech sounds better than adults, or have they simply been tested with more sensitive procedures? If infants do have greater discriminative capacities than adults, when does the decline occur and why?

The first problem that my colleagues and I faced was to find a testing procedure which could be used with infants, children of all ages, and adults. We could then begin a program of studies comparing their relative abilities to perceive the differences between phonetic contrasts of both native and nonnative languages.

The testing routine we chose is a variation of the so-called infant head turn procedure (for a complete description, see Kuhl 1987). Subjects are presented with several slightly different versions of the same phoneme (e.g., /ba/) repeated continuously at 2-sec intervals. On a random basis every four to twenty repetitions, a new phoneme is introduced. For example, a subject will hear "ba," "ba," "ba," "ba," "ba," "da," "da." Babies are conditioned to turn their heads toward the source of the sound when they detect the change from one phoneme to another (e.g., from "ba" to "da"). Correct head turns are reinforced with the activation of a little toy animal and with clapping and praise from the experimental assistant. Adults and children are tested the same way, except that they press a button instead of turning their heads when they detect a

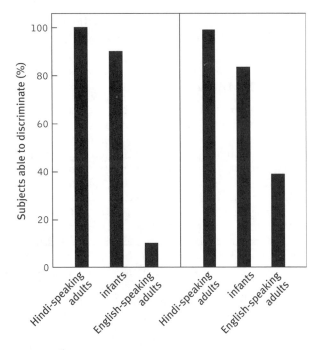

FIGURE 1

When tested on their ability to discriminate two Hindi syllables that are not used in English, six-to-eight-month-old infants from English-speaking families do nearly as well as Hindi-speaking adults. English-speaking adults, however, have great difficulty with this discrimination task, depending on the degree of difference from English sounds. The graph on the left shows a contrast involving two "t" sounds, one dental (i.e., made with the tip of the tongue touching the upper front teeth) and the other retroflex (made with the tongue curled back under the palate). This contrast is rare in the world's languages. The contrast in the graph on the right involves two kinds of voicing, a phenomenon that is less unusual and thus somewhat more recognizable to English-speaking adults. (After Werker et al. 1981.)

change in the phoneme, and the reinforcement is age-appropriate.

In the first series of experiments, we compared English-speaking adults, infants from English-speaking families, and Hindi-speaking adults on their ability to discriminate the /ba/-/da/ distinction, which is used in both Hindi and English, as well as two pairs of syllables that are used in Hindi but not in English (Werker et al. 1981). The two pairs of Hindi syllables were chosen on the basis of their relative difficulty. The first pair contrasts two "t" sounds that are not used in English. In English, we articulate "t" sounds by placing the tongue a bit behind the teeth at the alveolar ridge. In Hindi, there are two different "t" phonemes. One is produced by placing the tongue on the teeth (a dental t—written /t/). The other is produced by curling the tip

of the tongue back and placing it against the roof of the mouth (a retroflex t—written /T/). This contrast is not used in English, and is in fact very rare among the world's languages.

The second pair of Hindi syllables involves different categories of voicing—the timing of the release of a consonant and the amount of air released with the consonant. Although these phonemes, called /t^h/ and /d^h/, are not used in English, we had reason to believe that they might be easier for English-speaking adults to discriminate than the /t/-/T/ distinction. The timing difference between /t^h/ and /d^h/ spans the English /t/-/d/ boundary. Moreover, this contrast is more common among the world's languages.

The results of this study, which are presented in Figure 1, were consistent with the hypothesis of universal phonetic sensitivity in the young infant and a decline by adulthood. As expected, all subjects could discriminate /ba/ from /da/. Of more interest, the infants aged six to eight months performed like the Hindi adults and were able to discriminate both pairs of Hindi speech contrasts. The English-speaking adults, on the other hand, were considerably less able to make the Hindi distinctions, especially the difficult dental-retroflex one.

TIMING OF DEVELOPMENTAL CHANGES

The next series of experiments was aimed at determining when the decline in nonnative sensitivity occurs. It was originally believed that this decline would coincide with puberty, when, as Lenneberg (1967) claims, language flexibility decreases. However, our work showed that twelve-year-old English-speaking children were no more able to discriminate non-English syllables than were English-speaking adults (Werker and Tees 1983). We then tested eight- and four-year-old English-speaking children, and, to our surprise, even the four-year-olds could not discriminate the Hindi contrasts. Hindi-speaking four-year-olds, of course, showed no trouble with this discrimination.

Before testing children even younger than age four, we felt it was necessary to determine that the phenomenon of developmental loss extended to other languages. To this end, we chose a phonemic contrast from a North American Indian language of the Interior Salish family, called Nthlakapmx by native speakers in British Columbia but also referred to as Thompson.

North American Indian languages include many consonants produced in the back of the vocal tract, behind our English /k/ and /g/. The pair of sounds we chose contrasts a "k" sound produced at the velum with another "k" sound (written /q/) produced by raising the back of the tongue against the uvula. Both are glottalized—that is, there is an ejective portion (similar to a click) at the beginning of the release of the consonants.

Again, we compared English-speaking adults, infants from English-speaking families, and Nthlakapmx-speaking adults in their abilities to discriminate this pair of sounds (Werker and Tees 1984a). As was the case with the Hindi syllables, both the Nthlakapmx-speaking adults and the infants could discriminate the non-English phonemes, but the English-speaking adults could not.

We were now satisfied that there is at least some generality to the notion that young infants can discriminate across the whole phonetic inventory but that there is a developmental decline in this universal sensitivity. Our next series of experiments involved testing children between eight months and four years of age to try to determine just when the decline in sensitivity might start. It quickly became apparent

that something important was happening within the first year of life. We accordingly compared three groups of infants aged six to eight, eight to ten, and ten to twelve months. Half of each group were tested with the Hindi (/ta/-Ta/) and half with the Nthlakapmx (/k̓/-/q̓i/) contrast.

As shown in Figure 2, the majority of the six-to-eight-month-old infants from English-speaking families could discriminate the two non-English contrasts, whereas only about one-half of the eight-to-ten-month-olds could do so. Only two out of ten ten-to-twelve-months-olds could discriminate the Hindi contrast, and only one out of ten the Nthlakapmx. This provided strong evidence that the decline in universal phonetic sensitivity was occurring between six and twelve months of age. As a further test to see if this developmental change would be apparent within the same individuals, six infants from English-speaking families were tested at two-month intervals beginning when they were about six to eight months old. All six infants could discriminate both the Hindi and Nthlakapmx contrasts at the first testing, but by the third testing session, when they were ten to twelve months old, they were not able to discriminate either contrast.

To verify that the decline in nonnative sensitivity around ten to twelve months was a function of language experience, we tested a few infants from Hindi- and Nthlakapmx-speaking families when they reached eleven to twelve months old. As predicted, these infants were still able to discriminate their native contrasts, showing quite clearly that the decline observed in the infants from English-speaking families was a function of specific language experience. Since doing these studies, we have charted the decline between six and twelve months old using a computer-generated set of synthetic syllables which model another pair of Hindi sounds not used in English (Werker and Lalonde 1988).

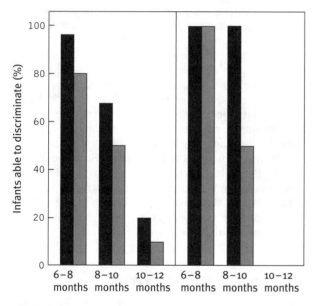

FIGURE 2

Infants show a decline in the universal phonetic sensitivity demonstrated in Figure 1 during the second half of their first year, as shown here in the results of experiments performed with babies from English-speaking families and involving non-English syllables from Hindi (dark gray bars) and Nthlakapmx, a language spoken by some native Indians in British Columbia (light gray bars). The graph on the left gives results from experiments with three groups of infants aged six to eight months, eight to ten months, and ten to twelve months. The graph on the right gives results from testing one group of infants three times at the appropriate ages. None of the latter group were able to discriminate either of the non-English contrasts when they were ten to twelve months old. (After Werker and Tees 1984a.)

HOW DOES EXPERIENCE AFFECT DEVELOPMENT?

A theoretical model for considering the possible effects of experience on perceptual development was suggested by Gottlieb in 1976. As expanded by both Gottlieb (1981) and Aslin (1981), the model includes several roles experience might—or might not—play, as shown in Figure 3.

Induction refers to cases in which the emergence and form of a perceptual capability depend entirely on environmental input. In this case, an infant would not show categorical perception of speech sounds without prior experience. Attunement refers to a situation in which experience influences the full development of a capability, enhancing the level of performance; for example, categorical boundaries

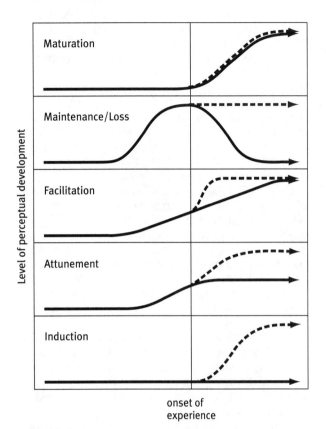

FIGURE 3

Researchers have suggested several roles that experience might—or might not—play in the development of particular perceptual capabilities. These possibilities are shown graphically here: **— — —** *curves represent development after the onset of experience, and* **———** *curves represent development in the absence of experience. Induction refers to cases in which a capability depends entirely on experience. Attunement refers to a situation in which experience makes possible the full development of a capability. In facilitation, experience affects only the rate of development of a capability. Maintenance/loss refers to the case in which a capability is fully developed before the onset of experience, but experience is necessary to maintain the capability. Maturation refers to the development of a capability independent of experience. The phenomenon of universal phonetic sensitivity followed by a narrowing of sensitivity to native language sounds appears to illustrate maintenance/loss, since it suggests that young infants can discriminate phonetic contrasts before they have gained experience listening but that experience with language is necessary to maintain the full ability. (After Aslin 1981; Gottlieb 1981.)*

between phonetic contrasts might be sharper with experience than without. In facilitation, experience affects the rate of development of a capability, but it does not affect the end point. If this role were valid, speech perception would improve even without listening experience, but hearing specific sounds would accelerate the rate of improvement. Maintenance loss refers to the case in which a perceptual ability is fully developed prior to the onset of specific experience, which is required to maintain that capability. Without adequate exposure an initial capability is lost. Finally, maturation refers to the unfolding of a perceptual capability independent of environmental exposure. According to this hypothetical possibility, the ability to discriminate speech sounds would mature regardless of amount or timing of exposure.

Our work is often interpreted as an illustration of maintenance/loss, since it suggests that young infants can discriminate phonetic contrasts before they have gained experience listening but that experience hearing the phones used in their own language is necessary to maintain the ability to discriminate at least some pairs of phones.

Support for this view was provided by another study in which we tested English-speaking adults who had been exposed to Hindi during the first couple of years of life and had learned their first words in Hindi but had little or no subsequent exposure. These subjects could discriminate the Hindi syllables much more easily than other English-speaking adults, and performed virtually as well as native Hindi speakers on the discrimination task (Tees and Werker 1984). This is consistent with the view that early experience functions to maintain perceptual abilities, suggesting that no further experience is necessary to maintain them into adulthood.

RECOVERY OF SENSITIVITY

Our early work led us to believe that the loss of nonnative sensitivity is difficult to reverse in adults. In one study, we tested English-speaking adults who had studied Hindi for various lengths of time. Adults who had studied Hindi for five years or more were able to discriminate the non-English Hindi syllables, but those who had studied Hindi for one year at the university level could not do so. In fact, even several hundred trials were insufficient to teach English-speaking adults to discriminate the more difficult Hindi contrasts (Tees and Werker 1984). This implies that while the ability is recoverable, considerable experience is required. Similar conclusions can be drawn from a study by MacKain and her colleagues (1981), who tested Japanese speakers learning English. Only after one year of intensive English training in the United States could they discriminate /ra/ from /la/.

The question still remained whether recovery of nonnative sensitivity results from new learning in adulthood or from a latent sensitivity. To explore this question, we asked English-speaking adults to discriminate both the full syllables of the difficult Hindi and Nthlakapmx phonemes and shortened portions of the syllables which do not sound like speech at all but contain the critical acoustic information specifying the difference between the phonemes (Werker and Tees 1984b). Subjects were first tested on the shortened stimuli and then on the full syllables. To our surprise, they were able to discriminate the shortened stimuli easily but were still not able to discriminate the full syllables, even immediately after hearing the relevant acoustic information in shortened form. This finding reveals that the auditory capacity for discriminating the acoustic components of these stimuli has not been lost but that it is difficult to apply when processing language-like sounds.

In a further set of experiments, we attempted to make English-speaking adults discriminate the full-syllable nonnative stimuli (Werker and Logan 1985). One task involved presenting adults with pairs of stimuli and asking them to decide simply if the stimuli were the same or different, a test that proved to be much more sensitive than the head turn procedure. In this "same/different" task, listeners have to compare only two stimuli at a time. Moreover, if the interval between the two stimuli is short enough, listeners can hold the first stimulus in auditory memory while comparing it to the second. In the head turn task, on the other hand, listeners have to compare each stimulus to a whole set of variable stimuli and judge whether it is a member of the same category.

We found that English-speaking adults could discriminate the Hindi syllables when tested in the same/different procedure, particularly after practice. Thus there was evidence that adults can discriminate nonnative contrasts if tested in a more sensitive procedure. Similar results have been reported by other researchers (Pisoni et al. 1982). This suggests that the developmental changes between infancy and adulthood should be considered a language-based reorganization of the categories of communicative sounds rather than an absolute loss of auditory sensitivity. The increasing reliance on language-specific categories accounts for the age-related decline, implying that maintenance has its effect at the level of linguistic categories rather than simple peripheral auditory sensitivity (see Best et al. 1988).

PARALLELS IN SPEECH PRODUCTION

It is interesting to compare our findings of developmental changes in speech perception to recent work on speech production. Although it is impossible to survey this substantial literature here, there appear to be systematic regularities in the repertoire of sounds produced at different stages of babbling. These regularities may reflect vocal tract and neuromuscular maturation, with phones appearing as a child develops the ability to articulate them (Locke 1983). In contrast to early work suggesting that the sounds produced during babbling gradually narrow to those that are used in the language-learning environment, recent research shows very little influence from the native language on vocal development during the babbling stage. This conclusion is particularly strong for consonants. However, it is clear that after the acquisition of the first word children's vocal productions start becoming differentiated on the basis of language experience. That is, once a child begins to talk, the sounds produced conform more and more closely to the subset of phones used in his native language. The stage at which these changes occur is consistent with our work showing universal sensitivity in early infancy followed by only language-specific sensitivity beginning around ten to twelve months.

This leads us to believe that just as a reorganization of language production is related to the emergence of the first spoken word, so too the reorganization of perceptual abilities may be related to the emergence of the ability to understand words. By the time he is one year old, a child understands a fair amount of spoken language, even though he may produce only a few words. We are currently conducting experiments to see if the reorganization of speech perception is related to the emerging ability to understand words. This work will add another piece to the solution of the puzzle of how early sensitivity to all language sounds becomes limited to the functional categories that are necessary for communicating in one's own language.

REFERENCES

Aslin, R. N. 1981. Experiential influences and sensitive periods in perceptual development: A unified model. In *Development of Perception*, ed. R. N. Aslin, J. R. Alberts, and M. R. Petersen, vol. 2, pp. 45–94. Academic Press.

Aslin, R. N., D. B. Pisoni, B. L. Hennessy, and A. J. Perey. 1981. Discrimination of voice onset time by human infants: New findings and implications for the effect of early experience. *Child Devel.* 52:1135–45.

Best, C. T., G. W. McRoberts, and N. N. Sithole. 1988. The phonological basis of perceptual loss for non-native contrasts: Maintenance of discrimination among Zulu clicks by English-speaking adults and infants. *J. Exper. Psychol.: Human Percept. Perform.* 14:345–60.

Eilers, R. E., W. I. Gavin, and D. K. Oller. 1982. Cross-linguistic perception in infancy: Early effects of linguistic experience. *J. Child Lang.* 9:289–302.

Eimas, P. D. 1975. Developmental studies in speech perception. In *Infant Perception: From Sensation to Cognition*, ed. L. B. Cohen and P. Salapatek, vol. 2, pp. 193–231. Academic Press.

Eimas, P. D., E. R. Siqueland, P. W. Jusczyk, and J. Vigorito. 1971. Speech perception in infants. *Science*, 171:303–06.

Gottlieb, G. 1976. The roles of experience in the development of behavior and the nervous system. In *Studies on the Development of Behavior and the Nervous System*, ed. G. Gottlieb, vol. 3, pp. 1–35. Academic Press.

_____ 1981. Roles of early experience in species-specific perceptual development. In *Development of Perception.* ed. R. N. Aslin, J. R. Alberts, and M. R. Petersen, vol. 1, pp. 5–44. Academic Press.

Kuhl, P. K. 1987. Perception of speech and sound in early infancy. In *Handbook of Infant Perception*, ed. P. Salapatek and L. Cohen, vol. 2., pp. 275–382. Academic Press.

Lasky, R. E., A. Syrdal-Lasky, and R. E. Klein. 1975. VOT discrimination by four to six and a half month old infants from Spanish environments. *J. Exper. Child Psychol.* 20:215–25.

Lenneberg, E. H. 1967. *Biological Foundations of Language.* Wiley.

Liberman, A. M., F. S. Cooper, D. P. Shankweiler, and M. Studdert-Kennedy. 1967. Perception of the speech code. *Psychol. Rev.* 74:431–61.

Lisker, L., and A. S. Abramson. 1970. The voicing dimension: Some experiments in comparative phonetics. In *Proceedings of the 6th International Congress of Phonetic Sciences*, pp. 563–67. Prague: Academia.

Locke, J. L. 1983. *Phonological Acquisition and Change.* Academic Press.

MacKain, K. S., C. T. Best, and W. Strange. 1981. Categorical perception of English /r/ and /l/ by Japanese bilinguals. *Appl. Psycholing.* 2:269–90.

Miyawaki, K., et al. 1975. An effect of linguistic experience: The discrimination of [r] and [l] by native speakers of Japanese and English. *Percept. Psychophy.* 18:331–40.

Pisoni, D. B., R. N. Aslin, A. J. Perey, and B. L. Hennessy. 1982. Some effects of laboratory training on identification and discrimination of voicing contrasts in stop consonants. *J. Exper. Psychol.: Human Percept. Perform.* 8:297–314.

Streeter, L. A. 1976. Language perception of two-month old infants shows effects of both innate mechanisms and experience. *Nature* 259:39–41.

Tees, R. C., and J. F. Werker. 1984. Perceptual flexibility: Maintenance or recovery of the ability to discriminate non-native speech sounds. *Can. J. Psychol.* 34:579–90.

Trehub, S. 1976. The discrimination of foreign speech contrasts by infants and adults. *Child Devel.* 47:466–72.

Werker, J. F., J. H. V. Gilbert, K. Humphrey, and R. C. Tees. 1981. Developmental aspects of cross-language speech perception. *Child Devel.* 52:349–53.

Werker, J. F., and C. E. Lalonde. 1988. The development of speech perception: Initial capabilities and the emergence of phonemic categories. *Devel. Psychol.* 24:672–83.

Werker, J. F., and J. S. Logan. 1985. Cross-language evidence for three factors in speech perception. *Percept. Psychophys.* 37:35–44.

Werker, J. F., and R. C. Tees. 1983. Developmental changes across childhood in the perception of non-active speech sounds. *Can. J. Psychol.* 37:278–86.

_____ 1984a. Cross-language speech perception: Evidence for perceptual reorganization during the first year of life. *Infant Behav. Devel.* 7:49–63.

_____ 1984b. Phonemic and phonetic factors in adult cross-language speech perception. *J. Acoustical Soc. Am.* 75:1866–78.

Questions

1. What are phones and how are they related to phonemes?
2. What role does categorical perception play in the development of language?
3. What laboratory procedure did Werker use to study infant perception of the difference between phonetic contrasts?
4. What does Figure 3 tell us about when in development phonetic discrimination occurs?
5. Is the ability to discriminate sounds that do not appear in a person's native language completely lost in infancy? Use evidence to support your answer.
6. These results suggest that one important development in the first year is a reorganization of speech-related functions in the brain. How do you think this process develops for children raised in bilingual homes?

14 Early Experience and Emotional Development: The Emergence of Wariness of Heights

JOSEPH J. CAMPOS · BENNETT I. BERTENTHAL · ROSANNE KERMOIAN

Why do infants who have just learned to crawl show no avoidance of heights? As unbelievable as it sounds, there is a gap in time between the beginning of crawling and fear of heights. However, once children become fearful of heights, they are quite afraid and this emotional response stays with them throughout life. What explains this pattern of development? In the early years of psychology, it was believed that humans had many instincts including fear of heights. Following from this, if fear of heights is built into the human physiology as an instinct, developmental changes would not occur. This was a long-standing assumption that was challenged by the following research, which shows that fear of heights is a learned emotional response.

In the article, Joseph J. Campos, Bennett I. Bertenthal, and Rosanne Kermoian describe their research on the relation between early locomotor experience and the development of fear. Several features of this research are noteworthy. First, the investigators needed to adapt a research technique used for studying crawling infants for use with infants who have not yet learned to crawl. Second, the investigators needed to devise an ecologically valid way of testing infant fear. And third, they needed to identify experiences that prelocomotor children have that may provide them with experiences similar to locomotion.

Only by solving these three problems were the investigators able to study the connection between locomotor experience and emotional development. The results are important because they clarify that fear of heights is a learned, not an instinctual, process and because they provide a direct link between perceptual and motor experience early in life and emotional development.

Because of its biological adaptive value, wariness of heights is widely believed to be innate or under maturational control. In this report, we present evidence contrary to this hypothesis, and show the importance of locomotor experience for emotional development. Four studies bearing on this conclusion have shown that (1) when age is held constant, locomotor experience accounts for wariness of heights; (2) "artificial" experience locomoting in a walker generates evidence of wariness of heights; (3) an orthopedically handicapped infant tested longitudinally did not show wariness of heights so long as he had no locomotor experience; and (4) regardless of the age when infants begin to crawl, it is the duration of locomotor experience and not age that predicts avoidance of heights. These findings suggest that when infants begin to crawl, experiences generated by locomotion make possible the development of wariness of heights.

Between 6 and 10 months of age, major changes occur in fearfulness in the human infant. During this period, some fears are shown for the first time, and many others show a step-function increase in prevalence (Bridges, 1932; Scarr & Salapatek, 1970; Sroufe, 1979). These changes in fearfulness occur so abruptly, involve so many different elicitors, and have such biologically adaptive value that many investigators propose

Reprinted with permission of Blackwell Publishers from *Psychological Science*, vol. 3, 1992, 61–64.
This research was supported by grants from the National Institutes of Health (HD-16195, HD-00695, and HD-25066) and from the John D. and Catherine T. MacArthur Foundation.

maturational explanations for this developmental shift (Emde, Gaensbauer, & Harmon, 1976; Kagan, Kearsley, & Zelazo, 1978). For such theorists, the development of neurophysiological structures (e.g., the frontal lobes) precedes and accounts for changes in affect.

In contrast to predominantly maturational explanations of developmental changes, Gottlieb (1983, 1991) proposed a model in which different types of experiences play an important role in developmental shifts. He emphasized that new developmental acquisitions, such as crawling, generate experiences that, in turn, create the conditions for further developmental changes. Gottlieb called such "bootstrapping" processes probabilistic epigenesis. In contrast to most current models of developmental transition, Gottlieb's approach stresses the possibility that, under some circumstances, psychological function may precede and account for development of neurophysiological structures.

There is evidence in the animal literature that a probabilistic epigenetic process plays a role in the development of wariness of heights. Held and Hein (1963), for instance, showed that dark-reared kittens given experience with active self-produced locomotion in an illuminated environment showed avoidance of heights, whereas dark-reared littermates given passive experience moving in the same environment manifested no such avoidance. In these studies, despite equivalent maturational states in the two groups of kittens, the experiences made possible by correlated visuomotor responses during active locomotion proved necessary to elicit wariness of heights.

So long as they are prelocomotor, human infants, despite their visual competence and absence of visual deprivation, may be functionally equivalent to Held and Hein's passively moved kittens. Crawling may generate or refine skills sufficient for the onset of wariness of heights. These skills may include improved calibration of distances, heightened sensitivity to visually specified self-motion, more consistent coordination of visual and vestibular stimulation, and increased awareness of emotional signals from significant others (Bertenthal & Campos, 1990; Campos, Hiatt, Ramsay, Henderson, & Svejda, 1978).

There is anecdotal evidence supporting a link between locomotor experience and development of wariness of heights in human infants. Parents commonly report that there is a phase following the acquisition of locomotion when infants show no avoidance of heights, and will go over the edge of a bed or other precipice if the caretaker is not vigilant. Parents also report that this phase of apparent fearlessness is followed by one in which wariness of heights becomes quite intense (Campos et al., 1978).

In sum, both the kitten research and the anecdotal human evidence suggest that wariness of heights is not simply a maturational phenomenon, to be expected even in the absence of experience. From the perspective of probabilistic epigenesis, locomotor experience may operate as an organizer of emotional development, serving either to induce wariness of heights (i.e., to produce a potent emotional state that would never emerge without such experience) or to facilitate its emergence (i.e., to bring it about earlier than it otherwise would appear). The research reported here represents an attempt to determine whether locomotor experience is indeed an organizer of the emergence of wariness of heights.

Pinpointing the role of locomotion in the emergence of wariness of heights in human infants requires solution of a number of methodological problems. One is the selection of an ecologically valid paradigm for testing wariness of heights. Another is the determination of an outcome measure that can be used with both prelocomotor and locomotor infants. A third is a means of determining whether locomotion is playing a role as a correlate, an antecedent, an inducer, or a facilitator of the onset of wariness of heights.

The ecologically valid paradigm we selected for testing was the visual cliff (Walk, 1966; Walk & Gibson, 1961)—a large, safety-glass-covered table with a solid textured surface placed immediately underneath the glass on one side (the "shallow" side) and a similar surface placed some 43 in. underneath the glass on the floor below on the other side (the "deep" side).

To equate task demands for prelocomotor and locomotor infants, we measured the infants' wariness reactions while they were slowly lowered toward either the deep or the shallow side of the cliff. This descent procedure not only allowed us to assess differences in wariness reactions as a function of locomotor experience in both prelocomotor and locomotor infants but also permitted us to assess an index of depth perception, that is, a visual placing response (the extension of the arms and hands in anticipation of contact with the shallow, but not the deep, surface of the cliff [Walters, 1981]).

To assess fearfulness with an index appropriate to both pre- and postlocomoting infants, we measured heart rate (HR) responses during the 3-s period of descent onto the surface of the cliff. Prior work had shown consistently that heart rate decelerates in infants who are in a state of nonfearful attentiveness, but accelerates when infants are showing either a defensive response (Graham & Clifton, 1966) or a precry state (Campos, Emde, Gaensbauer, & Henderson, 1975).

To relate self-produced locomotion to fearfulness, we used a number of converging research operations. One was an *age-held-constant design*, contrasting the performance of infants who were locomoting with those of the same age who were not yet locomoting; the second was an analog of an experiential *enrichment* manipulation, in which infants who were otherwise incapable of crawling or creeping were tested after they had a number of hours of experience moving about voluntarily in walker devices; the third was an analog of an experiential *deprivation* manipulation, in which an infant who was orthopedically handicapped, but otherwise normal, was tested longitudinally past the usual age of onset of crawling and again after the delayed acquisition of crawling; and the fourth was a *cross-sequential lag design* aimed at teasing apart the effects of age of onset of locomotion and of duration of locomotor experience on the infant's avoidance of crossing the deep or the shallow side of the cliff to the mother.

EXPERIMENT 1: HR RESPONSES OF PRELOCOMOTOR AND LOCOMOTOR INFANTS

In the first study, a total of 92 infants, half locomoting for an average of 5 weeks, were tested at 7.3 months of age. Telemetered HR, facial expressions (taped from a camera under the deep side of the cliff), and the visual placing response were recorded. Each infant was lowered to each side of the cliff by a female experimenter, with the mother in another room.

As predicted from the work of Held and Hein (1963), locomotor infants showed evidence of

wariness of heights, and prelocomotor infants did not. Only on deep trials did the HR of locomotor infants accelerate significantly from baselevels (by 5 beats/min), and differ significantly from the HR responses of prelocomotor infants. The HR responses of prelocomotor infants did not differ from baselevels on either the deep or shallow sides. Surprisingly, facial expressions did not differentiate testing conditions, perhaps because the descent minimized the opportunity to target these expressions to social figures.

In addition, every infant tested, regardless of locomotor status, showed visual placing responses on the shallow side, and no infant showed placing responses on the deep side of the cliff. Thus, all infants showed evidence for depth perception on the deep side, but only locomotor infants showed evidence of fear-related cardiac acceleration in response to heights.

EXPERIMENT 2: ACCELERATION OF LOCOMOTOR EXPERIENCE

Although correlated, the development of locomotion and the emergence of wariness of heights may be jointly determined by a third factor that brings about

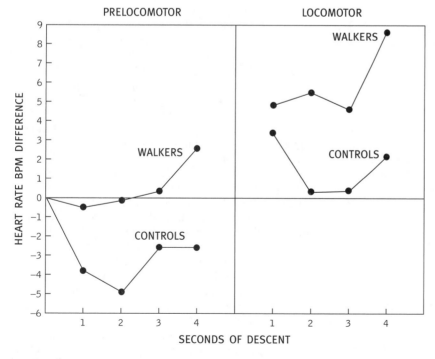

FIGURE 1

Heart rate response while the infant is lowered toward the deep side of the visual cliff as a function of locomotor experience. The left panel contrasts the performance of prelocomotor infants with and without "artificial" walker experience. The right panel contrasts the performance of crawling infants with and without "artificial" walker experience. Heart rate is expressed as difference from baseline in beats/min.

both changes. Disambiguation of this possibility required a means of providing "artificial" locomotor experience to infants who were not yet able to crawl. This manipulation was achieved by providing wheeled walkers to infants and testing them after their mothers had reported at least 32 hr of voluntary forward movement in the device.

Infants who received walkers were divided into two groups: prelocomotor walkers (N = 9M, 9F, Mean Age = 224 days, Walker Experience = 47 hr of voluntary forward movement) and locomotor walkers (N = 9M, 7F, Mean Age = 222 days, Walker Experience = 32 hr). The performance of infants in these two groups was compared with the performance of age-matched subjects, also divided into two groups: prelocomotor controls (N = 9M, 9F, Mean Age = 222 days) and locomotor controls (N = 9M, 7F, Mean Age = 222 days). The average duration of crawling experience was only 5 days in the locomotor walker and the locomotor control groups. All infants were tested using the same procedure as in the prior study. No shallow trials were administered in order to minimize subject loss due to the additional testing time required for such trials.

As revealed in Figure 1, the three groups of infants with any type of locomotor experience showed evidence of cardiac acceleration, whereas the prelocomotor control infants did not. It is noteworthy that all 16 infants in the locomotor walker group (who had a "double dosage" of locomotor experience consisting of walker training and some crawling) showed HR accelerations upon descent to the cliff. Planned comparisons revealed significant differences between (1) all walker infants and all controls, (2) all spontaneously locomoting infants and prelocomotor controls, and (3) prelocomotor walkers and prelocomotor controls. These findings show that the provision of "artificial" locomotor experience may facilitate or induce wariness of heights, even for infants who otherwise have little or no crawling experience. Locomotor experience thus appears to be an antecedent of the emergence of wariness.

EXPERIMENT 3: DEPRIVATION OF LOCOMOTOR EXPERIENCE

Although Experiment 2 showed that training in locomotion accelerates the onset of wariness of heights, it is possible that this response would eventually develop even in the absence of locomotor experience. To determine whether the delayed acquisition of crawling precedes the delayed emergence of wariness of heights, we longitudinally tested an infant with a peripheral handicap to locomotion. This infant was neurologically normal and had a Bayley Developmen-

tal Quotient of 126, but was born with two congenitally dislocated hips. After an early operation, he was placed in a full body cast. The infant was tested on the visual cliff monthly between 6 and 10 months of age using the procedures described above. While the infant was in the cast, he showed no evidence of crawling. At 8.5 months of age (i.e., 1.5 months after the normative age of onset of locomotion), the cast was removed, and the infant began crawling soon afterward.

This infant showed no evidence of differential cardiac responsiveness on the deep versus shallow side of the cliff until 10 months of age, at which time his HR accelerated markedly on the deep side, and decelerated on the shallow. Although we cannot generalize from a single case study, these data provide further support for the role of self-produced locomotion as a facilitator or inducer of wariness of heights.

EXPERIMENT 4: AGE OF ONSET OF LOCOMOTION VERSUS LOCOMOTOR EXPERIENCE

In the studies described so far, HR was used as an imperfect index of wariness. However, we felt that a study using behavioral avoidance was needed to confirm the link between locomotor experience and wariness of heights. We thus used the locomotor crossing test on the visual cliff, in which the infant is placed on the center of the cliff, and the mother is instructed to encourage the infant to cross to her over either the deep or the shallow side. In this study, we also assessed separately the effects of age of onset of crawling (early, normative, or late) and of duration of locomotor experience (11 or 41 days), as well as their interaction, using a longitudinal design.

The results of this study demonstrated a clear effect of locomotor experience independent of the age when self-produced locomotion first appeared. This effect of experience was evident with both nominal data (the proportion of infants who avoided descending onto the deep side of the cliff on the first test trial) and interval data (the latency to descend from the center board of the visual cliff onto the deep side on deep trials minus the latency to descend onto the shallow side on shallow trials). At whatever age the infant had begun to crawl, only 30% to 50% of infants avoided the deep side after 11 days of locomotor experience. However, after 41 days of locomotor experience, avoidance increased to 60% to 80% of infants. The latency data revealed a significant interaction of side of cliff with locomotor experience, but not a main effect of age, nor of the interaction of age with experience. The results of this study further suggest that locomotor experience paces the onset of wariness of heights.

PROCESSES UNDERLYING THE DEVELOPMENT OF WARINESS OF HEIGHTS

The pattern of findings obtained in these four studies, taken together with the animal studies by Held and Hein (1963), demonstrates a consistent relation between locomotor experience and wariness of heights. We propose the following interpretations for our findings.

We believe that crawling initially is a goal in itself, with affect solely linked to the success or failure of implementing the act of moving. Locomotion is initially not context dependent, and infants show no wariness of heights because the goal of moving is not coordinated with other goals, including the avoidance of threats. However, as a result of locomotor experience, infants acquire a sense of both the efficacy and the limitations of their own actions. Locomotion stops being an end in itself, and begins to be goal corrected and coordinated with the environmental surround. As a result, infants begin to show wariness of heights once locomotion becomes context dependent (cf. Bertenthal & Campos, 1990).

The context-dependency of the infants' actions may come about from falling and near-falling experiences that locomotion generates. Near-falls are particularly important because they are frequent, they elicit powerful emotional signals from the parent, and they set the stage for long-term retention of negative affect in such contexts.

There is still another means by which the infant can acquire a sense of wariness of depth with locomotion. While the infant moves about voluntarily, visual information specifying self-movement becomes more highly correlated with vestibular information specifying the same amount of self-movement (Bertenthal & Campos, 1990). Once expectancies related to the correlation of visual and vestibular information are formed, being lowered toward the deep side of the cliff creates a violation of the expected correlation. This violation results from the absence of visible texture near the infant when lowered toward the deep side of the cliff, relative to the shallow side. As a consequence, angular acceleration is not detected by the visual system, whereas it is detected by the vestibular system. This violation of expectation results in distress proportional to the magnitude of the violation. A test of this interpretation requires assessment of the establishment of visual-vestibular coordination as a function of locomotor experience and confirmation that wariness occurs in contexts that violate visual-vestibular coordination.

LOCOMOTOR EXPERIENCE AND OTHER EMOTIONAL CHANGES

The consequences of the development of self-produced locomotion for emotional development extend far beyond the domain of wariness of heights. Indeed, the onset of locomotion generates an entirely different emotional climate in the family. For instance, as psychoanalytic theories predict (e.g., Mahler, Pine, & Bergman, 1975), the onset of locomotion brings about a burgeoning of both positive and negative affect— positive affect because of the child's new levels of self-efficacy; negative affect because of the increases in frustration resulting from thwarting of the child's goals and because of the affective resonance that comes from increased parental expressions of prohibition (Campos, Kermoian, & Zumbahlen, in press). Locomotion is also crucial for the development of attachment (Ainsworth, Blehar, Waters, & Wall, 1978; Bowlby, 1973), because it makes physical proximity to the caregiver possible. With the formation of specific attachments, locomotion increases in significance as the child becomes better able to move independently toward novel and potentially frightening environments. Infants are also more sensitive to the location of the parent, more likely to show distress upon separation, and more likely to look to the parent in ambiguous situations.

Locomotion also brings about emotional changes in the parents. These changes include the increased pride (and sometimes sorrow) that the parents experience in their child's new mobility and independence and the new levels of anger parents direct at the baby when the baby begins to encounter forbidden objects. It seems clear from the findings obtained in this line of research that new levels of functioning in one behavioral domain can generate experiences that profoundly affect other developmental domains, including affective, social, cognitive, and sensorimotor ones (Kermoian & Campos, 1988). We thus propose that theoretical orientations like probabilistic epigenesis provide a novel, heuristic, and timely perspective for the study of emotional development.

REFERENCES

Ainsworth, M. D. S., Blehar, M., Waters, E., & Wall, S. (1978). *Patterns of attachment.* Hillsdale, NJ: Erlbaum.

Bertenthal, B., & Campos, J. J. (1990). A systems approach to the organizing effects of self-produced locomotion during infancy. In C. Rovee-Collier & L. P. Lipsitt (Eds.), *Advances in infancy research* (Vol. 6, pp. 1–60). Norwood, NJ: Ablex.

Bowlby, J. (1973). *Attachment and loss: Vol. 2. Separation.* New York: Basic Books.

Bridges, K. M. (1932). Emotional development in early infancy. *Child Development, 3,* 324–341.

Campos, J. J., Emde, R. N., Gaensbauer, T. J., & Henderson, C. (1975). Cardiac and behavioral interrelationships in the reactions of infants to strangers. *Developmental Psychology, 11*, 589–601.

Campos, J. J., Hiatt, S., Ramsay, D., Henderson, C., & Svejda, M. (1978). The emergence of fear of heights. In M. Lewis & L. Rosenblum (Eds.), *The development of affect* (pp. 149–182). New York: Plenum Press.

Campos, J. J., Kermoian, R., & Zumbahlen, R. M. (In press). In N. Eisenberg (Ed.), *New directions for child development.* San Francisco: Jossey-Bass.

Emde, R. N., Gaensbauer, T. J., & Harmon, R. J. (1976). Emotional expression in infancy: A biobehavioral study. *Psychological Issues* (Vol. 10, No. 37). New York: International Universities Press.

Gottlieb, G. (1983). The psychobiological approach to developmental issues. In P. Mussen (Ed.), *Handbook of child psychology: Vol. II. Infancy and developmental psychobiology* (4th ed.) (pp. 1–26). New York: Wiley.

Gottlieb, G. (1991). Experiential canalization of behavioral development: Theory. *Developmental Psychology, 27*, 4–13.

Graham, F. K., & Clifton, R. K. (1966). Heartrate change as a component of the orienting response. *Psychological Bulletin, 65*, 305–320.

Held, R. & Hein, A. (1963). Movement-produced stimulation in the development of visually guided behavior. *Journal of Comparative and Physiological Psychology, 56*, 872–876.

Kagan, J., Kearsley, R., & Zelazo, P. R. (1978). *Infancy: Its place in human development.* Cambridge, MA: Harvard University Press.

Kermoian, R., & Campos, J. J. (1988). Locomotor experience: A facilitator of spatial cognitive development. *Child Development, 59*, 908–917.

Mahler, M., Pine, F., & Bergman, A. (1975). *The psychological birth of the human infant.* New York: Basic Books.

Scarr, S., & Salapatek, P. (1970). Patterns of fear development during infancy. *Merrill-Palmer Quarterly, 16*, 53–90.

Sroufe, L. A. (1979). Socioemotional development. In J. Osofsky (Ed.), *Handbook of infant development* (pp. 462–516). New York: Wiley.

Walk, R. (1966). The development of depth perception in animals and human infants. *Monographs of the Society for Research in Child Development, 31* (Whole No. 5).

Walk, R., & Gibson, E. (1961). A comparative and analytical study of visual depth perception. *Psychological Monographs, 75* (15, Whole No. 5).

Walters, C. (1981). Development of the visual placing response in the human infant. *Journal of Experimental Child Psychology, 32*, 313–329.

QUESTIONS

1. What does it mean to say that new developmental acquisitions "bootstrap" further development?
2. What is the visual cliff and how is it used to study the development of depth perception and fear of heights?
3. How did the heart rate of locomotor and prelocomotor infants differ when they were lowered onto the two sides of the visual cliff?
4. Why was it important that Campos and his colleagues distinguish the development of awareness of heights from the development of wariness of heights?
5. If you were caring for two 6-month-olds, one who had been using a walker for a month or more and one who had no experience with walkers, would you have different concerns about keeping an eye on them?
6. If an infant were deprived of the ability to crawl or squirm from one place to another, do you think he or she would develop wariness of heights?

15 Patterns of Attachment in Two- and Three-Year-Olds in Normal Families and Families with Parental Depression

Marian Radke-Yarrow · E. Mark Cummings · Leon Kuczynski · Michael Chapman

A unique and universal characteristic of the human species is that human children have a lengthy period of dependence on adults. The theory of early social attachment focuses on the relationship between young children and their primary caregivers, and considers this process critical for organizing and supporting early socioemotional development.

In the following article a team of developmental psychologists led by Marian Radke-Yarrow used an experimental procedure known as the Strange Situation to study the attachment behaviors between depressed mothers and their children. Ideally, parents and children should be securely attached to one another. A securely attached child plays comfortably near the mother, does not need to check on her presence all the time, shows positive interest in strangers, and readily explores the environment. Such a child is upset when the mother leaves the room and greets the mother upon her return. Radke-Yarrow and colleagues hypothesized that maternal depression would disrupt the flow of this early relationship, and that this would leave depressed mothers and their children at risk for developing an unhealthy attachment relationship. Furthermore, the researchers also predicted that depressed mothers would model a depressive style of behavior that may then affect the development of the child's style of interacting with her and with others.

This research provides information about how the affective state of a parent not only influences parent-child interaction but may also influence the development of the child's own affective demeanor. Understanding the behavioral patterns that each partner brings to early social interactions is important for tracing the nature and outcome of the most important relationship in early child development.

Patterns of attachment were examined in normal and depressed mothers. Mother's diagnosis (bipolar, major unipolar, or minor depression, or no psychiatric disorder), self-reported current mood states, and affective behavior in interaction with the child were considered. A modified version of Ainsworth and Wittig's Strange Situation was used to assess attachment. Insecure (A, C, and A/C patterns) attachments were more common among children of mothers with a major depression (bipolar or unipolar) than among children of mothers

Reprinted with permission from *Child Development, 56*, 1985, 884–893. Copyright 1985 by the Society for Research in Child Development.

This work was supported by the National Institute of Mental Health, Bethesda, MD, and by the John D. and Catherine T. MacArthur Foundation, Research Network Award on the Transition from Infancy to Early Childhood, Chicago, IL. We wish to acknowledge the assistance of Judy Stillwell, Barbara Hollenbeck, Jonita Conners, Christine Kirby, Anne Mayfield, Wendy Rozario, and Rita Dettmers in the many phases of the research process. Requests for reprints should be sent to Marian Radke-Yarrow, Laboratory of Developmental Psychology, National Institute of Mental Health, Bldg. 15K, 9000 Rockville Pike, Bethesda, MD 20205.

with minor depression or among children of normal mothers. Insecure attachment was more frequent in children of mothers with bipolar depression than in children of mothers with unipolar depression. A/C attachments were associated with histories of most severe depression in the mother. In families in which mothers were depressed, depression in the father did not increase the likelihood of anxious attachment between mother and child. However, if mothers with a major affective disorder were without a husband in the household, risk of an insecure mother-child attachment was significantly increased. The mothers' expressed emotions (positive vs. negative) in interaction with their children in situations other than the Strange Situation, and independent of diagnosis, predicted patterns of attachment: mothers of insecurely attached children expressed more negative and less positive emotion. Mothers' self-reports of moods on the days they were observed were unrelated to attachment. Results are discussed in terms of the transmission of social and emotional disorders in relation to mothers' affective functioning.

Depression is known to aggregate in families, to be transmitted from one generation to the next. Significantly higher frequencies of psychopathology have been reported among children of parents with affective disorders than among children of normal parents, with a variety of mechanisms proposed as explanations (see reviews by Akisal & McKinney, 1975; Beardslee, Bemporad, Keller, & Klerman, 1983; Cytryn, McKnew, Zahn-Waxler, & Gershon, in press; Rutter & Garmezy, 1983). The likelihood of a genetic predisposition has been emphasized; and particularly for manic-depression, there is considerable evidence for biologically or genetically based transmission (see review by Meyersberg & Post, 1979). Although few investigators would rule out influences of environmental factors, such influences have not been extensively studied. Moreover, when the environment has been considered, both the conceptualizations and the methods used to assess its qualities have been inadequate. These deficiencies impose serious limitations on what is known about the role of environment and the interaction of genetic and environmental factors in the development of the offspring of depressed parents.

The depressed parent *is* the primary environment of the young child. The conditions of care and rearing that the parent provides must, of necessity, reflect the symptomatic behaviors of depression, the impairments that constitute the illness (emotional unavailability, sad affect, hopelessness, irritability, confusion, etc.). Although depressive illness does not present a homogeneous pattern of behaviors in every parent, the behaviors and mental status of the depressed person are all potentially interfering with the functions

and responsibilities of a caregiver and with the development of a good affective relationship with the child. The present study focuses on the quality of the affective bond that forms between mother and child under such conditions.

The quality of attachment between mother and child has been associated with the young child's adaptive and maladaptive behaviors in an impressively consistent succession of studies. Insecurely attached children, compared with those securely attached, have been found to be less competent in their relationships with peers and adults, more fearful of strangers, more prone to behavior problems, including social withdrawal and anxiety, and more dependent on adults (Arend, Gove, & Sroufe, 1979; Erickson, Sroufe, & Egeland, in press; LaFreniere & Sroufe, in press; Lieberman, 1977; Londerville & Main, 1981; Matas, Arend, & Sroufe, 1978; Pastor, 1981; Sroufe, Fox, & Pancake, 1983; Waters, Wippman, & Sroufe, 1979).

The literature on attachment identifies certain characteristics of mothering that are associated with the infant's secure attachment. These include the mother's responsivity, her emotional availability, and warm and accepting attitude toward the child (Ainsworth, Blehar, Waters, & Wall, 1978; Belsky, Rovine, & Taylor, 1984; Blehar, Lieberman, & Ainsworth, 1976; Londerville & Main, 1981; Main, Tomasini, & Tolan, in press; Stayton & Ainsworth, 1973; Tracy & Ainsworth, 1981). However, knowledge of the rearing environment at a level of detail and directness that allows examination of the processes through which a secure or insecure relationship develops and is maintained is very incomplete. This is particularly the case with regard to our understanding of the role of affective aspects of the environment in which the child is reared.

In the present study we have used parents' diagnoses of affective disorders (depression and manic-depression) and parental reports and expressions of their emotions and moods as indices of the affective quality of the child's rearing environment. How do attachment patterns in families with parental depression differ from patterns in normal families?

Research findings and theory support an expectation of increased attachment disturbances in the depressed families. A recent study of toddler-age offspring of manic-depressive parents shows attachment disturbances and early behavior problems (Gaensbauer, Harmon, Cytryn, & McKnew, 1984; Zahn-Waxler, Cummings, & McKnew, 1984; Yarrow, 1984). Bowlby (1969, 1973), Bretherton (in press), and Main, Kaplan, and Cassidy (in press) have hypothesized that early insecure attachment relationships result in children developing a fundamental view or working model of themselves as unlovable, and of others as rejecting and unresponsive. Some findings supportive of these expectations have been reported by Main and her colleagues (Cassidy & Main, 1983; Main, Kaplan,

| TABLE 1 | COMPARISONS OF DIAGNOSTIC GROUPS ON AGE, SEX, AND RACE | | | |

	Diagnostic Group		Major Affective Disorder	
Demographic Characteristics	Normal (N = 31)	Minor Depression (N = 12)	Unipolar Depression (N = 42)	Bipolar Depression (N = 14)
Age[a] (months)	31.9	31.4	30.4	36.0
Sex:				
Boys	13	7(1)[b]	24(4)[b] (2)[c]	3(2)[b]
Girls	18	5(2)[b]	18(3)[b] (3)[c]	11(4)[b](3)[c]
Race:				
White	24	12(3)[b]	34(6)[b] (1)[c]	12(6)[b] (3)[c]
Black	7	0	8(0)[b] (4)[c]	2(0)[b]
Hollingshead SES[d]	52.9	47.6	46.1	51.1

[a] Ranges in age are 25–39 months, 25–34 months, 16–44 months, and 30–47 months for the diagnostic groups, respectively.
[b] Number of families in which the father had a diagnosis of major depression.
[c] Number of families in which the father was not present.
[d] Ranges in SES in each of the groups, from low to high status, are 17–66, 34–64, 11–64.5, and 33.5–64, respectively.

& Cassidy, in press). Moreover, since the depressed parent is likely to be self-deprecating, it is quite possible that such views are conveyed to the child and extend to perceptions of the child.

If disturbed attachment patterns are characteristic of the offspring of affectively ill parents, a number of important research questions follow: (*a*) Within depressed and normal families, what are the parental behaviors that promote or interfere with the development of a secure attachment relationship? (*b*) Are the links between attachment patterns and child's (outcome) behavioral characteristics in the clinical population similar to the links found in nonclinical populations, or is the developmental course of the offspring of depressed parents more preprogrammed for maladaptive affective, cognitive, and social characteristics (i.e., more independent of environmental variables) than is the case for children of normal parents? (*c*) How may discordances (secure attachment and poor psychosocial development, or the obverse case) be explained?[1]

METHOD

SAMPLE

The sample consists of 99 children: 14 offspring of bipolar depressive (manic-depressive) mothers, 42 of mothers with major unipolar depression, 12 of moth-

ers with minor depression, and 31 of mothers with no history of affective disturbance.

Families (normal and depressed) were recruited by advertising for participants in a study of child rearing and development in healthy families and families in which the mother is depressed. Of the mothers who responded to announcements, approximately two-thirds wished to participate after learning more about the study. All volunteers were given a standard psychiatric interview, the Schedule for Affective Disorders and Schizophrenia (SADS) (Spitzer & Endicott, 1977). On the basis of the interview, families were selected who met specific diagnostic criteria, as well as criteria of SES, race, age, and sex of children. For a family to be selected for the normal group, both parents had to be present and had to be without a history of affective disorder. In families in which the mother had a diagnosis of depression, father's psychiatric status varied. Fathers could be with or without a diagnosis of depression; however, schizophrenic, alcoholic, and antisocial personalities were excluded. In eight families with major maternal depression, there was no father in the household. Of the families given psychiatric interviews, about half were screened out by us because they did not meet diagnostic requirements, or because their cell within the design was complete. Table 1 provides more information on the characteristics of the sample.

Families differed in terms of the percent of the child's lifetime in which the mother had episodes of

---

1. Data addressing these questions are being gathered in an ongoing study involving observations of parental and child behaviors at two periods in the child's life—at 2–3 years and at 5–6 years. The data reported here are from the first phase of this study.

depression. For bipolar mothers, the mean percent of the child's lifetime was 39.8 (range, 0%–100%); for mothers with unipolar depression, the mean percent was 61.6 (range, 0%–100%); and for mothers with minor depression, the mean percent was 13.7 (range, 0%–47%). (0 indicates mother's depression occurred before the child was born.)

Each mother who received a psychiatric diagnosis was rated on the severity of psychopathology on the Global Assessment Scale (GAS) (Spitzer, Gibbon, & Endicott, 1978). The mother is rated on her poorest functioning during the child's lifetime, on a continuous scale of 0 (needing continuous care and supervision) to 100 (superior functioning). The mean score for bipolar mothers was 47.6 (range, 15–65), for mothers with unipolar depression, 54.2 (range, 30–70), and for mothers with minor depression, 76.3 (range, 60–79). Mothers whose depression occurred before the child was born and could be rated for poorest functioning in their own lifetime ($N = 6$) had a mean rating of 43.7 (range, 1–65). Normal mothers are not given ratings. Treatments that mothers had received for affective illness were as follows: Seven had been hospitalized (three in the lifetime of their child), 25 were on drug treatment at some time (four currently), and 51 had sought professional help (19 were currently seeing a mental health professional).

PROCEDURE

The Strange Situation, developed by Ainsworth and Wittig (1969), was used in the present study to assess quality of attachment. The families came to the laboratory, an informal homelike apartment, for a series of half-days over a period of several weeks. Their behavior was observed (videotaped) over a variety of conditions constructed to approximate a range of natural rearing situations and demands. The Strange Situation was introduced in their first visit to the apartment. The procedure involves eight brief episodes in which the child's reactions to two separations from and reunions with the mother and to the presence of a stranger are observed. The sequence of episodes according to the individuals present is: (1) mother, child, and experimenter; (2) mother and child; (3) stranger, mother, and child; (4) stranger and child (separation from the mother); (5) mother and child (reunion with the mother); (6) child alone (separation from the mother); (7) stranger and child; and (8) mother and child (reunion with the mother). The traditional version of the Strange Situation was followed with two exceptions: (a) episode 3 was allowed to continue for 7 minutes instead of the usual 3, and the mother and also the stranger were asked to approach the child in a series of graded steps; (b) when the mother returned in episode 8, she brought with her a small case of toys, rather than returning empty-handed. The modifications were adaptations consistent with objectives of the larger study, in which (a) the child's capacities in familiar and unfamiliar interpersonal situations, and (b) the child's approach to a novel nonpersonal situation, were of interest.

Mother's current moods and emotions were assessed by self-report. An inventory of mood ratings, the Profile of Mood States (McNair, Lorr, & Droppleman, 1971), was filled out by the mother at the time of arrival for each laboratory visit.

Finally, the mothers' expressed affect was coded "live" during the Strange Situation and during subsequent half-day observations of mother-child interaction. The predominant emotions expressed were recorded on a minute-to-minute basis. Approximately 6 hours of the mother's affective behavior in the presence of her child was rated ($\overline{X} = 356.7$ min, SD = 3.8).

MEASURES

Assessment of the Quality of Attachment Ratings were made of interactive behaviors, including contact maintaining and proximity seeking, avoidance, resistance, search, and distance interaction. Two coders were given intensive training by one of the investigators, with whom reliability checks were also done. The mean Pearson product-moment reliability coefficient for ratings of interactive behaviors in the Strange Situation was .86 (range, .66–1.00) based on 50 Strange Situations coded by two independent observers. The percentage of interobserver agreement for classification of the quality of attachment was 96%. Coders of the attachment relationship did not take part in other aspects of the study and were blind to family diagnoses.

Quality of attachment was classified based on criteria outlined in Ainsworth et al. (1978). Consistent with the work of others, judgments of quality of attachment heavily emphasized responses to the two reunions with the mother. On the basis of studies of age changes in attachment behavior (Maccoby & Feldman, 1972; Marvin, 1972, 1977), we expected our 2–3-year-olds to show less proximity seeking and contact maintaining, but comparable levels of avoidance and resistance vis-à-vis the 12–18-month-olds on which this system was based. Accordingly, to obtain distributions of classifications as close to Ainsworth's as possible, avoidance and resistance were stressed in classification decisions. Children were classified as securely attached (B); insecurely attached, either insecure-ambivalent (C) or insecure-avoidant (A); or (3) insecurely attached, manifesting both ambivalence and avoidance (A/C).

The first three categories closely follow from Ainsworth et al. Secure children respond promptly to the mother on reunion, either by seeking proximity or physical contact with her, or by greeting her across a distance. Insecure-avoidant children ignore or avoid the mother on reunion. Insecure-ambivalent children resist contact with the mother on reunion, but may alternate this with proximity seeking. The fourth category (A/C), is not reported by Ainsworth et al., but is similar, although not identical, to Crittenden's A/C (1983) classification and Main and Weston's (1981) Unclassified category. These children showed moderate to high avoidance and moderate to high resistance during reunion, which served as the basis for classification, and most also displayed one or more of the following: "Affectless or sad with signs of depression," "Odd or atypical body posture or movement," and "Moderate to high proximity seeking." These responses were reported by those making attachment classifications, and by independent observers carefully reviewing the A/C tapes. Finally, one child of a mother diagnosed for current major depression could not be classified because his mother, responding to his protests, could not leave in either separation episode.

Analyses were conducted to determine the extent to which differences within the sample in age, sex, SES, and race might influence the interpretation of findings. The only age difference in interactive behaviors in the present study was a decline with age in contact-maintaining behavior during the two reunions with the mother: in episodes 5, $r(89) = -.25$, $p < .05$, and episode 8, $r(89) = -.50$, $p < .01$. There were no differences as a function of age in classifications (B, A, C, or A/C) of the quality of attachment. This is consistent with the findings from other research on age changes in attachment; children seldom show evidence of entering into qualitatively different forms of attachment relationships before 3 years of age (Marvin & Greenberg, 1982). Quality of attachment did not vary as a function of Hollingshead SES, whether calculated on a continuum or as a function of categories of status structure. Within the five categories of SES sta-

tus structure, disregarding diagnostic classifications, there was insecure attachment in four of the 10 families in the lowest two categories, in 16 of the 40 families in the middle two categories, and in 23 of the 48 families in the highest categories. Other studies have also failed to find differences in patterns of attachment as a function of social class (Schneider-Rosen & Cicchetti, 1984; Vaughn, Egeland, Sroufe, & Waters, 1979). Boys and girls and blacks and whites also did not differ significantly in the distribution of classifications of attachment. Subjects were collapsed across age, sex, race, and SES in further analyses.

Mothers' Self-report of Moods on the POMS Six mood scales from mothers' responses on the POMS were: (1) agreeable–hostile, (2) elated–depressed, (3) energetic–tired, (4) clearheaded–confused, (5) composed–anxious, and (6) confident–unsure. Scores were derived for each scale for each of 3 days in the laboratory apartment.

Mothers' Expressed Emotions Observed in Actions and Reactions in the Apartment Mothers' affects were scored, on a minute-by-minute basis, as cheerful–happy, tender–loving, tense–anxious, irritable–angry, sad–tearful, neutral–positive, or neutral–negative. The mean interobserver reliability, using the Kappa statistic (Bartko & Carpenter, 1976), which corrects for chance agreement, was .78. Because coders were not blind to mothers' diagnoses, a subset of sessions ($N = 21$) was coded from the videotapes by a coder who was blind to mothers' diagnoses. There was a high level of agreement; the mean intercoder reliability was Kappa = .79. Scores were derived for each of the affect categories by summing the number of minutes in which the emotion was observed, dividing by the total number of minutes of observation. Overall scores for any type of positive and any type of negative affect were also derived.

TABLE 2 **MATERNAL DIAGNOSTIC STATUS AND QUALITY OF ATTACHMENT RELATIONSHIP**

		Attachment (%)			
		Secure	**Insecure**		
Diagnostic Group	**N**	**B**	**A**	**C**	**A/C**
Normal	31	71 (22)[a]	29 (9)	0	0
Minor depression	12	75 (9)	17 (2)	8 (1)	0
Major affective disorder	55	45 (25)	31 (18)	4 (2)	20 (10)
Unipolar depression[b]	41	53 (22)	27 (11)	2 (1)	17 (7)
Bipolar	14	21 (3)	43 (7)	7 (1)	29 (3)

[a] Number of children receiving the classification.
[b] One child could not be classified, because his mother, responding to his extreme protests, would not leave in either separation episode.

RESULTS

MATERNAL DEPRESSION AND QUALITY OF ATTACHMENT

Distributions of attachment patterns by diagnostic groups are shown in Table 2. Insecure attachments were relatively infrequent in both the normal and minor depression groups (25%–30% of cases), and are comparable to rates reported in other studies of normal populations among younger children (e.g., Ainsworth et al., 1978; Waters, 1978). By contrast, insecure attachments were relatively frequent in families with major affective disorders (55% of cases), particularly among children of bipolar mothers (79%). Compared by means of tests of proportions (Hays, 1963), the difference between children of normal mothers and children of mothers with minor depression in incidence of insecure attachments was not significant, $z < 1$. There was a greater incidence of insecure attachments in families with major affective disorders than in normal families, $z = 2.33$, $p < .05$, or in families with minor depression, $z = 1.89$, $p < .10$ (all reported p values are two-tailed). Within the major affective disorders groups, insecure attachment was more frequent among children of bipolar mothers and among children of mothers with unipolar depression, $z = 2.08$, $p < .05$.

In 18 of the two-parent families with maternal depression, the father, too, had a diagnosis of depression. Forty-two percent of children in this group were insecurely attached, and 50% of the children within the depression group in which only the mother was depressed were insecurely attached, $z < 1$. Thus, whether mother only or both mother and father were depressed made no difference in the number of children with insecure attachments to mother. However, father's absence or presence did make a difference in the security of attachment to the mother. Because the number of families in which fathers were absent was small ($N < 10$), groups were compared by means of Fisher Exact Tests (Siegel, 1956). In the eight families (six girls and two boys) with major maternal depression and no father present, anxious attachment characterized seven of the children, a proportion higher than in families with major depression in which both parents were present, Fisher Exact Test, $p < .06$.

As noted earlier, a subgroup of children were classified as A/C. This classification occurred significantly more often among children of mothers with major affective disorders, Fisher Exact Test, $p < .01$. In fact, this pattern was observed only in children of mothers with a major affective disorder. Also, a disproportionate number of A/C's ($N = 4$) were in the single-parent major depression group.

TABLE 3   MOTHERS' AFFECTIVE FUNCTIONING IN THE CHILD'S LIFETIME AND QUALITY OF ATTACHMENT RELATIONSHIP

| | Attachment | | |
| | Secure | Insecure | |
Index	B	A or C	A/C
Percent of the child's lifetime mother is ill	26.5	25.9	79.7
Severity of mother's illness[a]	58.3	58.2	44.5
Treatment history[b]	.65	.73	1.60

[a] GAS scores varied from 0 (needing continuous care and supervision) to 100 (superior functioning); normal mothers are not given ratings.
[b] Number of forms of treatment received: hospitalization, drug therapy, psychotherapy; maximum score equals 3.

In further analyses of attachment and mother's depression, the percent of the child's lifetime in which the mother was ill, the severity (GAS) of her worst depressive episode, and her history of treatment for affective illness (number of forms of treatments received from among hospitalization, drug therapy, and psychotherapy) were considered. Analyses of variance with one between-subjects factor (attachment group) were performed for these indices: For the percent of the child's lifetime in which the mother was depressed, $F(2,91) = 8.96$, $p < .001$; for the severity of the mother's worst depressive episode, $F(2,56) = 4.68$, $p < .05$; and for the index of treatment history, $F(2,91) = 6.00$, $p < .005$. These relationships are shown in Table 3. Post-hoc Tukey tests were conducted to compare groups. Mothers of A/C children compared with mothers of children with B classifications or with A or C classifications had histories indicative of significantly more serious depression (all comparisons, $p < .05$). Mothers of B classification children and mothers of children with traditional insecure classifications (A or C) did not differ.

Next we examined the extent to which variables pertaining to mothers' depression contributed nonredundantly to prediction of attachment classification. For this analysis, three groups were distinguished: B, A or C, and A/C. The multiple correlation between attachment classification and maternal depression variables was $R = .38$, thus accounting for 15% of the variance in attachment classification. Stepwise multiple regression analyses indicated that mother's diagnosis was the best predictor, and the severity of her worst depressive episode was the second best predictor. Adding whether the father was absent into the analysis increased R to .47 and R^2 to 22%.

MOTHERS' CURRENT AFFECT AND QUALITY OF ATTACHMENT

To examine relations between mother's current emotions (disregarding diagnosis) and child's security of attachment, one-way analyses of variance with attachment group as the between-subjects factor were conducted for mother's self-assessed moods and for her expressed affect in interaction. There were no significant findings involving mothers' self-assessed moods. However, mothers' expressed emotions in interaction with their children during half-days in the apartment differentiated groups. Composite scores of positive and negative emotions showed that mothers of securely attached children expressed positive affect more often, and negative affect less often, than mothers of insecurely attached children (positive affect appeared in 80% and 69% of the minutes and negative affect in 18% and 31% of the minutes, respectively), $F's(1,80) \geq 4.02$, $p's < .05$. There were no significant differences between groups in expression of specific emotions.

Mothers' expressions of emotions and their diagnoses independently predicted attachment classification: Correlations between the percent of minutes rated positive or negative in affect and mother's diagnoses were nonsignificant. Multiple regression analyses indicated that mothers' general affective tone added significantly (5%) to the variance accounted for in attachment classification.

DISCUSSION

That affective illness of the mother may interfere with her ability to relate to her child in ways that promote a secure attachment is documented in these data. Depression decreased the likelihood of secure attachment between mother and child, at least as this is reflected in the child's responses to the mother in reunions after separation in the Strange Situation. Also, A/C patterns appear in children of mothers with major depression. The similarities with Crittenden's (1983) and Main and Weston's (1981) "unclassifiable" patterns observed among younger children are of interest. Crittenden's A/C's showed moderate to high avoidance and resistance, and most also showed some stereotypic or maladaptive behaviors, including "huddling on the floor," which might be interpreted as sadness. Main and Weston's "U's" showed extreme avoidance and distress, behaved "oddly" during the Strange Situation, and were affectless with signs of depression.

Another interesting parallel is that Crittenden's A/C's and those in the present study were found only among children of mothers with psychopathology: In Crittenden's study mothers were highly abusing, while our mothers were severely depressed. Mothers of Main and Weston's U's were unscreened for maternal psychopathology, so it is unclear whether psychopathology was a factor. These studies suggest that Ainsworth's classification system may not describe the entire range of patterns of attachment, and that important new patterns may be found in atypical samples. Another implication is that there is more than a dichotomy between security and insecurity; it may be necessary to distinguish between secure, insecure, and very insecure (A/C) patterns, or introduce more divisions along a dimension of anxiety (Crittenden, in press; Main, Kaplan, & Cassidy, in press). External validation is required, however, before any firm conclusions about the significance of new patterns can be drawn. The search for very insecure patterns may be complicated by the fact that they may vary as a function of the mothers' particular psychopathology or the age of the child.

The children of unipolar and bipolar depressed mothers had different patterns of attachment. Although children of mothers with major unipolar depression were more likely to be insecurely attached than children of mothers with no history of affective disturbance (47% vs. 29%), the difference in incidence of insecure attachment is not as great as with bipolar depression. Children of mothers with bipolar depression were more than twice as likely to be insecurely attached as children of normal mothers. This greater vulnerability in the bipolar families is consistent with existing evidence of a strong genetic component determining offspring development, as well as with an environmental interpretation that takes into account the difficulties posed not only by the severity of symptoms but also by the contrasting extremes and alternations in behavior in bipolar parents.

We know from the responses of depressed mothers on the SADS interview that their children had been exposed to episodes of maternal sad affect, hopelessness and helplessness, irritability, confusions, and, in bipolar depression, to these episodes alternating with periods of euphoria and grandiosity. It would be desirable to know the effects on the child of each of these patterns of behavior. We have suggestive evidence on the importance of various elements within these patterns. There is indication that, regardless of diagnosis, mothers' negative affective expression in interaction is associated with insecure attachment. Amount of exposure to disturbed affect was also associated with increased probability of a poor mother-child relationship. The significant relation between severity of disturbance and attachment classification suggests that mother's own ability to cope or to function well despite her disorder is one factor to be considered.

One can speculate concerning the effect of other depression-related behaviors. Consistent and positively responsive mothering has been repeatedly shown to be beneficial to the child in the literature of child development. To some degree, major depression precludes consistency of mothering, since depression is episodic (both unipolar and bipolar). Depressed mothers are likely, therefore, to be experienced by their children as unpredictable or inconsistent. Since confusion and preoccupations with self are conditions of depression, young children of depressed mothers are also likely to find their mothers unresponsive as well as physically and emotionally unavailable.

The hopeless and self-deprecating outlook of the parent who is severely depressed raises questions concerning another kind of possible impact on the child: How is this dimension of depression conveyed to the child, and with what effects? The research of Cummings, Zahn-Waxler, and Radke-Yarrow (1981), Klinnert, Campos, Sorce, Emde, and Svejda (1983), Radke-Yarrow and Zahn-Waxler (1984), and others has documented very young children's keen awareness of affective signals in others (in facial expressions, body language, and speech), whether or not the affect is directed to the child. What are the consequences of the exaggerated as well as the flat affect of depressed mothers for the cognitive and social-emotional aspects of the child's relationship with her? An important next step is to observe each of these aspects of maternal affect in interaction with the child in order to assess the child's responses to these encounters on a day-to-day basis.

We have been discussing the present findings as group differences between normal and depressed mothers. Not all mother-child pairs conform to the group difference. Normal mothers and mothers with a diagnosis of minor depression did not differ in frequencies of secure attachment (roughly three-fourths of the pairs were securely attached). The drop in the secure attachments to 53% in unipolar depression and 21% in bipolar depression, although impressive, still leaves "discordant" cases. Conditions outside the mother's illness-based behavior are surely contributory to the mother-child relationship. The attachment relationship, we assume, has contributions from the child. Since the present study provides information primarily on the mother component, the child's characteristics and coping mechanisms are unknowns.

One might assume that the father's relationship with the mother, his relationship with the child, and specifically his functioning when the mother is ill would be important. Although the present study has limited information concerning the father's role, the significance of father absence in increasing the frequency of insecure attachments throws some light on these questions. It suggests an interpretation in terms of the availability of an alternative attachment figure when the mother is ill. Bowlby (1969) has suggested that the effect of physical separation on attachment relationships depends in part on the physical availability of acceptable alternative figures during separation. In the case of maternal depression, when the mother may be emotionally unavailable, an available alternative paternal attachment figure appears to be important. In a related vein, the social supports available to the mother have been shown to be important in the quality of attachment relationship with the mother (Crockenberg, 1981). Social supports from father or others are likely to be important for depressed mothers in determining their ability to cope with their depression and with their role as parent. However, the findings suggest that whether the father has psychopathology may not be a critical factor in the social support provided by the father.

The father's illness was anticipated to be a factor influencing the child's relationship with the mother. It might be expected to influence the mother-child bond by virtue of its effects on both the mother's and child's well-being, as well as by its possible genetic contribution to the child's makeup. The expected effect of father's illness was not observed. It is possible that father's illness affected the child in other ways, which our data did not explore.

Research on the specific qualities of the rearing environment created for the child by parental pathology and on the conditions that moderate or modify the pathogenic aspects of parental rearing has a number of implications. If there are identifiably different rearing conditions associated with secure and insecure attachment in depressed families and with correspondingly good and poor child development, then there are implications for interpretations of epidemiological data. Questions could be raised as to the soundness of giving depressed parents specific probability statements about the likelihood of pathology in their children. Also, such data on rearing would provide instructive bases for interventions that would enhance the chances for adaptive development in the offspring of depressed parents.

REFERENCES

Ainsworth, M. D. S., Blehar, M. C., Waters, E., & Wall, S. (1978). *Patterns of attachment: A psychological study of the strange situation*. Hillsdale, NJ: Erlbaum.

Ainsworth, M. D. S., & Wittig, B. A. (1969). Attachment and exploratory behavior of one-year-olds in a Strange Situation. In B. M. Foss (Ed.), *Determinants of infant behavior* (Vol. 4, pp. 111–136). London: Methuen.

Akisal, H., & McKinney, W. (1975). Overview of recent research in depression: Integration of ten conceptual models into a comprehensive clinical frame. *Archives of General Psychiatry, 32*, 285–305.

Arend, R., Gove, F. L, & Sroufe, L. A. (1979). Continuity of individual adaptation from infancy to kindergarten: A predictive study of egoresiliency and curiosity in preschoolers. *Child Development, 50*, 950–959.

Bartko, J. J., & Carpenter, W. T. (1976). On the methods and theory of reliability. *Journal of Nervous and Mental Disease, 1976, 163*, 307–317.

Beardslee, W., Bemporad J., Keller, M., & Klerman G. (1983). Children of parents with major affective disorder: A review. *American Journal of Psychiatry*, 140(7), 825–832.

Belsky, J., Rovine, M., & Taylor, D. (1984). The Pennsylvania Infant and Family Development Project: III. The origins of individual differences in infant-mother attachment: Maternal and infant contributions. *Child Development, 55*, 718–728.

Blehar, M. C., Lieberman, A. F., & Ainsworth, M. D. S. (1976). Early face-to-face interaction and its relation to later infant-mother attachment. *Child Development, 48*, 182–194.

Bowlby, J. (1969). *Attachment and loss: Vol. 1. Attachment.* London: Hogarth.

Bowlby, J. (1973). *Attachment and loss: Vol. 2. Separation: Anxiety and anger.* New York: Basic.

Bretherton, I. (in press). Attachment theory: Retrospect and prospect. In I. Bretherton & E. Waters (Eds.), Growing points in attachment theory and research. *Monographs of the Society for Research in Child Development.*

Cassidy, J., & Main, M. (1983, March). *Secure attachment in infancy as a precursor of the ability to tolerate a brief laboratory separation at six years.* Paper presented at the Second World Congress of Infant Psychiatry, Cannes, France.

Crittenden, P. M. (1983, April). *Maltreated infants: Vulnerability and resilience.* Paper presented at the meeting of the Society for Research in Child Development, Detroit.

Crittenden, P. M. (in press). Social networks, quality of child-rearing, and child development. *Child Development.*

Crockenberg, S. B. (1981). Infant irritability, mother responsiveness, and social support influences on the security of infant-mother attachment. *Child Development, 52*, 857–865.

Cummings, E. M., Zahn-Waxler, C., & Radke-Yarrow, M. (1981). Young children's responses to expressions of anger and affection by others in the family. *Child Development, 52*, 1274–1282.

Cytryn, L., McKnew, D. H., Zahn-Waxler, C., & Gershon, E. S. (in press). Developmental issues in risk research: The offspring of affectively ill parents. In M. Rutter, C. E. Izard, & P. B. Read (Eds.), *Depression in children: Developmental perspectives.* New York: Guilford.

Erickson, M. F., Sroufe, L., & Egeland, B. (in press). The relationship between quality of attachment and behavior problems in preschool in a high risk sample. In I. Bretherton & E. Waters (Eds.), Growing points in attachment theory and research. *Monographs of the Society for Research in Child Development.*

Gaensbauer, T. J., Harmon, R. J., Cytryn, L., & McKnew, D. H. (1984). Social and affective development in children with a manic-depressive parent. *American Journal of Psychiatry, 141*, 223–229.

Hays, W. L (1963). *Statistics.* New York: Holt, Rinehart & Winston.

Klinnert, M., Campos, J., Sorce, J., Emde, R., & Svejda, M. (1983). Emotions as behavior regulators: Social referencing in infancy. In R. Plutchek & H. Kellerman (Eds.), *Emotions in early development: Vol. 2. The emotions.* New York: Academic Press.

LaFreniere, P., & Sroufe, L. A. (in press). Profiles of peer competence in the preschool: Interrelations among measures, influence of social ecology, and relation to attachment history. *Developmental Psychology.*

Lieberman, A. F. (1977). Preschoolers' competence with a peer: Influence of attachment and social experience. *Child Development, 48*, 1277–1287.

Londerville, S., & Main, M. (1981). Security of attachment, compliance, and maternal training methods in the second year of life. *Developmental Psychology, 17*, 289–299.

Maccoby, E., & Feldman, S. (1972). Mother-attachment and stranger-reactions in the third year of life. *Monographs of the Society for Research in Child Development, 37* (1, Serial No. 146).

Main, M., Kaplan, N., & Cassidy, J. (in press). Security in infancy, childhood, and adulthood: A move to the level of representation. In I. Bretherton & E. Waters (Eds.), Growing points in attachment theory and research. *Monographs of the Society for Research in Child Development.*

Main, J., Tomasini L., & Tolan, W. (in press). Differences among mothers of infants judged to differ in security. *Infant Behavior and Development.*

Main, M., & Weston, D. R. (1981). The quality of the toddlers' relationship to mother and father: Related to conflict behavior and the readiness to establish new relationships. *Child Development, 52*, 932–940.

Marvin, R. S. (1972). *Attachment and cooperative behavior in two-, three-, and four-year olds.* Unpublished doctoral dissertation, University of Chicago.

Marvin, R. S. (1977). An ethological-cognitive model for the attenuation of mother-child attachment behavior. In T. M. Alloway & L. Kramer (Eds.), *Advances in the study of communication and affect: Vol. 3. The development of social attachments* (pp. 25–29). New York: Plenum.

Marvin, R. S., & Greenberg, M. T. (1982). Preschoolers' changing conceptions of their mothers: A social-cognitive study of mother-child attachment. In D. Forbes & M. T. Greenberg (Eds.), *New directions in child development: Vol. 14. Developing plans for behavior* (pp. 47–60). San Francisco: Jossey-Bass.

Matas, L., Arend, R. E., & Sroufe, L. A. (1978). Continuity of adaptation in the second year: The relationship between quality of attachment and later competence. *Child Development, 49*, 547–556.

McNair, D. M., Lorr, M., & Droppleman, L. F. (1971). *POMS—Profile of mood states.* San Diego, CA: Educational and Industrial Testing Service.

Meyersberg, M. A., & Post, R. M. (1979). An holistic developmental view of neural and psychological processes: A neurobiological-psychoanalytic integration. *British Journal of Psychiatry, 135*, 139–155.

Pastor, D. L. (1981). The quality of mother-infant attachment and its relationship to toddlers' initial sociability with peers. *Developmental Psychology, 17,* 326–335.

Radke-Yarrow, M., & Zahn-Waxler, C. (1984). Roots, motives, and patternings in children's prosocial behavior. In E. Staub, D. Bar-Tal, J. Karylowski, & J. Reykowski (Eds.), *The development and maintenance of prosocial behavior. International perspectives on positive morality.* New York: Plenum.

Rutter, M., & Garmezy, N. (1983). Developmental psychopathology. In E. M. Hetherington (Ed.), P. H. Mussen (Series Ed.), *Handbook of child psychology: Vol. 4. Socialization, personality, and social development* (pp. 775–911). New York: Wiley.

Schneider-Rosen, K., & Cicchetti, D. (1984). The relationships between affect and cognition in maltreated infants: Quality of attachment and the development of self recognition. *Child Development, 55,* 648–658.

Siegel, S. (1956). *Nonparametric statistics.* New York: McGraw Hill.

Spitzer, R. L., & Endicott, J. (1977). *The schedule for affective disorders and schizophrenia: Lifetime version.* New York: New York State Psychiatric Institute, Biometrics Research.

Spitzer, R. L., Gibbon, M., & Endicott, J. (1978). *Global assessment scale.* New York: New York State Psychiatric Institute, Biometrics Research.

Sroufe, L. A., Fox, N. E., & Pancake, V. R. (1983). Attachment and dependency in developmental perspective. *Child Development, 54,* 1615–1627.

Stayton, D. J., & Ainsworth, M. D. S. (1973). Individual differences in infant responses to brief everyday separations as related to other infant and maternal behavior. *Developmental Psychology, 9,* 226–235.

Tracy, R., & Ainsworth, M. D. S. (1981). Maternal affectionate behavior and infant-mother attachment patterns. *Child Development, 52,* 1341–1343.

Vaughn, B., Egeland, B., Sroufe, L. A., & Waters, E. (1979). Individual differences in infant-mother attachment at twelve and eighteen months: Stability and change in families under stress. *Child Development, 50,* 971–975.

Waters, E. (1978). The reliability and stability of individual differences in infant-mother attachment. *Child Development, 49,* 483–494.

Waters, E., Wippman, J., & Sroufe, L. A. (1979). Attachment, positive affect, and competence in the peer group: Two studies in construct validation. *Child Development, 50,* 821–829.

Zahn-Waxler, C., Cummings, E. M., McKnew, D. H., & Radke-Yarrow, M. (1984). Affective arousal and social interactions in young children of manic-depressive parents. *Child Development, 55,* 112–122.

QUESTIONS

1. Why is secure attachment with a primary caregiver important for healthy development?
2. What modifications to the Strange Situation process were used in this research and why?
3. The investigators collected several different types of measures of maternal depression. Why did they do this?
4. Why are children of depressed mothers more likely to be insecurely attached to their mothers than children of mothers who are not depressed?
5. How might concurrent experience with another caregiver who is not depressed, such as the child's father or a day-care provider, affect the emotional development of a child with a depressed mother?
6. What child characteristics or behaviors might help young children cope with a mother who is depressed?

16 Facts, Fantasies and the Future of Child Care in the United States

Sandra Scarr · Deborah Phillips · Kathleen McCartney

Over the past twenty years women have entered the labor force in record numbers. The majority of these women have young children in need of supervision and care while their mothers are at work. This reality has posed enormous challenges for families and society. From a developmental perspective, several questions arise.

We know from research that early attachment with primary caregivers is critical to the child's well-being. Does care outside the home disrupt the formation or stability of this relationship? Does child care benefit young children in any way? For example, does it enhance language or cognitive or social development? The answers to these questions will determine the shape of child care in years to come.

In the following article, Sandra Scarr, Deborah Phillips, and Kathleen McCartney review research on this topic. They discuss what is known about how child care affects psychological development. They also raise important issues related to social policy about child care in the United States. This article is an excellent example of how theories of child development, empirical findings, and social policy can inform one another and be used to improve care for children and families.

Psychologists in both family practice and developmental research may be puzzled about the scientific status of research on child care as it affects children, parents, and caregivers. What conclusions can be reached about mothers in the labor force, about the advisability of various child care arrangements, about their short- and long-term consequences, and what advice do we as psychologists have to offer in the public interest to parents of infants and young children? In this article, we review research on child care, and discuss its implications for the nation and for psychology as a research enterprise and a helping profession.

Child care is now as essential to family life as the automobile and the refrigerator. As of 1986, the majority of families, including those with infants, require child care to support parental employment. Yet most families find it far easier to purchase quality cars and refrigerators than to buy good care for their children.

Contemporary realities about the need for child care, captured in statistics about family income, mens' wages, maternal employment, and labor force needs, have not produced a coherent national policy on parental leaves or on child care services for working parents (Kahn & Kamerman, 1987; Scarr, Phillips, & McCartney, 1989a). Instead, our society remains ambivalent about mothers who work and about children whose care is shared, part-time, with others (McCartney & Phillips, 1988). The cost of our reluctance to shed fantasies about children's needs and parents' obligations, particularly mothers' obligations, is the failure to develop constructive social policies.

Facts and fantasies about child care arrangements influence the thinking of psychologists, other experts, parents, and those who make child care policy. It is thus imperative to reassess our ideas about children's needs and maternal roles, based especially on research. The social and demographic facts that are affecting the growing reliance on child care are now well known. They encompass documentation of declines in family income (Greenstein, 1987), dramatic changes in family structure (Cherlin, 1988), rapid increases in maternal employment and projected

Reprinted with permission of Blackwell Publishers from *Psychological Science*, vol. 1, 1990, 26–35.

continuations of this trend (Hofferth & Phillips, 1987), and converging patterns of employment among mothers of all races and marital statuses (Kahn & Kamerman, 1987; Phillips, 1989). In this article we aim to dispel some of the fantasies that have prevented our nation from making appropriate provisions for the care of infants and young children, and to present research facts about child care. In conclusion, we take a brief look at current policy debates and at the future of child care that could emerge if we proceeded from facts about infants, mothers, and child care.

FANTASIES ABOUT MOTHERS

Science is, in part, a social construction (Scarr, 1985). As such, we sometimes construct fantasies about child development, the uses and implications of which can endure long beyond the time when conflicting evidence becomes available. This is most likely to occur when prior scientific results support strongly-held social values. We argue here that the field of psychology has constructed fantasies about the role of mothers in infant development that have impact on our views of child care. We label these beliefs *fantasies* because they are not supported by contemporary scientific evidence. Such fantasies can be found in thinking about mother-infant attachment, maternal deprivation, and the role of early experience for later development. The end result is that some of our fantasies about the mothers and infant development have contributed to our national ambivalence about child care as an acceptable childrearing environment.

FANTASIES ABOUT MOTHER-INFANT ATTACHMENT

Prevailing views about mother-infant attachment have their roots in psychoanalytic theory, Bowlby's theory (1951), and ethology. In some way, all these theories espouse "monotropism" (Smith, 1980), the idea that a single relationship with a special caregiver, typically the mother, is critical for physical and social nourishment. Psychiatrists and others from a psychoanalytic tradition have most often objected to the use of child care, especially in infancy, for this reason (Fraiberg, 1977; Goldstein, Freud, & Solnit, 1973). Yet, research reveals that infants can and do develop multiple attachment relationships: with fathers (Lamb, 1980), with other family members and close friends of the family (Schaffer, 1977), and with caregivers (Ainslie & Anderson, 1984; Farran & Ramey, 1977; Howes, Rodning, Galluzzo, & Myers, 1988). Moreover, we know that most infants become securely attached to their parents, even when they live with a full-time

caregiver in a kibbutz (Fox, 1977). Some research has shown that a secure attachment with a caregiver can buttress a child who otherwise might be at risk (Howes, Rodning, Galluzzo & Myers, 1988). Nevertheless, little is known about children's relationships with their caregivers, whose roles in children's lives must differ from those of parents, especially because of the high turnover rates of caregivers in the United States. An enduring child-adult relationship requires at least moderate stability in caregiving.

A number of studies have compared attachment relationships between infants and their mothers as a function of maternal employment or use of child care. Currently, there is a controversy concerning whether extensive child care during infancy is a risk to infants' attachments to their mothers (Belsky, 1988). But most infants require care while their mothers work. Should we view as a "risk factor" a small mean difference in attachment security (8%; Clarke-Stewart, 1989) between children as a function of maternal employment status or child care use? When children in child care seem to fare less well, child care is said to be a risk. When children in child care fare better on assessments of social competence, independence, or school readiness (e.g., Clarke-Stewart, 1984; Gunnarsson, 1978; Howes & Olenick, 1986; Howes & Stewart, 1987), no one is prepared to call care by mothers a risk factor. All forms of care have their strengths and weaknesses, although the effect sizes are likely to be small (for a thorough review of infant care, see Clarke-Stewart, 1989).

Few would disagree that maternal employment and child care are contextual issues (Bronfenbrenner, 1979, 1986), with many "ifs, ands, and buts" that depend upon the family and the child care situation. Unfortunately, expert advice to parents often fails to mention the size of effects, fails to acknowledge known moderators of effects, and fails to speculate on the possibility, indeed probability, of unknown moderators (Gerson, Alpert, & Richardson, 1984). A notable exception comes from Maurer & Maurer (1989):

> Developmental psychology knows much more about babies now than it knew even ten years ago. ... Consider, for instance, the effect upon the baby of the mother's going back to work. ... Studies on the topic abound, and every new one yields a flurry of pronouncements, either dire or reassuring depending on the results. But look at some of the factors involved here. A baby may be cared for in his own home, or in somebody else's home, or in a day care center, by either a relative or a stranger. The caretaker may be trained or untrained, and may be looking after one baby or several babies. The mother may be an overbearing woman and the caretaker easy-going, or vice

versa. The mother may be happy about going to work and relaxed about giving over her baby in the morning, or she may be distressed at having to leave him with someone else: either way she may communicate her emotions to the child. At home in the evening, the mother may not have time to play with the baby because she is swamped with housework, or the babysitter or her husband may do the housework, leaving her evenings free. Her husband may be unhappy about her returning to work, so their evenings with the child become tense, or her husband may support her. And, of course, babies differ in temperament from one to another, so they react differently to all these factors. Clearly, no one study can take all of this into account (pp. 207–208).

No study to date has taken into account this full complement of possible influences on children's development and family functioning.

Fantasies about Early Experience

The "romance of early experience" (Scarr & Arnett, 1987) has given us the assumption that infancy provides more potent and pervasive influences than does later human experience. Although evidence for modest relations between early experience and later development exists (Caspi, Elder, & Bem, 1987; Erickson, Sroufe, & Egeland, 1985; Fagan, 1984; Funder, Block, & Block, 1983; Sigman, Cohen, Beckwith, & Parmelee, 1986), we agree with Kagan's (1979) interpretation of the data, namely that continuity does not imply inevitability. The human organism is surprisingly resilient in the face of deleterious experiences and sufficiently malleable to "bounce back" given constructive inputs. Only the most pervasive and continuous detrimental experiences have lasting, negative effects on development (Clarke & Clarke, 1976; Ernst, 1988; Lerner, 1984). Although this fact is encouraging for developmentalists, it is discouraging for interventionists, because even the most intensive early interventions appear to require some follow-up services or lasting environmental changes to assure long-term gains (Rutter, 1979; Scarr & McCartney, 1988; Valentine & Stark, 1979).

As a consequence of growing evidence for malleability, the search for critical periods has shifted toward efforts to examine relations between early and later experience, and to elucidate the mechanisms by which individuals and their environments interact to promote continuities and discontinuities in development (Brim & Kagan, 1980; Lerner, 1984; Scarr & Weinberg, 1983; Wachs & Gruen, 1982). Research on the developmental implications of child care would benefit greatly from adopting this perspective.

Fantasies about Maternal Deprivation

Images about child care include for some the notion of deprivation of maternal care. Research on "maternal deprivation" reached an emotional climax in the 1950s, when Spitz (1945), Bowlby (1951), and others claimed that institutionalized infants were retarded intellectually and socially for lack of mothering. Re-analyses and reinterpretation of the evidence (Yarrow, 1961) found that it was, in fact, lack of sensory and affective stimulation in typical institutions that led to detrimental outcomes for the orphans. Infants need someone consistently there with whom to interact and to develop a trusting relationship, but that person does not have to be the child's biological mother.

Critics of child care sometimes write as though working parents abandon their infants as orphans. For example, the term, "maternal absence," was used to describe employed mothers in the title of a recent article in the prestigious journal, *Child Development* (Barglow, Vaughn & Molitor, 1987). The terms "maternal absence" and "maternal deprivation" seem uncomfortably close and both conjure up negative images. Some seem to forget that employed mothers are typically with their babies in the mornings, evenings, weekends, and holidays, which for most fully-employed workers constitutes about half of the child's waking time.[1] And, when the child is ill, mothers are more likely than other family members to stay at home with the child (Hughes & Galinsky, 1986).

There are moderators of effects in the maternal deprivation literature as well. In his comprehensive review, Rutter (1979) concluded that it is not separation alone but separation in conjunction with other risk factors, for example, family stress, that leads to later antisocial behavior in children. A recent study by Ernst (1988) in Switzerland demonstrates Rutter's point nicely. Ernst's longitudinal study of 137 children who spent their first years in residential nurseries showed no differences between these children and the general population in IQ and in popularity. These children were two to three times more likely to develop behavior and social disorders, however. Ernst's careful analyses revealed that it was not nursery status alone that accounted for the difference. Rather, risk was associated with psychosocial factors in the environment such as parental discord, psychosocial disorder in parents, and abuse.

Early deprivation often indicates that an unfavorable situation will continue. For example, one research team has conducted a retrospective study and found that care during infancy is associated with negative outcomes at age 8 (Vandell & Corasaniti, in press). Infant care was atypical 8 years ago from a demographic perspective (Hofferth & Phillips, 1987). Thus, we must ask the follow-up questions Ernst thought to ask about psychosocial factors in the environment that might be continuous. Was the use of infant child care 8 years ago an indicator of unfavorable circumstances that continue in childhood? A search for these moderators is most likely to advance our knowledge of any identified child care effects. The quality of maternal care, just like other child care arrangements, depends on many aspects of the home situation and mothers' mental health. The fantasy that mothers at home with young children provide the best possible care neglects the observation that some women at home full-time are lonely, depressed, and not functioning well (see Crosby, 1987; Scarr, Phillips & McCartney, 1989b). Although, surely, most mothers at home are well motivated to provide good and stimulating care, they have many responsibilities other than direct child care. Time-use studies show that mothers at home full-time with preschool children spend very little time in direct interaction with them. They spend less time playing educational games and talking with the children than in many other household activities (Hill & Stafford, 1978; Hoffman, 1984; Nock & Kingston, in press; Ziegler, 1983). Child caregivers, on the other hand, usually have a majority of their time to give to their charges, although they usually have more children to care for than a mother at home. There are trade-offs: Neither home care nor out-of-home care promises quality child care. In fact, employed mothers of infants and young children spend less time in total home activities than non-employed mothers (715 versus 930 minutes, summed across one workday and a Sunday), but their actual time with their *children* is much closer to that of non-employed mothers. The largest difference in time with young children is the distribution of time between weekdays and weekends, with employed mothers concentrating their child-time on the weekends. Employed mothers scrimp on housework and on their own leisure time, rather than on time with their children (Nock & Kingston, in press). Fathers with employed wives spend more time with their infants and preschool children than fathers with non-employed wives (580 versus 521 minutes; Nock & Kingston, in press). Thus, working parents do spend considerable time in both direct and indirect activities with their children. In addition, children of working parents have the attention of caregivers while their parents work.

RESEARCH FACTS ABOUT CHILD CARE AND CHILD DEVELOPMENT

Child care arrangements, like families, vary enormously in their abilities to promote children's development, to provide support for working families, and to give caregivers rewarding adult roles. In the research literature, however, child care is still cast as nonmaternal care by investigators who, in fact, rarely study variation in child care settings. Similarly, home care is treated uniformly as though all families were alike, and is assumed to be preferred to other child care arrangements. Thus studies often ignore the facts that families vary from abusive and neglectful of children's needs to supportive and loving systems that promote optimal development, and so do other child care arrangements. Actual child care arrangements vary from hiring a trained nanny or untrained babysitter in one's own home, to family day care in another person's home, to centers that care for more than 100 infants and children. Diversity in the quality of child care, at home and in other settings, is what matters for children. High-quality day care settings have in fact been shown to compensate for poor family environments (McCartney, Scarr, Phillips, & Grajek, 1985; Ramey, Bryant & Suarez, 1985) and, for low-income children, to promote better intellectual and social development than they would have experienced in their own homes.

DEVELOPMENTAL EFFECTS OF CHILD CARE

Fears about the effects of child care have centered on possible interference with infants' attachment to their mothers, on their later social development, and on their intellectual development.

Attachment Research The earliest research on child care asked whether or not caregivers replaced mothers as children's primary attachment figures. Concerns that daily prolonged separations from mother might weaken the mother-child bond were a direct heritage of the work on children in orphanages. But child care was not found to be a milder form of full-time institutionalization. Attachment was not adversely affected by enrollment in the university-based child care centers that provided the early child care samples. Bonds formed between children and their caregivers did not replace the mother-child attachment relationship (Belsky & Steinberg, 1978; Etaugh, 1980).

Now, almost twenty years later, the emergence of infant day care as a middle-class phenomenon among parents who themselves were reared at home by their mothers, has spawned an active debate about infant day care. The central issue here is whether full-time child care in the first year of life increases the probability of insecure attachments between mothers and infants. Some researchers have presented evidence that supports this claim (Belsky, 1986; Belsky, 1988; Belsky & Rovine, in press).

Other researchers have highlighted the many limitations of this new literature on infant day care (Clarke-Stewart, in press; Clarke-Stewart & Fein, 1983;

McCartney & Galanopoulos, 1988; Phillips, McCartney, Scarr, & Howes, 1987). The main limitation concerns the exclusive use of the Strange Situation (Ainsworth & Wittig, 1969) to assess attachment. Critics question whether this experimental laboratory procedure of separation from and reunion with mother is equally stressful for children with and without child care experience, because children with child care experience have daily experience with the supposed stressful procedure. Furthermore, studies with an attachment Q-sort measure (Waters & Deane, 1985) have failed to show differences between children in child care and children at home with mother (Belsky, personal communication, to K. McCartney, November 6, 1987; Weinraub, Jaeger, & Hoffman, in press). Finally, the practical significance of differences reported in the Strange Situation between child care and non-child care samples is minimal, despite press reports to the contrary (Clarke-Stewart, 1989).

Social Development   Although some studies have reported no differences in social behavior (Golden, Rosenbluth, Grossi, Policare, Freeman, & Brownlees, 1978; Kagan, Kearsley & Zelaso, 1978), others find that children who have attended child care are more socially competent (Clarke-Stewart, 1984; Gunnarsson, 1978; Howes & Olenick, 1986; Howes & Stewart, 1987; Ruopp, et al., 1979), and still others suggest lower levels of social competence (Haskins, 1985; Rubenstein, Howes, & Boyle, 1983). Positive outcomes include teacher and parent ratings of considerateness and sociability (Phillips, McCartney, & Scarr, 1987), observations of compliance and self regulation (Howes & Olenick, 1986), and observations of involvement and positive interactions with teachers (McCartney, 1984; Ruopp, Travers, Glantz, & Coelen, 1979; Vandell & Powers, 1983).

Negative outcomes of day care experience have emphasized aggression. For example, Haskins' (1985) study of graduates from the Abecedarian project, a high-quality intervention day care program, showed that teachers in the early elementary grades rated these children higher on scales of aggression than a control group that was not enrolled in the program. However, a subgroup of the control children who were enrolled in an equivalent amount of community-based child care were found to be among the least aggressive children in the study, thereby demonstrating that the effect was not due to child care per se. A change in the curriculum of the Abecedarian project decreased aggression by 80% (Finkelstein, 1982), and by third grade, all early effects had dissipated for the initial group (Bryant, personal communication, February 1988). Here again, the story of day care effects will eventually be told through an examination of moderators, such as quality, and of trends in behavior over time.

> Senate approval in June [1989] of the Act for Better Child Care (ABC) represents the first major effort by the federal government to address the nation's child care crisis since 1971 when President Nixon vetoed the Child Development Act. It is the first of several bills in progress that deal with the long-neglected issue.
> —from *Child Behavior and Development Letter* (Brown University), 1989, 5, 1.

Intellectual and Cognitive Development   Differences in intelligence between children in varying forms of day care and children cared for by their mothers have not been reported in most studies (Carew, 1980; Doyle & Somers, 1978; Kagan, Kearsley, & Zelaso, 1978; Robertson, 1982; Stith & Davis, 1984). Two studies, however, have reported that children in center care score higher on tests of cognitive competence (Clarke-Stewart, 1984; Rubenstein, Howes, & Boyle, 1981) than children in other types of child care settings. Similar evidence is provided by evaluations of early intervention programs (Lee, Brooks-Gunn, & Schnur, 1988; McCartney, Scarr, Phillips & Grajek, 1985; McKey, Condelli, Ganson, Barrett, McConkey & Plantz, 1985; Ramey & Haskins, 1981; Schweinhart & Weikart, 1980; Seitz, Apel, Rosenbaum, & Zigler, 1983), which indicate that carefully designed group programs can have substantial, and, in some cases lasting, positive effects on children's patterns of achievement.

In sum, there is near consensus among developmental psychologists and early childhood experts that child care per se does not constitute a risk factor in children's lives; rather, poor quality care and poor family environments can conspire to produce poor developmental outcomes (National Center for Clinical Infant Programs, 1988).

CHILD CARE AS A HETEROGENEOUS ENVIRONMENT

Contemporary developmental research has recognized the vast heterogeneity of child care and turned to the question of "what is *quality?*" in child care. Reliable indices of child care quality include caregiver-child ratio, group size, and caregiver training and experience. These variables, in turn, facilitate constructive and sensitive interactions among caregivers and children, which promote positive social and cognitive development (Phillips, 1987; Ruopp et al., 1979).

The caregiver-child ratio is related to decreased exposure to danger (Ruopp et al., 1979) and to increased language interactions in the child care setting. Both Bruner (1980) and Howes and Rubenstein (1985) report that children in centers with more adults per child engage in more talking and more playing. Another study (McCartney, 1984) has documented a link between verbal interaction with caregivers and children's language competence. Results of the National Day Care Study suggest that adequate ratios are particularly important for infants, with experts citing 1:4 as the threshold for good quality care.

Research on group size has revealed that the larger the group, the more management is necessary; the smaller the group, the more education and social interaction is possible. As first demonstrated in the National Day Care Study (Ruopp et al., 1979), caregivers in larger groups provide less social interaction and cognitive stimulation. Children in larger groups were found to be more apathetic and more distressed. These findings have since been replicated in other studies (Bruner, 1980; Howes, 1983; Howes & Rubenstein, 1985).

The research on caregiver training and education is particularly consistent. Not surprisingly, years of child-related education are associated with increased caregiver responsivity, positive affect, and ability to provide socially- and intellectually-stimulating experiences (Clarke-Stewart & Gruber, 1984; Howes, 1983; Ruopp et al., 1979; Stallings & Porter, 1980). These findings do not simply represent the effects of self-selection. Two intervention studies show that training leads to caregiver improvement (Arnett, 1989; Kaplan & Conn, 1984). Experience working with children cannot replace child-related training. Although Howes (1983) found an association between years of experience and responsiveness to children, the National Day Care Study (Ruopp et al., 1979) found that day care experience was associated with less social interaction and more apathy. Other studies have not found any important effects of experience per se (Phillips, McCartney, Scarr, & Howes, 1987; Stallings & Porter, 1980).

Research has also shown that many aspects of quality are correlated and that a good center is essentially one with good caregivers. Good caregivers are caring, able to read a baby's signals, and responsive to babies signals (McCartney, 1987). In fact, preschoolers perceive caregivers to provide the same caregiving functions as their mothers (Tephly & Elardo, 1984). The vast literature on mother-child interaction can also inform us of caregiving behaviors that are important. Although these behaviors are not legislatable, they are trainable.

Among the most recent indicators of quality to emerge from research is the stability of children's child care arrangements (Cummings, 1980; Howes & Olenick, 1986; Howes & Stewart, 1987). Children who experience multiple changes in caregivers and settings develop less optimally in social and language areas than children with stable child care, with effects lasting into the early school years (Howes, 1988). The importance of stable care stands in stark contrast with the alarmingly high turnover rates among child care workers. Between 1980 and 1990, 42% of all nonhousehold child care workers will need to be replaced each year, just to maintain the current supply of child care providers ("New Occupational," 1984). Low pay, lack of benefits, and stressful working conditions are the major reasons cited by child care workers who leave their jobs (Jorde-Bloom, 1987; Kontos & Stremmel, 1988; Whitebook, Howes, Darrah, & Friedman, 1982). Infants and young children cannot develop stable relationships with caregivers if they are faced with new caregivers every few weeks.

RELATIONS BETWEEN HOME AND CHILD CARE

In studies of typical child care, researchers can neither assign children randomly to child care nor assign parents to varying employment patterns. As a consequence, efforts to decipher the "effects" of child care are a methodological conundrum. Pre-existing family differences—in background, traits, and beliefs—are confounded with child care arrangements.

Recent research suggests that there may be interaction effects between family characteristics and child care arrangements in maternal anxiety (Hock, DeMeis & McBride, 1987), marital status and living arrangements (Scarr, Lande, & McCartney, 1989), such that good child care can compensate for poor home environments. There is also increasing evidence that the lowest income and most disorganized families (among the middle class) end up in the lowest quality child care programs (Howes & Olenick, 1986; Howes & Stewart, 1987; Lamb, Huang, Brookstein, Broberg, Hult, & Frodi, 1988). A number of other family variables might reasonably moderate effects, especially those related to family stress (Kontos & Wells, 1986).

A number of relationships may affect children's sense of security and thereby their adjustment. Belsky found that daughters with unemployed mothers were more likely to be insecurely attached to their fathers than daughters of employed mothers (Belsky & Rovine, in press). Using the attachment Q-sort (Waters & Deane, 1985), Howes and her colleagues (Howes, et al., 1988) have shown recently that both attachment security at home with mother and attachment security with the caregiver at day care are predictors of the child's positive interaction with caregivers and peers in day care. Interactions between family characteristics and child care have been found to affect development in the first 2 years of life. For example, Scarr, Lande, and McCartney (1989) reported negative main effects for typical center care (but not family day care) in the first 2 years of life on both intellectual and social/emotional ratings. The same children were also disadvantaged by being reared in single mother-headed households (but not in extended families with single mothers). Further, they found important inter-actions between households and center care, such that infants from single mother-headed households benefited from group care more than similar children in other kinds of care, including maternal care. By the age of 4 years, there were no effects of child care in the first 2 years or in the second 2 years on any child development outcome. Other research (McBride & Belsky, 1988; Weinraub, Jaeger & Hoffman, in press) has found that relations between maternal employ-ment and attachment vary according to maternal sat-isfaction with child care arrangements, role satisfac-tion, and coping skills. Studies such as these suggest that child care must be seen in the context of the child's family life before one can interpret any effects of child care per se.

FACTS ABOUT CHILD CARE POLICY

For the first time in a decade, child care is on the na-tional agenda. In 1988, more than 40 bills containing provisions for child care were introduced in the U.S. Congress (Robins, 1988). Driven largely by escalating rates of employment among non-poor, married moth-ers (Kahn & Kamerman, 1987), federal child care poli-cies have come under intense scrutiny and numerous proposals for restructuring the federal role have sur-faced. These range from "supply side" proposals that emphasize improvements in the current system of child care to "demand side" proposals that offer fami-lies additional tax subsidies for purchasing child care. Parental leave policies are also being debated. In addi-tion, the majority of states are now moving towards limited funding for school-based child care programs that typically are targeted at poor and/or disadvan-taged families (Marx & Seligson, 1988).

The same demographic trends that are influencing child care policy are also creating new goals for wel-fare reform effects. For low-income mothers, prevail-ing beliefs about maternal care have traditionally led us to favor policies that enable them to stay home with their babies, through child support and public assistance (e.g., Aid to Families with Dependent Chil-dren). But the new welfare reform bill (Family Support Act of 1988: P.L. 100–483), emphasizes training, em-ployment and women's attainment of economic inde-pendence rather than support for full-time mothering

(Phillips, in press). This shift in purpose is due largely to policymakers' recognition that the majority of mothers with preschool-age children are now in the labor force. Under these circumstances, it is difficult to justify the prior exemption from training and em-ployment programs for AFDC-eligible mothers with children under age 6. Unfortunately, even in the best of circumstances, the child care subsidies included in the Family Support Act are continued for only one year after mothers achieve the minimum wage jobs for which they are being trained.

The policy debate about child care is no longer about whether there will be support for child care or whether families will continue to rely on child care (Martinez, 1989). Instead, it has focused on relatively pragmatic questions about delivery systems, target populations, and financing. These questions, however, are not uncontroversial. For example, the high cost of market forms of child care and fears about nationaliz-ing our child care system have generated strong resis-tance to legislation that ties government subsidies to use of licensed programs (i.e., centers and regulated family day care homes) or that mandates federal day care standards. For these reasons, we are unlikely ever to see child care and leave policies in the United States that resemble European or Canadian policies (see Scarr, Phillips, & McCartney, 1989a). Considera-tions of "who should provide child care?" are now mired in an acrimonious debate involving the schools, community-based child care programs, and church-housed programs. And, on-going debates about whether government child care benefits should be re-served for the poor or also assist the non-poor, and about whether these benefits should purchase good quality child care (as in the Head Start program) or disregard consideration of quality are far from re-solved.

The child care policies that result from today's de-bate will constitute some adaptation to the realities of working parents. However, the effects of our na-tional ambivalence about working mothers will un-doubtedly be felt, as well. Prevailing beliefs that mothers of very young children belong at home and that child care problems are best solved privately will assure that any new child care policy is likely to re-main fragmented, marginal, and modestly funded. At a minimum, any generous policy that might actually create an incentive for those mothers who have a choice about working to use child care, will be avoided.

This is the political and social context on which research on child care has a bearing. The ways in which research questions are framed and the values that underlie our questions can challenge the as-sumptions that guide policy and promote policies that are based more on facts and less on fantasies.

THE FUTURE

RESEARCH ON CHILD CARE

Future research on child care influences will need to place more emphasis on the contexts in which families use child care services (Bronfenbrenner, 1986; McCartney & Galanopoulis, 1988). The ecology of child care includes the family, its choice of child care arrangements, its ability to pay for quality care, and its independent effects on child development. Contemporary researchers recognize the necessity of taking into account not only the quality of child care, but also the quality of the home environment, individual differences in children, and the history of children's experience with child care. Life is complicated, and thus requires complex models.

As part of the ecology of child care, research needs to examine the effects of the *un*availability of child care, particularly of the unavailability of good quality, consistent care. Similarly, we have no understanding of the effects of the virtual absence of parental leave policies in the United States (Scarr, Phillips, & McCartney, 1989b). What are the effects on children and families when parents do not have choices about when they return to work, and about the type and quality of the child care they offer their children?

Research on child care has also sampled a relatively narrow range of care types, with licensed centers and regulated family day care homes dominating the empirical literature. Even among center-based arrangements, we have neglected for-profit chains and centers that are exempted from state regulation (e.g., church-run centers in several states). Unregulated family day care homes and other types of care that are not covered by state licensing (e.g., nannies) are virtually unstudied. As a consequence, it is entirely possible that we have not sampled programs that represent the poorest quality care offered in this country.

Longitudinal research is necessary to determine which effects of child care are transitory and which represent enduring influences on development. So far, there are conflicting findings on the long term correlates of early child care arrangements (Scarr, Lande & McCartney, 1989; Scarr & McCartney, in preparation; Vandell & Corasaniti, in press; Vandell, Henderson & Wilson, in press).

At the very least, research is needed on: (1) the family and other mediators of development that correlate, augment, and interact with child care arrangements; (2) range of types and qualities of child care; and (3) longitudinal research on short and long term effects of child care on development, on families, and on caregivers. For these reasons, we can make few definitive statements at this time about the direct effects of child care on children. Rather, we have documented effects that appear to be caused by child care, but may be attributable to children's case histories, temperaments, families, or to complex interactions among these and other circumstances.

CONCLUSIONS

The discussion of fantasies about the nature of child care suggests that we need a closer look at the facts about children's, parents', and care providers' experiences in our current child care system—their discomforts and their satisfactions—to orient our research to the most pressing issues. As one of the reviewers of the article said,

> … in the circumstances prevailing in contemporary society, day care—far more often than not—plays an essential and crucial role as a support system that enables families to function and can provide important supplementary developmental experiences for children. To be sure, there are probably some circumstances, not yet fully understood, that involve some measure of risk, especially for very young children, and these risks need to be weighed, but they are hardly comparable in their probability and magnitude to those to which many children are exposed, through the unavailability of quality child care for thousands of families that desperately want and need it. (Bronfenbrenner, personal communication, December 1988)

For children, the most pressing issue is quality of care—care that will encourage and support all aspects of child development.

For parents, the most pressing issues are affordability and availability of consistent and dependable child care, and employment options that make the task of combining worker and parent roles less stressful.

For child care providers, the most pressing issues are staff wages and working conditions and public support for a system of high quality care that will meet the diverse needs of the working poor, minority families, middle income families, and even yuppie parents who want "the best."

For policy makers, at federal and state levels, the most pressing issues are how to fund a system of quality child care, regulate those aspects of quality that can be legislated and enforced, and coordinate efforts with the private sector and at all levels of government.

NOTE

1. Consider 5 working days/week for 49 weeks of the year: 1.5 hours in the morning, 3 hours of the child's waking time in the late afternoon and evening, for a sum of 4.5 of the approximately 14 hours of the child's

daily waking time. The caregiver accounts for approximately 9 hours of which 2 hours are typically spent in a nap. (A half hour is allocated for transportation.) The sum of the work-week hours for parents employed full-time is 1102; for caregivers, 1715.

To the parental sum, add week-ends (2 days/work week) for 49 weeks, sum of 1274. To that add 3 weeks of vacation time, and 10 days of personal and sick leave (for self and child) during the work week, a sum of 455.

By these calculations, typical, fully-employed parents spend 2831 hours with the child; caregivers spent approximately 1715.

REFERENCES

Ainslie, R. C., & Anderson, C. W. (1984). Day care children's relationships to their mothers and caregivers: An inquiry into the conditions for the development of attachment. In R. C. Ainslie (Ed.), *The child and the day care setting.* New York: Praeger.

Ainsworth, M., & Wittig, B. A. (1969). Attachment and exploratory behavior of one-year olds in a strange situation. In B. M. Foss (Ed.), *Determinants of infant behavior*, Vol. 4. London: Methuen.

Arnett, J. (1989). Issues and obstacles in the training of caregivers. In J. Lande, S. Scarr, & N. Gunzenhauser (Eds.), *Caring for children: Challenge to America* (pp. 241–256). Hillsdale, NJ: Erlbaum.

Barglow, P., Vaughn, B. E., & Molitor, N. (1987). Effects of maternal absence due to employment on the quality of infant-mother attachment in a low-risk sample. *Child Development, 58*, 945–954.

Belsky, J. (1986). Infant day care: A cause for concern? *Zero to Three, 6(5)*, 1–9.

Belsky, J. (1988). The "effects" of infant day care reconsidered. *Early Childhood Research Quarterly, 3*, 235–272.

Belsky, J., & Rovine, M. J. (in press). Nonmaternal care in the first year of life and the security of infant-parent attachment. *Child Development.*

Belsky, J., & Steinberg, L. D. (1978). The effects of daycare: A critical review. *Child Development, 49*, 929–949.

Bowlby, J. (1951). *Maternal care and mental health.* Geneva: World Health Organization.

Bronfenbrenner, U. (1979). *The ecology of human development: Experiments by nature and design.* Cambridge, MA: Harvard University Press.

Bronfenbrenner, U. (1986). Ecology of the family as a context for human development: Research perspectives. *Developmental Psychology, 22*, 723–742.

Brim, O. G., & Kagan, J. (1980). *Constancy and change in human development.* Cambridge, MA: Harvard University Press.

Bruner, J. (1980). *Under five in Britain.* London: Methuen.

Carew, J. (1980). Experience and the development of intelligence in young children. *Monographs of the Society for Research in Child Development, 45*, 6–7 (Serial No. 187).

Caspi, A., Elder, G. H., Jr., & Bem, D. J. (1987). Moving against the world: Life course patterns of explosive children. *Developmental Psychology, 23*, 308–313.

Cherlin, A. J. (Ed.). (1988). *The changing American family and public policy.* Washington, DC: The Urban Institute Press.

Clarke, A. M., & Clarke, A. D. B. (1976). *Early experience: Myth and evidence.* London: Open Books.

Clarke-Stewart, A. (1984). Day care: A new context for research and development. In M. Perlmutter (Ed.), *The Minnesota Symposia on Child Psychology: Vol. 27. Parent-child interaction and parent-child relations in child development* (pp. 61–100). Hillsdale, NJ: Erlbaum.

Clarke-Stewart, A. (1989). Infant day care: Malignant or maligned? *American Psychologist.*

Clarke-Stewart, A., & Fein, G. (1983). Early childhood programs. In P. H. Mussen (Series Ed.) & M. Haith and J. Campos (Vol. Eds.), *Handbook of child psychology: Vol. II. Infancy and developmental psychobiology* (pp. 917–1000). New York: Wiley.

Clarke-Stewart, A., & Gruber, C. (1984). Day care forms and features. In R. C. Ainslie (Ed.), *The child and the day care setting* (pp. 35–62). New York: Praeger.

Crosby, F. J. (Ed.). (1987). *Spouse, parent, worker: On gender and multiple roles.* New Haven: Yale University Press.

Cummings, E. H. (1980). Caregiver stability and day care. *Developmental Psychology, 16*, 31–37.

Doyle, A., & Somers, K. (1978). The effects of group and family day care on infant attachment behaviors. *Canadian Journal of Behavioral Science, 10*, 38–45.

Erickson, M. F., Sroufe, L. A., & Egeland, B. (1985). The relationship between quality of attachment and behavior problems in preschool in a high-risk sample. In I. Bertherton & E. Waters (Eds.), Growing points in attachment theory and research. *Monographs of the Society for Research in Child Development, 50*, 147–166.

Ernst, D. (1988). Are early childhood experiences overrated? A reassessment of maternal deprivation. *European Archives of Psychiatry and Neurological Sciences, 237*, 80–90.

Etaugh, C. (1980). Effects of nonmaternal care on children: Research evidence and popular views. *American Psychologist, 35*, 309–319.

Fagan, J. F. (1984). The intelligent infant: Theoretical implications. *Intelligence, 8*, 1–9.

Farran, D., & Ramsey, C. (1977). Infant day care and attachment behaviors toward mothers and teachers. *Child Development, 48*, 1112–1116.

Finkelstein, N. (1982). Aggression: Is it stimulated by day care? *Young Children, 37*, 3–9.

Fox, N. (1977). Attachment of kibbutz infants to mothers and metapelet. *Child Development, 48*, 1228–1239.

Fraiberg, S. (1977). *Every child's birthright: In defense of mothering.* New York: Basic Books.

Funder, D., Block, J. H., & Block, J. (1983). Delay of gratification: Some longitudinal personality correlates. *Journal of Personality and Social Psychology, 44*, 1198–1213.

Gerson, J., Alpert, J. L., & Richardson, M. (1984). Mothering: The view from psychological research. *Signs, 9*, 434–453.

Golden, M., Rosenbluth, L., Grossi, M. T., Policare, H. J., Freeman, H., Jr., & Brownlee, E. M. (1978). *The New York City infant day care study.* New York: Medical and Health Research Association of New York City.

Goldstein, J., Freud, A., & Solnit, A. J. (1973). *Beyond the best interests of the child.* New York: Free Press.

Greenstein, R. (1987). Testimony presented before the Income Security Task Force Committee on the Budget, U.S. House of Representatives, Washington, D.C., November 9, 1987.

Gunnarsson, L. (1978). *Children in day care and family care in Sweden* (Research Bulletin, No. 21). Gothenburg, Sweden: University of Gothenburg.

Haskins, R. (1985). Public school aggression among children with varying day care experience. *Child Development, 56,* 689–703.

Hill, C. R., & Stafford, F. P. (1978). Parental care of children: Time diary estimates of quantity, predictability, and variety. *Institute for Social Research Working Paper Series.* Ann Arbor: University of Michigan.

Hock, E., DeMeis, D., & McBride, S. (1987). Maternal separation anxiety: Its role in the balance of employment and motherhood in mothers of infants. In A. Gottfried, & A. Gottfried (Eds.), *Maternal employment and children's development: Longitudinal research* (pp. 191–229). New York: Plenum.

Hofferth, S. L., & Phillips, D. A. (1987). Child care in the United States, 1970 to 1995. *Journal of Marriage and the Family, 49,* 559–571.

Hoffman, L. W. (1984). Maternal employment and the child. In M. Perlmutter (Ed.), *The Minnesota Symposia on Child Psychology: Vol. 17. Parent child interaction and parent-child relations in development* (pp. 101–127). Hillsdale, NJ: Erlbaum.

Howes, C. (1983). Caregiver behavior in center and family day care. *Journal of Applied Developmental Psychology, 4,* 99–107.

Howes, C. (1988). Relations between early child care and schooling. *Developmental Psychology, 24,* 53–57.

Howes, C., and Olenick, M. (1986). Child care and family influences on compliance. *Child Development, 57,* 202–216.

Howes, C., Rodning, C., Galluzzo, D., & Myers, L. (1988). Attachment and child care: Relationships with mother and caregiver. *Early Childhood Research Quarterly, 3,* 403–416.

Howes, C., & Rubenstein, J. (1985). Determinants of toddlers' experience in daycare: Age of entry and quality of setting. *Child Care Quarterly, 14,* 140–151.

Howes, C., & Stewart, P. (1987). Child's play with adults, toys, and peers: An examination of family and child-care influences. *Developmental Psychology, 23,* 423–430.

Hughes, D., & Galinsky, E. (1986). Maternity, paternity, and parenting policies: How does the United States compare. In S. A. Hewlett, A. S. Ilchman, & J. J. Sweeney (Eds.), *Family and work: Bridging the gap* (pp. 53–66). Cambridge, MA: Ballinger.

Jorde-Bloom, P. (1987, April). *Factors influencing overall job commitment and facet satisfaction in early childhood work environments.* Paper presented at the meeting of the American Education Research Association, Washington, D.C.

Kagan, J. (1979). Family experience and the child's development. *American Psychologist, 34,* 886–891.

Kagan, J., Kearsley, R. B., & Zelaso, P. R. (1978). *Infancy: Its place in human development.* Cambridge, MA: Harvard University Press.

Kahn, A. J., & Kamerman, S. B. (1987). *Child care: Facing the hard choices.* Dover, MA; Auburn House.

Kaplan, M., & Conn, J. (1984). The effects of caregiver training on classroom setting and caregiver performance in eight community day care centers. *Child Study Journal, 14,* 79–93.

Kontos, S., & Stremmel, A. J. (1988). Caregivers' perceptions of working conditions in a child care environment. *Early Childhood Research Quarterly, 3,* 77–90.

Kontos, S., & Wells, W. (1986). Attitudes of caregivers and the day care experiences of families. *Early Childhood Research Quarterly, 1,* 47–67.

Lamb, M. (1980). The development of parent-infant attachments in the first two years of life. In F. Pederson (Ed.), *The father-infant relationship: Observational studies in the family setting.* New York: Praeger.

Lamb, M., Hwang, C., Bookstein, F. L., Broberg, A., Hult, G., & Frodi, M. (1988). Determinants of social competence in Swedish preschoolers. *Developmental Psychology, 24,* 58–70.

Lee, V. E., Brooks-Gunn, J., & Schnur, E. (1988). Does Head Start work? A 1-year follow-up comparison of disadvantaged children attending Head Start, no preschool, and other preschool programs. *Developmental Psychology, 24,* 210–222.

Lerner, R. M. (1984). *On the nature of human plasticity.* New York: Cambridge University Press.

Martinez, S. (1989). Child care and federal policy. In J. Lande, S. Scarr, & N. Gunzenhauser (Eds.), *Caring for children: Challenge to America* (pp. 111–124). Hillsdale, NJ: Erlbaum.

Marx, F., & Seligson, M. (1988). *The public school early childhood study. The state survey.* New York: Bank Street College of Education.

Maurer, C., & Maurer, D. (1988). *World of the newborn.* New York: Basic.

McBride, S., & Belsky, J. (1988). Characteristics, determinants, and consequences of maternal separation anxiety. *Developmental Psychology, 24,* 407–414.

McCartney, K. (1984). The effect of quality of day care environment upon children's language development. *Developmental Psychology, 20,* 244–260.

McCartney, K. (1987, July/August). Quality: A child's point of view. *Child Care Action News,* Newsletter of the Child Care Action Campaign, 4(4).

McCartney, K., & Galanopoulis, A. (1988). Child care and attachment: A new frontier the second time around. *American Journal of Orthopsychiatry, 58,* 16–24.

McCartney, K., & Phillips, D. (1988). Motherhood and child care. In B. Birns & D. Hay (Eds.), *Different faces of motherhood* (pp. 157–183). New York: Plenum Press.

McCartney, K., Scarr, S., Phillips, D., & Grajek, S. (1985). Day care as intervention: Comparisons of varying quality programs. *Journal of Applied Development Psychology, 6,* 247–260.

McKey, R. H., Condelli, L., Ganson, H., Barrett, B. J., McConkey, C., & Plantz, M. C. (1985). *The impact of Head Start on children, families, and communities: Final report of the Head Start evaluation, synthesis, and utilization project.* Washington, D.C.: CSR Inc.

National Center for Clinical Infant Programs. (1988). *Infants, Families and Child Care.* Washington, D.C.: Author. Brochure.

New occupational separation data improve estimates of job replacement needs. (1984, March). *Monthly Labor Review, 107(3),* 3–10.

Nock, S. L., & Kingston, P. W. (in press). Time with children: The impact of couples' work-time commitments. *Social Forces.*

Phillips, D. (Ed.). (1987). *Quality in child care: What does research tell us?* Washington, D.C.: National Association for the Education of Young Children.

Phillips, D. (1989). Future directions and need for child care in the United States. In J. S. Lande, S. Scarr, & N. Gunzenhauser (Eds.), *Caring for children: Challenge to America* (pp. 257–275). Hillsdale, NJ: Erlbaum.

Phillips, D. (in press). With a little help: Children in poverty and child care. In A. Huston (Ed.), *Children and Poverty.* New York: Cambridge University Press.

Phillips, D., McCartney, K., & Scarr, S. (1987). Child-care quality and children's social development. *Developmental Psychology, 23,* 537–543.

Phillips, D., McCartney, K., Scarr, S., & Howes, C. (1987, February). Selective view of infant day care research: A cause for concern! *Zero to Three, 7,* 18–21.

Ramey, C. T., Bryant, D. M., & Suarez, T. M. (1985). Preschool compensatory education and the modifiability of intelligence: A critical review. In D. Detterman (Ed.), *Current topics in human intelligence* (pp. 247–296). Norwood, NJ: Ablex.

Ramey, C. T., & Haskins, R. (1981). The causes and treatment of school failure: Insights from the Carolina Abecedarian Project. In M. J. Begab, H. C. Haywood, & H. L. Garber (Eds.), *Psychosocial influences in retarded performance: Strategies for improving competence.* Baltimore: University Park Press.

Robertson, A. (1982). Day care and children's response to adults. In E. Zigler & E. W. Gordon (Eds.), *Day care: Scientific and social policy issues* (pp. 152–173). Boston: Auburn House.

Robins, P. (1988). Child care and convenience: The effects of labor market entry cost on economic self-sufficiency among public housing residents. *Social Science Quarterly, 69,* 122–136.

Rubenstein, J., Howes, C., & Boyle, P. (1981). A two year follow-up of infants in community based day care. *Journal of Child Psychology and Psychiatry, 22,* 209–218.

Ruopp, R., Travers, J., Glantz, F., & Coelen, C. (1979). *Children at the center: Final results of the National Day Care Study.* Boston: Abt. Associates.

Rutter, M. (1979). Maternal deprivation, 1972–1978: New findings, new concepts, new approaches. *Child Development, 50,* 283–291.

Scarr, S. (1985). Constructing psychology: Making facts and fables for our times. *American Psychologist, 40,* 499–512.

Scarr, S., & Arnett, J. (1987). Malleability: Lessons from intervention and family studies. In J. J. Gallagher (Ed.), *The malleability of children* (pp. 71–84). New York: Brooke.

Scarr, S., Lande, J., & McCartney, K. (1989). Child care and the family: Cooperation and interaction. In J. Lande, S. Scarr,

& N. Gunzenhauser (Eds.), *Caring for children: The future of child care in the United States* (pp. 1–21). Hillsdale, NJ: Erlbaum.

Scarr, S., & McCartney, K. (in preparation). Follow-up studies of early child care experiences at school age.

Scarr, S., & McCartney, K. (1988). Far from home: An experimental evaluation of the mother-child home program in Bermuda. *Child Development, 59,* 531–543.

Scarr, S., Phillips, D., & McCartney, K. (1989a). Dilemmas of child care in the United States: Employed mothers and children at risk. *Canadian Psychology, 30(2),* 126–139.

Scarr, S., Phillips, D., & McCartney, K. (1989b). Working mothers and their families. *American Psychologist,* June.

Scarr, S., & Weinberg, R. A. (1983). The Minnesota adoption studies: Genetic differences and malleability. *Child Development, 54,* 260–267.

Schaffer, H. R. (1977). *Attachments.* Cambridge, MA: Harvard University Press.

Schweinhart, L., & Weikart, D. (1980). The effects of the Perry Preschool Program on youths through age 15. *Monographs of the High/Scope Educational Research Foundation No. 7.*

Seitz, V., Apfel, N., Rosenbaum, L., & Zigler, E. (1983). Long term effects of Projects Head Start and Follow Through: The New Haven Project. In Consortium for Longitudinal Studies, *As the twig is bent. Lasting effects of preschool programs* (pp. 299–332). Hillsdale, NJ: Erlbaum.

Sigman, M., Cohen, S. E., Beckwith, L., & Parmelee, A. H. (1986). Infant attention in relation to intellectual abilities in childhood. *Developmental Psychology, 22,* 788–792.

Smith, P. K. (1980). Shared care of young children: Alternative models to monotropism. *Merrill-Palmer Quarterly, 26,* 371–389.

Spitz, R. (1945). Hospitalism: An inquiry into the genesis of psychiatric conditions in early childhood. *Psychoanalytic Study of the Child, 1,* 53–74.

Stallings, J., & Porter, A. (1980, June). *National Day Care Home Study: Observation component* (Final Report of the National Day Care Home Study, Vol. III). Washington, DC: Dept. of Health, Education and Welfare.

Stith, S., & Davis, A. (1984). Employed mothers and family day care substitute caregivers. *Child Development, 55,* 1340–1348.

Tephly, J., & Elardo, R. (1984). Mothers and day care teachers: Young children's perceptions. *British Journal of Developmental Psychology, 2,* 251–256.

Valentine, J., & Stark, E. (1979). The social context of parent involvement in Head Start. In E. Zigler, & J. Valentine (Eds.), *Project Head Start: A legacy of the War on Poverty.* (pp. 291–314). New York: Free Press.

Vandell, D. L., & Corsaniti, M. A. (in press). Child care in the family: Complex contributions to child development. In K. McCartney (Ed.), *New directions in child development research, Vol. 20: The social ecology of child care.* New York: Jossey-Bass.

Vandell, D. L., Henderson, V. K., & Wilson, K. S. (in press). A longitudinal study of children with varying quality day care experiences. *Child Development.*

Vandell, D. L., & Powers, C. P. (1983). Day care quality and children's free play activities. *American Journal of Orthopsychiatry, 53,* 493–500.

Wachs, T. D., & Gruen, G. E. (1982). *Early experience and human development.* New York: Plenum Press.

Waters, E., & Deane, K. E. (1985). Defining and assessing individual differences in attachment relationships: Q-methodology and the organization of behaviors in infancy and childhood. In I. Bertherton & E. Waters (Eds.), Growing points in attachment theory and research. *Monographs of the Society for Research in Child Development, 50,* 41–65.

Weinraub, M., Jaeger, E., & Hoffman, L. (in press). Predicting infant outcome in families of employed and non-employed mothers. *Early Childhood Research Quarterly.*

Whitebook, M., Howes, C., Darrah, R., & Friedman, J. (1982). Caring for the caregivers: Staff burnout in child care. In L. Katz (Ed.), *Current topics in early childhood education* (Vol. 4, pp. 211–235). Norwood, NJ: Ablex.

Yarrow, L. (1961). Maternal deprivation: Toward an empirical and conceptual evaluation. *Psychological Bulletin, 58,* 459–490.

Ziegler, M. E. (1983). *Assessing parents' and children's time together.* Paper presented at the annual meeting of the Society for Research in Child Development, Detroit, Michigan.

QUESTIONS

1. Which views of childhood do Scarr, Phillips, and McCartney call fantasies? Why do they call these fantasies?
2. Critics of early child care often refer to the maternal deprivation literature to support their claims. What are some of the problems in doing this?
3. What characteristics do high quality child-care settings have?
4. Do children who are in child care have different types of attachment to their parents than children who are not in child care? Explain.
5. How does the social and cognitive development of children who are in child care differ from that of children who are not in child care?
6. What questions about child care does future research need to address?

PART III

Early Childhood

In much of the early research on child development, the age period from 2 to 5 was largely ignored. This may seem shocking since quite a bit of research attention is now directed toward this period, known as early childhood. The reasons why an entire age period was largely overlooked are many. Chief among them was great interest among psychologists and educators in the behaviors and skills of school-age children. This information was useful for designing curriculum and informing teachers about children's needs. Since children in the years of early childhood, at least until very recently, do not typically go to school, there was less pressing demand to describe their behaviors and skills. Furthermore, many of the concepts that researchers were interested in, ranging from cognitive skills such as logical thinking to social behavior such as peer relations, flourish in middle childhood but appear in only piecemeal form in early childhood. Consequently, school-age children were seen as having developed many of the skills that interested researchers and younger children were seen as not yet developed in these areas. And, so the reasoning goes, if they are not yet developed why study them?

In recent decades, this entire perspective has changed and an upsurge in interest in early childhood has emerged. This was, in part, fueled by theoretical views such as Vygotsky's that consider it more interesting and informative to study developmental processes as they are forming and changing, not after they are in place. If competencies are already in place, as many are in school-age children, they must develop in early childhood. This realization led to increased interest in how basic concepts, those that are the foundation of the intellectual skills evident in school-age children, originate.

At the same time as this realization occurred, there was increasing interest in the development of language and the role that language plays in social and cognitive development. Language is the most important intellectual tool that humans have. It organizes thinking and it connects people to one another. Progress in language development is extremely rapid over the years of early childhood, and this has enormous impact on all the other areas of development. Thus, better understanding of language development and use is critical to describing human development as a whole.

The five articles in this section describe some of the psychological changes that occur in early childhood. They describe cognitive changes (DeLoache, Miller, and

Rosengren; Avis and Harris), changes in language and communication (Bruner), and social changes (Farver and Howes; Maccoby) that occur during this period. These changes are those that set the stage for children's entry into the broader social and intellectual world of middle childhood.

17 From Communicating to Talking

JEROME S. BRUNER

Language develops rapidly in the early years of life. Over this time children are transformed from nontalking communicative companions to talkers in their own right. This transformation is fueled from many sources—biological, cognitive, and social. In the following article, Jerome Bruner discusses how these three aspects of language development are coordinated over the early years to support the development of children's communicative competence. He emphasizes the important role that social experience and organized cultural practices play in supporting language acquisition.

In this essay, Bruner offers a provocative discussion of how infant capabilities, human action, and social experience give both form and direction to language development. He introduces a concept, the language acquisition support system, which recognizes the important role that adult partners play in helping children develop linguistic competence.

Although this perspective represents the current conceptualization of language development, it is a far cry from earlier views that considered language as either a learned skill or a biologically endowed property of the species. Of particular note in this discussion is the important role that Bruner assigns to cultural practices in early language development. As children participate in the routine, goal-directed activities of everyday life, experiences in which language serves an important and instrumental role, they learn about language and develop language skills as participants in a larger language community. Furthermore, the fact that children have emotional ties to those around them serves to strengthen the interest and motivation that they bring to these language learning experiences.

If we are to consider the transition from prelinguistic communication to language, particularly with a concern for possible continuities, we had better begin by taking as close a look as we can at the so-called "original endowment" of human beings. Might that endowment affect the acquisition and early use of language? I do not mean simply the prelinguistic precursors of grammar or an "innate capacity" for language. The question must be a more general one. What predisposes a living being to use language and be changed by its use? Suppose we grant that there is some innate capacity to master language as a symbolic system, as Noam Chomsky urged, or even to be predisposed toward particular linguistic distinctions, as Derek Bickerton has recently proposed? Why is language used? After all, chimpanzees have some of the same capacities and they don't use them.

The awkward dilemma that plagues questions about the original nature and later growth of human faculties inheres in the unique nature of human competence. For human competence is both biological in origin and cultural in the means by which it finds expression. While the *capacity* for intelligent action has deep biological roots and a discernible evolutionary history, the *exercise* of that capacity depends upon man appropriating to himself modes of acting and thinking that exist not in his genes but in his culture. There is obviously something in "mind" or in "human nature" that mediates between the genes and the culture that makes it possible for the latter to be a prosthetic device for the realization of the former.

When we ask then about the endowment of human beings, the question we put must be twofold. We must ask not only about capacities, but also about how humans are aided in expressing them in the medium of culture. The two questions, of course, are inseparable, since human intellectual capacity necessarily evolved to fit man for using the very prosthetic devices that a culture develops and accumulates for the enablement of its members.

There is some point in studying early human capacities and their development in seemingly culture-less laboratories, as if they were simply expressions of man's biological dispositions and endowment. But we must also bear in mind that the idealization of this endowment depends on the tool kit of the culture, whatever we choose to do in the laboratory. The main trend of the last quarter century has been to look increasingly at the contexts that enable human beings to act as they do; increasingly, we can see the futility of considering human nature as a set of autonomous dispositions.

I can easily outline what seems to me, at least, to be "infant endowment" in the so-called cognitive sphere. But to do so relevantly I must focus on those aspects that fit and perhaps even compel human beings to operate in the culture. For I think that it is the requirement of *using* culture as a necessary form of coping that forces man to master language. Language is the means for interpreting and regulating the culture. The interpreting and negotiating start the moment the infant enters the human scene. It is at this stage of interpretation and negotiation that language acquisition is acted out. So I shall look at "endowment" from the point of view of how it equips the infant to come on stage in order to acquire the means for taking his place in culture.

INITIAL COGNITIVE ENDOWMENT

Let me begin with some more or less "firm" conclusions about perception, skill, and problem solving in the prelinguistic infant and consider how they might conceivably predispose the child to acquire "culture" through language.

The first of these conclusions is that much of the cognitive processing going on in infancy appears to operate in support of goal-directed activity. From the start, the human infant is *active* in seeking out regularities in the world about him. The child is active in a uniquely human way, converting experience into species-typical means-end structures. Let me begin with the unlikely example of nonnutritive sucking.

The human infant, like mammals generally, is equipped with a variety of biological processes that ensure initial feeding, initial attachment to a caretaker, initial sensory contact with the world—all quite well buffered to prevent the infant from overreacting. Nonnutritive sucking, an example of one of these buffering mechanisms, has the effect of relaxing large muscle groups, stilling movements of the gut, reducing the number of eye movements in response to excessively patterned visual fields, and in general assuring the maintenance of a moderate level of arousal in

the face of even a demanding environment. That much is probably "hard-wired."

But such sucking soon comes under the child's own control. Infants as young as five to six weeks are quite capable, we found, of sucking on a pacifier nipple in order to bring a visual display from blur into focus—increasing their rate of sucking well above baseline when the picture's focus is made contingent on speed of sucking. Sucking and looking, moreover, are coordinated to assure a good view. When babies suck to produce clarity, they suck as they look, and when they stop they soon learn to look away. The same infants, when their sucking in a later session produces blur, suck while looking away from the blurred picture their sucking is producing and desist from sucking while looking at the picture. (We should note, by the way, that infants do not like blurred pictures.)

The Czech pediatrician Hanus Papousek has reported the same capacity for coordination of action in another domain, head turning. He taught six-to-ten-week-old babies to turn their heads to the right (or the left) in order to activate an attractive set of flashing lights. The infants soon learned the required response and, indeed, could even be taught to turn twice to each side for the desired lights. With mastery, their reactions became quite economical: They turned just enough to bring on the lights. But more interesting still, as the experiment progressed and the light display became familiar, they looked at it only briefly, just enough of a glance to confirm that the lights had gone on as expected (following which there was often a smile) and would then begin visually exploring other features of the situation. Successful prediction seems finally to have been the rewarding feature of the situation. With habituation, performance deteriorated—prediction was no longer interesting.

The point is not that infants are cleverer than was suspected before. Rather, it is that their behavior from early on is guided by active means-end readiness and by search. To put it another way, more in keeping with our general point, the infant from the start is tuned to the coordinative requirements of action. He seems able to appreciate, so to speak, the structure of action and particularly the manner in which means and ends must be combined in achieving satisfactory outcomes—even such arbitrary means as sucking to produce changes in the visual world. He seems, moreover, to be sensitive to the requirements of prediction and, if Papousek's interpretation of the "smile of predictive pleasure" is to be taken seriously, to get active pleasure from successful prediction. Anyone who has bothered to ponder the pleasure infants derive from achieving repetitive, surefire prediction will appreciate this point.

To say that infants are also "social" is to be banal. They are geared to respond to the human voice, to the human face, to human action and gesture. Their means-end readiness is easily and quickly brought into coordination with the actions of their caretakers. The pioneering work of Daniel Stern and Berry Brazelton and their colleagues underlines how early and readily activated infants are by the adults with whom they interact and how quickly their means-end structuring encompasses the actions of another. The infant's principal "tool" for achieving his ends is another familiar human being. In this respect, human infants seem more socially interactive than any of the Great Apes, perhaps to the same degree that Great Apes are more socially interactive than Old or New World Monkeys, and this may be a function of their prolonged and uniquely dependent form of immaturity, as I have argued elsewhere.

Infants are, in a word, tuned to enter the world of human action. Obvious though the point may seem, we shall see that it has enormous consequences for the matter at hand. This leads directly to the second conclusion about infant "endowment."

It is obvious that an enormous amount of the activity of the child during the first year and a half of life is extraordinarily social and communicative. Social interaction appears to be both self-propelled and self-rewarding. Many students of infant behavior, like Tom Bower, have found that a social response to the infant is the most powerful reinforcer one can use in ordinary learning experiments. And withholding social response to the child's initiatives is one of the most disruptive things one can do to an infant—e.g., an unresponding face will soon produce tears. Even in the opening weeks of life the infant has the capacity to imitate facial and manual gestures (as Andrew Meltzoff has shown); they respond with distress if their mothers are masked during feeding; and, they show a sensitivity to expression in the mother by turn taking in vocalization when their level of arousal is moderate and by simultaneous expression when it is high.

While the child's attachment to the mother (or caretaker) is initially assured by a variety of innate response patterns, there very quickly develops a reciprocity that the infant comes to anticipate and count on. For example, if during play the mother assumes a sober immobile face, the infant shows fewer smiles and turns his head away from the mother more frequently than when the mother responds socially, as Edward Tronick and his colleagues have shown. The existence of such reciprocity—buttressed by the mother's increasing capacity to differentiate an infant's "reasons" for crying as well as by the infant's capacity to anticipate these consistencies—soon creates a form of mutual attention, a harmony or "intersubjectivity," whose importance we shall take up later.

In any case, a pattern of inborn initial social responses in the infant, elicited by a wide variety of effective signs from the mother—her heartbeat, the visual configuration of her face and particularly her eyes, her characteristic smell, the sound and rhythms of her voice—is soon converted into a very complex joint anticipatory system that converts initial biological attachment between mother and child into something more subtle and more sensitive to individual idiosyncracies and to forms of cultural practice.

The third conclusion is that much of early infant action takes place in constrained, familiar situations and shows a surprisingly high degree of order and "systematicity." Children spend most of their time doing a very limited number of things. Long periods are spent in reaching and taking, banging and looking, etc. Within any one of these restricted domains, there is striking "systematicity." Object play provides an example. A single act (like banging) is applied successively to a wide range of objects. Everything on which the child can get his hands is banged. Or the child tries out on a single object all the motor routines of which he or she is capable—grasping the object, banging it, throwing it to the floor, putting it in the mouth, putting it on top of the head, running it through the entire repertory.

Nobody has done better than Jean Piaget in characterizing this systematicity. The older view that pictured the infant as "random" in his actions and saw growth as consisting of becoming "coordinated" can no longer stand up to the evidence. Given the limits of the child's range of action, what occurs within that range is just as orderly and systematic as is adult behavior. There may be differences of opinion concerning the "rules" that govern this orderly behavior, but there can be no quarrel about its systematicity. Whether one adopts a Piagetian view of the matter or one more tuned to other theories, like Heinz Werner's, is, in light of the more general issues, quite irrelevant.

It is not the least surprising, in light of this conclusion, that infants enter the world of language and of culture with a readiness to find or invent systematic ways of dealing with social requirements and linguistic forms. The child reacts "culturally" with characteristic hypotheses about what is required and enters language with a readiness for order. We shall, of course, have much more to say about this later.

There are two important implications that follow from this. The first is obvious, though I do not recall ever having encountered the point. It is that from the start, the child becomes readily attuned to "making a lot out of a little" by combination. He typically works on varying a small set of elements to create a larger range of possibilities. Observations of early play behavior and of the infant's communicative efforts certainly confirm this "push" to generativeness, to combinatorial and variational efforts. Indeed, Ruth Weir's classic study of the child's spontaneous speech while alone in his crib after bedtime speaks volumes on this combinatorial readiness, as does Melissa Bowerman's on children's spontaneous speech errors.

The second implication is more social. The acquisition of prelinguistic and linguistic communication takes place, in the main, in the highly constrained settings to which we are referring. The child and his caretaker readily combine elements in these situations to extract meanings, assign interpretations, and infer intentions. A decade ago there was considerable debate among developmental linguists on whether in writing "grammars" of child speech one should use a method of "rich interpretation"—taking into account not only the child's actual speech but also the ongoing actions and other elements of the context in which speech was occurring. Today we take it for granted that one must do so. For it is precisely the combining of all elements in constrained situations (speech and nonspeech alike) that provides the road to communicative effectiveness. It is for this reason that I shall place such heavy emphasis on the role of "formats" in the child's entry into language.

A fourth conclusion about the nature of infant cognitive endowment is that its systematic character is surprisingly abstract. Infants during their first year appear to have rules for dealing with space, time, and even causation. A moving object that is transformed in appearance while it is moving behind a screen produces surprise when it reappears in a new guise. Objects that seem to be propelled in ways that *we* see as unnatural (e.g., without being touched by an approaching object) also produce surprise reactions in a three-month-old as well. Objects explored by touch alone are later recognized by vision alone. The infant's perceptual world, far from being a blooming, buzzing confusion, is rather orderly and organized by what seem like highly abstract rules.

Again, it was Piaget who most compellingly brought this "abstractness" to our attention in describing the logical structure of the child's search for invariance in his world—the search for what remains unchanged under the changing surface of appearance. And again, it is not important whether the "logic" that he attributed to this systematic action is correct or not. What is plain is that, whether Piagetian logical rules characterize early "operational behavior" or whether it can be better described by some more general logical system, we know that cognitively and communicatively there is from the start a capacity to "follow" abstract rules.

It is *not* the case that language, when it is encountered and then used, is the first instance of abstract rule following. It is not, for example, in language alone that the child makes such distinctions as those between specific and nonspecific, between states and processes, between "punctual" acts and recurrent ones, between causative and noncausative actions. These abstract distinctions, picked up with amazing

speed in language acquisition, have analogues in the child's way of ordering his world of experience. Language will serve to specify, amplify, and expand distinctions that the child has already about the world. But these abstract distinctions are already present, even without language.

These four cognitive "endowments"—means-end readiness, transactionality, systematicity, and abstractness—provide foundation processes that aid the child's language acquisition. None of them "generates" language, for language involves a set of phonological, syntactic, semantic, and illocutionary rules and maxims that constitute a problem space of their own. But linguistic or communicative hypotheses depend upon these capacities as enabling conditions. Language does not "grow out of" prior protophonological, protosyntactic, protosemantic, or protopragmatic knowledge. It requires a unique sensitivity to a patterned sound system, to grammatical constraints, to referential requirements, to communicative intentions, etc. Such sensitivity grows in the process of fulfilling certain general, nonlinguistic functions—predicting the environment, interacting transactionally, getting to goals with the aid of another, and the like. These functions are first fulfilled primitively if abstractly by prelinguistic communicative means. Such primitive procedures, I will argue, must reach requisite levels of functioning before *any* Language Acquisition Device (whether innate or acquired) can begin to generate "linguistic hypotheses."

ENTRY INTO LANGUAGE

We can turn now to the development of language per se. Learning a native language is an accomplishment within the grasp of any toddler, yet discovering how children do it has eluded generations of philosophers and linguists. Saint Augustine believed it was simple. Allegedly recollecting his own childhood, he said, "When they named any thing, and as they spoke turned towards it, I saw and remembered that they called what one would point out by the name they uttered. . . . And thus by constantly hearing words, as they occurred in various sentences, I collected gradually for what they stood; and having broken in my mouth to these signs, I thereby gave utterance to my will." But a look at children as they actually acquire language shows Saint Augustine to be far, far off target. Alas, he had a powerful effect both on his followers and on those who set out to refute him.

Developmental linguistics is now going through rough times that can be traced back to Saint Augustine as well as to the reactions against him. Let me recount a little history. Saint Augustine's view, perhaps because there was so little systematic research on language acquisition to refute it, prevailed for a long time. It was even put into modern dress. Its most recent "new look" was in the form of behaviorist "learning theory." In this view's terms, nothing particularly linguistic needed to be said about language. Language, like any other behavior, could be "explained" as just another set of responses. Its principles and its research paradigms were not derived from the phenomena of language but from "general behavior." Learning tasks, for example, were chosen to construct theories of learning so as to ensure that the learner had no predispositions toward or knowledge of the material to be learned. All was as if *ab initio*, transfer of response from one stimulus to another was assured by the similarity between stimuli. Language learning was assumed to be much like, say, nonsense syllable learning, except that it might be aided by imitation, the learner imitating the performance of the "model" and then being reinforced for correct performance. Its emphasis was on "words" rather than on grammar. Consequently, it missed out almost entirely in dealing with the combinatorial and generative effect of having a syntax that made possible the routine construction of sentences never before heard and that did not exist in adult speech to be imitated. A good example is the Pivot-Open class, P(0), construction of infant speech in which a common word or phrase is combined productively with other words as in *all-gone mummy, all-gone apple*, and even *all-gone bye-bye* (when mother and aunt finally end a prolonged farewell).

It is one of the mysteries of Kuhnian scientific paradigms that this empiricist approach to language acquisition persisted in psychology (if not in philosophy, where it was overturned by Frege and Wittgenstein) from its first enunciation by Saint Augustine to its most recent one in B. F. Skinner's *Verbal Behavior.* It would be fair to say that the persistence of the mindless behavioristic version of Augustinianism finally led to a readiness, even a reckless readiness, to be rid of it. For it was not only an inadequate account, but one that damped inquiry by its domination of "common sense." It set the stage for the Chomskyan revolution.

It was to Noam Chomsky's credit that he boldly proclaimed the old enterprise bankrupt. In its place he offered a challenging, if counterintuitive hypothesis based on nativism. He proposed that the acquisition of the *structure* of language depended upon a Language Acquisition Device (LAD) that had as its base a universal grammar or a "linguistic deep structure" that humans know innately and without learning. LAD was programmed to recognize in the surface structure of any natural language encountered its deep structure or universal grammar by virtue of the kinship between innate universal grammar and the grammar of any and all natural languages. LAD abstracted the grammatical realization rules of the local

language and thus enabled the aspirant speaker potentially to generate all the well-formed utterances possible in the language and none that were ill-formed. The universal grammatical categories that programmed LAD were in the innate structure of the mind. No prior nonlinguistic knowledge of the world was necessary, and no privileged communication with another speaker was required. Syntax was independent of knowledge of the world, of semantic meaning, and of communicative function. All the child needed was exposure to language, however fragmentary and uncontextualized his samples of it might be. Or more correctly, the acquisition of syntax could be conceived of as progressing with the assistance of whatever *minimum* world knowledge or privileged communication proved necessary. The only constraints on rate of linguistic development were psychological limitations on *performance*: the child's limited but growing attention and memory span, etc. Linguistic competence was there from the start, ready to express itself when performance constraints were extended by the growth of requisite skills.

It was an extreme view. But in a stroke it freed a generation of psycholinguists from the dogma of association-cum-imitation-cum-reinforcement. It turned attention to the problem of rule learning, even if it concentrated only on syntactic rules. By declaring learning theory dead as an explanation of language acquisition (one of the more premature obituaries of our times), it opened the way for a new account.

George Miller put it well. We now had *two* theories of language acquisition: one of them, empiricist associationism, was impossible; the other, nativism, was miraculous. But the void between the impossible and the miraculous was soon to be filled in, albeit untidily and partially.

To begin with, children in fact had and *needed* to have a working knowledge of the world before they acquired language. Such knowledge gave them semantic targets, so to speak, that "corresponded" in some fashion to the distinctions they acquired in their language. A knowledge of the world, appropriately organized in terms of a system of concepts, might give the child hints as to where distinctions could be expected to occur in the language, might even alert him to the distinctions. There were new efforts to develop a generative semantics out of which syntactical hypotheses could presumably be derived by the child. In an extreme form, generative semantics could argue that the concepts in terms of which the world was organized are the same as those that organize language. But even so, the *linguistic* distinctions still had to be mastered. These were not about the *world* but about morphology or syntax or whatever else characterized the linguistic *code.*

The issue of whether rules of *grammar* can somehow be inferred or generalized from the structure of our knowledge of the world is a very dark one. The strong form of the claim insists that syntax can be derived directly from nonlinguistic categories of knowledge in some way. Perhaps the best claim can be made for a case grammar. It is based on the reasonable claim that the concepts of action are innate and primitive. The aspiring language learner already knows the so called arguments of action: who performed the action, on what object, toward whom, where, by what instrument, and so on. In Charles Fillmore's phrase, "meanings are relativized to scenes," and this involves an "assignment of perspective." Particular phrases impose a perspective on the scene and sentence decisions are perspective decisions. If, for example, the agent of action is perspectively forefronted by some grammatical means such as being inserted as head word, the placement of the nominal that represents agency must be the "deep subject" of the sentence. This leaves many questions unanswered about how the child gets to the point of being able to put together sentences that assign his intended action perspectives to scenes.

The evidence for the semantic account was nonetheless interesting. Roger Brown pointed out, for example, that at the two-word stage of language acquisition more than three-quarters of the child's utterances embody only a half dozen semantic relations that are, at base, case or caselike relations—Agent-Action, Action-Object, Agent-Object, Possession, etc. Do these semantic relations generate the grammar of the language? Case notions of this kind, Fillmore tells us, "comprise a set of universal, presumably innate, concepts which identify certain types of judgments human beings are capable of making about the events that are going on around them . . . who did it, who it happened to, and what got changed." The basic structures are alleged to be these arguments of action, and different languages go about realizing them in different ways: by function words, by inflectional morphemes as in the case endings of Latin, by syntactic devices like passivization, and so on. Grammatical forms might then be the surface structures of language, depending for their acquisition on a prior understanding of deep semantic, indeed even protosemantic, concepts about action.

Patrica Greenfield then attempted to show that the earliest *one-word* utterances, richly interpreted in context, could also be explained as realizations of caselike concepts. And more recently Katherine Nelson has enriched the argument that children acquire language already equipped with concepts related to action: "The functional core model (FCM) essentially proposed that the child came to language with a store of familiar concepts of people and objects that were organized around the child's experience with these things. Because the child's experience was active, the dynamic aspects would be the most potent part of what the child came to know about the things experienced. It could be expected that the child would organize knowledge around what he could do with things and what they could do. In other words, knowledge of the world would be functionally organized from the child's point of view." To this earlier view she has now added a temporal dimension—the child's mastery of "scripts for event structures," a sequential structure of "causally and temporally linked acts with the actors and objects specified in the most general way." These scripts provide the child with a set of syntagmatic formats that permit him to organize his concepts sequentially into sentencelike forms such as those reported by Roger Brown. The capacity to do this rests upon a basic form of representation that the child uses from the start and gradually elaborates. In effect, it is what guides the formation of utterances beyond the one-word stage.

The role of world knowledge in generating or supporting language acquisition is now undergoing intensive study. But still another element has now been added—the pragmatic. It is the newest incursion into the gap between "impossible" and "miraculous" theories of language acquisition. In this view, the central idea is communicative intent: we communicate with some end in mind, some function to be fulfilled. We request or indicate or promise or threaten. Such functionalism had earlier been a strong thread in linguistics, but had been elbowed aside by a prevailing structuralism that, after Ferdinand de Saussure's monumental work, became the dominant mode.

New developments revived functionalism. The first was in the philosophy of language spearheaded by Ludwig Wittgenstein's use-based theory of meaning, formulated in his *Philosophical Investigations*, and then by the introduction of speech acts in Austin's *How to Do Things with Words*. Austin's argument (as already noted) was that an utterance cannot be analyzed out of the context of its use and its use must include the intention of the speaker and interpretation of that intention by the addressee in the light of communication conventions. A speaker may make a request by many alternative linguistic means, so long as he honors the conventions of his linguistic community. It may take on interrogative construction ("What time is it?"), or it may take the declarative form ("I wonder what time it is").

Roger Brown notes an interesting case with respect to this issue: in the protocols of Adam, he found that Adam's mother used the interrogative in two quite different ways, one as a request for action, the other as a request for information: "Why don't you . . . (e.g., play with your ball now)," and "Why are you playing with your ball?" Although Adam answered informational *why* questions with *Because*, there was no instance of his ever confusing an action and an information-seeking *why* question. He evidently recognized the differing intent of the two forms of utterance quite adequately from the start. He must have been learning speech acts rather than simply the *why* interrogative form.

This raises several questions about acquisition. It puts pragmatics into the middle of things. Is intent being decoded by the child? It would seem so. But linguistics usually defines its domain as "going from sound to sense." But what is "sense?" Do we in fact go from sound to intention, as John Searle proposed? A second question has to do with shared or conventional presuppositions. If children are acquiring notions about how to interpret the intentions encoded in utterances, they must be taking into account not only the structure of the utterance, but also the nature of the conditions that prevail just at the time the utterance is made. Speech acts have at least three kinds of conditions affecting their appropriateness or "felicity": a preparatory condition (laying appropriate ground for the utterance); an essential condition (meeting the logical conditions for performing a speech act, like, for example, being uninformed as a condition for asking for information related to a matter); and sincerity conditions (wishing to have the information that one asks for). They must also meet affiliative conditions: honoring the affiliation or relation between speaker and hearer, as in requesting rather than demanding when the interlocutor is not under obligation.

Paradoxically, the learning of speech acts may be easier and less mysterious than the learning either of syntax or semantics. For the child's syntactic errors are rarely followed by corrective feedback, and semantic feedback is often lax. But speech acts, on the contrary, get not only immediate feedback but also correction. Not surprising, then, that prelinguistic communicative acts precede lexico-grammatical speech in their appearance. Not surprising, then, that such primitive "speech act" patterns may serve as a kind of matrix in which lexico-grammatical achievements can be substituted for earlier gestural or vocal procedures.

In this view, entry into language is an entry into discourse that requires both members of a dialogue pair to interpret a communication and its intent. Learning a language, then, consists of learning not only the grammar of a particular language but also learning how to realize one's intentions by the appropriate use of that grammar.

The pragmatician's stress on intent requires a far more active role on the part of the adult in aiding the child's language acquisition than that of just being a "model." It requires that the adult be a consenting partner, willing to negotiate with the child. The negotiation has to do, probably, least with syntax, somewhat more with the semantic scope of the child's lexicon, and a very great deal with helping make intentions clear and making their expression fit the conditions and requirements of the "speech community," i.e., the culture.

And the research of the last several years—much of it summarized in Catherine Snow and Charles Ferguson's *Talking to Children*—does indeed indicate that parents play a far more active role in language acquisition than simply modeling the language and providing, so to speak, input for a Language Acquisition Device. The current phrase for it is "fine tuning." Parents speak at the level where their children can comprehend them and move ahead with remarkable sensitivity to their child's progress. The dilemma, as Roger Brown puts it, is how do you teach children to talk by talking baby talk with them at a level that they already understand? And the answer has got to be that the important thing is to keep communicating with them, for by so doing one allows them to learn how to extend the speech that they have into new contexts, how to meet the conditions on speech acts, how to maintain topics across turns, how to know what's worth talking about—how indeed to regulate language use.

So we can now recognize two ways of filling the gap between an impossible empiricist position and a miraculous nativist one. The child must master the conceptual structure of the world that language will map—the social world as well as the physical. He must also master the conventions for making his intentions clear by language.

SUPPORT FOR LANGUAGE ACQUISITION

The development of language, then, involves two people negotiating. Language is not encountered willy-nilly by the child; it is shaped to make communicative interaction effective—fine-tuned. If there is a Language Acquisition Device, the input to it is not a shower of spoken language but a highly interactive affair shaped, as we have already noted, by some sort of an adult Language Acquisition Support System.

After all, it is well known from a generation of research on another "innate" system, sexual behavior, that much experiential priming is necessary before innate sexual responses can be evoked by "appropriate" environmental events. Isolated animals are seriously retarded. By the same token, the recognition and the production of grammatical universals may similarly depend upon prior social and conceptual experience. Continuities between prelinguistic communication and later speech of the kind I alluded to earlier may, moreover, need an "arranged" input of adult speech if the child is to use his growing grasp of conceptual distinctions and communicative functions as guides to language use. I propose that this "arranging" of early speech interaction requires routinized and familiar settings, formats, for the child to comprehend what is going on, given his limited capacity for processing information. These routines constitute what I intend by a Language Acquisition Support System.

There are at least four ways in which such a Language Acquisition Support System helps assure continuity from prelinguistic to linguistic communication. Because there is such concentration on familiar and routine transactional formats, it becomes feasible for the adult partner to highlight those features of the world that are already salient to the child and that have a basic or simple grammatical form. Slobin has suggested, for example, that there are certain prototypical ways in which the child experiences the world: e.g., a "prototypical transitive event" in which "an animate agent is seen willfully . . . to bring about a physical and perceptible change of state or location in a patient by means of direct body contact." Events of this kind, we shall see, are a very frequent feature of mother-child formats, and it is of no small interest that in a variety of languages, as Slobin notes, they "are encoded in consistent grammatical form by age two." Slobin offers the interesting hypothesis "that [these] prototypical situations are encoded in the most basic grammatical forms available in a language." We shall encounter formats built around games and tasks involving both these prototypical means-end structures and canonical linguistic forms that seem almost designed to aid the child in spotting the referential correspondence between such utterances and such events.

Or to take another example, Bickerton has proposed that children are "bioprogrammed" to notice certain distinctions in real world events and to pick up (or even to invent) corresponding linguistic distinctions in order to communicate about them. His candidates are the distinctions (a) between specific and nonspecific events, (b) between state and process, (c) between "punctual" and continuous events, and (d) between causative and noncausative actions. And insofar as the "fine tuning" of adult interaction with a child concentrates on these distinctions—both in reality and in speech—the child is aided in moving from their conceptual expression to an appreciation of their appropriate linguistic representation. Again, they will be found to be frequent in the formats of the children we shall look at in detail.

A second way in which the adult helps the child through formatting is by encouraging and modeling lexical and phrasal substitutes for familiar gestural and vocal means for effecting various communicative functions. This is a feature of the child's gradual mastery of the request mode.

H. P. Grice takes it as a hallmark of mature language that the speaker not only has an intention to communicate, but that he also has *conventionalized* or "nonnatural" means for expressing his intention. The speaker, in his view, presupposes that his interlocutor will accept his means of communication and will infer his intention from them. The interlocutor presupposes the same thing about the speaker. Grice, concerned with adults, assumes all this to be quite conscious, if implicit.

An infant cannot at the prelinguistic outset be said to be participating in a conscious Gricean cycle when signaling conventionally in his games with his mother. That much selfconsciousness seems unlikely. But what we will find in the following chapters is that the mother acts as if he did. The child in turn soon comes to operate with some junior version of the Gricean cycle, awaiting his mother's "uptake" of his signaling.

In Katherine Nelson's terms, the young child soon acquires a small library of scripts and communicative procedures to go with them. They provide steady frameworks in which he learns effectively, by dint of interpretable feedback, how to make his communicative intentions plain. When he becomes "conscious" enough to be said to be operating in a Gricean cycle is, I think, a silly question.

What is striking is how early the child develops means to signal his focus of attention and his requests for assistance—to signal them by conventionalized means in the limited world of familiar formats. He has obviously picked up the gist of "nonnatural" or conventionalized signaling of his intentions before ever he has mastered the formal elements of lexico-grammatical speech. I think the reader will agree, in reading later chapters, that the functional framing of communication starts the child on his way to language proper. Thirdly, it is characteristic of play formats particularly that they are made of stipulative or constitutive "events" that are created by language and then recreated on demand by language. Later these formats take on the character of "pretend" situations. They are a rich source of opportunity for language learning and language use.

Finally, once the mother and child are launched into routinized formats, various psychological and linguistic processes are brought into play that generalize from one format to another. Naming, for example, appears first in indicating formats and then transfers to requesting formats. Indeed, the very notion of finding linguistic parallels for conceptual distinctions generalizes from one format to another. So too do such "abstract" ideas as segmentation, interchangeable roles, substitutive means—both in action and in speech.

These are the mundane procedures and events that constitute a Language Acquisition Support System, along with the elements of fine tuning that comprise "baby talk" exchanges.

QUESTIONS

1. What are the four cognitive endowments that children bring to language learning experiences?
2. Why is a behaviorist or learning approach inadequate for explaining language acquisition?
3. What is a language acquisition support system?
4. Why does Bruner argue that language acquisition primarily involves learning speech acts rather than grammar or semantics?
5. What role do adults play in children's language learning?
6. How does children's participation in routine events and scripts support the development of language?

18 The Credible Shrinking Room: Very Young Children's Performance with Symbolic and Nonsymbolic Relations

JUDY S. DeLOACHE · KEVIN F. MILLER · KARL S. ROSENGREN

A unique and important characteristic of human intelligence is the ability to create, understand, and manipulate symbols. A symbol is an arbitrary arrangement of things, either letters or numbers or images or objects, that refer to something else. Because symbols are arbitrary, we need to learn what particular symbols refer to. Although our brain is capable of processing symbols, we are not born with knowledge about the symbols we encounter in everyday life. Rather, we develop understanding of these symbols over the course of childhood.

Recently, Judy DeLoache, Kevin Miller, and Karl Rosengren have been studying children's early skill at understanding symbols by asking 2½-year-old children to find a toy in a room after seeing a tiny version of the toy hidden in a scale model of the room. In the study described in this article, they included a cleverly designed manipulation that allowed them to test a prominent hypothesis about early symbolic understanding. This hypothesis asserts that young children have difficulty understanding symbols because this understanding requires them to deal with two levels of representation simultaneously.

Their creative test of this hypothesis provides information about the early emergence of symbolic understanding, as well as support for this hypothesis. This research is important in that it demonstrates an important cognitive change of early childhood, one that lays the foundation for the development of more complex symbolic processing which is essential in all facets of learning and development.

Becoming a proficient symbol user is a universal developmental task in the first years of life, but detecting and mentally representing symbolic relations can be quite challenging for young children. To test the extent to which symbolic reasoning per se is problematic, we compared the performance of 2½-year-olds in symbolic and nonsymbolic versions of a search task. The children had to use their knowledge of the location of a toy hidden in a room to draw an inference about where to find a miniature toy in a scale model of the room (and vice versa). Children in the nonsymbolic condition believed a shrinking machine had caused the room to become the model. They were much more successful than children in the symbolic condition, for whom the model served as a symbol of the room. The results provide strong support for the role of dual representation in symbol understanding and use.

Reprinted by permission of Blackwell Publishers from *Psychological Science*, 8 (1997), pp. 308–313. Copyright © 1997 American Psychological Society.

Address correspondence to Judy DeLoache, Psychology Department, University of Illinois, 603 East Daniel, Champaign, IL 61820: e-mail: jdeloach@s.psych.uiuc.edu.

Acknowledgments The research reported here was supported in part by Grant HD-25271 from the National Institute of Child Health and Human Development. This article was completed while the first author was a fellow at the Center for Advanced Study in the Behavioral Sciences with financial support from the John D. and Catherine T. MacArthur Foundation. Grant No. 95-32005-0. We thank R. Baillargeon and G. Clore for helpful comments on this article and K. Anderson and N. Bryant for assistance in the research.

Nothing so distinguishes humans from other species as the creative and flexible use of symbols. Abstract concepts, reasoning, scientific discovery, and other uniquely human endeavors are made possible by language and a panoply of symbolic tools, including numbers, alphabets, maps, models, and various notational systems. The universality and centrality of symbolic representation in human cognition make understanding its origins a key developmental issue.

How do children master the symbolic artifacts of their culture? They must start by recognizing that certain entities should be interpreted and responded to primarily in terms of what they stand for—their referents—rather than themselves. This is obviously a major challenge in the case of completely arbitrary symbol—referent relations. Nothing about the appearance of a numeral or a printed word suggests what it represents. Hence, it is not surprising that children have to be explicitly taught and only gradually learn the abstract relations between numerals and quantities and between printed and spoken words.

In contrast, it is generally taken for granted that highly iconic symbols (i.e., symbols that resemble their referents) are understood easily and early. Recent research, however, reveals that this assumption is unwarranted: A high degree of similarity between a symbol and its referent is no guarantee that young children will appreciate the symbol—referent relation. For example, several studies have established that very young children often fail to detect the relation between a realistic scale model and the room it represents (DeLoache, 1987, 1989, 1991; DeLoache, Kolstad, & Anderson, 1991; Dow & Pick, 1992; Marzolf & DeLoache, 1994; Uttal, Schreiber, & DeLoache, 1995). Most 2$\frac{1}{2}$-year-old children give no evidence of understanding that the model and room are related or that what they know about one space can be used to draw an inference about the other. Children just a few months older (3-year-olds) readily exploit this symbol—referent relation.

Why is a highly iconic relation that is so transparent to older children and adults so opaque to very young children? Many theorists have characterized symbols as possessing dual reality (Gibson, 1979; Gregory, 1970; Potter, 1979). According to the *dual representation* hypothesis (DeLoache, 1987, 1991, 1995a, 1995b), it is the double nature of symbols that poses particular difficulty for young children. To understand and use a symbol, one must mentally represent both the symbol itself and its relation to the referent. Thus, one must achieve dual representation, thinking about the concrete features of the symbol and the abstract relation between it and something else at the same time.

According to this hypothesis, the more salient the concrete aspects of a symbol are, the more difficult it is to appreciate its abstract, symbolic nature. Thus,

young children's attention to a scale model as an interesting and attractive object makes it difficult for them to simultaneously think about its relation to something else. The philosopher Langer (1942) seemed to have something similar in mind when she noted that a peach would make a poor symbol because people care too much about the peach itself.

The research reported here constitutes an extremely stringent test of this hypothesis. We compared 2$\frac{1}{2}$-year-old children's performance in two tasks in which they had to detect and exploit the relation between a scale model and a room. In both tasks, children had to use their knowledge of where a toy was hidden in one space to infer where to find an analogous toy in the other space. In one task, there was a symbolic relation between the model and the room, whereas the other task involved a nonsymbolic relation between the same two entities. If achieving dual representation is a key obstacle in early symbolic reasoning, then performance should be superior in the nonsymbolic task, which does not require dual representation. We made this prediction even though the nonsymbolic task involved convincing children of an impossible scenario—that a machine could cause the room to shrink into the model.

Our reasoning was that if a child believes that the model is the large room after having been shrunk, then there is no symbolic relation between the two spaces; to the credulous child, the model simply *is* the room (albeit dramatically different in size). Thus, if the room is shrunk after a large toy has been hidden in it, finding a miniature toy in the model is, from the child's perspective, primarily a memory task. Dual representation is not necessary. Note that in both tasks, children must use the correspondence between the hiding places in the two spaces; their memory representation of the toy hidden behind a full-sized chair in the room must lead them to search behind the miniature chair in the model. In the symbolic task, the child knows there are two chairs, so he or she must represent the relation between them. In the nonsymbolic task, however, the child thinks there is only one chair. Superior performance in the nonsymbolic, shrinking-room task would thus provide strong support for the dual representation hypothesis.

METHOD

SUBJECTS

The subjects included 15 children (29–32 months, $M = 30$ months) in the symbolic condition and 17 (29–33 months, $M = 31$ months) in the nonsymbolic condition. Names of potential subjects came from files of birth announcements in the local newspaper, and the majority of the children were middle class and white.

MATERIALS

The same two spaces were used for both tasks. The larger space was a tentlike portable room (1.9 m × 2.5 m) constructed of plastic pipes supporting white fabric walls (1.9 m high) with a brown cardboard floor. The smaller space was a scale model (48.3 cm × 62.9 cm, with walls 38.1 cm high) of the portable room, constructed of the same materials. The room held several items of furniture (fabric-covered chair, dresser, set of shelves, basket, etc.); the model contained miniature versions of these items that were highly similar in appearance (e.g., same fabric on the chairs) to their larger counterparts. The relative size and spatial arrangement of the objects were the same in the two spaces, and the model was always in the same spatial orientation as the room. This model and room have been used in several previous studies (DeLoache et al., 1991; Marzolf & DeLoache, 1994). Figures 1a, 1b, and 1c show the arrangement of the room and model for the two tasks.

PROCEDURE

Symbolic task   In this task (which was very similar to that used in the previously cited model studies), each child was given an orientation that began with the introduction of two troll dolls referred to as "Big Terry" (21 cm high) and "Little Terry" (5 cm). The correspondence between the room (described as "Big Terry's room") and the model ("Little Terry's room") and between all of the objects within them was fully and explicitly described and demonstrated by the experimenter.

On the first of four experimental trials, the child watched as the experimenter hid the larger doll somewhere in the room (e.g., behind the chair, in the basket). The child was told that the smaller toy would be hidden in the "same place" in the model. The child waited (10–15 s) as the miniature toy was hidden in the model in the adjoining area (Fig. 1a) and was then encouraged to retrieve it. The experimenter reminded the child of the corresponding locations of the two toys: "Can you find Little Terry? Remember, he's hiding in the same place in his little room where Big Terry's hiding in his big room." If the child failed to find the toy on his or her first search, increasingly direct prompts were given until the child retrieved the toy. On the second trial, the hiding event occurred in the model instead of the room. Thus, the child

watched as the miniature toy was hidden in the model, and he or she was then asked to retrieve the larger toy from the room. The space in which the hiding event occurred again alternated for the third and fourth trials.[1]

To succeed, children in the symbolic task had to realize that the room and model were related. If they did, they could figure out where to search for the target toy, even though they had not actually seen it being hidden. If they failed to represent the model–room relation, they had no way of knowing where to search. Based on numerous previous studies with this basic task, we expected a low level of performance from our 2½-year-old subjects (DeLoache, 1987, 1989, 1991; DeLoache et al., 1991; Dow & Pick, 1992; Marzolf & DeLoache, 1994).

Nonsymbolic task   The initial arrangement for this task is shown in Figure 1b. In the orientation to the task, each child was introduced to "Terry" (the larger troll doll) and to "Terry's room" (the portable room). In the ensuing practice trial, the child watched as the experimenter hid the troll in the room and then waited for a count of 5 before searching. The children always succeeded in this simple memory-based retrieval (100% correct).

Next, the child was shown a "machine that can shrink toys" (actually an oscilloscope with flashing green lights—the solid rectangle in Fig. 1b). The troll doll was placed in front of it, a switch was turned on, and the child and experimenter retreated to an adjoining area and closed the door to the lab. During a delay of approximately 10 s, the child heard a tape of computer-generated tones, which were described as the "sounds the shrinking machine makes while it's working." When the sounds stopped, the child returned to the lab to find a miniature troll (5 cm high) in the place the larger one had previously occupied. Figures 1d and 1e depict the shrinking machine with the troll before and after the shrinking event.

The child was then told that the machine could also make the troll get larger, and the process was repeated in reverse, ending with the large troll again standing in front of the machine. For the final part of the orientation, the same shrinking and enlarging demonstrations were performed with "Terry's room." The shrinking machine was aimed at the room, and the child and experimenter waited in the adjoining area, listening to a longer (38-s) tape of the same computer sounds. When the door to the lab was opened,

---

1. There were two major differences between the current symbolic task and the standard model task used in previous research: First, the hiding event alternated from trial to trial between model and room. In the standard task, it always occurs in one space or the other for a given child. In studies in which half the children see the hiding event in the room and the other half in the model, there has never been any difference in performance as a function of this variable. Second, in the standard task, children always perform two retrievals: For example, after seeing the toy being hidden in the model, they first search for the larger toy in the room and then return to the model to retrieve the toy they originally observed being hidden. However, the performance of the 2½-year-olds tested in the current study did not differ from that of a group tested in the standard model task using all the same materials.

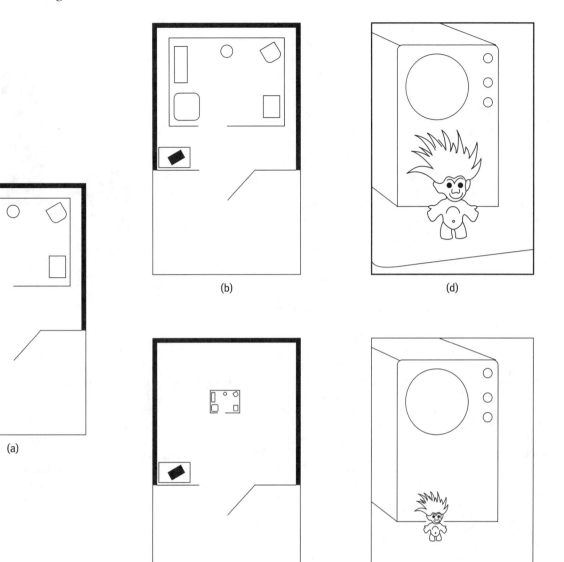

FIGURE 1

Physical arrangements for the symbolic and nonsymbolic tasks. For the symbolic task (a), the portable room was located in a large lab, surrounded on three sides by opaque curtains (represented by heavy lines); the model was located in an adjoining area. The nonsymbolic task began with the arrangement shown in (b); before the first shrinking event, the portable room was located in the lab, partially surrounded by curtains, just as it was for the symbolic task. The only difference was the presence of the shrinking machine, represented by the dark rectangle, sitting on a table. In the aftermath of the shrinking event, depicted in (c), the model sat in the middle of the area previously occupied by the portable room. The sketches in (d) and (e) show Terry the Troll before and after the demonstration shrinking event.

the scale model was revealed sitting in the middle of the area previously occupied by the room (Fig. 1c). The sight of the small model in place of the large room was very dramatic. The process was then repeated in reverse, resulting in the room replacing the model.[2]

---

2. An elaborate scenario supported the shrinking and enlarging events. When the child first saw the artificial room, it was surrounded on three sides by black curtains, which were visible only on the sides in front of the portable room (Fig. 1b).

On the first of four trials, the child watched as the larger doll was hidden in the room (the same hiding places were used as in the symbolic task), and the child was instructed to remember where it was hidden. After a 38-s delay, again spent waiting in the adjoining area listening to the sounds of the shrinking machine, the child entered the lab, where the model had replaced the portable room. The child was encouraged to find the doll: "Can you find Terry? Remember where we hid him? That's where he's hiding." The miniature troll was, of course, hidden in the model in the place that corresponded to where the child had seen the larger troll being hidden in the room. On two of the four trials, the room and large troll were shrunk, alternating with two trials in which the model and miniature troll were enlarged. A different hiding place was used on each trial.

To assess the extent to which the children accepted our shrinking-machine scenario, the experimenter and each child's accompanying parent independently rated the child on a 5-point scale, with 1 indicating that the child "firmly believed" that the machine really did shrink the objects and 5 indicating that the child "firmly did not believe" it. The average ratings were 1.1 and 1.5 for the experimenter and parents, respectively. There was only one child that the observing adults judged to be at all skeptical. The children generally reacted to the shrinking events with interest and pleasure, but not astonishment. Several children made revealing comments, such as "I want to make it big [little] again," and, while listening to the sounds of the shrinking machine, "It's working to make it big." In addition, when the children later told other family members about the session, they typically talked about the troll or the room "getting little." None ever described the situation as pretend or as a trick. We therefore feel confident that our subjects believed that the model and room were actually the same thing, which means that the shrinking-room task was, as intended, nonsymbolic (involving an identity rather than a symbolic relation).[3]

We wish to emphasize that it is unlikely that the a priori prediction of superior performance in the nonsymbolic task would be made on any basis other than the dual representation hypothesis. Indeed, various aspects of the procedures would lead to the opposite expectation. For example, getting and keeping tod-

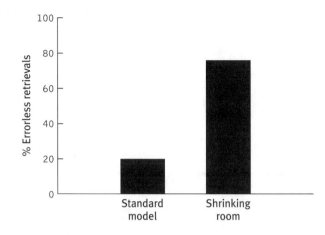

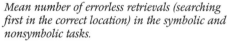

FIGURE 2

Mean number of errorless retrievals (searching first in the correct location) in the symbolic and nonsymbolic tasks.

dlers motivated in experimental situations is always a challenge; and the shrinking-room task was more complicated, required more verbal communication, and took longer than the standard symbolic task. In addition, the delay between the hiding event and the opportunity to search for the toy was substantially longer in the shrinking-room task (ca. 50–60 s) than in the standard symbolic task (ca. 10–15 s). Delays between hiding and retrieval are known to cause the performance of even older children to deteriorate dramatically in the standard model task (Uttal et al., 1995).

RESULTS

The critical question was whether performance in the nonsymbolic (shrinking-room) condition would be superior to performance in the symbolic (model) condition. Figure 2 shows the mean number of errorless retrievals (searching first at the correct location) achieved in the two tasks.

The children in the symbolic task achieved a mean of only 0.8 errorless retrievals over four trials ($SE = 0.2$), a rate not different from chance. (We con-

For each shrinking event, as soon as the child had left the lab, one assistant turned on a tape recorder to begin the shrinking-machine sounds (thereby concealing any noises made in the lab). Two other assistants pulled the artificial room behind the curtains, and the first placed the model, with the miniature troll in the appropriate position, in the center of the space formerly occupied by the room. In the enlarging events, the model was replaced by the room.

3. The parents of all the participants in this study were fully informed of the procedures to be followed, and a parent was present throughout each experimental session. The children's assent was always obtained before the sessions began. After the completion of their sessions, the children in the nonsymbolic (shrinking-room) condition were debriefed: They were shown the two dolls and the model and room together, and the experimenter explained that the machine did not really shrink or enlarge them.

servatively estimated chance at 25%, based on our use of four hiding places; however, it is actually lower because there are additional possible hiding places.) Individual performance in this task was similarly poor: Six of the 15 children never found the toy, and 6 retrieved it only once. No child succeeded on more than two of the four trials. These children understood that they were supposed to search for a hidden toy on each trial, and they were happy to do so, but they apparently failed to realize that their knowledge of one space could be applied to the other.

The poor performance of the children in the symbolic task (19%) is exactly what would be expected from previous model studies. In research in our own and other labs using a variety of different models and rooms, $2^1/_2$-year-olds reliably average around 20% successful retrievals.

In contrast, children in the nonsymbolic task were very successful. Performance in the nonsymbolic (shrinking-room) condition was well above chance—3.1 errorless retrievals ($SE = 0.2$)—and significantly better than the performance of the children in the symbolic condition. Twelve of the 17 subjects achieved three or more errorless retrievals, and 7 of those had perfect scores. The difference between the two tasks was the only significant result in a 2 (task) $\times$ 2 (gender) analysis of variance, $F(1, 28) = 51.5$, $p < .0001$. Performance did not differ on trials in which the hiding event occurred in the room and the child searched in the model versus trials in which the hiding and search spaces were the reverse.

The main result of this study has been replicated, both in an additional study with $2^1/_2$-year-olds and in two studies in which the same logic was applied to a different age group. Using two different, more difficult versions of the model task, we found the same pattern of results with 3-year-olds as occurred with the $2^1/_2$-year-olds in the present study—significantly better performance in the nonsymbolic, shrinking-room version than in the symbolic model task (DeLoache, 1995a; Marzolf, 1994).

DISCUSSION

We conclude that a major challenge to detecting and using symbolic relations stems from their inherent dual reality and the necessity of achieving dual representation (DeLoache, 1987, 1995a, 1995b). The model task was more difficult than the shrinking-room task because the former required dual representation, whereas the latter eliminated the need for it. The research reported here provides strong support for a theoretical account of early symbol understanding and use in which young children's ability to use symbols is considered to be limited by several factors, a key one being the difficulty of achieving dual repre-

sentation (DeLoache, 1995a, 1995b). Relatively limited information processing capacity makes it difficult for younger children to keep two representations active at the same time, and limited cognitive flexibility makes it especially difficult for them to mentally represent a single entity in two different ways.

The study reported here provides especially strong support against criticism of this theoretical account of early symbol use. It has been claimed that the use of a symbol such as a scale model requires nothing more than simply detecting some kind of correspondence between the symbol and referent (Blades & Spencer, 1994; Lillard, 1993; Perner, 1991). One claim is that the child succeeds on each trial by noticing that the current hiding place of the miniature toy corresponds to the full-sized hiding place of the larger toy, without ever appreciating the higher level relation between the two spaces.

The simple correspondence view cannot explain the current results. For one thing, it offers no account of how children's performance depends on the kind of relation that must be represented. In both tasks, corresponding items in the two spaces must be mentally linked; memory for the object concealing the original toy must support a search at the corresponding object. The challenge in the nonsymbolic task is simply to recognize that object in its new form. The challenge in the symbolic task is to represent the relation between that object and the other one it stands for.

Furthermore, simply detecting the correspondence between matching items does not support successful performance in the symbolic task. In a recent study (DeLoache, 1995a), $2^1/_2$-year-old children readily matched the items in the room to the corresponding items in the model, yet still failed the subsequent standard model task. Establishing object correspondences is thus necessary but not sufficient for reasoning from one space to the other. Although the simple correspondence account has the appearance of parsimony, because it posits a lower level explanation than dual representation, it cannot account for results presented here and elsewhere in support of dual representation (DeLoache, 1991; Marzolf & DeLoache, 1994).

At the most general level, the research reported here indicates that it is the nature of a child's mental representation of the relation between two entities that governs the child's ability to reason from one to the other. Very young children can reason successfully based on an identity relation, even when it results from the complex and novel scenario of a shrinking machine. They fail to appreciate a symbolic relation between the same two entities, even though it is explained and demonstrated. Despite the importance and universality of symbolization, very young children are quite conservative when it comes to interpreting novel objects as symbols.

The dual representation hypothesis, which received strong support from the study reported here, has important practical implications. For example, it calls into question the assumption commonly made by educators that children will readily comprehend the meaning of manipulables—concrete objects used to instantiate abstract mathematical concepts (Uttal, Scudder, & DeLoache, 1997). One must take care to ensure that children appreciate the relation between, for example, the size of blocks and numerical quantities before using the blocks for teaching purposes. Similar doubt is cast on the widespread practice of using anatomically explicit dolls to interview young children in child-abuse investigations. Young children's difficulty with dual representation suggests that the relevant self–doll relation may not be clear to them; if so, using dolls may not be helpful and might even be counterproductive. Recent research has supported this conjecture: Several studies have reported no advantage to using dolls to interview 3-year-old children about events they have experienced (Bruck, Ceci, Francoeur, & Renick, 1995; DeLoache, Anderson, & Smith, 1995; DeLoache & Marzolf, 1995; Goodman & Aman, 1990; Gordon et al., 1993).

One other aspect of the results reported here merits attention. The $2^1/_2$-year-old children had no difficulty dealing with the size transformations supposedly effected by the shrinking machine. This finding is consistent with research showing that very young children represent and rely on geometric features of a space (Hermer & Spelke, 1994). The children's ability to mentally scale the two spaces in the present research may have been assisted by the fact that the size transformations preserved the geometric properties of the original space, including its overall shape, the relative sizes and positions of the objects, and the distances among them.

Spatial representations other than scale models also pose problems for young children. Only with difficulty can 3-year-olds use a simple map to locate a hidden object, and their ability to do so is easily disrupted (Bluestein & Acredolo, 1979). Older preschool children often fail to interpret aerial photographs consistently (Liben & Downs, 1992); they may, for example, describe one feature of an aerial photo correctly as a river but another as a piece of cheese. Thus, figuring out the nature and use of spatial symbols is a persistent challenge for young children.

The current study, along with other research on the early understanding and use of symbols, makes it clear that one can never assume that young children will detect a given symbol–referent relation, no matter how transparent that relation seems to adults or older children. Young children may perceive and form a meaningful interpretation of both the symbol and the entity it stands for without representing the relation between them.

REFERENCES

Blades, M., & Spencer, C. (1994). The development of children's ability to use spatial representations. In H. Reese (Ed.)., *Advances in child development and behavior* (Vol. 25, pp. 157–199). New York: Academic Press.

Bluestein, N., & Acredolo, L. (1979). Developmental change in map reading skills. *Child Development, 50,* 691–697.

Bruck, M., Ceci, S. J., Francoeur, E., & Renick, A. (1995). Anatomically detailed dolls do not facilitate preschoolers, reports of a pediatric examination involving genital touching. *Journal of Experimental Psychology: Applied, 1,* 95–109.

DeLoache, J. S. (1987). Rapid change in the symbolic functioning of very young children. *Science, 238,* 1556–1557.

DeLoache, J. S. (1989). Young children's understanding of the correspondence between a scale model and a larger space. *Cognitive Development, 4,* 121–139.

DeLoache, J. S. (1991). Symbolic functioning in very young children: Understanding of pictures and models. *Child Development, 62,* 736–752.

DeLoache, J. S. (1995a). Early symbolic understanding and use. In D. Medin (Ed.), *The psychology of learning and motivation* (Vol. 33, pp. 65–114). New York: Academic Press.

DeLoache, J. S. (1995b). Early understanding and use of symbols. *Current Directions in Psychological Science, 4,* 109–113.

DeLoache, J. S., Anderson, K., & Smith, C. M. (1995, April). *Interviewing children about real-life events.* Paper presented at the annual meeting of the Society for Research in Child Development, Indianapolis, IN.

DeLoache, J. S., Kolstad, D. V., & Anderson, K. N. (1991). Physical similarity and young children's understanding of scale models. *Child Development, 62,* 111–126.

DeLoache, J. S., & Marzolf, D. P. (1995). The use of dolls to interview young children. *Journal of Experimental Child Psychology, 60,* 155–173.

Dow, G. A., & Pick, H. L. (1992). Young children's use of models and photographs as spatial representations. *Cognitive Development, 7,* 351–363.

Gibson, J. J. (1979). *The ecological approach to visual perception.* Boston: Houghton Mifflin.

Goodman, G. S., & Aman, C. (1990). Children's use of anatomically detailed dolls to recount an event. *Child Development, 61,* 1859–1871.

Gordon, B. N., Ornstein, P. A., Nida, R. E., Follmer, A., Crenshaw, M. C., & Albert, G. (1993). Does the use of dolls facilitate children's memory of visits to the doctor? *Applied Cognitive Psychology, 7,* 459–474.

Gregory, R. L. (1970). *The intelligent eye.* New York: McGraw-Hill.

Hermer, L., & Spelke, E. (1994). A geometric process for spatial reorientation in young children. *Nature, 370,* 57–69.

Langer, S. K. (1942). *Philosophy in a new key.* Cambridge, MA: Harvard University Press.

Liben, L. L., & Downs, R. M. (1992). Developing an understanding of graphic representations in children and adults: The case of GEO-Graphics. *Cognitive Development, 7,* 331–349.

Lillard, A. S. (1993). Pretend play skills and the child's theory of mind. *Child Development, 64,* 348–371.

Marzolf, D. P. (1994, April). *Representing and mapping relations in a symbolic task.* Paper presented at the International Conference on Infant Studies, Paris.

Marzolf, D. P., & DeLoache, J. S. (1994). Transfer in young children's understanding of spatial representations. *Child Development, 64,* 1–15.

Perner, J. (1991). *Understanding the representational mind.* Cambridge, MA: Bradford Books/MIT Press.

Potter, M. C. (1979). Mundane symbolism: The relations among objects, names, and ideas. In N. R. Smith & M. B. Franklin (Eds.), *Symbolic functioning in childhood* (pp. 41–65). Hillsdale, NJ: Erlbaum.

Uttal, D. H., Schreiber, J. C., & DeLoache, J. S. (1995). Waiting to use a symbol: The effects of delay on children's use of models. *Child Development, 66,* 1875–1891.

Uttal, D. H., Scudder, K. V., & DeLoache, J. S. (1997). Manipulatives as symbols: A new perspective on the use of concrete objects to teach mathematics. *Journal of Applied Developmental Psychology, 18,* 37–54.

QUESTIONS

1. What are symbols and why are they difficult for young children to understand?
2. What manipulation did the investigators use to test the dual representation hypothesis?
3. What effect did shrinking the room have on the performance of 2-1/2-year-olds in this task?
4. Do you agree with the reasoning that if a child believes the model is actually the large room that had been shrunk, they do not need symbolic representation to find the toy? Why or why not?
5. What developmental changes do you think explain children's increasing skill over early childhood in understanding symbols?
6. What implications do these findings have for the use of anatomically correct dolls in interviewing young children in legal cases involving child sexual abuse?

19 Belief-Desire Reasoning among Baka Children: Evidence for a Universal Conception of Mind

JEREMY AVIS · PAUL L. HARRIS

There has been much interest among researchers in when and how children come to understand the mind and how it works. This area of study, known as theory of mind, covers topics ranging from the development of the ability to distinguish appearance from reality to children's understanding of dreams, false beliefs, and desires.

Most research on children's theory of mind has been conducted with children in Western communities in which discussion about the mind, its uses, and what people think are common. Children in Western communities are not only privy to conversations about the mind from an early age, they are encouraged by parents to participate in these conversations. Parents often ask children what they are thinking about, what other people believe, and about all kinds of mentalistic constructs like dreams and imaginary friends. Research along these lines reveals that much changes from age 2 to age 6 in children's understanding of the mind, and this change is assumed to be universal.

Despite an assumption of universality, it was an open question as to whether children in non-Western communities have a similar developmental course. To address this question, Jeremy Avis and Paul L. Harris conducted a study with children in the Baka community, a hunter-gatherer group that lives in Cameroon in west-central Africa. The investigators adapted an experimental procedure for use in this community that focuses on children's understanding of the mental state of another person. Children between the ages of 2 and 6 years participated. This research was time consuming and difficult to conduct. However, it provides a window into a developmental process that only examination of children reared in very different sociocultural circumstances can provide. As such, it is a nice example of the utility of cross-cultural investigation for advancing developmental theory.

Children of the Baka, a group of pygmies living in the rain forests of southeast Cameroon, were tested for their conception of mind. Specifically, they were invited to move a desirable food from its container to a hiding place in the absence of the adult preparing the food and then predict the likely reactions of the adult on his return. A majority of older children (n = 17; mean age 5 years) correctly predicted that the adult would approach the original but now empty container, would feel happy rather than sad before lifting its cover, and sad rather than happy after discovering the disappearance of the food. A minority of younger children (n = 17; mean age 3¹/₂ years) were also systematically correct for all 3 predictions. The results provide support for the claim that belief-desire reasoning is universally acquired in childhood.

Reprinted by permission of Blackwell Publishers from *Child Development*, 62 (1991), pp. 460–467. Copyright © 1991 by the Society for Research in Child Development.

This research would not have been possible without the presence of Shaunagh Willman of Sydney, Australia. Sincere thanks also go to Philip Agland of Dja River Films, Clinton Robinson of SIL, and Dr Paul Nkwi of the Ministry of Education and Scientific Research in Yaounde. Financial help was given by both the Clive Pare Memorial Fund and the OKS Benevolent Fund. Finally, the most profound gratitude and thanks go to the people of Sakwe and Lupe camps. Reprints may be obtained from P. L. Harris, Department of Experimental Psychology, South Parks Rd., Oxford, OXl 3UD, U.K.

Recent evidence has shown that young children adopt a mentalistic framework for predicting and explaining human action and emotion (Astington, Harris, & Olson, 1988; Harris, 1989). Children rapidly understand that what people do or feel cannot be predicted solely from the situation facing them but must be related to the desires and beliefs they bring to the situation. By the age of 3 years, children appreciate that when people want an object they will seek to secure it; if they succeed, they will feel happy; if they fail, they will feel sad and continue their efforts (Harris, Johnson, Hutton, Andrews, & Cooke, 1989; Wellman & Bartsch, 1988; Yuill, 1984). By the age of 4–5 years, children also understand the impact of beliefs on action and emotion; they appreciate that people usually act so as to approach their goal but may sometimes go in the wrong direction if their beliefs about the location of the goal are mistaken; moreover, people feel happy or sad depending on whether they expect to get what they want, irrespective of whether that expectation conforms to the objective situation (Hadwin & Perner, in press; Harris et al., 1989; Perner, Leekam, & Wimmer, 1987; Wimmer & Perner, 1983).

The above studies were carried out in Western Europe and North America, using a variety of paradigms. It is tempting to conclude, therefore, that such a mentalistic framework is universally adopted in early childhood. Indeed, the most contentious issue in the study of children's conception of mind is not whether children do adopt that framework but rather whether the timetable sketched above is too conservative (Chandler, Fritz, & Hala, 1989; Perner, in press; Sodian, Taylor, Harris, & Perner, 1991, in this issue; Wellman, 1990). However, a brief excursion outside the confines of developmental psychology reveals considerable disagreement about the status and ubiquity of belief-desire reasoning.

Confidence in its universality has been emphatically expressed within the philosophy of mind. For example, Fodor (1987) says that the predisposition to explain human behavior in terms of intentional mental states (notably beliefs and desires) is innate and universal: "There is, so far as I know, no human group that doesn't explain behaviour by imputing beliefs and desires to the behaviour. (And if an anthropologist claimed to have found such a group, I wouldn't believe him.)"

Anthropologists whom Fodor would presumably disbelieve are not far to seek. In his classic monograph on the Dinka of southern Sudan, Lienhardt (1961) writes: "The Dinka have no conception which at all corresponds to our popular modern conception of the 'mind,' as mediating and, as it were storing up the experiences of the self. . . . What we should call the "memories" of experiences, and regard therefore as in some way intrinsic to the remembering person . . . appear to the Dinka as exteriorly acting upon him."

Since few developmental psychologists are committed to Fodor's unabashed nativism, it is reasonable to ask whether children everywhere do adopt the same mentalistic framework to predict action and emotion. As a first step, the present study was carried out among 2–6-year-old children of the Baka, a preliterate hunter-gatherer people of southeast Cameroon. The procedure was tailored to local practices familiar to the children. They watched while an adult cooked some tasty fruit kernels, placed them in a covered bowl, and went away for a few minutes. In his absence, children were prompted by another adult to remove the kernels from the bowl and hide them. They were then asked about the likely reactions of the first adult on his return. Where would he look for the kernels? How would he feel immediately *before* lifting the lid of the bowl? And how would he feel *after* lifting the lid. The first and second questions required children to anticipate the impact of a mistaken belief on action and emotion, respectively. The third question required children to anticipate the impact of a frustrated desire on emotion.

METHOD

Setting. Testing took place among the Baka, a pygmy people who live in the rain forests of southeast Cameroon. Baka society corresponds to what anthropologists have variously described as an egalitarian/prestige-avoidance culture (Bahuchet, 1985). Food is obtained through hunting, gathering, and fishing in different parts of the forest, depending on the season. The Baka also work for part of the year on the plantations of the more sedentary surrounding tribes, such as the Bagandou. Nevertheless, the culture still largely follows the traditional hunter-gatherer pattern (see Agland, 1987; Silcock, 1988). References and invocations to the forest god (Komba), visitations by the potentially malevolent spirit (Jengi), observation of ritual dances and initiation rites, and accusations of sorcery are key components of Baka cultural life.

Experimenters. Initially, testing was attempted by two Europeans who spoke enough Baka to administer the test questions. However, the children were unused to the presence of outsiders and often did little more than echo the questions. Efforts to recruit local adults as experimenters also proved unsuccessful because the notion of exact (and seemingly pointless) repetition of the test questions was alien to them.

Two Baka visitors to the camp eventually served as primary experimenters. They differed from the permanent members of the group in that they lived a sedentary life for part of the year near the only road in the region. They returned to the camp for important events (on this occasion, the birth of a child and an initiation ritual). Nevertheless, they were well known to many of the children tested and indeed related to them. Unlike the other adults, they had been to school and could read and write French. In addition to carrying out the testing, they helped to produce a grammatically correct wording in Baka of the questions put to the children.

Subjects. Like their parents, none of the Baka children tested had been to school and none could read. Baka children spend much of their time at play, often in the miniature play village (Ndabala) behind the main camp; there they practice the arts of hut building, spear shaping, and fire making. They also participate in the practical tasks of camp life. Children as young as 5 years may be seen fetching and carrying water or food and bathing and minding younger siblings.

A total of 48 children were tested from four Baka camps within a comfortable walking distance of one another. Of these, six were discarded because the two local experimenters were still gaining familiarity with the questioning procedure and posed the questions incorrectly. A further eight children were discarded because they were either distracted or upset during the procedure and gave only one answer or none at all to the three key questions. The remaining 34 children were equally divided into a younger group and an older group. The younger children (nine males and eight females) ranged from an estimated 2 years 11 months to 4 years 3 months (mean 3 years 6 months), while the older children ranged from an estimated 4 years 4 months to 6 years 1 month (mean 5 years 0 months).

Considerable effort was made to assess the children's ages accurately. On arrival in the camp, children were rank ordered for apparent age from youngest to oldest with the help of a camp elder. Next, adult members of the camp and the two local experimenters helped to identify the year and season in which each potential subject was born. Year of birth was often pinpointed by reference to recent salient events (e.g., the poisoning of the mayor in a nearby sous-prefecture; the last initiation ceremony). Seasons were identified by their distinctive weather pattern. There are four seasons in southeast Cameroon, each marked by a distinctive temperature and rainfall. Within each season, associated activities (e.g., planting, harvesting, coffee reckoning, dam fishing) helped to pinpoint the date of birth. Such activities take place in different parts of the forest and served as a helpful mnemonic for the time of birth of a particular child. Finally, the two local experimenters could translate from the seasonal calendar of the Baka into the Western Calendar. In addition, they themselves could remember the births of some of the children to within a couple of weeks.

These procedures meant that each child's age could be established with respect to year, season, and nearest seasonal activity. Errors were unlikely to be biased toward systematic underestimation or overestimation. Hence, the estimates of mean ages are likely to be correct to within 1 or 2 months despite possible mistakes in identifying the exact month of birth for individual children.

Procedure. Testing took place in the cooking area of a native hut: this allowed the experimental procedure to be embedded in practices that were familiar to Baka children. The two experimenters (Mopfana and Mobissa) sat around a star-shaped fire. Mopfana cooked wild mango kernels (a favorite delicacy) on a baking tray positioned over the fire. Beside the fire stood a bowl with a lid and a cooking pot with a lid. Subjects' replies were tape-recorded for later analysis with a tie-pin microphone concealed in a drum or gathering basket. The first three children at each new camp were also watched through a peephole in the side of the hut by J.A. to check that all was going as planned.

The mother was called and brought the child into the hut. She stayed to keep the child calm and relaxed and occasionally repeated a question to the child if he or she failed to reply. The child sat either on the knee of Mobissa or its mother and watched while Mopfana took the kernels off the fire and placed them in the bowl. He then said (theatrically): "Now take a look at these tasty kernels I've got cooking here—they're so sweet, so sugary, so amazingly delicious! Yum, Yum! Before I eat them, I'll just go over to the mbanjo [male meeting-place] for a quick smoke and a chat. I'll be back soon to eat them." He then covered the bowl with a lid, went out of the hut to the mbanjo, and arranged the next subject with its mother.

Mobissa, who (by virtue of his age) was higher in status than the adolescent Mopfana, then said: "Mopfana has gone to the mbanjo. He can't see what we're doing. Come on, let's play a game. Take the kernels from the bowl and hide them. Where do you think we should hide them?"

He waited for the child to act. If the child did not hide the kernels, Mobissa said: "Put them in the pot." Once the child had hidden the kernels, he said: "There, the kernels are in the pot" (or wherever the child has chosen) and proceeded to ask Test Questions 1–3: (1) "When Mopfana comes back, where will he look for the kernels, in the bowl or in the pot?" (or wherever the child had chosen). (2) "Before Mopfana lifts the lid of the bowl will his heart feel good or bad?" (Note that if a child had answered Question 1 wrongly, Mobissa first recapped the situation, explaining that Mopfana would look in the bowl, where he had left the kernels, before posing Questions 2 and 3.)

(3) "After he lifts the lid, will his heart feel good or bad?" Children were praised regardless of their responses and then allowed to go.

RESULTS

The tapes were decoded in two stages. An initial sample was decoded at the camp by two Europeans with the help of Mobissa and Mopfana. The remainder was decoded (by the same two Europeans) on their return. Children were scored in terms of where they hid the kernels and whether they gave correct replies to Questions 1–3. Children gave unambiguous replies (that could be readily coded as right or wrong) or they gave no reply at all. There were no coding disagreements.

Hiding the Kernels. Within each age group, 15 (out of 17) children hid the kernels appropriately in response to Mobissa's prompt. Children spontaneously chose a variety of locations to serve as hiding places: the nearby pot, Mobissa's clothes, their own hand, under the meat smoker, and in a basket. The remaining four children needed further prompting; they took up Mobissa's suggestion that they hide the kernels in the pot.

Questions 1–3. Children were scored as correct if they designated the bowl as the place where Mopfana would look on his return for Question 1, if they predicted that he would be happy rather than sad prior to lifting the lid for question 2, and if they predicted that he would be sad rather than happy after lifting the lid for Question 3. Children who gave no reply were scored as incorrect.

Occasionally, it seemed likely that children were wrong not through lack of understanding but because they had taken other considerations into account. One 5-year-old explicitly voiced such a possibility. She explained that the cook would remain happy even after discovering the empty bowl because he would be given the kernels to eat eventually. Despite its plausibility, this reply was scored as incorrect. Tables 1 and 2 report individual replies to each question in the younger and older group, respectively.

A clear majority of older children were accurate on all three questions, whereas younger children produced more errors. Chi-square tests confirmed that significantly more than half of the older children were correct for each question: Question 1, $\chi^2(1) = 13.24$, $p < .001$; questions 2 and 3, $\chi^2(1) = 7.12$, $p < .01$. The performance of younger children did not exceed chance on any of the three questions: Questions 1 and 2, $\chi^2(1) = 1.47$, N.S.; Question 3, $\chi^2(1) = 2.88$, $p < .1$.

The older group produced an overall mean of 2.59 (out of 3) correct replies and the younger group an overall mean of 2.00 (out of 3). A t test showed that

TABLE 1   RESPONSES OF INDIVIDUAL CHILDREN IN THE YOUNGER GROUP AS A FUNCTION OF QUESTION

Name	Age	Sex	1	2	3
Etika	2.11	M	1	1	1
Njumbo 1	2.11	F	1	1	1
Layano	3.1	F	0	0	1
Lakala	3.1	F	1	1	1
Mondindo	3.1	F	1	1	1
Marie	3.2	F	1	1	0[a]
Nina	3.3	F	1	0	1
Ndouma	3.4	F	0[a]	1	0[b]
Toji 1	3.6	M	0	0	0[b]
Kpongo	3.7	M	1	1	1
Ngoma	3.7	M	0[a]	1	1
Toji 2	3.8	M	1	1	1
Njumbo 2	3.11	M	0	0	1
Mandongo 1	4.0	F	1	0	1
Papa	4.1	M	0	1	0
Lose	4.3	M	1	1	0
Mandongo 2	4.3	M	1	0	1
Total			11	11	12

[a]No response treated as a wrong answer.
[b]Prompted to hide pfeke.

the older group was more accurate than the younger group, $t(32) = 2.17$, $p < .05$.

Although the younger group performed poorly on each question, and worse than the older group, it was clear that a minority of the younger group did well. Six- younger children and 12 older children were correct on all three questions. Two binomial tests were carried out, making the assumption that the chance probability of three correct replies by any individual child was one in eight (0.125). The number of children who were completely correct exceeded chance for each age group (younger group, $p < .014$; older group, $p < .000001$).

Strictly speaking, a test of belief-based reasoning should be confined to Questions 1 and 2, since Question 3 could be answered simply by understanding Mopfana's desire for kernels, irrespective of his beliefs about their whereabouts. Accordingly, replies to Questions 1 and 2 were examined with the binomial test, making the assumption that any individual child might be expected to produce two correct replies with a probability of one in four (0.25). Eight younger children ($p < .04$) and 14 older children ($p < .0001$) were correct on both questions.

TABLE 2   RESPONSES OF INDIVIDUAL CHILDREN IN THE OLDER GROUP AS A FUNCTION OF QUESTION

Name	Age	Sex	Question 1	2	3
Aiké	4.4	F	1	1	1
Anja	4.4	M	1	1	1[a]
Kindango	4.6	F	1	1	1
Owomenjeo	4.6	M	1	1	1
Mandeke	4.7	F	1	1	1[a]
Medo	4.9	F	1	1	1
Maboi	4.10	F	1	1	0
Ano	4.11	M	1	1	1
Linga 1	5.0	M	1	0	1
Mougondo	5.0	M	1	1	1
Nendomma	5.1	F	1	1	1
Lengaé	5.1	F	1	1	1
Njumbo	5.2	F	1	1	0[b]
Ngembi	5.4	M	1	1	1
Linga 2	5.7	M	0	0	1
Buno	6.0	F	1	0	1
Ndjeboute	6.1	M	1	1	0
Total			16	14	14

[a]Prompted where to hide pfeke.
[b]Expected cook to get kernels eventually.

For Questions 1 and 2, the older group produced a mean of 1.77 correct replies and the younger group a mean of 1.29 correct replies. A t test showed that the older group was more accurate than the younger group, $t(32) = 2.073$, $p < .05$.

In summary, most of the older children could engage in belief-desire reasoning. There was also evidence that a minority of the younger children could do so. However, there was an age change in accuracy of performance.

DISCUSSION

The performance of the older children was very systematic. They performed above chance on each question, and the majority gave correct replies for all three questions. Younger children were less accurate overall, but a minority gave correct replies to all three questions.

It is possible to offer ad hoc explanations for correct replies to individual questions, but correct performance on all three questions provides strong evidence for accurate psychological attributions. For example, children might have predicted that the returning adult would go to the bowl not because they understood his mistaken belief but because they expected him to mechanically repeat his earlier response of approaching the bowl. Yet correct anticipation of his emotional reactions (Questions 2 and 3) could not be achieved in terms of such response repetition because correct answers called for different replies to the two questions. Similarly, although predictions of happiness prior to opening the bowl (Question 2) might be based on the assumption that the adult would eventually eat and enjoy the kernels not on any insight into his mistaken belief about what would be found in the bowl, such an assumption would lead to incorrect replies to Question 3.

Thus, by the age of 4–5 years, Baka children are good at predicting a person's action and emotion in terms of his or her beliefs and desires about a situation rather than in terms of the objective situation itself. Indeed, it is possible that the test questions occasionally led to an underestimate of this competence. Recall that one 5-year-old explained that Mopfana would be happy even on finding the bowl empty because he would eventually receive the kernels anyway. Some of the 6-year-olds who gave incorrect answers may have adduced similar considerations instead of taking the questions at face value.

Competence at belief-desire reasoning is also found in some 3-year-olds but is less widespread. These results are consistent with findings among Western children (Hadwin & Perner, in press; Harris et al., 1989; Wellman & Bartsch, 1988; Wimmer & Perner, 1983). In one respect, the results for the 3-year-olds are unexpected. In several experiments with false belief tasks, 3-year-old Western children have performed below chance (see Perner et al., 1987, Table 5). Nevertheless, this has not been a consistent finding. For example, Perner et al. (1987, Experiment 2) and Gopnik and Astington (1988, Experiments 1 and 2) found that 3-year-olds performed at chance on false belief tasks, and Freeman, Lewis, and Doherty (in press) report above-chance performance. The safest conclusion, therefore, is that most tasks reveal an improvement from 3 to 5 years in the ability to take false beliefs into account, although the exact level of performance fluctuates from one task to another. The present results are consistent with this conclusion.

Experiments in the Orient had already suggested that reasoning about mistaken beliefs might show a similar age change across diverse cultures. Flavell, Zhang, Zou, Dong, and Qi (1983) tested 3–5-year-olds in mainland China on a task in which they examined a fake object (e.g., a sponge painted to look like a rock) and then stated what it really was and how it looked. This task also requires a distinction to be made between reality and the belief that someone might hold about that reality, given limited perceptual access. Three-year-olds were unable to answer the two questions correctly, whereas 5-year-olds succeeded. These results paralleled those obtained with children in the United States (Flavell, 1986).

Similarly, Gardner, Harris, Ohmoto, and Hamazaki (1988) tested Japanese children on their understanding of the distinction between real and apparent emotion, using similar stories to those given to U.S. and U.K. children in earlier studies. Despite marked differences in cultural norms regarding the expression of emotion (Ekman, 1973), a similar age change was obtained in each setting (Harris & Gross, 1988).

It should be emphasized, however, that the children in these earlier cross-cultural studies had all been to school or preschool and were living in industrialized, literate cultures. Not so for Baka children. They grow up in a preliterate society still largely following an ancient hunter-gatherer lifestyle and they have no experience of schooling. The fact that belief-desire reasoning emerges at approximately the same age in such diverse settings strengthens the claim that this mode of reasoning is a universal feature of normal human development.

If this claim is accepted, how can it be reconciled with the radically different conceptions of mind described by social anthropologists for different cultures (Heelas & Lock, 1981; Lienhardt, 1961)? Three possible resolutions of this apparent conflict may be considered. First, it could be argued that it is too early to extrapolate from the limited amount of developmental research conducted hitherto, even if it includes children from preliterate as well as advanced, industrialized cultures. Future studies might show that although belief-desire reasoning is found in diverse cultures, it is far from universal. Like the subject-verb-object sentence structure, it might be a common but far from ubiquitous human strategy.

A second possibility is that cultural variation in the conceptualization of mental states is more apparent than real. The very familiarity of belief-desire reasoning might render it transparent and virtually invisible to social anthropologists in search of more exotic modes of thought. For example, a representation of the spirit Jengi (a Baka male disguised in raffia robes) visits the Baka village. The men seek to mislead the women by treating this representation as the actual spirit and "protect" the women from Jengi, who supposedly eats women. Although this practice can be analyzed at one level in terms of the distinctive cosmology and gender roles of the Baka, it also illustrates how the men seek to use misleading appearances and false beliefs in their relations with the women.

Thus, adults and children everywhere might have recourse to a universal beliefdesire framework, even in thinking about distinctive cultural practices. Apparent differences in the way that mental states are conceived might emerge only in response to puzzling or leading questions about the ultimate nature and source of mental states. Recent developmental evidence illustrates this possibility. Young children systematically distinguish mental entities from real entities if asked whether such entities can be seen or touched (Harris, Brown, Marriott, Whittall, & Harmon, in press; Wellman & Estes, 1986), yet they appear to confuse dreams and images with real entities when asked traditional Piagetian questions about their source (Estes, Wellman, & Woolley, 1989).

The third possibility is that genuine cultural variation in the way that mental states are conceived does exist, but these diverse conceptions elaborate upon rather than displace a universal assent to certain core concepts, notably beliefs and desires. Of the three possibilities considered, this seems the most plausible. It grants a fundamental role to belief-desire reasoning in the everyday prediction and explanation of action. At the same time, it leaves open the possibility that particular cultures elaborate sections of that theory in distinct ways. For example, although it seems likely that children in all cultures will arrive at a basic distinction between events that have really occurred and those that have been dreamt about, they may disagree about the status of dream events. In some cultures, they may be taken to reflect emotional conflicts; in others (including the Baka), they may sometimes be taken as prognostications of future events.

This formulation suggests an interesting agenda for future research. The present study has examined only one facet of the child's conception of mind: the use of belief-desire reasoning. Its results imply that other rapidly acquired concepts—for example, the distinction between mental entities and real entities (Wellman & Estes, 1986) and the distinction between accidental and intended actions (Poulin-Dubois & Schultz, 1988)—will also be universal acquisitions. It also implies that at some point in development children will begin to elaborate culture-specific ideas around those core assumptions.

References

Agland, P. (1987). *Baka: People of the rainforest* [an ethnographic film]. Dja River Films.

Astington, J. W., Harris, P. L., & Olson, D. R. (1988). *Developing theories of mind.* Cambridge: Cambridge University Press.

Bahuchet, S. (1985). *Les Pygmées Aka et la fôret centrafricaine.* Paris: Selaf.

Chandler, M., Fritz, A. S., & Hala, S. (1989). Small-scale deceit: Deception as a marker of two-, three-, and four-year-olds' early theories of mind. *Child Development,* **60,** 1263–1277.

Ekman, P. (1973). *Darwin and facial expression: A century of research in review.* New York: Academic Press.

Estes, D., Wellman, H. M., & Woolley, J. D. (1989). Children's understanding of mental phenomena. In H. W. Reese (Ed.),

Advances in child development and behavior (pp. 41–87). San Diego: Academic Press.

Flavell, J. H. (1986). The development of children's knowledge about the appearance-reality distinction. *American Psychologist*, **41**, 418–425.

Flavell, J. H., Zhang, X-D, Zou, H., Dong, Q., & Qi, S. (1983). A comparison of the appearance-reality distinction in the People's Republic of China and the United States. *Cognitive Psychology*, **15**, 459–466.

Fodor, J. (1987). *Psychosemantics.* Cambridge, MA: Bradford, MIT.

Freeman, N. H., Lewis, C., & Doherty, M. J. (in press). Preschoolers' grasp of a desire for knowledge in a false-belief prediction: Practical intelligence and verbal report. *British Journal of Developmental Psychology*.

Gardner, D., Harris, P. L., Ohmoto, M., & Hamasaki, T. (1988). Japanese children's understanding of the distinction between real and apparent emotion. *International Journal of Behavioral Development*, **11**, 203–218.

Gopnik, A., & Astington. J. (1988). Children's understanding of representational change and its relation to the understanding of false-belief and the appearance-reality distinction. *Child Development*, **59**, 26–37.

Hadwin, J., & Perner, J. (in press). Pleased and surprised: Children's cognitive theory of emotion. *British Journal of Developmental Psychology*.

Harris, P. L. (1989). *Children and emotion: The development of psychological understanding.* Oxford: Basil Blackwell.

Harris, P. L., Brown, E., Marriott, C., Whittall, S., & Harmon, S. (in press). Monsters, ghosts and witches: Testing the limits of the fantasy-reality distinction. *British Journal of Developmental Psychology*.

Harris, P. L., & Gross, D. (1988). Children's understanding of real and apparent emotion. In J. W. Astington, P. L. Harris, & D. R. Olson (Eds.), *Developing theories of mind* (pp. 295–314). Cambridge: Cambridge University Press.

Harris, P. L., Johnson, C. N., Hutton, D., Andrews, G., &

Cooke, T. (1989). Young children's theory of mind and emotion. *Cognition and Emotion*, **3**, 379–400.

Heelas, P., & Lock, A. (1981). *Indigenous psychologies.* London: Academic Press.

Lienhardt, G. (1961). *Divinity and experience: The religion of the Dinka.* Oxford: Clarendon Press.

Perner, J. (in press). *Understanding the representational mind.* Cambridge, MA: Bradford, MIT.

Perner, J., Leekam, S. R., & Wimmer, H. (1987). Three-year-olds' difficulty with false belief: The case for a conceptual deficit. *British Journal of Developmental Psychology*, **5**, 125–137.

Poulin-Dubois, D., & Shultz, T. R. (1988). The development of the understanding of human behavior: From agency to intentionality. In J. W. Astington, P. L. Harris, & D. R. Olson (Eds.), *Developing theories of mind* (pp. 109–125). Cambridge: Cambridge University Press.

Silcock, L. (1988). *Baka: People of the rainforest.* London: Channel 4 Television Broadcasting Support Services.

Sodian, B., Taylor, C., Harris, P. L., & Perner, J. (1991). Early deception and the child's theory of mind: False trails and genuine markers. *Child Development*, **62**, 468–483.

Wellman, H. M. (1990). *Children's theories of mind.* Cambridge, MA: Bradford, MIT.

Wellman, H. M., & Bartsch, K. (1988). Young children's reasoning about beliefs. *Cognition*, **30**, 239–277.

Wellman, H. M., & Estes, D. (1986). Early understanding of mental entities: A reexamination of childhood realism. *Child Development*, **57**, 910–923.

Wimmer, H., & Perner, J. (1983). Beliefs about beliefs: Representation and constraining function of wrong beliefs in young children's understanding of deception. *Cognition*, **13**, 103–128.

Yuill, N. (1984). Young children's coordination of motive and outcome in judgements of satisfaction and morality. *British Journal of Developmental Psychology*, **2**, 73–81.

QUESTIONS

1. Why is understanding the beliefs and desires of other people important to human functioning?
2. Do you think it made any difference in the children's responses that the experimenters were familiar to the community rather than outsiders? How?
3. What procedures were used to determine the children's ages? Why was this necessary?
4. On what questions did younger and older children differ?
5. What do the results indicate about the universal status of belief-desire reasoning and its development in early childhood?
6. Do you think these results will help revise earlier anthropological views about non-Western people having limited reasoning about mental states? Why or why not?

20 Cultural Differences in American and Mexican Mother-Child Pretend Play

JoAnn Farver · Carollee Howes

Piaget, Vygotsky, Freud, Erikson, and many other early psychologists were very interested in children's play. This is because play provides children with many different opportunities for development. These opportunities range from practicing cognitive and social skills to learning how to regulate emotions.

Until recently, research on children's play has concentrated on the play behaviors of middle-class children in Western communities. In the past few years, research by developmental psychologists has expanded to include studies of children's play in many communities throughout the world. This research has revealed much similarity in children's play, suggesting that this general type of activity is linked to some basic developmental processes. However, some variation in children's play across cultural communities has also been found. These variations stem from many sources, including cultural values, practices of social interaction, and the resources available to support and guide children's play.

In this article, JoAnn Farver and Carollee Howes compare the play of mothers and toddlers in two cultural communities, in the United States and Mexico. This research reveals interesting differences in the play in these two groups. The investigators make it clear that these differences are best understood when they are considered in relation to the broader social and cultural values of the community.

Toddler-age children's play with their mothers (n = 60) was videotaped in the U.S. and Mexico. Episodes were examined for pretend play, mutual involvement in social play, joint involvement in cooperative social pretend play, and maternal play behaviors. Contextual features were observed, recorded, and analyzed using an activity setting model. Mothers were interviewed about their value of children's play behavior. Although children's pretend play and mother-child mutual involvement increased with age in the two cultures, American mother-child pairs accounted for the greater proportion of interactive social play and pretend play episodes. There were also cultural differences in behaviors that mothers used to structure play and in mothers' value of children's play. The findings suggest that mothers guide the development of their children's play according to their particular cultural norms, which poses a theoretical challenge to the current notion that mothers are the primary facilitators of children's early pretend play.

American and Mexican young children's pretend play with their mothers was investigated, with the primary objective of understanding how culture influences the way in which mothers and their children engage in and express pretend play. Most research on children's early symbolic development and play behavior

Reprinted by permission of the authors and Wayne State University Press from *Merrill-Palmer Quarterly*, 39 (1993), pp. 344–358. Copyright © 1993 by Wayne State University Press, Detroit, Michigan.

The research is based on a dissertation submitted by J. M. Farver in partial fulfillment of the requirements for the doctoral degree in the Graduate School of Education, University of California, Los Angeles. The study was supported by grants from the University of California, Los Angeles, Chicano Studies Program, and the Organization of American States, Washington, DC. The authors gratefully acknowledge the families who participated in this study. A special thanks to the Menzie family, and to the Mexican field assistants, Patricia Rodriques, Victor Guerrero, and Evelyn Aron, who helped with coding the data and establishing reliability. Correspondence may be sent to J. M. Farver, Department of Psychology, SGM 501, University of Southern California, Los Angeles, CA 90089-1061.

TABLE 1   FEATURES OF AMERICAN AND MEXICAN ACTIVITY SETTINGS

	American	Mexican
Personnel available	Mothers[a]	Mothers[f]
	Toddlers	Toddlers
	Siblings	Siblings
		Extended family
		Neighbors
		Older children
Nature of tasks and activities performed	Formal play with educational outcomes[b]	Informal play in work contexts[g]
	Mother joins child's activities	Child joins mother's activities
Purpose of tasks	Prepare for school[c]	Prepare for work[h]
Cultural goals, values, and beliefs	Independence[d]	Interdependence[i]
	Individual autonomy	Family orientation
	Self-confidence	Cooperation
	Cognitive skills	Social skills
Scripts governing interactions	Parents help child learn[e]	Parents model desired behavior[j]
	Child learns through adult's efforts at teaching in play	Child learns by observing and imitating adult behavior in work

[a]Rogoff, Mistry, Göncü, & Mosier, 1991; Whiting & Edwards, 1988.
[b]Haight & Miller, 1991; Miller & Garvey, 1984; Whiting & Edwards, 1988.
[c]Bradley & Caldwell, 1984; Levenstein, 1986, in press; LeVine, 1980; White, 1980.
[d]Hoffman, 1988; Lawton, Fowell, Schuler, & Madsen, 1984; LeVine, 1980; Richman, Miller, & Solomon, 1988; Whiting & Edwards, 1988.
[e]Levenstein, 1986, in press; LeVine, 1980.
[f.g.h]Romney & Romney, 1966; Whiting & Edwards, 1988; Zukow, 1989.
[i]Bronstein-Burrows, 1981; Diáz-Guerrero, 1975; Falicov & Karrer, 1980; Holtzman, 1982; Holtzman, Diáz-Guerrero, Swartz, & Tapia, 1969; Kagan, 1981; Kagan & Ember, 1975; Keefe, Padrilla, & Carlos, 1979; Peñalosa, 1968; Ramírez, 1967; Ramírez & Price-Williams, 1974.
[j]Bronstein-Burrows, 1981; Ramírez & Castañeda, 1974.

has been based on white, middle-class Western samples. As result, cultural and social-class differences in children's play have been interpreted as signs of deficiency rather than variation (Feitelson, 1977; Smilansky, 1968). In the present study, the data base was broadened by comparing mother-child play in two different cultural contexts to allow general inferences to be made about the role of culture in development. The study also provides information about similarities and variations in developmental processes across particular contexts in which development occurs.

According to Western theorists, young children's pretend play originates in early interaction with parents. Werner and Kaplan (1963) claimed that it is the child's initial desire to share the object world with the mother that motivates the earliest attempts at communication and marks the beginning of internalized symbolic processes. According to this theory, early pretend play begins during the child's active experimentation with objects and in the seeking of confirmation of the developing symbols from the mother. In Western studies of early play behavior, it is proposed that mothers facilitate young children's beginning attempts at pretense. As mothers provide suggestions and communicate the rules of playing pretend, children incorporate the maternal guidance into play sequences and gradually begin to construct pretend scripts and enact roles. During play, mothers and children coordinate their actions and, with maternal assistance, children can perform beyond their existing level of competence (Haight & Miller, 1991; Miller, & Garvey, 1984; O'Connell & Bretherton, 1984; Slade, 1987).

Although research indicates that mothers structure or scaffold children's early pretend play, it is unclear whether these findings are generalizable to mothers and children in different cultures. In other societies, children may have few opportunities to play with their mothers. Mothers may not have time to spend in specific child-centered activities involving play. Children's play may not be considered to be a valuable, productive activity, or entering and managing children's play may be culturally inappropriate adult behavior. Cultural variations in mother-child communication styles also may influence their collaboration in play. Such culture-specific factors may affect a mother's inclination to play with her child, her scaffolding behavior, and the partner's involvement in pretend play.

To examine the influence of culture in shaping mother-child pretend play, an activity setting approach was used here. This approach is derived from Soviet activity theory (Leont'ev, 1981) and the Whiting behavior-setting concept (Whiting & Edwards, 1988), and is elaborated in Weisner and Gallimore's work (Tharp & Gallimore, 1988; Weisner, Gallimore, & Jordan, 1988). The model emphasizes the Vygotsky (1978) notion that children's development cannot be understood apart from the wider social milieu. Ecological factors as well as the economic and social organization of a community influence families' daily routines, individuals with whom they interact, activities in which they engage, and scripts that guide their behavior (Whiting & Edwards, 1988).

To compare American and Mexican mother-child play along similar contextual or environmental dimensions, variables that potentially influence mother-child interaction and play behavior were isolated. Features of American and Mexican activity settings, as derived from the research literature, are elaborated in Table 1.

Based on differences in the American and Mexican activity setting features, it was predicted that American children, reared in single family homes where mothers are available and customary play companions, display more symbolic level play with objects and engage in more frequent and more complex episodes of shared pretend play with their mothers than do Mexican children, who live in extended families and have rare opportunities to formally play with their mothers.

A second hypothesis is that cultural differences in childrearing goals and practices and the mother's value of play activity affect the behaviors which mothers use to scaffold children's pretend play. American mothers, who value play, emphasize the early development of cognitive skill, and promote children's independent effort, were expected to make frequent suggestions for fantasy play, to support their children's efforts at pretense, and to use an implicit style of guidance (defined as providing verbal support and following their children's lead in play). Mexican mothers, who place little or no value on play and emphasize direction, modeling, and imitation in shared daily activity, were expected to make few suggestions for fantasy play, to rarely use praise or approval as reinforcement, and to use an explicit style of guidance (defined as organizing and directing play activity).

METHOD

SUBJECTS

The participants were 60 children and their mothers: 30 Anglo-American and 30 Mexican, 10 from each culture, at ages 18, 24, and 36 months. Half of each age group were girls. Criterion for selection was that the child was at least a second-born. American families were contacted by flyers posted at neighborhood parks and by word of mouth. Mexican families were recruited by an assistant who was a resident of the community.

The American sample of white, working-class families came from an economically depressed county in northern California. Nuclear family households contained from two to five children ($M = 2.45$), ranging in age from 6 months to 12 years. Fathers were employed in the building trades, as truck drivers, retail store clerks, and similar occupations. Mothers did not work outside the home. Most mothers reported that, given their level of training and education, they could not earn enough money to both afford childcare and make a significant contribution to family income.

The Spanish-speaking Mexican Mestizo sample came from a town of about 5,000 residents located on the Pacific Coast 1,700 miles south of the U. S. border. Households consisted of intact families (i.e., both parents were living in the home) with two to five children ($M = 3.3$ children), ranging in age from infancy to 10 years. The nuclear families were embedded in an extended kinship cluster that included grandparents and/or paternal siblings and their children.

The Mexican community was selected because the predominant socioeconomic status closely approximated the American working-class sample. Although no universal measure of social class is comparable across societies, Mexican sociologists claim that parallels can be drawn between the American class system and the Mexican (Alba, 1982; Balán, 1973; Eckstein, 1989; Suárez, 1978). Mexican sociologists distinguish working-class status from white-collar professionals who are considered to be middle-class (*clase media*), and the lower class (*clase humilde*) landless peasants (*campesinos*), informal sector day laborers, unskilled and semiskilled workers, who inhabit squatter settlements and tenements (*vecindades*), by using indices of skilled labor union affiliation, work stability, home ownership, desire for upward mobility, and primary-level education of 6 years (Balán, 1973; Eckstein, 1989; Suárez, 1978).

Mexican fathers in this sample were employed in unionized (*syndicados*) construction-related jobs (tile setters, masons, and concrete finishers), as automobile mechanics, wrought iron workers, craftsmen, or truck drivers. Mothers were occupied with household maintenance. During interviews and conversations, parents expressed the desire to improve their economic standing and occupational opportunities and education for their children. Most older siblings were enrolled in or had attended the community's "kinder" program (preschool for 4- and 5-year-olds).

All Mexican families held the title to their land. Their houses were lowcost, but solidly built and of middle-class style, with separate rooms for cooking, sleeping, and everyday living. Houses were furnished with stoves, refrigerators, and television sets, and nearly all had indoor plumbing.

PROCEDURE

Qualitative and quantitative research methods were used in both cultures. The qualitative data collection began first and continued throughout the study with the intent to describe ethnographically the family life, childrearing practices, and the characteristics of the activity settings that the children typically inhabited.

To minimize subjects' reactivity to the observer's presence in the Mexican setting, the researcher spent considerable time in the community prior to data collection. Each family was observed in and around their homes for a total of 8 hours. Observations were unstructured so that family behavior might be as self-motivated and spontaneous as possible. The observer attempted to be unobtrusive while recording detailed field notes of their daily routines and activities.

Field notes were compiled and analyzed using the grounded theory method developed by sociologists Glaser and Strauss (1967), an inductive approach that consists of jointly collecting, categorizing, coding, and analyzing the data to allow theories to emerge. These emerging theories then can be systematically tested, provisionally verified, discarded, or reformulated simultaneously as data collection proceeds. The strength of this approach is that it allows the researcher to uncover patterns in participant behavior as it occurs in context. Thus, the researcher does not enter the setting with preconceived notions, possibly ignoring important variables.

In the quantitative procedure, mothers and children of both cultures were videotaped as they played with a bag of wooden shapes in their home for about 20 min. The wooden shapes included human, animal, and tree figures, various arched and flat rectangular pieces, square blocks, and a wooden train connected by magnets. The purpose of the shapes was to provide opportunities for pretense without introducing "toys" from the American culture to the Mexican and vice

versa. Because the shapes were novel in Mexico, and, by maternal report, very different from toys and blocks in the American homes, children in both cultures were allowed to play with the shapes for 20 min prior to the videotaping. In both cultures, mothers were told that the study was about how mothers and children play. Mothers were asked to "Play with your child in anyway you want" (*Juege con su nino de la manera en que usted le gusta*).

At the end of the data collection, mothers were interviewed about their views of children's play. All observations, interviews, and videotaping of the children and their families in both cultures were conducted by the first author.

CODING AND MEASURES

Videotapes were fully transcribed and then segmented into play episodes. An episode began when either partner touched an object or verbally interacted with the partner in the immediate environment. An episode ended when participants were no longer involved in play (e.g., either partner's attention was directed away for more than 30 s, or either partner moved away) or the theme of the play changed. The use of a different shape constituted a change in theme, unless the shapes were used in relationship to each other. For example, placing an animal shape on a tall stack of blocks was considered related to the ongoing theme of "stacking blocks." Sustained attention to, or introduction of, another shape into play, or an announced suggestion for a different play theme signaled the beginning of a new episode.

Level of Play with Objects. Each episode was coded once for the focal child's highest level of object play by using a scale adopted from that of O'Connell and Bretherton (1984). *Exploratory play* consisted of all manipulative behaviors such as handling, throwing, banging, or mouthing the objects, or touching one shape to another. *Combinational play* included putting objects together, stacking the shapes, making spatial configurations, or grouping shapes by function or color. *Symbolic play* was coded when children used the shapes to represent other objects or activities, and included conventional or functional uses of the shapes, such as giving a horse shape a "ride" on the train, object substitution (using a block for a bed), and the use of an independent agent (making the human shapes walk or talk).

Mutual Involvement in Social Play. Each episode was coded for the presence or absence of mutual involvement in social play by using a measure adopted from a study by Howes (1980). Mutual involvement was coded when partners directed social bids to each other (smiled, vocalized, offered or received object, helped with task) and/or engaged in complementary and reciprocal activities with mutual awareness (e.g., child offered a shape, mother took it and offered it back).

Joint Involvement in Cooperative Social Pretend Play. Episodes containing symbolic level play were selected and coded for partners' joint involvement in cooperative pretend play by using a measure adopted from that of Howes (1985). Cooperative pretend play was coded when both partners performed fantasy actions in the context of ongoing social play, which indicated that they assumed complementary pretend roles (e.g., mother-baby).

Maternal Behaviors in Play. Fifteen maternal play behaviors, derived from observations of the activity settings and judged to be salient in the two cultures, were coded for the number of times each occurred during an episode. These behaviors were clustered to form four broad maternal scaffolding behaviors. Labeling objects, directing play, correcting child, setting stage for play, attracting child's attention, and providing a model were clustered to represent *explicit guidance*. These were times when mothers explicitly organized and directed play activity and children followed their lead. Requesting help, giving help, joining child's play, describing child's behavior, and describing own behavior, were combined to represent *implicit guidance*. Here, mothers provided interpretative commentary, kept their partner informed about what they were doing, and followed their children's lead in play. Praising and encouraging independence were clustered to form *support child's effort*. Suggesting symbolic play and using paralinguistic cues to animate play objects were combined to represent *suggest fantasy play*.

Reliability. Videotapes were coded by the bilingual first author and a bicultural, bilingual assistant who was uninformed of the children's ages and the goals of the study. The first author trained the assistant by using six videotapes (one for each age level in each culture). To establish reliability, six additional tapes were randomly selected and coded independently by the first author and the assistant. Cohen's kappas for rater agreement on identifying episodes, coding level of object play, mother-child involvement in social play, and cooperative pretend play, and determining the 15 maternal behaviors and their clustering and coding, ranged from .91 to .96 for the American dyads, and from .82 to .90 for the Mexican dyads. Similar reliability checks performed midway and at the end of the coding ranged from .95 to .97.

Because the data were collected by the first author, careful attention was given to training and establishing reliability with the assistant. To avoid experimenter bias, the assistant's codings of the videotapes were used in the data analysis.

MATERNAL INTERVIEWS

During the interviews, mothers were asked open-ended questions about the value that they placed on children's play behavior and who was their child's most common play partner. In both cultures, mothers' responses about the most important value of play fell into three main types: child's amusement, mutual enjoyment, and educational benefits. The four common play partners were mothers, fathers, siblings, and unrelated children. Mothers rated the importance of play on a 3-point scale: *not important, somewhat important,* and *very important.*

Cohen's kappas for agreement between the first author and the assistant on categorizing and coding of the three maternal interview questions ranged from .97 to .99 for the American sample, and from .94 to .98 for the Mexican sample.

RESULTS

NUMBER OF EPISODES

There were 782 mother-child play episodes in the two cultures (U.S., $M = 12.06$, $SD = 4.33$; Mexico, $M = 11.76$, $SD = 2.95$). An analysis of variance (ANOVA) comparing the number of episodes by age and culture was not significant.

SYMBOLIC LEVEL PLAY, MUTUAL INVOLVEMENT, AND COOPERATIVE PRETEND PLAY

Proportions were calculated for the frequencies of symbolic level object play, mother-child mutual involvement in social play, and mother-child cooperative social pretend play by dividing each measure by the total number of episodes. To avoid violating the assumptions of ANOVAS proportional variables, an arcsine transformation was conducted. Proportions were compared using three separate 3(Age) $\times$ 2 (Culture) $\times$ 2(Sex) ANOVAs. Because no main effects or interactions were found for sex, it was dropped from further analyses.

Significant main effects appeared for age and culture. Proportions of symbolic level play, $F(2, 44) = 6.75$, $p < .01$; partner's mutual involvement, $F(2, 44) = 4.28$, $p < .01$; and cooperative pretend play, $F(2, 44) = 5.54$, $p < .05$, all increased with age. Scheffé post hoc tests ($p < .05$) comparing age groups showed more symbolic level play, partner involvement, and cooperative pretend play among 36-month-olds than 18-month-olds. American children accounted for the greater proportion of symbolic play with objects, $F(1, 44) = 9.71$, $p < .01$. American mother-child dyads had a greater proportion of episodes with mutual involvement, $F(1, 44) = 6.27$, $p < .05$, and cooperative pretend play, $F(1, 44) = 3.79$, $p < .05$, than did Mexican dyads.

MATERNAL PLAY BEHAVIORS

To examine the behaviors that mothers used to structure children's play and to understand how maternal behaviors differ by age and culture, four ANOVAs, 3(Age) × 2(Culture), were conducted. No significant main effects or interactions were found for age. However, significant main effects appeared for culture. American mothers used more implicit guidance (U.S., $M = 40.00$, $SD = 21.09$; Mexico, $M = 19.80$, $SD = 13.25$), $F(1, 58) = 19.31$, $p < .001$; supported child's effort (U.S., $M = 6.30$, $SD = 5.71$; Mexico, $M = 1.57$, $SD = 3.92$), $F(1, 58) = 13.54$, $p < .001$; and suggested fantasy (U.S., $M = 16.83$, $SD = 15.02$; Mexico, $M = 8.50$, $SD = 10.53$), $F(1, 58) = 6.92$, $p < .01$, than did Mexican mothers. Mexican mothers used more explicit guidance (Mexico, $M = 53.46$, $SD = 24.42$; U.S., $M = 36.26$, $SD = 16.69$), $F(1, 58) = 10.44$, $p < .01$, than did American mothers.

MATERNAL INTERVIEWS

Answers in each category were summed and compared by culture. The majority of the American mothers believed that play was very important and provided educational benefits for children. The most common play partners were mothers and siblings. In contrast, the majority of the Mexican mothers considered play to be an unimportant and children's amusement. The most common play partners were siblings and other children.

In summary, many American mothers interpreted the play task as a teaching opportunity whereas some simply played. Mothers who saw their role as a teacher tended to sit back from the play activity while offering commentary on the child's actions and providing suggestions for play. Other mothers used a question-and-answer format to talk about the physical properties of the shapes and used praise to reward correct answers. All mothers made frequent suggestions for play and provided assistance when necessary or requested by their child. Mothers who tended to play rather than teach their child suggested symbolic play themes, engaged in role play, and animated human figures and vehicle shapes using paralinguistic cues. In contrast, a few Mexican mothers made suggestions for symbolic play and animated the shapes, whereas others drew their children's attention to the properties of the shapes and then handed them individually to their children to examine.

Some American mothers reported that they frequently played with their children because it was mutually enjoyable, whereas others said they believed that children derived some benefit from it. In contrast, Mexican mothers rarely sat down to play formally with their children. Although, the Mexican mothers in this study did not discourage children's play, and said they enjoyed their children's playful efforts at modeling their behavior, they did not attach any particular value to play activity nor did they be-

TABLE 2   PROPORTION OF TOTAL EPISODES OF SYMBOLIC LEVEL PLAY, MOTHER-CHILD MUTUAL INVOLVEMENT, AND COOPERATIVE PRETEND PLAY BY AGE AND CULTURE

| | Age in Months | | | | | | F | | |
| | 18 | | 24 | | 36 | | | | |
	%	SD	%	SD	%	SD	Culture	Age	Age × Culture
Symbolic play									
U.S.	.34	(.22)	.42	(.35)	.58	(.27)	9.71**	6.75**	1.43
Mexico	.04	(.05)	.37	(.27)	.34	(.19)			
Mutual involvement									
U.S.	.65	(.39)	.88	(.11)	1.00	(.02)	6.27**	4.28*	1.60
Mexico	.63	(.15)	.74	(.19)	.71	(.34)			
Cooperative pretend									
U.S.	.01	(.05)	.02	(.06)	.44	(.41)	3.79*	5.54**	5.01**
Mexico	.00	(.00)	.11	(.31)	.05	(.12)			

Note. In all cases, Scheffé tests indicated age 36 mo. > 18 mo.
*$p < .05$. **$p < .01$.

TABLE 3 CULTURAL DIFFERENCES IN FREQUENCIES OF MATERNAL BELIEFS ABOUT PLAY, ITS IMPORTANCE, AND MOST COMMON PLAY PARTNERS

	Culture	
	U.S. (n = 30)	Mexico (n = 30)
Value of Play		
Child's amusement	2	27
Mutual enjoyment	8	0
Educational benefits	20	3
Importance		
None	0	27
Somewhat	5	3
Very	25	0
Play Partners		
Mother	18	0
Father	2	0
Siblings	10	20
Unrelated children	0	10

lieve it was important for them to play with their children.

DISCUSSION

The results support the initial assumption that cultural variations in activity-setting components are associated with not only the frequency and the expression of mother-child play, but also the contexts in which play occurs. In the American setting, where play activity is valued for its educational benefits, mothers spent time directly organizing children's play activities by providing objects and ideas for play as well as engaging in the play itself. Mothers' facilitation of the play contexts seemed to enhance their children's expression of symbolic level play and the frequency of joint cooperative pretend play.

In contrast, mother-child play was not a common feature of the Mexican setting. In the Mexican community, unlike the American community, children's symbolic or pretend play behavior does not originate in interaction with adults. When asked to play, these Mexican mothers readily complied, but their play became explicit teaching which was based on a work model rather than a play activity setting model. Mexican mother-child interactive play took place in the context of shared work activity rather than in more structured, child-centered pretend play situations that

are characteristic of American culture. For example, in the American setting mothers and their children were observed dressing dolls and putting them in baby-doll carriages, whereas, in the Mexican context, mothers and children played with real babies.

This finding is a challenge to the emphasis that Western researchers have placed on the mother-child relationship in facilitating children's early efforts at pretense. Results from a subsequent comparison of mother- and sibling-child play in the same two settings (Farver, in press) suggest that, in this particular Mexican environment, play develops in the context of sibling interaction. Sibling caretaking and mixed-age group play experiences may provide opportunities for Mexican older siblings to develop skills in directing play with younger siblings. In turn, younger children may begin to acquire skills and knowledge by participating in play activities with more competent partners. The scaffolding or supporting of play provided by a more skilled partner may be essential to the development of children's play, but who does the scaffolding and how it gets done may be culture-specific.

Differences found in the mother-child play and social interaction among the Mexican families should not be construed as cultural deficiencies. Instead, cultural differences apparent in the maternal play behaviors may be related to culture-specific childrearing practices that serve adaptive functions. In both cultures, mothers modified their children's play behavior toward goals and values that were consistent with their patterns of coping with the surrounding environment.

The issue of a possible confound of social class and culture is an important one. Based on the work of Mexican sociologists, relative to the current class structure within Mexico today these families can be considered working class. Although the living conditions of the Mexican families are more "humble" than those of the American families, based on the data reported here it is suggested that cultural values and childrearing practices, rather than material conditions, influence mother-child play.

The use of a single, 20-min quantitative procedure raises two issues. The first concerns the interdependence of the setting and the individual. That is, by asking mothers to play with unfamiliar toys are they being removed from their context and, therefore, do their activities become meaningless? A subsequent analysis of mother-child play with the same subjects in a natural play context suggests not. This research yielded results similar to the structured mother-child "toy play" procedure presented here (Farver, 1991).

The second issue concerns the representativeness of a short 20-min play session. The data reported here were only one part of a larger study examining children's play alone and with multiple partners in toy (shape) play and free-play contexts. Two hours of videotaped play for each child are the bases of the generalizations made here.

In spite of the attempts to balance social class, to collect qualitative observations to inform the quantitative data, and to use "culture free" toys, alternative interpretations of the results are possible. The sample size was small and the communities discussed here represent only two examples of Mexican and American societies. Also, a considerable range of intracultural variability and a great variety of individual differences exist in any cultural group. Therefore, these results need to be replicated in other samples.

REFERENCES

Alba, F. (1982). *The population of Mexico: Trends, issues, and policies*. NJ: Transaction Press.

Balán, J. (1973). *Migration, occupational structure and social mobility*. Mexico City: National Autonomous University of Mexico Press.

Bradley, R., & Caldwell, B. (1984). The relation of infants' home environment to achievement test performance in first grade: A follow-up study. *Child Development, 55*, 803–809.

Bronstein-Burrows, P. (1981). Patterns of parent behavior: A cross-cultural study. *Merrill-Palmer Quarterly, 27*, 129–143.

Diáz-Guerrero, R. (1975). *Psychology of the Mexican: Culture and personality*. Austin: University of Texas Press.

Eckstein, S. (1989). *The poverty of revolution*. Princeton, NJ: Princeton University Press.

Falicov, C. J., & Karrer, B. M. (1980). Cultural variations in the family life cycle: The Mexican-American family. In E. Carter & M. Goldrick (Eds.), *The family life cycle: A framework for family therapy*. New York: Gardner.

Farver, J. (1991, April). Free play activities of American and Mexican mother-child pairs. In L. Beizer & P. Miller (Chairs), *Cultural dimensions of pretend play in infancy and early childhood*. Symposium conducted at the meeting of the Society for Research in Child Development, Seattle, WA.

Farver, J. (in press). Cultural differences in scaffolding play: A comparison of American and Mexican mother-child and sibling-child pairs. In K. MacDonald (Ed.), *Parents and children playing*. Albany, NY: SUNY Press.

Feitelson, D. (1977). Cross-cultural studies of representational play. In B. Tizard & D. Harvey (Eds.), *The biology of play*. Suffolk, England: Levenham Press.

Glaser, B., & Strauss, A. (1967). *The discovery of grounded theory*. New York: Aldine.

Haight, W., & Miller, P. (1991, April). Belief systems that frame and inform middle-class parents' participation in their young children's pretend play. In L. Beizer & P. Miller (Chairs), *Cultural dimensions of pretend play in infancy and early childhood*. Symposium conducted at the meeting of the Society for Research in Child Development, Seattle, WA.

Hoffman, L. (1988). Cross-cultural differences in childrearing goals. In R. LeVine, P. Miller, & M. Maxwell (Eds.), *Parental behavior in diverse societies: New directions for child development*. San Francisco: Jossey-Bass.

Holtzman, W. (1982). Cross-cultural comparisons of personality development in Mexico and the United States. In D. Wagner & H. Stevenson (Eds.), *Cultural perspectives on child development*. San Francisco: Freeman.

Holtzman, W., Díaz-Guerrero, R., Swartz, J., & Tapia, L. (1969). Cross-cultural longitudinal research on child development: Studies of American and Mexican school children. In J. P. Hill (Ed.), *Minnesota Symposia on Child Psychology*. Minneapolis: University of Minnesota Press.

Howes, C. (1980). Peer play scale as an index of complexity of social interaction. *Developmental Psychology, 16*, 371–372.

Howes, C. (1985). Sharing fantasy: Social pretend play in toddlers. *Child Development, 56*, 1253–1258.

Kagan, S. (1981). Ecology and the acculturation of cognitive and social styles among Mexican-American children. *Hispanic Journal of Behavioral Sciences, 3*, 111–144.

Kagan, S., & Ember, P. (1975). Maternal response to success and failure of Anglo-American, Mexican-American and Mexican children. *Child Development, 46*, 452–458.

Keefe, S., Padrilla, A., & Carlos, M. (1979). The Mexican-American extended family as an emotional support system. *Human Organization, 38*, 144–152.

Lawton, J., Fowell, N., Schuler, A., & Madsen, M. (1984). Parents' perceptions of actual and ideal childrearing practices. *Journal of Genetic Psychology, 145*, 77–87.

Leont'ev, A. N. (1981). The problem of activity in psychology. In J. Wertsch (Ed.), *The concept of activity in Soviet psychology*. Armank, NY: Sharpe.

Levenstein, P. (1986). Mother-child interaction and children's educational achievement. In A. Gottfried & C. Brown (Eds.), *Play interactions: The contributions of play materials and parental involvement to children's development*. Boston: Lexington.

Levenstein, P. (in press). The necessary lightness of mother-child play. In K. MacDonald (Ed.), *Parents and children playing*. Albany: SUNY Press.

Levine, R. A. (1980). *Anthropology and child development: New directions for child development*. San Francisco: Jossey-Bass.

Miller, P., & Garvey, C. (1984). Mother-baby role play: Its origins in social support. In I. Bretherton (Ed.), *Symbolic play*. New York: Academic Press.

O'Connell, B., & Bretherton, I. (1984). Toddlers' play, alone and with mothers. In I. Bretherton (Ed.), *Symbolic play*. New York: Academic Press.

Peñalosa, P. (1968). Mexican family roles. *Journal of Marriage and the Family, 30*, 680–689.

Ramírez, M. (1967). Identification with Mexican family values and authoritarianism in Mexican-Americans. *Journal of Social Psychology, 73*, 3–11.

Ramírez, M., & Castañeda, A. (1974). *Cultural democracy, bicognitive development and education*. New York: Academic Press.

Ramírez, M., & Price-Williams, D. (1974). Cognitive styles in children: Two Mexican communities. *Interamerican Journal of Psychology, 8*, 93–101.

Richman, A., Miller, P., & Solomon, M. (1988). The socialization of infants in suburban Boston. In R. LeVine, P. Miller, & M. Maxwell (Eds.), *Parental behavior in diverse societies: New directions for child development*. San Francisco: Jossey-Bass.

Rogoff, B., Mistry, J., Göncü, A., & Mosier, C. (1991). Cultural variation in the role relations of toddlers and their families. In M. Bornstein (Ed.), *Cultural approaches to parenting*. Hillsdale, NJ: Erlbaum.

Romney, K., & Romney, R. (1966). *The Mixtecans of Juxtlahuaca*. New York: Wiley.

Slade, A. (1987). A longitudinal study of maternal involvement and symbolic play. *Child Development, 58*, 367–375.

Smilansky, S. (1968). *The effect of sociodramatic play on disadvantaged school children*. New York: Wiley.

Suárez, E. C. (1978). *Stratification and social mobility in Mexico City*. Mexico City: National Autonomous University of Mexico Press.

Tharp, R., & Gallimore, R. (1988). *Rousing minds to life*. Cambridge: Cambridge University Press.

Vygotsky, L. (1978). *Mind in society*. Cambridge: Cambridge University Press.

Weisner, T., Gallimore R., & Jordan, C. (1988). Unpacking cultural effects on classroom learning: Native Hawaiian peer assistance and child generated activity. *Education and Anthropology Quarterly, 19*, 327–353.

Werner, H., & Kaplan, B. (1963). *Symbol formation*. New York: Wiley.

White, B. L. (1980). *A parent's guide to the first three years*. Trenton: Prentice-Hall.

Whiting, B., & Edwards, C. P. (1988). *Children of different worlds: The formation of social behavior*. Cambridge: Harvard University Press.

Zukow, P. (1989). *Sibling interaction across cultures*. New York: Springer-Verlag.

QUESTIONS

1. According to traditional Western theories of development, how does pretend play in young children originate?
2. What is an activity-setting approach to research in child development?
3. Examine the features of American and Mexican activity settings for child development. What are the common features in these two communities? What features differ?
4. What did Farver and Howes do to minimize the impact of observing the families in the Mexican setting? Do you think this was a good thing to do? Why?
5. What types of play were significantly different in these two communities?
6. How do the different play patterns observed in these two communities relate to the cultural values in each setting? What does this tell us about the role of play in child socialization?

21 Gender and Relationships: A Developmental Account

ELEANOR MACCOBY

Gender-related differences in human behavior have been of interest to psychologists for generations. One of the main questions asked by developmentalists about these differences is how they originate. The behavior of young children provides some of the best evidence for answering this question. Observing the activities of children during the preschool and early school years indicates that many gender-related behaviors begin to appear during this time.

Eleanor Maccoby has spent her career studying young children's social relationships and development, and she has taken particular interest in the topic of gender differences in relationships. One observation she finds especially intriguing is that gender-related behaviors are more evident when children are observed in groups than when children are tested individually. This suggests that something about social experience is critical to the expression, and perhaps the development of, gender-related behaviors.

To pursue this topic, the following article explores the role of social relationships in the development and organization of gender-related behaviors. Maccoby argues that peers, especially other-sex peers, play a pivotal role in the development and maintenance of these behaviors. This is an interesting perspective in that it is contrary to the long-standing view that experience with parents shapes children's gender-typed behaviors.

This article argues that behavioral differentiation of the sexes is minimal when children are observed or tested individually. Sex differences emerge primarily in social situations, and their nature varies with the gender composition of dyads and groups. Children find same-sex play partners more compatible, and they segregate themselves into same-sex groups, in which distinctive interaction styles emerge. These styles are described. As children move into adolescence, the patterns they developed in their childhood same-sex groups are carried over into cross-sex encounters in which girls' styles put them at a disadvantage. Patterns of mutual influence can become more symmetrical in intimate male-female dyads, but the distinctive styles of the two sexes can still be seen in such dyads and are subsequently manifested in the roles and relationships of parenthood. The implications of these continuities are considered.

Historically, the way we psychologists think about the psychology of gender has grown out of our thinking about individual differences. We are accustomed to assessing a wide variety of attributes and skills and giving scores to individuals based on their standing relative to other individuals in a sample population. On most psychological attributes, we see wide variation among individuals, and a major focus of research has been the effort to identify correlates or sources of this variation. Commonly, what we have done is to classify individuals by some antecedent variable, such as age or some aspect of their environment, to determine how much of the variance among individuals in their performance on a given task can be accounted for by this so-called *antecedent* or *independent* variable. Despite the fact that hermaphrodites exist, almost every individual is either clearly male or clearly female. What could be more natural for psychologists than to ask how much variance among individuals is accounted for by this beautifully binary factor?

Fifteen years ago, Carol Jacklin and I put out a book summarizing the work on sex differences that had come out of the individual differences perspective (Maccoby & Jacklin, 1974). We felt at that time that the yield was thin. That is, there were very few attributes on which the average values for the two sexes differed consistently. Furthermore, even when consistent differences were found, the amount of variance accounted for by sex was small, relative to the amount of variation within each sex. Our conclusions fitted in quite well with the feminist zeitgeist of the times, when most feminists were taking a minimalist position, urging that the two sexes were basically alike and that any differences were either illusions in the eye of the beholder or reversible outcomes of social shaping. Our conclusions were challenged as having both overstated the case for sex differences (Tieger, 1980) and for having understated it (Block, 1976).

In the last 15 years, work on sex differences has become more methodologically sophisticated, with greater use of meta analyses to reveal not only the direction of sex differences but quantitative estimates of their magnitude. In my judgment, the conclusions are still quite similar to those Jacklin and I arrived at in 1974: There are still some replicable sex differences, of moderate magnitude, in performance on tests of mathematical and spatial abilities, although sex differences in verbal abilities have faded. Other aspects of intellectual performance continue to show gender equality. When it comes to attributes in the personality-social domain, results are particularly sparse and inconsistent. Studies continue to find that men are more often agents of aggression than are women (Eagly, 1987; Huston, 1985; Maccoby & Jacklin, 1980). Eagly (1983, 1987) reported in addition that women are more easily influenced than men and that men are more altruistic in the sense that they are more likely to offer help to others. In general, however, personality traits measured as characteristics of individuals do not appear to differ systematically by sex (Huston, 1985). This no doubt reflects in part the fact that male and female persons really are much alike, and their lives are governed mainly by the attributes that all persons in a given culture have in common. Nevertheless, I believe that the null findings coming out of comparisons of male and female individuals on personality measures are partly illusory. That is, they are an artifact of our historical reliance on an individual differences perspective. Social behavior, as many have pointed out, is never a function of the individual alone. It is a function of the interaction between two or more persons. Individuals behave differently with different partners. There are certain important ways in which gender is implicated in social behavior—ways that may be obscured or missed altogether when behavior is summed across all categories of social partners.

An illustration is found in a study of social interaction between previously unacquainted pairs of young children (mean age, 33 months; Jacklin & Maccoby, 1978). In some pairs, the children had same-sex play partners; in others, the pair was made up of a boy and a girl. Observers recorded the social behavior of each child on a time-sampling basis. Each child received a score for total social behavior directed toward the partner. This score included both positive and negative behaviors (e.g., offering a toy and grabbing a toy; hugging and pushing; vocally greeting, inviting, protesting, or prohibiting). There was no overall sex difference in the amount of social behavior when this was evaluated without regard to sex of partner. But there was a powerful interaction between sex of the subject and that of the partner: Children of each sex had much higher levels of social behavior when playing with a same-sex partner than when playing with a child of the other sex. This result is consistent with the findings of Wasserman and Stern (1978) that when asked to approach another child, children as young as age three stopped farther away when the other child was of the opposite sex, indicating awareness of gender similarity or difference, and wariness toward the other sex.

The number of time intervals during which a child was simply standing passively watching the partner play with the toys was also scored. There was no overall sex difference in the frequency of this behavior, but the behavior of girls was greatly affected by the sex of the partner. With other girls, passive behavior seldom occurred; indeed, in girl–girl pairs it occurred less often than it did in boy–boy pairs. However when paired with boys, girls frequently stood on the sidelines and let the boys monopolize the toys. Clearly, the little girls in this study were not more passive than the little boys in any overall, trait-like sense. Passivity in these girls could be understood only in relation to the characteristics of their interactive partners. It was a characteristic of girls in cross-sex dyads. This conclusion may not seem especially novel because for many years we have known that social behavior is situationally specific. However, the point here is that interactive behavior is not just situationally specific, but that it depends on the gender category membership of the participants. We can account for a good deal more of the behavior if we know the gender mix of dyads, and this probably holds true for larger groups as well.

An implication of our results was that if children at this early age found same-sex play partners more compatible, they ought to prefer same-sex partners when they entered group settings that included children of both sexes. There were already many indications in the literature that children do have same-sex playmate preferences, but there clearly was a need for more systematic attention to the degree of sex segregation that prevails in naturally occurring children's groups at different ages. As part of a longitudinal study of children from birth to age six, Jacklin and I did time-sampled behavioral observation of approximately 100 children on their preschool playgrounds, and again two years later when the children were playing during school recess periods (Maccoby & Jacklin, 1987). Same-sex playmate preference was clearly apparent in preschool when the children were approximately $4\frac{1}{2}$. At this age, the children were spending nearly 3 times as much time with same-sex play partners as with children of the other sex. By age $6\frac{1}{2}$, the preference had grown much stronger. At this time, the children were spending 11 times as much time with same-sex as with opposite-sex partners.

Elsewhere we have reviewed the literature on playmate choices (Maccoby, 1988; Maccoby & Jacklin, 1987), and here I will simply summarize what I believe the existing body of research shows:

1. Gender segregation is a widespread phenomenon. It is found in all the cultural settings in which children are in social groups large enough to permit choice.

2. The sex difference in the gender of preferred playmates is large in absolute magnitude, compared to sex differences found when children are observed or tested in nonsocial situations.

3. In a few instances, attempts have been made to break down children's preferences for interacting with other same-sex children. It has been found that the preferences are difficult to change.

4. Children choose same-sex playmates spontaneously in situations in which they are not under pressure from adults to do so. In modern co-educational schools, segregation is more marked in situations that have not been structured by adults than in those that have (e.g., Eisenhart & Holland, 1983). Segregation is situationally specific, and the two sexes can interact comfortably under certain conditions, for example, in an absorbing joint task, when structures and roles are set up by adults, or in non-public settings (Thorne, 1986).

5. Gender segregation is not closely linked to involvement in sex-typed activities. Preschool children spend a great deal of their time engaged in activities that are gender neutral, and segregation prevails in these activities as well as when they are playing with dolls or trucks.

6. Tendencies to prefer same-sex playmates can be seen among three-year-olds and at even earlier ages under some conditions. But the preferences increase in strength between preschool and school and are maintained at a high level between the ages of 6 and at least age 11.

7. The research base is thin, but so far it appears that a child's tendency to prefer same-sex playmates has little to do with that child's standing on measures of individual differences. In particular, it appears to be unrelated to measures of masculinity or femininity and also to measures of gender schematicity (Powlishta, 1989).

Why do we see such pronounced attraction to same-sex peers and avoidance of other-sex peers in childhood? Elsewhere I have summarized evidence pointing to two factors that seem to be important in the preschool years (Maccoby, 1988). The first is the rough-and-tumble play style characteristic of boys and their orientation toward issues of competition and dominance. These aspects of male–male interaction appear to be somewhat aversive to most girls. At least, girls are made wary by male play styles. The second factor of importance is that girls find it difficult to influence boys. Some important work by Serbin and colleagues (Serbin, Sprafkin, Elman, & Doyle, 1984) indicates that between the ages of $3\frac{1}{2}$ and $5\frac{1}{2}$, children greatly increase the frequency of their attempts to influence their play partners. This indicates that children are learning to integrate their activities with those of others so as to be able to carry out coordinated activities. Serbin and colleagues found that the increase in influence attempts by girls was almost entirely an increase in making polite suggestions to others, whereas among boys the increase took the form of more use of direct demands. Furthermore, during this formative two-year period just before school entry, boys were becoming less and less responsive to polite suggestions, so that the style being progressively adopted by girls was progressively less effective with boys. Girls' influence style was effective with each other and was well adapted to interaction with teachers and other adults.

These asymmetries in influence patterns were presaged in our study with 33-month-old children: We found then that boys were unresponsive to the vocal prohibitions of female partners (in that they did not withdraw), although they would respond when a vocal prohibition was issued by a male partner. Girls were responsive to one another and to a male partner's prohibitions. Fagot (1985) also reported that boys are "reinforced" by the reactions of male peers—in the sense that they modify their behavior following a male peer's reaction—but that their behavior appears not to be affected by a female's response.

My hypothesis is that girls find it aversive to try to interact with someone who is unresponsive and that they begin to avoid such partners. Students of power and bargaining have long been aware of the importance of reciprocity in human relations. Pruitt (1976) said, "Influence and power are omnipresent in human affairs. Indeed, groups cannot possibly function unless their members can influence one another" (p. 343). From this standpoint, it becomes clear why boys and girls have difficulty forming groups that include children of both sexes.

Why do little boys not accept influence from little girls? Psychologists almost automatically look to the nuclear family for the origins of behavior patterns seen in young children. It is plausible that boys may have been more reinforced for power assertive behavior by their parents, and girls more for politeness, although the evidence for such differential socialization pressure has proved difficult to come by. However, it is less easy to imagine how or why parents should reinforce boys for being unresponsive to *girls*. Perhaps it is a matter of observational learning: Children may have observed that between their two parents, their fathers are more influential than their mothers. I am skeptical about such an explanation. In the first place, mothers exercise a good deal of managerial authority within the households in which children live, and it is common for fathers to defer to their judgment in matters concerning the children. Or, parents form a coalition, and in the eyes of the children they become a joint authority, so that it makes little difference to them whether it is a mother or a father who is wielding authority at any given time. Furthermore, the asymmetry in children's cross-sex influence with their peers appears to have its origins at quite an early age—earlier, I would suggest, than children have a very clear idea about the connection between their own sex and that of the same-sex parent. In other words, it seems quite unlikely that little boys ignore girls' influence attempts because little girls remind them of their mothers. I think we simply do not know why girls' influence styles are ineffective with boys, but the fact that they are has important implications for a variety of social behaviors, not just for segregation.

Here are some examples from recent studies. Powlishta (1987) observed preschool-aged boy–girl pairs competing for a scarce resource. The children were brought to a playroom in the nursery school and were given an opportunity to watch cartoons through a movie-viewer that could only be accessed by one child at a time. Powlishta found that when the two children were alone together in the playroom, the boys got more than their share of access to the movie-viewer. When there was an adult present, however, this was no longer the case. The adult's presence appeared to inhibit the boys' more power-assertive techniques and resulted in girls having at least equal access.

This study points to a reason why girls may not only avoid playing with boys but may also stay nearer to a teacher or other adult. Following up on this possibility, Greeno (1989) brought four-child groups of kindergarten and first-grade children into a large playroom equipped with attractive toys. Some of the quartets were all-boy groups, some all-girl groups, and some were made up of two boys and two girls. A female adult sat at one end of the room, and halfway through the play session, moved to a seat at the other end of the room. The question posed for this study was: Would girls move closer to the teacher when boys were present than when they were not? Would the sex composition of a play group make any difference to the locations taken up by the boys? The results were that in all-girl groups, girls actually took up locations *farther* from the adult than did boys in all-boy groups. When two boys were present, however, the two girls were significantly closer to the adult than were the boys, who tended to remain at intermediate distances. When the adult changed position halfway through the session, boys' locations did not change, and this was true whether there were girls present or not. Girls in all-girl groups tended to move in the opposite direction when the adult moved, maintaining distance between themselves and the adult; when boys were present, however, the girls tended to move *with* the adult, staying relatively close. It is worth noting, incidentally, that in all the mixed-sex groups except one, segregation was extreme; both boys and girls behaved as though there was only one playmate available to them, rather than three.

There are some fairly far-reaching implications of this study. Previous observational studies in preschools had indicated that girls are often found in locations closer to the teacher than are boys. These studies have been done in mixed-sex nursery school groups. Girls' proximity seeking toward adults has often been interpreted as a reflection of some general affiliative trait in girls and perhaps as a reflection of some aspect of early socialization that has bound them more closely to caregivers. We see in the Greeno study that proximity seeking toward adults was *not* a general trait in girls. It was a function of the gender composition of the group of other children present as potential interaction partners. The behavior of girls implied that they found the presence of boys to be less aversive when an adult was nearby. It was as though they realized that the rough, power-assertive behavior of boys was likely to be moderated in the presence of adults, and indeed, there is evidence that they were right.

We have been exploring some aspects of girls' avoidance of interaction with boys. Less is known about why boys avoid interaction with girls, but the fact is that they do. In fact, their cross-sex avoidance appears to be even stronger. Thus, during middle childhood both boys and girls spend considerable portions of their social play time in groups of their own sex. This might not matter much for future relationships were it not for the fact that fairly distinctive styles of interaction develop in all-boy and all-girl groups. Thus, the segregated play groups constitute powerful socialization environments in which children acquire distinctive interaction skills that are adapted to same-sex partners. Sex-typed modes of interaction become consolidated, and I wish to argue that the distinctive patterns developed by the two sexes at this time have implications for the same-sex and cross-sex relationships that individuals form as they enter adolescence and adulthood.

It behooves us, then, to examine in somewhat more detail the nature of the interactive milieus that prevail in all-boy and all-girl groups. Elsewhere I have reviewed some of the findings of studies in which these two kinds of groups have been observed (Maccoby, 1988). Here I will briefly summarize what we know.

The two sexes engage in fairly different kinds of activities and games (Huston, 1985). Boys play in somewhat larger groups, on the average, and their play is rougher (Humphreys & Smith, 1987) and takes up more space. Boys more often play in the streets and other public places; girls more often congregate in private homes or yards. Girls tend to form close, intimate friendships with one or two other girls, and these friendships are marked by the sharing of confidences (Kraft & Vraa, 1975). Boys' friendships, on the other hand, are more oriented around mutual interests in activities (Erwin, 1985). The breakup of girls' friendships is usually attended by more intense emotional reactions than is the case for boys.

For our present purposes, the most interesting thing about all-boy and all-girl groups is the divergence in the interactive styles that develop in them. In male groups, there is more concern with issues of dominance. Several psycholinguists have recorded the verbal exchanges that occur in these groups, and Maltz and Borker (1983) summarized the findings of several studies as follows: Boys in their groups are more likely than girls in all-girl groups to interrupt one another; use commands, threats, or boasts of authority; refuse to comply with another child's demand; give information; heckle a speaker; tell jokes or suspenseful stories; top someone else's story; or call another child names. Girls in all-girl groups, on the other hand, are more likely than boys to express agreement with what another speaker has just said, pause to give another girl a chance to speak, or when starting a speaking turn, acknowledge a point previously made by another speaker. This account indicates that among boys, speech serves largely egoistic functions and is used to establish and protect an individual's turf. Among girls, conversation is a more socially binding process.

In the past five years, analysts of discourse have done additional work on the kinds of interactive processes that are seen among girls, as compared with those among boys. The summary offered by Maltz and Borker has been both supported and extended.

Sachs (1987) reported that girls soften their directives to partners, apparently attempting to keep them involved in a process of planning a play sequence, while boys are more likely simply to tell their partners what to do. Leaper (1989) observed children aged five and seven and found that verbal exchanges among girls more often take the form of what he called "collaborative speech acts" that involve positive reciprocity, whereas among boys, speech acts are more controlling and include more negative reciprocity. Miller and colleagues (Miller, Danaher, & Forbes, 1986) found that there was more conflict in boys' groups, and given that conflict had occurred, girls were more likely to use "conflict mitigating strategies," whereas boys more often used threats and physical force. Sheldon (1989) reported that when girls talk, they seem to have a double agenda: to be "nice" and sustain social relationships, while at the same time working to achieve their own individual ends. For boys, the agenda is more often the single one of self-assertion. Sheldon (1989) has noted that in interactions among themselves, girls are *not* unassertive. Rather, girls do successfully pursue their own ends, but they do so while toning down coercion and dominance, trying to bring about agreement, and restoring or maintaining group functioning. It should be noted that boys' confrontational style does not necessarily impede effective group functioning, as evidenced by boys' ability to cooperate with teammates for sports. A second point is that although researchers' own gender has been found to influence to some degree the kinds of questions posed and the answers obtained, the summary provided here includes the work of both male and female researchers, and their findings are consistent with one another.

As children move into adolescence and adulthood, what happens to the interactive styles that they developed in their largely segregated childhood groups? A first point to note is that despite the powerful attraction to members of the opposite sex in adolescence, gender segregation by no means disappears. Young people continue to spend a good portion of their social time with same-sex partners. In adulthood, there is extensive gender segregation in workplaces (Reskin, 1984), and in some societies and some social-class or ethnic groups, leisure time also is largely spent with same-sex others even after marriage. The literature on the nature of the interactions that occur among same-sex partners in adolescence and adulthood is quite extensive and cannot be reviewed here. Suffice it to say in summary that there is now considerable evidence that the interactive patterns found in sex-homogeneous dyads or groups in adolescence and adulthood are very similar to those that prevailed in the gender-segregated groups of childhood (e.g., Aries, 1976; Carli, 1989; Cowan, Drinkard, & MacGavin, 1984; Savin-Williams, 1979).

How can we summarize what it is that boys and girls, or men and women, are doing in their respective groups that distinguishes these groups from one another? There have been a number of efforts to find the major dimensions that best describe variations in interactive styles. Falbo and Peplau (1980) have factor analyzed a battery of measures and have identified two dimensions: one called direct versus indirect, the other unilateral versus bilateral. Hauser et al. (1987) have distinguished what they called *enabling* interactive styles from *constricting* or *restrictive* ones, and I believe this distinction fits the styles of the two sexes especially well. A restrictive style is one that tends to derail the interaction—to inhibit the partner or cause the partner to withdraw, thus shortening the interaction or bringing it to an end. Examples are threatening a partner, directly contradicting or interrupting, topping the partner's story, boasting, or engaging in other forms of self-display. Enabling or facilitative styles are those, such as acknowledging another's comment or expressing agreement, that support whatever the partner is doing and tend to keep the interaction going. I want to suggest that it is because women and girls use more enabling styles that they are able to form more intimate and more integrated relationships. Also I think it likely that it is the male concern for turf and dominance—that is, with not showing weakness to other men and boys—that underlies their restrictive interaction style and their lack of self-disclosure.

Carli (1989) has recently found that in discussions between pairs of adults, individuals are more easily influenced by a partner if that partner has just expressed agreement with them. In this work, women were quite successful in influencing one another in same-sex dyads, whereas pairs of men were less so. The sex difference was fully accounted for by the fact that men's male partners did not express agreement as often. Eagly (1987) has summarized data from a large number of studies on women's and men's susceptibility to influence and has found women to be somewhat more susceptible. Carli's work suggests that this tendency may not be a general female personality trait of "suggestibility" but may reflect the fact that women more often interact with other women who tend to express reciprocal agreement. Carli's finding resonates with some work with young children interacting with their mothers. Mary Parpal and I (Parpal & Maccoby, 1985) found that children were more compliant to a mother's demands if the two had previously engaged in a game in which the child was allowed to give directions that the mother followed. In other words, maternal compliance set up a system of reciprocity in which the child also complied. I submit that the same principle applies in adult interactions and that among women, influence is achieved in part by being open to influence from the partner.

Boys and men, on the other hand, although less successful in influencing one another in dyads, develop group structures—well-defined roles in games, dominance hierarchies, and team spirit—that appear to enable them to function effectively in groups. One may suppose that the male directive interactive style is less likely to derail interaction if and when group structural forces are in place. In other words, men and boys may *need* group structure more than women and girls do. However, this hypothesis has yet to be tested in research. In any case, boys and men in their groups have more opportunity to learn how to function within hierarchical structures than do women and girls in theirs.

We have seen that throughout much of childhood and into adolescence and adulthood as well, people spend a good deal of their social time interacting with others of their own gender, and they continue to use distinctive interaction styles in these settings. What happens, then, when individuals from these two distinctive "cultures" attempt to interact with one another? People of both sexes are faced with a relatively unfamiliar situation to which they must adapt. Young women are less likely to receive the reciprocal agreement, opportunities to talk, and so on that they have learned to expect when interacting with female partners. Men have been accustomed to counter-dominance and competitive reactions to their own power assertions, and they now find themselves with partners who agree with them and otherwise offer enabling responses. It seems evident that this new partnership should be easier to adapt to for men than for women. There is evidence that men fall in love faster and report feeling more in love than do women early in intimate relationships (Huston & Ashmore, 1986). Furthermore, the higher rates of depression in females have their onset in adolescence, when rates of cross-sex interaction rise (Nolen-Hoeksema, in press). Although these phenomena are no doubt multidetermined, the asymmetries in interaction styles may contribute to them.

To some degree, men appear to bring to bear much the same kind of techniques in mixed-sex groups that they are accustomed to using in same-sex groups. If the group is attempting some sort of joint problem solving or is carrying out a joint task, men do more initiating, directing, and interrupting than do women. Men's voices are louder and are more listened to than women's voices by both sexes (West & Zimmerman, 1985); men are more likely than women to lose interest in a taped message if it is spoken in a woman's rather than a man's voice (Robinson & MacArthur, 1982). Men are less influenced by the opinions of other group members than are women. Perhaps as a consequence of their greater assertiveness, men have more influence on the group process (Lockheed, 1985; Pugh & Wahrman, 1983), just as they did in childhood. Eagly and colleagues (Eagly, Wood, & Fishbaugh, 1981) have drawn our attention to an important point about cross-sex interaction in groups: The greater resistance of men to being influenced by other group members is found only when the men are under surveillance, that is, if others know whether they have yielded to their partners' influence attempts. I suggest that it is especially the monitoring by other *men* that inhibits men from entering into reciprocal influence with partners. When other men are present, men appear to feel that they must guard their dominance status and not comply too readily lest it be interpreted as weakness.

Women's behavior in mixed groups is more complex. There is some work indicating that they adapt by becoming more like men—that they raise their voices, interrupt, and otherwise become more assertive than they would be when interacting with women (Carli, 1989; Hall & Braunwald, 1981). On the other hand, there is also evidence that they carry over some of their well-practiced female-style behaviors, sometimes in exaggerated form. Women may wait for a turn to speak that does not come, and thus they may end up talking less than they would in a women's group. They smile more than the men do, agree more often with what others have said, and give nonverbal signals of attentiveness to what others— perhaps especially the men—are saying (Duncan & Fiske, 1977). In some writings this female behavior has been referred to as "silent applause."

Eagly (1987) reported a meta-analysis of behavior of the two sexes in groups (mainly mixed-sex groups) that were performing joint tasks. She found a consistent tendency for men to engage in more task behavior—giving and receiving information, suggestions, and opinions (see also Aries, 1982)—whereas women are more likely to engage in socioemotional behaviors that support positive affective relations within the group. Which style contributes more to effective group process? It depends. Wood, Polek, and Aiken (1985) have compared the performance of all-female and all-male groups on different kinds of tasks, finding that groups of women have more success on tasks that require discussion and negotiation, whereas male groups do better on tasks where success depends on the volume of ideas being generated. Overall, it appears that *both* styles are productive, though in different ways.

There is evidence that women feel at a disadvantage in mixed-sex interaction. For example, Hogg and Turner (1987) set up a debate between two young men taking one position and two young women taking another. The outcomes in this situation were contrasted with a situation in which young men and women were debating against same-sex partners. After the cross-sex debate, the self-esteem of the young men rose, but that of the young women declined. Fur-

thermore, the men liked their women opponents better after debating with them, whereas the women liked the men less. In other words, the encounter in most cases was a pleasurable experience for the men, but not for the women. Another example comes from the work of Davis (1978), who set up get-acquainted sessions between pairs of young men and women. He found that the men took control of the interaction, dictating the pace at which intimacy increased, whereas the women adapted themselves to the pace set by the men. The women reported later, however, that they had been uncomfortable about not being able to control the sequence of events, and they did not enjoy the encounter as much as the men did.

In adolescence and early adulthood, the powerful forces of sexual attraction come into play. When couples are beginning to fall in love, or even when they are merely entertaining the possibility of developing an intimate relationship, each is motivated to please the other, and each sends signals implying "Your wish is my command." There is evidence that whichever member of a couple is more attractive, or less in love, is at an advantage and is more able to influence the partner than vice versa (Peplau, 1979). The influence patterns based on the power of interpersonal attraction are not distinct in terms of gender; that is, it may be either the man or the woman in a courting relationship who has the influence advantage. When first meeting, or in the early stages of the acquaintance process, women still may feel at some disadvantage, as shown in the Davis study, but this situation need not last. Work done in the 1960s indicated that in many couples, as relationships become deeper and more enduring, any overall asymmetry in influence diminishes greatly (Heiss, 1962; Leik, 1963; Shaw & Sadler, 1965). Most couples develop a relationship that is based on communality rather than exchange bargaining. That is, they have many shared goals and work jointly to achieve them. They do not need to argue over turf because they have the same turf. In well-functioning married couples, both members of the pair strive to avoid conflict, and indeed there is evidence that the men on average are even more conflict-avoidant than the women (Gottman & Levenson, 1988; Kelley et al., 1978). Nevertheless, there are still carry-overs of the different interactive styles males and females have acquired at earlier points in the life cycle. Women seem to expend greater effort toward maintaining harmonious moods (Huston & Ashmore, 1986, p. 177). With intimate cross-sex partners, men use more direct styles of influence, and women use more indirect ones. Furthermore, women are more likely to withdraw (become silent, cold, and distant) and/or take unilateral action in order to get their way in a dispute (Falbo & Peplau, 1980), strategies that we suspect may reflect their greater difficulty in influencing a male partner through direct negotiation.

Space limitations do not allow considering in any depth the next set of important relationships that human beings form: that between parents and children. Let me simply say that I think there is evidence for the following: The interaction styles that women have developed in interaction with girls and other women serve them well when they become mothers. Especially when children are young, women enter into deeper levels of reciprocity with their children than do men (e.g., Gleason, 1987; Maccoby & Jacklin, 1983) and communicate with them better. On the other hand, especially after the first two years, children need firm direction as well as warmth and reciprocity, and fathers' styles may contribute especially well to this aspect of parenting. The relationship women develop with young children seems to depend very little on whether they are dealing with a son or a daughter; it builds on maternal response to the characteristics and needs of early childhood that are found in both boys and girls to similar degrees. Fathers, having a less intimate relationship with individual children, treat young boys and girls in a somewhat more gendered way (Siegal, 1987). As children approach middle childhood and interact with same-sex other children, they develop the interactive styles characteristic of their sex, and their parents more and more interact with them as they have always done with same-sex or opposite-sex others. That is, mothers and daughters develop greater intimacy and reciprocity; fathers and sons exhibit more friendly rivalry and joking, more joint interest in masculine activities, and more rough play. Nevertheless, there are many aspects of the relationships between parents and children that do not depend on the gender of either the parent or the child.

Obviously, as the scene unfolds across generations, it is very difficult to identify the point in the developmental cycle at which the interactional styles of the two sexes begin to diverge, and more important, to identify the forces that cause them to diverge. In my view, processes within the nuclear family have been given too much credit—or too much blame—for this aspect of sex-typing. I doubt that the development of distinctive interactive styles has much to do with the fact that children are parented primarily by women, as some have claimed (Chodorow, 1978; Gilligan, 1982), and it seems likely to me that children's "identification" with the same-sex parent is more a consequence than a cause of children's acquisition of sex-typed interaction styles. I would place most of the emphasis on the peer group as the setting in which children first discover the compatibility of same-sex others, in which boys first discover the requirements of maintaining one's status in the male hierarchy, and in which the gender of one's partners becomes supremely important. We do not have a clear answer to the ultimate question of why the segregated peer groups function as they do. We need now to think about how it can be answered. The answer is important if we are to adapt ourselves successfully to the rapid changes in the roles and relationships of the two sexes that are occurring in modern societies.

REFERENCES

Aries, E. (1976). Interaction patterns and themes of male, female, and mixed groups. *Small Group Behavior, 7*, 7–18.

Aries, E. J. (1982). Verbal and nonverbal behavior in single-sex and mixed-sex groups: Are traditional sex roles changing? *Psychological Reports, 51*, 127–134.

Block, J. H. (1976). Debatable conclusions about sex differences. *Contemporary Psychology, 21*, 517–522.

Carli, L. L. (1989). Gender differences in interaction style and influence. *Journal of Personality and Social Psychology, 56*, 565–576.

Chodorow, N. (1978). *The reproduction of mothering.* Berkeley, CA: University of California Press.

Cowan, C., Drinkard, J., & MacGavin, L. (1984). The effects of target, age and gender on use of power strategies. *Journal of Personality and Social Psychology, 47*, 1391–1398.

Davis, J. D. (1978). When boy meets girl: Sex roles and the negotiation of intimacy in an acquaintance exercise. *Journal of Personality and Social Psychology, 36*, 684–692.

Duncan, S., Jr., & Fiske, D. W. (1977). *Face-to-face interaction: Research, methods and theory.* Hillsdale, NJ: Erlbaum.

Eagly, A. H. (1983). Gender and social influence. *American Psychologist, 38*, 971–981.

Eagly, A. H. (1987). *Sex differences in social behavior: A social role interpretation.* Hillsdale, NJ: Erlbaum.

Eagly, A. H., Wood, W., & Fishbaugh, L. (1981). Sex differences in conformity: Surveillance by the group as a determinant of male non-conformity. *Journal of Personality and Social Psychology, 40*, 384–394.

Eisenhart, M. A., & Holland, D. C. (1983). Learning gender from peers: The role of peer group in the cultural transmission of gender. *Human Organization, 42*, 321–332.

Erwin, P. (1985). Similarity of attitudes and constructs in children's friendships. *Journal of Experimental Child Psychology, 40*, 470–485.

Fagot, B. I. (1985). Beyond the reinforcement principle: Another step toward understanding sex roles. *Developmental Psychology, 21*, 1097–1104.

Falbo, T. & Peplau, L. A. (1980). Power strategies in intimate relationships. *Journal of Personality and Social Psychology, 38*, 618–628.

Gilligan, C. (1982). *In a different voice: Psychological theory and women's development.* Cambridge, MA: Harvard University Press.

Gleason, J. B. (1987). Sex differences in parent-child interaction. In S. U. Phillips, S. Steele, & C. Tanz (Eds.), *Language, gender and sex in comparative perspective* (pp. 189–199). Cambridge, England: Cambridge University Press.

Gottman, J. M., & Levenson, R. W. (1988). The social psychophysiology of marriage. In P. Roller & M. A. Fitzpatrick (Eds.),

Perspectives on marital interaction (pp. 182–200). New York: Taylor & Francis.

Greeno, C. G. (1989). *Gender differences in children's proximity to adults*. Unpublished doctoral dissertation, Stanford University, Stanford, CA.

Hall, J. A., & Braunwald, K. G. (1981). Gender cues in conversation. *Journal of Personality and Social Psychology, 40,* 99–110.

Hauser, S. T., Powers, S. I., Weiss-Perry, B., Follansbee, D. J., Rajapark, D., & Greene, W. M. (1987). *The constraining and enabling coding system manual*. Unpublished manuscript.

Heiss, J. S. (1962). Degree of intimacy and male-female interaction. *Sociometry, 25,* 197–208.

Hogg, M. A., & Turner, J. C. (1987). Intergroup behavior, self stereotyping and the salience of social categories. *British Journal of Social Psychology, 26,* 325–340.

Humphreys, A. P., & Smith, P. K. (1987). Rough and tumble friendship and dominance in school children: Evidence for continuity and change with age in middle childhood. *Child Development, 58,* 201–212.

Huston, A. C. (1985). The development of sex-typing: Themes from recent research. *Developmental Review, 5,* 1–17.

Huston, T. L., & Ashmore, R. D. (1986). Women and men in personal relationship. In R. D. Ashmore & R. K. Del Boca (Eds.), *The social psychology of female-male relations*. New York: Academic Press.

Jacklin, C. N., & Maccoby, E. E. (1978). Social behavior at 33 months in same-sex and mixed-sex dyads. *Child Development, 49,* 557–569.

Kelley, H. H., Cunningham, J. D., Grisham, J. A., Lefebvre, L. M., Sink, C. R., & Yablon, G. (1978). Sex differences in comments made during conflict in close relationships. *Sex Roles, 4,* 473–491.

Kraft, L. W., & Vraa, C. W. (1975). Sex composition of groups and pattern of self-disclosure by high school females. *Psychological Reports, 37,* 733–734.

Leaper, C. (1989). *The sequencing of power and involvement in boys' and girls' talk*. Unpublished manuscript (under review), University of California, Santa Cruz.

Leik, R. K. (1963). Instrumentality and emotionality in family interaction. *Sociometry, 26,* 131–145.

Lockheed, M. E. (1985). Sex and social influence: A meta-analysis guided by theory. In J. Berger & M. Zelditch (Eds.), *Status, attributions, and rewards* (pp. 406–429). San Francisco, CA: Jossey-Bass.

Maccoby, E. E. (1988). Gender as a social category. *Developmental Psychology, 26,* 755–765.

Maccoby, E. E., & Jacklin, C. N. (1974). *The psychology of sex differences*. Stanford, CA: Stanford University Press.

Maccoby, E. E., & Jacklin, C. N. (1980). Sex differences in aggression: A rejoinder and reprise. *Child Development, 51,* 964–980.

Maccoby, E. E., & Jacklin, C. N. (1983). The "person" characteristics of children and the family as environment. In D. Magnusson & V. L. Allen (Eds.), *Human development: An interactional perspective* (pp. 76–92). New York: Academic Press.

Maccoby, E. E., & Jacklin, C. N. (1987). Gender segregation in childhood. In H. W. Reese (Ed.), *Advances in child development and behavior*. (Vol. 20, pp. 239–288). New York: Academic Press.

Maltz, D. N., & Borker, R. A. (1983). A cultural approach to male-female miscommunication. In John A. Gumperz (Ed.), *Language and social identity* (pp. 195–216). New York: Cambridge University Press.

Miller, P., Danaher, D., & Forbes, D. (1986). Sex-related strategies for coping with interpersonal conflict in children aged five and seven. *Developmental Psychology, 22,* 543–548.

Nolen-Hoeksema, S. (in press). *Sex differences in depression*. Stanford, CA: Stanford University Press.

Parpal, M., & Maccoby, E. E. (1985). Maternal responsiveness and subsequent child compliance. *Child Development, 56,* 1326–1334.

Peplau, A. (1979). Power in dating relationships. In J. Freeman (Ed.), *Women: A feminist perspective* (pp. 121–137). Palo Alto, CA: Mayfield.

Powlishta, K. K. (1987, April). *The social context of cross-sex interactions*. Paper presented at biennial meeting of the Society for Research in Child Development, Baltimore, MD.

Powlishta, K. K. (1989). *Salience of group membership: The case of gender*. Unpublished doctoral dissertation, Stanford University, Stanford, CA.

Pruitt, D. G. (1976). Power and bargaining. In B. Seidenberg & A. Snadowsky (Eds.), *Social psychology: An introduction* (pp. 343–375). New York: Free Press.

Pugh, M. D., & Wahrman, R. (1983). Neutralizing sexism in mixed-sex groups: Do women have to be better than men? *American Journal of Sociology, 88,* 746–761.

Reskin, B. F. (Ed.). (1984). *Sex segregation in the workplace: Trends, explanations and remedies*. Washington, DC: National Academy Press.

Robinson, J., & McArthur, L. Z. (1982). Impact of salient vocal qualities on causal attribution for a speaker's behavior. *Journal of Personality and Social Psychology, 43,* 236–247.

Sachs, J. (1987). Preschool boys' and girls' language use in pretend play. In S. U. Phillips, S. Steele, & C. Tanz (Eds.), *Language, gender and sex in comparative perspective* (pp. 178–188). Cambridge, England: Cambridge University Press.

Savin-Williams, R. C. (1979). Dominance hierarchies in groups of early adolescents, *Child Development, 50,* 923–935.

Serbin, L. A., Sprafkin, C., Elman, M., & Doyle, A. (1984). The early development of sex differentiated patterns of social influence. *Canadian Journal of Social Science, 14,* 350–363.

Shaw, M. E., & Sadler, O. W. (1965). Interaction patterns in heterosexual dyads varying in degree of intimacy. *Journal of Social Psychology, 66,* 345–351.

Sheldon, A. (1989, April). *Conflict talk: Sociolinguistic challenges to self-assertion and how young girls meet them*. Paper presented at the biennial meeting of the Society for Research in Child Development, Kansas City.

Siegal, M. (1987). Are sons and daughters treated more differently by fathers than mothers? *Developmental Review, 7,* 183–209.

Thorne, B. (1986). Girls and boys together, but mostly apart. In W. W. Hartup & L. Rubin (Eds.), *Relationships and development* (pp. 167–184). Hillsdale, NJ: Erlbaum.

Tieger, T. (1980). On the biological basis of sex differences in aggression. *Child Development, 51,* 943–963.

Wasserman, G. A., & Stern, D. N. (1978). An early manifestation of differential behavior toward children of the same and opposite sex. *Journal of Genetic Psychology, 133,* 129–137.

West, C., & Zimmerman, D. H. (1985). Gender, language and discourse. In T. A. van Dijk (Ed.), *Handbook of discourse analysis: Vol. 4. Discourse analysis in society* (pp. 103–124). London: Academic Press.

Wood, W., Polek, D., & Aiken, C. (1985). Sex differences in group task performance. *Journal of Personality and Social Psychology, 48,* 63–71.

QUESTIONS

1. According to psychological research, how do males and females differ?
2. Why are children's behaviors more sex-typed when they play with a child of the same sex than with a child of the other sex?
3. What patterns of gender segregation appear between the ages of 4 and 6 years?
4. What do children's attempts to influence their play partners have to do with the development of gender-related behaviors?
5. How does the presence of an adult affect the sex-typed behaviors of girls and boys?
6. What implications do these results have for whether children should be in same-sex or mixed-sex classrooms in the early years of school?

PART IV
Middle Childhood

The ages from 7 to 12 are the years of middle childhood. Around the world this is recognized as a wonderful and exciting period of children's lives. In all cultures, middle childhood is the time when children lose their baby teeth, are involved in activities that remove them from constant adult supervision, and are held responsible for their own actions. All these changes are made possible because children have increased physical skills, which allow them to help out more at home and at school. Also, their increased intellectual capacities allow children to engage in more difficult activities, follow more complex directions, and keep better track of what they are doing. However, cognitive change during this period is not an all-or-nothing process. The article by Siegler in this section discusses variability in children's thinking skills, especially their strategy use, as characteristic of cognitive development during this period.

Although the most obvious changes during this period are in physical and intellectual growth, children's social life is also changing dramatically. Children are spending more time with other children, mostly age mates, and these interactions can provide opportunities for intellectual development. The article by Duran and Gauvain examines this topic. Children's experiences with peers also begin to take on more emotional complexity. Children learn to communicate and modulate their emotions in ways that are socially accepted. The article by Davis discusses research on this developmental process. Also during middle childhood, most children find increasing satisfaction in peer relationships. However, this process is easier for some children than others. The article by Crick and Ladd concentrates on children who have difficulties in peer relationships.

The most salient institution children experience during middle childhood is school. Although school is supposed to enhance children's intellectual competence, cultural variation in the academic performance of children suggests that opportunities in the classroom to develop cognitive skills differ to a great degree. This issue is discussed in detail in the article by Stigler and Stevenson. Finally, an article on intelligence by Neisser et al. is included in this section. Although this topic is not unique to this age group, it is an increasingly important facet of an individual's experience in middle childhood. Our understanding of intelligence and IQ is far from complete, as this article makes clear.

Together, these articles describe the period of middle childhood as one in which children's developing cognitive skills are increasingly integrated with the intellectual, social, and emotional life of the community in which they live. Maturity carries with it increased expectations and responsibilities toward the group, and it is in middle childhood that the first steps of this lifelong process appear.

22 Cognitive Variability: A Key to Understanding Cognitive Development

ROBERT S. SIEGLER

An information-processing approach to cognitive development conceives of this process as the gradual learning of new and more complex skills. Because young children have fewer skills than older children and adults, researchers who adopt this approach are especially interested in the ways in which young children overcome their cognitive limitations to solve problems. This has led to research on the development and use of strategies to solve problems.

In recent years, Robert S. Siegler has studied cognitive development by looking very closely at the strategies children use to understand and solve problems. This research has led to the discovery that children do not, at any given point in development, have only one way of understanding or solving a problem. Rather, children's thinking may contain a variety of problem-solving techniques or strategies. Furthermore, Siegler observed that variability in strategy use often precedes cognitive change. This observation led Siegler to suggest that variability may hold the key for unlocking one of the most difficult, yet most interesting, development questions: How does change occur?

In this article, Siegler reviews his position on the role of variability and cognitive development and discusses data that support this point of view. This perspective holds promise for an area of study that has for a long time struggled with describing mechanisms of change. Perhaps, as Siegler suggests, progress on this front has been impeded by a too narrow depiction of what children know or have available to them as thinking tools at any given point in development.

Among the most remarkable characteristics of human beings is how much our thinking changes with age. When we compare the thinking of an infant, a toddler, an elementary school student, and an adolescent, the magnitude of the change is immediately apparent. Accounting for how these changes occur is perhaps the central goal of researchers who study cognitive development.

Alongside this agreement about the importance of the goal of determining how change occurs, however, is agreement that we traditionally have not done very well in meeting it. In most models of cognitive development, children are depicted as thinking or acting in a certain way for a prolonged period of time, then undergoing a brief, rather mysterious, transition, and then thinking or acting in a different way for another prolonged period. For example, on the classic conservation-of-liquid quantity problem, children are depicted as believing for several years that pouring water into a taller, thinner beaker changes the amount of water; then undergoing a short period of cognitive conflict, in which they are not sure about the effects of pouring the water; and then realizing that pouring does not affect the amount of liquid. How children get from the earlier to the later understanding is described only superficially.

Critiques of the inadequacy of such accounts have been leveled most often at stage models such as Piaget's. The problem, however, is far more pervasive. Regardless of whether the particular approach

Reprinted with permission from the author and Blackwell Publishers from *Current Directions in Psychological Science,* 3, (1994), pp. 1–5. Copyright © 1994 by the American Psychological Society.

Preparation of this article was made possible by grants from the Spencer Foundation, the National Institutes of Health, and the Mellon Foundation to the author. Special thanks go to Kevin Crowley for his careful readings and excellent suggestions regarding the article.

describes development in terms of stages, rules, strategies, or theories; regardless of whether the focus is on reasoning about the physical or the social world; regardless of the age group of central interest, most theories place static states at center stage and change processes either in the wings or offstage altogether. Thus, 3-year-olds are said to have nonrepresentational theories of mind and 5-year-olds representational ones; 5-year-olds to have absolute views about justice and 10-year-olds relativistic ones; 10-year-olds to be incapable and 15-year-olds capable of true scientific reasoning. The emphasis in almost all cognitive-developmental theories has been on identifying sequences of one-to-one correspondences between ages and ways of thinking or acting, rather that on specifying how the changes occur.

If developmentalists are so interested in change processes, why would the topic be given such cursory treatment in most contemporary theories? Part of the problem is that studying change is inherently difficult. It poses all the conceptual and methodological demands of studying performance at any one time, and imposes the added demands of determining what is changing and how the change is being accomplished.

An additional part of the difficulty, however, may be self-imposed. In our efforts to describe differences among age groups in as simple, dramatic, and memorable terms as possible, we may unwittingly have made understanding change more difficult than it needs to be. In particular, portraying children's thinking and knowledge as monolithic for several years at a time creates a need to explain the wide gulfs between the successive hypothesized understandings—even though such gulfs may not exist. The typical depictions make change a rare, almost exotic, event that demands an exceptional explanation. If children of a given age have for several years had a particular understanding, why would they suddenly form a different understanding, and why would they regularly form it at a particular age? The problem is exacerbated by the fact that for many of the competencies of interest, generally relevant experience is available at all ages and specifically relevant experience at none. Children see liquids poured into containers of different dimensions at all ages—and are not ordinarily told at any age that the amount of liquid remains the same after pouring as before. Why, then, would they consistently have one concept of liquid quantity conservation at age 5 and a different one at age 7?

Recognition of the unwelcome side effects of the one-to-one depictions of cognitive growth has led to a new generation of research that focuses directly on changes in children's thinking. This research has documented large-scale variability in children's thinking and suggests that the variability contributes directly to cognitive growth.

PERVASIVE VARIABILITY

Variability in children's thinking exists at every level—not just between children of different ages, or between different children of the same age, but also within an individual solving a set of related problems, within an individual solving the same problem twice, and even within an individual on a single trial.

VARIABILITY WITHIN AN INDIVIDUAL SOLVING RELATED PROBLEMS

Detailed analyses of tasks on which one-to-one correspondences between age and way of thinking have been postulated indicate that children's thinking is generally much more variable than past depictions have suggested. To cite an example from language development, rather than young children passing through a stage in which they always overregularize past tense forms (e.g., saying "goed" and "eated" rather than "went" and "ate"), children at all ages between $2\frac{1}{2}$ and 5 years produce both substantial numbers of overregularized forms and substantial numbers of correct ones. The variability throughout this age range is present for a single child followed throughout the period, as well as for groups of children sampled at a single age. Adding to the variability, children often produce more than one incorrect form of a given verb; on different occasions, a given child will say, "I ate it," "I eated it," and "I ated it."[1]

Similar variability has been found in the development of memory strategies. Contrary to the widely cited model that 5-year-olds do not rehearse and 8-year-olds do, trial-by-trial assessments indicate that the majority of children of both ages sometimes do and sometimes do not rehearse.[2] The percentage of trials on which they rehearse increases with age, but, again, there is variability throughout the age range.

Conceptual development evidences the same pattern. Despite claims that 5-year-olds think of number conservation solely in terms of the lengths of the rows, trial-by-trial assessments indicate that most 5-year-olds sometimes rely on the lengths of the rows, sometimes rely on the type of transformation, and sometimes use other strategies such as counting or pairing.[3] Again, the frequency of reliance on these ways of thinking changes with age, but most 5-year-olds' judgments and verbal explanations indicate several different ways of thinking about the concept.

Development of problem-solving skills provides yet more evidence for such within-subject cognitive variability. Contradicting models in which preschoolers are said to use the sum strategy (counting from 1) to solve simple addition problems and in which first through third graders are said to use the min strategy (counting from the larger addend, as when solving $3 + 6$ by counting "6, 7, 8, 9") to solve them, children of all these ages use a variety of strategies. In one study, most children presented a set of addition problems used at least three different strategies on different problems, and most children examined in a more extensive microlongitudinal study used at least five distinct strategies.[4]

VARIABILITY WITHIN AN INDIVIDUAL SOLVING A SINGLE PROBLEM TWICE

The variability within individual children cannot be reduced to children using different strategies on different problems. Even presented the identical problem twice within a single session, or on 2 successive days, children use different strategies on roughly one third of the pairs of trials in addition, time-telling, and block-building tasks.[5] This variability within individuals within problems cannot be explained by learning; in these studies, children used the strategy that appeared more advanced almost as often for the first presentation of a problem as for the second (roughly 45% vs. 55%).

VARIABILITY WITHIN A SINGLE TRIAL

In the limiting case, variability has been found even within an individual solving a particular problem on a single trial. This type of variability has been reported by investigators interested in the relation between children's hand gestures and verbal explanations. In these studies, children often express one type of understanding through the gestures and a quite different understanding through the explanations.[6] For example, on number conservation problems, children may express a reliance on relative lengths of the rows in their hand gestures, while at the same time verbally expressing reliance on the type of transformation, or vice versa.

These findings suggest that cognitive change is better thought of in terms of changing distributions of ways of thinking than in terms of sudden shifts from one way of thinking to another. The types of descriptions of change that emerge from such analyses are illustrated in Figures 1 and 2. Figure 1 shows

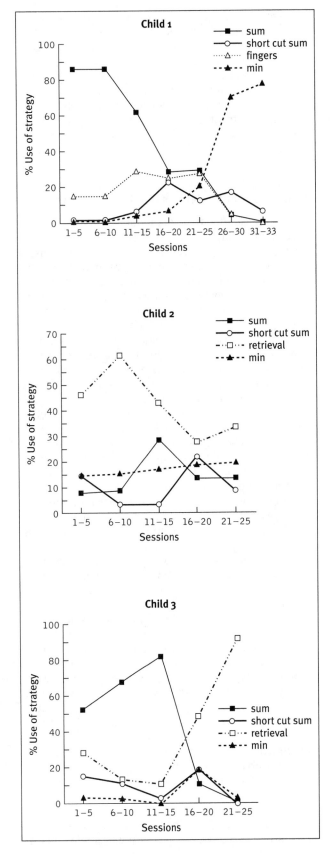

FIGURE 1

Changes in distributions of addition strategies of 3 children over roughly 30 sessions conducted over a 3-month period. Notice the variability that is present within each child's performance within each block of sessions, as well as the changes in distributions of strategy use over the course of the study (data from Siegler and Jenkins[4]).

changes in 3 children's addition strategies over a 3-month period;[4] Figure 2 shows changes in a child's map-drawing strategies over a 2-year period.[7] Similar changes in distributions of strategies have been found in studies of conceptual understanding, memory strategies, problem solving, and language. In all these domains, cognitive development involves changing distributions of approaches, rather than discontinuous movements from one way of thinking to another.

VARIABILITY AND COGNITIVE CHANGE

Variability is not just an incidental feature of thinking; it appears to play a critical role in promoting cognitive change. Several types of evidence converge on this conclusion. One comes from observations of children in the process of discovering new strategies. Both the trials immediately before a discovery and the trial on which the discovery is made frequently involve especially variable behavior—disfluencies, unclear references, long pauses, and unusual gestures.[4] A second type of empirical evidence linking variability to cognitive change involves analyses of which children are most likely to make discoveries. Children whose verbal explanations and gestures reflect different initial misunderstandings of number conservation and of numerical equivalence problems $(a + b + c = \_ + c)$ are more likely to make discoveries subsequently than are children whose explanations and gestures reflect the same initial misunderstanding.[6] Similarly, children whose pretest explanations reflect varied ways of thinking are more likely to learn from instruction regarding the meaning of the equal sign in mathematics than are children whose pretest explanations reflect crisp, specific misunderstandings.[8]

A different type of evidence for the contribution of variability to cognitive change comes from formal models of development. Theorists who differ in many particular assumptions have found that modeling change requires both mechanisms that produce variability and mechanisms that produce adaptive choices among the variants. Connectionist models of development are based on connection strengths among processing units varying at all points in learning, from initial, randomly varying strengths to final, asymptotic level; change occurs through redistributions of the varying connection strengths. Dynamic systems models also treat variability as a fundamental property of development; they aim to explain how local variability gives to global regularities. Similarly, recent symbolic-processing models of development focus on how varying strategies, analogies, and other higher order units come to be used increasingly in the situations in which they are most effective. At a less formal level, operant conditioning models, evolu-

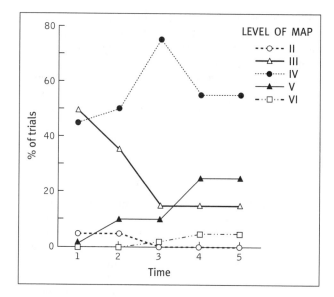

FIGURE 2

Changes in distributions of map-drawing approaches across five sessions, conducted over a 2-year period. Higher numbers indicate more advanced levels of map drawing; thus, Level IV maps are more advanced than Level III ones (data from Feldman[7]).

tionarily based models, and generate-and-test models are all based on the assumption that change occurs through selection processes operating on omnipresent, spontaneously produced variability in behavior.[9]

A striking empirical finding about the variability in children's thinking, and one that is important for its ability to contribute to cognitive development, is the constrained quality of the variations that children generate. Far from conforming to a trial-and-error model, in which all types of variations might be expected, the new approaches that children attempt consistently conform to the principles that define legal strategies in the domain (except when children are forced to solve problems for which they do not possess any adequate strategy). For example, in a 30-session study of preschoolers' discovery of new addition strategies, none of the children ever attempted strategies that violated the principles underlying addition.[4] They invented legitimate new strategies, such as the min strategy, but never illegitimate ones, such as adding the smaller addend to itself or counting from the larger addend the number of times indicated by the first addend. The question is how they limit their newly generated strategies to legal forms.

One possibility is that even before discovering new strategies, children often understand the goals that legitimate strategies in the domain must satisfy.

Such understanding would allow them, without trial and error, to discriminate between legitimate new strategies that meet the essential goals and illegitimate strategies that do not. A very recent study revealed that children possessed such knowledge in both of the domains that were examined—simple addition and tic-tac-toe.[10] In simple addition, children who had not yet discovered the min strategy nonetheless judged that strategy (demonstrated by the experimenter) to be as smart as the strategy they themselves most often used—counting from 1—and significantly smarter than an equally novel but illegitimate strategy that the experimenter demonstrated. In tic-tac-toe, children rated a novel strategy that they did not yet use—forking—as even smarter than the strategy they themselves usually employed—trying to complete a single row or column. Ability to anticipate the value of untried strategies may promote cognitive growth by filtering out unpromising possibilities and thus channeling innovations in potentially useful directions.

CONCLUSIONS

Thinking is far more variable than usually depicted. In the past, researchers have usually ignored such variability or viewed it as a bother. This stance has led to subjects being given practice periods, not so the especially variable behavior in those periods can be studied, but so that it can be discarded, in order that it not obscure the more orderly patterns in later performance. When such variability has been explicitly noted at all, it has usually been viewed as an unfortunate limitation of human beings, a kind of design defect, something to be overcome through practice. Computers, robots, and other machines not subject to this flaw can perform many tasks more accurately than people can. Presumably, people's performance would also be enhanced if it were less variable.

This view of variability as detracting from efficient performance misses at least half the story, though. The variability of cognition and action allows us to discover a great deal about the environments toward which the thinking and action are directed. Our difficulty in reproducing the way we pronounced a word in an unfamiliar foreign language may lead to some even less adequate pronunciations in the short run, but in the longer run may lead us to generate and then learn better pronunciations. Likewise, our inability to give a colloquium in the same words twice, even when we want to, may lead to some parts being less clear than in the best of our previous presentations, but it also allows us to observe audience reaction to new lines of argument and to learn which ones are best received. In general, cognitive variability may lead to performance never incorporating on any one occasion all the best features of previous performance, but also may be critical to our becoming increasingly proficient over time.

If cognitive variability does indeed facilitate learning, it would be adaptive if such variability were most pronounced when learning, rather than efficient performance, is most important—that is, in infancy and early childhood. This appears to be the case. Across many domains, expertise brings with it decreasingly variable performance. To the extent that young children are "universal novices," their lack of expertise alone would lead to their performance being more variable than that of older children and adults. A number of cognitive neuroscientists have hypothesized that above and beyond such effects of practice, the process of synaptogenesis, which results in children from roughly birth to age 7 having far more synaptic connections than older children and adults, may contribute both to the high variability of early behavior and to young children's special ability to acquire language, perceptual skills, and other competencies under abnormal organismic and environmental conditions.[11] That is, young children's greater variability at the neural level seems to allow them to learn useful behaviors under a greater range of circumstances. The general lesson seems to be that explicitly recognizing the great variability of infants' and young children's thinking, and attempting to explain how it is generated and constrained, will advance our understanding of the central mystery about cognitive development—how change occurs.

NOTES

1. S. A. Kuczaj, The acquisition of regular and irregular past tense forms, *Journal of Verbal Learning and Verbal Behavior, 16*, 589–600 (1977).
2. K. McGilly and R. S. Siegler, The influence of encoding and strategic knowledge on children's choices among serial recall strategies, *Developmental Psychology, 26*, 939–941 (1990).
3. R. S. Siegler, *A microgenetic study of number conservation*, manuscript in preparation, Carnegie Mellon University, Pittsburgh (1993).
4. R. S. Siegler and E. Jenkins, *How Children Discover New Strategies* (Erlbaum, Hillsdale, NJ, 1989).
5. R. S. Siegler and K. McGilly, Strategy choices in children's time-telling, in *Time and Human Cognition: A Life Span Perspective*, I. Levin and D. Zakay, Eds. (Elsevier Science, Amsterdam, 1989); R. S. Siegler and J. Shrager, Strategy choices in addition and subtraction: How do children know what to do? in *The Origins of Cognitive Skills*, C. Sophian, Ed. (Erlbaum, Hillsdale, NJ, 1984); A.C. Wilkinson, Partial knowledge and self-correction: Developmental studies of a quantitative concept, *Developmental Psychology, 18*, 876–893 (1982).
6. R. B. Church and S. Goldin-Meadow, The mismatch between gesture and speech as an index of transitional

knowledge, *Cognition, 23*, 43–71 (1986); S. Goldin-Meadow and M. W. Alibali, Transitions in concept acquisition: Using the hand to read the mind, *Psychological Review* (in press).

7. D. H. Feldman, *Beyond Universals in Cognitive Development* (Ablex, Norwood, NJ, 1980).

8. T. Graham and M. Perry, Indexing transitional knowledge, *Developmental Psychology, 29, 779–788* (1993).

9. For examples of these perspectives, see D. T. Campbell, Evolutionary epistemology, in *The Philosophy of Karl Popper*, Vol. 14, P. A. Schilpp, Ed. (Open Court, La Salle, IL, 1974); J. L. McClelland and E. Jenkins, Nature, nurture, and connections: Implications of connectionist models for cognitive development, in *Architectures for Intelligence*, K. Van Lehn, Ed. (Erlbaum, Hillsdale, NJ, 1991); L. B. Smith and E. Thelen, Eds., *Dynamical Systems in Development: Applications* (Bradford Books, Cambridge, MA, in press); B. F. Skinner, Selection by consequences, *Science, 213*, 509–504 (1981).

10. R. S. Siegler and K. Crowley, Goal sketches constrain children's strategy discoveries, *Cognitive Psychology* (in press).

11. P. S. Goldman-Rakic, development of cortical circuitry and cognitive function, *Child Development*, 58, 609–622 (1987); W.T. Greenough, J.E. Black, and C. Wallace, Experience and brain development, *Child Development, 58, 539–559* (1987).

QUESTIONS

1. Why, according to Siegler, has it been difficult for cognitive developmental psychologists to study the process of mental change?
2. What is one example that Siegler uses to support his claim that variability exists in an individual's problem-solving efforts?
3. Are you surprised that children sometimes use different strategies to solve the same problem on two different trials? Why? What assumption about cognitive development does this observation challenge?
4. Why is it important to Siegler that the variations that children use to solve a problem are not simply different attempts based on trial and error?
5. What may be the neurological basis for cognitive variability between birth and 7 years of age?
6. How, according to Siegler, might variability in thinking lead to cognitive change?

23 The Role of Age versus Expertise in Peer Collaboration during Joint Planning

RUTH T. DURAN · MARY GAUVAIN

Over the last two decades there have been many research efforts to understand the social foundations of cognitive development. Much of this research has concentrated on social interaction between adults and children or peers as a source of cognitive growth.

The following article by Ruth T. Duran and Mary Gauvain is about peer collaboration and cognitive development, a topic that was of much interest to both Piaget and Vygotsky. Their similar interest does not mean that they held like views on this, however. Piaget felt that collaboration between children who were nearly equal in their understanding would instigate cognitive change, whereas Vygotsky emphasized collaboration between novice and expert peers as conducive to mental growth.

In this study, the interaction between experts and novices is the focus. Despite extensive research on this type of pairing, several questions remain. One of these has to do with the role of expertise versus child age during peer collaboration on a cognitive task that involves planning. One of the difficulties in studying the influence of expertise on children's learning from peer interaction is that expertise is often confounded with child age. Because child age is usually an index of social status, this further complicates the picture. This research uses a design that teases these variables apart, and results indicate that age and expertise do, indeed, make different contributions to the social process of cognitive development when peers work together.

This study examined the role of age and expertise in influencing collaboration during joint planning. The collaborative patterns of 7-year-old expert planners working with 5-year-old novice planners were compared to 5-year-old experts collaborating with same-age novices on delivery tasks requiring reverse sequencing strategies. Novices who planned with same-age experts had more involvement in the task than novices in cross-age dyads, and individual posttest performance of the novices was related to the extent to which novices were involved in the collaborative task. Furthermore, the posttest performance of children who planned with same-age experts, but not older experts, was significantly better than same-age children in a related study using this same task who did not previously collaborate with a peer. Results suggest that cognitive gains are achieved when children collaborate with peers who are more expert in the problem-solving activity, particularly when there is substantial involvement by the novice, and that this is more likely for 5-year-old children when partners are of the same age rather than of different ages. The relation of social facilitation to cognitive development is discussed, with particular attention to the role of social comparison processes in explaining the age patterns found.

Reprinted with permission from the authors and Academic Press from *Journal of Experimental Child Psychology*, 55 (1993), pp. 227–242. Copyright © 1993 by Academic Press.

This article is based on a senior thesis submitted by the first author to Claremont McKenna College in partial fulfillment of the requirements of a B.A. degree. We are grateful to the children of Condit School, Mary B. Eyre Children's School, and Sycamore Elementary for giving us a chance to work with and learn from them. We also acknowledge the assistance of Laurie Jones, Mark Costanzo, and Paul Huard on this project. Comments by Phil Costanzo and Alex Siegel greatly improved our understanding of the data and are much appreciated. Correspondence and reprint requests should be addressed to Mary Gauvain, Department of Psychology, University of California, Riverside, Riverside, CA 92521.

Over the past two decades the contribution of peer interaction to children's cognitive development has received increased attention as researchers acknowledge the value of peer experiences on learning and problem solving. Peer interaction facilitates learning because partners often contribute new information, define and restructure a problem in a way that is familiar, and generate discussions that lead to the selection of the most effective problem-solving strategy (Azmitia & Perlmutter, 1989). Thus, through mutual feedback, evaluation, and debate, peers motivate one another to abandon misconceptions and search for better solutions. The present study is intended to broaden our understanding of the effects of peer collaboration on children's thinking by examining age and expertise as mediators of social influence on children's planning skills. Of particular interest is whether age-related status affects cognitive interaction by a novice and expert on a planning task.

Much of the recent research on peer collaboration identifies two theories to account for the facilitation of cognition: Piaget's structural perspective and Vygotsky's sociohistorical perspective. Piaget (1948) and Vygotsky (1978) shared the view that children are active participants in their development, and both emphasized that children learn and develop their thinking processes by interacting with both objects and people. Although Piaget's primary concern was the development of the individual in relation to the physical properties of the world, he did believe that discussion between children plays a role in cognitive development and proposed that cognitive conflict between peers was a mechanism for the social facilitation of cognition. For Piaget, peer interaction is conducive to cognitive development because of the relatively symmetrical nature of peer interaction, i.e., relatively little cognitive and social distance between peers, compared to asymmetric interactions, i.e., those occurring between children and adults or between peers of higher cognitive or social status (Azmitia & Perlmutter, 1989). According to Piaget (1948), children are likely to conform to rules that they do not fully understand because of this asymmetry in adult–child interactions and will tend to agree with the adult, who has more power and knowledge, without examining the ideas themselves. When a peer has a different perspective, no asymmetry of power exists, and thus partners are more likely to participate in the problem-solving process.

Vygotsky (1978) placed greater emphasis on the role of asymmetrical relationships, focusing on the role of guidance by a person who has achieved a level of expertise beyond that of the child. During guided participation (Rogoff, 1990), more experienced social members use sociocultural tools, like language, to encourage thinking in less experienced members beyond what they are capable of on their own. Vygot-sky's emphasis on interaction with more mature partners, such as adults or skilled peers, is therefore, essential to his theory (Tudge & Rogoff, 1989).

To help clarify these theoretical differences, researchers have investigated the influence of peers with varying expertise on children's learning. Researchers have found that cognitive development can be attained both by pairing children of different skills, e.g., nonconservers with conservers (e.g., Murray, 1982; Perret-Clermont, 1980), as well as by pairing children at approximately the same cognitive level (Glachan & Light, 1982). Yet Azmitia (1988) found that children at the same level make little progress. And Ellis and Rogoff (1986) showed that more capable peers are not necessarily effective teachers in promoting certain skills. Thus, despite extensive investigations in recent years regarding the influence of peer collaboration on cognitive development, the merit of conflict versus guidance is still under scrutiny. This inquiry is not independent of concerns about the relative skill or expertise of the partners in promoting cognitive growth. Unfortunately, these issues are difficult to disentangle since age and expertise are often confounded in research on peer interaction.

In fact, in many studies individual differences in expertise are assumed to correspond to age differences (Ellis & Gauvain, 1992). Although this may be a reasonable assumption, expertise on particular tasks should not necessarily be assumed to correlate with age, especially ages that are somewhat close developmentally, e.g., 5- and 7-year-old children. Preassessments of children's ability on tasks independent of age are essential to establishing skill level and assigning children to dyads.

A related concern is the influence of differential age on peer involvement during interaction. Recall that Piaget cautioned that interaction with adults may be less effective than with peers due to inherent restrictions of the adult–child status differential. Such cautions may also be relevant to peer interaction in which peers are of the same versus different ages. Research in social development indicates quite clearly that child age is correlated with social status and dominance (Blurton Jones, 1972; Grusec & Lytton, 1988). This suggests that even in peer collaboration, age-related status may play an important role in how partners participate in the interaction. Since age and expertise, even when preassessed, are typically confounded in peer collaboration research, it remains unclear as to how age-related status may affect peer interaction.

In order to reconcile Piaget and Vygotsky's views it is necessary to explore further the variables involved in social interaction such as the relative age and expertise of the social partners and the different mechanisms influencing the social facilitation of cognition. One of the goals of the present study is to examine the processes proposed by Vygotsky and

Piaget, such as cognitive conflict and guidance by an expert, that may promote cognitive development, with particular attention to the differential influence of age and expertise on the process and outcome of peer collaboration during joint planning. The study focuses on joint planning because research suggests that children's metacognitive skills, such as planning, are likely to benefit from social interaction (e.g., Hartup, 1985; Rogoff, Gauvain, & Gardner, 1987; Wertsch, McNamee, McLane, & Budwig, 1980).

In the present study, the role of collaboration between children and their more experienced peers in affecting skill in planning was investigated. In particular, the influence of age on novice and expert involvement in the task was studied by comparing the interactional process when children planned with an expert of the same age versus one who was older. Based on findings from earlier research (see Azmitia & Perlmutter, 1989), we expected that novices would improve their planning skills when planning with experts, and the benefits attained from interaction would transfer to the novice's subsequent individual performance. However, it was also expected that the relative ages of the partners would influence the degree to which the novice participated in the task. Novices collaborating with same-age experts were expected to be more involved in the process of planning because, as research in social development suggests, collaboration between children of the same age is less marked by dominance and is therefore less emotionally threatening than corrective advice from adults or older children (Damon, 1984). Because previous research has not established the mechanisms of social interaction that promote cognitive development, this study also investigated the different mechanisms of social interaction. In particular, this study examined conflict between the partners, observational learning by the novice, and guidance by the expert. These processes may influence the likelihood that children will learn through collaboration, however, their use may be related to whether the partners are of the same or different ages.

METHOD

SUBJECTS

Seventy 5- and 7-year-old children from three elementary schools serving middle-income populations were pretested to obtain 16 5-year-old novice planners ($M = 5.5$ years; range = 5.2–5.9 years), 8 5-year-old expert planners ($M = 5.5$ years; range = 5.2–5.9 years), and 8 7-year-old expert planners ($M = 7.5$ years; range = 7.2–7.9 years). During the interactive sessions, novice planners were assigned randomly to either a 5- or 7-year-old expert planner of the same sex. Thus, in the final group there were 8 mixed ability, cross-age

dyads and 8 mixed ability, same-age dyads with an equal number of boys and girls in each condition.

TASKS AND MATERIALS

Three tasks, designed by Gauvain (1992), were used for the planning tasks. Each task involved sequencing and delivering five items to locations in a village drawn on 22 × 28-in. (55.9 × 71.1 cm) poster board using a small delivery truck. Solution of the problems required a reverse sequencing strategy, i.e., the delivery vehicles were constructed so that only the next item to be delivered could be removed at any time. Consequently, each problem required advance planning of the entire sequence of items for delivery to be successfully accomplished. The tasks combine some of the elements of planning tasks used by Gauvain and Rogoff (1989) in their research on planning skills and by Boder (1978) in his research on the development of children's skill at reverse sequencing. Each child participated in an individual pretest and a collaborative session, and novices also participated in an individual posttest.

Pretest Task.   The pretest involved delivering mail to houses. This drawing on the poster board contained a post office, a one-way street sign, an oval street route, and five homes (three orange and two blue homes) lined along the one-way road. Materials included five letters (three orange and two blue) that corresponded to the homes according to color and a red toy wagon for delivering the letters from the post office to the homes (Fig. 1).

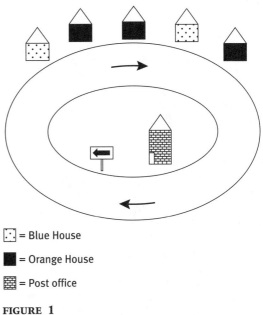

[·] = Blue House

■ = Orange House

▦ = Post office

FIGURE 1
Mail delivery task used in the pretest.

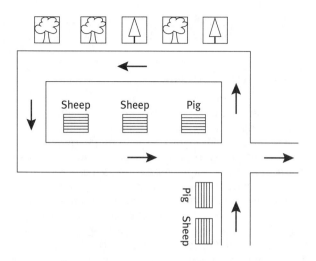

FIGURE 2
Farm delivery task used in the interactional session.

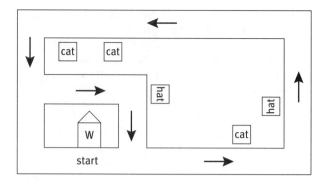

FIGURE 3
Warehouse delivery task used in the posttest.

Collaborative Task.   Children planning collaboratively were asked to deliver farm items to areas in a farm scene depicted on a poster board. Task materials included a poster board on which was drawn a diagram of a farm with pictures of three sheep pens, two pig pens, and a field indicating where three shrubs and two trees were to be planted. Animal pens and planting fields were identified with stickers of the items. Wooden blocks in the shape of the animals (three sheep and two pigs) and the plants (three shrubs and two trees) were delivered to assigned areas in the farm using a wooden truck designed to fit the blocks. Two deliveries were conducted using this scene. The first delivery involved the trees and shrubs and the second the pigs and sheep (Fig. 2).

Posttest Task.   The scene depicted on the poster board for the posttest contained two hat stores, three cat stores, and a warehouse. Cards labeled with stickers of hats or cats and the same wagon used in the pretest were also used (Fig. 3).

PROCEDURE

The children were asked to perform three planning tasks. The first task, the mail delivery, was the easiest of the four and was used as the pretest. Based on their performance, the children were identified as either an expert (the child successfully completed the pretest in three or fewer delivery attempts) or a novice (more than three delivery attempts were needed) using normative scores for these tasks obtained from a study that examined the development of children's planning skills (Gauvain, 1992). Children were considered novice planners if their pretest performance exceeded

the mean number of trials required for successful completion of the task for their age group. Novices were then paired randomly with either a 5-year-old expert planner or a 7-year-old expert planner for the Farm Delivery. After the collaborative task, the novice was given a posttest similar to, but more difficult than, the pretest. The collaborative sessions took place the same day as the posttest. All of the sessions were videotaped at the children's school in a quiet space where the child could not be distracted or observed by others.

Pretest Task: Mail Delivery.   The experimenter placed the poster board on the table in front of the child. The experimenter explained that the drawing contained a small village, and pointed out the post office, one-way road, and houses, and then asked the child to identify the two types of houses. The child was also asked to trace a finger along the direction of travel indicated for the one-way road. Then the experimenter explained to the child that he or she was to deliver a letter to each of the houses, and the color of the letter was to match the color of the house. The letters were then placed at the post office in random order and the child was shown a wagon and told that it was to be used for the delivery. The experimenter then explained the rules for mail delivery: (1) only one letter from the wagon, the top one, may be removed at a time; (2) the road is one-way so the wagon cannot be backed up; (3) the mail is to be delivered to all the houses in one trip; and (4) if during delivery the child discovers that the arrangement of the letters in the wagon is incorrect, all the letters and the wagon are to be brought back to the Post Office, rearranged, and delivered again. The experimenter asked the child if he or she understood the rules and asked if there were any questions. If the child violated the rules during the delivery, the experimenter reiterated them and asked the child to continue. Upon completion, the experimenter told the child that he or she did a good job.

Collaborative Session: Farm Delivery. The experimenter placed the poster board on the table facing the children, and told the children that in this task they were to deliver items to a farm. The experimenter described the illustrations on the board: the road, especially the one-way signs, and the fields and pens. The procedure for delivery was explained, with the experimenter pointing out that there would be two different deliveries. First the children were to deliver the trees and shrubs (Delivery One) and then they would deliver the animals (Delivery Two). The experimenter then introduced the items to be delivered and explained that only one item was to go to each delivery point. The experimenter identified where each item went and explained to the children that they were to deliver to the front of the fields and pens. The children were then shown the delivery truck and the experimenter explained how to load and unload items. The starting position for the truck was identified, and then the rules were explained: (1) the road is one-way and therefore the truck cannot back up; (2) the truck is low on gas, so it can go around the road once for each delivery; (3) the children are to work together; and (4) if, during a delivery, they feel that the truck is loaded incorrectly, they are to collect all the items and return to the starting position and reload the truck. The experimenter asked the children if they understood the rules and procedure and asked if there were any questions. The children were then instructed to begin the task. If the children violated the rules, the experimenter repeated them, and then instructed the children to continue with the task. Upon completion, the children were complimented on their work.

Posttest Task: Warehouse Delivery. The novice was asked to do one more delivery task. The experimenter placed the poster board used in the posttest in front of the child and introduced the illustrations, including the road, especially the one-way markings, the warehouse, and stores. The experimenter pointed out that there were two different types of stores, those that sold cats and those that sold hats. The child was then given cards with stickers of cats or hats on them and asked to deliver them to the stores using the toy wagon. The same rules in the mail delivery task applied in the posttest and were repeated. If the child violated the rules, the experimenter explained the rules again, and asked the child to continue. After the posttest was completed, the child was complimented on his or her work.

CODING

Performance was coded for plan effectiveness and for the use of planning strategies. The extent of each partners' involvement in the task during the interactional trial was coded, as was the interactional process used by the children to convey or ascertain planning relevant information. Mechanisms of social interaction included observational learning, i.e., the amount of time the novices observed the expert performing the task; guidance by the expert, including physical intervention, directives and suggestions, and positive support; and conflicting statements or disagreements. Three (19%) of the 16 tapes were coded independently by two coders, yielding ϕ correlation reliabilities ranging from .64 to 1.0.

Plan Effectiveness. To assess the children's pretest, interaction, and posttest performance, the number of delivery attempts made, including the final successful delivery and any partial or instructional attempts, were recorded. Thus, the higher the number of delivery attempts, the less effective the planning performance. On the pretest, children who delivered the mail in three or less trials were considered experts, while those children who took more than three trials were considered novices. This was based on the performance in another study (Gauvain, 1992) of a sample of 5-year-olds on this same pretest in which the average number of trials for successful completion was 3.16 ($SD = 2.8$, $n = 16$).

Planning Strategies. This includes statements regarding task strategy and was coded during joint planning. Strategy statements include both general task strategy statements, such as how to do the task in an efficient or planful way, and specific strategy statements, concerning strategic handling of individual task moves. Examples of general task strategy statements are "Let's put the last one on first" or "You have to load it the opposite way to deliver it right." Statements such as "What about this one next?" and "The tree goes here" are examples of specific task strategies.

Partners' Task Involvement. Each of the items selected for loading in the Farm Delivery Task was coded according to whether the novice on his or her own, the expert on his or her own, or the novice and expert together chose the item, loaded the item into the truck, and delivered the item.

Interactional Process. Three different measures reflecting the various theoretical emphases in the peer literature were used to assess the interactional process the partners used to convey or ascertain task-relevant information. *Observational learning* was the total number of seconds novices spent observing their expert partners perform the task. *Guidance by the expert* was coded as either physical intervention, which was any physical interference by the expert of the novice's activity by manipulating an object or person, e.g., the expert putting his or her hand on the novice's hand; directives and suggestion, that is the expert verbally telling or suggesting to the novice what to do; and positive support, which included positive statements and physical gestures by the expert that recognize progress by the novice on the task and/or promote continuance. *Conflict* included statements of disagreements about the choice, arrangement, or handling of an item.

RESULTS

Analysis of variance (ANOVA) was used to compare the performance and social interactional processes of children collaborating with same-age expert peers versus older expert peers.

PLANNING DURING COLLABORATION

There were no differences in planning effectiveness, i.e., the number of delivery attempts children required to perform the tasks successfully, between the two groups in either farm delivery. Peers in same-age dyads required an average of 1.5 trials to complete Delivery One and 4.1 trials to complete Delivery Two successfully. Peers in cross-age dyads required an average of 1.4 trials to complete Delivery One and 2.7 to complete Delivery Two successfully.

The most interesting differences emerged in relation to partner involvement and the interactional process. Novices planning with same-age experts were more involved in the three task operations, choosing, loading, and delivering items ($M = 40.25$, $SD = 25.94$),

during the two trials of the interaction than novices working with older experts ($M = 19.87$, $SD = 15.89$), $F(1, 16) = 5.43$, $p < .05$. (Because the conditions of homogeneity of variance was violated, a log base-10 transformation was used in this analysis.) Novices in same-age dyads were responsible, on average, for 32% of these task operations and novices in cross-age dyads were responsible for an average of 26% of these task operations. (Table 1 contains the means for these variables by group for each of the two farm deliveries.) Experts in same-age dyads were responsible for an average of 51% of the task operations, and experts in cross-age dyads were responsible, on average, for 55%. The remaining 17 and 18%, respectively, were shared by the two partners. Thus, the hypothesis that novices planning with same-age experts would be more involved in the task than novices planning with older experts was supported.

Vygotsky proposed that the experienced partner would adjust the problem-solving process so that, with experience, the learner would be able to participate in increasingly more complex aspects of the solution. Examination of the novice's participation from Delivery One (the easier of the two deliveries) to Delivery Two of the Farm Task reveals that novices planning with same-age experts increased in their participation from Delivery One, when they were responsible for an average of 29% of the task operations, to Delivery Two, when they were responsible for an average of 35% of the task operations, $t(7) = 1.82$, $p = .05$. In contrast, participation of the novices in cross-age dyads decreased as the task became more

TABLE 1   MEANS (AND STANDARD DEVIATIONS) FOR PERCENTAGE INVOLVEMENT BY NOVICES AND EXPERTS AND INTERACTIONAL PROCESS BY GROUP FOR THE INTERACTION TASK

Group	Same-age dyads		Cross-age dyads	
Variable	Delivery 1	Delivery 2	Delivery 1	Delivery 2
Partners' task involvement				
Novice only	28.6 (11.4)	34.6 (16.1)	29.8 (13.2)	22.9 (17.2)
Expert only	52.4 (15.0)	49.9 (15.3)	51.1 (18.2)	58.5 (19.6)
Both novice and expert	19.0 (10.4)	15.4 (7.7)	19.0 (6.7)	18.6 (7.2)
Guidance by an expert				
Physical intervention	1.4 (.7)	3.2 (3.4)	1.4 (.5)	1.6 (1.4)
Directives and suggestions	2.9 (2.2)	5.6 (5.3)	2.6 (2.2)	3.1 (2.5)
Positive support	1.6 (.7)	5.1 (4.7)	1.5 (.8)	1.2 (.5)
Observational learning				
(in seconds)	22.0 (27.1)	50.0 (98.9)	19.0 (16.7)	18.4 (33.2)
Conflict	2.5 (1.9)	4.2 (4.4)	1.1 (.3)	2.2 (1.3)

difficult, from a mean of 30% to a mean of 23%, $t(7) = -2.61$, $p = .02$.

Although the total amount of guidance by the expert on the Farm Task did not differ between the two groups, when the two deliveries are considered separately, we find that during the second delivery 5-year-old experts provided more positive support ($M = 5.12$, $SD = 4.7$), $F(1, 16) = 5.37$, $p = .05$, for the novices than 7-year-old experts ($M = 1.25$, $SD = .46$). In addition, conflict during the second delivery was somewhat greater in the same-age dyads, $F(1, 16) = 3.23$, $p = .09$. (See means for these variables in Table 1.) It appears that same-age experts not only fostered more participation by the novice as he or she gained experience, these experts also supported their agemates more during the joint task. However, novices and experts of the same age also tended to challenge each other more than when partners were of different ages. Finally, due to the variance within the groups, they did not differ in terms of the time spent by the novice observing the expert perform the task.

Same-age dyads were not significantly different from cross-age dyads in number of strategy statements made by the expert. Experts in the same-age dyads produced an average of 14.4 strategy statements and those in cross-age dyads produced an average of 7.7 strategy statements. Novices in same-age dyads produced slightly more strategy statements (an average of 8.4) than novices in cross-age dyads (an average of 4.0), $F(1, 16) = 4.01$, $p = .06$, suggesting that, in addition to greater participation in task operations, collaborating with a same-age peer may also facilitate greater involvement by the novice in strategy formation.

Taken together, these results indicate that peer interaction differs when partners are of the same versus different ages. Novices planning with same-age experts were more involved in the task and experienced more support and challenge from same-age partners who were more expert at the task than did novices planning with older experts. Age-related dynamics appear to be an influential factor in the process of peer cognitive interaction. We now examine the relationship of the interactional process in these two groups to the novices' individual posttest performances to investigate whether these dynamics are related to what novices learn from collaborating with an expert.

RELATION OF COLLABORATION TO POSTTEST PLANNING PERFORMANCE

Pearson correlation coefficients were calculated to determine whether the interaction related to posttest performance and whether these relationships differed across the two groups. It was found that the number of trials required by novices to complete the posttest successfully was related to partner involvement during the interaction. More involvement by the novice in choosing, loading, and delivering items during the collaborative tasks was related to more effective planning on the posttest, $r(16) = -.49$, $p < .05$. (Recall that better planning performance is indicated by fewer trials.) And, mirroring this, greater involvement by the expert during the interaction was related to less effective planning by the novice on the posttest, $r(16) = .56$, $p < .05$.

When the two farm deliveries are considered separately, we find that for the novices in the same-age dyads, the number of trials required to complete the posttest was related to the total instances of guidance by the expert in delivery two, $r(8) = -.78$, $p < .05$. That is, for children in same-age dyads only, the extent to which the expert offered assistance to the novice was related to better performance on the posttest. Thus, Vygotsky's suggestion that interaction with those who are more expert would foster guidance and cognitive support was supported in the same-age dyads only. Since there were no differences between groups in the amount of guidance by the experts, perhaps other factors, such as involvement of the novice, which was greater in same-age dyads, bolstered the effectiveness of the experts' assistance during joint planning.

Further support for the importance of learner involvement in the task emerged in t tests comparing the posttest scores (number of delivery trials to complete the task) of the children in this study with the posttest scores of 5-year-old children in a study using this same task but who did not collaborate with a peer prior to the posttest (Gauvain, 1992). It was found that only the children who collaborated with the same-age experts, but not those who collaborated with older experts, performed significantly better than children who did not collaborate, $t(24) = 2.18$, $p < .05$. The mean number of trials to complete the posttest successfully for 5-year-old children who planned with same-age experts was 2.37 ($SD = 1.30$, $n = 8$) and the mean for the children who planned alone prior to the posttest was 4.75 ($SD = 3.94$, $n = 16$). The mean number of trials for 5-year-old children who planned previously with an older expert was 3.37 ($SD = 1.85$, $n = 8$), which does not differ significantly from the children who planned with the same-age experts or who planned entirely on their own. This suggests that collaboration between novices and experts of the same-age, but not of different ages, may lead to more successful planning than when children plan independently.

DISCUSSION

The purpose of this study was to examine the effects of age versus expertise in facilitating the development of children's planning skills during joint planning. It was hypothesized that the age of the expert partner would influence the involvement of the novice, which in turn would affect the extent of learning. The results support this prediction. Novices who planned with same-age experts were more involved in the task than novices who planned with older experts. Furthermore, novices who collaborated with same-age experts performed significantly better in later individual planning than children who did not collaborate prior to performing the same task. This difference did not appear for novices who planned with older experts. Finally, guidance by the expert, although not significantly different between the two groups, was related to later individual planning for novices who previously planned with same-age experts but not for novices who previously planned with older experts.

These findings support Vygotsky's (1978) general contention that cognitive development may benefit from opportunities available in the social context. However, they extend this view by suggesting factors that may influence this process. Although the results indicate that collaboration between novice and expert planners can lead to the development of the novice's skills, exposure to expertise was not sufficient for explaining the cognitive gains resulting from the social situation. The extent to which the novices were involved in the task influenced learning, however, the extent of novice involvement was affected by the relative age of the social partners. Perhaps novices who planned with same-age experts did not perceive as much social and cognitive distance between themselves and the experts compared to novices who planned with older experts. Children may feel more comfortable collaborating with experts of the same age and even perceive the partner's skills as attainable.

Another possibility, related to the first, is that experts in cross-age dyads dominate the interaction and do not allow their novice partners to participate in the problem-solving process. Recall that the data showed that the experts in the cross-age group were responsible, on average, for 55% of the task operations, while their novice partners were responsible for only 26% of the operations (compared with 51% involvement for experts and 32% for novices in same-age dyads). Furthermore, after examining the novices' participation from Delivery One, the easier of the two deliveries, to Delivery Two of the interaction, it was found that novices planning with same-age experts increased their participation, whereas participation of the novices in cross-age dyads decreased as the task became more difficult. These patterns, as well as the finding that the 5-year-old experts provided more positive support for their partners in Delivery Two, raise the possibility that the 5-year-old experts were more sensitive to the learner's needs and capabilities, and therefore allowed their novice partners to be more involved in the task as they gained experience. Of course, the related interpretation is that 5-year-old

novices are more likely to allow older experts to dominate the interaction than same-age experts. The marginally significant difference in conflict between the two groups, with greater conflict in same-age dyads, supports this interpretation. More frequent bids for dominance by older children and acceptance of these by younger children are reciprocal processes, that, by definition, are more likely to appear in mixed-age pairs.

Of the mechanisms that are hypothesized to facilitate cognitive growth — conflict, guided participation, and observational learning — only guidance by an expert was found to mediate learning. However, guidance was only effective for 5-year-old novices planning with same-age experts, who also had greater involvement in the task. Thus, guided participation in conjunction with increased task involvement facilitated learning for the novice when planning with a same-age, but more expert peer. Piaget hypothesized that conflict between children mediates cognitive growth. In this study, the amount of conflict between social partners was minimal, although it was somewhat greater among same-age peers who did not share the same skill at planning. This suggests that in interactions where partners are not equal in skill but equal in age, mechanisms such as guidance and extent of participation may be more central than conflict for social facilitation to occur.

Although these results further our understanding of the role of social experience in cognitive development, they are less useful for explaining why the conditional effects for age were obtained and whether these effects are specific to the ages studied here or represent a more general finding. Research on the development of social comparison processes by Ruble and colleagues (Feldman & Ruble, 1988; Ruble, Boggiano, Feldman, & Loebl, 1980; Ruble & Frey, 1987) suggests a possible answer to these questions. When children collaborate with more experienced partners, opportunities arise for them to make ability comparisons between themselves and their partners that may be useful for defining their behavior as well as for directing future performances. Studies conducted in Ruble's lab have shown that child age influences the occurrence and the nature of these comparisons. During social interaction, 5-to 6-year-old children, the same age as the novices in the present study, are primarily oriented toward same-age peers as a source of social comparison, whereas older children and adults are more likely to select "upward" comparisons as a source for self-evaluation. Stated more generally, the meaning of different people in social cognitive processes, like social comparison, is a function of age-related developmental processes. In this research, same-age experts may have constituted an ideal arrangement for mediating social cognitive effects for 5-to 6-year-old novices, thereby reflecting age-specific processes of social comparison rather than more general principles of social facilitation across childhood. To explore this suggestion further, research that varies the ages of the novices in addition to that of the experts is needed. Since the ages of 7 to 9 years have been found (e.g., see Ruble & Frey, 1987) to be particularly important for refining processes of social comparison, such research may reveal whether these ages are also critical junctures in processes of social facilitation.

In sum, this research investigated the influence of peer interaction on cognitive development by examining differences in children's planning when they planned with an expert of the same age or an expert who was older. In previous research on peer collaboration, age and expertise have typically been confounded. Rather than suggesting that simply the presence of an expert partner promotes cognitive development, this study points to age-related status and behaviors as mediating the process and outcome of peer interaction on problem-solving tasks. In addition to the extent of task involvement by the novice and guidance by the expert, which were greater in same-age dyads, facilitation effects for young children may also be driven by opportunities during collaboration for children to make social comparisons. These findings suggest that further understanding of how the sociocognitive processes of guided participation, conflict, and observational learning relate to and integrate with processes of social comparison over the course of development is essential for unpacking the mechanisms whereby social interaction may promote or impede cognitive growth.

REFERENCES

Azmitia, M. (1988). Peer interaction and problem solving: When are two heads better than one? *Child Development*, **59**, 87–96.

Azmitia, M., & Perlmutter, M. (1989). Social influences on children's cognition: State of the art and future directions. In H. Reese (Ed.), *Advances in child development and behavior* (Vol. 22, pp. 89–144). San Diego, CA: Academic Press.

Blurton Jones, N. (1972). *Ethological studies of child behavior.* London: Cambridge University Press.

Boder, A. (1978). Etude de la composition d'un ordre inverse: Hypothese dur la coordination de deux sources de controle du raisonnement. *Archives de Psychologie*, **46**, 87–113.

Damon, W. (1984). Peer education: The untapped potential. *Journal of Applied Developmental Psychology*, **5**, 331–343.

Ellis, S., & Gauvain, M. (1992). Social and cultural influences on children's collaborative interactions. In L. T. Winegar and J. Valsiner (Eds.), *Children's development within social context: Vol. 2. Research and methodology* (pp. 155–180). Hillsdale, NJ: Erlbaum.

Ellis, S., & Rogoff, B. (1986). Problem solving in children's management of instruction. In E. Mueller and C. R. Cooper (Eds.), *Process and outcome in peer relationships* (pp. 301–325). New York: Academic Press.

Feldman, N. S., & Ruble, D. N. (1988). The effect of personal relevance on psychological inference: A developmental analysis. *Child Development*, **59**, 1339–1352.

Gauvain, M. (1992). *The development of planning skills.* Unpublished manuscript, University of California, Riverside.

Gauvain, M., & Rogoff, B. (1989). Collaborative problem solving and children's planning skills. *Developmental Psychology*, **25**, 139–151.

Glachan, M., & Light, P. (1982). Peer interaction and learning: Can two ways make a right? In G. Butterworth & P. Light (Eds.), *Social cognition: Studies of the development of understanding* (pp. 238–262). Chicago: University of Chicago Press.

Grusec, J. E., & Lytton, H. (1988). *Social development: History, theory, and research.* New York: Springer-Verlag.

Hartup, W. (1985). Relationships and their significance in cognitive development. In R. Hinde & A. Perret-Clermont (Eds.), *Relationships and cognitive development* (pp. 66–82). Oxford: Oxford University Press.

Mueller, E., & Cooper, C. R. (Eds.). (1986). *Process and outcome in peer relationships.* New York: Academic Press.

Murray, F. B. (1982). Teaching through social conflict. *Contemporary Educational Psychology*, **7**, 257–271.

Perret-Clermont, A. N. (1980). *Social interaction and cognitive development in children.* London: Academic Press.

Piaget, J. (1948). *The moral judgement of the child.* IL: Free Press.

Piaget, J. (1983). Piaget's theory. In W. Kessen (Ed.), *History, theory, and methods*: Vol. 1. *Handbook of Child Psychology* (pp. 294–356). New York: Wiley.

Rogoff, B. (1990). *Apprenticeship in thinking: Cognitive development in social context.* New York: Oxford University Press.

Rogoff, B., Gauvain, M., & Gardner, W. P. (1987). *Children's adjustment of plans to circumstances.* In S. L. Friedman, E. K. Scholnick, & R. R. Cocking (Eds.), *The role of planning in psychological development* (pp. 303–320). London: Cambridge University Press.

Ruble, D. N., Boggiano, A. K., Feldman, N. S., & Loebl, J. H. (1980). A developmental analysis of the role of social comparison in self-evaluation. *Developmental Psychology*, **16**, 105–115.

Ruble, D. N., & Frey, K. S. (1987). Social comparison and self-evaluation in the classroom: Developmental changes in knowledge and function. In J. C. Masters & W. P. Smith (Eds.), *Social comparison, social justice, relative deprivation* (pp. 81–104). Hillsdale, NJ: Erlbaum.

Tudge, J. R. H., & Rogoff, B. (1989). Peer influences on cognitive development: Piagetian and Vygotskian perspectives. In M. Bornstein and J. Bruner (Eds.). *Interaction in human development* (pp. 17–40). Hillsdale, NJ: Erlbaum.

Vygotsky, L. S. (1978). *Mind and society.* Cambridge, MA: Harvard University Press.

Wertsch, J. V., McNamee, G. D., McLane J. B., & Budwig, N. A. (1980). The adult–child dyad as a problem-solving system. *Child Development*, **51**, 1215–1221.

Questions

1. Why are expertise and age often confounded in cognitive developmental research involving peers?
2. Why were novices who worked with same-age experts expected to learn more about planning after collaborating with a peer than novices who worked with older experts?
3. What patterns of partner involvement appeared in the two social groupings (young novice–young expert vs. younger novice–older expert)?
4. How did guidance and conflict differ in these two groups?
5. How does developmental change in the process of social comparison help explain these results?
6. Whose view of peer collaboration and cognitive development was supported, Piaget's or Vygotsky's? Explain.

24 Children's Perceptions of Their Peer Experiences: Attributions, Loneliness, Social Anxiety, and Social Avoidance

NICKI R. CRICK · GARY W. LADD

Children's social relations with peers during middle childhood has been the subject of much research on social development. Although this topic is interesting in its own right, it also has much practical significance. Children's relations with peers during this time are some of the best predictors of healthy adjustment in adulthood. Therefore, better understanding of how children formulate relationships with peers and what happens when they don't is critical.

Research has shown that difficulties with peers can take many forms. For some children, these difficulties are manifest in acting-out behaviors, such as bullying and other forms of aggression. For other children, these difficulties register in internalized behaviors, such as loneliness, social anxiety, and social avoidance. This article by Nicki R. Crick and Gary W. Ladd concentrates on the latter group of children, those who appear to internalize their problems with peers. It examines the ways in which children who take this approach explain or attribute the outcomes of their peer experiences. Results identify two attributional patterns among these children that have different outcomes for children's adjustment.

In this study, Crick and Ladd provide a nice demonstration of some of the techniques used to study peer relations. These include a sociometric assessment to establish children's social status. They also used a pencil and paper measure to assess children's perceptions of loneliness, social anxiety, and social avoidance, as well as the children's attributions. Correlation analyses were used to study the interrelations of these variables.

In this study, 338 3rd and 5th graders completed a sociometric questionnaire and 3 instruments designed to assess their feelings of loneliness, social anxiety, social avoidance, and their attributions for social outcomes. Results showed that children's feelings and attributions varied as a function of peer status, gender, and grade. For example, compared with peers, rejected children reported higher levels of loneliness and were more likely to attribute relationship failures to external causes. Children's feelings were also significantly related to their attributions about social events. Popular, average, and controversial status children who were socially distressed exhibited a non-self-serving attributional style, whereas distressed rejected children exhibited a self-serving attributional pattern. Neglected children who were distressed exhibited elements of both of these attributional styles.

Reprinted by permission of the authors and the American Psychological Association from *Developmental Psychology*, 29 (1993), pp. 244–254. Copyright© 1993 by the American Psychological Association.

Nicki R. Crick, Division of Human Development and Family Studies, University of Illinois at Urbana-Champaign; Gary W. Ladd, Bureau of Educational Research, University of Illinois at Urbana-Champaign.

Portions of this article were presented at the meeting of the American Educational Research Association in April 1992, in San Francisco. We thank Barbara O'Donnel, Cheryl Nicholson, Theresa Morey, and Nancy Hollett-Wright for assistance with data collection and compilation.

Correspondence concerning this article should be addressed to Nicki R. Crick, Division of Human Development and Family Studies, 1105 West Nevada Street, University of Illinois, Urbana, Illinois 61801.

Because poor peer relationships have been associated with difficulties in development (see Parker & Asher, 1987), children with social adjustment problems have been the focus of numerous investigations in recent years. Much of this work has been concerned with identifying the behavioral and social–cognitive correlates of peer rejection (e.g., Crick & Ladd, 1990; Dodge, 1983; Renshaw & Asher, 1983), and this information has often been used to design appropriate interventions for children experiencing peer difficulties (e.g., Bierman & Furman, 1984; Ladd, 1981; Oden & Asher, 1977). Children are typically selected for such interventions on the basis of behavioral observation (e.g., those who behave aggressively) or through others' assessments of the child's social competence (e.g., peer sociometric nominations). Until recently, the relation between the researcher's or peers' perspective and the children's own perceptions of their social problems had not been considered.

Information regarding the emotional distress experienced by some children in social situations is important in several respects. As Hymel and Franke (1985) have argued, such information provides children with a "voice" in their possible selection for intervention procedures. Asher and colleagues (Asher & Williams, 1987; Asher, Zelis, Parker, & Bruene, 1991) have found that, given the opportunity, a large percentage of elementary school-age children will use this voice to ask for help with peer problems. Information about the child's perspective may also provide the researcher or clinician with clues as to which children will be most likely to benefit from intervention. Children who are unhappy with their social situation are likely to be more motivated than their peers to learn new social skills that may improve their relationships. In addition, as we have argued elsewhere (Ladd & Crick, 1989), information about children's feelings regarding their social experiences may enhance our understanding of the processes underlying children's social problems. For example, some children who appear socially incompetent may experience feelings of social anxiety that contribute to their inability to interact effectively. For these children, an understanding of their feelings in social situations may be crucial in delineating possible sources and contributors to their peer difficulties.

Feelings of loneliness, social anxiety, and preferences for peer avoidance have been proposed as important indicators of children's perceptions of distress or dissatisfaction within the peer group (e.g., Asher & Wheeler, 1985; Hymel & Franke, 1985). To date, only a few studies exist that have explored these indicators. Assessment of children's loneliness began when Asher and his colleagues (Asher, Hymel, & Renshaw, 1984) constructed a loneliness questionnaire appropriate for use with third- through sixth-grade children. These authors provide convincing evidence of

the measure's satisfactory psychometric properties. In their initial study using the questionnaire, Asher et al. found that third- through sixth-grade unpopular children reported significantly higher levels of loneliness than their popular peers. In a subsequent study of children in the same age group, Asher and Wheeler (1985) distinguished between subgroups of unpopular children (i.e., rejected and neglected) and found that rejected children reported higher levels of loneliness than their more popular peers whereas neglected children did not. This finding has been replicated in several other samples (Asher & Williams, 1987; Cassidy & Asher, 1992; Parkhurst & Asher, 1992).

Research on children's feelings of social anxiety (i.e., feelings of anxiousness experienced specifically during peer interaction) and preferences for social avoidance has been delayed by the absence of reliable and valid measures. However, Franke and Hymel (cf. Franke & Hymel, 1984; Hymel & Franke, 1985) have developed an instrument to assess children's social avoidance and social anxiety that appears to have sound psychometric properties (e.g., high test–retest reliability, an interpretable and replicable factor structure, and evidence supportive of construct validity—see Franke & Hymel, 1984, 1987; Hymel & Franke, 1985).

Franke and Hymel (1984) used this instrument and the Asher et al. (1984) loneliness measure to survey third- through sixth-grade popular and unpopular children. Results showed that unpopular girls reported significantly higher levels of social anxiety and loneliness than did popular girls. In addition, loneliness was significantly related to social anxiety for girls and to social avoidance for both boys and girls. This study represents an important first step in the study of children's feelings of social anxiety and peer avoidance. However, further research is needed in which neglected children (those who are largely ignored by peers), rejected children (those who are actively disliked by peers), and controversial children (those who are highly liked by some peers and highly disliked by other peers) are identified—three distinct and important groups of children (Asher & Wheeler, 1985; Coie, Dodge, & Coppottelli, 1982; Hymel & Rubin, 1985). These groups were targeted in a study of social anxiety by LaGreca, Dandes, Wick, Shaw, and Stone (1988). However, these authors used a status classification system that has been shown to be less than optimal for the identification of neglected and controversial children (Asher & Dodge, 1986). Thus, the degree to which rejected, neglected, and controversial status children experience social anxiety is still unclear. The first goal of the present study was to compare the social feelings (i.e., social anxiety, social avoidance, and loneliness) of these groups of children with those of their popular and average status peers.

A second goal of the study was to assess the number of children in each status group who report multiple forms of distress. Feeling bad about one's peer experiences in a number of ways (e.g., anxious plus lonely) may be more upsetting for children than feeling bad about only one aspect of one's peer experiences (e.g., anxious). Multiple forms of distress may also pose more serious risks to children's long-term health and development (Rutter, 1979) and thus warrant further research attention. Consequently, it seemed important to identify the percentage of children in each sociometric status group who may be experiencing multiple forms of distress.

Asher et al. (1984) have pointed out that feelings about one's social relationships are subjective experiences. Consequently, the relation between peer status (a nonsubjective indicator of social adjustment) and children's feelings of loneliness, social anxiety, and so on is far from perfect. Although some important between-group status differences have been noted in the previously described research on children's social feelings, close scrutiny of these investigations shows that a large degree of within-group variation is also apparent. For example, some children who are popular with peers report extremely high levels of loneliness, whereas some rejected children report extremely low levels. Thus, there appear to be large individual differences in children's social feelings within status groups that have not yet been explained (Asher & Wheeler, 1985).

Clearly, the relation between children's social adjustment and their feelings about their peer experiences is a complex one. Asher and his colleagues have recently proposed that this relation might be better understood through an examination of children's attributions regarding the causes of social outcomes (Asher et al., 1984; Asher, Parkhurst, Hymel, & Williams, 1990). In two recent papers, specific theoretical linkages among peer status, social feelings, and children's attributions have been proposed (Crick & Dodge, 1992; Ladd & Crick, 1989). According to these authors, children's social feelings develop during the course of peer interaction as they attempt to interpret social events (e.g., peers' reactions and attitudes toward them). Part of this interpretation process involves figuring why particular social events have occurred (i.e., making attributions). Thus, children's social feelings and their attributions for social outcomes are related social–cognitive and affective processes, both of which are dependent to some degree on the types of peer encounters that children experience. Consequently, socially distressed children in one status group are likely to be faced with a different attributional task than are children in another group, primarily because their peer experiences differ. For example, a lonely popular child and a lonely rejected child may each make attributions about social events

that support their negative views of the peer environment. However, those attributions are based on different "data sets" for each child (primarily successful peer interactions for the popular child and primarily unsuccessful peer interactions for the rejected child).

Because there is little prior research in which children's social feelings, attributions for social outcomes, and peer status have all been assessed in a single study, information about the proposed theoretical linkages is lacking. Thus, in the present study, our third goal was to test the hypothesis that children's feelings are related to their attributions about social outcomes and that this relation varies within each status group.

Previous work suggests that the locus of children's attributions (e.g., external or internal) may be an important dimension for understanding the relations among peer status, social feelings, and social attributions. For example, prior investigations have shown a relation between low peer status and internal attributions for social failure (Ames, Ames, & Garrison, 1977; Goetz & Dweck, 1980; Hymel et al., 1983, Study 1), and external attributions for social success (Ames et al., 1977; Hymel et al., 1983, Study 1). In the Hymel et al. study, which was a 2-year project, this finding was not replicated in the second year. Because these studies did not distinguish among social status groups (e.g., rejected vs. neglected), these findings were not used as a basis for generating specific a priori hypotheses in the present study.

In this investigation, children's internal (e.g., the outcome was caused by the self), external (e.g., the outcome was caused by the peer), and mutual (e.g., the outcome was caused by an interaction between the self and peer) attributions were assessed, categories that were adapted from those used by Ames et al. (1977). It was expected that the mutual category, one that is not commonly used in studies of children's attributions, might be useful in identifying groups of children who think about social interactions in relatively mature ways. This was expected because attributions of mutual causation seem to call for recognition of the transactional nature of relationships, an interpretation that appears more complex than those that simply involve blaming a peer or the self. Specifically, we hypothesized that older children would make more mutual attributions than younger children.

To assess children's feelings of distress regarding their peer relationships, we used the Asher and Wheeler (1985) loneliness scale and the Franke and Hymel (1984) social anxiety and avoidance scale. To assess children's attributions, we constructed an instrument that measures the locus of children's attributions for social outcomes. Previous investigators of children's attributions have typically examined two general types of social outcomes: positive (i.e., social success) and negative (i.e., social failure or rejection; see Ladd & Crick, 1989, for a review). However, recent research shows that at least two specific kinds of positive and negative social outcomes are salient to children (Crick & Ladd, 1990): (a) instrumental outcomes (e.g., whether or not a peer does what you want them to do) and relational outcomes (e.g., whether or not a peer likes you). Based on these findings, children's attributions for both instrumental and relational outcomes were assessed in the present study. Because the self-perception and attribution measures are relatively new, a fourth goal of the present study was to investigate the psychometric adequacy of each measure.

METHOD

SUBJECTS

A total of 338 children from five midwestern elementary schools served as subjects. The sample included 175 third graders (79 girls and 96 boys) and 164 fifth graders (79 girls and 85 boys) from 12 third- and 11 fifth-grade classrooms. Mean age was 9.5 years for the third graders and 11.4 years for the fifth graders. Each subject had parental consent to participate in the project.

SOCIOMETRIC ASSESSMENT

Within each of the classrooms, subjects were asked to nominate up to three classmates they liked to play with most at school (positive nominations) and up to three classmates they liked to play with least at school (negative nominations). The positive and negative nominations children received from their classmates were used to identify five sociometric status groups—popular, average, neglected, rejected, and controversial children—using the procedure described by Coie and Dodge (1983), except for those in the average group, who were identified using the criteria described by Coie et al. (1982). First, the number of positive nominations (p) and the number of negative nominations (n) received by each child were standardized within each classroom. These standardized scores were then used to create two new variables, social preference ($Zp - Zn$) and social impact ($Zp + Zn$). Children's scores for each of these two variables were again standardized within each classroom. We used the standardized scores for social impact, social preference, number of positive nominations, and number of negative nominations to determine each child's social status according to the following criteria: (a) Popular children received a social preference score greater than 1.0, a positive nomination score greater than 0, and a negative nomination score less than 0; (b) average children received a social preference score

less than .5 and greater than −.5; (c) neglected children received a social impact score of less than −1.0, a positive nomination score less than 0, and a negative nomination score less than 0; (d) rejected children received a social preference score less than −1.0, a negative nomination score greater than 0, and a positive nomination score less than 0; and (e) controversial children received a social impact score greater than 1.0, a negative nomination score greater than 0, and a positive nomination score greater than 0.

This procedure resulted in the identification of 49 popular (27 third and 22 fifth graders), 76 average (44 third and 32 fifth graders), 42 neglected (19 third and 23 fifth graders), 59 rejected (30 third and 29 fifth graders), and 19 controversial (9 third and 10 fifth graders) children. Children not classified by this scheme completed the questionnaires, but their data were not included in the subsequent analyses.

LONELINESS, SOCIAL ANXIETY, AND SOCIAL AVOIDANCE SCALES

The Franke and Hymel (1984) social anxiety and social avoidance scale for children consists of six items that assess social anxiety (e.g., "I usually feel nervous when I meet someone for the first time") and six items that assess social avoidance (e.g., "I really like doing things with other kids"). Possible responses to each item range from 1(*not at all true about me*) to 5 (*always true about me*). Following the procedures described by Franke and Hymel, children's responses to the six items for each subscale were summed to yield two total subscale scores (i.e., one for anxiety and one for avoidance), each of which could range from 6 (*low anxiety/avoidance*) to 30 (*high anxiety/avoidance*). Children's total scores were used in subsequent analyses.

The Asher and Wheeler (1985) loneliness inventory consists of 16 items that assess children's feelings of loneliness and social dissatisfaction (e.g., "It's hard for me to make friends") and 8 filler items (e.g., "I like to read"). Possible responses to each item range from 1 (*not at all true about me*) to 5 (*always true about me*). Following the method outlined by Asher and Wheeler, children's responses to the 16 loneliness items were summed to yield a total scale score that could range from 16 (*low loneliness*) to 80 (*high loneliness*). Each child's total score was used in subsequent analyses. Children's responses to the 8 filler items were not analyzed.

ATTRIBUTION INSTRUMENT

In contrast to prior research in which forced-choice questionnaires have sometimes been used (e.g., Ames et al., 1977), the attribution instrument used in the present study allowed children to rate the likelihood of multiple causes for each outcome presented. Because social situations are typically complex and often influenced to some degree by multiple causal agents, this method was used so that complex views of social events could be more validly assessed (i.e., instead of forcing children with complex perspectives to select only one cause as has been done in much of the prior research). Thus, with this method, children could indicate that more than one cause was applicable in a particular instance. For example, a child could indicate that negative outcomes are sometimes due to the peer and sometimes due to the self (i.e., they could rate both the internal and the external outcomes as "sometimes the reason" for the outcome).

The attribution instrument used in the present study consists of 20 social outcomes, 5 for each of the four outcome categories (i.e., positive–instrumental; negative–instrumental; positive–relational; and negative–relational). For each of the outcomes, three possible causes are described that vary according to the locus of the attribution (i.e., internal, external, or mutual). Example items are given in the Appendix, one for each of the four outcome categories.

Children respond to the measure by rating how often each outcome might occur to them as a result of each of the three possible causes. Each rating is done with respect to a 5-point scale that varies from 1 (*this is never the reason*) to 5 (*this is always the reason*). Children received scores per outcome, one for each of the three locus categories. Children's scores were summed across the five similar items within each outcome type and locus type (individual item scores could range from 0 to 25), resulting in a total of 12 scores per child for the entire measure.

To examine the internal consistency of children's responses to the attribution items, we computed Cronbach's alpha. The measure proved to be reliable, with $\alpha = .83$. Alphas were also computed for the individual subscales, and only those with internal consistency sufficient for five-item scales (i.e., those with $\alpha \geq .5$) were retained for use in subsequent analyses. All but 2 (external positive–relational outcomes and external positive–instrumental outcomes) of the 12 subscales met this criteria (for the remaining subscales, $\alpha = .5 - .6$ range).

ADMINISTRATION OF THE INSTRUMENTS

The three instruments were group administered within each classroom or each grade level in a school during two separate sessions. Order of presentation of the measures was randomized within grade level. Before the administration of each instrument, children were first taught to use the response scale through the use of several practice items (e.g., "I like to eat spinach"). Then the first item of the instrument and the possible responses were read aloud to the group by one of the administrators. The administrator continued to read items out loud until it seemed apparent that the children could complete the remaining items on their own. Teams of two to four trained examiners (depending on the group size) monitored children's responses during testing to ensure that they understood the tasks and used the response formats correctly.

RESULTS

Before conducting subsequent analyses, we first assessed the psychometric adequacy of the loneliness, social anxiety, and peer avoidance measures for the present sample of children. To examine the internal consistency of children's responses to the items contained in the three instruments, we first computed Cronbach's alpha. All three measures proved to be reliable, with $\alpha = .90, .70,$ and $.79$ for the loneliness, social anxiety, and social avoidance scales, respectively. Intermeasure correlations were also examined to ensure that the measures were not redundant. For the entire population, results showed that children's loneliness scores were only low to moderately correlated with their avoidance ($r = .49, p < .01$) and anxiety ($r = .25, p < .01$) scores. Children's avoidance and anxiety scores were uncorrelated ($r = .07, ns$). Correlations done separately for girls and boys yielded findings similar to those found by Franke and Hymel (1984); that is, loneliness was significantly related to anxiety for girls ($r = .31, p < .001$) and to avoidance for both sexes ($r = .36, p < .001$ and $r = .52, p < .001$ for girls and boys, respectively).

We also attempted to replicate the factor structure of the loneliness and social anxiety/avoidance instruments using the same analyses reported by Asher and colleagues (Asher et al., 1984; Asher & Wheeler, 1985) and Franke and Hymel (1984). Children's responses to the items on each of the two instruments were subjected to a principal-components factor analysis.

The factor analysis done on children's responses to the loneliness scale (quartimax rotation) produced findings that were nearly identical to those reported by Asher and Wheeler (1985). A primary factor was extracted that accounted for 26.7% of the variation in the scores and consisted of the 16 loneliness items (loadings ranged from .50 to .76 with the exception of one item that had a loading of .32). One filler item (i.e., "I play sports a lot") loaded moderately (.34) on the loneliness factor, a finding that is consistent with results reported by Asher and Wheeler. Following the procedures outlined by these authors, we did not use the sports filler item in computing children's loneliness scores in the present study.

TABLE 1   CHILDREN'S LONELINESS, ANXIETY, AND ATTRIBUTION SCORES BY SOCIOMETRIC STATUS

Measure	Status group				
	Popular	Average	Neglected	Rejected	Controversial
Loneliness					
M	27.86	32.30	32.38	39.66	31.47
SD	8.48	9.27	12.86	13.21	6.32
Anxiety					
M	17.35	18.95	16.83	18.85	18.63
SD	4.51	4.74	4.55	4.95	3.73
IPR					
M	18.22	18.20	17.46	17.32	16.42
SD	3.04	3.05	2.63	3.83	3.06
MPR					
M	18.57	18.17	17.76	17.33	16.37
SD	2.80	3.06	2.97	3.01	3.61
INR					
M	12.10	11.09	11.12	12.11	11.37
SD	3.89	3.19	3.41	4.02	2.75
ENR					
M	12.84	13.78	13.80	14.79	12.11
SD	2.85	3.40	3.30	4.11	2.69
MNR					
M	14.41	14.28	13.79	14.46	14.68
SD	3.51	3.61	3.51	4.13	3.97
IPI					
M	16.67	16.52	16.52	15.61	15.28
SD	3.36	2.98	3.02	3.44	4.34
MPI					
M	17.06	17.18	16.07	16.82	16.47
SD	3.03	2.97	3.33	3.24	3.20
INI					
M	11.67	11.19	11.26	12.19	11.58
SD	3.14	3.64	3.62	3.26	3.47
ENI					
M	14.24	13.59	14.02	14.73	13.84
SD	2.72	2.98	3.65	3.52	3.02
MNI					
M	13.47	13.64	13.17	14.58	14.00
SD	3.13	3.34	4.09	4.00	4.08

Note. IPR = internal, positive–relational; MPR = mutual, positive–relational; INR = internal, negative–relational; ENR = external, negative–relational; MNR = mutual, negative–relational; IPI = internal, positive–instrumental; MPI = mutual, positive–instrumental; INI = internal, negative–instrumental; ENI = external, negative–instrumental; MNI = mutual, negative–instrumental. Because of low subscale reliability, scores for external attributions about positive events (external, positive–relational and external, positive–instrumental) are not included in the table.

The factor analysis done on children's responses to the social anxiety and social avoidance scale (varimax rotation) was highly consistent with those reported by Franke and Hymel (1984). The analysis produced two distinct factors. The avoidance items loaded on the first factor (loadings ranged from .58 to .77), and the anxiety items loaded on the second factor (loadings ranged from .40 to .71). The avoidance factor accounted for 25.2% of the variation in children's scores, and the anxiety factor accounted for 20.4% of the variation in scores. Cross-loadings were insubstantial for both factors.

STATUS DIFFERENCES IN CHILDREN'S FEELINGS AND ATTRIBUTIONS

To assess possible group differences in children's perceptions of loneliness, social avoidance, and social anxiety, we conducted three 2 (grade) $\times$ 2 (sex) $\times$ 5 (sociometric status) between-subjects analyses of variance (ANOVAs) on children's responses to each scale.[1] To assess possible group differences in children's attributions, four 2 (grade) $\times$ 2 (sex) $\times$ 5 (sociometric status) between-subject multivariate analyses of variance (MANOVAs) were conducted (one for each outcome category) in which children's scores for the internal, external, and mutual attribution categories served as the variates (all three variates were not included in every set of analyses because two subscales were dropped after prior analyses showed them to be unreliable). These overall analyses were then followed by tests of simple effects and Duncan post hoc tests where appropriate.

Children's Perceptions of Loneliness. The ANOVA, done on children's loneliness scores, resulted in a significant effect of sociometric status, $F(4, 225) = 8.80$, $p < .001$, and a marginally significant effect of grade, $F(1, 225) = 3.45$, $p < .07$. Inspection of the main effect means for grade showed that third graders ($M = 34.29$, $SD = 11.31$) tended to report higher levels of loneliness than did fifth graders ($M = 31.85$, $SD = 11.34$). A Duncan post hoc test ($p = .05$), done on the status means, showed that rejected children reported significantly higher levels of loneliness than their popular, average, neglected, and controversial peers (see Table 1 for cell means and standard deviations).

Children's Perceptions of Social Avoidance. The ANOVA done on children's responses to the social avoidance subscale yielded significant effects due to grade, $F(1, 225) = 8.33$, $p < .01$. Inspection of the

main effect means for grade revealed that third graders ($M = 12.98$, $SD = 4.67$) reported significantly more social avoidance than fifth graders ($M = 11.43$, $SD = 4.27$).

Children's Perceptions of Social Anxiety. The ANOVA done on children's reported levels of social anxiety resulted in significant effects for grade, $F(1, 225) = 9.76$, $p < .01$; sex, $F(1, 225) = 4.91$, $p < .05$; sociometric status, $F(4, 225) = 2.38$, $p \le .05$; and grade by sex, $F(1, 225) = 4.30$, $p < .05$. A Duncan post hoc test ($p = .05$), done on the status means, revealed that neglected children reported significantly lower levels of anxiety than average and rejected children (see Table 1 for cell means and standard deviations). Neglected children's scores, although lower, did not differ statistically from those of popular children or controversial children. Inspection of the cell means for the main effects of sex and grade showed that girls ($M = 19.03$, $SD = 4.49$) and fifth graders ($M = 19.20$, $SD = 4.33$) reported significantly more social anxiety than boys ($M = 17.54$, $SD = 4.77$) and third graders ($M = 17.34$, $SD = 4.84$), respectively. However, these main effects are qualified by a significant interaction of sex and grade. This interaction was investigated through a Duncan post hoc test ($p = .05$) of the cell means. This analysis revealed that fifth-grade girls ($M = 20.54$, $SD = 4.23$) reported significantly higher levels of social anxiety than the other three groups (third-grade boys: $M = 17.27$, $SD = 5.27$; third-grade girls: $M = 17.45$, $SD = 4.23$; and fifth-grade boys: $M = 17.90$, $SD = 4.06$).

Children's Attributions. The MANOVA done on children's attribution scores for the negative, relational outcomes yielded a significant multivariate effect for sociometric status. Wilks's lambda (3, 0, 108 1/2) = .89, $p < .05$, and a significant follow-up univariate test for the external attribution category, $F(4, 221) = 3.66$, $p < .01$. A Duncan post hoc test showed that rejected children were more likely than popular and controversial children to attribute negative, relational outcomes to peers (see Table 1 for cell means and standard deviations).

The MANOVA done on children's attribution scores for the positive, relational outcomes yielded a marginally significant multivariate test for sociometric status, Wilks's lambda (2, 1/2, 109) = .94, $p \le .06$, and for grade, Wilks's lambda (1, 0, 109) = .98, $p < .08$. However, univariate tests for status were significant for the internal attribution category, $F(4, 221) = 2.68$, $p < .05$, and for the mutual attribution category, $F(4,$

---

[1]A univariate, rather than a multivariate, approach to analyses was taken for two reasons: (a) intercorrelations of the measures did not appear high enough to mandate a multivariate approach, and (b) we wanted to replicate the analyses used in prior research (i.e., univariate ANOVAs) to test the generalizability of the results obtained with the feeling measures across samples.

221) = 2.75, $p < .05$. Duncan post hoc tests showed the following (refer to Table 1 for cell means and standard deviations). Controversial children were less likely than average status peers to attribute positive, relational outcomes to themselves. Also, controversial children were less likely than popular and average children to attribute positive, relational outcomes to mutual causes. Univariate tests for grade showed a significant effect for the mutual attribution category, $F(1, 221) = 3.87$, $p \leq .05$. Inspection of cell means indicated that fifth graders ($M = 18.22$, $SD = 2.81$) were more likely than third graders ($M = 17.49$, $SD = 3.26$) to attribute positive, relational outcomes to mutual causes.

The MANOVA done on children's attribution scores for negative, instrumental outcomes yielded a significant multivariate effect for grade, Wilks's lambda (1, 1/2, 109) = .96, $p < .05$. Univariate tests showed a significant effect for the mutual attribution category, $F(1, 222) = 4.10$, $p < .05$. Inspection of cell means revealed that fifth graders ($M = 14.28$, $SD = 3.57$) were more likely than third graders ($M = 13.31$, $SD = 3.71$) to attribute negative, instrumental outcomes to mutual causes.

The MANOVA done on children's attribution scores for positive, instrumental outcomes yielded a significant multivariate effect for the Grade × Sex × Sociometric Status interaction. Wilks's lambda (3, 0, 108 1/2) = .90, $p < .05$. Univariate tests showed a significant effect for the internal, attribution category, $F(4, 221) = 2.49$, $p < .05$. Follow-up tests (simple effects ANOVAs and Duncan post hoc tests) showed that third-grade, popular boys ($M = 15.35$, $SD = 3.22$) were less likely than fifth-grade, popular boys ($M = 17.79$, $SD = 3.38$) and third-grade, popular girls ($M = 18.40$, $SD = 1.65$) to attribute positive, instrumental outcomes to themselves.

STATUS GROUP MEMBERSHIP OF HIGH-VERSUS LOW-DISTRESS CHILDREN

To provide an overall assessment of the number of children in each status group who may be experiencing multiple forms of distress, we identified a group of high-distress children. Specifically, children were classified as in the high-distress category if they had scores greater than a half a standard deviation above the mean on at least two of the three perception measures.[2] Table 2 shows the percentage of children in each status group belonging to the high-distress cate-

gory. A chi-square analysis was performed for this contingency table (i.e., frequencies in the high-distress vs. nonhigh-distress groups), and the test was significant, $\chi^2(4, N = 245) = 15.13$, $p < .01$. Tests on cell proportions (Bruning & Kintz, 1977; z tests for proportions in which rejected, neglected, and controversial children were each compared with average

TABLE 2   FREQUENCY AND PERCENTAGE OF CHILDREN REPORTING RELATIVELY HIGH LEVELS OF DISTRESS

Status group	n	Frequency	%
Popular	49	8	16.3
Average	76	19	25.0
Neglected	42	10	23.8
Rejected	59	26	44.1
Controversial	19	2	10.5

TABLE 3   INTERCORRELATIONS FOR THE FEELING MEASURES BY STATUS GROUP

Status group	Avoidance	Anxiety
Popular (n = 49)		
Loneliness	.515**	.226
Avoidance		.069
Average (n = 76)		
Loneliness	.428**	.334*
Avoidance		.194
Neglected (n = 42)		
Loneliness	.560**	.428*
Avoidance		.031
Rejected (n = 59)		
Loneliness	.440**	.178
Avoidance		.030
Controversial (n = 19)		
Loneliness	.022	.102
Avoidance		.149

*$p < .01$.   **$p < .001$.

---

[2]A more extreme group of high-distress children was also identified. This group included children with scores greater than 1 standard deviation above the mean on at least two of the three perception measures. Analyses conducted for this second set of classifications yielded the same results as those reported in the text for the original set of classifications (i.e., significantly more rejected than popular or average children were classified as highly distressed, $z = 3.02$, $p < .01$ and $z = 3.47$, $p < .001$, respectively).

and popular children) revealed that significantly more rejected than popular and average children were classified as highly distressed (rejected vs. average: $z = 2.36$, $p < .05$; rejected vs. popular: $z = 3.10$, $p < .01$).

RELATIONS AMONG ATTRIBUTIONS, FEELINGS, AND PEER STATUS

First, the intercorrelations of the feeling measures were examined separately for each status group with a series of two-tailed correlations (see Table 3).[3] Results indicate that, for all status groups except controversial children, loneliness was significantly related to social avoidance. Also, for average and neglected children, loneliness was significantly related to social anxiety.

Second, the relations among children's feelings about their social experiences and their attributions for social outcomes were examined through a series of two-tailed correlations, conducted separately for each of the four status groups (see footnote 3). Results of these analyses are contained in Tables 4 and 5. To minimize Type I error, we used a conservative significance level ($p < .01$).

Results indicate that children's feelings are significantly related to their attributions. As predicted, these relations appear to vary within each sociometric status group. More specifically, for popular children, feeling lonely is negatively related to taking credit for relationship successes. For rejected children, wanting to avoid peers is positively related to blaming others when relationships fail. For average children, feeling lonely is positively related to blam-

---

TABLE 4 TWO-TAILED CORRELATIONS BY STATUS GROUP FOR RELATIONAL OUTCOMES

Status group	IPR	MPR	INR	ENR	MNR
Popular ($n = 49$)					
Loneliness	−.508**	−.306	.248	−.224	−.187
Avoidance	−.205	−.245	.176	−.066	.031
Anxiety	.038	.009	−.172	−.230	−.214
Average ($n = 76$)					
Loneliness	−.266	−.234	.432**	.267	.107
Avoidance	−.106	−.230	.220	.136	.208
Anxiety	.080	.146	−.051	−.009	.284
Neglected ($n = 42$)					
Loneliness	−.592**	−.276	.172	.351	.198
Avoidance	−.472*	−.173	.217	.416*	.420*
Anxiety	−.174	.052	.017	−.066	−.129
Rejected ($n = 59$)					
Loneliness	−.102	−.001	.096	.252	.097
Avoidance	−.080	−.023	.128	.393*	.220
Anxiety	−.127	.057	−.078	.009	−.084
Controversial ($n = 19$)					
Loneliness	.015	−.019	−.352	.053	−.410
Avoidance	.029	−.122	.294	−.600*	.090
Anxiety	.204	.279	−.046	−.057	.314

Note. IPR = internal, positive–relational; MPR = mutual, positive–relational; INR = internal, negative–relational; ENR = external, negative–relational; MNR = mutual, negative–relational.
*$p < .01$. **$p < .001$.

---

[3]To assess the possible impact of grade, we performed an additional set of these analyses in which grade was partialed from each of the feeling and attributional variables before the calculation of the correlations. These analyses yielded partial correlations comparable with the correlations reported in Tables 3, 4, and 5.

TABLE 5   TWO-TAILED CORRELATIONS BY STATUS GROUP FOR INSTRUMENTAL OUTCOMES

Status group	IPI	MPI	INI	ENI	MNI
Popular (n = 49)					
Loneliness	−.201	−.246	.277	.134	−.011
Avoidance	−.106	−.052	.256	.079	.037
Anxiety	.063	.246	−.171	−.185	−.063
Average (n = 76)					
Loneliness	−.243	−.186	.411**	.113	.354*
Avoidance	−.279	−.229	.327*	.045	.205
Anxiety	.052	.018	−.132	−.026	.066
Neglected (n = 42)					
Loneliness	−.495*	−.377	.286	.351	.274
Avoidance	−.452*	−.195	.426*	.425*	.390
Anxiety	−.014	−.088	.002	−.104	−.253
Rejected (n = 59)					
Loneliness	−.124	.245	.094	.228	−.021
Avoidance	−.092	−.187	−.002	.340	.209
Anxiety	.124	.095	−.102	.037	−.074
Controversial (n = 19)					
Loneliness	−.100	−.029	.100	−.081	−.176
Avoidance	.131	−.377	.572*	−.226	−.128
Anxiety	.454	.386	−.044	.201	.468

Note. IPI = internal, positive−instrumental; MPI = mutual, positive−instrumental; INI = internal, negative−instrumental; ENI = external, negative−instrumental; MNI = mutual, negative−instrumental.

$*p < .01.$ $**p < .001.$

ing the self for relationship failures and blaming the self or the interaction between the self and other (mutual attributions) for instrumental failures. For neglected children, feeling lonely is negatively related to taking credit for relational and instrumental successes. Also, for this group, wanting to avoid peers is negatively related to taking credit for relational and instrumental successes; positively related to blaming others and the interaction between the self and others for relationship failures; and positively related to blaming the self and others for instrumental failures. For controversial children, wanting to avoid peers is negatively related to blaming others for relationship failures and positively related to blaming the self for instrumental failures.

DISCUSSION

Results of the present study provide initial evidence for proposed theoretical linkages among social status, social distress, and children's attributions for social events (Asher et al., 1990; Ladd & Crick, 1989). In addition, they provide additional support for the psychometric soundness of the Asher and Wheeler (1985) loneliness scale and the Franke and Hymel (1984) social anxiety and social avoidance scale.

Results from the social distress measures yielded a unique pattern of results for the three status groups that are typically characterized as having social problems (i.e., rejected, neglected, and controversial status children). Findings for the controversial children showed that, as a group, they are not more socially distressed than other children. In fact, results of the multiple distress analyses showed that, compared with other status groups (including popular children), the controversial group had the smallest proportion of members who could be classified as multiply distressed. Thus, even though they are actively disliked by some peers, it appears that most controversial status children are relatively happy and comfortable with their peer relationships.

Similarly, the findings for the neglected group showed that they are not greatly distressed by their relative lack of relationships within the peer group (i.e., as a group, they reported relatively low levels of loneliness and social anxiety and had few members classified as multiply distressed), results that are consistent with research by Rubin, Hymel, LeMare, and Rowden (1989). Unlike rejected children, neglected children tend to be positively nominated by at least one peer (Coie & Dodge, 1983). Perhaps neglected children are satisfied with less prominent positions in the peer culture or may be less interested than other children in extensive social ties (e.g., developing relationships with large numbers of peers). As Solano (1986) has suggested, having few friends is not necessarily associated with feeling lonely, and even one positive relationship may reduce various forms of interpersonal distress (cf. Asher et al., 1990). Perhaps this is the case for neglected children.

In contrast to controversial and neglected children, rejected children exhibited relatively high levels of social distress (i.e., they reported significantly higher levels of loneliness than all other groups and had the largest percentage of members who could be classified as experiencing multiple forms of distress). Given that rejected children live in a social environment in which most of their peers dislike them, it is not surprising that they tend to feel lonely or to experience more than one form of distress. Because peer rejection is often an overt phenomenon (i.e., ridicule and rejecting behavior tends to be expressed openly in children's peer groups), rejected children may become keenly aware of their peers' negative sentiments toward them and feel distressed about their relative lack of positive relationships and abundance of negative relationships. Moreover, this potential awareness, coupled with the fact that rejected status is a relatively stable condition in children's peer groups (Coie & Dodge, 1983), may cause children to anticipate similar treatment from peers in the future. Support for these ideas is provided by the findings from the attribution measure. That is, rejected children were more likely than other children to view peers as the cause of their social difficulties (e.g., because other kids are mean). This result is consistent with previous research showing hostile attributional biases (i.e., the tendency to infer hostile intent to peers) in rejected children (e.g., Dodge & Frame, 1982; Waas, 1988; see Crick & Dodge, 1992, for a review).

Results of the present investigation show that, consistent with prior research, status groups differ significantly in the degree to which they are distressed about their social experiences (i.e., significant between-group variation is apparent). However, this research also demonstrates that, as predicted, considerable within-status group variation in social distress is also present (e.g., 16% of the popular children reported relatively high levels of distress, and 56% of the rejected children did not report high levels of distress). More important, it provides evidence that this within-group variation is significantly related to children's attributions for social events, a link that has been proposed previously (Asher et al., 1990; Ladd & Crick, 1989) but has not been emprically investigated.

Two distinct attributional patterns were apparent for the present sample, both of which can be interpreted within a conceptual framework adapted from attributional research with adults. Numerous investigations of adults have demonstrated that most individuals attribute positive events to themselves and negative events to external causes, a "self-serving" or self-protective bias that helps to maintain self-esteem (Miller & Ross, 1975). However, in contrast, distressed adults exhibit what has been called a "non-self-serving" bias (Asher et al., 1990); that is, they blame themselves for failures and they fail to take credit for social successes (e.g., Anderson, Horowitz, & French, 1983; Sweeney, Anderson, & Bailey, 1986). This attributional style is likely to lead to decreases in self-esteem and to heightened feelings of distress.

The present findings provide evidence that the attributional patterns found in prior studies for distressed versus nondistressed adults are also applicable to children (i.e., low social distress was associated with a self-serving attributional style for relational events, whereas high social distress was associated with a non-self-serving attributional style in the present research). However, these patterns appear to be specific to popular, average, and controversial status children only (i.e., neglected and rejected children exhibited different patterns). Thus, these findings are consistent with the idea that popular, average, and controversial children who feel socially distressed (who differ from neglected and rejected children in that they are all liked by peers to at least a moderate degree) may feel bad about their peer experiences partly because they interpret social interactions in a nonadaptive manner (i.e., in a way that fails to buffer them from negative conclusions about the self). This is a significant finding, because it demonstrates that being liked by peers (e.g., or even being extremely well liked as in the case of popular children) is not necessarily sufficient for emotional well-being; that is, an adaptive attributional style may also be required that facilitates enjoyment of social successes and adequate coping with social failures. For example, it appears that popular children, despite their high degree of acceptance in the peer group, must also be able to recognize their own role in producing their social successes in order to be satisfied with their peer relationships. Thus, it may be necessary in future research to include both subjective measures of social adjustment (e.g., social distress instruments) and the more traditional objective measures (e.g., peer status) to adequately identify children with problematic peer relationships.

In contrast to the attributional style of distressed popular, average, and controversial status children, distressed children who were rejected by peers exhibited a self-serving attributional style for relational outcomes (i.e., greater distress was associated with blaming peers for negative relational events). Unlike popular, average, and controversial status children, those who are rejected have more reason, from an objective standpoint, to feel distressed about their interactions with peers (i.e., because they are actively disliked by most peers and also lack positive peer relationships). It seems likely that admitting to social problems may be considerably more difficult for rejected children (i.e., because their difficulties are much more serious and long lasting) than for children who are better liked. As a result, those rejected children who are willing to acknowledge (or are aware of) their social problems may develop a self-protective, defensive way of thinking about those problems in order to cope with overly painful feelings (i.e., they may have a greater need than other children to avoid blaming themselves when they experience social failures and social distress). If so, they may develop a self-serving attributional style that allows them to interpret rejection experiences (which they are likely to encounter often) in a manner that is relatively nonthreatening to their self-esteem. Unfortunately, these types of attributions may also prevent distressed rejected children from acknowledging their own role in the creation of their social difficulties.

Findings for the neglected group showed that they exhibited elements of both of the previously described attributional patterns. For this group, social distress was associated with a non-self-serving attributional style for positive relational and instrumental events (i.e., loneliness and peer avoidance were both associated with not taking credit for positive outcomes) and a self-serving attributional style for negative relational events (i.e., peer avoidance was associated with blaming peers for negative relational outcomes). Thus, it appears that distressed neglected children, who are similar to rejected children in that they lack positive peer relationships, also interpret negative relational events in a self-protective manner. However, it appears that this protectiveness does not extend to their interpretations of social successes. In addition, assessment of neglected children's attributions for negative outcomes that were instrumental in nature showed that those who were distressed exhibited elements of both the self-serving and the non-self-serving attributional style for these outcomes (i.e., they blamed both the self and peers for these events). In this study, negative instrumental outcomes involved being ignored or thwarted by peers (e.g., "a kid you know does not listen when you talk"), situations that are likely to require assertiveness in order to improve one's effectiveness. Given that neglected children have been characterized as relatively submissive (see Coie, Dodge, & Kupersmidt, 1990, for a review), perhaps those neglected children who feel distressed are aware of their skill deficits in this area (and take

some of the blame for these instrumental failures). However, it appears that they are not taking all of the blame for these difficulties, because they also identify peers as a source of their problems.

The overall pattern of results for neglected children, particularly the significant associations of social distress with multiple causes, suggests two explanations. First, distressed children in this group may be uncertain as to why they are experiencing social problems. This is a plausible rationale given that, more than any other group, neglected children are unlikely to receive direct feedback from peers regarding their social standing (because they are largely ignored by peers: cf. Sobol & Earn, 1985). Thus, those who feel socially distressed, when faced with an attribution task, may conclude that many of the presented causes of social events are reasonable. Second, it is possible that distressed neglected children simply make attributions that are more complex than those of their peers (and thus they recognize that social events may have multiple causes).

Evaluation of grade and sex effects in the present study supported the hypothesized relations. The finding that fifth graders reported greater social anxiety than third graders is consistent with evidence suggesting that preadolescents are more concerned than younger children with self-presentational factors typically associated with social anxiety (e.g., evaluation of their behavior by peers: Elkind, 1980). Also, as predicted, fifth graders in the present sample were more likely than third graders to attribute social outcomes to mutual causes. This finding likely reflects children's growing awareness with advancing age of the transactional nature of social outcomes. That is, older children may be better able to take into account the complexities of social interaction that rarely depend solely on one's own actions or those of the peer but also may be caused by the type of relationship one has with the peer. These results also provide evidence that the mutual attribution category is an important one for research with these age groups.

The gender differences in social distress found in the present study are similar to those found by Franke and Hymel (1984): That is, girls in both studies reported higher levels of anxiety than boys. Also, the findings reported here indicate that the difference between boys and girls may become more pronounced as children get older. Franke and Hymel proposed that boys may actually feel as anxious as girls in social situations but may be more reluctant than girls to admit it. Strayer (1986) suggested a second interpretation: that girls are more likely than boys to cite interpersonal events as causes of emotions. Thus, it may be that social situations serve as a source of anxiety for girls more often than for boys.

It is important to note that rejected children's tendency to blame peers for negative, relational outcomes in the present study could be viewed as inconsistent with the attributional pattern displayed by low-status children in three other studies (i.e., internal attributions for social failure and external attributions for social success—Ames et al., 1977; Goetz & Dweck, 1980; Hymel et al., 1983). However, important methodological differences between these prior investigations and the present study likely account for seemingly discrepant results. Specifically, these include (a) differences in the methods used to assess attributions (e.g., in the present study, children rated the likelihood of multiple causes for each outcome, whereas in the Ames et al. study, children were asked to choose only one cause per outcome); (b) differences in the ways that comparison groups have been identified (i.e., prior studies did not make a distinction between neglected and rejected children); and (c) differences in the types of social events that have been presented to children to elicit their attributions (i.e., in prior studies, two general types of social events—positive and negative—have been presented to children, whereas the events used to elicit attributions in the present research were much more specific in nature; see Hymel et al., 1983, for a similar discussion).

Given the recent trend toward the study of behaviorally distinct subgroups of rejected children (e.g., Asher & Williams, 1987; Crick, 1991; Parkhurst, Roedel, Bendixen, & Potenza, 1991), one possible direction for future research would be to assess the relations among social distress and attributions for subgroups of rejected-aggressive and rejected-withdrawn children. Thus far, researchers have assessed either the attributions or the levels of social distress exhibited by children within these subgroups (but not both variables within a single study), and these investigations have yielded null or inconsistent findings (Hymel et al., 1983; Quiggle, Garber, Panak, & Dodge, 1992; cf. Asher et al., 1990). It is possible that meaningful results would be obtained if the analytic approach used in the present study is adapted for use in future research (i.e., if the relation between attributions and social feelings is assessed independently for behaviorally distinct subgroups of rejected children).

The large discrepancy found in the present study between the degree of distress reported by neglected, controversial, and rejected children (i.e., three groups sometimes thought to be experiencing social difficulties) provides further support for the distinctiveness of the peer experiences of these three groups. Results also provide evidence that children who have been categorically labeled as socially adjusted in prior investigations (i.e., popular or average status children) are not necessarily "protected" from feelings of social distress and problematic peer relationships. These findings highlight the importance of considering children's own assessments of "how things are going for them socially" instead of relying solely on external sources of information (e.g., peers, teachers, and researchers) in distinguishing children who are experiencing peer problems from those who are not.

REFERENCES

Ames, R., Ames, C., & Garrison, W. (1977). Children's causal ascriptions for positive and negative interpersonal outcomes. *Psychological Reports, 41,* 595–602.

Anderson, C. A., Horowitz, L. M., & French, R. (1983). Attributional style of lonely and depressed people. *Journal of Personality and Social Psychology, 45,* 127–136.

Asher, S. R., & Dodge, K. A. (1986). Identifying children who are rejected by their peers. *Developmental Psychology, 22,* 444–449.

Asher, S. R., Hymel, S., & Renshaw, P. D. (1984). Loneliness in children. *Child Development, 55,* 1457–1464.

Asher, S. R., Parkhurst, J. T., Hymel, S., & Williams, G. A. (1990). Peer rejection and loneliness in childhood. In S. R. Asher & J. D. Coie, *Peer rejection in childhood* (pp. 253–273). New York: Cambridge University Press.

Asher, S. R., & Wheeler, V. A. (1985). Children's loneliness: A comparison of rejected and neglected peer status. *Journal of Consulting and Clinical Psychology, 53,* 500–505.

Asher, S. R., & Williams, G. A. (1987, April). New approaches to identifying rejected children at school. In G. W. Ladd (Chair). *Identification and treatment of socially rejected children in school settings.* Symposium conducted at the annual meetings of the American Educational Research Association, Washington, DC.

Asher, S. R., Zelis, K. M., Parker, J. G., & Bruene, C. M. (1991, April). *Self-referral for peer relationship problems among aggressive and withdrawn low-accepted children.* Paper presented at the meeting of the Society for Research in Child Development, Seattle, WA.

Bierman, K. L., & Furman, W. (1984). The effects of social skill training and peer involvement on the social adjustment of preadolescents. *Child Development, 55,* 151–162.

Bruning, J. L., & Kintz, B. L. (1977). *Computational handbook of statistics.* Glenview, IL: Scott, Foresman.

Cassidy, J., & Asher, S. R. (1992). Loneliness and peer relations in young children. *Child Development, 63,* 350–365.

Coie, J. D., & Dodge, K. A. (1983). Continuities and changes in children's social status: A five-year longitudinal study. *Merrill-Palmer Quarterly, 29,* 261–281.

Coie, J. D., Dodge, K. A., & Coppotelli, H. (1982). Dimensions and types of status: A cross-age perspective. *Developmental Psychology, 18,* 557–570.

Coie, J. D., Dodge, K. A., & Kupersmidt, J. (1990). Peer group behavior and social status. In S. R. Asher & J. D. Coie (Eds.), *Peer rejection in childhood* (pp. 17–59). New York: Cambridge University Press.

Crick, N. R. (1991, April). Subgroups of neglected and rejected children. In J. T. Parkhurst & D. L. Rabiner (Chairs), *The behavioral characteristics and the subjective experience of aggressive and withdrawn/submissive rejected children.* Symposium conducted at the meeting of the Society for Research in Child Development, Seattle, WA.

Crick, N. R., & Dodge, K. A. (1992). *A review and reformulation of social-information-processing mechanisms in children's social adjustment.* Manuscript submitted for publication.

Crick, N. R., & Ladd, G. W. (1990). Children's perceptions of the outcomes of social strategies: Do the ends justify being mean? *Developmental Psychology, 26,* 612–620.

Dodge, K. A. (1983). Behavioral antecedents of peer social status. *Child Development, 54,* 1386–1399.

Dodge, K. A., & Frame, C. L. (1982). Social cognitive biases and deficits in aggressive boys. *Child Development, 53,* 620–635.

Elkind, D. (1980). Strategic interactions in early adolescence. In J. Adelson (Ed.), *Handbook of adolescent psychology* (pp. 432–444). New York: Wiley.

Franke, S., & Hymel, S. (1984, May). *Social anxiety in children: The development of self-report measures.* Paper presented at the third biennial meeting of the University of Waterloo Conference on Child Development, Waterloo, Ontario, Canada.

Franke, S., & Hymel, S. (1987). *Social anxiety and social avoidance in children: The development of a self-report measure.* Unpublished manuscript, Department of Psychology, University of Waterloo, Ontario, Canada.

Goetz, T. W., & Dweck, C. S. (1980). Learned helplessness in social situations. *Journal of Personality and Social Psychology, 39,* 246–255.

Hymel, S., & Franke, S. (1985). Children's peer relations: Assessing self-perceptions. In B. H. Schneider, K. H. Rubin, & J. E. Ledingham (Eds.), *Children's peer relations: Issues in assessment and intervention* (pp. 75–92). New York: Springer-Verlag.

Hymel, S., Freignang, R., Franke, S., Both, L., Bream, L., & Bory, S. (1983, April). *Children's attributions for social situations: Variations as a function of social status and self-perception variables.* Paper presented at the annual meeting of the Canadian Psychological Association, Winnipeg, Manitoba, Canada.

Hymel, S., & Rubin, K. H. (1985). Children with peer relationship and social skill problems: Conceptual, methodological, and developmental issues. In G. J. Whitehurst (Ed.). *Annals of child development* (Vol. 2, pp. 251–297). Greenwich, CT: JAI Press.

Ladd, G. W. (1981). Effectiveness of a social learning model for enhancing children's social interaction and peer acceptance. *Child Development, 52,* 171–178.

Ladd, G. W., & Crick, N. R. (1989). Probing the psychological environment: Children's cognitions, perceptions, and feelings in the peer culture. In C. Ames & M. Maehr (Eds.), *Advances in motivation and achievement: Motivation enhancing environments* (Vol. 6, pp. 1–44). Greenwich, CT: JAI Press.

LaGreca, A. M., Dandes, S. K., Wick, P., Shaw, K., & Stone, W. L. (1988). Development of the social anxiety scale for children: Reliability and concurrent validity. *Journal of Clinical Child Psychology, 17,* 84–91.

Miller, D., & Ross, M. (1975). Self-serving bias in the attribution of causality: Fact or fiction? *Psychological Bulletin, 82,* 213–225.

Oden, S., & Asher, S. R. (1977). Coaching children in social skills for friendship making. *Child Development, 48,* 495–506.

Parker, J., & Asher, S. R. (1987). Peer acceptance and later personal adjustment: Are low-accepted children "at risk"? *Psychological Bulletin, 102,* 357–389.

Parkhurst, J. T., & Asher, S. R. (1992). Peer rejection in middle school: Subgroup differences in behavior, loneliness, and interpersonal concerns. *Developmental Psychology, 28,* 231–241.

Parkhurst, J. T., Roedel, T. D., Bendixen, L. D., & Potenza, M. T. (1991, April). Subgroups of rejected middle school students: Their behavioral characteristics, friendships, and social concerns. In J. T. Parkhurst & D. L. Rabiner (Chairs), *The behavioral characteristics and the subjective experience of aggressive and withdrawn/submissive rejected children.* Symposium conducted at the meeting of the Society for Research in Child Development, Seattle, WA.

Quiggle, N., Garber, J., Panak, W. F., & Dodge, K. A. (1992). Social-information processing in aggressive and depressed children. *Child Development, 63,* 1305–1320.

Renshaw, P. D., & Asher, S. R. (1983). Children's goals and strategies for social interaction. *Merrill-Palmer Quarterly, 29,* 353–374.

Rubin, K. R., Hymel, S., LeMare, L., & Rowden, L. (1989). Children experiencing social difficulties: Sociometric neglect reconsidered. *Canadian Journal of Behavioral Science, 21,* 94–111.

Rutter, M. (1979). Maternal deprivation, 1972–1978: New findings, new concepts, new approaches. *Child Development, 50,* 283–305.

Sobol, M. P., & Earn, B. M. (1985). Assessment of children's attributions for social experiences: Implications for social skills training. In B. H. Schneider, K. H. Rubin, & J. E. Ledingham (Eds.), *Children's peer relations: Issues in assessment and intervention* (pp. 93–110). New York: Springer-Verlag.

Solano, C. H. (1986). People without friends: Loneliness and its alternatives. In V. J. Derlaga & B. A. Winstead (Eds.), *Friendship and social interaction* (pp. 227–246). New York: Springer-Verlag.

Strayer, J. (1986). Children's attributions regarding the situational determinants of emotion in self and others. *Developmental Psychology, 22,* 649–654.

Sweeney, P. D., Anderson, K., & Bailey, S. (1986). Attributional style in depression: A meta-analytic review. *Journal of Personality and Social Psychology, 50,* 974–991.

Waas, G. A. (1988). Social attributional biases of peer-rejected and aggressive children. *Child Development, 59,* 969–992.

Appendix
Example Attribution Items by Outcome Category

Positive, Relational Item

Imagine that a kid you know wants to be your friend. How often would this happen because:

a.   You are easy to get along with. (internal attribution)

b. The other kid likes to have a lot of friends. (external attribution)

c. You and the other kid like to do things together. (mutual attribution)

NEGATIVE, RELATIONAL ITEM

Imagine that a kid you know does not like you very much. How often would this happen because:

a. You and the other kid do not have fun together. (mutual)

b. You do things that bother kids sometimes. (internal)

c. The other kid does not like very many people. (external)

POSITIVE, INSTRUMENTAL ITEM

Imagine that a kid you know does what you tell them to do. How often would this happen because:

a. You and the other kid do things for each other sometimes. (mutual)

b. You are good at getting kids to do what you want. (internal)

c. The other kid likes to do things for people. (external)

NEGATIVE, INSTRUMENTAL ITEM

Imagine that a kid you know will not let you have something you ask for. How often would this happen because:

a. You and the other kid do not share with each other. (mutual)

b. The other kid is hard to get along with. (external)

c. You do not ask for things in a nice way. (internal)

QUESTIONS

1. Why is it important to ask children themselves about their social experiences and what may be the causes of these experiences?
2. How are loneliness, social anxiety, and social avoidance similar? How are they different?
3. Why are attributions of mutual causality more common among older children than younger children? What consequence does this developmental change have for peer relations?
4. How were children's attributions of social outcomes assessed?
5. Why do you think that rejected children are more likely to attribute negative outcomes to peers?
6. What implications do these results have for helping children who have difficulties with peers?

25 How Asian Teachers Polish Each Lesson to Perfection

JAMES W. STIGLER · HAROLD W. STEVENSON

Much attention has been directed recently to the educational performance of children in the United States relative to that of children in other societies. These comparisons indicate that U.S. children fall far behind Asian students in the areas of mathematics and sciences. There have been many attempts to understand these patterns, but the most successful by far has been the analysis conducted by James W. Stigler and Harold W. Stevenson that focuses on children's experiences in the classroom in China, Japan, and the United States.

This research examines the educational practices and goals in the three communities, and observations indicate that both the processes and outcomes of schooling reflect deeply held cultural values. The research suggests that modeling U.S. classrooms after those in other cultures will not necessarily benefit children in the absence of the supporting cultural context from which these practices derive meaning and direction.

This research is important for several reasons. It connects children's everyday experiences in the classroom to learning and performance outcomes. Although this seems like an obvious step, the classroom context, especially across cultural communities, has rarely been examined in enough detail to determine how different classroom practices affect children's learning. The research is also an excellent example of cultural psychology in that it studies children and their experiences in relation to the cultural context in which development occurs.

Although there is no overall difference in intelligence, the differences in mathematical achievement of American children and their Asian counterparts are staggering.[1]

Let us look first at the results of a study we conducted in 120 classrooms in three cities: Taipei (Taiwan); Sendai (Japan); and the Minneapolis metropolitan area. First and fifth graders from representative schools in these cities were given a test of mathematics that required computation and problem solving. Among the one hundred first graders in the three locations who received the lowest scores, fifty-eight were American children; among the one hundred lowest-scoring fifth graders, sixty-seven were American children. Among the top one hundred first graders in mathematics, there were only fifteen American children. And only one American child appeared among the top one hundred fifth graders. The highest-scoring American classroom obtained an average score lower than that of the lowest-scoring Japanese classroom and of all but one of the twenty classrooms in Taipei. In whatever way we looked at the data, the poor performance of American children was evident.

These data are startling, but no more so than the results of a study that involved 40 first- and 40 fifth-

Reprinted with permission from the authors and the American Federation of Teachers from *American Educator*, Spring, 1992, pp. 12–20, 43–47. Copyright © 1992 by the American Federation of Teachers. This article is an excerpt from H. S. Stevenson and J. S. Stigler, *The Learning Gap: Why Our Schools Are Failing and What We Can Learn from Japanese and Chinese Education*, New York: Summit Books, 1992.

Note: The research described in this article has been funded by grants from the National Institute of Mental Health, the National Science Foundation, and the W.T. Grant Foundation. The research is the result of collaboration with a large group of colleagues in China, Japan, Taiwan, and the United States who have worked together for the past decade. We are indebted to each of these colleagues and are especially grateful to Shinying Lee of the University of Michigan who has been a major contributor to the research described in this article.

grade classrooms in the metropolitan area of Chicago—a very representative sample of the city and the suburbs of Cook County—and twenty-two classes in each of these grades in metropolitan Beijing (China). In this study, children were given a battery of mathematics tasks that included diverse problems, such as estimating the distance between a tree and a hidden treasure on a map, deciding who won a race on the basis of data in a graph, trying to explain subtraction to visiting Martians, or calculating the sum of nineteen and forty-five. There was no area in which the American children were competitive with those from China. The Chinese children's superiority appeared in complex tasks involving the application of knowledge as well as in the routines of computation. When fifth graders were asked, for example, how many members of a stamp club with twenty-four members collected only foreign stamps if five-sixths of the members did so, 59 percent of Beijing children, but only 9 percent of the Chicago children produced the correct answer. On a computation test, only 2.2 percent of the Chinese fifth graders scored at or below the mean for their American counterparts. All of the twenty Chicago area schools had average scores on the fifth-grade geometry test that were below those of the Beijing schools. The results from all these tasks paint a bleak picture of American children's competencies in mathematics.[2]

The poor performance of American students compels us to try to understand the reasons why. We have written extensively elsewhere about the cultural differences in attitudes toward learning and toward the importance of effort vs. innate ability and about the substantially greater amounts of time Japanese and Chinese students devote to academic activities in general and to the study of math in particular.[3] Important as these factors are, they do not tell the whole story. For that we have to take a close look inside the classrooms of Japan, China, and the United States to see how mathematics is actually taught in the three cultures.

LESSONS NOT LECTURES

If we were asked briefly to characterize classes in Japan and China, we would say that they consist of coherent lessons that are presented in a thoughtful, relaxed, and nonauthoritarian manner. Teachers frequently rely on students as sources of information. Lessons are oriented toward problem solving rather than rote mastery of facts and procedures and utilize many different types of representational materials. The role assumed by the teacher is that of knowledgeable guide, rather than that of prime dispenser of information and arbiter of what is correct. There is frequent verbal interaction in the classroom as the teacher attempts to stimulate students to produce, explain, and evaluate solutions to problems. These

characteristics contradict stereotypes held by most Westerners about Asian teaching practices. Lessons are not rote; they are not filled with drill. Teachers do not spend large amounts of time lecturing but attempt to lead the children in productive interactions and discussions. And the children are not the passive automata depicted in Western descriptions but active participants in the learning process.

We begin by discussing what we mean by the coherence of a lesson. One way to think of a lesson is by using the analog of a story. A good story is highly organized; it has a beginning, a middle, and an end; and it follows a protagonist who meets challenges and resolves problems that arise along the way. Above all, a good story engages the reader's interest in a series of interconnected events, which are best understood in the context of the events that precede and follow it.

Such a concept of a lesson guides the organization of instruction in Asia. The curricula are defined in terms of coherent lessons, each carefully designed to fill a forty- to fifty-minute class period with sustained attention to the development of some concept or skill. Like a good story, the lesson has an introduction, a conclusion, and a consistent theme.

We can illustrate what we are talking about with this account of a fifth-grade Japanese mathematics class:

> The teacher walks in carrying a large paper bag full of clinking glass. Entering the classroom with a large paper bag is highly unusual, and by the time she has placed the bag on her desk the students are regarding her with rapt attention. What's in the bag? She begins to pull items out of the bag, placing them, one-by-one, on her desk. She removes a pitcher and a vase. A beer bottle evokes laughter and surprise. She soon has six containers lined up on her desk. The children continue to watch intently, glancing back and forth at each other as they seek to understand the purpose of this display.

> The teacher, looking thoughtfully at the containers, poses a question: "I wonder which one would hold the most water?" Hands go up, and the teacher calls on different students to give their guesses: "the pitcher," "the beer bottle," "the teapot." The teacher stands aside and ponders: "Some of you said one thing, others said something different. You don't agree with each other. There must be some way we can find out who is correct. How can we know who is correct?" Interest is high, and the discussion continues.

> The students soon agree that to find out how much each container holds they will need to fill the containers with something. How about water? The teacher finds some buckets and sends several

children out to fill them with water. When they return, the teacher says: "Now what do we do?" Again there is a discussion, and after several minutes the children decide that they will need to use a smaller container to measure how much water fits into each of the larger containers. They decide on a drinking cup, and one of the students warns that they all have to fill each cup to the same level—otherwise the measure won't be the same for all of the groups.

At this point the teacher divides the class into their groups (*han*) and gives each group one of the containers and a drinking cup. Each group fills its container, counts how many cups of water it holds, and writes the result in a notebook. When all of the groups have completed the task, the teacher calls on the leader of each group to report on the group's findings and notes the results on the blackboard. She has written the names of the containers in a column on the left and a scale from 1 to 6 along the bottom. Pitcher, 4.5 cups; vase, 3 cups; beer bottle, 1.5 cups; and so on. As each group makes its report the teacher draws a bar representing the amount, in cups, the container holds.

Finally, the teacher returns to the question she posed at the beginning of the lesson: Which container holds the most water? She reviews how they were able to solve the problem and points out that the answer is now contained in the bar graph on the board. She then arranges the containers on the table in order according to how much they hold and writes a rank order on each container, from 1 to 6. She ends the class with a brief review of what they have done. No definitions of ordinate and abscissa, no discussion of how to make a graph preceded the example—these all became obvious in the course of the lesson, and only at the end did the teacher mention the terms that describe the horizontal and vertical axes of the graph they had made.

With one carefully crafted problem, this Japanese teacher has guided her students to discover—and most likely to remember—several important concepts. As this article unfolds, we hope to demonstrate that this example of how well-designed Asian class lessons are is not an isolated one; to the contrary, it is the norm. And as we hope to further demonstrate, excellent class lessons do not come effortlessly or magically. Asian teachers are not born great teachers; they and the lessons they develop require careful nurturing and constant refinement. The practice of teaching in Japan and China is more uniformly perfected than it is in the United States because their systems of education are structured to encourage teaching excel-

lence to develop and flourish. Ours is not. We will take up the question of why and what can be done about this later in the piece. But first, we present a more detailed look at what Asian lessons are like.

COHERENCE BROKEN

Asian lessons almost always begin with a practical problem, such as the example we have just given, or with a word problem written on the blackboard. Asian teachers, to a much greater degree than American teachers, give coherence to their lessons by introducing the lesson with a word problem.

It is not uncommon for the Asian teacher to organize the entire lesson around the solution to this single problem. The teacher leads the children to recognize what is known and what is unknown and directs the students' attention to the critical parts of the problem. Teachers are careful to see that the problem is understood by all of the children, and even mechanics, such as mathematical computation, are presented in the context of solving a problem.

Before ending the lesson, the teacher reviews what has been learned and relates it to the problem she posed at the beginning of the lesson. American teachers are much less likely than Asian teachers to begin and end lessons in this way. For example, we found that fifth-grade teachers in Beijing spent eight times as long at the end of the class period summarizing the lessons as did those in the Chicago metropolitan area.

Now contrast the Japanese math lesson described above with a fifth-grade American mathematics classroom that we recently visited. Immediately after getting the students' attention, the teacher pointed out that today was Tuesday, "band day," and that all students in the band should go to the band room. "Those of you doing the news report today should meet over there in the corner," he continued. He then began the mathematics class with the remaining students by reviewing the solution to a computation problem that had been included in the previous day's homework. After this brief review, the teacher directed the students' attention to the blackboard, where the day's assignment had been written. From this point on, the teacher spent most of the rest of the period walking about the room monitoring the children's work, talking to individual children about questions or errors, and uttering "shushes" whenever the students began talking among themselves.

This example is typical of the American classrooms we have visited, classrooms where students spend more time in transition and less in academic activities, more time working on their own and less being instructed by the teacher; where teachers spend much of their time working with individual students and attending to matters of discipline; and where the shape of a coherent lesson is often hard to discern.

American lessons are often disrupted by irrelevant interruptions. These serve to break the continuity of the lesson and add to children's difficulty in perceiving the lesson as a coherent whole. In our American observations, the teacher interrupted the flow of the lesson with an interlude of irrelevant comments or the class was interrupted by someone else in 20 percent of all first-grade lessons and 47 percent of all fifth-grade lessons. This occurred less than 10 percent of the time at both grade levels in Sendai, Taipei, and Beijing. In fact, no interruptions of either type were recorded during the eighty hours of observation in Beijing fifth-grade classrooms. The mathematics lesson in one of the American classrooms we visited was interrupted every morning by a woman from the cafeteria who polled the children about their lunch plans and collected money from those who planned to eat the hot lunch. Interruptions, as well as inefficient transitions from one activity to another, make it difficult to sustain a coherent lesson throughout the class period.

Coherence is also disrupted when teachers shift frequently from one topic to another. This occurred often in the American classrooms we observed. The teacher might begin with a segment on measurement, then proceed to a segment on simple addition, then to a segment on telling time, and then to a second segment on addition. These segments constitute a math class, but they are hardly a coherent lesson. Such changes in topic were responsible for 21 percent of the changes in segments that we observed in American classrooms but accounted for only 4 percent of the changes in segments in Japanese classrooms.

Teachers frequently capitalize on variety as a means of capturing children's interest. This may explain why American teachers shift topics so frequently within the lesson. Asian teachers also seek variety, but they tend to introduce new activities instead of new topics. Shifts in materials do not necessarily pose a threat to coherence. For example, the coherence of a lesson does not diminish when the teacher shifts from working with numerals to working with concrete objects, if both are used to represent the same subtraction problem. Shifting the topic, on the other hand, introduces variety, but at the risk of destroying the coherence of the lesson.

CLASSROOM ORGANIZATION

Elementary school classrooms are typically organized in one of three ways: the whole class is working as a unit; the class is divided into a number of small groups; or children work individually. In our observa-

tions, we noted when the child was receiving instruction or assistance from the teacher and when the student was working on his own. The child was considered to be receiving instruction whenever the teacher was the leader of the activity, whether it involved the whole class, a small group, or only the individual child.

Looking at the classroom in this manner led us to one of our most pronounced findings: Although the number of children in Asian classes is significantly greater than the number in American classes, Asian students received much more instruction from their teachers than American students. In Taiwan, the teacher was the leader of the child's activity 90 percent of the time, as opposed to 74 percent in Japan, and only 46 percent in the United States. No one was leading instruction 9 percent of the time in Taiwan, 26 percent in Japan, and an astonishing 51 percent of the time in the United States (see Figure 1). Even American first graders actually spent more time on their own than they did participating in an activity led by the teacher.

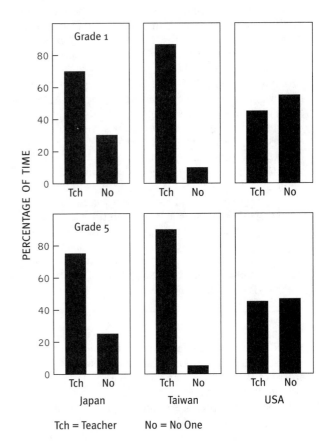

FIGURE 1

Percentage of time students spent in activity led by teacher and by no one.

How We Made Sure We Were Looking at Representative Schools

Frequent reports on television and in books and newspapers purport to depict what happens inside Japanese and Chinese classrooms. These reports usually are based on impressions gathered during brief visits to classrooms—most likely classrooms that the visitor's contacts in Asia have preselected. As a result, it is difficult to gauge the generality of what was seen and reported. Without observing large, representative samples of schools and teachers, it is impossible to characterize the teaching practices of any culture.

The descriptions that we present are based on two large observational studies of first-and fifth-grade classrooms that we conducted in Japan, Taiwan, China, and the United States. In contrast to informal observations, the strength of formal studies such as ours is that the observations are made according to consistent rules about where, when, and what to observe.

In the first study, our observers were in classrooms for a total of over four thousand hours—over a thousand class periods in 20 first- and fifth-grade classrooms in each of three cities: Sendai, Japan; Taipei, Taiwan; and Minneapolis, Minnesota.[1] Our second study took place in two hundred classrooms, forty each in Sendai and Taipei, plus forty in Beijing, China, and eighty in the Chicago metropolitan area of the United States.[2] Care was taken to choose schools that were representative. Our Chicago metropolitan area sample—the urban and suburban areas that make up Cook County—included schools that are predominantly white, black, Hispanic, and ethnically mixed; schools that draw from upper, middle, and lower socioeconomic groups; schools that are public and private; and schools that are urban and suburban.

Observers visited each classroom four times over a one-to two-week period, yielding a total of eight hundred hours of observations. The observers, who were residents of each city, wrote down as much as they could about what transpired during each mathematics class. Tape recordings made during the classes assisted the observers in filling in any missing information. These detailed narrative accounts of what transpired in the classrooms yielded even richer information than we obtained in the first study, where the observers followed predefined categories for coding behavior during the course of observations.

After the narrative records had been translated into English, we divided each observation into segments, which we defined as beginning each time there was a change in topic, materials, or activity. For example, a segment began when students put away their textbooks and began working on a worksheet or when the teacher stopped lecturing and asked some of the students to write their solutions to a problem on the blackboard.

Both studies focused on mathematics classes rather than on classes in subjects such as reading, where cultural differences in teaching practices may be more strongly determined by the content of what is being taught. For example, it is likely that the processes of teaching and learning about the multiplication of fractions transcend cultural differences, whereas teaching children how to read Chinese characters may require different approaches from those used to teach children to read an alphabetic language.

References

1. Stevenson, H. W., Stigler, J. W., Lucker, G. W., Lee, S. Y., Hsu, C. C., & Kitamura, S. (1987). Classroom behavior and achievement of Japanese, Chinese, and American children. In R. Glaser (Ed.), *Advances in instructional psychology.* Hillsdale NJ: Erlbaum.
2. Stigler, J. W., & Perry, M. (1990). Mathematics learning in Japanese, Chinese, and American classrooms. In Stigler, J. W., Shweder, R. A., & Herdt, G. (Eds.), *Cultural psychology: Essays on comparative human development.* Cambridge, Cambridge University Press. pp. 328–356.

One of the reasons American children received less instruction is that American teachers spent 13 percent of their time in the mathematics classes not working with any students, something that happened only 6 percent of the time in Japan and 9 percent in Taiwan. (As we will see later, American teachers have to steal class time to attend to the multitude of chores involving preparation, assessment, and administration because so little nonteaching time is available for them during the day.)

A much more critical factor in the erosion of instructional time was the amount of time American teachers were involved with individuals or small groups. American children spend 10 percent of their time in small groups and 47 percent of their time working individually. Much of the 87 percent of the time American teachers were working with their students was spent with these individual students or small groups, rather than with the class as a whole. When teachers provide individual instruction, they must leave the rest of the class unattended, so instructional time for all remaining children is reduced.

Children can learn without a teacher. Nevertheless, it seems likely that they could profit from having their teacher as the leader of their activities more than half of the time they are in the classroom. It is the incredibly large amounts of time that American children are left unassisted and the effect that unattended time has on the coherence of the larger lesson that is the problem.

When children must work alone for long periods of time without guidance or reaction from the teacher, they begin to lose focus on the purpose of their activity. Asian teachers not only assign less seatwork than American teachers, they also use seatwork differently. Chinese and Japanese teachers tend to use short, frequent periods of seatwork, alternating between group discussion of problems and time for children to work problems on their own. Seatwork is thereby embedded into the lesson. After they work individually or in small groups on a problem, Asian students are called upon to present and defend the solutions they came up with. Thus, instruction, practice, and evaluation are tightly interwoven into a coherent whole. In contrast, the average length of seatwork in American fifth-grade classrooms was almost twice as long as it was in Asian classrooms. And, instead of embedding seatwork into the ongoing back and forth of the lesson, American teachers tend to relegate it to one long period at the end of the class, where it becomes little more than a time for repetitious practice. In Chicago, 59 percent of all fifth-grade lessons ended with a period of seatwork, compared with 23 percent in Sendai and 14 percent in Taipei. American teachers often do not discuss the work or its connection to the goal of the lesson, or even evaluate its accuracy. Seatwork was never evaluated or discussed in 48 percent of all American fifth-grade classes we observed, compared to less than 3 percent of Japanese classes and 6 percent of Taiwan classes.

Since Asian students spend so much of their time in whole-group work, we need to say a word about that format. Whole-class instruction in the United States has gotten a somewhat bad reputation. It has become associated with too much teacher talk and too many passive, tuned-out students. But as we will see in more detail as we continue our description of Asian classrooms, whole-class instruction in Japan and China is a very lively, engaging enterprise. Asian teachers do not spend large amounts of time lecturing. They present interesting problems; they pose provocative questions; they probe and guide. The students work hard, generating multiple approaches to a solution, explaining the rationale behind their methods, and making good use of wrong answers.

HANDLING DIVERSITY

The organization of American elementary school classrooms is based on the assumption that whole-group instruction cannot accommodate students' diverse abilities and levels of achievement; thus, large amounts of whole-class time are given up so that the teacher can work individually with students. Asian educators are more comfortable in the belief that all children, with proper effort, can take advantage of a uniform educational experience, and so they are able to focus on providing the same high-quality experience to all students. Our results suggest that American educators need to question their long-held assumption that an individualized learning experience is inherently a higher-quality, more effective experience than is a whole-class learning experience. Although it may be true that an equal amount of time with a teacher may be more effective in a one-on-one situation than in a large-group situation, we must realize that the result of individualized instruction, given realistic financial constraints, is to drastically reduce the amount of teacher instruction every child receives.

Japanese and Chinese teachers recognize individual differences among students, but they handle that diversity in a very different way. First, as we will see in more detail later, they have much greater amounts of nonteaching time than do American teachers, and part of that time is available for working with individual students. They may spend extra time with slower students or ask faster students to assist them, but they focus their lesson on teaching all children regardless of apparent differences in ability or developmental readiness. Before we discuss how they do that in a whole-group setting, we need to first address the question of whether American classrooms are more diverse than Asian ones, thus potentially rendering whole-class instruction more difficult.

Whenever we discuss our research on teaching practices, someone in the audience inevitably reminds us that Japan and China are nations with relatively homogeneous populations while the United States is the melting pot of the world. How could we expect that practices used in Asian societies could possibly be relevant for the American context, where diversity is the rule in race, ethnicity, language, and social class?

What impedes teaching is the uneven preparation of children for the academic tasks that must be accomplished. It is diversity in children's educational backgrounds, not in their social and cultural backgrounds, that poses the greatest problems in teaching. Although the United States is culturally more diverse than Japan or China, we have found no more diversity at the classroom level in the educational level of American than of Asian students. The key factor is that, in the United States, educational and cultural diversity are positively related, leading some persons to the inappropriate conclusion that it is ethnic and cultural diversity, rather than educational diversity, that leads to the difficulties faced by American teachers.

It is true, for example, that there is greater variability in mathematics achievement among American than among Japanese children, but this does not mean that the differences are evident in any particular classroom. Variability in the United States exists to a large extent across neighborhoods and schools (rather than within them). Within individual classrooms, the variability in levels of academic achievement differs little between the United States and Japan, Taiwan, or China. It is wrong to argue that diversity within classrooms is an American problem. Teachers everywhere must deal with students who vary in their knowledge and motivation.

Tracking does not exist in Asian elementary schools. Children are never separated into different classrooms according to their presumed levels of intellectual ability. This egalitarian philosophy carries over to organization within the classroom. Children are not separated into reading groups according to their ability; there is no division of the class into groups differentiated by the rate at which they proceed through their mathematics books. No children leave the classroom for special classes, such as those designed for children who have been diagnosed as having learning disabilities.

How do teachers in Asian classrooms handle diversity in students' knowledge and skills? For one thing, they typically use a variety of approaches in their teaching, allowing students who may not understand one approach the opportunity to experience other approaches to presenting the material. Periods of recitation are alternated with periods in which children work for short periods on practice problems. Explanations by the teacher are interspersed with periods in which children work with concrete materials or struggle to come up with their own solutions to problems. There is continuous change from one mode of presentation, one type of representation, and one type of teaching method to another.

Asian teaching practices thrive in the face of diversity, and some practices can depend on diversity for their effectiveness. Asking students to suggest alternative solutions to a problem, for example, works best when students have had experience in generating a variety of solutions. Incorrect solutions, which are typically dismissed by the American teacher, become topics for discussion in Asian classrooms, and all students can learn from this discussion. Thus, while American schools attempt to solve the problems of diversity by segregating children into different groups or different classrooms, and by spending large amounts of regular class time working with individual students, Asian teachers believe that the only way they can cope with

the problem is by devising teaching techniques that accommodate the different interests and backgrounds of the children in their classrooms.

Asian teachers also exploit the fact that the same instruction can affect different students in different ways, something that may be overlooked by American teachers. In this sense, Asian teachers subscribe to what would be considered in the West to be a "constructivist" view of learning. According to this view, knowledge is regarded as something that must be constructed by the child rather than as a set of facts and skills that can be imparted by the teacher. Because children are engaged in their own construction of knowledge, some of the major tasks for the teacher are to pose provocative questions, to allow adequate time for reflection, and to vary teaching techniques so that they are responsive to differences in students' prior experience. Through such practices, Asian teachers are able to accommodate individual differences in learning, even though instruction is not tailored to each student.

USE OF REAL-WORLD PROBLEMS AND OBJECTS

Elementary school mathematics is often defined in terms of mathematical symbols and their manipulation; for example, children must learn the place-value system of numeration and the operations for manipulating numerals to add, subtract, multiply, and divide. In addition, children must be able to apply these symbols and operations to solving problems. In order to accomplish these goals, teachers rely primarily on two powerful tools for representing mathematics: language and the manipulation of concrete objects. How effectively teachers use these forms of representation plays a critical role in determining how well children will understand mathematics.

One common function of language is in defining terms and stating rules for performing mathematical operations. A second, broader function is the use of language as a means of connecting mathematical operations to the real world and of integrating what children know about mathematics. We find that American elementary school teachers are more prone to use language to define terms and state rules than are Asian teachers, who, in their efforts to make mathematics meaningful, use language to clarify different aspects of mathematics and to intergrate what children know about mathematics with the demands of real-world problems. Here is an example of what we mean by a class in which the teacher defines terms and states rules:

An American teacher announces that the lesson today concerns fractions. Fractions are defined and she names the numerator and denominator. "What do we call this?" she then asks. "And this?" After assuring herself that the children understand the meaning of the terms, she spends the rest of the lesson teaching them to apply the rules for forming fractions.

Asian teachers tend to reverse the procedure. They focus initially on interpreting and relating a real-world problem to the quantification that is necessary for a mathematical solution and then to define terms and state rules. In the following example, a third-grade teacher in Japan was also teaching a lesson that introduced the notation system for fractions.

> The lesson began with the teacher posing the question of how many liters of juice (colored water) were contained in a large beaker. "More than one liter," answered one child. "One and a half liters," answered another. After several children had made guesses, the teacher suggested that they pour the juice into some one-liter beakers and see. Horizontal lines on each beaker divided it into thirds. The juice filled one beaker and part of a second. The teacher pointed out that the water came up to the first line on the second beaker—only one of the three parts was full. The procedure was repeated with a second set of beakers to illustrate the concept of one-half. After stating that there had been one and one-out-of-three liters of juice in the first big beaker and one and one-out-of-two liters in the second, the teacher wrote the fractions on the board. He continued the lesson by asking the children how to represent two parts out of three, two parts out of five, and so forth. Near the end of the period he mentioned the term "fraction" for the first time and attached names to the numerator and the denominator.
>
> He ended the lesson by summarizing how fractions can be used to represent the parts of a whole.

In the second example, the concept of fractions emerged from a meaningful experience; in the first, it was introduced initially as an abstract concept. The terms and operations in the second example flowed naturally from the teacher's questions and discussion; in the first, language was used primarily for defining and summarizing rules. Mathematics ultimately requires abstract representation, but young children understand such representation more readily if it is derived from meaningful experience than if it results from learning definitions and rules.

Asian teachers generally are more likely than American teachers to engage their students, even very young ones, in the discussion of mathematical concepts. The kind of verbal discussion we find in American classrooms is more short-answer in nature, oriented, for example, toward clarifying the correct way to implement a computational procedure.

Teachers ask questions for different reasons in the United States and in Japan. In the United States, the purpose of a question is to get an answer. In Japan, teachers pose questions to stimulate thought. A Japanese teacher considers a question to be a poor one if it elicits an immediate answer, for this indicates that students were not challenged to think. One teacher we interviewed told us of discussions she had with her fellow teachers on how to improve teaching practices. "What do you talk about?" we wondered. "A great deal of time," she reported, "is spent talking about questions we can pose to the class—which wordings work best to get students involved in thinking and discussing the material. One good question can keep a whole class going for a long time; a bad one produces little more than a simple answer."

In one memorable example recorded by our observers, a Japanese first-grade teacher began her class by posing the question to one of her students: "Would you explain the difference between what we learned in yesterday's lesson and what you came across in preparing for today's lesson?" The young student thought for a long time, but then answered the question intelligently, a performance that undoubtedly enhanced his understanding of both lessons.

CONCRETE REPRESENTATIONS

Every elementary school student in Sendai possesses a "Math Set," a box of colorful, well-designed materials for teaching mathematical concepts: tiles, clock, ruler, checkerboard, colored triangles, beads, and many other attractive objects.

In Taipei, every classroom is equipped with a similar, but larger, set of such objects. In Beijing, where there is much less money available for purchasing such materials, teachers improvise with colored paper, wax fruit, plates, and other easily obtained objects. In all cases, these concrete objects are considered to be critically important tools for teaching mathematics, for it is through manipulating these objects that children can form important links between real-world problems and abstract mathematical notations.

American teachers are much less likely than Chinese or Japanese teachers to use concrete objects. At fifth grade, for example, Sendai teachers were nearly twice as likely to use concrete objects as the Chicago area teachers, and Taipei teachers were nearly five times as likely. There was also a subtle, but important, difference in the way Asian and American teachers used concrete objects. Japanese teachers, for example, use the items in the Math Set throughout the elementary school years and introduced small tiles in a high percentage of the lessons we observed in the first grade. American teachers seek variety and may use Popsicle sticks in one lesson, and in another, marbles, Cheerios, M&Ms, checkers, poker chips, or plastic animals. The American view is that objects should be varied in order to maintain children's interest. The Asian view is that using a variety of representational materials may confuse children, and thereby make it more difficult for them to use the objects for the representation and solution of mathematics problems. Having learned to add with tiles makes multiplication easier to understand when the same tiles are used.

Through the skillful use of concrete objects, teachers are able to teach elementary school children to understand and solve problems that are not introduced in American curricula until much later. An example occurred in a fourth-grade mathematics lesson we observed in Japan. The problem the teacher posed is a difficult one for fourth graders, and its solution is generally not taught in the United States until much later. This is the problem:

> There are a total of thirty-eight children in Akira's class. There are six more boys than there are girls. How many boys and how many girls are in the class?

This lesson began with a discussion of the problem and with the children proposing ways to solve it. After the discussion, the teacher handed each child two strips of paper, one six units longer than the other, and told the class that the strips would be used to help them think about the problem. One slip represented the number of girls in the class and the other represented the number of boys. By lining the strips next to each other, the children could see that the degree to which the longer one protruded beyond the shorter one represented 6 boys. The procedure for solving the problem then unfolded as the teacher, through skillful questioning, led the children to the solution: The number of girls was found by taking the total of both strips, subtracting 6 to make the strips of equal length, and then dividing by 2. The number of boys could be found, of course, by adding 6 to the number of girls. With this concrete visual representation of the problem and careful guidance from the teacher, even fourth graders were able to understand the problem and its solution.

STUDENTS CONSTRUCT MULTIPLE SOLUTIONS

A common Western stereotype is that the Asian teacher is an authoritarian purveyor of information, one who expects students to listen and memorize correct answers or correct procedures rather than to construct knowledge themselves. This may or may not be an accurate description of Asian high school teachers,[4] but, as we have seen in previous examples, it does not describe the dozens of elementary school teachers that we have observed.

Chinese and Japanese teachers rely on students to generate ideas and evaluate the correctness of the ideas. The possibility that they will be called upon to state their own solution as well as to evaluate what another student has proposed keeps Asian students alert, but this technique has two other important functions. First, it engages students in the lesson, increasing their motivation by making them feel they are participants in a group process. Second, it conveys a more realistic impression of how knowledge is acquired. Mathematics, for example, is a body of knowledge that has evolved gradually through a process of argument and proof. Learning to argue about mathematical ideas is fundamental to understanding mathematics. Chinese and Japanese children begin learning these skills in the first grade; many American elementary school students are never exposed to them.

We can illustrate the way Asian teachers use students' ideas with the following example. A fifth-grade teacher in Taiwan began her mathematics lesson by calling attention to a six-sided figure she had drawn on the blackboard. She asked the students how they might go about finding the area of the shaded region. "I don't want you to tell me what the actual area is, just tell me the approach you would use to solve the problem. Think of as many different ways as you can of ways you could determine the area that I have drawn in yellow chalk." She allowed the students several minutes to work in small groups and then called upon a child from each group to describe the group's solution. After each proposal, many of which were quite complex, the teacher asked members of the other groups whether the procedure described could yield a correct answer. After several different procedures had been suggested, the teacher moved on to a second problem with a different embedded figure and repeated the process. Neither teacher nor students actually carried out a solution to the problem until all of the alternative solutions had been discussed. The lesson ended with the teacher affirming the importance of coming up with multiple solutions. "After all," she said, "we face many problems every day in the real world. We have to remember that there is not only one way we can solve each problem."

American teachers are less likely to give students opportunities to respond at such length. Although a great deal of interaction appears to occur in American classrooms—with teachers and students posing questions and giving answers—American teachers generally pose questions that are answerable with a yes or no or with a short phrase. They seek a correct answer and continue calling on students until one produces it. "Since we can't subtract 8 from 6," says an American teacher, "we have to . . . what?" Hands go up, the teacher calls on a girl who says "Borrow." "Correct," the teacher replies. This kind of interchange does not establish the student as a valid source of information, for the final arbiter of the correctness of the student's opinions is still the teacher. The situation is very different in Asian classrooms, where children are likely to be asked to explain their answers and other children are then called upon to evaluate their correctness.

Clear evidence of these differing beliefs about the roles of students and teachers appears in the observations of how teachers evaluate students' responses. The most frequent form of evaluation used by American teachers was praise, a technique that was rarely used in either Taiwan or Japan. In Japan, evaluation most frequently took the form of a discussion of children's errors.

Praise serves to cut off discussion and to highlight the teacher's role as the authority. It also encourages children to be satisfied with their performance rather than informing them about where they need improvement. Discussing errors, on the other hand, encourages argument and justification and involves students in the exciting quest of assessing the strengths and weaknesses of the various alternative solutions that have been proposed.

Why are American teachers often reluctant to encourage students to participate at greater length during mathematics lessons? One possibility is that they feel insecure about the depth of their own mathematical training. Placing more emphasis on students' explanations necessarily requires teachers to relinquish some control over the direction the lesson will take. This can be a frightening prospect to a teacher who is unprepared to evaluate the validity of novel ideas that students inevitably propose.

USING ERRORS EFFECTIVELY

We have been struck by the different reactions of Asian and American teachers to children's errors. For Americans, errors tend to be interpreted as an indication of failure in learning the lesson. For Chinese and Japanese, they are an index of what still needs to be learned. These divergent interpretations result in very different reactions to the display of errors—embarrassment on the part of the American children, calm acceptance by Asian children. They also result in differences in the manner in which teachers utilize errors as effective means of instruction.

We visited a fifth-grade classroom in Japan the first day the teacher introduced the problem of adding fractions with unequal denominators. The problem was a simple one: adding one-third and one-half. The

children were told to solve the problem and that the class would then review the different solutions.

After everyone appeared to have completed the task, the teacher called on one of the students to give his answer and to explain his solution. "The answer is two-fifths," he stated. Pointing first to the numerators and then to the denominators, he explained: "One plus one is two; three plus two is five. The answer is two-fifths." Without comment, the teacher asked another boy for his solution. "Two point one plus three point one, when changed into a fraction adds up to two-fifths." The children in the classroom looked puzzled. The teacher, unperturbed, asked a third student for her solution. "The answer is five-sixths." The student went on to explain how she had found the common denominator, changed the fractions so that each had this denominator, and then added them.

The teacher returned to the first solution. "How many of you think this solution is correct?" Most agreed that it was not. She used the opportunity to direct the children's attention to reasons why the solution was incorrect. "Which is larger, two-fifths or one-half?" The class agreed that it was one-half. "It is strange, isn't it, that you could add a number to one-half and get a number that is smaller than one-half." She went on to explain how the procedure the child used would result in the odd situation where, when one-half was added to one-half, the answer yielded is one-half. In a similarly careful, interactive manner, she discussed how the second boy had confused fractions with decimals to come up with his surprising answer. Rather than ignoring the incorrect solutions and concentrating her attention on the correct solution, the teacher capitalized on the errors the children made in order to dispel two common misperceptions about fractions.

We have not observed American teachers responding to children's errors so inventively. Perhaps because of the strong influence of behavioristic teaching that conditions should be arranged so that the learner avoids errors and makes only a reinforceable response, American teachers place little emphasis on the constructive use of errors as a teaching technique. It seems likely, however, that learning about what is wrong may hasten children's understanding of why the correct procedures are appropriate.

WHY NOT HERE?

Few who have visited urban classrooms in Asia would disagree that the great majority of Chinese and Japanese teachers are highly skilled professionals. Their dedication is legendary; what is often not appreciated is how thoughtfully and adroitly they guide children through the vast amount of material that they must master during the six years of elementary school. We, of course, witnessed examples of excellent lessons in American classrooms. And there are of course individual differences among Asian teachers. But what has impressed us in our personal observations and in the data from our observational studies is how remarkably well most Asian teachers teach. It is the *widespread* excellence of Asian class lessons, the high level of performance of the *average* teacher, that is so stunning.

The techniques used by Chinese and Japanese teachers are not new to the teaching profession—nor are they foreign or exotic. In fact, they are the types of techniques often recommended by American educators. What the Japanese and Chinese examples demonstrate so compellingly is that when widely implemented, such practices can produce extraordinary outcomes.

Unfortunately, these techniques have not been broadly applied in the United States. Why? One reason, as we have discussed, is the Asian belief that the whole-group lesson, if done well, can be made to work for every child. With that assumption, Asian teachers can focus on the perfection of that lesson. However, even if American educators shared that belief, it would be difficult for them to achieve anything near the broad-based high quality that we observed in Asian classrooms. This is not the fault of American teachers. The fault lies with a system that prepares them inadequately and then exhausts them physically, emotionally, and intellectually while denying them the collegial interaction that every profession relies upon for the growth and refinement of its knowledge base.

The first major obstacle to the widespread development and execution of excellent lessons in America is the fact that American teachers are overworked. It is inconceivable that American teachers, by themselves, would be able to organize lively, vivid, coherent lessons under a regimen that requires that they teach hour after hour every day throughout the school year. Preparing lessons that require the discovery of knowledge and the construction of understanding takes time. Teaching them effectively requires energy. Both are in very short supply for most American teachers.

Being an elementary school teacher in the United States at the end of the twentieth century is extraordinarily difficult, and the demands made by American society exhaust even the most energetic among them. "I'm dancing as fast as I can," one teacher summarized her feelings about her job, "but with all the things that I'm supposed to do, I just can't keep up."

The full realization of how little time American teachers have when they are not directly in charge of children became clear to us during a meeting in Beijing. We were discussing the teachers' workday. When we informed the Chinese teachers that American teachers are responsible for their classes all day long,

with only an hour or less outside the classroom each day, they looked incredulous. How could any teacher be expected to do a good job when there is no time outside of class to prepare and correct lessons, work with individual children, consult with other teachers, and attend to all of the matters that arise in a typical day at school! Beijing teachers teach no more than three hours a day, unless the teacher is a homeroom teacher, in which case, the total is four hours. During the first three grades, the teaching assignment includes both reading and mathematics; for the upper three grades of elementary school, teachers specialize in one of these subjects. They spend the rest of their day at school carrying out all of their other responsibilities to their students and to the school. The situation is similar in Japan. According to our estimate, Japanese elementary school teachers are in charge of classes only 60 percent of the time they are at school.

The large amounts of nonteaching time at school are available to Asian teachers because of two factors. The first concerns the number of teachers typically assigned to Asian schools. Although class sizes are considerably larger in Asia, the student-to-teacher ratio within a school does not differ greatly from that in the United States. By having more students in each class and the same number of teachers in the school, all teachers can have fewer teaching hours. Time is freed up for teachers to meet and work together on a daily basis, to prepare lessons for the next day, to work with individual children, and to attend staff meetings.

The second factor increasing the time available to Japanese and Chinese teachers at school is that they spend more hours at school each day than do American teachers. In our study, for example, teachers in Sendai and Taipei spent an average of 9.5 and 9.1 hours per day, respectively, compared to only 7.3 hours for the American teachers. Asian teachers arrive at school early and stay late, which gives them time to meet together and to work with children who need extra help. Most American teachers, in contrast, arrive at school shortly before classes begin and leave not long after they end. This does not mean a shorter work week for American teachers. What it does mean is that they must devote their evenings to working alone on the next day's lessons, further increasing their sense of isolation.

LEARNING FROM EACH OTHER

The second reason Asian classes are so well crafted is that there is a very systematic effort to pass on the accumulated wisdom of teaching practice to each new generation of teachers and to keep perfecting that practice by providing teachers the opportunities to continually learn from each other.

Americans often act as if good teachers are born, not made. We hear this from both teachers and parents. They seem to believe that good teaching happens if the teacher has a knack with children, gets along well with them, and keeps them reasonably attentive and enthusiastic about learning. It is a commonly accepted truism in many colleges of education that teaching is an art and that students cannot be taught how to teach.

Perhaps because of this belief, students emerge from American colleges of education with little training in how to design and teach effective lessons. It is assumed that teachers will discover this for themselves. Courses in teaching methods are designed to serve a different purpose. On the one hand, they present theories of learning and cognitive development. Although the students are able to quote the major tenets of the theorists currently in vogue, the theories remain as broad generalizations that are difficult to apply to the everyday tasks that they will face as classroom teachers. At the opposite extreme, these methods courses provide education students with lists of specific suggestions for activities and materials that are easy to use and that children should enjoy (for example, pieces of breakfast cereal make handy counters for teaching basic number facts). Teachers are faced, therefore, with information that is either too general to be applied readily or so specific that it has only limited usefulness. Because of this, American teachers complain that most of what they know had to be learned by themselves, alone, on the job.

In Asia, graduates of teacher training programs are still considered to be novices who need the guidance and support of their experienced colleagues. In the United States, training comes to a near halt after the teachers acquire their teaching certificates. American teachers may take additional coursework in the evenings or during summer vacations, or they may attend district or citywide workshops from time to time. But these opportunities are not considered to be an essential part of the American system of teacher training.

In Japan, the system of teacher training is much like an apprenticeship under the guidance of experienced colleagues. The teacher's first year of employment marks the beginning of a lengthy and elaborate training process. By Japanese law, beginning teachers must receive a minimum of twenty days of inservice training during their first year on the job.[5] Supervising the inservice training are master teachers, selected for their teaching ability and their willingness to assist their young colleagues. During one-year leaves of absence from their own classrooms, they observe the beginner in the classroom and offer suggestions for improvement.

In addition to this early tutelage in teaching techniques, Japanese teachers, beginners as well as seasoned teachers, are required to continually perfect their teaching skills through interaction with other teachers. One mechanism is through meetings organized by the vice principal and head teachers of their own school. These experienced professionals assume responsibility for advising and guiding their young colleagues. The head teachers organize meetings to discuss teaching techniques and to devise lesson plans and handouts. These meetings are supplemented by informal districtwide study groups and courses at municipal or prefectural education centers.[6]

A glimpse at what takes place in these study groups is provided in a conversation we recently had with a Japanese teacher. She and her colleagues spend a good deal of their time together working on lesson plans. After they finish a plan, one teacher from the group teaches the lesson to her students while the other teachers look on. Afterward, the group meets again to criticize the teacher's performance and to make suggestions for how the lesson could be improved. In her school, there is an annual "teaching fair." Teachers from other schools are invited to visit the school and observe the lessons being taught. The visitors rate the lessons, and the teacher with the best lesson is declared the winner.

In addition, national television in Japan presents programs that show how master teachers handle particular lessons or concepts. In Taiwan, such demonstrations are available on sets of videotapes that cover the whole curriculum.

Making use of lessons that have been honed over time does not mean that the Asian teacher simply mimics what she sees. As with great actors or musicians, the substance of the curriculum becomes the script or the score; the goal is to perform the role or piece as effectively and creatively as possible. Rather than executing the curriculum as a mere routine, the skilled teacher strives to perfect the presentation of each lesson. She uses the teaching techniques she has learned and imposes her own interpretation on these techniques in a manner that she thinks will interest and motivate her pupils.

Of course, teachers find it easier to share helpful tips and techniques among themselves when they are all teaching the same lesson at about the same time. The fact that Taiwan, Japan, and China each has a national curriculum that provides a common focus is a significant factor in teacher interaction. Not only do we have no national curriculum in the United States, but the curriculum may not be consistent within a city or even within a single school. American textbooks, with a spiral curriculum that repeats topics year after year and with a profusion of material about each topic, force teachers to omit some of each year's material. Even when teachers use the same textbook, their classes differ according to which topics they choose to skip and in the pace with which they proceed through the text. As a result, American teachers have less incentive than Asian teachers to share experiences with each other or to benefit from the successes and failures that others have had in teaching particular lessons.

Adding further to the sense of isolation is the fact that American teachers, unlike other professionals, do not share a common body of knowledge and experience. The courses offered at different universities and colleges vary, and even among their required courses, there is often little common content from college to college. Student teaching, the only other activity in which all budding teachers participate, is a solitary endeavor shared only with the regular classroom teacher and perhaps a few fellow student teachers.

Opportunities for Asian teachers to learn from each other are influenced, in part, by the physical arrangements of the schools. In Japanese and Chinese schools, a large room in each school is designed as a teachers' room, and each teacher is assigned a desk in this room. It is here that they spend their time away from the classroom preparing lessons, correcting students' papers, and discussing teaching techniques. American teachers, isolated in their own classrooms, find it much harder to discuss their work with colleagues. Their desk and teaching materials are in their own classrooms, and the only common space available to teachers is usually a cramped room that often houses supplies and the school's duplicating facilities, along with a few chairs and a coffee machine. Rarely do teachers have enough time in their visits to this room to engage in serious discussions of educational policy or teaching practices.

Critics argue that the problems facing the American teacher are unique and that it is futile to consider what Japanese and Chinese teaching are like in seeking solutions to educational problems in the United States. One of the frequent arguments is that the students in the typical Asian classroom share a common language and culture, are well disciplined and attentive, and are not distracted by family crises and their own personal problems, whereas the typical American teacher is often faced with a diverse, burdened, distracted group of students. To be sure, the conditions encountered by teachers differ greatly among these societies. Week after week, American teachers must cope with children who present them with complex, wrenching personal problems. But much of what gives American classrooms their aura of disarray and disorganization may be traced to how schools are organized and teachers are trained as well as to characteristics of the children.

It is easy to blame teachers for the problems confronting American education, and this is something that the American public is prone to do. The accusation is unfair. We cannot blame teachers when we deprive them of adequate training and yet expect that on their own they will become innovative teachers; when we cast them in the roles of surrogate parents, counselors, and psychotherapists and still expect them to be effective teachers; and when we keep them so busy in the classroom that they have little time or opportunity for professional development once they have joined the ranks of the teaching profession.

Surely the most immediate and pressing task in educating young students is to create a new type of school environment, one where great lessons are a commonplace occurrence. In order to do this, we must ask how we can institute reforms that will make it possible for American teachers to practice their profession under conditions that are as favorable for their own professional development and for the education of children as those that exist in Asia.

References

1. The superior academic achievement of Chinese and Japanese children sometimes leads to speculation that they are brighter than American children. This possibility has been supported in a few reports that have received attention in the popular press and in several scientific journals. What has not been reported or widely understood is that, without exception, the studies contending that differences in intelligence are responsible for differences in academic performance have failed to meet acceptable standards of scientific inquiry. In fact, studies that have reported differences in I.Q. scores between Asian and American children have been flawed conceptually and methodologically. Their major defects are nonequivalent tests used in the different locations and noncomparable samples of children. To determine the cognitive abilities of children in the three cultures, we needed tests that were linguistically comparable and culturally unbiased. These requirements preclude reliance on tests translated from one language to another or the evaluation of children in one country on the basis of norms obtained in another country. We assembled a team with members from each of the three cultures, and they developed ten cognitive tasks falling into traditional "verbal" and "performance" categories. The test results revealed no evidence of overall differences in the cognitive functioning of American, Chinese, and Japanese children. There was no tendency for children from any of the three cultures to achieve significantly higher average scores on all the tasks. Children in each culture had strengths and weaknesses, but by the fifth grade of elementary school, the most notable feature of children's cognitive performance was the similarity in level and variability of their scores. [Stevenson, H. W., Stigler, J. W., Lee, S. Y., Lucker, G. W., Kitamura, S., & Hsu, C. C. (1985). Cognitive performance and academic achievement of Japanese, Chinese, and American children. *Child Development*, 56, 718–734.]

2. Stevenson, H. W. (1990). Adapting to school: Children in Beijing and Chicago. *Annual Report*. Stanford CA: Cen-

ter for Advanced Study in the Behavioral Sciences. Stevenson, H. W., Lee, S., Chen, C., Lummis, M., Stigler, J., Fan, L., & Ge, F. (1990). Mathematics achievement of children in China and the United States. *Child Development*, 61, 1053–1066. Stevenson, H. W., Stigler, J. W., & Lee, S.Y (1986). Mathematics achievement of Chinese, Japanese, and American children. *Science*, 231, 693–699. Stigler, J. W., Lee, S. Y., & Stevenson, H. W. (1990). *Mathematical knowledge.* Reston, VA: National Council of Teachers of Mathematics.

3. Stevenson, H. W., Lee, S. Y., Chen C., Stigler, J. W., Hsu, C. C., & Kitamura, S. (1990). Contexts of achievement. *Monographs of the Society for Research in Child Development.* Serial No. 221, 55, Nos. 1–2.
4. Rohlen, T. P. (1983). *Japan's High Schools.* Berkeley: University of California Press.
5. Dorfman, C. H. (Ed.) (1987). *Japanese Education Today.* Washington, D.C.: U.S. Department of Education.
6. Ibid.

Questions

1. What are three classroom practices that are different in the United States, Japan, and China and how do these affect what children learn about mathematics in school?
2. How is instructional time eroded in U.S. classrooms? What can be done to change this?
3. Stigler and Stevenson found that the use of real-world problems and objects helps children learn mathematics better than more abstract references. Why do you think real-world problems help students learn?
4. Why is it a problem when the majority of class time is spent on individual seat work as opposed to group instruction or activities?
5. How do differences in cultural values in these three communities lead to a different interpretation and use of children's errors in the classroom?
6. What would need to be changed in teacher training and support in the United States for teachers here to use the teaching techniques practiced by teachers in Japan and China?

26 Gender Differences in Masking Negative Emotions: Ability or Motivation?

TERESA L. DAVIS

The development of emotional competence takes place over the course of childhood. With increasing age, children gain more control over their emotions, as well as control over communicating their emotional state to others. One interesting question about this process pertains to gender differences.

Among adults, females are generally considered to be more emotionally expressive than males. This suggests either that females have higher emotional arousal than males or that females and males have similar arousal levels but that females display a higher level of arousal than males. The latter interpretation suggests that males have more control than females in displaying their emotional state.

In the following article, Teresa L. Davis addresses this question and provides data that undermine both of these possibilities. She used a classic paradigm, the disappointing gift task, to study emotional expressiveness in boys and girls at two different ages in middle childhood. The results tell an interesting story about the emergence of male and female differences in emotional display. They also point to the powerful influence of gender socialization and social expectations on how children learn to express their feelings to others.

Research has demonstrated that boys display greater negative affect than girls when they receive a disappointing gift. In this study, ability and motivation were investigated as possible reasons for the gender differences. First-and 3rd-grade children's emotion dissimulation in a disappointing gift task was compared with their degree of dissimulation in a highly motivating game task that required the same ability (masking disappointment with a positive expression) but involved a self-gain motive. If boys are motivated, can they hide their disappointment as well as girls? Boys reduced their expression of negative affect in the game task; however, they still showed higher levels of negativity than did the girls. Perhaps because of socialization experiences, girls have more practice in hiding disappointment and, therefore, are better skilled. Girls also showed higher levels of social monitoring behaviors than boys, and younger girls demonstrated the greatest number of tension behaviors.

Adults and children are capable of presenting to others affective displays that differ from the emotions they are really experiencing. Studies of the development of spontaneous regulation of emotional displays suggest that this ability develops early, being

---

Reprinted by permission of the author and the American Psychological Association from *Developmental Psychology*, 31 (1995), pp. 660–667. Copyright © 1995 by the American Psychological Association.

This research was supported by a National Institute of Child Health and Human Development traineeship awarded to the Department of Psychology, University of Florida (National Research Service Award 1T32HD07318).

I wish to thank Scott A. Miller and Patricia H. Miller for their valuable comments on earlier versions of this article and James Algina for statistical consultation. I am also grateful to Janice Wachtel, Yonette Hassell, Mindy Yoskin, and Barbara Quinones for assisting with data collection and to the children of Stephen Foster elementary school for their participation in this project.

Correspondence concerning this article should be addressed to Teresa L. Davis, who is now at Department of Psychology, Box 87, Middle Tennessee State University, Murfreesboro, Tennessee 37132.

demonstrated even by preschool children (Cole, 1986; Reissland & Harris, 1991), and may improve with age (Saarni, 1984). The degree of emotion dissimulation demonstrated, at least in some situations, also seems to be related to the gender of the child (Cole, 1986; Saarni, 1984).

Children's spontaneous use of display rules or the principles that guide the expression of emotion has been examined primarily through a *disappointing gift* paradigm developed by Saarni (1984). This paradigm evokes a culturally defined display rule, "You should look pleased when you receive a gift even if you don't like it," requiring the masking of the child's true emotion. In Saarni's (1984) study, first-, third-, and fifth-grade children received an attractive gift for their participation in the evaluation of workbooks, and then, in a later session, they received a disappointing "baby gift." The number of positive, negative, and transitional behaviors (those that were minimally positive or were suggestive of uncertainty) was measured.

Saarni (1984) found a marginally significant age effect, with older children, especially girls, expressing more positive facial and vocal behaviors on receipt of the disappointing gift compared with younger children. The other major finding was a gender difference in response to the disappointing gift, with girls' behaviors appearing less negative than boys'. The older two age groups of girls responded equally positively to the attractive and unattractive gifts. Third- and fifth-grade boys also displayed more transitional behaviors than girls of the same age.

In a similar study using preschool, first-grade, and third-grade children, Cole (1986) did not find an age effect. She did, however, replicate Saarni's (1984) gender finding. In a followup study, Cole further explored whether the preschool girls were actually feeling disappointment by comparing the expressions of preschool girls who opened a disappointing gift in the presence of an experimenter with girls who opened the gift while the experimenter was absent. More disappointment was expressed when the experimenter was absent, suggesting that these young girls were indeed hiding their feelings of unhappiness.

The purpose of the present study was to investigate the possible reasons for the effects of gender found in this type of task. Saarni (1984) has suggested three possible explanations. These explanations are linked to the three components necessary to effectively use a display rule: The children must have knowledge of the rule, must be able to produce the expression, and must be motivated to hide their true emotions.

The first explanation for the gender effect, differences in knowledge, is not supported by the literature. Studies using picture story tasks find that although the understanding of display rules increases between the ages of 4 and 10 years for both boys and girls, there are no differences in knowledge on the basis of gender (Friend & Davis, 1993; Gnepp & Hess, 1986; Harris, Donnelly, Gabriell, & Pitt-Watson, 1986; Saarni, 1979). In addition, these studies suggest that hiding disappointment in a gift situation is one of the earliest understood display rules and should be well known by the older children in the disappointing gift studies.

A second plausible reason for the gender effect could be a difference in the abilities of boys and girls to produce the positive expression (Saarni, 1984) or perhaps prevent the negative emotion from showing. Although research on adults suggests that women may be better encoders (or producers) of emotional cues than men (Buck, Miller, & Caul, 1974; Hall, 1979; Rotter & Rotter, 1988), studies with children as encoders often find that the identification of emotions based on facial expressions is not affected by the gender of the child displaying the feeling (Felleman, Barden, Carlson, Rosenberg, & Masters, 1983; Morency & Krauss, 1982).

Posing the positive expression is only one part of masking disappointment. The child must also prevent the real emotion from showing. Shennum and Bugental (1982) asked 6- to 12-year-olds to hide their emotions. When the task was to mask dislike with happy expressions, no sex differences were found. In contrast to these results, Feldman, Jenkins, and Popoola (1979) found that girls were better able to look pleased while drinking sour fruit juice than boys. These studies indicate that there is some question about whether girls are better at masking negative emotions.

A third possible explanation for gender differences involves differing levels of motivation between boys and girls. For example, Saarni (1984) suggested that there may be more social pressure for girls to act nice. Consistent with this view, Banerjee and Eggleston (1993) found that parents of preschoolers expect girls to be more restricted in their emotional displays than boys and also expect girls to use more sophisticated mentalistic strategies to control their emotions. Because of these different cultural expectations, girls may be more motivated to hide their disappointment than boys.

Of the three components necessary for display rule use—knowledge, ability to pose facial expressions, and motivation—the gender differences noted in the disappointing gift paradigm are most probably related to ability and motivation. Both of these possibilities are investigated.

In the present study, children's ability to mask disappointment with happiness was compared on two tasks. Each child participated in a disappointing gift task that was modeled after the Saarni (1984) and Cole (1986) studies and also in a game task. The game required the same ability as the disappointing gift task (immediately masking disappointment with happiness), but the motivation for doing so was self-interest (winning the game). The game was designed to discover whether gender differences disappear in a situation in which boys and girls are highly motivated to hide their disappointment. As in the gift task, the children received a positive item and then a disappointing one. To keep the attractive prize, the child had to appear to like the second, unattractive one. This game differs from most of the emotion-masking research in which a child is simply asked to act and has little to explicitly gain or lose by his or her actions. In this game, the child could win or lose an attractive prize depending on his or her ability to mask disappointment.

It was expected that the results of the disappointing gift task would replicate those of previous studies. Girls would demonstrate less negativity than boys when receiving a disappointing gift and would respond equally positively to the positive and negative gifts. It was also expected that if the primary difference between the two sexes is the ability to pose the positive expression and suppress the negative one, then the same pattern of performance would appear in both tasks (game and disappointing gift) – girls would show fewer negative and more positive behaviors than boys. However, if motivation is the important difference between the performance of girls and boys, one would expect to see girls masking negative emotions more successfully than boys on the prosocial gift task but both sexes performing equally well on the self-interest game task.

In addition, two other behavior categories were explored in this study. Saarni (1992) extended her previous scoring system (Saarni, 1984) to include social monitoring and tension behaviors. Behaviors indicating that the children were attempting to control their expressions but were not entirely successful (such as a mumbled "thank you") were coded as social monitoring behaviors. The tension behavior category included indicators of anxiety (such as twisting in chair). This study is the first to investigate these two separate behavior categories in a situation involving the masking of disappointment.

METHOD

PARTICIPANTS

The participants were 64 children: 32 first graders (16 girls and 16 boys: $M = 6$ years 11 months) and 32 third graders (16 girls and 16 boys: $M = 9$ years 3 months). The children were predominantly from middle-class families and were recruited through the public school system by means of a letter to the parents. Seven of the children were members of ethnic minority groups. First and third graders were selected to be consistent with the age groups in the previous two studies that demonstrated the gender difference.

Younger children were considered; however, pilot testing indicated that they had difficulty understanding the game task.

MATERIALS

Various segments of the interview were videotaped by using a camera in view of the children. The children were not aware of when they were being taped and when the camera was off. The camera was introduced to the children at the beginning of the interview, and most of them paid little attention to it after showing some initial interest.

PROCEDURE

The children were interviewed individually in a four-part session at their elementary school by one of two pairs of female experimenters used in the study. Each pair interviewed an equal number of children of each gender and at each grade level. Within each pair, the experimenters alternated between the role of Experimenter 1 and Experimenter 2 (counterbalanced across grade and gender). The order of presentation of the gift and game tasks was also counterbalanced.

At the beginning of the testing session, the child was introduced to Experimenter 1, who asked the child to rank order 10 items. The items included a range of desirable (e.g., "smelly" Magic Markers and glow-in-the-dark Super Balls) and less desirable (e.g., plastic spoons and teething rings) objects. The children were told that the experimenter wanted to see what types of items children of different ages liked. The children's two lowest-ranked and two highest-ranked items were used in the study. The highest-ranked item was always paired with the 9th-ranked item, and the 2nd-ranked item was always paired with the lowest-ranked item. The pairs of items used in each task (1st and 9th, 2nd and 10th) were counterbalanced across tasks (gift and game) and gender and grade. The child was then escorted to a different part of the room and was given the game and gift tasks.

Disappointing Gift Task.   Experimenter 2 explained that she was interested in how children liked different types of workbooks. The children were told that if they would work a problem and help evaluate the workbook, they would receive a gift for their effort and help. The child was then told that the session would be videotaped so that the experimenter could see how children work on problems. The experimenter helped the child pick out a problem to work. After the child finished the problem, the experimenter asked a few questions regarding difficulty of the workbook and comparison to classroom work. The child was then thanked and given a gift. The child was asked to unwrap the gift at the table.

The first gift was always either the child's first or second choice. For the next 10 s, the examiner made eye contact with the child but did not stare, maintained a neutral expression, and did not interact with the child to avoid leading the child's facial expression. The children were then asked to help with a second workbook problem. The procedure was repeated except that the gift the child received was one of his or her least favorite items. Experimenter 2 then thanked the child and exited the room.

Experimenter 1 (who had been taping) then interviewed the child about the gifts that were received. This interview was based on the method used in Cole's (1986) study. The children were first asked which gift they liked better. They were then asked if they felt more happy or more sad when they unwrapped each gift. If they indicated that they felt happy about the disappointing gift, they were prompted: "I thought that __ was your last choice. Some children would feel sad about receiving this prize and some would not. I want to know how you really feel."

Game Task.   Experimenter 1 told the children that she wanted to play a new game with them to see if it was the kind of game children their age like to play. The children were told they were being videotaped to see how children play the game. Experimenter 2 brought in two boxes, set them in front of the child, and then operated the camera. The boxes opened toward the child, and Experimenter 1 could not see what was in them. The rules were explained to the child as follows:

> Inside each box is a prize. I cannot see the prize from here, so only you know what is in the box. The way this game works is that you will look into the blue box first and then you will look up at me. Then you will look into the red box and look at me. OK? To win the game, you want to try to *trick* me. If you trick me then you get to keep both prizes. If you don't then I get both prizes back. This is how you trick me: There may be two prizes that you really like in the boxes or there may be one prize you like a little better. To win the game, you want to act like you like both of the prizes very much. You want to look happy when you look at me. If you look like you like both prizes very much, then you get to keep both of the prizes. But, if I can tell you don't like one of the prizes in the box, then I get both the prizes back and you don't get to keep any. OK, let's make sure you understand. What are you going to do first? How do you want to look when you look at me? And if I can tell that you don't like a prize, what happens?

When the children indicated that they understood, the game began. The children were told to look

in the first box and then look up at the experimenter. They were also told they could say anything that they wanted to as long as they did not name the item in the box. The children looked at the experimenter for 10 s before being told to proceed to the next box.

The first box the children opened contained an attractive prize. The second box contained a least-favorite item. The children needed to look happy in spite of this to win the game and keep the first prize. At the end of the game, all of the children were told that they did very well and would get to keep both prizes. Experimenter 1 then asked the children the same questions about the prizes that were asked about the gifts (i.e., which the child liked better and how the child felt about receiving each). The children were then allowed to trade in the prizes that they did not want for others. They were told that we might not be able to trade in prizes for all of the children but today we happened to have extras. We asked them not to tell the others that they got to trade in their prizes. They were then asked if they had heard about the experiment from any of the other children and what specifically they had heard.

SCORING

A behavior coding system developed by Saarni (1992) was used. This system is similar to the one used in Saarni's 1984 study and involves observing behaviors such as facial expressions, vocalizations, gazing, and selected body movements. In Saarni's 1984 coding system, behaviors were coded as positive, negative, or transitional. The behaviors coded into the first two categories were obvious positive or negative displays. Behaviors coded into the transitional category were those that seemed to indicate an understanding that some degree of expressive control was required, but the children were not yet executing the control properly. Some of these behaviors suggested that the children felt anxious, such as shifting in their seats; other behaviors appeared to be attempts at expressive control, such as fake smiles. In Saarni's (1992) new system, transitional behaviors have been further divided into two types: social monitoring behaviors and tension behaviors. The responses coded into the social monitoring category are minimally positive in affect or suggestive of attempts at control, and those in the tension category indicate uneasiness and stress. The Appendix lists the types of behaviors that were coded into each category.

The 10 s following the exposure to each gift and prize were scored (four 10-s segments per child). The time interval began when the child first made eye contact with the prize or gift and was analyzed with a frame-by-frame technique. Each child received a score for each dimension (positive, negative, social monitoring, and tension) for each of the four segments (16 scores for each child). Two taped segments had to be dropped from the analysis. One first-grade boy dropped his disappointing gift on the floor when he opened it and thus was under the table retrieving it during the 10-s taping period. A third-grade boy looked into the first box in the game task before he was given the instructions.

The scores consisted of a frequency count of the number of behaviors on each dimension the observer counted. Repeated instances of the same behavior were not counted toward the frequency totals (Saarni, 1984, 1992). Two individuals who were unaware of the methodology and purpose of the study coded each tape. Using the Spearman–Brown formula, the interrater reliability was $r = .87$ for the positive dimension, $r = .77$ for the negative dimension, $r = .78$ for the social monitoring dimension, and $r = .76$ for the tension dimension. Disagreements were resolved by discussion.

RESULTS

Preliminary analyses indicated that there were no main effects or interactions involving task order or experimenter pair. Therefore, these variables were not included. All analysis of variance (ANOVA) results were calculated using the PROC/GLM procedure in SAS.

DISAPPOINTING GIFT TASK

The results of the positive and negative behaviors were first analyzed for the gift condition only in order to explore the replication of previous findings on disappointing gift tasks. Preliminary analyses indicated that there was no effect of grade on the number of positive or negative behaviors; therefore, this variable was dropped from further analyses. A 2 × 2 (Sex × Valence: positive gift/disappointing gift) ANOVA on the number of positive expressions indicated a main effect of valence, $F(1, 61) = 14.90$, $p < .001$. The children responded more positively to the attractive gift ($M = 2.05$) than they did to the disappointing gift ($M = 1.34$).

Because specific predictions were made regarding gender, planned pairwise comparisons were made contrasting positive expressions in the attractive and disappointing gift conditions for boys and girls separately. There was a significant decrease in positive behaviors expressed by boys in the disappointing ($M = 1.23$) versus the attractive ($M = 2.13$) gift condition, $F(1, 30) = 12.10$, $p < .002$. However, for the girls the difference was not significant (disappointing gift condition, $M = 1.44$; attractive gift condition, $M = 1.97$).

The same ANOVA on negative emotions also indicated a main effect of valence, $F(1, 61) = 27.83$,

$p < .001$. Children expressed a greater number of negative behaviors when they received a disappointing gift ($M = 2.71$) than when they received an attractive gift ($M = 1.76$). The valence main effect was qualified by a Sex × Valence interaction, $F(1, 61) = 4.52$, $p < .04$. In the attractive gift condition, there was no difference in the negative expressions of boys ($M = 1.77$) and girls ($M = 1.75$); however, when the children received a disappointing gift, the number of negative expressions did differ, $F(1, 61) = 5.60$, $p < .02$, with boys ($M = 3.10$) demonstrating a greater number than girls ($M = 2.31$).

These results are consistent with those found in other studies using this paradigm. The girls in this study showed the same degree of positivity when receiving either a disappointing gift or an attractive gift. The boys, however, showed a decrease in positive behaviors in the disappointing gift situation and also demonstrated more negative behaviors than girls when receiving a disappointing gift.

A COMPARISON OF THE DISAPPOINTING GIFT AND GAME TASKS

Performance in the game task was compared to performance on the disappointing gift task to investigate the influence of ability and motivation on children's masking of negative emotions. Because the children never said "thank you" in the game task, the children's scores on the gift task were recalculated excluding this item. The adjusted scores were used in all analyses comparing the gift and game tasks. The means for the game task and the adjusted means for the gift task are presented in Table 1. The four dimensions of emotional expression were analyzed separately. Preliminary analyses indicated no main effects or interactions involving grade for the positive and negative dimensions; therefore, grade was not included in the analyses on these two dimensions.

A 2 × 2 × 2 (Sex × Valence × Task: game/gift) ANOVA on the number of positive expressions indicated a main effect of task, $F(1, 60) = 8.31$, $p < .005$. Children were more positive in the game task ($M = 2.20$) than in the gift task ($M = 1.69$). There was also a valence main effect, $F(1, 60) = 12.59$, $p < .001$, with a greater number of positive expressions when the gift/prize was attractive ($M = 2.19$) than when the gift/prize was disappointing ($M = 1.70$).

The same analysis on the number of negative expressions indicated three significant main effects: task, valence, and sex. The task main effect, $F(1, 60) = 32.31$, $p < .001$, indicated that a greater number of negative behaviors were expressed in the gift task ($M = 2.23$) than in the game task ($M = .69$). For valence, $F(1, 60) = 15.17$, $p < .001$, more negativity was expressed when a disappointing gift/prize was received ($M = 1.74$) than when an attractive gift/prize

TABLE 1 MEAN NUMBERS OF POSITIVE AND NEGATIVE BEHAVIORS EXPRESSED AS A FUNCTION OF TASK, GENDER, AND VALENCE

	Sex of child			
	Male		Female	
Condition	M	SD	M	SD
Positive behaviors				
Gift				
Attractive	2.06	1.57	1.84	1.72
Disappointing	1.23	1.27	1.41	1.50
Game				
Attractive prize	2.10	1.26	2.53	1.34
Disappointing prize	1.93	1.52	2.21	1.54
Negative behaviors				
Gift				
Attractive	1.10	0.71	1.06	1.07
Disappointing	2.23	1.47	1.53	0.95
Game				
Attractive prize	.73	0.83	.50	0.67
Disappointing prize	1.06	1.11	.50	0.84

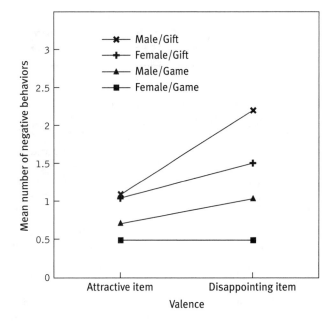

FIGURE 1

Mean number of negative behaviors as a function of gender, task, and valence.

was received ($M = 1.18$). The gender main effect, $F(1, 60) = 7.41$, $p < .008$, showed that boys expressed more negativity ($M = 1.66$) than did girls ($M = 1.26$).

These main effects were qualified by two interactions (see Figure 1). Follow-up t tests on a Task × Valence interaction, $F(1, 60) = 11.80$, $p < .001$, indicated that on the gift task there were more negative behaviors expressed when receiving the disappointing gift ($M = 1.76$) than when receiving the attractive gift ($M = 2.71$), $t(61) = 4.50$, $p < .001$. However, in the game task, there was no difference in the number of negative behaviors expressed when either the attractive or disappointing gift was received ($Ms = .61$ and .78, respectively).

A significant Sex × Valence interaction was also found, $F(1, 60) = 4.03$, $p < .05$. There was no difference in the negative behavior of boys and girls when an attractive gift/prize was received ($Ms = 1.24$ and 1.12, respectively). There was a significant difference in the number of negative behaviors expressed by boys and girls when a negative gift/prize was received, $F(1, 60) = 9.16$, $p < .004$, with girls expressing fewer negative behaviors ($M = 1.40$) than boys ($M = 2.08$). The negative behavior of girls did not differ based on whether a negative or positive item was received. However, boys were significantly more negative when they received a disappointing versus an attractive gift/prize, $t(30) = 3.32$, $p < .002$. These findings indicate that girls were better than boys at suppressing negative expressions not only in the gift task but also in the game task.

The means for the social monitoring and tension behaviors are presented in Table 2. Preliminary analyses indicated that grade was not significant for the social monitoring behaviors; therefore, this variable was not included. A 2 × 2 × 2 (Sex × Valence × Task: game/gift) ANOVA on the number of social monitoring behaviors indicated a main effect of task, $F(1, 60) = 23.15$, $p < .001$. The number of social monitoring behaviors was higher in the game task ($M = 2.05$) than in the gift task ($M = 1.45$). There was also a significant effect of sex, $F(1, 60) = 8.59$, $p < .005$, with girls showing a higher degree of social monitoring ($M = 1.97$) than boys ($M = 1.54$).

A 2 × 2 × 2 × 2 (Sex × Valence × Grade × Task: game/gift) ANOVA on the number of tension behaviors indicated main effects of valence and sex. The valence main effect, $F(1, 58) = 4.63$, $p < .04$, showed that tension behaviors were higher when the children received a disappointing gift/prize ($M = 3.03$) than when they received a positive gift/prize ($M = 2.72$). The sex main effect, $F(1, 58) = 11.89$, $p < .001$, indicated that girls ($M = 3.33$) demonstrated more tension behaviors than boys ($M = 2.42$). A marginal Sex × Grade interaction, $F(1, 58) = 3.14$, $p < .08$, suggests that for girls there is a significant difference between first ($M = 3.81$) and third ($M = 2.86$) graders,

TABLE 2   MEAN NUMBERS OF SOCIAL MONITORING AND TENSION BEHAVIORS EXPRESSED AS A FUNCTION OF TASK, VALENCE, GRADE, AND GENDER

| | Grade 1 | | | | Grade 3 | | | |
| | Male | | Female | | Male | | Female | |
Task	M	SD	M	SD	M	SD	M	SD
	Social monitoring behaviors							
Gift								
Attractive	1.07	0.80	1.62	0.96	1.47	0.74	1.75	1.24
Disappointing	1.13	0.83	1.37	0.89	1.40	1.35	1.81	1.11
Game								
Attractive prize	1.86	0.63	2.31	0.70	1.73	0.96	2.12	1.02
Disappointing prize	1.46	0.92	2.37	0.89	2.20	0.68	2.38	0.62
	Tension behaviors							
Gift								
Attractive	2.06	1.79	3.12	1.75	2.13	1.24	2.69	1.30
Disappointing	2.80	1.47	3.81	2.34	2.53	0.99	3.31	2.30
Game								
Attractive prize	2.40	1.68	4.25	2.05	2.80	2.07	2.37	1.45
Disappointing prize	2.47	1.96	4.06	1.65	2.20	1.21	3.06	1.65

$F(1, 30) = 6.65$, $p < .02$. For boys, there was no significant difference based on grade (first-grade boys: $M = 2.43$; third-grade boys: $M = 2.42$). The youngest girls demonstrated the greatest number of tension behaviors.

TRADING OF GIFTS AND STATEMENTS OF POSITIVE AND NEGATIVE FEELINGS

The children's trading behavior and their descriptions of their feelings about receiving the gifts and prizes suggested that they were more disappointed with the unattractive items than with the attractive ones. When allowed to trade their gifts and prizes at the end of the session, all of the children except 3 kept their attractive items. Most of the children, however, decided to trade the negative gifts and prizes they had been given. A categorical modeling analysis (CATMOD in SAS) indicated that there were no significant differences in the percentage of boys (84%) who traded and the percentage of girls (90%) who traded their disappointing gifts. For the negative prizes in the game task, all of the boys traded the prize and all but 7 of the girls traded.

The children all stated that they felt happy about receiving the attractive gifts and prizes. More children stated that they felt sad (70%) rather than happy (30%) when they received the unattractive items. Using the children's responses after their answer had been probed, a 2 × 2 (Sex × Task: game vs. gift)

CATMOD analysis on the children's probed responses indicated that there were no effects of sex or task. Although not all of the children were willing to admit that they felt sad when they received the disappointing item, there were no sex or task differences that would suggest one gender was more disappointed than the other or that the items in one task were more or less disappointing than the items in the other.

DISCUSSION

Consistent with previous research, gender differences in emotional expression were found in the disappointing gift task. The girls expressed fewer negative behaviors than the boys on receipt of an unattractive gift. The two groups did not differ in the degree of positive and negative expressiveness when receiving an attractive gift. Consistent with Cole (1986), no age differences were found.

The present study extended the previous findings in several ways. First, this study explored the importance of motivation and ability as possible explanations for the gender differences in emotional expression found in a disappointing gift situation. When the children's dissimulation in the disappointing gift task was compared with their performance in a motivating game task, two interesting findings emerged. First, negativity was reduced a great deal for both boys and girls in the game task, suggesting that motivation was playing a role in the degree of emotion dissimulation. Second, and perhaps more interestingly, even though the absolute level of negativity expressed was greatly depressed in the game task, the boys still were not as capable of suppressing negative expressions in response to a disappointing item as were the girls. Girls may be more skilled at this type of emotion dissimulation.

The two tasks, gift and game, did differ in that the children needed to spontaneously access the display rule in the gift condition whereas they were told the rule in the game condition. However, of interest was the ability to hide spontaneously felt disappointment with happiness. The game task seemed an adequate elicitor of that ability.

Gender differences were also found for social monitoring and tension behaviors. The girls in this study seemed to be more involved in social monitoring than the boys, regardless of whether they were receiving a positive or negative item. There was also a higher degree of social monitoring for both genders in the game task. The tension behaviors were higher when children received negative gifts and prizes. The girls showed more tension behaviors than the boys, but this was found primarily for the younger girls.

There are several possible explanations for the gender differences found in this study. Some explanations emphasize a biological basis for differences. For example, there may be differences in brain structure that may affect emotional expressiveness, or women could be endowed with a greater innate capacity for learning to communicate nonverbally (see Blanck, Buck, & Rosenthal, 1986; Hall, 1979). Other explanations have focused primarily on socialization practices. If society exerts more pressure on girls to "act nice," then perhaps girls have spent more time hiding certain negative feelings and this experience has led to increased ability. Boys, even when trying hard, cannot do as well because they have had less practice than girls. Greater pressure for girls to be compliant and act nice may also have led to higher levels of social monitoring and to greater levels of tension behaviors, especially for the younger girls who may have less confidence in their abilities to regulate their negative feelings.

There is some evidence that parents socialize their children's emotional expressiveness differently depending on the gender of the child. Malatesta and Haviland (1982) found that mothers responded to the emotional displays of boys and girls differently beginning in the first year of life. Mothers showed more contingent smiling to the smiles of infant boys and were more likely to match the emotional behavior of boys than girls. As previously discussed, Banerjee and Eggleston (1993) have demonstrated that parents of preschool children expect girls to show more control of their emotions than boys, and they expect girls to

use more sophisticated emotional control strategies. Other studies, however, have indicated that parents believe they encourage their sons to control their feelings to a greater degree than their daughters (Block, 1979), and parents are more emotionally responsive to their daughters in negative emotion-eliciting situations (Fabes et al., 1994).

In addition, boys and girls have different expectations about how their genuine displays of emotion will be responded to by adults. Boys expect more disapproval for expressing sadness than girls and expect less disapproval than girls for expressing anger (Fuchs & Thelen, 1988: Perry, Perry, & Weiss, 1989). It is clear that more research is needed to further investigate the socialization patterns of parents regarding their children's control of emotional displays.

The biosocial interactionist view suggests that perhaps biological differences in male and female individuals interact with factors in the social environment leading to gender differences (Kenrick, 1987). For example, research suggests that sex differences may exist on the approach–avoidance dimension of temperament (Rothbart, 1989). This difference may affect social–emotional development. If girls are more likely to show inhibition of approach, then parents may be more successful in their attempts to socialize impulsive actions, such as emotional displays (see Rothbart, 1989). In another type of interactive effect, Fabes et al. (1994) have demonstrated that socialization practices may also be influenced by the mother's perception of the child's level of emotional responsiveness.

The interaction of child characteristics and socialization could be further explored by investigating children's spontaneous masking of emotions other than disappointment. An emotional display difference that is based on differences in temperament between boys and girls would lead to the expectation that boys would have more difficulty masking other types of emotions at least in the early years. However, a finding that gender differences vary across different kinds of emotions would be consistent with the socialization practices explanation. Also consistent with the socialization explanation are findings that gender differences in emotion dissimulation in a disappointing gift context are not found in all cultures (Josephs, 1993). Even within American culture, Gross and Richardson (1993) have demonstrated that emotion dissimulation in a disappointing gift task differs on the basis of whether the children are in the presence of a same-sex or opposite-sex peer.

The joint influence of child characteristics and socialization may lead to different developmental patterns in emotional dissimulation. For example, if socialization pressures are the same for both genders but one gender is more sensitive to these pressures (e.g., because of temperamental differences), then one may see the gender difference decreasing as children get older. However, if socialization pressures are different for boys and girls for certain emotional displays such as sadness, then one may see gender differences widening in older children. There is also the possibility that socialization processes may lead eventually to less global but more context-specific differences in emotion dissimulation. For example, Saarni (1988) found that older girls more than younger girls or boys prefer to express their true emotions to peers rather than to adults.

The present study begins to explore the roles of motivation and skill in an emotion dissimulation situation. The design used in this study to examine the contributions of motivation and skill could be applied to the masking of other emotions or even reported gender differences in other behavioral domains. In addition, it is clear that within each gender there is a great deal of variability in emotion dissimulation. As discussed, various individual difference variables may be interacting with the socialization process. This paradigm could be used to explore a variety of variables potentially important to children's masking of emotions including degree of empathy, temperament, level of social monitoring, and family expressiveness.

REFERENCES

Banerjee, M., & Eggleston, R. (1993, March). *Preschoolers' and parents' understanding of emotion regulation.* Paper presented at the meetings of the Society for Research in Child Development, New Orleans, LA.

Blanck, P. D., Buck, R., & Rosenthal, R. (Eds.), (1986). *Nonverbal communication in the clinical context.* University Park: Pennsylvania State University Press.

Block, J. H. (1979). Another look at sex differentiation in the socialization behaviors of mothers and fathers. In J. Sherman & F. L. Denmark (Eds.), *Psychology of women: Future directions in research* (pp. 29–87). New York: Psychological Dimensions.

Buck, R., Miller, R. E., & Caul, W. F. (1974). Sex, personality, and physiological variables in the communication of affect via facial expression. *Journal of Personality and Social Psychology, 30,* 587–596.

Cole, P. M. (1986). Children's spontaneous control of facial expression. *Child Development, 57,* 1309–1321.

Fabes, R. A., Eisenberg, N., Karbon, M., Bernzweig, J., Speer, A. L., & Carlo, G. (1994). Socialization of children's vicarious emotional responding and prosocial behavior: Relations with mothers' perceptions of children's emotional reactivity. *Developmental Psychology, 30,* 44–55.

Feldman, R., Jenkins, L., & Popoola, O. (1979). Detection of deception in adults and children via facial expressions. *Child Development, 50,* 350–355.

Felleman, E. S., Barden, R. C., Carlson, C. R., Rosenberg, L., & Masters, J. C. (1983). Children's and adults' recognition of spontaneous and posed emotional expressions in young children. *Developmental Psychology, 19,* 405–413.

Friend, M., & Davis, T. L. (1993). The appearance-reality distinction: Children's understanding of the physical and affective domains. *Developmental Psychology, 29,* 907–914.

Fuchs, D., & Thelen, M. (1988). Children's expected interpersonal consequences of communicating their affective state and reported likelihood of expression. *Child Development, 59,* 1314–1322.

Gnepp, J., & Hess, D. L. (1986). Children's understanding of verbal and facial display rules. *Developmental Psychology, 22,* 103–108.

Gross, D., & Richardson, A. (1993, March). *Emotional-expressive behavior in children: Social context effects.* Paper presented at the meetings of the Society for Research in Child Development. New Orleans, LA.

Hall, J. A. (1979). Gender, gender roles and nonverbal communication skills. In R. Rosenthal (Ed.), *Skill in nonverbal communication* (pp. 32–67). Cambridge, MA: Oelgeschlager, Gunn & Hain.

Harris, P. L., Donnelly, K., Gabriell, R. G., & Pitt-Watson, R. (1986). Children's understanding of the distinction between real and apparent emotion. *Child Development, 57,* 895–909.

Josephs, I. E. (1993, March). *The development of display rules: Do you understand what you already do?* Paper presented at the meetings of the Society for Research in Child Development, New Orleans, LA.

Kenrick, D. T. (1987). Gender, genes, and the social environment: A biosocial interactionist perspective. In P. Shaver & C. Hendrick (Eds.). *Sex and gender: Review of personality and social psychology* (Vol. 7, pp. 14–43). London: Sage.

Malatesta, C. Z., & Haviland, J. M. (1982). Learning display rules: The socialization of emotion expression in infancy. *Child Development, 53,* 991–1003.

Morency, N. L., & Krauss, R. M. (1982). Children's nonverbal encoding and decoding of affect. In R. S. Feldman (Ed.), *Development of nonverbal behavior in children* (pp. 181–199). New York: Springer-Verlag.

Perry, D., Perry, L., & Weiss, R. (1989). Sex differences in the consequences that children anticipate for aggression. *Developmental Psychology, 25,* 312–319.

Reissland, N., & Harris, P. (1991). Children's use of display rules in pride-eliciting situations. *British Journal of Developmental Psychology, 9,* 431–435.

Rothbart, M. K. (1989). Temperament and development. In G. A. Kohnstamm. J. E. Bates, & M. K. Rothbart (Eds.), *Temperament in childhood* (pp. 187–247). New York: Wiley.

Rotter, N. G., & Rotter, G. S. (1988). Sex-differences in the encoding and decoding of negative facial emotions. *Journal of Nonverbal Behavior, 12,* 139–148.

Saarni, C. (1979). Children's understanding of display rules for expressive behavior. *Developmental Psychology, 15,* 424–429.

Saarni, C. (1984). An observational study of children's attempts to monitor their expressive behavior. *Child Development, 55,* 1504–1513.

Saarni, C. (1988). Children's understanding of the interpersonal consequences of dissemblance of nonverbal emotional expressive behavior. *Journal of Nonverbal Behavior, 12,* 275–294.

Saarni, C. (1992). Children's emotional-expressive behaviors as regulators of others' happy and sad emotional states. In N. Eisenberg & R. A. Fabes (Eds.), *New directions for child development: Vol. 55, Emotion and its regulation in early development* (pp. 91–106). San Francisco: Jossey-Bass.

SAS Institute Inc. (1985). *SAS® user's guide: Statistics*, (5th edition). Cary, NC: Author.

Shennum, W. A., & Bugental, D. B. (1982). The development of control over affective expression in nonverbal behavior. In R. S. Feldman (Ed.), *Development of nonverbal behavior in children* (pp. 101–122). New York: Springer-Verlag.

APPENDIX
DIMENSIONS OF EXPRESSIVE BEHAVIOR

POSITIVE BEHAVIORS

Relaxed broad smile (teeth showing), closed lip smile

Enthusiastic "Thank you"

Arched brows as in positive surprise

Smiling eye contact with experimenter

Eye crinkle while smiling

Positive verbal comments

Positive tone of voice

Giggling, laughing

Leans forward

Uses expressive hand gestures while talking

NEGATIVE BEHAVIORS

Tense, square-looking smile (lips open, teeth may show)

Down-turned mouth (as in frown or grimace)

Avoids eye contact

Knit brows

Leans backward

Sharp breath exhalation, snorting, groaning

Sighing

Omitted "Thank you"

Negative verbal comments

Negative tone of voice

SOCIAL MONITORING BEHAVIORS

Slight and/or closed lip smile

Staring at experimenter

Tilts head

Faint or mumbled "Thank you"

Questioning vocalization

Abrupt onset/offset of smile

Rapid glances at experimenter when neither is speaking

TENSION BEHAVIORS

Pressing, pursing, biting, or sucking of lips

Bites or mouths clothing

Cheek puffing

Prolonged tongue protrusions

Jaw wiggling, rotating, thrusting, etc.

Nose wrinkle

Rapid, nervous blinking

Looking around room or at ceiling in a scanning fashion

Face, nose touching or scratching

Finger(s) in mouth, on lips, or nail biting

Touches/scratches hair, scalp, ears, etc.

Touches/scratches upper or lower torso

Hides hands (in pockets, sleeves, sits on)

Rubs eyes

Finger rubbing or scratching

Holds or folds hands or arms together

Hand wringing, twisting

Covers face (or part of face) with hand(s)

Stands up during session

Shrugs

Twisting, shifting, sinking in chair

Pumps up/down in seat

Stretching

QUESTIONS

1. What is the disappointing gift task and what is it used to study?
2. Why did Davis think it was important to tease apart ability and motivation in the display of negative emotions by boys and girls?
3. Why do girls show more positive emotions and social monitoring than boys on these tasks?
4. Why do boys show more negative emotions and less social responsiveness on these tasks?
5. What does the data presented in Figure 1 indicate about the role for motivation in the emotional display of boys and girls?
6. Few age differences appeared in this study. One difference was that younger girls showed more tension behaviors when receiving a disappointing gift than the other three groups of children. What do you think these age-related patterns indicate about the development of masking negative emotions?

27 Intelligence: Knowns and Unknowns

Ulric Neisser · Gwyneth Boodoo · Thomas J. Bouchard, Jr. · A. Wade
Boykin · Nathan Brody · Stephen J. Ceci · Diane F. Halpern · John C.
Loehlin · Robert Perloff · Robert J. Sternberg · Susana Urbina

Of the many individual differences that distinguish one person from another, none has produced a stormier and more prolonged debate than intelligence. During the entire twentieth century psychologists have sought valid measures of children's intelligence that would not be influenced by family background or cultural origin. Unfortunately, this effort has met with limited success, and has fueled an ongoing debate.

The following article is part of a report commissioned by the American Psychological Association and written by a team of scholars knowledgeable about the construct and study of intelligence. The group was convened to respond to questions raised in the mid-1990s in the book *The Bell Curve*. In this book, ethnic differences in IQ were attributed to biological differences in intellectual capacity.

As the reports explains, answers to some of these questions are known and indicate that nurture and environment are powerful forces in organizing and directing human intelligence. Answers to other questions remain unknown. These "unknowns" will undoubtedly set the research agenda in the area of intelligence for decades to come. In the meantime, the debate continues on this important, and controversial, area of development.

In the fall of 1994, the publication of Richard Herrnstein and Charles Murray's book The Bell Curve *sparked a new round of debate about the meaning of intelligence test scores and the nature of intelligence. The debate was characterized by strong assertions as well as by strong feelings. Unfortunately, those assertions often revealed serious misunderstandings of what has (and has not) been demonstrated by scientific research in this field. Although a great deal is now known, the issues remain complex and in many cases still unresolved. Another unfortunate aspect of the debate was that many participants made little effort to distinguish scientific issues from political ones. Research findings were often* assessed not so much on their merits or their scientific standing as on their supposed political implications. In such a climate, individuals who wish to make their own judgments find it hard to know what to believe.

Reviewing the intelligence debate at its meeting of November 1994, the Board of Scientific Affairs (BSA) of the American Psychological Association (APA) concluded that there was urgent need for an authoritative report on these issues—one that all sides could use as a basis for discussion. Acting by unanimous vote, BSA established a Task Force charged with preparing such a report. Ulric Neisser, Professor of Psychology at Emory University and a member of BSA, was appointed Chair.

Reprinted and adapted by permission of the American Psychological Association from *American Psychologist*, 51 (1996), pp. 77–101. Copyright © 1996 by the American Psychological Association.

    This is a "Report of a Task Force Established by the American Psychological Association."

    The Task Force appreciates the contributions of many members of the APA Board of Scientific Affairs (BSA) and the APA Board for the Advancement of Psychology in the Public Interest (BAPPI), who made helpful comments on a preliminary draft of this report. We also wish to acknowledge the indispensable logistical support of the APA Science Directorate during the preparation of the report itself.

    Correspondence concerning the report should be addressed to Ulric Neisser, Department of Psychology, Emory University, Atlanta, GA 30322. Electronic mail may be sent via Internet to neisser@fsl.psy.emory.edu.

The APA Board on the Advancement of Psychology in the Public Interest, which was consulted extensively during this process, nominated one member of the Task Force; the Committee on Psychological Tests and Assessment nominated another; a third was nominated by the Council of Representatives. Other members were chosen by an extended consultative process, with the aim of representing a broad range of expertise and opinion.

The Task Force met twice, in January and March of 1995. Between and after these meetings, drafts of the various sections were circulated, revised, and revised yet again. Disputes were resolved by discussion. As a result, the report presented here has the unanimous support of the entire Task Force.

1. CONCEPTS OF INTELLIGENCE

Individuals differ from one another in their ability to understand complex ideas, to adapt effectively to the environment, to learn from experience, to engage in various forms of reasoning, to overcome obstacles by taking thought. Although these individual differences can be substantial, they are never entirely consistent: A given person's intellectual performance will vary on different occasions, in different domains, as judged by different criteria. Concepts of "intelligence" are attempts to clarify and organize this complex set of phenomena. Although considerable clarity has been achieved in some areas, no such conceptualization has yet answered all the important questions and none commands universal assent. Indeed, when two dozen prominent theorists were recently asked to define intelligence, they gave two dozen somewhat different definitions (Sternberg & Detterman, 1986). Such disagreements are not cause for dismay. Scientific research rarely begins with fully agreed definitions, though it may eventually lead to them.

. . . Several current theorists argue that there are many different "intelligences" (systems of abilities), Only a few of which can be captured by standard psychometric tests. Others emphasize the role of culture, both in establishing different conceptions of intelligence and in influencing the acquisition of intellectual skills. Developmental psychologists, taking yet another direction, often focus more on the processes by which all children come to think intelligently than on measuring individual differences among them. There is also a new interest in the neural and biological bases of intelligence, a field of research that seems certain to expand in the next few years.

In this brief report, we focus on a limited and rather specific set of questions:

[Note from eds.: Because we have not included the text of this article in its entirety, please see Neisser et al. (1996). Intelligence: Knowns and Unknowns. *American Psychologist, 51*(2), 77–101, for further discussion of these different approaches to intelligence. We include the description of the psychometric approach to aid in interpreting the later sections.]

- What are the significant conceptualizations of intelligence at this time? (Section 1)

- What do intelligence test scores mean, what do they predict, and how well do they predict it? (Section 2)

- Why do individuals differ in intelligence, and especially in their scores on intelligence tests? Our discussion of these questions implicates both genetic factors (Section 3) and environmental factors (Section 4).

- Do various ethnic groups display different patterns of performance on intelligence tests, and if so what might explain those differences? (Section 5)

- What significant scientific issues are presently unresolved? (Section 6)

Public discussion of these issues has been especially vigorous since the 1994 publication of Herrnstein and Murray's *The Bell Curve*, a controversial volume which stimulated many equally controversial reviews and replies. Nevertheless, we do not directly enter that debate. Herrnstein and Murray (and many of their critics) have gone well beyond the scientific findings, making explicit recommendations on various aspects of public policy. Our concern here, however, is with science rather than policy. The charge to our Task Force was to prepare a dispassionate survey of the state of the art: to make clear what has been scientifically established, what is presently in dispute, and what is still unknown. In fulfilling that charge, the only recommendations we shall make are for further research and calmer debate.

THE PSYCHOMETRIC APPROACH

Ever since Alfred Binet's great success in devising tests to distinguish mentally retarded children from those with behavior problems, psychometric instruments have played an important part in European and American life. Tests are used for many purposes, such as selection, diagnosis, and evaluation. Many of the most widely used tests are not intended to measure intelligence itself but some closely related construct: scholastic aptitude, school achievement, specific abilities, etc. Such tests are especially important for selection purposes. For preparatory school, it's the SSAT; for college, the SAT or ACT; for graduate school, the GRE; for medical school, the MCAT; for law school, the LSAT; for business school, the GMAT. Scores on intelligence-related tests matter, and the stakes can be high.

Intelligence Tests. Tests of intelligence itself (in the psychometric sense) come in many forms. Some use only a single type of item or question: examples include the Peabody Picture Vocabulary Test (a measure of children's verbal intelligence) and Raven's Progressive Matrices (a nonverbal, untimed test that requires inductive reasoning about perceptual patterns). Although such instruments are useful for specific purposes, the more familiar measures of general intelligence—such as the Wechsler tests and the Stanford-Binet—include many different types of items, both verbal and nonverbal. Test-takers may be asked to give the meanings of words, to complete a series of pictures, to indicate which of several words does not belong with the others, and the like. Their performance can then be scored to yield several subscores as well as an overall score.

By convention, overall intelligence test scores are usually converted to a scale in which the mean is 100 and the standard deviation is 15. (The standard deviation is a measure of the variability of the distribution of scores.) Approximately 95% of the population has scores within two standard deviations of the mean, i.e., between 70 and 130. For historical reasons, the term "IQ" is often used to describe scores on tests of intelligence. It originally referred to an "Intelligence Quotient" that was formed by dividing a so-called mental age by a chronological age, but this procedure is no longer used.

Intercorrelations Among Tests. Individuals rarely perform equally well on all the different kinds of items included in a test of intelligence. One person may do relatively better on verbal than on spatial items, for example, while another may show the opposite pattern. Nevertheless, subtests measuring different abilities tend to be positively correlated: people who score high on one such subtest are likely to be above average on others as well. These complex patterns of correlation can be clarified by factor analysis, but the results of such analyses are often controversial themselves. Some theorists (e.g., Spearman, 1927) have emphasized the importance of a general factor, g, which represents what all the tests have in common; others (e.g., Thurstone, 1938) focus on more specific group factors such as memory, verbal comprehension, or number facility. As we shall see in Section 2, one common view today envisages something like a hierarchy of factors with g at the apex. But there is no full agreement on what g actually means: it has been described as a mere statistical regularity (Thomson, 1939), a kind of mental energy (Spearman, 1927), a generalized abstract reasoning ability (Gustafsson, 1984), or an index measure of neural processing speed (Reed & Jensen, 1992).

There have been many disputes over the utility of IQ and g. Some theorists are critical of the entire psychometric approach (e.g., Ceci, 1990; Gardner, 1983; Gould, 1978), while others regard it as firmly established (e.g., Carroll, 1993; Eysenck, 1973; Herrnstein & Murray, 1994; Jensen, 1972). The critics do not dispute the stability of test scores, nor the fact that they predict certain forms of achievement—especially school achievement—rather effectively (see Section 2). They do argue, however, that to base a concept of intelligence on test scores alone is to ignore many important aspects of mental ability.

. . .

2. INTELLIGENCE TESTS AND THEIR CORRELATES

The correlation coefficient, r, can be computed whenever the scores in a sample are paired in some way. Typically this is because each individual is measured twice: he or she takes the same test on two occasions, or takes two different tests, or has both a test score and some criterion measure such as grade point average or job performance. (In Section 3 we consider cases where the paired scores are those of two different individuals, such as twins or parent and child.) The value of r measures the degree of relationship between the two sets of scores in a convenient way, by assessing how well one of them (computationally it doesn't matter which one) could be used to predict the value of the other. Its sign indicates the direction of relationship: when r is negative, high scores on one measure predict low scores on the other. Its magnitude indicates the strength of the relationship. If $r = 0$, there is no relation at all; if r is 1 (or -1), one score can be used to predict the other score perfectly. Moreover, the square of r has a particular meaning in cases where we are concerned with predicting one variable from another. When $r = .50$, for example, r^2 is .25: this means (given certain linear assumptions) that 25% of the variance in one set of scores is predictable from the correlated values of the other set, while the remaining 75% is not.

BASIC CHARACTERISTICS OF TEST SCORES

Stability. Intelligence test scores are fairly stable during development. When Jones and Bayley (1941) tested a sample of children annually throughout childhood and adolescence, for example, scores obtained at age 18 were correlated $r = .77$ with scores that had been obtained at age 6 and $r = .89$ with scores from age 12. When scores were averaged across several successive tests to remove short-term fluctuations, the correlations were even higher. The mean for ages 17 and 18 was correlated $r = .86$ with the mean for ages 5, 6, and 7, and $r = .96$ with the mean for ages 11, 12, and 13. (For comparable findings in a more recent study, see Moffitt, Caspi, Harkness, & Silva, 1993.) Nevertheless, IQ scores do change over time. In the same study (Jones & Bayley, 1941), the average change between age 12 and age 17 was 7.1 IQ points: some individuals changed as much as 18 points. . . .

It is important to understand what remains stable and what changes in the development of intelligence. A child whose IQ score remains the same from age 6 to age 18 does not exhibit the same performance throughout that period. On the contrary, steady gains in general knowledge, vocabulary, reasoning ability, etc. will be apparent. What does *not* change is his or her score in comparison to that of other individuals of the same age. A six-year-old with an IQ of 100 is at the mean of six-year-olds; an 18-year-old with that score is at the mean of 18-year-olds.

Factors and *g*. As noted in Section 1, the patterns of intercorrelation among tests (i.e., among different kinds of items) are complex. Some pairs of tests are much more closely related than others, but all such correlations are typically positive and form what is called a "positive manifold." Spearman (1927) showed that in any such manifold, some portion of the variance of scores on each test can be mathematically attributed to a "general factor," or *g*. Given this analysis, the overall pattern of correlations can be roughly described as produced by individual differences in *g* plus differences in the specific abilities sampled by particular tests. In addition, however, there are usually patterns of intercorrelation among groups of tests. These commonalities, which played only a small role in Spearman's analysis, were emphasized by other theorists. Thurstone (1938), for example, proposed an analysis based primarily on the concept of group factors.

While some psychologists today still regard *g* as the most fundamental measure of intelligence (e.g., Jensen, 1980), others prefer to emphasize the distinctive profile of strengths and weaknesses present in each person's performance. A recently published review identifies over 70 different abilities that can be distinguished by currently available tests (Carroll, 1993). One way to represent this structure is in terms of a hierarchical arrangement with a general intelligence factor at the apex and various more specialized abilities arrayed below it. Such a summary merely acknowledges that performance levels on different tests are correlated; it is consistent with, but does not prove, the hypothesis that a common factor such as *g* underlies those correlations. Different specialized abilities might also be correlated for other reasons, such as the effects of education. Thus while the *g*-based factor hierarchy is the most widely accepted current view of the structure of abilities, some theorists regard it as misleading (Ceci, 1990). Moreover, as noted in Section 1, a wide range of human abilities—including many that seem to have intellectual components—are outside the domain of standard psychometric tests.

TESTS AS PREDICTORS

School Performance. Intelligence tests were originally devised by Alfred Binet to measure children's ability to succeed in school. They do in fact predict school performance fairly well: the correlation between IQ scores and grades is about .50. They also predict scores on school achievement tests, designed to measure knowledge of the curriculum. Note, however, that correlations of this magnitude account for only about 25% of the overall variance. Successful school learning depends on many personal characteristics other than intelligence, such as persistence, interest in school, and willingness to study. The encouragement for academic achievement that is received from peers, family, and teachers may also be important, together with more general cultural factors (see Section 5).

Years of Education. Some children stay in school longer than others; many go on to college and perhaps beyond. Two variables that can be measured as early as elementary school correlate with the total amount of education individuals will obtain: test scores and social class background. Correlations between IQ scores and total years of education are about .55, implying that differences in psychometric intelligence account for about 30% of the outcome variance. The correlations of years of education with social class background (as indexed by the occupation/education of a child's parents) are also positive, but somewhat lower.

There are a number of reasons why children with higher test scores tend to get more education. They are likely to get good grades, and to be encouraged by teachers and counselors; often they are placed in "college preparatory" classes, where they make friends who may also encourage them. In general, they are likely to find the process of education rewarding in a way that many low-scoring children do not (Rehberg & Rosenthal, 1978). These influences are not omnipotent: some high scoring children do drop out of school. Many personal and social characteristics other than psychometric intelligence determine academic success and interest, and social privilege may also play a role. Nevertheless, test scores are the best single predictor of an individual's years of education. . . .

Social Status and Income. How well do IQ scores (which can be obtained before individuals enter the labor force) predict such outcome measures as the social status or income of adults? This question is complex, in part because another variable also predicts such outcomes: namely, the socioeconomic status (SES) of one's parents. Unsurprisingly, children of privileged families are more likely to attain high social status than those whose parents are poor and less educated. These two predictors (IQ and parental SES) are by no means independent of one another; the correlation between them is around .33 (White, 1982).

One way to look at these relationships is to begin with SES. According to Jencks (1979), measures of parental SES predict about one-third of the variance in young adults' social status and about one-fifth of the variance in their income. About half of this predictive effectiveness depends on the fact that the SES of parents also predicts children's intelligence test scores, which have their own predictive value for social outcomes; the other half comes about in other ways.

We can also begin with IQ scores, which by themselves account for about one-fourth of the social status variance and one-sixth of the income variance. Statistical controls for parental SES eliminate only about a quarter of this predictive power. One way to conceptualize this effect is by comparing the occupational status (or income) of adult brothers who grew up in the same family and hence have the same parental SES. In such cases, the brother with the higher adolescent IQ score is likely to have the higher adult social status and income (Jencks, 1979). This effect, in turn, is substantially mediated by education: the brother with the higher test scores is likely to get more schooling, and hence to be better credentialled as he enters the workplace. . . .

Job Performance.   Scores on intelligence tests predict various measures of job performance: supervisor ratings, work samples, etc. Such correlations, which typically lie between $r = .30$ and $r = .50$, are partly restricted by the limited reliability of those measures themselves. They become higher when r is statistically corrected for this unreliability: in one survey of relevant studies (Hunter, 1983), the mean of the corrected correlations was .54. This implies that, across a wide range of occupations, intelligence test performance accounts for some 29% of the variance in job performance. . . .

Social Outcomes.   Psychometric intelligence is negatively correlated with certain socially undesirable outcomes. For example, children with high test scores are less likely than lower-scoring children to engage in juvenile crime. In one study, Moffitt, Gabrielli, Mednick, and Schulsinger (1981) found a correlation of $-.19$ between IQ scores and number of juvenile offenses in a large Danish sample; with social class controlled, the correlation dropped to $-.17$. The correlations for most "negative outcome" variables are typically smaller than .20, which means that test scores are as-

sociated with less than 4% of their total variance. It is important to realize that the causal links between psychometric ability and social outcomes may be indirect. Children who are unsuccessful in—and hence alienated from—school may be more likely to engage in delinquent behaviors for that very reason, compared to other children who enjoy school and are doing well.

In summary, intelligence test scores predict a wide range of social outcomes with varying degrees of success. Correlations are highest for school achievement, where they account for about a quarter of the variance. They are somewhat lower for job performance, and very low for negatively valued outcomes such as criminality. In general, intelligence tests measure only some of the many personal characteristics that are relevant to life in contemporary America. Those characteristics are never the only influence on outcomes, though in the case of school performance they may well be the strongest.

TEST SCORES AND MEASURES OF PROCESSING SPEED

Many recent studies show that the speeds with which people perform very simple perceptual and cognitive tasks are correlated with psychometric intelligence (for reviews see Ceci, 1990; Deary, 1995; Vernon, 1987). In general, people with higher intelligence test scores tend to apprehend, scan, retrieve, and respond to stimuli more quickly than those who score lower.

. . .

Problems of Interpretation.   Some researchers believe that psychometric intelligence, especially g, depends directly on what may be called the "neural efficiency" of the brain (Eysenck, 1986; Vernon, 1987). They regard the observed correlations between test scores and measures of processing speed as evidence for their view. If choice reaction times, inspection times, and VEP latencies actually do reflect the speed of basic neural processes, such correlations are only to be expected. In fact, however, the observed patterns of correlation are rarely as simple as this hypothesis would predict. Moreover, it is quite possible that high- and low-IQ individuals differ in other ways that affect speeded performance (cf. Ceci, 1990). Those variables include motivation, response criteria (emphasis on speed vs. accuracy), perceptual strategies (cf. Mackenzie et al., 1991), attentional strategies, and—in some cases—differential familiarity with the material itself. Finally, we do not yet know the direction of causation that underlies such correlations. Do high levels of "neural efficiency" promote the development of intelligence, or do more intelligent people simply find faster ways to carry out perceptual tasks? Or both? These questions are still open.

3. THE GENES AND INTELLIGENCE

. . . We focus here on the relative contributions of genes and environments to individual differences in particular traits. To avoid misunderstanding, it must be emphasized from the outset that gene action always involves an environment—at least a biochemical environment, and often an ecological one. (For humans, that ecology is usually interpersonal or cultural.) Thus all genetic effects on the development of observable traits are potentially modifiable by environmental input, though the practicability of making such modifications may be another matter. Conversely, all environmental effects on trait development involve the genes or structures to which the genes have contributed. Thus there is always a genetic aspect to the effects of the environment (cf. Plomin & Bergeman, 1991).

RESULTS FOR IQ SCORES

Parameter Estimates.   Across the ordinary range of environments in modern Western societies, a sizable part of the variation in intelligence test scores is associated with genetic differences among individuals. Quantitative estimates vary from one study to another, because many are based on small or selective samples. If one simply combines all available correlations in a single analysis, the heritability (h^2) works out to about .50 and the between-family variance (c^2) to about .25 (e.g., Chipuer, Rovine, & Plomin, 1990; Loehlin, 1989). These overall figures are misleading, however, because most of the relevant studies have been done with children. We now know that the heritability of IQ changes with age: h^2 goes up and c^2 goes down from infancy to adulthood (McCartney, Harris, & Bernieri, 1990; McGue, Bouchard, Iacono, & Lykken, 1993). In childhood h^2 and c^2 for IQ are of the order of .45 and .35; by late adolescence h^2 is around .75 and c^2 is quite low (zero in some studies). Substantial environmental variance remains, but it primarily reflects within-family rather than between-family differences.

These adult parameter estimates are based on a number of independent studies. The correlation between MZ twins reared apart, which directly estimates $h2$, ranged from .68 to .78 in five studies involving adult samples from Europe and the United States (McGue et al., 1993). The correlation between unrelated children reared together in adoptive families, which directly estimates c^2, was approximately zero for adolescents in two adoption studies (Loehlin,

Horn, & Willerman, 1989; Scarr & Weinberg, 1978) and .19 in a third (the Minnesota transracial adoption study: Scarr, Weinberg, & Waldman, 1993).

These particular estimates derive from samples in which the lowest socioeconomic levels were underrepresented (i.e., there were few very poor families), so the range of between-family differences was smaller than in the population as a whole. This means that we should be cautious in generalizing the findings for between-family effects across the entire social spectrum. The samples were also mostly White, but available data suggest that twin and sibling correlations in African American and similarly selected White samples are more often comparable than not (Loehlin, Lindzey, & Spuhler, 1975).

Why should individual differences in intelligence (as measured by test scores) reflect genetic differences more strongly in adults than they do in children? One possibility is that as individuals grow older their transactions with their environments are increasingly influenced by the characteristics that they bring to those environments themselves, decreasingly by the conditions imposed by family life and social origins. Older persons are in a better position to select their own effective environments, a form of genotype-environment correlation. In any case the popular view that genetic influences on the development of a trait are essentially frozen at conception while the effects of the early environment cumulate inexorably is quite misleading, at least for the trait of psychometric intelligence.

Implications.   Estimates of h^2 and c^2 for IQ (or any other trait) are descriptive statistics for the populations studied. (In this respect they are like means and standard deviations.) They are outcome measures, summarizing the results of a great many diverse, intricate, individually variable events and processes, but they can nevertheless be quite useful. They can tell us how much of the variation in a given trait the genes and family environments explain, and changes in them place some constraints on theories of how this occurs. On the other hand they have little to say about specific mechanisms, i.e., about how genetic and environmental differences get translated into individual physiological and psychological differences. Many psychologists and neuroscientists are actively studying such processes; data on heritabilities may give them ideas about what to look for and where or when to look for it.

A common error is to assume that because something is heritable it is necessarily unchangeable. This is wrong. Heritability does not imply immutability. As previously noted, heritable traits can depend on learning, and they may be subject to other environmental effects as well. The value of h^2 can change if the distribution of environments (or genes) in the population is substantially altered. On the other hand, there can be effective environmental changes that do not change heritability at all. If the environment relevant to a given trait improves in a way that affects all members of the population equally, the mean value of the trait will rise without any change in its heritability (because the differences among individuals in the population will stay the same). This has evidently happened for height: the heritability of stature is high, but average heights continue to increase (Olivier, 1980). Something of the sort may also be taking place for IQ scores—the so-called "Flynn effect" discussed in Section 4. . . .

4. ENVIRONMENTAL EFFECTS ON INTELLIGENCE

The "environment" includes a wide range of influences on intelligence. Some of those variables affect whole populations, while others contribute to individual differences within a given group. Some of them are social, some are biological; at this point some are still mysterious. It may also happen that the proper interpretation of an environmental variable requires the simultaneous consideration of genetic effects. Nevertheless, a good deal of solid information is available.

SOCIAL VARIABLES

It is obvious that the cultural environment—how people live, what they value, what they do—has a significant effect on the intellectual skills developed by individuals. Rice farmers in Liberia are good at estimating quantities of rice (Gay & Cole, 1967); children in Botswana, accustomed to story-telling, have excellent memories for stories (Dube, 1982). Both these groups were far ahead of American controls on the tasks in question. On the other hand Americans and other Westernized groups typically outperform members of traditional societies on psychometric tests, even those designed to be "culture-fair."

Cultures typically differ from one another in so many ways that particular differences can rarely be ascribed to single causes. Even comparisons between subpopulations can be difficult to interpret. If we find that middle-class and poor Americans differ in their scores on intelligence tests, it is easy to suppose that the environmental difference has caused the IQ difference (i.e., that growing up in the middle class produces higher psychometric intelligence than growing up poor). But there may also be an opposite direction of causation: individuals can come to be in one environment or another because of differences in their own abilities. Waller (1971) has shown, for example, that adult sons whose IQ scores are above those of

their fathers tend to have higher social-class status than those fathers; conversely, sons with IQ scores below their fathers' tend to have lower social-class status. Since all the subjects grew up with their fathers, the IQ differences in this study cannot have resulted from class-related differences in childhood experience. Rather, those differences (or other factors correlated with them) seem to have had an influence on the status that they achieved. Such a result is not surprising, given the relation between test scores and years of education reviewed in Section 2.

Occupation. In Section 2 we noted that intelligence test scores predict occupational level, not only because some occupations require more intelligence than others but also because admission to many professions depends on test scores in the first place. There can also be an effect in the opposite direction, i.e., workplaces may affect the intelligence of those who work in them. Kohn and Schooler (1973), who interviewed some 3,000 men in various occupations (farmers, managers, machinists, porters, etc.), argued that more "complex" jobs produce more "intellectual flexibility" in the individuals who hold them. Although the issue of direction of effects was not fully resolved in their study—and perhaps not even in its longitudinal follow-up (Kohn & Schooler, 1983)—this remains a plausible suggestion. . . .

Schooling. Attendance at school is both a dependent and an independent variable in relation to intelligence. On the one hand, children with higher test scores are less likely to drop out and more likely to be promoted from grade to grade and then to attend college. Thus the number of years of education that adults complete is roughly predictable from their childhood scores on intelligence tests. On the other hand, schooling itself changes mental abilities, including those abilities measured on psychometric tests. This is obvious for tests like the SAT that are explicitly designed to assess school learning, but it is almost equally true of intelligence tests themselves. . . .

Schools affect intelligence in several ways, most obviously by transmitting information. The answers to questions like "Who wrote Hamlet?" and "What is the boiling point of water?" are typically learned in school, where some pupils learn them more easily and thoroughly than others. Perhaps at least as important are certain general skills and attitudes: systematic problem-solving, abstract thinking, categorization, sustained attention to material of little intrinsic interest, and repeated manipulation of basic symbols and operations. There is no doubt that schools promote and permit the development of significant intellectual skills, which develop to different extents in different children. It is because tests of intelligence draw on many of those same skills that they predict school achievement as well as they do.

To achieve these results, the school experience must meet at least some minimum standard of quality. In very poor schools, children may learn so little that they fall farther behind the national IQ norms for every year of attendance. When this happens, older siblings have systematically lower scores than their younger counterparts. This pattern of scores appeared in at least one rural Georgia school system in the 1970s (Jensen, 1977). Before desegregation, it must have been characteristic of many of the schools attended by Black pupils in the South. In a study based on Black children who had moved to Philadelphia at various ages during this period, Lee (1951) found that their IQ scores went up more than half a point for each year that they were enrolled in the Philadelphia system.

Interventions.   Intelligence test scores reflect a child's standing relative to others in his or her age cohort. Very poor or interrupted schooling can lower that standing substantially; are there also ways to raise it? In fact many interventions have been shown to raise test scores and mental ability "in the short run" (i.e., while the program itself was in progress), but long-run gains have proved more elusive. One noteworthy example of (at least short-run) success was the Venezuelan Intelligence Project (Herrnstein, Nickerson, de Sanchez, & Swets, 1986), in which hundreds of seventh-grade children from under-privileged backgrounds in that country were exposed to an extensive, theoretically-based curriculum focused on thinking skills. The intervention produced substantial gains on a wide range of tests, but there has been no follow-up.

Children who participate in "Head Start" and similar programs are exposed to various school-related materials and experiences for one or two years. Their test scores often go up during the course of the program, but these gains fade with time. By the end of elementary school, there are usually no significant IQ or achievement-test differences between children who have been in such programs and controls who have not. There may, however, be other differences. Follow-up studies suggest that children who participated in such programs as preschoolers are less likely to be assigned to special education, less likely to be held back in grade, and more likely to finish high school than matched controls (Consortium for Longitudinal Studies, 1983; Darlington, 1986; but see Locurto, 1991).

More extensive interventions might be expected to produce larger and more lasting effects, but few such programs have been evaluated systematically. One of the more successful is the Carolina Abecedarian Project (Campbell & Ramey, 1994), which provided a group of children with enriched environments from early infancy through preschool and also maintained appropriate controls. The test scores of the enrichment-group children were already higher than those of controls at age two; they were still some 5 points higher at age 12, seven years after the end of the intervention. Importantly, the enrichment group also outperformed the controls in academic achievement.

Family Environment.   No one doubts that normal child development requires a certain minimum level of responsible care. Severely deprived, neglectful, or abusive environments must have negative effects on a great many aspects—including intellectual aspects—of development. Beyond that minimum, however, the role of family experience is now in serious dispute (Baumrind, 1993; Jackson, 1993; Scarr, 1992, 1993). Psychometric intelligence is a case in point. Do differences between children's family environments (within the normal range) produce differences in their intelligence test performance? The problem here is to disentangle causation from correlation. There is no doubt that such variables as resources of the home (Gottfried, 1984) and parents' use of language (Hart & Risley, 1992, in press) are correlated with children's IQ scores, but such correlations may be mediated by genetic as well as (or instead of) environmental factors. . . .

BIOLOGICAL VARIABLES

Every individual has a biological as well as a social environment, one that begins in the womb and extends throughout life. Many aspects of that environment can affect intellectual development. We now know that a number of biological factors—malnutrition, exposure to toxic substances, various prenatal and perinatal stressors—result in lowered psychometric intelligence under at least some conditions.

Nutrition.   There has been only one major study of the effects of prenatal malnutrition (i.e., malnutrition of the mother during pregnancy) on long-term intellectual development. Stein, Susser, Saenger, and Marolla (1975) analyzed the test scores of Dutch 19-year-old males in relation to a wartime famine that had occurred in the winter of 1944–45, just before their birth. In this very large sample (made possible by a universal military induction requirement), exposure to the famine had no effect on adult intelligence. Note, however, that the famine itself lasted only a few months; the subjects were exposed to it prenatally but not after birth.

In contrast, prolonged malnutrition during childhood does have long-term intellectual effects. These have not been easy to establish, in part because many other unfavorable socioeconomic conditions are often associated with chronic malnutrition (Ricciuti, 1993;

but cf. Sigman, 1995). In one intervention study, however, preschoolers in two Guatemalan villages (where undernourishment is common) were given ad lib access to a protein dietary supplement for several years. A decade later, many of these children (namely, those from the poorest socioeconomic levels) scored significantly higher on school-related achievement tests than comparable controls (Pollitt, Gorman, Engle, Martorell, & Rivera, 1993). It is worth noting that the effects of poor nutrition on intelligence may well be indirect. Malnourished children are typically less responsive to adults, less motivated to learn, and less active in exploration than their more adequately nourished counterparts. . . .

Lead. Certain toxins have well-established negative effects on intelligence. Exposure to lead is one such factor. In one long-term study (Baghurst et al., 1992; McMichael et al., 1988), the blood lead levels of children growing up near a lead smelting plant were substantially and negatively correlated with intelligence test scores throughout childhood. No "threshold dose" for the effect of lead appears in such studies. Although ambient lead levels in the United States have been reduced in recent years, there is reason to believe that some American children—especially those in inner cities—may still be at risk from this source (cf. Needleman, Geiger, & Frank, 1985).

Alcohol. Extensive prenatal exposure to alcohol (which occurs if the mother drinks heavily during pregnancy) can give rise to fetal alcohol syndrome, which includes mental retardation as well as a range of physical symptoms. Smaller "doses" of prenatal alcohol may have negative effects on intelligence even when the full syndrome does not appear. Streissguth, Barr, Sampson, Darby, and Martin (1989) found that mothers who reported consuming more than 1.5 oz. of alcohol daily during pregnancy had children who scored some 5 points below controls at age four. Prenatal exposure to aspirin and antibiotics had similar negative effects in this study.

Perinatal Factors. Complications at delivery and other negative perinatal factors may have serious consequences for development. Nevertheless, because they occur only rarely, they contribute relatively little to the population variance of intelligence (Broman, Nichols, & Kennedy, 1975). Down's syndrome, a chromosomal abnormality that produces serious mental retardation, is also rare enough to have little impact on the overall distribution of test scores.

The correlation between birth weight and later intelligence deserves particular discussion. In some cases low birth weight simply reflects premature delivery; in others, the infant's size is below normal for its gestational age. Both factors apparently contribute to the tendency of low-birth-weight infants to have

lower test scores in later childhood (Lubchenko, 1976). These correlations are small, ranging from .05 to .13 in different groups (Broman et al., 1975). The effects of low birth weight are substantial only when it is very low indeed (less than 1,500 gm). Premature babies born at these very low birth weights are behind controls on most developmental measures; they often have severe or permanent intellectual deficits (Rosetti, 1986).

CONTINUOUSLY RISING TEST SCORES

Perhaps the most striking of all environmental effects is the steady worldwide rise in intelligence test performance. Although many psychometricians had noted these gains, it was James Flynn (1984, 1987) who first described them systematically. His analysis shows that performance has been going up ever since testing began. The "Flynn effect" is now very well documented, not only in the United States but in many other technologically advanced countries. The average gain is about 3 IQ points per decade—more than a full standard deviation since, say, 1940.

Although it is simplest to describe the gains as increases in population IQ, this is not exactly what happens. Most intelligence tests are "restandardized" from time to time, in part to keep up with these very gains. As part of this process the mean score of the new standardization sample is typically set to 100 again, so the increase more or less disappears from view. In this context, the Flynn effect means that if 20 years have passed since the last time the test was standardized, people who now score 100 on the new version would probably average about 106 on the old one.

The sheer extent of these increases is remarkable, and the rate of gain may even be increasing. The scores of 19-year-olds in the Netherlands, for example, went up more than 8 points—over half a standard deviation—between 1972 and 1982. What's more, the largest gains appear on the types of tests that were specifically designed to be free of cultural influence (Flynn, 1987). One of these is Raven's Progressive Matrices, an untimed nonverbal test that many psychometricians regard as a good measure of *g.*

These steady gains in intelligence test performance have not always been accompanied by corresponding gains in school achievement. Indeed, the relation between intelligence and achievement test scores can be complex. This is especially true for the Scholastic Aptitude Test (SAT), in part because the ability range of the students who take the SAT has broadened over time. That change explains some portion—not all—of the prolonged decline in SAT scores that took place from the mid-1960s to the early 1980s, even as IQ scores were continuing to rise

(Flynn, 1984). Meanwhile, however, other more representative measures show that school achievement levels have held steady or in some cases actually increased (Herrnstein & Murray, 1994). The National Assessment of Educational Progress (NAEP), for example, shows that the average reading and math achievement of American 13- and 17-year-olds improved somewhat from the early 1970s to 1990 (Grissmer, Kirby, Berends, & Williamson, 1994). An analysis of these data by ethnic group, reported in Section 5, shows that this small overall increase actually reflects very substantial gains by Blacks and Latinos combined with little or no gain by Whites.

The consistent IQ gains documented by Flynn seem much too large to result from simple increases in test sophistication. Their cause is presently unknown, but three interpretations deserve our consideration. Perhaps the most plausible of these is based on the striking cultural differences between successive generations. Daily life and occupational experience both seem more "complex" (Kohn & Schooler, 1973) today than in the time of our parents and grandparents. The population is increasingly urbanized; television exposes us to more information and more perspectives on more topics than ever before; children stay in school longer; and almost everyone seems to be encountering new forms of experience. These changes in the complexity of life may have produced corresponding changes in complexity of mind, and hence in certain psychometric abilities.

A different hypothesis attributes the gains to modern improvements in nutrition. Lynn (1990) points out that large nutritionally-based increases in height have occurred during the same period as the IQ gains: perhaps there have been increases in brain size as well. As we have seen, however, the effects of nutrition on intelligence are themselves not firmly established.

The third interpretation addresses the very definition of intelligence. Flynn himself believes that real intelligence—whatever it may be—cannot have increased as much as these data would suggest. Consider, for example, the number of individuals who have IQ scores of 140 or more. (This is slightly above the cutoff used by L. M. Terman [1925] in his famous longitudinal study of "genius.") In 1952 only 0.38% of Dutch test takers had IQs over 140; in 1982, scored by the same norms, 9.12% exceeded this figure! Judging by these criteria, the Netherlands should now be experiencing "a cultural renaissance too great to be overlooked" (Flynn, 1987, p. 187). So too should France, Norway, the United States, and many other countries. Because Flynn (1987) finds this conclusion implausible or absurd, he argues that what has risen cannot be intelligence itself but only a minor sort of "abstract problem solving ability." The issue remains unresolved. . . .

5. GROUP DIFFERENCES

Group means have no direct implications for individuals. What matters for the next person you meet (to the extent that test scores matter at all) is that person's own particular score, not the mean of some reference group to which he or she happens to belong. The commitment to evaluate people on their own individual merit is central to a democratic society. It also makes quantitative sense. The distributions of different groups inevitably overlap, with the range of scores within any one group always wider than the mean differences between any two groups. In the case of intelligence test scores, the variance attributable to individual differences far exceeds the variance related to group membership (Jensen, 1980). . . .

Besides European Americans ("Whites"), the ethnic groups to be considered are Chinese and Japanese Americans, Hispanic Americans ("Latinos"), Native Americans ("Indians"), and African Americans ("Blacks"). These groups (we avoid the term "race") are defined and self-defined by social conventions based on ethnic origin as well as on observable physical characteristics such as skin color. None of them are internally homogeneous. Asian Americans, for example, may have roots in many different cultures: not only China and Japan but also Korea, Laos, Vietnam, the Philippines, India, and Pakistan. Hispanic Americans, who share a common linguistic tradition, actually differ along many cultural dimensions. In their own minds they may be less "Latinos" than Puerto Ricans, Mexican Americans, Cuban Americans, or representatives of other Latin cultures. "Native American" is an even more diverse category, including a great many culturally distinct tribes living in a wide range of environments.

. . .

MEAN SCORES OF DIFFERENT ETHNIC GROUPS

Asian Americans.   In the years since the Second World War, Asian Americans—especially those of Chinese and Japanese extraction—have compiled an outstanding record of academic and professional achievement. This record is reflected in school grades, in scores on content-oriented achievement tests like the SAT and GRE, and especially in the disproportionate representation of Asian Americans in many sciences and professions. Although it is often supposed that these achievements reflect correspondingly high intelligence test scores, this is not the case. In more than a dozen studies from the 1960s and 1970s analyzed by Flynn (1991), the mean IQs of Japanese and Chinese American children were always around 97 or 98; none was over 100. Even Lynn (1993), who argues for a slightly higher figure, concedes that the achievements of these Asian Americans far outstrip what might have been expected on the basis of their test scores.

It may be worth noting that the interpretation of test scores obtained by Asians in Asia has been controversial in its own right. Lynn (1982) reported a mean Japanese IQ of 111 while Flynn (1991) estimated it to be between 101 and 105. Stevenson et al. (1985), comparing the intelligence-test performance of children in Japan, Taiwan, and the United States, found no substantive differences at all. Given the general problems of cross-cultural comparison, there is no reason to expect precision or stability in such estimates. Nevertheless, some interest attaches to these particular comparisons: they show that the well-established differences in school achievement among the same three groups (Chinese and Japanese children are much better at math than American children) do not simply reflect differences in psychometric intelligence. Stevenson, Lee, and Stigler (1986) suggest that they result from structural differences in the schools of the three nations as well as from varying cultural attitudes toward learning itself. It is also possible that spatial ability—in which Japanese and Chinese obtain somewhat higher scores than Americans—plays a particular role in the learning of mathematics. . . .

Hispanic Americans. Hispanic immigrants have come to America from many countries. In 1993, the largest Latino groups in the continental United States were Mexican Americans (64%), Puerto Ricans (11%), Central and South Americans (13%), and Cubans (5%) (U.S. Bureau of the Census, 1994). There are very substantial cultural differences among these nationality groups, as well as differences in academic achievement (Duran, 1983; United States National Commission for Employment Policy, 1982). Taken together, Latinos make up the second largest and the fastest-growing minority group in America (Davis, Haub, & Willette, 1983; Eyde, 1992).

In the United States, the mean intelligence test scores of Hispanics typically lie between those of Blacks and Whites. There are also differences in the patterning of scores across different abilities and subtests (Hennessy & Merrifield, 1978; Lesser, Fifer, & Clark, 1965). Linguistic factors play a particularly important role for Hispanic Americans, who may know relatively little English. (By one estimate, 25% of Puerto Ricans and Mexican Americans and at least 40% of Cubans speak English "not well" or "not at all" [Rodriguez, 1992]). Even those who describe themselves as bilingual may be at a disadvantage if Spanish was their first and best-learned language. It is not surprising that Latino children typically score higher on the performance than on the verbal subtests of the English-based Wechsler Intelligence Scale for Children–Revised (WISC–R; Kaufman, 1994). Nevertheless, the predictive validity of Latino test scores is not negligible. In young children, the WISC–R has reasonably high correlations with school achievement measures (McShane & Cook, 1985). For high school students of moderate to high English proficiency, standard aptitude tests predict first-year college grades about as well as they do for non-Hispanic Whites (Pennock-Roman, 1992).

Native Americans. There are a great many culturally distinct North American Indian tribes (Driver, 1969), speaking some 200 different languages (Leap, 1981). Many Native Americans live on reservations, which themselves represent a great variety of ecological and cultural settings. Many others presently live in metropolitan areas (Brandt, 1984). Although few generalizations can be appropriate across so wide a range, two or three points seem fairly well established. The first is a specific relation between ecology and cognition: the Inuit (Eskimo) and other groups that live in the arctic tend to have particularly high visual-spatial skills. (For a review see McShane & Berry, 1988.) Moreover, there seem to be no substantial sex differences in those skills (Berry, 1974). It seems likely that this represents an adaptation—genetic or learned or both—to the difficult hunting, traveling, and living conditions that characterize the arctic environment.

On the average, Indian children obtain relatively low scores on tests of verbal intelligence, which are often administered in school settings. The result is a performance-test/verbal-test discrepancy similar to that exhibited by Hispanic Americans and other groups whose first language is generally not English. Moreover, many Indian children suffer from chronic middle-ear infection (otitis media), which is "the leading identifiable disease among Indians since record-keeping began in 1962" (McShane & Plas, 1984a, p. 84). Hearing loss can have marked negative effects on verbal test performance (McShane & Plas, 1984b).

African Americans. The relatively low mean of the distribution of African American intelligence test scores has been discussed for many years. Although studies using different tests and samples yield a range of results, the Black mean is typically about one standard deviation (about 15 points) below that of Whites (Jensen, 1980; Loehlin et al., 1975; Reynolds et al., 1987). The difference is largest on those tests (verbal or nonverbal) that best represent the general intelligence factor g (Jensen, 1985). It is possible, however, that this differential is diminishing. In the most recent restandardization of the Stanford-Binet test, the Black/White differential was 13 points for younger children and 10 points for older children (Thorndike, Hagen, & Sattler, 1986). In several other studies of children since 1980, the Black mean has consistently been over 90 and the differential has been in single digits (Vincent, 1991). Larger and more definitive studies are needed before this trend can be regarded as established.

Another reason to think the IQ mean might be changing is that the Black/White differential in *achievement* scores has diminished substantially in the last few years. Consider, for example, the mathematics achievement of 17-year-olds as measured by the National Assessment of Educational Progress (NAEP). The differential between Black and White scores, about 1.1 standard deviations as recently as 1978, had shrunk to .65 *SD* by 1990 (Grissmer et al., 1994) because of Black gains. Hispanics showed similar but smaller gains; there was little change in the scores of Whites. Other assessments of school achievement also show substantial recent gains in the performance of minority children.

In their own analysis of these gains, Grissmer et al. (1994) cite both demographic factors and the effects of public policy. They found the level of parents' education to be a particularly good predictor of children's school achievement; that level increased for all groups between 1970 and 1990, but most sharply for Blacks. Family size was another good predictor (children from smaller families tend to achieve higher scores); here too, the largest change over time was among Blacks. Above and beyond these demographic effects, Grissmer et al. believe that some of the gains can be attributed to the many specific programs, geared to the education of minority children, that were implemented during that period.

Test Bias.   It is often argued that the lower mean scores of African Americans reflect a bias in the intelligence tests themselves. This argument is right in one sense of "bias" but wrong in another. To see the first of these, consider how the term is used in probability theory. When a coin comes up heads consistently for any reason it is said to be "biased," regardless of any consequences that the outcome may or may not have. In this sense the Black/White score differential is *ipso facto* evidence of what may be called "outcome bias." African Americans are subject to outcome bias not only with respect to tests but along many dimensions of American life. They have the short end of nearly every stick: average income, representation in high-level occupations, health and health care, death rate, confrontations with the legal system, and so on. With this situation in mind, some critics regard the test score differential as just another example of a pervasive outcome bias that characterizes our society as a whole (Jackson, 1975; Mercer, 1984). Although there is a sense in which they are right, this critique ignores the particular social purpose that tests are designed to serve.

From an educational point of view, the chief function of mental tests is as *predictors* (Section 2). Intelligence tests predict school performance fairly well, at least in American schools as they are now constituted. Similarly, achievement tests are fairly good predictors of performance in college and postgraduate settings. Considered in this light, the relevant question is whether the tests have a "predictive bias" against Blacks. Such a bias would exist if African American performance on the criterion variables (school achievement, college GPA, etc.) were systematically higher than the same subjects' test scores would predict. This is not the case. The actual regression lines (which show the mean criterion performance for individuals who got various scores on the predictor) for Blacks do not lie above those for Whites; there is even a slight tendency in the other direction (Jensen, 1980; Reynolds & Brown, 1984). Considered as predictors of future performance, the tests do not seem to be biased against African Americans.

Characteristics of Tests.   It has been suggested that various aspects of the way tests are formulated and administered may put African Americans at a disadvantage. The language of testing is a standard form of English with which some Blacks may not be familiar; specific vocabulary items are often unfamiliar to Black children; the tests are often given by White examiners rather than by more familiar Black teachers; African Americans may not be motivated to work hard on tests that so clearly reflect White values; the time demands of some tests may be alien to Black culture. (Similar suggestions have been made in connection with the test performance of Hispanic Americans, e.g., Rodriguez, 1992.) Many of these suggestions are plausible, and such mechanisms may play a role in particular cases. Controlled studies have shown, however, that none of them contributes substantially to the Black/White differential under discussion here (Jensen, 1980; Reynolds & Brown, 1984; for a different view see Helms, 1992). Moreover, efforts to devise reliable and valid tests that would minimize disadvantages of this kind have been unsuccessful.

INTERPRETING GROUP DIFFERENCES

If group differences in test performance do not result from the simple forms of bias reviewed above, what is responsible for them? The fact is that we do not know. Various explanations have been proposed, but none is generally accepted. It is clear, however, that these differences—whatever their origin—are well within the range of effect sizes that can be produced by environmental factors. The Black/White differential amounts to one standard deviation or less, and we know that environmental factors have recently raised mean test scores in many populations by at least that much

(Flynn, 1987: see Section 4). To be sure, the "Flynn effect" is itself poorly understood: it may reflect generational changes in culture, improved nutrition, or other factors as yet unknown. Whatever may be responsible for it, we cannot exclude the possibility that the same factors play a role in contemporary group differences.

Socioeconomic Factors.   Several specific environmental/cultural explanations of those differences have been proposed. All of them refer to the general life situation in which contemporary African Americans find themselves, but that situation can be described in several different ways. The simplest such hypothesis can be framed in economic terms. On the average, Blacks have lower incomes than Whites; a much higher proportion of them are poor. It is plausible to suppose that many inevitable aspects of poverty—poor nutrition, frequently inadequate prenatal care, lack of intellectual resources—have negative effects on children's developing intelligence. Indeed, the correlation between "socioeconomic status" (SES) and scores on intelligence tests is well-known (White, 1982).

Several considerations suggest that this cannot be the whole explanation. For one thing, the Black/White differential in test scores is not eliminated when groups or individuals are matched for SES (Loehlin et al., 1975). Moreover, the data reviewed in Section 4 suggest that—if we exclude extreme conditions—nutrition and other biological factors that may vary with SES account for relatively little of the variance in such scores. Finally, the (relatively weak) relationship between test scores and income is much more complex than a simple SES hypothesis would suggest. The living conditions of children result in part from the accomplishments of their parents: If the skills measured by psychometric tests actually matter for those accomplishments, intelligence is affecting SES rather than the other way around. We do not know the magnitude of these various effects in various populations, but it is clear that no model in which "SES" directly determines "IQ" will do.

A more fundamental difficulty with explanations based on economics alone appears from a different perspective. To imagine that any simple income- and education-based index can adequately describe the situation of African Americans is to ignore important categories of experience. The sense of belonging to a group with a distinctive culture—one that has long been the target of oppression—and the awareness or anticipation of racial discrimination are profound personal experiences, not just aspects of socioeconomic status. Some of these more deeply rooted differences are addressed by other hypotheses, based on caste and culture.

Caste-like Minorities.   Most discussions of this issue treat Black/White differences as aspects of a uniquely

"American dilemma" (Myrdal, 1944). The fact is, however, that comparably disadvantaged groups exist in many countries: the Maori in New Zealand, scheduled castes ("untouchables") in India, non-European Jews in Israel, the Burakumin in Japan. All these are "caste-like" (Ogbu, 1978) or "involuntary" (Ogbu, 1994) minorities. John Ogbu distinguishes this status from that of "autonomous" minorities who are not politically or economically subordinated (like Amish or Mormons in the United States), and from that of "immigrant" or "voluntary" minorities who initially came to their new homes with positive expectations. Immigrant minorities expect their situations to improve; they tend to compare themselves favorably with peers in the old country, not unfavorably with members of the dominant majority. In contrast, to be born into a caste-like minority is to grow up firmly convinced that one's life will eventually be restricted to a small and poorly-rewarded set of social roles.

Distinctions of caste are not always linked to perceptions of race. In some countries lower and upper caste groups differ by appearance and are assumed to be racially distinct; in others they are not. The social and educational consequences are the same in both cases. All over the world, the children of caste-like minorities do less well in school than upper-caste children and drop out sooner. Where there are data, they have usually been found to have lower test scores as well.

In explaining these findings, Ogbu (1978) argues that the children of caste-like minorities do not have "effort optimism," i.e., the conviction that hard work (especially hard schoolwork) and serious commitment on their part will actually be rewarded. As a result they ignore or reject the forms of learning that are offered in school. Indeed they may practice a sort of cultural inversion, deliberately rejecting certain behaviors (such as academic achievement or other forms of "acting White") that are seen as characteristic of the dominant group. While the extent to which the attitudes described by Ogbu (1978, 1994) are responsible for African American test scores and school achievement has not been empirically established, it does seem that familiar problems can take on quite a different look when they are viewed from an international perspective.

African American Culture.   According to Boykin (1986, 1994), there is a fundamental conflict between certain aspects of African American culture on the one hand and the implicit cultural commitments of most American schools on the other. "When children are ordered to do their own work, arrive at their own individual answers, work only with their own materials, they are being sent cultural messages. When children come to believe that getting up and moving about the classroom is inappropriate, they are being sent powerful cultural messages. When children come to confine their 'learning' to consistently bracketed time periods, when they are consistently prompted to tell what they know and not how they feel, when they are led to believe that they are completely responsible for their own success and failure, when they are required to consistently put forth considerable effort for effort's sake on tedious and personally irrelevant tasks . . . then they are pervasively having cultural lessons imposed on them" (1994, p. 125).

In Boykin's view, the combination of constriction and competition that most American schools demand of their pupils conflicts with certain themes in the "deep structure" of African American culture. That culture includes an emphasis on such aspects of experience as spirituality, harmony, movement, verve, affect, expressive individualism, communalism, orality, and a socially defined time perspective (Boykin, 1986, 1994). While it is not shared by all African Americans to the same degree, its accessibility and familiarity give it a profound influence.

The result of this cultural conflict, in Boykin's view, is that many Black children become alienated from both the process and the products of the education to which they are exposed. One aspect of that process, now an intrinsic aspect of the culture of most American schools, is the psychometric enterprise itself. He argues (Boykin, 1994) that the successful education of African American children will require an approach that is less concerned with talent sorting and assessment, more concerned with talent development.

One further factor should not be overlooked. Only a single generation has passed since the Civil Rights movement opened new doors for African Americans, and many forms of discrimination are still all too familiar in their experience today. Hard enough to bear in its own right, discrimination is also a sharp reminder of a still more intolerable past. It would be rash indeed to assume that those experiences, and that historical legacy, have no impact on intellectual development.

The Genetic Hypothesis.   It is sometimes suggested that the Black/White differential in psychometric intelligence is partly due to genetic differences (Jensen, 1972). There is not much direct evidence on this point, but what little there is fails to support the genetic hypothesis. One piece of evidence comes from a study of the children of American soldiers stationed in Germany after the Second World War (Eyferth, 1961): there was no mean difference between the test scores of those children whose fathers were White and those whose fathers were Black. (For a discussion of possible confounds in this study, see Flynn, 1980.) Moreover, several studies have used blood-group methods to estimate the degree of African ancestry of

American Blacks; there were no significant correlations between those estimates and IQ scores (Loehlin, Vandenberg, & Osborne, 1973; Scarr, Pakstis, Katz, & Barker, 1977).

It is clear (Section 3) that genes make a substantial contribution to individual differences in intelligence test scores, at least in the White population. The fact is, however, that the high heritability of a trait within a given group has no necessary implications for the source of a difference between groups (Loehlin et al., 1975). This is now generally understood (e.g., Herrnstein & Murray, 1994). But even though no such implication is *necessary*, some have argued that a high value of h^2 makes a genetic contribution to group differences more *plausible*. Does it?

That depends on one's assessment of the actual difference between the two environments. Consider Lewontin's (1970) well-known example of seeds from the same genetically variable stock that are planted in two different fields. If the plants in field X are fertilized appropriately while key nutrients are withheld from those in field Y, we have produced an entirely environmental group difference. This example works (i.e., h^2 is genuinely irrelevant to the differential between the fields) because the differences between the effective environments of X and Y are both large and consistent. Are the environmental and cultural situations of American Blacks and Whites also substantially and consistently different—different enough to make this a good analogy? If so, the within-group heritability of IQ scores is irrelevant to the issue. Or are those situations similar enough to suggest that the analogy is inappropriate, and that one can plausibly generalize from within-group heritabilities? Thus the issue ultimately comes down to a personal judgment: How different are the relevant life experiences of Whites and Blacks in the United States today? At present, this question has no scientific answer.

6. SUMMARY AND CONCLUSIONS

. . .

It is customary to conclude surveys like this one with a summary of what has been established. Indeed, much is now known about intelligence. A near-century of research, most of it based on psychometric methods, has produced an impressive body of findings. Although we have tried to do justice to those findings in this report, it seems appropriate to conclude on a different note. In this contentious arena, our most useful role may be to remind our readers that many of the critical questions about intelligence are still unanswered. Here are a few of those questions:

1.   Differences in genetic endowment contribute substantially to individual differences in (psycho-

metric) intelligence, but the pathway by which genes produce their effects is still unknown. The impact of genetic differences appears to increase with age, but we do not know why.

2. Environmental factors also contribute substantially to the development of intelligence, but we do not clearly understand what those factors are or how they work. Attendance at school is certainly important, for example, but we do not know what aspects of schooling are critical.

3. The role of nutrition in intelligence remains obscure. Severe childhood malnutrition has clear negative effects, but the hypothesis that particular "micronutrients" may affect intelligence in otherwise adequately-fed populations has not yet been convincingly demonstrated.

4. There are significant correlations between measures of information-processing speed and psychometric intelligence, but the overall pattern of these findings yields no easy theoretical interpretation.

5. Mean scores on intelligence tests are rising steadily. They have gone up a full standard deviation in the last 50 years or so, and the rate of gain may be increasing. No one is sure why these gains are happening or what they mean.

6. The differential between the mean intelligence test scores of Blacks and Whites (about one standard deviation, although it may be diminishing) does not result from any obvious biases in test construction and administration, nor does it simply reflect differences in socioeconomic status. Explanations based on factors of caste and culture may be appropriate, but so far have little direct empirical support. There is certainly no such support for a genetic interpretation. At present, no one knows what causes this differential.

7. It is widely agreed that standardized tests do not sample all forms of intelligence. Obvious examples include creativity, wisdom, practical sense, and social sensitivity; there are surely others. Despite the importance of these abilities we know very little about them: how they develop, what factors influence that development, how they are related to more traditional measures.

In a field where so many issues are unresolved and so many questions unanswered, the confident tone that has characterized most of the debate on these topics is clearly out of place. The study of intelligence does not need politicized assertions and recriminations; it needs self-restraint, reflection, and a great deal more research. The questions that remain are socially as well as scientifically important. There is no reason to think them unanswerable, but finding the answers will require a shared and sustained effort as well as the commitment of substantial scientific resources. Just such a commitment is what we strongly recommend.

REFERENCES

Baghurst, P. A., McMichael, A. J., Wigg, N. R., Vimpani, G. V., Robertson, E. F., Roberts, R. J., & Tong, S. L. (1992). Environmental exposure to lead and children's intelligence at the age of seven years: The Port Pirie cohort study. *New England Journal of Medicine, 327*, 1279–1284.

Baumrind, D. (1993). The average expectable environment is not good enough: A response to Scarr. *Child Development, 64*, 1299–1317.

Berry, J. W. (1974). Ecological and cultural factors in spatial perceptual development. In J. W. Berry & P. R. Dasen (Eds.), *Culture and cognition: Readings in cross-cultural psychology* (pp. 129–140). London: Methuen.

Boykin, A. W. (1986). The triple quandary and the schooling of Afro-American children. In U. Neisser (Ed.), *The school achievement of minority children* (pp. 57–92). Hillsdale, NJ: Erlbaum.

Boykin, A. W. (1994). Harvesting talent and culture: African-American children and educational reform. In R. Rossi (Ed.), *Schools and students at risk* (pp. 116–138). New York: Teachers College Press.

Brandt, E. A. (1984). The cognitive functioning of American Indian children: A critique of McShane and Plas. *School Psychology Review, 13*, 74–82.

Broman, S. H., Nichols, P. L., & Kennedy, W. A. (1975). *Preschool IQ: Prenatal and early developmental correlates.* Hillsdale. NJ: Erlbaum.

Campbell, F. A., & Ramey, C. T. (1994). Effects of early intervention on intellectual and academic achievement: A follow-up study of children from low-income families. *Child Development, 65*, 684–698.

Carroll, J. B. (1993). *Human cognitive abilities: A survey of factor-analytic studies.* Cambridge, England: University of Cambridge Press.

Ceci, S. J. (1990). *On intelligence . . . more or less: A bioecological treatise on intellectual development.* Englewood Cliffs, NJ: Prentice Hall.

Chipuer, H. M., Rovine, M., & Plomin, R. (1990). LISREL modelling: Genetic and environmental influences on IQ revisited. *Intelligence, 14*, 11–29.

Consortium for Longitudinal Studies. (1983). *As the twig is bent . . . lasting effects of preschool programs.* Hillsdale, NJ: Erlbaum.

Darlington, R. B. (1986). Long-term effects of preschool programs. In U. Neisser (Ed.), *The school achievement of minority children* (pp. 159–167). Hillsdale, NJ: Erlbaum.

Davis, C., Haub, C., & Willette, J. (1983). U.S. Hispanics: Changing the face of America. *Population Bulletin, 38*(No. 3).

Deary, I. J. (1995). Auditory inspection time and intelligence: What is the causal direction? *Developmental Psychology, 31*, 237–250.

Driver, H. E. (1969). *Indians of North America*. Chicago: University of Chicago Press.

Dube, E. F. (1982). Literacy, cultural familiarity, and "intelligence" as determinants of story recall. In U. Neisser (Ed.), *Memory observed: Remembering in natural contexts* (pp. 274–292). New York: Freeman.

Duran, R. P. (1983). *Hispanics' education and background: Prediction of college achievement*. New York: College Entrance Examination Board.

Eyde, L. D. (1992). Introduction to the testing of Hispanics in industry and research. In K. F. Geisinger (Ed.), *Psychological testing of Hispanics* (pp. 167–172). Washington. DC: American Psychological Association.

Eyferth, K. (1961). Leistungen verchiedener Gruppen von Besatzungskindern Hamburg-Wechsler Intelligentztest fur Kinder (HAWIK) [The performance of different groups of occupation children in the Hamburg-Wechsler Intelligence Test for Children]. *Archive fur die gesamte Psychologie, 113*, 222–241.

Eysenck, H. (1973). *The measurement of intelligence*. Baltimore: Williams & Wilkins.

Eysenck, H. J. (1986). Inspection time and intelligence: A historical introduction. *Personality and Individual Differences, 7*, 603–607.

Flynn, J. R. (1980). *Race, IQ, and Jensen*. London: Routledge & Kegan Paul.

Flynn, J. R. (1984). The mean IQ of Americans: Massive gains 1932 to 1978. *Psychological Bulletin, 95*, 29–51.

Flynn, J. R. (1987). Massive IQ gains in 14 nations: What IQ tests really measure. *Psychological Bulletin, 101*, 171–191.

Flynn, J. R. (1991). *Asian-Americans: Achievement beyond IQ*. Hillsdale, NJ: Erlbaum.

Gardner, H. (1983). *Frames of mind: The theory of multiple intelligences*. New York: Basic Books.

Gay, J., & Cole, M. (1967). *The new mathematics and an old culture: A study of learning among the Kpelle of Liberia*. New York: Holt, Rhinehart & Winston.

Gottfried, A. W. (Ed.). (1984). *Home environment and early cognitive development: Longitudinal research*. New York: Academic Press.

Gould, S. J. (1978). Morton's ranking of races by cranial capacity: Unconscious manipulation of data may be a scientific norm. *Science, 200*, 503–509.

Grissmer, D. W., Kirby, S. N., Berends, M., & Williamson, S. (1994). *Student achievement and the changing American family*. Santa Monica, CA: RAND Corporation.

Gustafsson, J.-E. (1984). A unifying model for the structure of intellectual abilities. *Intelligence, 8*, 179–203.

Hart, B., & Risley, T. R. (1992). American parenting of language-learning children: Persisting differences in family-child interactions observed in natural home environments. *Developmental Psychology, 28*, 1096–1105.

Hart, B., & Risley, T. R. (in press). *Meaningful differences in the everyday experience of young American children*. Baltimore: P. H. Brookes.

Helms, J. E. (1992). Why is there no study of cultural equivalence in standardized cognitive ability testing? *American Psychologist, 47*, 1083–1101.

Hennessy, J. J., & Merrifield, P. R. (1978). Ethnicity and sex distinctions in patterns of aptitude factor scores in a sample of urban high school seniors. *American Educational Research Journal, 15*, 385–389.

Herrnstein, R. J., & Murray, C. (1994). *The bell curve: Intelligence and class structure in American life*. New York: Free Press.

Herrnstein, R. J., Nickerson R. S., de Sanchez, M., & Swets, J. A. (1986). Teaching thinking skills. *American Psychologist, 41*, 1279–1289.

Hunter, J. E. (1983). A causal analysis of cognitive ability, job knowledge, job performance, and supervisor ratings. In F. Landy, S. Zedeck, & J. Cleveland (Eds.), *Performance measurement and theory* (pp. 257–266). Hillsdale, NJ: Erlbaum.

Jackson, G. D. (1975). On the report of the Ad Hoc Committee on Educational Uses of Tests with Disadvantaged Students: Another psychological view from the Association of Black Psychologists. *American Psychologist, 30*, 88–93.

Jackson, J. F. (1993). Human behavioral genetics, Scarr's theory, and her views on interventions: A critical review and commentary on their implications for African American children. *Child Development, 64*, 1318–1332.

Jencks, C. (1979). *Who gets ahead? The determinants of economic success in America*. New York: Basic Books.

Jensen, A. R. (1972). *Genetics and education*. New York: Harper & Row.

Jensen, A. R. (1977). Cumulative deficit in IQ of Blacks in the rural South. *Developmental Psychology, 13*, 184–191.

Jensen, A. R. (1980). *Bias in mental testing*. New York: Free Press.

Jensen, A. R. (1985). The nature of the black-white difference on various psychometric tests: Spearman's hypothesis. *Behavioral and Brain Sciences, 8*, 193–263.

Jones, H. E., and Bayley, N. (1941). The Berkeley Growth Study. *Child Development, 12*, 167–173.

Kaufman, A. S. (1994). *Intelligent testing with the WISC-III*. New York: Wiley.

Kohn, M. L., & Schooler, C. (1973). Occupational experience and psychological functioning: An assessment of reciprocal effects. *American Sociological Review, 38*, 97–118.

Kohn, M. L., & Schooler, C. (1983). *Work and personality: An inquiry into the impact of social stratification*. Norwood, NJ: Ablex.

Leap, W. L. (1981). American Indian languages. In C. Ferguson & S. B. Heath (Eds.), *Language in the USA*. Cambridge, England: Cambridge University Press.

Lee, E. S. (1951). Negro intelligence and selective migration: A Philadelphia test of the Klineberg hypothesis. *American Sociological Review, 16*, 227–232.

Lesser, G. S., Fifer, G., & Clark, D. H. (1965). Mental abilities of children from different social-class and cultural groups. *Monographs of the Society for Research in Child Development, 30* (Whole No. 102).

Lewontin, R. (1970). Race and intelligence. *Bulletin of the Atomic Scientists, 26*, 2–8.

Locurto, C. (1991). Beyond IQ in preschool programs? *Intelligence, 15*, 295–312.

Loehlin, J. C. (1989). Partitioning environmental and genetic contributions to behavioral development. *American Psychologist, 10*, 1285–1292.

Loehlin, J. C., Horn, J. M., & Willerman, L. (1989). Modeling IQ change: Evidence from the Texas Adoption Project. *Child Development, 60*, 993–1004.

Loehlin, J. C., Lindzey, G., & Spuhler, J. N. (1975). *Race differences in intelligence*. New York: Freeman.

Loehlin, J. C., Vandenberg, S. G., & Osborne, R. T. (1973). Blood group genes and Negro-White ability differences. *Behavior Genetics, 3*, 263–270.

Lubchenko, L. O. (1976). *The high-risk infant*. Philadelphia: Saunders.

Lynn, R. (1982). IQ, in Japan and the United States shows a growing disparity. *Nature, 297*, 222–223.

Lynn, R. (1990). The role of nutrition in secular increases in intelligence. *Personality and Individual Differences, 11*, 273–285.

Lynn, R. (1993). Oriental Americans: Their IQ, educational attainment, and socio-economic status. *Personality and Individual Differences, 15*, 237–242.

Mackenzie, B., Molloy, E., Martin, F., Lovegrove, W., & McNicol, D. (1991). Inspection time and the content of simple tasks: A framework for research on speed of information processing. *Australian Journal of Psychology, 43*, 37–43.

McCartney, K., Harris, M. J., & Bernieri, F. (1990). Growing up and growing apart: A developmental meta-analysis of twin studies. *Psychological Bulletin, 107*, 226–237.

McGue, M., Bouchard, T. J., Jr., Iacono, W. G., & Lykken, D. T. (1993). Behavioral genetics of cognitive ability: A life-span perspective. In R. Plomin & G. E. McClearn (Eds.). *Nature, nurture, & psychology* (pp. 59–76). Washington, DC: American Psychological Association.

McMichael, A. J., Baghurst, P. A., Wigg, N. R., Vimpani, G. V., Robertson, E. F., & Roberts, R. J. (1988). Port Pirie cohort study: Environmental exposure to lead and children's abilities at the age of four years. *New England Journal of Medicine, 319*, 468–475.

McShane, D. A., & Berry, J. W. (1988). Native North Americans: Indian and Inuit abilities. In S. H. Irvine & J. W. Berry (Eds.). *Human abilities in cultural context* (pp. 385–426). New York: Cambridge University Press.

McShane, D. A., & Cook, V. J. (1985). Transcultural intellectual assessment: Performance by Hispanics on the Wechsler Scales. In B. B. Wolman (Ed.), *Handbook of intelligence: Theories, measurements, and applications*. New York: Wiley.

McShane, D. A., & Plas, J. M. (1984a). Response to a critique of the McShane & Plas review of American Indian performance on the Wechsler Intelligence Scales. *School Psychology Review, 13*, 83–88.

McShane, D. A., & Plas, J. M. (1984b). The cognitive functioning of American Indian children: Moving from the WISC to the WISC-R. *School Psychology Review, 13*, 61–73.

Mercer, J. R. (1984). What is a racially and culturally nondiscriminatory test? A sociological and pluralistic perspective.

In C. R. Reynolds & R. T. Brown (Eds.), *Perspectives on bias in mental testing*. New York: Plenum Press.

Moffitt, T. E., Caspi, A., Harkness, A. R., & Silva, P. A. (1993). The natural history of change in intellectual performance: Who changes? How much? Is it meaningful? *Journal of Child Psychology and Psychiatry, 34*, 455–506.

Moffitt, T. E., Gabrielli, W. F., Mednick, S. A., & Schulsinger, F. (1981). Socioeconomic status, IQ, and delinquency. *Journal of Abnormal Psychology, 90*, 152–156.

Myrdal, G. (1944). *An American dilemma: The Negro problem and modern democracy*. New York: Harper.

Needleman, H. L., Geiger, S. K., & Frank, R. (1985). Lead and IQ scores: A reanalysis. *Science, 227*, 701–704.

Ogbu, J. U. (1978). *Minority education and caste: The American system in cross-cultural perspective*. New York: Academic Press.

Ogbu, J. U. (1994). From cultural differences to differences in cultural frames of references. In P. M. Greenfield & R. R. Cocking (Eds.), *Cross-cultural roots of minority child development* (pp. 365–391). Hillsdale, NJ: Erlbaum.

Olivier, G. (1980). The increase of stature in France. *Journal of Human Evolution, 9*, 645–649.

Pennock-Roman, M. (1992). Interpreting test performance in selective admissions for Hispanic students. In K. F. Geisinger (Ed.), *Psychological testing of Hispanics* (pp. 95–135). Washington, DC: American Psychological Association.

Plomin, R., & Bergeman, C. S. (1991). The nature of nurture: Genetic influence on "environmental" measures. *Behavioral and Brain Sciences, 14*, 373–427.

Pollitt, E., Gorman, K. S., Engle, P. L., Martorell, R., & Rivera, J. (1993). Early supplementary feeding and cognition. *Monographs of the Society for Research in Child Development, 58* (Serial No. 235).

Reed, T. E., & Jensen, A. R. (1992). Conduction velocity in a brain nerve pathway of normal adults correlates with intelligence level. *Intelligence, 16*, 259–272.

Rehberg, R. A., & Rosenthal, E. R. (1978). *Class and merit in the American high school*. New York: Longman.

Reynolds, C. R., & Brown, R. T. (1984). Bias in mental testing: An introduction to the issues. In C. R. Reynolds & R. T. Brown (Eds.), *Perspectives on bias in mental testing* (pp. 1–39). New York: Plenum Press.

Reynolds, C. R., Chastain, R. L., Kaufman, A. S., & McLean, J. E. (1987). Demographic characteristics and IQ among adults: Analysis of the WAIS-R standardization sample as a function of the stratification variables. *Journal of School Psychology, 25*, 323–342.

Ricciuti, H. N. (1993). Nutrition and mental development. *Current Directions in Psychological Science, 2*, 43–46.

Rodriguez, O. (1992). Introduction to technical and societal issues in the psychological testing of Hispanics. In K. F. Geisinger (Ed.), *Psychological testing of Hispanics* (pp. 11–15). Washington, DC: American Psychological Association.

Rosetti, L. (1986). *High risk infants: Identification, assessment, and intervention*. Boston: Little Brown.

Scarr, S. (1992). Developmental theories for the 1990s: Development and individual differences. *Child Development, 63*, 1–19.

Scarr, S. (1993). Biological and cultural diversity: The legacy of Darwin for development. *Child Development, 64,* 1333–1353.

Scarr, S., Pakstis, A. J., Katz, S. H., & Barker, W. B. (1977). Absence of a relationship between degree of White ancestry and intellectual skills within a Black population. *Human Genetics, 39,* 69–86.

Scarr, S., & Weinberg, R. A. (1978). The influence of "family background" on intellectual attainment. *American Sociological Review, 43,* 674–692.

Scarr, S., Weinberg, R. A., & Waldman, I. D. (1993). IQ correlations in transracial adoptive families. *Intelligence, 17,* 541–555.

Sigman, M. (1995). Nutrition and child development: More food for thought. *Current Directions in Psychological Science, 4,* 52–55.

Spearman, C. (1927). *The abilities of man.* New York: Macmillan.

Stein, Z., Susser, M., Saenger, G., & Marolla, F. (1975). *Famine and human development: The Dutch hunger winter of 1944–45.* New York: Oxford University Press.

Sternberg, R. J., & Detterman, D. K. (Eds.). (1986). *What is intelligence? Contemporary viewpoints on its nature and definition.* Norwood, NJ: Ablex.

Stevenson, H. W., Lee, S. Y., & Stigler, J. W. (1986). Mathematics achievement of Chinese, Japanese, and American children. *Science, 231,* 693–699.

Stevenson, H. W., Stigler, J. W., Lee, S. Y., Lucker, G. W., Kitamura, S., & Hsu, C. C. (1985). Cognitive performance and academic achievement of Japanese, Chinese, and American children. *Child Development, 56,* 718–734.

Streissguth, A. P., Barr, H. M., Sampson, P. D., Darby, B. L., & Martin, D. C. (1989). IQ at age 4 in relation to maternal alcohol use and smoking during pregnancy. *Developmental Psychology, 25,* 3–11.

Terman, L. M. (1925). *Genetic studies of genius: Mental and physical traits of a thousand gifted children.* Stanford, CA: Stanford University Press.

Thomson, G. H. (1939). *The factorial analysis of human ability.* Boston: Houghton Mifflin.

Thorndike, R. L., Hagen, E. P., & Sattler, J. M. (1986). *Stanford-Binet intelligence scale: Fourth edition (Technical Manual).* Chicago: Riverside.

Thurstone, L. L. (1938). *Primary mental abilities.* Chicago: University of Chicago Press.

United States Bureau of the Census. (1994). *The Hispanic population of the United States: March 1993* (Current Population Reports, Series P20–475). Washington, DC: Author.

United States National Commission for Employment Policy. (1982). *Hispanics and jobs: Barriers to progress* (Report No. 14). Washington, DC: Author.

Vernon, P. A. (1987). *Speed of information processing and intelligence.* Norwood, NJ: Ablex.

Vincent, K. R. (1991). Black/White IQ differences: Does age make the difference? *Journal of Clinical Psychology, 47,* 266–270.

Waller, J. H. (1971). Achievement and social mobility: Relationships among IQ score, education, and occupation in two generations. *Social Biology, 18,* 252–259.

White, K. R. (1982). The relation between socioeconomic status and academic achievement. *Psychological Bulletin, 91,* 461–481.

QUESTIONS

1. What is intelligence?
2. Why is stability in intelligence considered an important characteristic of an IQ test score?
3. What do IQ tests predict well? What do they not predict very well?
4. What does research on environmental effects on intelligence indicate about the nature of human intelligence?
5. Why have IQ test scores increased over the twentieth century?
6. How does Lewontin's (1970) example of genetically identical seeds growing up in different fields relate to the debate about ethnic differences in IQ?

PART V
Adolescence

Adolescence is a period that is difficult to define. In many ways, it is a cultural construction. That is, whether adolescence is demarcated as a unique stage depends on the culture in which a child lives. Not only is the presence of adolescence as a distinct stage variable across cultures, the duration of adolescence, when it does occur, varies. In Western communities, adolescence is a fairly long period. It ranges from about 11 years of age until the end of the teens. Sometimes adolescence even stretches beyond the teen years for those who are still dependent on their parents in their early twenties. In many non-Western communities, adolescence is often a fairly short period of time, usually ending with an abrupt transition after puberty to participation in adult responsibilities such as marriage or work life.

Research on adolescence cuts across many topics. The general tenor of the research for a long time has been problem-focused. That is, adolescence is seen as a time of much duress and problems of adjusting. The articles in this section address this issue in a variety of ways. One, by Arnett, reexamines the question of whether adolescence is, in fact, a time of storm and stress. Another article, by Wolfson and Carskadon, revisits assumptions about biological change in this age group by studying the adolescent sleep/wake cycle. Two articles study adolescent–parent relations. One, by Chapell and Overton, focuses on parental influences on cognitive development and test performance during this period. The other, by Fuligni, studies the relation between culture, the adolescent's bids for autonomy, and conflict with parents. Finally, the article by Patterson, DeBaryshe, and Ramsey explores the origins of adolescent delinquency by looking more closely at family processes that precede this type of problem behavior.

All of these articles make it clear that adolescence is a time of rapid physical, cognitive, and emotional change that is greatly influenced by the social and cultural context in which the adolescent lives. What society expects of and tolerates of its members who are just on the verge of maturity reflects the values and goals of the culture. These values and goals are implicit in the interactions and experiences adolescents have, especially with their parents. As you will see, not all adolescent–parent relationships are the same, and some pose more challenges to adolescent adjustment than others.

28 Adolescent Storm and Stress, Reconsidered

JEFFREY JENSEN ARNETT

The study of adolescence has been filled for decades with controversy. There are disagreements about whether it is a "true" period of development or simply an artifact of modern times. There are disagreements about the cause(s) of adolescence: Is it instigated by biological or social or cognitive changes? There are disagreements about when adolescence begins and when it ends: Does it begin when the first signs of puberty appear or is it regulated by certain social passages, like entering junior high or high school? Does it end at high school graduation, or age 20, or marriage, or college graduation?

One long-standing disagreement among psychologists concerns the nature of adolescence. The first American developmental psychologist, G. Stanley Hall, called adolescence a time of "storm and stress." This conceptualization of adolescence has stuck, especially in the public sphere. But what is the status of this view from a research perspective?

This article by Jeffrey Jensen Arnett discusses the history and research evidence on the topic of adolescent storm and stress. Current research generally supports this view, though the notion of what is meant by storm and stress has changed substantially over the years. This article is a reminder that some of the oldest ideas in psychology are often the most interesting, as well as the hardest to understand.

G. S. Hall's (1904) view that adolescence is a period of heightened "storm and stress" is reconsidered in light of contemporary research. The author provides a brief history of the storm-and-stress view and examines 3 key aspects of this view: conflict with parents, mood disruptions, and risk behavior. In all 3 areas, evidence supports a modified storm-and-stress view that takes into account individual differences and cultural variations. Not all adolescents experience storm and stress, but storm and stress is more likely during adolescence than at other ages. Adolescent storm and stress tends to be lower in traditional cultures than in the West but may increase as globalization increases individualism. Similar issues apply to minority cultures in American society. Finally, although the general public is sometimes portrayed by scholars as having a stereotypical view of adolescent storm and stress, both scholars and the general public appear to support a modified storm-and-stress view.

Nearly 100 years after G. Stanley Hall (1904) proposed that adolescence is inherently a time of storm and stress, his view continues to be addressed by psychologists. For the most part, contemporary psychologists reject the view that adolescent storm and stress is universal and inevitable (e.g., Eccles et al., 1993; Offer & Schonert-Reichl, 1992; Petersen et al., 1993; Steinberg & Levine, 1997). However, the storm-and-stress view is usually invoked by psychologists only in passing, in the course of addressing some other topic. Rarely has the storm-and-stress view been considered directly, and rarely have its merits and limitations been evaluated in depth.

Reprinted by permission of the author and the American Psychological Association from *American Psychologist*, 54 (1999), pp. 317–326. Copyright © 1999 by the American Psychological Association.

Editor's note: Ann S. Masten served as action editor for this article.

Author's note: I thank Christy Buchanan, Lene Jensen, and Reed Larson for their insightful comments and suggestions.

Correspondence concerning this article should be addressed to Jeffrey Jensen Arnett, Department of Human Development, University of Maryland, 3304 Benjamin Building, College Park, MD 20742. Electronic mail may be sent to arnett@wam.umd.edu.

Hall initiated the scientific study of adolescence, and since his time (especially in the past 20 years), research on adolescence has produced a great deal of information that bears on the question of adolescent storm and stress. As the centennial of Hall's (1904) landmark two-volume work approaches, this may be an appropriate time to evaluate the merits of the view for which he is best known today. I argue here that a case can be made for the validity of a modified storm-and-stress view. The claim that adolescent storm and stress is characteristic of all adolescents and that the source of it is purely biological is clearly false. However, evidence supports the existence of some degree of storm and stress—at least for adolescents in the middle-class American majority culture—with respect to conflict with parents, mood disruptions, and risk behavior. Not all adolescents experience storm and stress in these areas, but adolescence is the period when storm and stress is *more likely* to occur than at other ages. I emphasize that there are individual differences among adolescents in the extent to which they exhibit storm and stress and that there are cultural variations in the pervasiveness of adolescent storm and stress.

STORM AND STRESS: A BRIEF HISTORY

Hall (1904) was the first to consider the storm-and-stress issue explicitly and formally in relation to adolescent development, but he was not the first in the history of Western thought to remark on the emotional and behavioral distinctiveness of adolescence. Aristotle stated that youth "are heated by Nature as drunken men by wine." Socrates characterized youth as inclined to "contradict their parents" and "tyrannize their teachers." Rousseau relied on a stormy metaphor in describing adolescence: "As the roaring of the waves precedes the tempest, so the murmur of rising passions announces the tumultuous change. . . . Keep your hand upon the helm," he advised parents, "or all is lost" (Rousseau, 1762/1962, pp. 172–173).

Around the time Rousseau was writing, an influential genre of German literature was developing, known as "sturm und drang" literature—roughly translated as "storm and stress." The quintessential work of the genre was Goethe's (1774/1989) *The Sorrows of Young Werther*, a story about a young man who commits suicide in despair over his doomed love for a married woman. There were numerous other stories at the time that depicted youthful anguish and angst. The genre gave rise to popular use of the term "storm and stress," which Hall (1904) adopted a century later when writing his magnum opus on adolescent development.

Hall (1904) favored the Lamarckian evolutionary ideas that were considered by many prominent thinkers in the early 20th century (Freud and Jung included) to be a better explanation of evolution than Darwin's theory of natural selection. In Lamarck's now-discredited theory, evolution takes place as a result of accumulated experience. Organisms pass on their characteristics from one generation to the next not in the form of genes (which were unknown at the time Lamarck and Darwin devised their theories), but in the form of *memories and acquired characteristics*. Thus, Hall, considering development during adolescence, judged it to be "suggestive of some ancient period of storm and stress" (1904, Vol. 1, p. xiii). In his view, there must have been a period of human evolution that was extremely difficult and tumultuous: the memory of that period had been passed ever since from one generation to the next and was *recapitulated* in the development of each individual as the storm and stress of adolescent development. To Hall, this legacy of storm and stress was particularly evident in adolescents' tendency to question and contradict their parents, in their mood disruptions, and in their propensity for reckless and antisocial behavior.

Although Hall is often portrayed as depicting adolescent storm and stress as universal and biological, in fact his view was more nuanced. He acknowledged individual differences, noting for example that conflict with parents was more likely for adolescents with "ruder natures" (1904, Vol. 2, p. 79). Also, he believed that a *tendency* toward storm and stress in adolescence was universal and biologically based, but that culture influenced adolescents' expression and experience of it. He saw storm and stress as more likely to occur in the United States of his day than in "older lands with more conservative traditions" (1904, Vol. 1, p. xvi). In his view, the storm and stress of American adolescence was aggravated by growing urbanization, with all its temptations to vice, and by the clash between the sedentary quality of urban life and what he saw as adolescents' inherent need for activity and exploration. Hall also believed that adolescent storm and stress in his time was aggravated by the failure of home, school, and religious organizations to recognize the true nature and potential perils of adolescence and to adapt their institutions accordingly, a view not unlike that of many more recent scholars (e.g., Eccles et al., 1993; Simmons & Blythe, 1987).

In the century since Hall's work established adolescence as an area of scientific study, the debate over adolescent storm and stress has simmered steadily and boiled to the surface periodically. Anthropologists, led by Margaret Mead (1928), countered the claim that a tendency toward storm and stress in adolescence is universal and biological by describing non-Western cultures in which adolescence was neither stormy nor stressful. In contrast, psychoanalytic theorists, particularly Anna Freud (1946, 1958, 1968, 1969), have been the most outspoken proponents of the storm-and-stress view. Like Hall, psychoanalytic theorists viewed adolescent storm and stress as rooted in the recapitulation of earlier experiences, but as a recapitulation of ontogenetic Oedipal conflicts from early childhood rather than phylogenetic epochs (Blos, 1962). This recapitulation of Oedipal conflicts provoked emotional volatility (as the adolescent ego attempted to gain ascendancy over resurgent instinctual drives), depressed mood (as the adolescent mourned the renunciation of the Oedipal parent), and conflict with parents (in the course of making this renunciation: Blos, 1962). Furthermore, the resurgence of instinctual drives was regarded as likely to be acted out in "dissocial, even criminal" behavior (Freud, 1968, p. 18).

Anna Freud (1958, 1968, 1969) viewed adolescents who did not experience storm and stress with great suspicion, claiming that their outward calm concealed the inward reality that they must have "built up excessive defenses against their drive activities and are now crippled by the results" (1968, p. 15). She, much more than Hall, viewed storm and stress as universal and immutable, to the extent that its absence signified psychopathology: "To be normal during the adolescent period is by itself abnormal" (1958, p. 267).

In recent decades, two types of studies concerning adolescent storm and stress have appeared. A handful of studies, mostly by Buchanan and Holmbeck (Buchanan, 1998; Buchanan et al., 1990; Buchanan & Holmbeck, 1998; Holmbeck & Hill, 1988; Offer, Ostrov, & Howard, 1981), have focused on public perceptions of adolescence as a time of storm and stress. These studies (using American middle-class samples) have consistently found that most people in the American majority culture perceive adolescence as a time of relative storm and stress. For example, Buchanan et al. (1990) found that the majority of both parents and teachers agreed with statements such as "early adolescence is a difficult time of life for children and their parents/teachers." Buchanan and Holmbeck (1998) reported that college students and parents of early adolescents viewed adolescents as more likely than elementary school children to have problems such as symptoms of internalizing disorders (e.g., anxiousness, insecurity, and depression) and risk taking/rebelliousness (e.g., recklessness, impulsivity, and rudeness). Similarly, the majority of college students surveyed by Holmbeck and Hill (1988) agreed with statements such as "adolescents frequently fight with their parents."

A second type of contemporary study has addressed the actual occurrence of adolescent storm and stress, in the specific areas of conflict with parents (Gecas & Seff, 1990; Steinberg, 1987), emotional volatility (Larson & Richards, 1994), negative affect (Brooks-Gunn & Warren, 1989; Buchanan, Eccles, & Becker, 1992; Petersen et al., 1993), and risk behavior (Arnett, 1992; Moffitt, 1993). Storm and stress tends to be mentioned in these studies not as the primary focus but in the course of addressing another topic. Consistently, these studies reject the claim—usually attributed to Hall—that adolescent storm and stress is universal and find only weak support for the claim that it is biologically based. However, the studies also consistently support a modified storm-and-stress thesis that adolescence is a time when various types of problems are *more likely* to arise than at other ages. The primary goal of this article is to draw together the evidence from these areas and to present an argument for the validity of the modified storm-and-stress thesis.

DEFINING STORM AND STRESS

It is important at this point to address directly the question of what is included under the concept of adolescent storm and stress. Taking historical and theoretical views in combination with contemporary research, the core of the storm-and-stress view seems to be the idea that adolescence is a period of life that is *difficult* (Buchanan et al., 1990)—more difficult in some ways than other periods of life and difficult for adolescents as well as for the people around them. This idea, that adolescence is difficult, includes three key elements:

1. *Conflict with parents.* Adolescents have a tendency to be rebellious and to resist adult authority. In particular, adolescence is a time when conflict with parents is especially high.

2. *Mood disruptions.* Adolescents tend to be more volatile emotionally than either children or adults. They experience more extremes of mood and more swings of mood from one extreme to the other. They also experience more frequent episodes of depressed mood.

3. *Risk behavior.* Adolescents have higher rates of reckless, norm-breaking, and antisocial behavior than either children or adults. Adolescents are more likely to cause disruptions of the social order and to engage in behavior that carries the potential for harm to themselves and/or the people around them.

This is not an all-inclusive list of the possible elements of adolescent storm and stress. Occasionally, storm and stress has been discussed in terms of other elements such as school difficulties (Eccles et al., 1993) and self-image (Offer & Offer, 1975). However, the three elements discussed here appear consistently in the writings of Hall (1904), the anthropologists

(Mead, 1928), the psychoanalysts (Blos, 1962; Freud, 1968, 1969), and contemporary scholars (e.g., Buchanan, 1998; Eccles et al., 1993; Offer & Schonert-Reichl, 1992; Petersen et al., 1993; Steinberg & Levine, 1997). Thus, these three elements are the focus of this article.

Before proceeding, one more comment is in order about the length of adolescence. Hall (1904, Vol. 1, p. xix) viewed adolescence and its accompanying storm and stress as lasting through the early twenties. Other observers of adolescent storm and stress, from Aristotle to the present, have applied their comments not just to early adolescence but to a middle and late adolescence/emerging adulthood extending through the late teens and early twenties (see Kett, 1977). Here, I too consider the evidence related to the storm-and-stress view for an extended adolescent age range. Different elements of storm and stress have different peaks—conflict with parents in early adolescence (Paikoff & Brooks-Gunn, 1991), mood disruptions in midadolescence (Petersen et al., 1993), and risk behavior in late adolescence and emerging adulthood (Arnett, 1992, 1999). Each of these elements represents a different kind of difficulty to be experienced, for adolescents as well as for those around them. It is in combination that they create a perception of adolescence as a difficult period of life.

I now consider each of the three elements of the storm-and-stress view, in order of their developmental peak during adolescence: conflict with parents, mood disruptions, and risk behavior.

Conflict with Parents

Hall (1904) viewed adolescence as a time when "the wisdom and advice of parents and teachers is overtopped, and in ruder natures may be met by blank contradiction" (Vol. 2, p. 79). He viewed this as due not only to human evolutionary history but also to the incompatibility between adolescents' need for independence and the fact that "parents still think of their offspring as mere children, and tighten the rein where they should loosen it" (Vol. 2, p. 384). Contemporary studies have established that conflict with parents increases in early adolescence, compared with preadolescence, and typically remains high for a couple of years before declining in late adolescence (Laursen, Coy, & Collins, 1998; Paikoff & Brooks-Gunn, 1991; Smetana, 1989). A recent meta-analysis by Laursen et al. (1998) concluded that within adolescence, conflict frequency is highest in early adolescence and conflict intensity is highest in midadolescence. One naturalistic study of early adolescents' conflicts with parents and siblings reported a rate of 2 conflicts every three days, or 20 per month (Montemayor & Hanson, 1985). During the same time that the number of daily conflicts between parents and

their early adolescent children increases (compared with preadolescence), declines occur in the amount of time they spend together and in their reports of emotional closeness (Larson & Richards, 1994). Conflict is especially frequent and intense between mothers and early adolescent daughters (Collins, 1990).

This conflict makes adolescence difficult not just for adolescents but for their parents. Parents tend to perceive adolescence as the most difficult stage of their children's development (Buchanan et al., 1990; Pasley & Gecas, 1984; Small, Cornelius, & Eastman, 1983). However, it should be added that there are substantial individual differences, and there are many parents and adolescents between whom there is little conflict, even if overall rates of conflict between parents and children rise in adolescence. Conflict between parents and adolescents is more likely when the adolescent is experiencing depressed mood (Cole & McPherson, 1993), when the adolescent is experiencing other problems such as substance abuse (Petersen, 1988), and when the adolescent is an early-maturing girl (Buchanan et al., 1992).

Almost without exception, contemporary scholars emphasize that higher rates of conflict with parents in adolescence do not indicate a serious or enduring breach in parent–adolescent relationships (e.g., Hill & Holmbeck, 1987; Montemayor, 1986; Offer & Offer, 1975; Rutter, Graham, Chadwick & Yule, 1976; Steinberg & Levine, 1997). Even amidst relatively high conflict, parents and adolescents tend to report that overall their relationships are good, that they share a wide range of core values, and that they retain a considerable amount of mutual affection and attachment. The conflicts tend to be over apparently mundane issues such as personal appearance, dating, curfews, and the like (Smetana, 1988). Even if they disagree on these issues, they tend to agree on more serious issues such as the value of honesty and the importance of education.

This point seems well-established by research, but it does not mean that adolescence is not a difficult time for both adolescents and their parents as a result of their minor but frequent conflicts. A useful connection could be made here to the literature on stress. This literature provides substantial evidence that it does not take cataclysmic events such as loss of employment or the death of a loved one to induce the experience of high stress. On the contrary, many people experience a high degree of stress from an accumulation of minor irritations and aggravations, the "daily hassles" of life (Kohn, Lafreniere, & Gurevich, 1991; Taylor, 1991). Thus, for parents and adolescents, it may be true that their frequent conflicts tend to concern relatively mundane day-to-day issues. However, it may be that the "hassle" of these frequent conflicts is substantially responsible for perceptions that adolescence is a difficult time.

Furthermore, the principal issues of conflict between adolescents and their parents may not be as trivial as they seem on the surface. Conflicts between adolescents and their parents often concern issues such as when adolescents should begin dating and whom they should date, where they should be allowed to go, and how late they should stay out. All of these issues can serve as proxies for arguments over more serious issues such as substance use, automobile driving safety, and sex. By restricting when adolescents can date and with whom, parents indirectly restrict adolescents' sexual opportunities. By attempting to restrict where adolescents can go and how late they should stay out, parents may be attempting to limit adolescents' access to alcohol and drugs, to shield adolescents from the potentially dangerous combination of substance use and automobile driving, and to restrict adolescents' opportunities for sexual exploration.

Sexual issues may be especially likely to be argued about in this indirect way, through issues that seem mundane (and therefore safe for discussion) on the surface. No clear mores currently exist in American society concerning the sexual behavior of unmarried young people in their teens (Michael, Gagnon, Laumann, & Kolata, 1994). Because of this lack of social consensus, parents of adolescents are left with many questions that admit no easy answers. Few would agree that sexual intercourse is permissible for 13 year olds, but beyond this the questions grow more complex. Is kissing OK for 13 year olds? When do necking and petting become permissible? At what age should dating be allowed, in light of the fact that it may lead to kissing, necking, petting, and more? If intercourse is not permissible for 13 year olds, what about for 16 or 17 year olds? For the most part, American parents prefer not to discuss these issues—or any other sexual issues—directly with their children (Jones et al., 1986). Yet even parents who believe in giving their adolescents a substantial degree of autonomy may not feel that they can simply leave sexual decisions to their adolescents, particularly in a time when AIDS and other sexually transmitted diseases are prevalent (Eccles et al., 1993). The result is that parents and their adolescents argue about seemingly trivial issues (such as whether dating should be allowed as early as age 13 or whether a 17 year old's curfew should be at midnight or at 1 a.m.) that may be proxies for arguments over complex and sensitive sexual issues.

Some scholars (e.g., Steinberg, 1990) have suggested that conflict between adolescents and their parents is actually beneficial to adolescents' development, because it promotes the development of individuation and autonomy within the context of a warm relationship. This may be true, but high conflict may make adolescence a difficult time for adolescents and their parents even if the conflict ultimately has benefits.

MOOD DISRUPTIONS

The claim of a link between adolescence and extremes of emotion (especially negative) is perhaps the most ancient and enduring part of the storm-and-stress view. Hall (1904) viewed adolescence as "the age of . . . rapid fluctuation of moods" (Vol. 1, p. xv), with extremes of both elation and depressed mood. What does contemporary research tell us about whether adolescence is distinguished by high emotional volatility and a tendency toward negative moods? In general, studies that have assessed mood at frequent intervals have found that adolescents do indeed report greater extremes of mood and more frequent changes of mood, compared with preadolescents or adults. Also, a number of large longitudinal studies concur that negative affect increases in the transition from preadolescence to adolescence (see Buchanan et al., 1992, for a review).

One of the most interesting and enlightening lines of research on this topic in recent years has involved studies using the Experience Sampling Method (ESM; e.g., Csikszentmihalyi & Larson, 1984; Larson & Ham, 1993; Larson & Richards, 1994). Also known as the "beeper method," this research entails having adolescents (and others) carry beepers throughout the day and having them record their thoughts, behavior, and emotions when they are beeped at random times. This method has provided an unprecedented look into the daily lives of adolescents, including how their emotions vary in the course of a day and how these variations compare with the emotions recorded by preadolescents and adults using the same method.

The results of this research indicate that there is truth to the storm-and-stress claim that adolescence is a time of greater mood disruptions. Adolescents report experiencing extremes of emotion (positive as well as negative, but especially negative) more often than their parents do (Larson & Richards, 1994; also see Larson, Csikszentmihalyi, & Graef, 1980). They report feeling "self-conscious" and "embarrassed" two to three times more often than their parents and are also more likely to feel awkward, lonely, nervous, and ignored. Adolescents also report greater mood disruptions when compared with preadolescents. Comparing preadolescent fifth graders with adolescent ninth graders, Larson and Richards (1994) described the emotional "fall from grace" that occurs in that interval, as the proportion of time experienced as "very happy" declines by 50%, and similar declines take place in reports of feeling "great," "proud," and "in control." The result is an overall "deflation of childhood happiness" (p. 85) as childhood ends and adolescence begins.

Larson and Richards (1994) saw this increase in mood disruptions as due to cognitive and environmental factors rather than pubertal changes. They noted that there is little relationship in their data between pubertal stage and mood disruptions. Rather, adolescents' newly developed capacities for abstract reasoning "allow them to see beneath the surface of situations and envision hidden and more long-lasting threats to their well-being" (p. 86). Larson and Richards also argued that the experience of multiple life changes and personal transitions during adolescence (such as the onset of puberty, changing schools, and beginning to date) contributes to adolescents' mood disruptions. However, Larson and Richards emphasized that it is not just that adolescents experience potentially stressful events, but *how* they experience and interpret them, that underlies their mood disruptions. Even in response to the same or similar events, adolescents report more extreme and negative moods than preadolescents or adults.

In addition to the ESM studies, other studies have found negative moods to be prevalent in adolescence, especially for girls. In their review of adolescent depression, Petersen et al. (1993) described a "midadolescence peak" (p. 157) that has been reported in studies of age differences in depressed mood, indicating that adolescents have higher rates of depressed mood than either children or adults. Petersen et al. analyzed 14 studies of nonclinical samples of adolescents and concluded that depressed mood ("above which a score is thought to be predictive of clinical depression," p. 157) applied to over one third of adolescents at any given time.

Adolescents vary in the degree to which they experience mood disruptions. A variety of factors have been found to make mood disruptions in adolescence more likely, including low popularity with peers, poor school performance, and family problems such as marital discord and parental divorce (Petersen et al., 1993). The more negative life events adolescents experience, the more likely they are to experience mood disruptions (Brooks-Gunn & Warren, 1989). Although these individual differences should be kept in mind, overall the results of research indicate support for the storm-and-stress view that adolescence is more likely than other age periods to be a time of emotional difficulty.

RISK BEHAVIOR

At the beginning of a scene in "The Winter's Tale," Shakespeare (1623/1995) has an older man deliver a soliloquy about the youth of his day. "I would that there were no age between ten and three-and-twenty, or that youth would sleep out the rest," he grumbles, "for there is nothing in between but getting wenches with child, wronging the ancientry,

stealing, fighting . . . " (Act III, Scene 3). This lament should ring familiar to anyone living in Western societies in recent centuries and to people in many other societies as well. Adolescence has long been associated with heightened rates of antisocial, norm-breaking, and criminal behavior, particularly for boys. Hall (1904) included this as part of his view of adolescent storm and stress, agreeing that "a period of semicriminality is normal for all healthy [adolescent] boys" (Vol. 1, p. 404).

Contemporary research confirms that in the United States and other Western countries, the teens and early twenties are the years of highest prevalence of a variety of types of risk behavior (i.e., behavior that carries the potential for harm to self and/or others). This pattern exists for crime as well as for behavior such as substance use, risky automobile driving, and risky sexual behavior (Arnett, 1992; Moffitt, 1993). Unlike conflict with parents or mood disruptions, rates of risk behavior peak in late adolescence/emerging adulthood rather than early or middle adolescence (Arnett, 1999). Rates of crime rise in the teens until peaking at age 18, then drop steeply (Gottfredson & Hirschi, 1990). Rates of most types of substance use peak at about age 20 (Johnston, O'Malley, & Bachman, 1994). Rates of automobile accidents and fatalities are highest in the late teens (U.S. Department of Transportation, 1995). Rates of sexually transmitted diseases (STDs) peak in the early twenties (Stein, Newcomb, & Bentler, 1994), and two thirds of all STDs are contracted by people who are under 25 years old (Hatcher, Trussell, Stewart, & Stewart, 1994).

The variety of respects in which adolescents engage in risk behavior at greater rates than children or adults lends further validity to the perception of adolescence as a difficult time, a time of storm and stress. Although adolescents generally experience their participation in risk behavior as pleasurable (Arnett, 1992; Lyng, 1993), suffering the consequences of such behavior—contact with the legal system, treatment for an STD, involvement in an automobile accident, and so forth—is likely to be experienced as difficult. Furthermore, it is understandable that parents may find it difficult to watch their children pass through the ages when such behavior is most likely to occur.

In this area, as with conflict with parents and mood disruptions, it is important to recognize individual differences. Adolescents vary a great deal in the extent to which they participate in risk behavior. To some extent, these differences are forecast by behavior prior to adolescence. Persons who exhibit behavior problems in childhood are especially likely to engage in risk behavior as adolescents (Moffitt, 1993). Individual differences in characteristics such as sensation seeking and impulsivity also contribute to individual differences in risk behavior during adolescence (Arnett, 1992; Zuckerman, 1983). Nevertheless, although not all adolescents engage in risk behavior, the majority of adolescents take part occasionally in risk behavior of one kind or another (Arnett, 1992; Moffitt, 1993). This lends substantial credence to the view that adolescence is a period of storm and stress.

WHY STORM AND STRESS?

Even if we accept the argument that adolescence is a time of heightened tendency toward storm and stress, the question of why this should be so remains. To what extent do the roots of storm and stress lie in the biological changes that take place in the course of puberty? To what extent are the roots cultural, with adolescent storm and stress being especially pronounced in cultures that value individualism?

Current evidence indicates that biological changes make some contribution. With respect to mood disruptions, reviews of the effects of hormones on adolescents' moods have concluded that the dramatic hormonal changes that accompany puberty contribute to emotional volatility (Buchanan et al., 1992) and negative moods (Brooks-Gunn, Graber, & Paikoff, 1994), particularly in early adolescence when the rate of hormonal change is steepest. However, scholars in this area emphasize that the hormonal contribution to adolescent mood disruptions appears to be small and tends to exist only in interaction with other factors (Brooks-Gunn et al., 1994; Brooks-Gunn & Warren, 1989; Susman, 1997).

More generally, with respect to mood disruptions as well as with respect to conflict with parents and risk behavior, too little is known about the role of biological factors to make definitive statements at this point about the role they may play in adolescent storm and stress. Numerous possibilities exist concerning biological influences on storm and stress and the interaction between biological and cultural factors. For example, recently a phenomenon called *delayed phase preference* has been identified (Carskadon, Vieria, & Acebo, 1993), which is a tendency, based in the biological changes of puberty, for adolescents to prefer staying up until relatively late at night and sleeping until relatively late in the morning. Does the cultural practice of requiring adolescents to get up in the early morning to attend school—even earlier than young children—result for some adolescents in a sleep-deprived state that may contribute to mood disruptions and more frequent conflict with parents? Other possible biological contributors to adolescent storm and stress include genes that may become active in adolescence and increase the likelihood of mood disruptions, as well as biological bases for developmental changes in characteristics such as emotional regulation (mood disruptions), aggressiveness (conflict with parents), and sensation seeking (risk behavior).

Even with the limitations that exist in the knowledge of biological contributions to adolescent storm and stress, it is clear that the biological changes of puberty do not make adolescent storm and stress universal and inevitable. This is easily and unmistakably demonstrated by the fact that not all cultures experience the same levels of adolescent storm and stress, and some evidently do not experience it at all. Margaret Mead's (1928) original assertion to this effect has more recently been confirmed by Schlegel and Barry (1991), in their analysis of adolescence in 186 "traditional" (preindustrial) cultures worldwide. They reported that most traditional cultures experience less storm and stress among their adolescents, compared with the West.

A key difference between traditional cultures and the West, as Schlegel and Barry (1991) observed, is the degree of *independence* allowed by adults and expected by adolescents. In the majority cultures of the West, because of cultural values of individualism, it is taken for granted by adolescents and their parents (as well as by most Western social scientists) that children should become independent from their parents during the course of adolescence and should attain full independence by the end of adolescence. A substantial amount of adolescent storm and stress arises from regulating the pace of adolescents' growing independence (Steinberg, 1987). Differences of opinion over the proper pace of this process are a source of conflict between adolescents and their parents, and part of parents' perception of adolescence as difficult results from their concern that adolescents' growing independence may lead to participation in risk behavior (Pasley & Gecas, 1984). In contrast, independence for adolescents is less likely to be expected by adolescents and their parents in traditional cultures, so it is less likely to be a source of adolescent storm and stress (Dasen, in press).

Even in traditional cultures, adolescent storm and stress is not unknown. Biological changes in combination with changing family obligations and changing economic responsibilities are common to adolescence virtually everywhere and inherently involve new challenges and—for some adolescents, at least—difficulty (Dasen, in press). Some ethnographies on adolescence describe conceptions in traditional cultures of adolescence as a time of mood disruptions (e.g., Davis & Davis, 1989; Kirkpatrick, 1987). It should also be noted that differences exist among traditional cultures, with cultures that exclude adolescent boys from the activities of men being more likely to have problems with their adolescent boys than cultures in which boys take part daily in men's activities (Schlegel & Barry, 1991). Nevertheless, adolescent storm and stress is generally more common in the industrialized societies of the West than in traditional cultures.

However, all over the world, traditional cultures are becoming integrated into the global economy and are being influenced by Western (especially American) cultures through growing economic ties and through exposure to Western movies, music, and television (Barber, 1995). Within traditional cultures, adolescents are often the most enthusiastic consumers of Western media (Barber, 1995; Schlegel, in press), and evidence shows that adolescents may embrace the individualism of the West more readily than their parents do (Feldman, Mont-Reynaud, & Rosenthal, 1992). A potentially rich topic for research in the coming years would be to monitor changes in the degree of adolescent storm and stress in traditional cultures as globalization proceeds.

The limited evidence available so far indicates that adolescents in traditional cultures often are able to maintain their traditional values and practices—including low conflict with parents and low rates of risk behavior—even as they become avid consumers of Western popular culture (Feldman et al., 1992; Feldman, Rosenthal, Mont-Reynaud, Leung, & Lau, 1991; Schlegel, in press). However, it remains to be seen whether adolescents' adherence to traditional ways and their low levels of storm and stress will be sustained as globalization increasingly changes the nature of their daily experience. For adolescents in traditional cultures, the results of globalization include more time in school, more time with peers, less time spent with their parents and other adults, and more time for media-oriented leisure (Schlegel, in press). All of these changes mean greater independence for adolescents, greater emphasis on their individual development, and less emphasis on their obligations to others. If it is true that cultural values of individualism lie at the heart of adolescent storm and stress, then it seems likely that adolescence in traditional cultures will become more stormy and stressful in the ways described here as the influence of the West increases (Dasen, in press).

This does not mean that storm and stress is likely to increase in all respects for all adolescents in traditional cultures. Individual differences will undoubtedly exist, as they do in the West. Indeed, increased individualism means broadening the boundaries of socialization, so that a greater range of individual differences is allowed expression (Arnett, 1995). Furthermore, the increased individualism fostered by globalization is likely to result in benefits for adolescents, along with increased storm and stress. Cultural changes toward globalization and individualism are likely to mean that adolescents in traditional cultures will have a greater range of educational and occupational opportunities than previously and that these choices will be less constrained by gender and other factors (Dasen, in press; Noble, Cover, & Yanagishita, 1996). However, the cost may be greater adolescent

storm and stress. It is even possible that storm and stress will become more characteristic of adolescence in traditional cultures than in the West, because adolescents in rapidly changing societies will be confronted with multiple changes not only in their immediate lives but in their societies as well (Dasen, in press).

Similar issues exist within American society. Currently, there is evidence that adolescent storm and stress may be more likely in the majority culture—the largely White middle class—than in other cultures that are part of American society. For example, parent–adolescent conflict has been found to be more frequent in White middle-class families than in Mexican American families (Suarez-Orozco & Suarez-Orozco, 1996). In the same way that values of individualism make adolescent storm and stress more likely in the American majority culture compared with non-Western traditional cultures, a similar difference in values may make storm and stress more likely in the American majority culture than in certain minority cultures that are part of American society. And in the same way that adolescence in traditional cultures may become more stormy and stressful as the influence of the West increases, adolescents in American minority cultures may exhibit storm and stress to the extent that they adopt the individualistic values of the American majority culture.

Thus, it might be expected that adolescent storm and stress will increase with the number of generations an adolescent's family has been in the United States. Among Asian American adolescents, for example, it has been found that the greater the number of generations their families have been in the United States, the more likely the adolescents are to exhibit aspects of storm and stress (Fletcher & Steinberg, 1994; Steinberg, 1996; also see Rosenthal, 1984). However, as with the issues involving traditional cultures, the direct exploration of storm-and-stress issues involving adolescents in American minority cultures has been minimal thus far and represents a promising area for further investigation.

SCHOLARS AND STEREOTYPES

When adolescent storm and stress is discussed by contemporary scholars on adolescence, it is generally in the context of the scholars expressing concern over the "stereotype" or "myth" of adolescent storm and stress that is perceived to exist among parents, teachers, and the general public (Buchanan et al., 1990; Holmbeck & Hill, 1988; Offer & Schonert-Reichl, 1992; Petersen et al., 1993; Steinberg & Levine, 1997). Scholars contrast these popular perceptions of adolescence as a difficult time with their own research findings that adolescence is not difficult for all adolescents in all respects and that the biological changes of puberty are not strongly related to any storm and stress that does exist in adolescence.

One of the implications of the argument presented here is that the findings of the scholars and the conception of adolescence held by nonscholars in American society may not be so far apart after all. With respect to conflict with parents, mood disruptions, and risk behavior, the results of scholars' research indicate that adolescence is stormy and stressful for many American adolescents and for the people around them. It is true that this research also indicates that there are substantial individual differences in these difficulties and that storm and stress is by no means universal and inevitable. However, there is no indication that most people in the American public see storm and stress as universal and inevitable. On the contrary, the studies that have investigated perceptions of storm and stress inquire about people's perceptions of adolescents *in general*. People's responses endorsing storm-and-stress statements indicate simply that they see storm and stress as characteristic of adolescents taken as a group, not that it is characteristic of all adolescents without exception (Buchanan, 1998; Buchanan et al., 1990; Buchanan & Holmbeck, 1998; Holmbeck & Hill, 1988).

People tend to see adolescence as a time of life that is more likely than other times of life to involve difficulties such as conflict with parents, mood disruptions, and risk behavior, and scholars' research supports this modified storm-and-stress view of adolescence rather than contradicting it. Contemporary scholars disagree not so much with the American public or even with G. Stanley Hall (1904), but mainly with the psychoanalytic theorists of the past, particularly Anna Freud (1946, 1958, 1968, 1969), who can truly be said to have claimed that adolescent storm and stress is universal and inevitable. The one storm-and-stress issue on which scholars and the general public seem genuinely to disagree is the meaning and significance of parent–adolescent conflict, which scholars concede is common but tend to deprecate as being over trivial and mundane issues. However, as I have argued, there may be more merit to the popular view on this topic than scholars have acknowledged.

One reason for scholars' concern over public beliefs about adolescent storm and stress is that they fear such beliefs could have negative consequences. Some scholars speculate that storm-and-stress beliefs may lead parents to adopt authoritarian parenting techniques as a way of thwarting the storm and stress they anticipate in their adolescents (Holmbeck, 1996). Others fear that if storm and stress is regarded as normative, adolescents with serious problems will not get the attention and help they need because their problems will be dismissed as normal for adolescence (Offer & Schonert-Reichl. 1992; Petersen et al., 1993).

These concerns are legitimate and are well-taken. However, there are also concerns that arise from underrating the likelihood of storm and stress, and benefits that can result from expecting adolescence to be a time of storm and stress. Although it is true that if adolescence is expected to be a time of "turmoil" there may be adolescents whose problems go unrecognized and untreated, it is also true that if adolescence is expected to be no more difficult than childhood, then adolescents who are experiencing normal difficulties may be seen as pathological and in need of treatment.

Also, expecting adolescence to be difficult could have positive effects. Anticipating adolescent storm and stress may inspire parents and teachers to think ahead about how to approach potential problems of adolescence if they arise. Furthermore, parents, teachers, adolescents, and others who expect adolescence to be difficult may be pleasantly surprised when a particular adolescent shows few or no difficulties, as will be the case for many adolescents because there are considerable individual differences in the storm and stress they experience (Buchanan, 1998).

CONCLUSION

Adolescent storm and stress is not simply a myth that has captured the popular imagination but a real part of life for many adolescents and their parents in contemporary American society. Although the extreme portrayal of adolescent storm and stress by certain psychoanalytic theorists (Freud, 1958, 1968, 1969) is a caricature of normal adolescent development, there is support for Hall's (1904) view that a tendency toward some aspects of storm and stress exists in adolescence. In their conflicts with parents, in their mood disruptions, and in their higher rates of a variety of types of risk behavior, many adolescents exhibit a heightened degree of storm and stress compared with other periods of life. Their parents, too, often experience difficulty—from increased conflict when their children are in early adolescence, from mood disruptions during midadolescence, and from anxiety over the increased possibility of risk behavior when their children are in late adolescence. However, storm and stress in adolescence is not something written indelibly into the human life course. On the contrary, there are cultural differences in storm and stress, and within cultures there are individual differences in the extent to which adolescents exhibit the different aspects of it.

Finally, to view adolescence as a time of storm and stress is not to say that adolescence is characterized only by storm and stress. Even amidst the storm and stress of adolescence, most adolescents take pleasure in many aspects of their lives, are satisfied with most of their relationships most of the time, and are hopeful about the future (Offer & Schonert-Reichl, 1992). G. S. Hall (1904) saw adolescence as stormy and stressful, but also as "the birthday of the imagination" (Vol. 1, p. 313) and "the best decade of life" (Vol. 1, p. xviii), when "the life of feeling has its prime" (Vol. 1, p. 59). The paradox of adolescence is that it can be at once a time of storm and stress and a time of exuberant growth.

REFERENCES

Arnett, J. (1992). Reckless behavior in adolescence: A developmental perspective. *Developmental Review, 12,* 339–373.

Arnett, J. J. (1995). Broad and narrow socialization: The family in the context of a cultural theory. *Journal of Marriage and the Family, 57,* 617–628.

Arnett, J. (1999). *Emerging adulthood: A conception of development from the late teens through the twenties.* Manuscript submitted for publication.

Barber, B. R. (1995). *Jihad vs. McWorld: How globalism and tribalism are reshaping the world.* New York: Ballantine.

Blos, P. (1962). *On adolescence: A psychoanalytic interpretation.* New York: Free Press.

Brooks-Gunn, J., Graber, J. A., & Paikoff, R. L. (1994). Studying links between hormones and negative affect: Models and measures. *Journal of Research on Adolescence, 4,* 469–486.

Brooks-Gunn, J., & Warren, M. P. (1989). Biological and social contributions to negative affect in young adolescent girls. *Child Development, 60,* 40–55.

Buchanan, C. M. (1998). *Parents' category-based beliefs about adolescence: Links to expectations for one's own child.* Manuscript submitted for publication.

Buchanan, C. M., Eccles, J., & Becker, J. (1992). Are adolescents the victims of raging hormones? Evidence for activational effects of hormones on moods and behavior at adolescence. *Psychological Bulletin, 111,* 62–107.

Buchanan, C. M., Eccles, J. S., Flanagan, C., Midgley, C., Feldlaufer, H., & Harold, R. D. (1990). Parents' and teachers' beliefs about adolescents: Effects of sex and experience. *Journal of Youth & Adolescence, 19,* 363–394.

Buchanan, C. M., & Holmbeck, G. N. (1998). Measuring beliefs about adolescent personality and behavior. *Journal of Youth & Adolescence, 27,* 609–629.

Carskadon, M., Vieria, C., & Acebo, C. (1993). Association between puberty and delayed phase preference. *Sleep, 16,* 258–262.

Cole, D. A., & McPherson, A. E. (1993). Relation of family subsystems to adolescent depression: Implementing a new family assessment strategy. *Journal of Family Psychology, 7,* 119–133.

Collins, W. A. (1990). Parent–child relationships in the transition to adolescence: Continuity and change in interaction, affect, and cognition. In R. Montemayor, G. R. Adams, & T. P. Gullotta (Eds.), *From childhood to adolescence: A transitional period?* (pp. 85–106). Newbury Park, CA: Sage.

Csikszentmihalyi, M., & Larson, R. W. (1984). *Being adolescent: Conflict and growth in the teenage years.* New York: Basic Books.

Dasen, P. (in press). Rapid social change and the turmoil of adolescence: A cross-cultural perspective. *World Psychology.*

Davis, S. S., & Davis, D. A. (1989). *Adolescence in a Moroccan town.* New Brunswick, NJ: Rutgers.

Eccles, J. S., Midgely, C., Wigfield, A., Buchanan, C. M., Reuman, D., Flanagan, C., & MacIver, D. (1993). Development during adolescence: The impact of stage-environment fit on young adolescents' experiences in schools and in families. *American Psychologist, 48,* 90–101.

Feldman, S. S., Mont-Reynaud, R., & Rosenthal, D. A. (1992). When East moves West: The acculturation of values of Chinese adolescents in the U. S. and Australia. *Journal of Research on Adolescence, 2,* 147–175.

Feldman, S. S., Rosenthal, D. A., Mont-Reynaud, R., Leung, K., & Lau, S. (1991). Ain't misbehavin': Adolescent values and family environments as correlates of adolescent misconduct in Australia, Hong Kong, and the United States. *Journal of Research on Adolescence, 1,* 109–134.

Fletcher, A., & Steinberg, L. (1994, February). *Generational status and country of origin as influences on psychological adjustment of Asian-American adolescents.* Paper presented at the biennial meeting of the Society for Research on Adolescence, San Diego, CA.

Freud, A. (1946). *The ego and the mechanisms of defense.* New York: International Universities Press.

Freud, A. (1958). Adolescence. *Psychoanalytic Study of the Child, 15,* 255–278.

Freud, A. (1968). Adolescence. In A. E. Winder & D. Angus (Eds.), *Adolescence: Contemporary studies* (pp. 13–24). New York: American Book.

Freud, A. (1969). Adolescence as a developmental disturbance. In G. Caplan & S. Lebovici (Eds.), *Adolescence: Psychosocial perspectives* (pp. 5–10). New York: Basic Books.

Gecas, V., & Seff, M. A. (1990). Families and adolescents: A review of the 1980s. *Journal of Marriage and the Family, 52,* 941–958.

Goethe, J. W. von. (1989). *The sorrows of young werther, by Johann Wolfgang von Goethe* (M. Hulse, Trans.). London: Penguin. (Original work published 1774)

Gottfredson, M. R., & Hirschi, T. (1990). *A general theory of crime.* Stanford, CA: Stanford University Press.

Hall, G. S. (1904). *Adolescence: Its psychology and its relation to physiology, anthropology, sociology, sex, crime, religion, and education* (Vols. I & II). Englewood Cliffs, NJ: Prentice-Hall.

Hatcher, R. A., Trussell, J., Stewart, F., & Stewart, G. (1994). *Contraceptive technology.* New York: Irvington.

Hill, J., & Holmbeck, G. (1987). Disagreements about rules in families with seventh-grade girls and boys. *Journal of Youth & Adolescence, 16,* 221–246.

Holmbeck, G. N. (1996). A model of family relational transformations during the transition to adolescence: Parent-adolescent conflict and adaptation. In J. A. Graber, J. Brooks-Gunn, & A. C. Petersen (Eds.), *Transitions through adolescence: Interpersonal domains and context* (pp. 167–199). Mahwah, NJ: Erlbaum.

Holmbeck, G., & Hill, J. (1988). Storm and stress beliefs about adolescence: Prevalence, self-reported antecedents, and effects of an undergraduate course. *Journal of Youth & Adolescence, 17*, 285–306.

Johnston, L. D., O'Malley, P. M., & Bachman, J. G. (1994). *National survey results on drug use from the Monitoring the Future study, 1975–1993* (NIH Publication No. 94-3810). Washington, DC: U.S. Government Printing Office.

Jones, E. F., Forrest, J. D., Goldman, N., Henshaw, S., Lincoln, R., Rosoff, J. I., Westoff, C. F., & Wulf, D. (1986). *Teenage pregnancy in industrialized countries.* New Haven, CT: Yale University Press.

Kett, J. F. (1977). *Rites of passage: Adolescence in America, 1790 to the present.* New York: Basic Books.

Kirkpatrick, J. (1987). *Taure'are'a:* A liminal category and passage to Marquesan adulthood. *Ethos, 15*, 382–405.

Kohn, P. M., Lafreniere, K., & Gurevich, M. (1991). Hassles, health, and personality. *Journal of Personality and Social Psychology, 61*, 478–482.

Larson, R. W., Csikszentmihalyi, M., & Graef, R. (1980). Mood variability and the psycho-social adjustment of adolescents. *Journal of Youth & Adolescence, 9*, 469–490.

Larson, R., & Ham, M. (1993). Stress and "storm and stress" in early adolescence: The relationship of negative life events with dysphoric affect. *Developmental Psychology, 29*, 130–140.

Larson, R., & Richards, M. H. (1994). *Divergent realities: The emotional lives of mothers, fathers, and adolescents.* New York: Basic Books.

Laursen, B., Coy, K. C., & Collins, W. A. (1998). Reconsidering changes in parent–child conflict across adolescence: A meta-analysis. *Child Development, 69*, 817–832.

Lyng, S. (1993). Dysfunctional risk taking: Criminal behavior as edgework. In N. J. Bell & R. W. Bell (Eds.), *Adolescent risk taking* (pp. 107–130). Newbury Park, CA: Sage.

Mead, M. (1928). *Coming of age in Samoa.* New York: Morrow.

Michael, R. T., Gagnon, J. H., Laumann, E. O., & Kolata, G. (1994). *Sex in America.* Boston: Little, Brown.

Moffitt, T. (1993). Adolescence-limited and life-course persistent antisocial behavior: A developmental taxonomy. *Psychological Review, 100*, 674–701.

Montemayor, R. (1986). Family variation in adolescent storm and stress. *Journal of Adolescent Research, 1*, 15–31.

Montemayor, R., & Hanson, E. (1985). A naturalistic view of conflict between adolescents and their parents and siblings. *Journal of Early Adolescents, 5*, 23–30.

Noble, J., Cover, J., & Yanagishita, M. (1996). *The world's youth.* Washington, DC: Population Reference Bureau.

Offer, D., & Offer, J. B. (1975). *From teenage to young manhood.* New York: Basic Books.

Offer, D., Ostrov, E., & Howard, K. I. (1981). The mental health professional's concept of the normal adolescent. *Archives of General Psychiatry, 38*, 149–153.

Offer, D., & Schonert-Reichl, K. A. (1992). Debunking the myths of adolescence: Findings from recent research. *Journal of the American Academy of Child & Adolescent Psychiatry, 31*, 1003–1014.

Paikoff, R., & Brooks-Gunn, J. (1991). Do parent–child relationships change during puberty? *Psychological Bulletin, 110*, 47–66.

Pasley, K., & Gecas, V. (1984). Stresses and satisfactions of the parental role. *Personnel and Guidance Journal, 2*, 400–404.

Petersen, A. C. (1988). Adolescent development. *Annual Review of Psychology, 39*, 583–607.

Petersen, A. C., Compas, B. E., Brooks-Gunn, J., Stemmler, M., Ey, S., & Grant, K. E. (1993). Depression in adolescence. *American Psychologist, 48*, 155–168.

Rosenthal, D. A. (1984). Intergenerational conflict and culture: A study of immigrant and nonimmigrant adolescents and their parents. *Genetic Psychology Monographs, 109*, 53–75.

Rousseau, J. J. (1962). *The Emile of Jean Jacques Rousseau.* (W. Boyd, Ed. & Trans.). New York: Teachers College Press, Columbia University. (Original work published 1762)

Rutter, M., Graham, P., Chadwick, F., Yule, W. (1976). Adolescent turmoil: Fact or fiction? *Journal of Child Psychiatry and Psychology, 17*, 35–56.

Schlegel, A. (in press). The global spread of adolescent culture. In L. Crockett & R. K. Silbereisen (Eds.), *Negotiating adolescence in a time of social change.* Cambridge, England: Cambridge University Press.

Schlegel, A., & Barry, H., III. (1991). *Adolescence: An anthropological inquiry.* New York: Free Press.

Simmons, R., & Blythe, D. (1987). *Moving into adolescence: The impact of pubertal change and school context.* Hawthorn, NY: Aldine de Gruyter.

Small, S. A., Cornelius, S., & Eastman, G. (1983, August). *Parenting adolescent children: A period of adult storm and stress?* Paper presented at the 91st Annual Meeting of the American Psychological Association, Anaheim, CA.

Smetana, J. G. (1988). Concepts of self and social convention: Adolescents' and parents' reasoning about hypothetical and actual family conflicts. In M. Gunnar & W. A. Collins (Eds.), *Minnesota Symposium on Child Psychology* (Vol. 21, pp. 79–122). Hillsdale, NJ: Erlbaum.

Smetana, J. G. (1989). Adolescents' and parents' reasoning about actual family conflict. *Child Development, 60*, 1052–1067.

Stein, J. A., Newcomb, M. D., & Bentler, P. M. (1994). Psychosocial correlates and predictors of AIDS risk behaviors, abortion, and drug use among a community sample of young adult women. *Health Psychology, 13*, 308–318.

Steinberg, L. (1987). Family processes in adolescence: A developmental perspective. *Family Therapy, 14*, 77–86.

Steinberg, L. (1990). Autonomy, conflict, and harmony in the family relationship. In S. Feldman & G. Elliott (Eds.), *At the threshold: The developing adolescent* (pp. 255–276). Cambridge, MA: Harvard University Press.

Steinberg, L. (1996). *Beyond the classroom: Why school reform has failed and what parents need to do.* New York: Simon & Schuster.

Steinberg, L., & Levine, A. (1997). *You and your adolescent: A parents' guide for ages 10 to 20.* New York: Harper Perennial.

Suarez-Orozco, C., & Suarez-Orozco, M. (1996). *Transforma-*

tions: Migration, family life and achievement motivation among Latino adolescents. Palo Alto, CA: Stanford University Press.

Susman, E. J. (1997). Modeling developmental complexity in adolescence: Hormones and behavior in context. *Journal of Research on Adolescence, 7,* 283–306.

Taylor, S. E. (1991). *Health psychology* (2nd ed.). New York: McGraw-Hill.

U. S. Department of Transportation. (1995). *Understanding youthful risk taking and driving.* (DOT Publication No. HS 808-318). Springfield, VA: National Technical Information Service.

Zuckerman, M. (Ed.). (1983). *Biological bases of sensation seeking, impulsivity, and anxiety.* Hillsdale, NJ: Erlbaum.

QUESTIONS

1. What three key elements are always included in the notion of adolescent storm and stress?
2. When are conflicts between adolescents and their parents the highest? Is there a developmental explanation for this?
3. What factors are related to whether or not an adolescent is a risk taker?
4. Are biological changes at puberty the cause of storm and stress in adolescence? Why or why not?
5. Why do you think adolescents in non-Western communities are the most enthusiastic consumers in their own societies of Western media? What cultural consequences might this have?
6. In your view, is the public justified in considering adolescence a time of storm and stress?

29 Sleep Schedules and Daytime Functioning in Adolescents

AMY R. WOLFSON · MARY A. CARSKADON

High school typically begins about 7:30 or 8:00 A.M. and students shuffle into class very tired. Teachers notice the fatigued looks on the students' faces and tell them that they should not stay up so late and get more sleep. If this sounds familiar to you, you are not alone. Adolescents have complained for years that school begins too early, but these complaints have been dismissed because adolescents were seen as the cause of the problem because they stay up too late. Is this interpretation true? Recent research on adolescent body rhythms casts doubt on this. It suggests that this sleep/wake/fatigue cycle is actually part of the biological growth process, a process that is part of pubertal development.

In this article by Amy R. Wolfson and Mary A. Carskadon, research is described that examined the sleep/wake patterns of adolescents. What did the researchers learn? Adolescents' sleep needs are, in fact, different from those of adults. And, as a result, the schedule that adolescents are made to keep because of school and other demands on their time impacts their daily functioning to a significant degree.

Perhaps in the near future this research will lead to practical changes in adolescent daily lives, especially concerning when school begins. Changes along these lines would support, rather than strain, development during this period of growth.

Sleep and waking behaviors change significantly during the adolescent years. The objective of this study was to describe the relation between adolescents' sleep/wake habits, characteristics of students (age, sex, school), and daytime functioning (mood, school performance, and behavior). A Sleep Habits Survey was administered in homeroom classes to 3,120 high school students at 4 public high schools from 3 Rhode Island school districts. Self-reported total sleep times (school and weekend nights) decreased by 40–50 min across ages 13–19, ps <.001. The sleep loss was due to increasingly later bedtimes, whereas rise times were more consistent across ages. Students who described themselves as struggling or failing school (C's, D's/F's) reported that on school nights they obtain about 25 min less sleep and go to bed an average of 40 min later than A and B students, ps < .001. In addition, students with worse grades reported greater weekend delays of sleep schedule than did those with better grades. Furthermore, this study examined a priori defined adequate sleep habit groups versus less than adequate sleep habit groups on their daytime functioning. Students in the short school-night total sleep group (< 6 hr 45 min) and/or large weekend bedtime delay group (> 120 min) reported increased daytime sleepiness, depressive mood, and sleep/wake behavior problems, ps < .05, versus those sleeping longer

Reprinted by permission of Blackwell Publishers from *Child Development*, 69 (1998), pp. 875–887. Copyright © 1998 by the Society for Research in Child Development.

Acknowledgments. This study was supported by funds from the National Institutes of Health, MH 45945. We thank Camille Brown, Catherine Darley, Francois Garand, Liza Kelly, Eric Kravitz, Christopher Monti, Orna Tzischinsky, and Beth Yoder for their assistance in gathering and coding data, and Christine Acebo and Ronald Seifer for their assistance regarding data analysis and interpretation of results. We would also like to thank the participating school districts in Rhode Island.

Addresses and affiliations. Corresponding author: Amy R. Wolfson, College of the Holy Cross, Department of Psychology, Worcester, MA 01610; e-mail: AWolfson@Holycross.edu. Mary A. Craskadon is at Brown University School of Medicine.

than 8 hr 15 min with less than 60 min weekend delay. Altogether, most of the adolescents surveyed do not get enough sleep, and their sleep loss interferes with daytime functioning.

INTRODUCTION

Adolescence is a time of important physical, cognitive, emotional, and social change when the behaviors in one developmental stage are constantly challenged by new abilities, insights, and expectations of the next stage. Sleep is a primary aspect of adolescent development. The way adolescents sleep critically influences their ability to think, behave, and feel during daytime hours. Likewise, daytime activities, changes in the environment, and individual factors can have significant effects on adolescents' sleeping patterns. Over the last 2 decades, researchers, teachers, parents, and adolescents themselves, have consistently reported that they are not getting enough sleep (Carskadon, 1990a; Carskadon, Harvey, Duke, Anders, & Dement, 1980; Price, Coates, Thoresen, & Grinstead, 1978; Strauch & Meier, 1988).

Although laboratory data demonstrate that adolescents probably do not have a decreased need for sleep during puberty (Carskadon, 1990a; Carskadon et al., 1980; Carskadon, Orav, & Dement, 1983), survey and field studies show that teenagers usually obtain much less sleep than school-age children, from 10 hr during middle childhood to less than 7.5–8 hours by age 16 (Allen, 1992; Carskadon, 1982, 1990a; Williams, Karacan, & Hursch, 1974). Although sleeping less than when younger, over 54% of high school students in a Swiss study (Strauch & Meier, 1988) endorsed a *wish for more sleep.*

A consistent finding in studies of adolescent sleep patterns is that they tend to stay up late. Price et al. (1978), for example, found that 60% of the eleventh and twelfth graders whom they surveyed stated that they "enjoyed staying up late." Another large survey study found that 45% of tenth to twelfth graders go to bed after midnight on school nights, and 90% retire later than midnight on weekends (Carskadon & Mancuso, 1988). Another consistent report (Bearpark & Michie, 1987; Petta, Carskadon, & Dement, 1984; Strauch & Meier, 1988) is that weekend total sleep times average 30–60 min more than school-night sleep times in 10- to 13/14-year-olds, and this difference increases to over 2 hr by age 18. Such data are usually interpreted as indicating that teenagers do not get enough sleep on school nights and then extend sleep on weekend nights to pay back a sleep debt. The most obvious explanation for the adolescent sleep debt appears to be a pattern of insufficient school-night sleep resulting from a combination of early school start times,

late afternoon/evening jobs and activities, academic and social pressures, and a physiological sleep requirement that does not decrease with puberty (Carskadon, 1990b; Manber et al., 1995; Wolfson et al., 1995).

Many factors contribute to or are affected by increased daytime sleepiness and inconsistent sleep schedules during the junior high and senior high school years. In the sections below, we review several key issues.

PUBERTY: SLEEP NEED, DAYTIME SLEEPINESS, AND CIRCADIAN PHASE DELAY

Several important changes directly affecting sleep patterns occur during the pubertal years. One feature that seems not to change or to change in an unexpected direction is sleep need. A 6-year longitudinal summer sleep laboratory study of Carskadon and colleagues (1980) held the opportunity for sleep constant at 10 hr in children who were 10, 11, or 12 years old at their first 3 night assessment. The research hypothesis was that with age, the youngsters would sleep less, reaching a normal adult sleep length of 7.5 or 8 hr by the late teens. In fact, the sleep quantity remained consistent at approximately 9.2 hours across all pubertal stages. Thus, these data clarified that sleep need is not reduced during adolescence. The longitudinal study of Carskadon and colleagues (1980) simultaneously demonstrated that daytime sleep tendency was increased at midpuberty. In other words, even though the amount of nocturnal sleep consumed by the adolescents did not decline during puberty, their midday sleepiness increased significantly at midpuberty and remained at that level (Carskadon et al., 1980, 1983). This finding was based on physician assessment of puberty using Tanner staging (Tanner, 1962) and a sensitive laboratory measure of sleepiness, the Multiple Sleep Latency Test (MSLT; Carskadon et al., 1986).

A significant change in the timing of behavior across adolescent development is a tendency to stay up later at night and to sleep in later in the morning than preadolescents, that is, to delay the phase of sleep (Carskadon, Vieira, & Acebo, 1993; Dahl & Carskadon, 1995). One manifestation of this process is that adolescents' sleep patterns on weekends show a considerable delay (as well as lengthening) versus weekdays, with sleep onset and offset both occurring significantly later. This sleep phase shift is attributed to psychosocial factors and to biological changes that take place during puberty. For example, in the longitudinal study described above, as children reached puberty, they were less likely to wake up on their own, and laboratory staff needed to wake them up

(Carskadon et al., 1980). In fact, they likely would have slept more than 9 hr if undisturbed.

Carskadon and her colleagues have shown that this adolescent tendency to phase delay may be augmented by a biological process accompanying puberty. An association between self-reported puberty scores (Carskadon & Acebo, 1993) and phase preference (morningness/eveningness) scores of over 400 pre- and early pubertal sixth graders showed a delay of phase preference correlated with maturation stage (Carskadon et al., 1993). Morningness/eveningness is a construct developed to estimate phase tendencies from self-descriptions. Morning persons tend to arise early in the morning and have difficulty staying up late whereas night persons have difficulty getting up early in the morning and prefer staying up late. Whereas most people are somewhere between these extremes, the cohort value shifts during adolescence (Andrade, Benedito-Silva, & Domenice, 1993; Ishihara, Honma, & Miyake, 1990). A recent study examined the circadian timing system more directly in early adolescents by measuring the timing of melatonin secretion, for the first time demonstrating a biological phase delay in association with puberty and in the absence of psychosocial factors (Carskadon, Acebo, Richardson, Tate, & Seifer, 1997).

ENVIRONMENTAL CONSTRAINT: SCHOOL START TIME

Many U.S. school districts start school earlier at academic transitions, for example, elementary to junior high school and junior high school to senior high school. Earlier high school start time is a major externally imposed constraint on teenagers' sleep-wake schedules; for most teens waking up to go to school is neither spontaneous nor negotiable. Early morning school demands often significantly constrict the hours available for sleep. For example, Szymczak, Jasinska, Pawlak, and Swierzykowska (1993) followed Polish students aged 10 and 14 years for over a year and found that all slept longer on weekends and during vacations as a result of waking up later. These investigators concluded that the school duty schedule was the predominant determinant of awakening times for these students. Similarly, several surveys of high school students found that students who start school at 7:30 A.M. or earlier obtain less total sleep on school nights due to earlier rise times (Allen, 1991; Allen & Mirabile, 1989; Carskadon & Mancuso, 1988).

In a preliminary laboratory/field study, we evaluated the impact of a 65 min advance in school start time on 15 ninth graders across the transition to tenth grade (Carskadon, Wolfson, Tzischinsky, & Acebo, 1995; Wolfson et al., 1995). The initial findings demonstrated that students slept an average of 40

min less in tenth grade compared with ninth grade due to earlier rise times, and they displayed an increase in MSLT measured daytime sleepiness. In addition, evening type students had more difficulty adjusting to the earlier start time than did morning types, and higher scores on the externalizing behavior problems scale (Youth Self-Report; Achenbach, 1991) were associated with less total sleep and later bedtimes (Brown et al., 1995; Wolfson et al., 1995).

DAYTIME BEHAVIORS

Very little research has assessed the relation between adolescents' sleep patterns and their daytime behaviors. Although studies have concluded that associations between sleep/wake patterns and daytime functioning exist, the direction of this relation is not clear. Clinical experience shows that adolescents who have trouble adapting to new school schedules and other changes (e.g., new bedtimes and rise times, increased activities during the day, increased academic demands) may develop problematic sleeping behaviors leading to chronic sleepiness. Several studies indicate an association between sleep and stress. For example, a number of studies have found that sleep-disturbed elementary school-age children experience a greater number of stresses (e.g., maternal absence due to work/school; family illness/accident; maternal depressed mood) than non-sleep-disturbed children (Kataria, Swanson, & Trevathan, 1987). Likewise, sleepy elementary school-age children may have poorer coping behaviors (e.g., more difficulty recognizing, appraising, and adapting to stressful situations) and display more behavior problems at home and in school (Fisher & Rinehart, 1990; Wolfson et al., 1995).

ACADEMIC PERFORMANCE

Sleepy adolescents—that is, those with inadequate sleep—may also encounter more academic difficulties. Several surveys of sample sizes ranging from 50 to 200 high school students reported that more total sleep, earlier bedtimes, and later weekday rise times are associated with better grades in school (Allen, 1992; Link & Ancoli-Israel, 1995; Manber et al., 1995). Epstein, Chillag, and Lavie (1995) surveyed Israeli elementary, junior high, and senior high school students and reported that less total sleep time was associated with daytime fatigue, inability to concentrate in school, and a tendency to doze off in class. Persistent sleep problems have also been associated with learning difficulties throughout the school years (Quine, 1992). Studies of excessive sleepiness in adolescents due to narcolepsy or sleep apnea have also reported negative effects on learning, school performance, and behavior (Dahl, Holttum, & Trubnick, 1994; Guilleminault, Winkle, & Korobkin, 1982).

SUMMARY OF FACTORS IMPOSING ON ADOLESCENTS' SLEEP/WAKE PATTERNS

The interplay among sleep/wake schedules, circadian rhythms, and behavior during adolescence results in an increasing pressure on the nocturnal sleep period, producing insufficient sleep in many teenagers and, ultimately, changes in daytime functioning (Carskadon, 1995). For preadolescents, parents are more likely to set bedtimes, school begins later in the morning, and societal expectations favor long sleep. Prepubescent children are thus more likely to have earlier bedtimes and to wake up before the school day begins (Petta et al., 1984). In contrast, due to behavioral factors (social, academic, work-related), environmental constraints (school schedule), and circadian variables (pubertal phase delay), teenagers have later bedtimes, earlier rise times, and therefore, decreased time available to sleep (Carskadon, 1995). As a result, adolescents get to bed late, have difficulty waking up in the morning, and struggle to stay alert and to function successfully during the daytime.

Unfortunately, previous studies of adolescents' lifestyles (e.g., Hendry, Glendinning, Shucksmith, Love, & Scott, 1994) have failed to factor in these important developmental changes in sleep/wake patterns, and unanswered questions remain regarding the developmental changes in adolescent sleep/wake habits, the impact of adolescents' sleep habits on their daytime functioning (e.g., school performance), and the influence of the environment (e.g., school schedules) on teenagers' sleep. The present study examines more closely adolescents' sleep/wake habits and their association with several daytime behaviors using data from a large-scale survey. Such data are useful to assess generalizability of findings; furthermore, a large sample provides an opportunity to accentuate meaningful findings by setting the effect size (Cohen, 1988) and by examining extreme groups from the larger sample (Kagan, Resnick, & Gibbons, 1989).

The chief goal of this study is to document the association between adolescents' sleep/wake habits and daytime sleepiness, high school grades, depressed mood, and other daytime behaviors. Our study has three objectives: (1) to describe age, sex, and school differences in sleep/wake patterns; (2) to characterize the relation between self-reported high school grades and sleep/wake schedules; and (3) to compare daytime functioning in students on schedules we define a priori as *adequate* versus those adopting *less than adequate* schedules.

METHOD

MEASURES

In the fall of 1994, an eight page School Sleep Habits Survey was administered in homeroom classes to high school students at four public high schools from three Rhode Island school districts. School start times ranged from 7:10 A.M. to 7:30 A.M. All students who wanted to complete the survey did so unless their parent/guardian refused consent. The survey items queried students about usual sleeping and waking behaviors over the past 2 weeks. Chief variables include school-night and weekend night total sleep time (TST), bedtime, and rise time. To assess *sleep schedule regularity*, two additional sleep variables were derived: *weekend delay* is the difference between weekend bedtime and school-night bedtime, and *weekend oversleep* is the difference between weekend total sleep time and school-night total sleep time.

The survey also covered school performance (self-reported grades in school) and scales assessing daytime sleepiness, sleep/wake behavior problems (Carskadon, Seifer, & Acebo, 1991), and depressive mood (Kandel & Davies, 1982). School performance was assessed by asking students, "Are your grades mostly A's, A's and B's, B's, B's and C's, C's, C's and D's, D's, or D's and F's?" These data were collapsed into four categories (mostly A's or A's/B's; mostly B's or B's/C's; mostly C's or C's/D's; mostly D's/F's).

The sleepiness scale consisted of total responses to items asking whether the respondent had struggled to stay awake (fought sleep) or fallen asleep in 10 different situations in the last 2 weeks, such as in conversation, while studying, in class at school, and so on (Carskadon et al., 1991). The respondent was asked to rate his or her answer on a scale of 1 to 4 (1 = no to 4 = both struggled to stay awake and fallen asleep). Scores on the sleepiness scale range from 10 to 40 and coefficient alpha was .70.

The sleep/wake behavior problems scale included 10 items asking frequency of indicators of erratic sleep/wake behaviors over the course of the last 2 weeks (e.g., arrived late to class because you overslept, stayed up past 3:00 A.M., needed more than one reminder to get up in the A.M., had an extremely hard time falling asleep, and so on; Carskadon et al., 1991). High school students were asked to rate the frequency of the particular behavior on a 5 point scale from everyday/night to never (5 = everyday, 1 = never). Scores range from 10 to 50, and coefficient alpha for the sleep/wake behaviors scale was .75.

The depressive mood scale (Kandel & Davies, 1982) queried the high school students as to how often they were bothered or troubled by certain situations in the last 2 weeks. It consists of six items (e.g., feeling unhappy, sad, or depressed; feeling hopeless about the future), and three response categories were provided, ranging from not at all to somewhat too much (e.g., scored 1 to 3, respectively). The index of depressive mood was based on a total score and has high internal reliability (coefficient alpha was .79 for this sample and .79 in the original study; Kandel & Davies, 1982). The Pearson correlation between the Kandel and Davies six item, depressive mood scale and the SCL-90 scale is .72, and prior studies demonstrated that the scale has high test-retest reliability with adolescent samples ($r = .76$) over 5–6 month intervals (Kandel & Davies, 1982).

PARTICIPANTS

The survey was completed anonymously by 3,120 students, 395 students at School A (rural), 1,077 at School B (urban), 745 at School C (suburban), and 903 at School D (suburban) (48% boys, 52% girls). The sample in Schools B and C comprised grades 10–12, whereas Schools A and D had ninth to twelfth graders. Approximately 8% of the students from schools A, C, and D and 17% from School B were eligible for free or reduced price lunches (State of Rhode Island Department of Education, 1994). Overall, the response rate was 88%. The students' ages ranged from 13 to 19 years (age 13–14, $n = 336$, age 15, $n = 858$, age 16, $n = 919$, age 17–19, $n = 988$). Over 91% of the students from Schools A, C, D reported that they were European American, whereas School B was more diverse (75% European American, 25% multiracial). On average, 81% of the students from all four schools reported that they live with both parents; 46% have older siblings, and 63% have younger siblings living in their homes. Eighty-six percent of their mothers *and* fathers were employed.

STATISTICAL METHODS

The findings are presented in three sections: (1) changes in sleep/wake habits according to age, sex, and school; (2) relation between high school grades and sleep/wake habits; and (3) an analysis of the differences in daytime functioning for students in extreme groups on several sleep parameters: short versus long school-night total sleep time, short versus long weekend oversleep, and small versus large weekend delay.

In the first two sections, multivariate analyses of variance (MANOVA) were used to examine age, sex, school, and grades in relation to the sleep/wake variables: total sleep time, bedtime, rise time, weekend delay, and weekend oversleep. Three multivariate analyses were computed: (1) school-night sleep variables, (2) weekend sleep variables, and (3) weekend delay and weekend oversleep. When significant multivariate effects were found, univariate effects were

then examined using Bonferroni tests to determine significant group mean differences.

The large sample size in this study raises the possibility of finding many *statistically* significant results that have very small effect sizes, thus running the risk of overinterpreting inconsequential relations. To address this potential problem, we use an effect size criterion in addition to a statistical significance criterion for discussion and interpretation of those results most likely to prove meaningful in the long run. In the results section that follows, we restrict our discussion to those significant findings that also have effect sizes between what Cohen (1988) characterizes as small and medium. Specifically, a correlation of .20 is the effect size criterion, which is slightly smaller than the midpoint of Cohen's small ($r = .10$) and medium ($r = .30$) effects in terms of variance explained. For analysis of group differences, effects where two groups differ by more than one-third of the sample standard deviation are considered. Again, this is slightly lower than the midpoint between small ($d = .20$) and medium ($d = .50$) effect sizes (Cohen, 1988). (Note that we do not calculate exact effect sizes for our more complex analyses but simply wish to have a reasonable criterion for further consideration of effects most likely to have generalizable implications.) All *statistically* significant results, regardless of effect size, are noted in the tables that accompany the text.

RESULTS

SLEEP/WAKE PATTERNS CHANGE ACROSS HIGH SCHOOL AGE GROUPS

Our analysis of age-related affects grouped data by four age ranges; Table 1 presents means, standard deviations, and F values for the sleep variables according to age. All school-night sleep variables were affected by age, multivariate $F(9, 6571) = 22.49$, $p < .001$. Specifically, average total sleep time decreased by approximately 40 min across the four age groups, $p < .001$, average school-night bedtimes were about 45 min later, $p < .001$, and average rise times about 10 min later, $p < .001$. Reported weekend sleep habits also showed age-related changes, multivariate $F(9, 6327) = 21.28$, $p < .001$. Average weekend total sleep time declined by about 50 min across the age groups, $p < .001$, as weekend night bedtimes shifted increasingly later, $p < .001$, differing by about 1 hr between the youngest and oldest teenagers. Weekend rise times did not change with age. Overall, weekend delay and weekend oversleep changed between ages 13 and 19, multivariate $F(6, 5060) = 3.93$, $p < .01$. Although this multivariate F is statistically significant, age group differences for weekend delay and weekend oversleep were too small (on the order of .1 SD) to meet our effect size criterion.

TABLE 1   MEANS AND STANDARD DEVIATIONS FOR SCHOOL-NIGHT AND WEEKEND SLEEP VARIABLES BY AGE

Sleep/Wake Variable	13–14 Years ($n = 336$)	15 Years ($n = 858$)	16 Years ($n = 919$)	17–19 Years ($n = 988$)	F Value	Bonferroni
School-night TST	462	449	435	424	24.13***	14, 15 > 16 > 17
	(67)	(66)	(68)	(66)		
School-night bedtime	10:05 P.M.	10:20 P.M.	10:37 P.M.	10:51 P.M.	53.54***	14 < 15 < 16 < 17
	(49)	(55)	(58)	(58)		
School-night rise time	5:59 A.M.	6:00 A.M.	6:05 A.M.	6:10 A.M.	19.47***	14, 15 < 16 < 17
	(24)	(25)	(29)	(31)		
Weekend TST	567	564	549	518	32.53***	14, 15 > 16 > 17
	(100)	(104)	(108)	(114)		
Weekend bedtime	11:54 P.M.	12:06 A.M.	12:30 A.M.	12:49 A.M.	42.33***	14, 15 < 16 < 17
	(94)	(83)	(82)	(80)		
Weekend rise time	9:22 A.M.	9:40 A.M.	9:46 A.M.	9:32 A.M.	ns	. . .
	(85)	(104)	(107)	(107)		
Weekend oversleep	104	115	112	95	5.80**⁻	. . .
	(102)	(112)	(116)	(114)		
Weekend delay	89	88	92	95	ns	. . .
	(71)	(66)	(65)	(68)		

Note: TST refers to total sleep time (minutes). Weekend oversleep is the difference between weekend and school-night total sleep times and weekend delay is the difference between weekend and school-night bedtimes. Standard deviations in parentheses, are in minutes; TST, weekend oversleep, and weekend delay are in minutes as well.

**$p < .01$;   ***$p < .001$;   ⁻does not meet effect size criterion (e.g., effects where two groups differ by more than one-third of the sample standard deviation).

Although all four high schools had similarly early school start times (between 7:10 A.M. and 7:30 A.M.), students' school-night sleep habits varied among the schools, multivariate $F(9, 6571) = 12.76$, $p < .001$, due to differences in rise times, $p < .001$. In particular, students who attended the school with the earliest school start time (7:10) reported earlier rise times than students at the other schools (School A: $M = 5:53$ versus Schools B, C, D: $Ms = 6:04–6:09$, $ps < .01$). Although school differences occurred in reported average total sleep times and bedtimes, these group differences did not meet effect size criterion. Weekend sleep also varied among schools, multivariate $F(9, 6327) = 4.74$, $p < .001$; however, univariate differences for total sleep time, bedtime, and rise time did not meet our effect size criterion. Additionally, small differences among the schools on weekend delay and weekend oversleep were not meaningful based on the effect size criterion.

Few sex differences were identified. Female students reported different school-night sleep habits than their male peers, multivariate $F(3, 2700) = 41.36$, $p < .001$, due to female students reporting waking up earlier than males: females, $M = 5:58$ versus males,

$M = 6:10$, $F(1, 2702) = 100.81$, $p < .001$. Boys and girls did not differ on reported school-night bedtimes, nor total sleep times. Overall, female students had greater weekend delays and weekend oversleeps than the male students, multivariate $F(2, 2530) = 6.67$, $p < .001$; however, univariate differences did not meet the effect size criterion. Female and male high school students did not report significant differences in weekend total sleep times, bedtimes, or rise times. The overall sample distributions of sleep patterns are displayed in Figure 1.

ACADEMIC PERFORMANCE AND SLEEP HABITS

Table 2 [on page 260] presents the analyses of sleep habits based on self-reported academic performance. In general, students with higher grades reported longer and more regular sleep, multivariate $F(9, 6571) = 8.91$, $p < .001$. Specifically, they reported more total sleep, $p < .001$, and earlier bedtimes, $p < .001$, on school nights than did students with lower grades. Post hoc analysis showed that these differences distin-

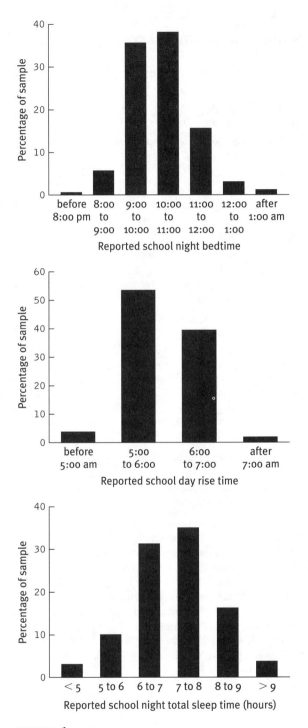

FIGURE 1

Sample distributions of sleep patterns

A and B students reported earlier bedtimes and earlier rise times than did C and D/F students, $ps < .001$; however, self-reported grades did not distinguish the students on reported weekend total sleep. Finally, students with worse grades reported greater weekend delays of sleep schedule than did those with better grades, multivariate $F(6, 5060) = 18.22$, $p < .001$. Thus, C and D/F students reported going to bed on average about 2.3 hr later on weekends than on school nights versus a difference of about 1.8 hr for the A and B students, $ps < .001$. Students with D/F's reported longer weekend oversleeps than A, B, or C students; however, these differences did not meet the effect size criterion.

DAYTIME FUNCTIONING OF STUDENTS WHO ADOPT *ADEQUATE* VERSUS *LESS THAN ADEQUATE* SLEEP HABITS

Data presented in the previous sections demonstrate that older high school students sleep less and have later bedtimes than younger students, and those who report a poor academic performance are more likely to sleep less, go to bed later, and have more irregular sleep/wake habits. These descriptive findings, however, do not explain whether especially short amounts of sleep and/or irregular schedules are associated with changes in daytime functioning. To describe more thoroughly the high school students who are obtaining minimal sleep and/or who have irregular sleep schedules, we examined a priori defined groups based on sleep variables that have been cited previously as having an impact on behavior, deriving our values from empirical data (Carskadon et al., 1980, 1983; Carskadon, Keenan, & Dement, 1987). Other potentially important factors (e.g., history of sleep disorders), may covary with these, but data from our survey focused on total sleep and school-night versus weekend schedule changes.

The *extreme* groups of students were defined as follows: long (≥ 8 hr 15 min) versus short (≤ 6 hr 45 min) school-night total sleep time; large (≥ 120 min) versus small (≤ 60 min) weekend delay; or high (> 120 min) versus low (< 60 min) weekend oversleep. High school students who had longer total sleep times, small weekend delays, or low weekend oversleeps were defined as having adopted *adequate* sleep habits, whereas students with shorter sleep times, large weekend delays or high weekend oversleeps were defined as having adopted *less than adequate* sleep habits. We compared these *extreme* groups on daytime and nighttime functioning. Table 3 [on page 261] displays means, standard deviations, and F values for depressive mood, sleepiness, and sleep/wake behavior problems for each of the sleep variable groups. (The demographic breakdown of these groups reflected the larger

guished students reporting C's and worse from those reporting mostly B's or better. Students' weekend sleep habits also differed according to self-reported grades, multivariate $F(9, 6327) = 18.79$, $p < .001$. Specifically,

TABLE 2   MEANS AND STANDARD DEVIATIONS FOR SCHOOL-NIGHT AND WEEKEND SLEEP VARIABLES BY GRADES

| Sleep/Wake Variables | Self-Reported Grades | | | | F Value | Bonferroni |
	Mostly A's or A's/B's (n = 1,238)	Mostly B's or B's/C's (n = 1,371)	Mostly C's or C's/D's (n = 390)	Mostly D's/F's (n = 61)		
School-night TST	442 (62)	441 (66)	424 (74)	408 (94)	16.66***	A, B > C, D/F
School-night bedtime	10:27 P.M. (53)	10:32 P.M. (56)	10:52 P.M. (65)	11:22 P.M. (81)	24.58***	A, B < C, D/F
School-night rise time	6:02 A.M. (25)	6:05 A.M. (29)	6:10 A.M. (34)	6:09 A.M. (31)	ns	. . .
Weekend TST	547 (100)	547 (109)	534 (124)	549 (137)	ns	. . .
Weekend bedtime	12:06 A.M. (78)	12:29 A.M. (82)	1:09 A.M. (97)	1:33 A.M. (93)	51.32***	A < B < C, D/F
Weekend rise time	9:21 A.M. (97)	9:43 A.M. (103)	9:59 A.M. (113)	10:33 A.M. (160)	24.10***	A < B < C, D/F
Weekend oversleep	105 (101)	108 (114)	109 (130)	137 (159)	3.32*–	A, B, C < D/F
Weekend delay	99 (68)	117 (72)	137 (77)	133 (80)	26.53***	A < B < C, D/F

Note: TST refers to total sleep time (minutes). Weekend oversleep is the difference between weekend and school-night total sleep times, and weekend delay is the difference between weekend and school-night bedtimes. Standard deviations, in parentheses, are in minutes; TST, weekend oversleep, and weekend delay are in minutes as well.

$*p < .05$; $**p < .01$; $***p < .001$; – does not meet effect size criterion (e.g., effects where two groups differ by more than one-third of the sample standard deviation).

sample on age, sex, and school attendance.) Separate analyses of variance were calculated for each dependent variable (depressive mood, level of sleepiness, and sleep/wake behavior problems), with school-night total sleep time, weekend delay, weekend oversleep, and sex as independent variables. Age was analyzed as a covariate in these analyses.

Overall, adolescents who were in the groups defined as *less than adequate* sleep habits reported increased behavioral difficulties in comparison to those we defined as *adequate sleepers*. Thus, students in the short total sleep group reported more sleep/wake behavior problems, such as arrived late to class because of oversleeping, tired or dragged out nearly every day, needed more than one reminder to get up, $ps < .01$, higher levels of depressive mood, $ps < .001$, and greater sleepiness, $ps < .001$, than those in the long sleep group. Similarly, adolescents in the large weekend delay group described more sleep/wake behavior problems, $ps < .01$, and greater daytime sleepiness, $ps < .05$, but no difference in depressed mood from those with small weekend delays. One exception was that the female students with large weekend delays

reported increased depressive mood levels, $p < .05$. Adolescents in the high weekend oversleep group reported more sleep/wake behavior problems, $p < .001$, but no differences in depressed mood or sleepiness from those in the low oversleep group. No sex differences were found in self-reported sleep/wake behavior problems; however, females reported higher levels of depressed mood: females, $M = 11.04$, $SD = 2.91$ versus males, $M = 9.20$, $SD = 2.68$, $p < .001$, and daytime sleepiness: females, $M = 15.26$, $SD = 3.59$ versus males, $M = 14.67$, $SD = 4.16$, $p \leq .01$, than did males.

DISCUSSION

The principal aim of this research was to assess the relation between adolescents' sleep/wake habits and their daytime functioning. The relatively high response rate (88%) obtained in this school-based study allows us to consider our findings representative of adolescents enrolled in moderate to large public high schools in this geographical region. The use of a self-

TABLE 3 MEANS, STANDARD DEVIATIONS, AND ANALYSIS OF VARIANCE FOR DAYTIME BEHAVIOR SCALES FOR *ADEQUATE* VERSUS *LESS THAN ADEQUATE* SLEEPERS

| Daytime Functioning Variables | Weekend Delay | | Weekend Oversleep | | School-Night TST | | F Values Sleep Variables | | | | | |
| | | | | | | | Delay | | Oversleep | | TST | |
	#60 (n = 887)	$120 (n = 928)	,60 (n = 972)	.120 (n = 1,411)	$495 (n = 959)	#405 (n = 1,207)	M	F	M	F	M	F
Depressive mood	10.13 (2.94)	10.35 (2.97)	9.92 (2.85)	10.42 (2.99)	9.48 (2.76)	10.79 (3.00)	ns	3.89*	ns	ns	10.80***	12.94***
Sleepiness	14.63 (3.71)	15.29 (3.98)	14.76 (3.82)	15.23 (3.81)	14.03 (3.51)	15.86 (4.01)	4.37*	6.45**	ns	ns	19.79***	29.77***
Sleep/wake behavior problems	19.10 (6.61)	21.80 (7.16)	19.33 (6.83)	21.22 (7.18)	18.48 (6.63)	22.17 (7.01)	13.17***	47.20***	17.83***	7.93**	16.15***	28.70***

Note: Weekend delay small = ≤60 min, large = ≥120 min; weekend oversleep short = <60 min, long = >120 min, and school-night TST long = ≥8 hr 45 min, short = ≤6 hr 15 min. M = effect for males, F = effect for females.

*p < .05; **p < .01; ***p < .001.

report questionnaire enabled us to gather timely information from a large student population.

High School Students' Sleep Loss and Irregular Sleep/Wake Schedules

In particular, this sample of over 3,000 high school students reported lower total sleep (school and weekend nights) across ages 13–19. On school nights, the mean total sleep decreased from 7 hr 42 min to 7 hr 4 min. Similarly, average weekend total sleep decreased from 9 hr 20 min to 8 hr 38 min. The sleep loss is due to increasingly later bedtimes in older teens, whereas rise times remain more consistent. The sleep habits of the students attending the four different high schools showed minimal differences, with the exception of school day rise time, which was significantly earlier for students attending the school with the earliest start time. Although the difference between 7:10 and 7:30 may appear slight, the impact on sleep patterns was meaningful.

Remarkably few differences were found between male and female high school students' sleep/wake patterns. Female adolescents reported that they woke up 12 min earlier than their male peers on school mornings, a finding consistent with an earlier survey of high school students (Carskadon, 1990b) and a study of junior high school students in Taiwan (Gau & Soong, 1995). In the Gau et al. sample, however, the junior high school girls also reported less total sleep than the boys. We speculate that adolescent girls may be getting up earlier because they require more time to prepare for school and/or for family responsibilities.

Taken together, we conclude that most of these adolescents do not get enough sleep. Our laboratory data indicate that optimal sleep length is about 9.2 hr in adolescents (Carskadon et al., 1980). Although individual differences in sleep need are likely, we note that 87% of our sample responded that they need more sleep than they get (median self-reported sleep need = 9 hr). Forty percent of the students reported that they went to bed after 11:00 P.M. on school nights, and 91% went to bed after 11:00 P.M. (67% after midnight) on weekends. Furthermore, 26% reported that they usually sleep 6.5 hr or less, and only 15% reported sleeping 8.5 hr or more on school nights (median = 7.5 hr). Nearly 70% of the students reported weekend delays of 60 min or more; on average, they reported oversleeping on weekends by nearly 1 hr and 50 min. Ninety-one percent of these high school students rise at 6:30 A.M. or earlier on school mornings, and 72% awaken at 9:00 A.M. or later on weekends.

These high school students' reported sleep/wake schedules are consistent with the major trends in the field: (1) self-reported nocturnal sleep time declines across the adolescent years; (2) bedtimes during high school become later; and (3) teenagers show large variations between weekend and school-night sleep schedules (e.g., Carskadon, 1990a; Strauch & Meier, 1988; Szymczak et al., 1993). In comparison to data from Rhode Island high school students surveyed 8 years earlier, these students reported on average approximately 15–20 min less sleep per night on school nights, principally reflecting earlier rising times (Carskadon, 1990a). The developmental and secular trends raise concerns about patterns that may have negative effects on teenagers' waking behavior.

Not assessed in this survey is the impact of family factors on sleep patterns. In the past, we have shown that parents tend to relinquish control of bedtime while increasing involvement with rising time as youngsters pass into adolescence (Carskadon, 1990a). In this particular sample, only 5.1% of students reported that parents set bedtimes on school nights; thus, the great majority of these youngsters set their own bedtime agenda. Over 80% of youngsters in this survey come from two-parent households in which both parents are employed, and we saw no differences between this cohort and those from single-parent homes on the major sleep variables. We propose that the biological and psychosocial processes favoring sleep delay in teens collides with early rising times mandated by schools and that even in the most well-regulated families the capacity for adequate adjustments may be limited.

Sleep/Wake Habits and School Performance

Our data support and extend findings from Kowalski and Allen (1995) and Link and Ancoli-Israel (1995) that students who described themselves as struggling or failing school (i.e., obtaining C's, D's/F's) report that they obtain less sleep, have later bedtimes, and have more irregular sleep/wake schedules than students who report better grades (i.e., A's, B's). In the Link and Ancoli-Israel survey of 150 high school students, students with self-reported higher grade point averages (GPA) slept more at night and reported less daytime sleepiness than students with lower GPAs. One explanation for these results is that students who get more sleep and maintain more consistent school/weekend sleep schedules obtain better grades because of their ability to be more alert and to pay greater attention in class and on homework. In contrast, Gau et al. (1995) found that younger students (junior high school age) on a highly competitive academic track reported shorter school and weekend night total sleep times, later bedtimes, and decreased daytime alertness than students in an alternative, less competitive program. Our data do not show a one-to-one relation between sleep patterns and grades. Certainly some students are able to function in school quite well with short amounts of sleep but may pay a price in other ways. Many students, however, may be too impaired by insufficient sleep to cope optimally with school demands. A major limitation of all of these studies is that they involve self-report; additional laboratory and field research are needed to clarify the direction of the relations among sleep loss, irregular sleep schedules, and academic performance and to assess other moderating and mediating variables, such as coping strategies, family rules, class schedules, and type of academic work.

ADDITIONAL CONSEQUENCES OF POOR SLEEP/WAKE HABITS

We have attempted to describe more thoroughly certain consequences of insufficient sleep and irregular sleep/wake schedules on adolescents' functioning by comparing extreme groups of students who reported patterns we defined as *adequate* versus *less than adequate* sleep/wake patterns. Students with short school-night sleep reported increased levels of depressed mood, daytime sleepiness, and problematic sleep behaviors in comparison to longer sleepers. Likewise, students with more irregular sleep schedules had more behavior problems. These data suggest that high school students with inadequate total sleep and/or irregular school-night to weekend sleep/wake schedules may struggle with daytime behavior problems. We interpret these findings to indicate that poor sleep habits influence behavior and mood, acknowledging that in certain youngsters the cause-effect arrow may go in the opposite direction.

Researchers are just beginning to compile evidence relating emotional well-being to sleep patterns. Our findings showing that teenagers with very short and irregular sleep/wake patterns have more daytime difficulties support the work of Morrison, McGee, and Stanton (1992), who compared four groups of 13- and 15-year-olds in New Zealand: those with no sleep problems, those indicating they needed more sleep only, those reporting difficulties falling asleep or maintaining sleep, and those with multiple sleep problems. These investigators found that adolescents in the sleep-problem groups were more anxious, had higher levels of depression, and had lower social competence than those in the no-sleep-problem group. Similarly, Carskadon et al. (1991) found that a pattern of short sleep in college-bound high school seniors was associated with reports of sleepiness and sleep problems in males and females, and with anxiety and depression in females. Moreover, in a study calling for ninth to twelfth graders to reduce their habitual sleep by 2 hr over 5 consecutive nights, dysphoric mood changes occurred during the reduced sleep period on both daily and weekly depressive mood scales (Carskadon et al., 1989).

We hypothesize that if adolescents had the opportunity to obtain more sleep each night, they would experience fewer fluctuations in daily mood and fewer behavioral difficulties. In essence, we propose that adolescent moodiness may be in part a repercussion of insufficient sleep. The tendency for some adolescents to have reduced nocturnal sleep times and irregular schedules may have consequences that extend beyond daytime sleepiness to feelings of depression. On the other hand, depressed adolescents may be more inclined toward insufficient sleep and irregular schedules (Dahl et al., 1996). Additional in-depth laboratory and field assessment studies to probe the interplay between context, sleep/wake patterns, and daytime functioning of adolescents may enable us to tease apart some of these factors.

CAVEATS AND IMPLICATIONS

We are very concerned about the important information that we have obtained from this large sample of high school students; however, certain caveats pertain. First, it is difficult to evaluate how representative the sample was, although the congruence between our findings and those from prior research (e.g., Carskadon, 1990a; Strauch & Meier, 1988) strongly suggest that the sample was quite typical. Whether our results hold for adolescents drawn from a wider socioeconomic and cultural background is an important issue for future studies. Second, the results of this study are based entirely on the adolescents' self-reports and suffer limitations because data are retrospective, based only on the last 2 weeks, and subjective. Multiple sources of measurement such as parent and teacher ratings, school record data, standardized test batteries, and sleep laboratory recordings would provide a more comprehensive and possibly more reliable assessment than the current study. Our previous experience in laboratory studies indicate that such self-report data are well correlated with data obtained from daily sleep diaries or continuous activity monitoring, although we have not made a formal comparison. On the other hand, in a study of tenth grade students that included 2 weeks of diaries and activity monitoring followed by a laboratory assessment, we found an average sleep length on school nights of 6 hr, 53 min ($SD = 39$), very similar to self-report (Carskadon, Acebo, Wolfson, Tzischinsky, & Darley, 1997).

Third, because the survey was conducted in one geographic area, some caution should be taken in generalizing the findings. Fourth, because the study design was cross-sectional, no conclusions about long-term development and ramifications of inadequate sleep can be drawn. Future investigations should gather several weeks of sleep and behavioral data and consider following high school students over several years. Finally, because the data are cross-sectional it is difficult to demonstrate causal direction. Models that include parameters different than those included in the present study (e.g., home structure, parenting styles, school schedules, and so forth) could also account for variation in grades and/or sleep/wake schedules. Nevertheless, the present study extends the research on adolescent sleep in several ways: (1) to a large population of public, high school students; (2) to a broader understanding of the association between sleep/wake habits, emotional well-being, and school performance in high school students from ages 13 to 19; and (3) to a clearer conceptualization of the risks for adolescents who obtain short amounts of sleep and/or experience erratic weekday-weekend sleep schedules on their daytime performance and mood.

Although self-report surveys have clear limitations, the implications of these data seem undeniable. First, schools need to take an active role and to examine sleep in the context of academic grades, test scores, truancy, behavioral difficulties, and other aspects of daytime functioning and adolescent development. Second, investigators in other fields who are concerned with adolescent development and well-being need to add the insights regarding adolescents' sleep into their studies and clinical work. Third, researchers, practitioners, and educators need to take interdisciplinary approaches to understanding and promoting the academic, health, and behavioral well-being of adolescents.

Adolescents confront a multitude of vulnerabilities, uncertainties, and changes. This developmental period is extremely eventful in terms of physiological, cognitive, and psychosocial development. Undoubtedly, most adolescents require more than 7 hr, 20 min (sample mean) of sleep to cope optimally with academic demands, social pressures, driving, and job responsibilities. Although adolescents may be differentially affected by pubertal changes in sleep/wake patterns, school start times, and academic responsibilities, the excessive sleepiness consequent to insufficient, erratic sleep is a potentially serious factor for adolescent development and behavioral well-being. The magnitude of the problem has been unrecognized because adolescent sleepiness is so widespread that it almost seems normal (Carskadon, 1990a). Steinberg and Darling (1994), Petersen, Silbereisen, and Soerensen (1993) and others have emphasized the importance of studying the context of adolescent development. The development of adolescent sleeping patterns cannot be understood without taking into account school schedules and other contexts; likewise, adolescent development (psychosocial, cognitive, emotional) cannot be fully examined without considering sleep/wake factors.

REFERENCES

Achenbach, T. (1991). *Manual for the Youth Self-Report and 1991 profile.* Burlington: University of Vermont Department of Psychiatry.

Allen, R. (1991). School-week sleep lag: Sleep problems with earlier starting of senior high schools. *Sleep Research, 20,* 198.

Allen, R. (1992). Social factors associated with the amount of school week sleep lag for seniors in an early starting suburban high school. *Sleep Research, 21,* 114.

Allen, R., & Mirabile, J. (1989). Self-reported sleep-wake patterns for students during the school year from two different senior high schools. *Sleep Research, 18,* 132.

Andrade, M. M., Benedito-Silva, E. E., & Domenice, S. (1993). Sleep characteristics of adolescents: A longitudinal study. *Journal of Adolescent Health, 14,* 401–406.

Bearpark, H. M., & Michie, P. T. (1987). Prevalence of sleep/wake disturbances in Sydney adolescents. *Sleep Research, 16,* 304.

Brown, C., Tzischinsky, O., Wolfson, A., Acebo, C., Wicks, J., Darley, C., & Carskadon, M. A. (1995). Circadian phase preference and adjustment to the high school transition. *Sleep Research, 24,* 90.

Carskadon, M. A. (1982). The second decade. In C. Guilleminault (Ed.), *Sleeping and waking disorders: Indications and techniques.* Menlo Park: Addison-Wesley.

Carskadon, M. A. (1990a). Patterns of sleep and sleepiness in adolescents. *Pediatrician, 17,* 5–12.

Carskadon, M. A. (1990b). Adolescent sleepiness: Increased risk in a high-risk population. *Alcohol, Drugs, and Driving, 5/6,* 317–328.

Carskadon, M. A. (1995). Sleep's place in teenagers' lives. *Proceedings of the Biennial Meeting of the Society for Research in Child Development,* p. 32 (abstract).

Carskadon, M. A., & Acebo, C. (1993). A self-administered rating scale for pubertal development. *Journal of Adolescent Health Care, 14,* 190–195.

Carskadon, M. A., Acebo, C., Richardson, G. S., Tate, B. A., & Seifer, R. (1997). Long nights protocol: Access to circadian parameters in adolescents. *Journal of Biological Rhythms, 12,* 278–289.

Carskadon, M. A., Acebo, C., Wolfson, A., Tzischinsky, O., & Darley, C. (1997). REM sleep on MSLTS in high school students is related to circadian phase. *Sleep Research, 26,* 705.

Carskadon, M. A., Dement, W. C., Mitler, M. M., Roth, T., Westbrook, P. R., & Keenan, S. (1986). Guidelines for the Multiple Sleep Latency Test (MSLT): A standard measure of sleepiness. *Sleep, 9,* 519–524.

Carskadon, M. A., Harvey, K., Duke, P., Anders, T. F., & Dement, W. C. (1980). Pubertal changes in daytime sleepiness. *Sleep, 2,* 453–460.

Carskadon, M. A., Keenan, S., & Dement, W. C. (1987). Nighttime sleep and daytime sleep tendency in preadolescents. In

C. Guilleminault (Ed.), *Sleep and its disorders in children.* New York: Raven Press.

Carskadon, M. A., & Mancuso, J. (1988). Sleep habits in high school adolescents: Boarding versus day students. *Sleep Research, 17,* 74.

Carskadon, M. A., Orav, E. J., & Dement, W. C. (1983). Evolution of sleep and daytime sleepiness in adolescents. In C. Guilleminault & E. Lugaresi (Eds.), *Sleep/wake disorders: Natural history, epidemiology, and long-term evolution* (pp. 201–216). New York: Raven Press.

Carskadon, M. A., Rosekind, M. R., Galli, J., Sohn, J., Herman, K. B., & Davis, S. S. (1989). Adolescent sleepiness during sleep restriction in the natural environment. *Sleep Research, 18,* 115.

Carskadon, M. A., Seifer, R., & Acebo, C. (1991). Reliability of six scales in a sleep questionnaire for adolescents. *Sleep Research, 20,* 421.

Carskadon, M. A., Vieira, C., & Acebo, C., (1993). Association between puberty and delayed phase preference. *Sleep, 16,* 258–262.

Carskadon, M. A., Wolfson, A., Tzischinsky, O., & Acebo, C. (1995). Early school schedules modify adolescent sleepiness. *Sleep Research, 24,* 92.

Cohen, J. (1988). *Statistical Power Analysis for the Behavioral Sciences.* Hillsdale, NJ: Erlbaum.

Dahl, R. E., & Carskadon, M. A. (1995). Sleep in its disorders in adolescence. In R. Ferber & M. Kryger (Eds.), *Principles and practice of sleep medicine in the child.* Philadelphia: WB Saunders.

Dahl, R. E., Holttum, J., & Trubnick, L. (1994). A clinical picture of childhood and adolescent narcolepsy. *Journal of the American Academy of Child and Adolescent Psychiatry, 33,* 834–841.

Dahl, R. E., Ryan, N. D., Matty, M. K., Birmaher, B., Alshabbout, M., Williamson, D. E., & Kupfer, D. J. (1996). Sleep onset abnormalities in depressed adolescents. *Biological Psychiatry, 39,* 400–410.

Epstein, R., Chillag, N., & Lavie, P. (1995). Sleep habits of children and adolescents in Israel: The influence of starting time of school. *Sleep Research, 24a,* 432.

Fisher, B. E., & Rinehart, S. (1990). Stress, arousal, psychopathology and temperament: A multidimensional approach to sleep disturbance in children. *Personality and Individual Differences, 11,* 431–438.

Gau, S-F., & Soong, W-T. (1995). Sleep problems of junior high school students in Taipei. *Sleep, 18,* 667–673.

Guilleminault, C., Winkle, R., & Korobkin, R. (1982). Children and nocturnal snoring: Evaluation of the effects of sleep related respiratory resistive load and daytime functioning. *European Journal of Pediatrics, 139,* 165–171.

Hendry, L. B., Glendinning, A., Shucksmith, J., Love, J., & Scott, J. (1994). The developmental context of adolescent lifestyles. In R. K. Silbereisen & T. Eberhard (Eds.), *Adolescence in context: The interplay of family, school, peers, and work in adjustment* (pp. 66–81). New York: Springer-Verlag.

Ishihara, K., Honma, Y., & Miyake, S. (1990). Investigation of the children's version of the morningness-eveningness questionnaire with primary and junior high school pupils in Japan. *Perceptual and Motor Skills, 71,* 1353–1354.

Kagan, J., Resnick, J. S., & Gibbons, J. (1989). Inhibited and uninhibited types of children. *Child Development, 60,* 838–845.

Kandel, D. B., & Davies, M. (1982). Epidemiology of depressive mood in adolescents. *Archives of General Psychiatry, 39,* 1205–1212.

Kataria, S., Swanson, M. S., & Trevathan, G. E. (1987). Persistence of sleep disturbances in preschool children. *Pediatrics, 110,* 642–646.

Kowalski, N., & Allen, R. (1995). School sleep lag is less but persists with a very late starting high school. *Sleep Research, 24,* 124.

Link, S. C., & Ancoli-Israel, S. (1995). Sleep and the teenager. *Sleep Research, 24a,* 184.

Manber, R., Pardee, R. E., Bootzin, R. R., Kuo, T., Rider, A. M., Rider, S. P., & Bergstrom, L. (1995). Changing sleep patterns in adolescence. *Sleep Research, 24,* 106.

Morrison, D. N., McGee, R., & Stanton, W. R. (1992). Sleep problems in adolescence. *Journal of the American Academy of Child and Adolescent Psychiatry, 31,* 94–99.

Peterson, A. C., Silbereisen, R. K., & Soerensen, S. (1993). Adolescent development: A global perspective. In W. Meeus, M. de Goede, W. Kox, & K. Hurrelmann (Eds.), *Adolescence, careers and cultures* (pp. 1–34). New York: De Gruyter.

Petta, D., Carskadon, M. A., & Dement, W. C. (1984). Sleep habits in children aged 7–13 years. *Sleep Research, 13,* 86.

Price, V. A., Coates, T. J., Thoresen, C. E., & Grinstead, O. A. (1978). Prevalence and correlates of poor sleep among adolescents. *American Journal of Diseases of Children, 132,* 583–586.

Quine, L. (1992). Severity of sleep problems in children with severe learning difficulties: Description and correlates. *Journal of Community and Applied Social Psychology, 2,* 247–268.

State of Rhode Island Department of Education. (1994). *Rhode Island Public Schools 1994 District Profiles.* Providence: Rhode Island Department of Elementary and Secondary Education.

Steinberg, L., & Darling, N. (1994). The broader context of social influence in adolescence. In R. K. Silbereisen & T. Eberhard (Eds.), *Adolescence in context: The interplay of family, school, peers, and work in adjustment* (pp. 25–45). New York: Springer-Verlag.

Strauch, I., & Meier, B. (1988). Sleep need in adolescents: A longitudinal approach. *Sleep, 11,* 378–386.

Szymczak, J. T., Jasinska, M., Pawlak, E., & Swierzykowska, M. (1993). Annual and weekly changes in the sleep-wake rhythm of school children. *Sleep, 16,* 433–435.

Tanner, J. M. (1962). *Growth in adolescence.* Oxford: Blackwell.

Williams, R., Karacan, I., & Hursch, C. (1974). *EEG of human sleep.* New York: Wiley & Sons.

Wolfson, A. R., Tzischinsky, O., Brown, C., Darley, C., Acebo, C., & Carskadon, M. (1995). Sleep, behavior, and stress at the transition to senior high school. *Sleep Research, 24,* 115.

QUESTIONS

1. What biological changes in sleep schedules and demands occur in adolescence?
2. What environmental factors affect the adolescent's sleep/wake patterns?
3. What changes occur in adolescent sleep schedules from age 13 to age 19?
4. How does adolescent sleep affect academic performance?
5. Do high school students with less than adequate amounts of sleep suffer? How?
6. What policy implications are suggested by this research? Do you think such changes would be easy or difficult to implement? Why?

30 Development of Logical Reasoning in the Context of Parental Style and Test Anxiety

MARK S. CHAPELL · WILLIS F. OVERTON

Among the many changes that occur in adolescence, cognitive or intellectual changes rank among the most important. These changes permit adolescents to think in more complex, abstract, and hypothetical ways than ever before. Piaget characterized the thinking that develops in adolescence as formal operational thought. By this he meant that adolescents were capable of performing logical operations that are formal or abstract in nature. Therefore, topics like abstract mathematics and scientific reasoning are now possible.

Despite general support for this view, many factors have emerged from research on formal operations that indicate that this type of thinking is greatly affected by social and experiential factors. In the following article, research by Mark S. Chapell and Willis F. Overton examines formal operational reasoning in relation to the parenting style that children experience in the family. Different parenting styles provide different opportunities and support for cognitive development. This research was designed to test the hypothesis that an authoritative or democratic style is the most supportive of cognitive development in the adolescent years. In addition to formal reasoning and parenting style, the researchers added another variable to their analysis, test anxiety. They predicted that test anxiety would relate to both parenting style and cognitive performance on a deductive reasoning task.

This research provides interesting answers to these questions. It also illustrates how a conceptual approach to cognitive development can be integrated with the developmental demands and experiences of a particular age group to yield insight into the social–cognitive aspects of development.

The development of reasoning during adolescence was examined, and the relationship of parental style and test anxiety to reasoning performance was explored. Participants were 120 students, 40 each in the sixth, tenth, and twelfth grades, classified into authoritative or nonauthoritative and high or low test-anxiety groups. They were administered 10 deductive reasoning problems. As predicted, tenth and twelfth graders demonstrated significantly more advanced reasoning than did sixth graders. As expected, authoritative parenting was related to more advanced reasoning performance and lower test anxiety than was nonauthoritative parenting. Further, low test anxiety was related to more advanced reasoning performance than was high test anxiety. Results are discussed in terms of contextual factors in logical reasoning.

Over the past several years, a body of evidence has emerged to support the position that deductive reasoning shows a developmental progression that culminates in a high level of performance by age 18 (Overton, 1990). This progression appears to hold for both cross-sectional (Overton, Ward, Noveck, Black, & O'Brien, 1987; Ward & Overton, 1990) and longitudinal samples (Reene & Overton, 1989). It is becoming increasingly apparent that by late adolescence this competence to reason in deductive fashion has been

Reprinted by permission of the authors and Wayne State University Press from Merrill-Palmer Quarterly, 44 (1998), pp. 141–156. Copyright © 1998 by Wayne State University Press, Detroit, MI.

Correspondence concerning this article may be sent to either Mark S. Chapell or Willis F. Overton, Department of Psychology, Temple University, Philadelphia, PA 19122. Electronic mail may be sent via Internet to Overton@VM.Temple.edu established. However, it is also becoming more apparent that the expression of this competence is mediated by a number of factors, including attachment representation (Jacobsen, Edelstein, & Hofmann, 1994), cognitive style (Neimark, 1975; Overton, Byrnes, & O'Brien, 1985), sex-role identity and learned helplessness (Overton & Meehan, 1982), and information-processing capacity (Niaz, 1991). Thus, although the ability to reason deductively may be available, there are significant individual differences in the expression of this competence. In the present study the development of reasoning across adolescence is investigated further and two potentially significant mediators of the expression of reasoning competence are explored: parental style and test anxiety.

Vygotsky and Piaget agree that social interaction promotes cognitive development, and where Piaget can be read as focusing on the individual while respecting the social, Vygotsky's focus is on the social, while respecting the individual (Overton, 1994). For Piaget (1928), cognitive socialization through discussion and the exchange of ideas begins in earnest with the onset of concrete operational thought. At this time, the individual's capacity to consider the logic of other points of view first emerges. The later development of formal operational thought in adolescence—when individuals can logically examine their own thought as well as the thought of others—may also be facilitated by social interaction. As Piaget suggests (1972):

> The formation and completion of cognitive structures imply a whole series of exchanges and a stimulating environment; the formation of operations always requires a favorable environment for 'co-operation', that is to say, operations carried out in common (e.g., the role of discussion, mutual criticism or support, problems raised as the result of exchanges of information, heightened curiosity due to the cultural influence of a social group, etc.). (p. 8)

The parent–child relationship is a fundamental social context where children and adolescents might regularly have the opportunity to engage in the intellectually constructive give-and-take described by Piaget. The quality and quantity of communication between parents and children has been thought to be influenced by a variety of factors, one of the most well-defined and well-researched of which is parenting style (Maccoby & Martin, 1983).

Baumrind (1967, 1971) identified three basic child-rearing styles, which she termed authoritative, authoritarian, and permissive parenting. Maccoby and Martin (1983) redefined and expanded this categorization and classified parents as high or low on each of two dimensions—responsiveness and demandingness—yielding a total of four parenting styles: (a) authoritative, (b) authoritarian, (c) indulgent, and (d) neglectful parents. Across alternative conceptualizations of parenting style, investigators (Baumrind, 1991; Darling & Steinberg, 1993; Maccoby & Martin, 1983) have consistently characterized authoritative parenting as a responsive, supportive, democratic yet demanding context. This style, through regular, well-reasoned, bidirectional communication, supplies to and expects from children and adolescents a great deal of thought. Authoritative parenting has been associated with a wide variety of positive childhood and adolescent outcomes (Baumrind, 1991; Darling & Steinberg, 1993; Maccoby & Martin, 1983), and would seem to offer the sort of cooperative social environment described by Piaget as facilitative to the development of formal thought. This hypothesis, first suggested by Gray (1990), has yet to be tested.

In contrast to the authoritative style, nonauthoritative parents, including authoritarian, indulgent and neglectful parents (Steinberg, Mounts, Lamborn, & Dornbusch, 1991), have been identified as either less responsive and supportive of children and adolescents, less demanding, or both. These conditions would be expected to be less effective in promoting cognitive development than those provided by authoritative parents. As a consequence, in this study of the relationship between parenting style and cognitive development the hypothesis is explored that adolescents with authoritative parents have more advanced reasoning performance than those with nonauthoritative parents.

The second factor in this study hypothesized to be related to logical reasoning performance is test anxiety. According to the competence-procedure model of logical reasoning (Overton, 1990, 1991), access to and application of formal reasoning competence is mediated by a variety of "real-time" processing procedures or strategies. Thus, for example, processing procedures such as metacognitive strategies have been shown to facilitate access to logical competence and enhance deductive reasoning problem-solving performance (Pollack, Overton, Rosenfeld, & Rosenfeld, 1995; Takahashi & Overton, 1996). By the same token, factors that interfere with logical processing strategies should inhibit access to logical competence and degrade problem-solving performance. One such source of interference with real-time logical processing strategies may be test anxiety.

Test anxiety has been shown to have a negative effect on performance in a variety of evaluative situations, resulting in lowered scores on problem-solving tasks, IQ tests, aptitude and achievement tests, and reduced school grade point average (Hembree, 1988). According to the cognitive interference model of test anxiety (Sarason, 1978; Wine, 1971, 1981), persons high in test anxiety perform more poorly on cognitive tasks than do less anxious persons due to interference provided by task-irrelevant thinking, worry, and negative self-evaluation. Studies of elementary and secondary school students have consistently shown that test anxiety is related to excessive off-task thinking, negative intrusive thoughts, and worry (Beidel & Turner, 1988; Comunian, 1993; Hembree, 1988; King, Mietz, Tinney, & Ollendick, 1995; Prins, Groot, & Hanewald, 1994; Zatz & Chassin, 1985), and the ability to minimize off-task thoughts during tests has been associated with lower test anxiety and improved performance (Denney, 1980; Hembree, 1988; Tryon, 1980). Deductive reasoning problems constitute a demanding test, and, particularly when used with students in schools, are likely to elicit test anxiety, which may degrade the processing strategies used to access and apply formal reasoning competence. Here we explore the hypothesis that adolescents with low test anxiety have more advanced reasoning performance than those with high test anxiety.

The final problem of interest to be addressed in this study is the possible relationship of parenting styles and test anxiety. Hill (1972, 1980) theorized that children of very critical parents, with unrealistically high expectations, might develop anxiety during the preschool years. As these children advance in school, they may become afraid to fail in evaluative situations for fear of parental criticism. Krohne (1980, 1990) also has advanced a theory of parental influence on children's test anxiety, a two-process model that predicts children with restrictive or inconsistent parents develop more test anxiety than do those with supportive parents. Studies by Krohne and colleagues (Krohne, 1990, 1992) with children 8 to 14 years of age have supported this prediction.

Nonauthoritative parents, including authoritarian, indulgent, and neglectful parents, closely resemble those theorized by Hill (1972, 1980) and Krohne (1980, 1990) to have children with test anxiety problems. By contrast, authoritative parenting has been related consistently, cross-sectionally, and longitudinally (Baumrind, 1991; Lamborn, Mounts, Steinberg, & Dornbusch, 1991; Steinberg, Lamborn, Darling, Mounts, & Dornbusch, 1994) to higher adolescent academic achievement and less adolescent stress than nonauthoritative parenting. In this study we explore the hypothesis that adolescents with authoritative parents have lower test anxiety than do those with nonauthoritative parents.

In summary, the primary goals of this study are to examine the development of deductive reasoning across adolescence, and to explore the relationship of parental style and test anxiety to reasoning performance. It is expected that reasoning performance improves during adolescence; that authoritative parenting is associated with more advanced adolescent reasoning performance; and that test anxiety is associated with lower reasoning performance. It is further predicted that authoritative parenting will be associated with lower adolescent test anxiety than nonauthoritative parenting.

METHOD

PARTICIPANTS

Forty students (20 male, 20 female) in each of the sixth grade ($M = 12.2$ years, $SD = 5.6$ months), tenth grade ($M = 15.9$ years, $SD = 6.2$ months), and twelfth grade ($M = 17.9$ years, $SD = 6.4$ months) participated voluntarily in the study ($N = 120$). The sample was upper middle class, 79% European American, 11% African American, 6% Asian American, 4% Hispanic American, drawn from a private school in the suburban Philadelphia area.

PROCEDURE

Participants were tested in small groups of 4 to 10 in their school classrooms. Participants were administered Overton's (1990) version of Wason's selection task, followed by a parenting style measure and a test anxiety measure.

MEASURES

Selection Task. The selection task (Overton, 1990) is composed of a series of 10 conditional propositions ("If p, then q"). Formal deductive understanding of an implication ("If p, then q") requires the recognition that particular instances of the antecedent and consequent clauses of a sentence are either permissible, not permissible, or indeterminate. The selection task requires this recognition and coordination between permissible and impermissible instances, and thus constitutes a valid measure of deductive reasoning. It should be noted that some have claimed that the selection task assesses pragmatic reasoning or permission schemes (Cheng & Holyoak, 1985). This issue is discussed in detail by Overton (1990). Further, however, recent empirical evidence (Foltz, Overton, & Ricco, 1995) has demonstrated a close relationship between Overton's Selection task and deductive reasoning on other tasks, and Rasch-scaling analysis (Mueller, Reene, & Overton, 1994) of Overton's Selection task indicates that the task forms a unidimensional construct and that no more than two problems (e.g., the driving problem and the beer problem) could be accounted for by reasoning other than formal reasoning. Selection task test booklets were constructed containing an instruction page, one warm-up problem, and 10 conditional reasoning problems. Each problem was presented on a separate page and all problems were in the conditional "if p, then q" form (see Table 1).

TABLE 1 SELECTION TASK CONDITIONAL PROPOSITION STATEMENTS

If a person is swimming in the public pool, then a lifeguard is present.*
If a student is watching television, then the student's homework is finished.
If a person is drinking beer, then the person is 21 years of age.
If a person is driving a motor vehicle, then he/she must be over 16 years of age.
If a student is caught running in the halls, then the student must be punished.
If a person is retired from work, then he/she is over 55 years of age.
If a student strikes a teacher, then the student is suspended.
If a person has a handgun, then the handgun must be registered.
If a drunken driver kills someone, then the driver must be charged with murder.
If a child with AIDs attends school, then the child has the community's approval.
If a girl under 14 years old has an abortion, then she must have her parents' permission.

---

*Warm-up problem

Using the warm-up problem as an example, the format of each page was as follows: At the top of the page were four response alternatives depicted as rectangular boxes with information printed inside about a situation. These response alternatives corresponded to the affirmation of "p" (i.e., swimming), the affirmation of "q" (i.e., lifeguard), the denial of "p" (i.e., sunbathing), and the denial of "q" (i.e., no lifeguard). Below these alternatives were the following instructions: "Each of the above cards has information about four different people at the public pool. One side of each card shows the person's behavior at the pool. One side of each card shows whether or not a lifeguard is present. Remember, you can only see one side of each card. Here is a rule: IF A PERSON IS SWIMMING IN THE PUBLIC POOL, THEN A LIFEGUARD IS PRESENT. If you could turn the cards over and see the information on the other side, which card or cards would you select to prove with certainty that the rule is being broken?" Space was provided below the boxes for the participant's choice.

The instruction page informed the participant that the booklet contained several problems and that each presented a rule. They were further informed that for each problem, they were to determine whether the rule was being broken. The experimenter read the instructions aloud while the participant read along silently. Participants were then given the warm-up problem, which was followed by verbal feedback concerning the correct responses (feedback was not given on test trials). Verbal feedback consisted only of pointing out the correct responses, and did not involve any further discussion. The order of response alternatives was randomized across problems, and the problem order was randomized across participants, with the exception of the standard warm-up problem.

Selection Task Scoring. A general solution score, giving partial credit for partial solutions, was used as the main dependent measure. For each problem participants received one point for each of the following: choosing "p," choosing "not q," not choosing "not p," not choosing "q," yielding a total possible score with a range of 0 to 40 points, across the 10 problems.

The correct logical response to selection task problems is the selection of the "p" and the "not q" alternatives while not selecting the "not p" or the "q" alternatives. This selection combination, which is called the complete falsification solution, was used as a second dependent variable. A score of 1 point was given for each problem when this solution was selected, and 0 points were given for any other response. Based on prior research (Foltz et al., 1995; Overton et al., 1987; Ward & Overton, 1990), a consistency criterion of 6 or more complete falsification solutions out of 10 problems was used to categorize the individual as having attained a formal reasoning status.

Parenting Style Measure. The parenting style measure (Steinberg et al., 1991) was used to classify participants into groups having authoritative or nonauthoritative parents. This perceived parenting style measure consists of three scales where adolescents report on their parents' practices: a parental acceptance and involvement scale (10 items; α = .72); a parental strictness and supervision scale (9 items; α = .76), and a psychological autonomy granting scale (12 items; α = .72). Composite scores were calculated for each of the three parenting dimensions. Following the classification procedure established by Steinberg et al. (1991), parents who scored above the sample median on all three scales were classified as authoritative, whereas parents who scored below the median on one or more scales were classified as nonauthoritative, a group that includes a variety of family types, including authoritarian, indulgent and neglectful families. In this sample, 31% of the parents ($n = 37$) were rated as authoritative, and 69% ($n = 83$) were rated as nonauthoritative.

Four more distinctive, "pure" parenting style classifications, including authoritative, authoritarian, indulgent, and neglectful parents, also were defined, following the procedures of Lamborn et al. (1991). In this sample, 43% of the families ($N = 51$) were characterized by a "pure" parenting style. Authoritative parents ($n = 20$) were those scoring in the top tertile on both the acceptance/involvement and strictness/supervision subscales. Authoritarian parents ($n = 9$) were those scoring in the lowest tetile on involvement but in the highest tertile on strictness. Indulgent parents ($n = 7$) scored in the highest tertile on involvement and in the lowest tertile on strictness. Neglectful parents ($n = 15$) scored in the lowest tertile on both involvement and strictness.

Test Anxiety Measure. Median scores on the Test Anxiety Inventory (TAI) were used to classify participants into high ($n = 60$, $M = 44.8$, $SD = 8.95$) or low ($n = 60$, $M = 28$, $SD = 3.64$) test anxiety groups. The TAI (Spielberger, 1980) is a self-report instrument recommended for use and used widely with college, high school and middle school students (DeVito, 1984). The TAI consists of 20 items or statements ($\alpha = .90$). Each statement is followed by a 1- to 4-point Likert-type scale where respondents indicate how often they have experienced the reaction to tests described in the statement, yielding a total test anxiety score ranging from a low of 20 to a maximum of 80 points. Test-retest reliabilities of $r = .81$ for 1-month periods are reported for the TAI (Spielberger, 1980).

RESULTS

In order to test the main developmental and individual differences hypotheses, a 3 (Grade) × 2 (Parental style) × 2 (Test anxiety) ANOVA, adjusted for unequal cell sizes, was computed on the general solution scores (see Table 2). Given an a priori alpha level of .05 for all statistical tests, there were significant main effects for grade, $F(2, 108) = 3.09$, $p < .05$; parental style, $F(1, 108) = 22.21$, $p < .001$, and test anxiety, $F(1, 108) = 7.26$, $p < .01$. Tukey post hoc comparisons showed that, as expected, both twelfth graders ($M = 35.4$, $SD = 4.9$) and tenth graders ($M = 34.4$, $SD = 5.1$) scored higher than sixth graders ($M = 31.7$, $SD = 6.7$), $p < .05$. Additionally, as predicted, adolescents with authoritative parents ($M = 38$, $SD = 4.2$) scored higher than those with nonauthoritative parents ($M = 32$, $SD = 5.7$), $p < .001$, and adolescents with low test anxiety ($M = 36.2$, $SD = 4.5$) scored higher than those with high test anxiety ($M = 31.4$, $SD = 6.1$), $p < .001$. There were no significant interactions. Gender differences in reasoning performance did not achieve significance, and there were no significant interactions between gender and other variables.

To further test the main hypotheses, a 3 (Grade) × 2 (Parental style) × 2 (Test anxiety) ANOVA, adjusted for unequal cell sizes, was computed on the complete falsification scores (see Table 3). There were significant main effects for grade, $F(2, 108) = 4.65$, $p < .02$; parental style, $F(1, 108) = 18.07$, $p < .001$, and test anxiety, $F(1, 108) = 10.63$, $p < .01$. Tukey post hoc comparisons showed that, as expected, both twelfth graders ($M = 7.5$, $SD = 2.81$) and tenth graders ($M = 6.7$, $SD = 2.86$) scored higher than sixth graders ($M = 5.1$, $SD = 3.6$), $p < .05$. Additionally, as predicted, adolescents with authoritative parents ($M = 8.68$, $SD = 2$) scored higher than those with nonauthoritative parents ($M = 5.46$, $SD = 3.22$), $p < .001$, and adolescents with low test anxiety ($M = 7.87$, $SD = 2.34$) scored

TABLE 2   GENERAL SOLUTION SCORES FOR SIXTH, TENTH, AND TWELFTH GRADERS BY TEST ANXIETY LEVELS AND PARENTING STYLES

	Sixth grade			Tenth grade			Twelfth grade		
	M	*SD*	*n*	*M*	*SD*	*n*	*M*	*SD*	*n*
Test anxiety									
Low	36.0	6.1	16	36.0	3.8	21	36.7	4.2	24
High	29.1	6.2	24	32.7	5.5	19	33.5	5.3	16
Parenting style									
Authoritative	37	4.5	12	38.4	2.9	11	38.4	2.4	14
Nonauthoritative	29.4	5.2	28	32.9	5.1	29	33.8	5.2	26

TABLE 3 TOTAL COMPLETE FALSIFICATION SOLUTIONS FOR SIXTH, TENTH, AND TWELFTH GRADERS BY TEST ANXIETY LEVELS AND PARENTING STYLES

	Sixth grade			Tenth grade			Twelfth grade		
	M	*SD*	*n*	*M*	*SD*	*n*	*M*	*SD*	*n*
Test anxiety									
Low	7.5	2.8	16	7.8	1.9	21	8.2	2.3	24
High	3.4	3.2	24	5.5	3.2	19	6.4	3.1	16
Parenting style									
Authoritative	7.8	2.9	12	8.9	1.1	11	9.2	1.2	14
Nonauthoritative	4.1	3.2	28	5.9	2.9	29	6.6	3.0	26

higher than those with high test anxiety ($M = 4.98$, $SD = 3.42$), $p < .001$. There were no significant interactions.

A final developmental comparison was made by examining the consistency with which participants in each grade gave the logically correct complete falsification solution. Based on the consistency criterion of 6 out of 10 complete falsification solutions used previously to indicate the attainment of formal reasoning (Foltz et al., 1995; Overton et al., 1987; Ward & Overton, 1990), 48% of sixth graders, 70% of tenth graders, and 80% of twelfth graders were categorized as formal deductive reasoners, a developmental progression consistent with the findings of Ward and Overton (1990). A test for the difference between two proportions indicated that both the twelfth grade ($z = 3.02$, $p < .001$), and tenth grade ($z = 2.04$, $p < .05$), contained more formal reasoners than did the sixth grade.

The formal reasoning criterion also was used to further examine the relationship between logical reasoning, parenting style, and test anxiety. Of adolescents with authoritative parents, 95% were rated as formal reasoners, compared to 53% of those with nonauthoritative parents, $z = 4.48$, $p < .001$. Of adolescents with low test anxiety, 82% reasoned at the formal level compared to 47% of those with high test anxiety, $z = 3.96$, $p < .001$.

There was no significant interaction between parenting style and test anxiety. In order to further examine the relationship between these variables, a one-way ANOVA was computed on the Test Anxiety Inventory scores of the four "pure" parenting style groups. In this sample, 43% of the families ($N = 51$) were characterized by "pure" parenting styles: authoritative ($n = 20$), authoritarian ($n = 9$), indulgent ($n = 7$), and neglectful ($n = 15$). There was a significant main effect, $F(3, 47) = 4.71$, $p < .01$. Tukey-Kramer post hoc comparisons revealed that adolescents with authoritative parents ($M = 31.1$, $SD = 7.6$) had signifi-

cantly less test anxiety than those with neglectful ($M = 43.4$, $SD = 8.8$) or indulgent parents ($M = 41.1$, $SD = 10.1$), $p < .05$. Differences between the group with authoritarian parents ($M = 34$, $SD = 8.4$) and the other groups were not significant.

Given that the predicted relationship between parenting style and test anxiety emerged only when the most discriminating, sample-reducing parenting style classification method was used, it is clear that a much larger sample is needed to fully test for the presence of the hypothesized interaction. Nevertheless, the fact that a significant relationship did emerge suggests that these variables may be correlated enough to make analysis by multiple regression preferable to that by ANOVA, because multiple regression is a method designed for such colinearity (Allison, Gorman, & Primavera, 1993). In order to test this possibility, a multiple regression was computed using general solution scores as the dependent variable, and grade,

TABLE 4 REGRESSION MODEL PREDICTING GENERAL SOLUTION SCORES

	Standardized		
	β weight	*B*	$t(116)$
Independent variable			
Grade	.20	1.43	2.65*
Parenting style	.39	4.94	5.02**
Test anxiety	−.26	−2.99	−3.25*
Summary statistics			
Multiple $R = .59$			
$R^2 = .35$			
$F(3, 116) = 20.56**$			

*$p < .01$. **$p < .001$.

parenting style, and test anxiety as the predictor variables (see Table 4).

Results of this analysis confirmed that grade ($\beta = .20$, $p < .01$), parenting style ($\beta = .39$, $p < .001$), and test anxiety ($\beta = -.26$, $p < .01$) did independently predict logical reasoning scores.

DISCUSSION

The results of this study support earlier findings that suggested logical reasoning, as measured with the selection task, improves across adolescence (Byrnes & Overton, 1988; Overton et al., 1987; Ward & Overton, 1990). As predicted, reasoning performance consistently improved from the sixth grade through the twelfth grade. Whereas less than half of early-adolescent sixth graders had attained formal reasoning status, a full 80% of late adolescent twelfth graders were categorized as formal reasoners. The use in this study of a sample that is representative ethnically suggests that this pattern of results will generalize well to a larger population, although the absence of any measure of SES may limit the external validity of this study.

The finding that almost all adolescents with authoritative parents were categorized as formal reasoners, compared to only half of those with nonauthoritative parents, suggests that authoritative parenting may consitute a context, a milieu in which adolescents are successfully encouraged to explore and expand their developing capacity for logical thought. These results are consistent with those of Baumrind (1991), Dornbusch, Ritter, Leiderman, Roberts, and Fraleigh (1987), and Steinberg, Lamborn, Dornbusch, and Darling (1992), who found that authoritative parenting was related to greater adolescent motivation to excel, and higher adolescent math and verbal achievement and school grade-point average than was less authoritative parenting. Further, these results provide support for the general Piagetian position that social factors play an important role in the process of individual cognitive development (Lourenço & Machado, 1996).

As predicted, adolescents with low test anxiety scored significantly higher on the selection task than did those with high test anxiety. This result suggests that test anxiety may degrade the effectiveness of processing procedures and strategies theorized to permit access to formal reasoning competence, according to the competence-procedure model of logical reasoning (Overton, 1990, 1991). Given that test anxiety diminishes the academic performance of an estimated 20% to 25% of all American elementary and secondary school students (Hill & Wigfield, 1984), the results of this study further suggest that investigations of adolescent deductive reasoning which do not take the negative effects of test anxiety into account may significantly underestimate reasoning performance in this population.

The finding that adolescents from authoritative families had less test anxiety than those from many nonauthoritative families generally supports the theory of Krohne (1980, 1990), and is consistent with previous research showing that authoritative parenting is related to less adolescent stress than nonauthoritative parenting (Baumrind, 1991; Lamborn et al., 1991; Steinberg et al., 1994). Because the relationship between parenting style and test anxiety emerged only when the most stringent, sample-reducing parenting style classification method was used, however, this finding should be regarded as tentative, and needs to be reexamined in a study with a much larger sample. Given that test anxiety has a serious negative impact on children beginning as early as the first grade, and peaks by the fourth grade (Hembree, 1988), future studies of the relationship between parenting styles and test anxiety should also include elementary school-age children.

In conclusion, the results of this study provide further support for the position that logical reasoning performance improves across adolescence. These results also suggest that authoritative parenting is related to more advanced reasoning performance and lower test anxiety than nonauthoritative parenting, and that low test anxiety is related to more advanced reasoning performance than high test anxiety.

REFERENCES

Allison, D. B., Gorman, B. S., & Primavera, L. H. (1993). Some of the most common questions asked of statistical consultants: Our favorite responses and recommended readings. *Genetic, Social, and General Psychology Monographs, 113*, 155–185.

Baumrind, D. (1967). Child care practices anteceding three patterns of preschool behavior. *Genetic Psychology Monographs, 75*, 43–88.

Baumrind, D. (1971). Current patterns of parental authority. *Developmental Psychology Monographs, 4*, 1–103.

Baumrind, D. (1991). The influence of parenting style on adolescent competence and substance use. *Journal of Early Adolescence, 11*, 56–95.

Beidel, D. C., & Turner, S. T. (1988). Comorbidity of test anxiety and other anxiety disorders in children. *Journal of Abnormal Child Psychology, 16*, 275–287.

Byrnes, J. P., & Overton, W. F. (1988). Reasoning about logical connectives: A developmental analysis. *Journal of Experimental Child Psychology, 46*, 194–218.

Cheng, P. W., & Holyoak, K. J. (1985). Pragmatic reasoning schemas. *Cognitive Psychology, 17*, 391–416.

Comunian, A. L. (1993). Anxiety, cognitive interference, and school performance of Italian children. *Psychological Reports, 73*, 747–754.

Darling, N., & Steinberg, L. (1993). Parenting style as context: An integrative model. *Psychological Bulletin, 113*, 487–496.

Denney, D. R. (1980). Self-control approaches to the treatment of test anxiety. In I. G. Sarason (Ed.), *Test anxiety: Theory, research and applications*. Hillsdale, NJ: Erlbaum.

DeVito, A. J. (1984). Test anxiety inventory. In D. J. Keyser & R. C. Sweetland (Eds.), *Test critiques*. New York: Test Corporation of America.

Dornbusch, S. M., Ritter, P. L., Leiderman, P. H., Roberts, D. F., & Fraleigh, M. J. (1987). The relation of parenting style to adolescent school performance. *Child Development, 58*, 1244–1257.

Foltz, C., Overton, W. F., & Ricco, R. B. (1995). Adolescent development from inductive to deductive problem solving strategies. *Journal of Experimental Child Psychology, 59*, 179–195.

Gray, W. G. (1990). Formal operational thought. In W. F. Overton (Ed.), *Reasoning, necessity, and logic: Developmental perspectives*. Hillsdale, NJ: Erlbaum.

Hembree, R. (1988). Correlates, causes, effects, and treatment of test anxiety. *Review of Educational Research, 58*, 47–77.

Hill, K. T. (1972). Anxiety in the evaluative context. In W. W. Hartup (Ed.), *The young child* (Vol. 2). Washington, DC: National Association for the Education of Young Children.

Hill, K. T. (1980). Motivation, evaluation, and educational testing policy. In L. J. Fyans (Ed.), *Achievement motivation: Recent trends in theory and research*. New York: Plenum.

Hill, K. T., & Wigfield, A. (1984). Test anxiety: A major educational problem and what can be done about it. *The Elementary School Journal, 85*, 105–121.

Jacobsen, T., Edelstein, W., & Hofmann, V. (1994). A longitudinal study of the relation between representations of attachment in childhood and cognitive functioning in childhood and adolescence. *Developmental Psychology, 30*, 112–124.

King, N. J., Mietz, A., Tinney, L., & Ollendick, T. H. (1995). Psychopathology and cognition in adolescents experiencing severe test anxiety. *Journal of Clinical Child Psychology, 24*, 49–54.

Krohne, H. W. (1980). Parental childrearing behavior and the development of anxiety and coping strategies in children. In I. G. Sarason & C. D. Spielberger (Eds.), *Stress and anxiety* (Vol. 7). Washington, DC: Hemisphere.

Krohne, H. W. (1990). Parental childrearing and anxiety development. In K. Hurrelmann & F. Losel (Eds.), *Health hazards in adolescence*. Berlin: Walter de Gruyter.

Krohne, H. W. (1992). Developmental conditions of anxiety and coping: A two-process model of child-rearing effects. In K. A. Hagtvet & T. B. Johnsen (Eds.), *Advances in test anxiety research: Vol. 7*. Lisse: Swets & Zeitlinger.

Lamborn, S., Mounts, N., Steinberg, L., & Dornbusch, S. (1991). Patterns of competence and adjustment among adolescents from authoritative, authoritarian, indulgent, and neglectful homes. *Child Development, 62*, 1049–1065.

Lourenço, O., & Machado, A. (1996). In defense of Piaget's theory: A reply to 10 common criticisms. *Psychological Review, 103*, 143–164.

Maccoby, E. D., & Martin, J. A. (1983). Socialization in the context of the family: Parent-child interaction. In P. H.

Mussen (Series Ed.) & E. M. Hetherington (Vol. Ed.), *Handbook of child psychology: Vol. 4. Socialization, personality, and social development* (4th ed.). New York: Wiley.

Mueller, U., Reene, K., & Overton, W. F. (1994, June). *Rasch-scaling of a deductive reasoning task*. Paper presented at the meeting of the Jean Piaget Society, Chicago, IL.

Neimark, E. D. (1975). Longitudinal development of formal operations thought. *Genetic Psychology Monographs, 91*, 171–225.

Niaz, M. (1991). Correlates of formal operational reasoning: A neo-Piagetian analysis. *Journal of Research in Science Teaching, 28*, 19–40.

Overton, W. F. (1990). Competence and procedures: Constraints on the development of logical reasoning. In W. F. Overton (Ed.) *Reasoning, necessity, and logic: Developmental perspectives*. Hillsdale, NJ: Erlbaum.

Overton, W. F. (1991). Competence, procedures, and hardware: Conceptual and empirical considerations. In M. Chapman & M. Chandler (Eds.), *Criteria for competence: Controversies in the assessment of children's abilities*. Hillsdale, NJ: Erlbaum.

Overton, W. F. (1994). Contexts of meaning: The computational and the embodied mind. In W. F. Overton & D. S. Palermo (Eds.), *The nature and ontogenesis of meaning*. Hillsdale, NJ: Erlbaum.

Overton, W. F., Byrnes, J. P., & O'Brien, D. P. (1985). Developmental and individual differences in conditional reasoning: The role of contradiction training and cognitive style. *Developmental Psychology, 21*, 692–701.

Overton, W. F., & Meehan, A. M. (1982). Individual differences in formal operational thought: Sex role and learned helplessness. *Child Development, 53*, 1536–1543.

Overton, W. F., Ward, S. L., Noveck, I. A., Black, J., & O'Brien, D. P. (1987). Form and content in the development of deductive reasoning. *Developmental Psychology, 23*, 22–30.

Piaget, J. (1928). *Judgment and reasoning of the child*. New York: Harcourt Brace Jovanovich.

Piaget, J. (1972). Intellectual evolution from adolescence to adulthood. *Human Development, 15*, 1–12.

Pollack, R. D., Overton, W. F., Rosenfeld, A., & Rosenfeld, R. (1995). Formal reasoning in late adulthood: The role of semantic content and metacognitive strategy. *Journal of Adult Development, 2*, 1–14.

Prins, P. J. M., Groot, M. J. M., & Hanewald, G. J. F. P. (1994). Cognition in test-anxious children: The role of on-task and coping cognition reconsidered. *Journal of Consulting and Clinical Psychology, 62*, 404–409.

Reene, K. J., & Overton, W. F. (1989, April). *Longitudinal investigation of adolescent deductive reasoning*. Paper presented at the meeting of the Society for Research in Child Development, Kansas City, MO.

Sarason, I. G. (1978). The Test Anxiety Scale: Concept and research. In C. D. Spielberger & I. G. Sarason (Eds.), *Stress and anxiety* (Vol. 5). Washington, DC: Hemisphere.

Spielberger, C. D. (1980). *Preliminary professional manual for the Test Anxiety Inventory (TAI)*. Palo Alto, CA: Consulting Psychologists Press.

Steinberg, L., Lamborn, S. D., Darling, N., Mounts, N. S., & Dornbusch, S. M. (1994). Over-time changes in adjustment and competence among adolescents from authoritative, authoritarian, indulgent, and neglectful families. *Child Development, 65*, 754–770.

Steinberg, L., Lamborn, S. D., Dornbusch, S. M., & Darling, N. (1992). Impact of parenting practices on adolescent achievement: Authoritative parenting, school involvement, and encouragement to succeed. *Child Development, 63*, 1266–1281.

Steinberg, L., Mounts, N., Lamborn, S., & Dornbusch, S. (1991). Authoritative parenting and adolescent adjustment across varied ecological niches. *Journal of Research on Adolescence, 1*, 19–36.

Takahashi, M., & Overton, W. F. (1996). Formal reasoning in Japanese older adults: The role of metacognitive strategy, task content, and social factors. *Journal of Adult Development, 3*, 81–91.

Tryon, G. S. (1980). The measurement and treatment of test anxiety. *Review of Educational Research, 50*, 343–372.

Ward, S. L., & Overton, W. F. (1990). Semantic familiarity, relevance, and the development of deductive reasoning. *Developmental Psychology, 26*, 488–493.

Wine, J. (1971). Test anxiety and direction of attention. *Psychological Bulletin, 76*, 92–104.

Wine, J. (1981). Evaluation anxiety: A cognitive-attentional construct. In H. W. Krohne & L. Laux (Eds.), *Achievement, stress, and anxiety*. New York: Hemisphere.

Zatz, S., & Chassin, L. (1985). Cognitions of test-anxious children under naturalistic test-taking conditions. *Journal of Consulting and Clinical Psychology, 53*, 393–401.

QUESTIONS

1. What are the four basic child rearing styles described by Maccoby and Martin?
2. Why is authoritative parenting hypothesized to be the most supportive style for cognitive development during adolescence?
3. What is test anxiety and why does it have a negative effect on performance?
4. What type of cognition or thinking was tested in this study and how was it assessed?
5. Who had the least test anxiety among the adolescents in the sample?
6. What do these results suggest about cognitive development and intellectual performance during the adolescent years?

31

Authority, Autonomy, and Parent–Adolescent Conflict and Cohesion: A Study of Adolescents from Mexican, Chinese, Filipino, and European Backgrounds

ANDREW J. FULIGNI

Adolescents and their parents often have conflict over the adolescent's bids for independence or autonomy. An adolescent may want to do something, but his or her parents may feel that the youth is not yet ready to do it. Because cultures have different values and expectations about adolescent independence and its development, it may be that adolescent–parent conflict about the adolescent's bids for independence has a different timing or course in different cultural communities.

Andrew J. Fuligni investigated this hypothesis by comparing adolescent–parent conflict in European-American families where independence is heavily emphasized with adolescent–parent conflict in three other cultural communities in the United States in which independence is not as heavily emphasized. This study involved a very large sample of high school students. The students were asked about their beliefs and expectations for autonomy and the amount of conflict they have with their parents around this issue.

The results reveal interesting relations between ethnicity, generational status, adolescent gender, and parent–adolescent conflict regarding autonomy. This research is a good example of how the family context and culture mediate adolescent development.

This study examined whether parent–child conflict and cohesion during adolescence vary among families characterized as having different cultural traditions regarding parental authority and individual autonomy. Approximately 1,000 American adolescents from immigrant and native-born families with Mexican, Chinese, Filipino, and European backgrounds reported on their beliefs, expectations, and relationships with parents; longitudinal data were available for approximately 350 of these youths. Despite holding different beliefs about parental authority and individual autonomy, adolescents from all generations and cultural backgrounds reported similar levels of conflict and cohesion with their parents. Discussion focuses on the relative

Reprinted by permission of the authors and the American Psychological Association from *Developmental Psychology*, 34 (1998), pp. 782–792. Copyright © 1998 by the American Psychological Association.

This article is based in part on a doctoral dissertation submitted by Andrew J. Fuligni to the University of Michigan. Portions of this article were presented at meetings of the Society for Research in Child Development, 1995, and the Society for Research on Adolescence, 1994. Support for this research has been provided by the William T. Grant Foundation and the Horace H. Rackham Graduate School at the University of Michigan.

I would like to thank those who assisted with the collection and processing of the data as well as the schools and their students for their participation. I am also grateful to David Almeida for reading an earlier version of the article.

Correspondence concerning this article should be addressed to Andrew J. Fuligni, Department of Psychology, New York University, New York, New York 10003.

importance of cultural beliefs and social settings in shaping the nature of parent–child relationships during adolescence.

In recent years, the prevailing portrait of parent–adolescent relationships has moved from an emphasis on an inevitable estrangement to a view that families adjust and maintain their relationships to accommodate the increasingly mature adolescent. Despite the shift in emphasis, developmentalists have consistently seen changes in parent–child conflict and cohesion as being associated with the critical development of adolescent autonomy. If these changes are indeed tied to autonomy, then parent–child relationships during adolescence may have an important cultural basis. To the extent that individual autonomy varies as a developmental imperative among cultural groups, the occurrence of parent–adolescent conflict and cohesion may also differ. Yet it is unclear whether this would be the case within a single society, especially if the dominant social settings do not support the maintenance of traditional cultural norms of adolescent autonomy and parental authority.

The majority of research on the changes in parent–child relationships during adolescence has been conducted with American families of European origin. Results suggest that the transition into adolescence introduces a certain amount of disruption into the relationships between children and their parents (Collins & Russell, 1991; Paikoff & Brooks-Gunn, 1991). In particular, small to moderate increases in conflict and declines in cohesion between children and their parents have been reported in many studies, though the findings regarding conflict tend to be less consistent than those regarding cohesion (see Laursen & Collins, 1994, for a discussion of this issue). Most of the increase in conflict, when documented, tends to be between adolescents and their mothers, whereas a decline in cohesion may occur most often between adolescents and their fathers (Collins & Russell, 1991; Steinberg, 1990). Evidence for differences according to the gender of the child is unclear.

The changes in parent–child relationships are thought to be instigated by adolescents' growing desire to increase their sense of autonomy and independence. Children become less satisfied with parents' authority over their personal lives and activities as they enter adolescence (Smetana, 1988). At the same time, they become more willing to openly disagree with their parents, which may lead to heightened conflict (Youniss & Smollar, 1985). Many of these contentious exchanges concern parents' regulation of adolescents' everyday lives, such as curfew rules and monitoring adolescents' activities with friends (Collins & Russell, 1991; Smetana, 1988). The early to middle adolescent years represent a time of heightened orientation toward peers, and children of this age often desire less parental control over their lives so that they can increase their involvement with their friends (Steinberg & Silverberg, 1986).

Despite the disruptions during early to middle adolescence, most parents and adolescents avoid the stormy estrangement that was once thought to be inevitable. A majority of adolescents provide a generally positive assessment of their relationships with their parents (Hill & Holmbeck, 1986). After middle adolescence, conflict begins to decline through late adolescence (Laursen & Collins, 1994). Although perhaps not as dependent on their parents as they were earlier in life, older adolescents still see their parents as their primary sources of support and advice regarding important aspects of their lives such as schooling and future employment (Douvan & Adelson, 1966).

Considering these latter findings, many developmentalists interpret the disruptions during early to middle adolescence as the beginning of a transformation of parent–child relationships that is necessary for healthy adolescent development. Together, modest amounts of conflict and emotional distancing help to transform parent–child relationships from the parent-dominated quality of childhood to a more egalitarian and interdependent quality of adulthood (Collins, 1990). If they are not excessive, disagreements with parents enable adolescents to form and argue for their own ideas and opinions (Cooper, 1988). Although complete detachment from parents is clearly not advantageous (Ryan & Lynch, 1989), establishing a degree of independence within continued supportive parent–child relationships is thought to be the most conducive process for healthy adolescent development (Grotevant & Cooper, 1986).

The findings and interpretations of parent–adolescent relationships within European American families pose an interesting question. If parent–child conflict and emotional distancing are a function of the development of adolescents' autonomy, would they occur within families in which individual autonomy has traditionally not been as important a task of adolescent development? Through a dramatic rise in immigration in the last 30 years, the United States has an increasing number of families from cultures that have traditionally placed a different emphasis on individual autonomy. The three largest immigrant groups—those with Mexican, Chinese, and Filipino backgrounds—have all been characterized as possessing traditions of respecting parental authority and downplaying individual autonomy in the service of family cohesion and solidarity. Many observers have cited the existence of these norms within Mexican and Chinese families, emphasizing the importance of parent–child hierarchies and the obligations of children to their families (e.g., Chilman, 1993; Harrison, Wilson, Pine, Chan, & Buriel, 1990; Ho, 1981; Shon & Ja, 1982).

Although little has been written about the nature of Filipino families, the few scholars who have described these families highlight a deference to authority, a desire to avoid confrontation, and an emphasis on family commitment and cohesion (Uba, 1994).

Empirical studies have rarely been conducted to determine whether families indeed hold these values and whether these beliefs influence members' relationships with one another (Harrison et al., 1990). Yet if Mexican, Chinese, and Filipino families do downplay individual autonomy, then this norm may have particular relevance for the nature of parent–child relationships during adolescence. If the value of individual autonomy contributes to the moderate disruptions in European American family relationships, then the deemphasis of adolescent autonomy within these other cultural groups may lead to smaller increases in conflict and emotional distancing. This is because the extent to which individual autonomy is endorsed should influence specific beliefs and expectations that can affect the ways in which adolescents and their parents relate to one another.

First, the value of individual autonomy can have important implications for adolescents' beliefs about parental authority. When autonomy is emphasized, children begin to question the purview of parental authority as they enter adolescence. A strong sense of family obligation coupled with a firm family hierarchy, however, leads to a great respect for parental authority (Harrison et al., 1990). For example, the hierarchical relationship between parents and children in many Chinese families traditionally should remain much the same through adolescence and adulthood, in part because of Confucian principles that dictate children should obey their parents their entire lives (Ho, 1981). Mexican and Filipino families also emphasize the importance of respecting the purview of parental authority, though perhaps not as strongly as traditional Chinese families (Chilman, 1993; Uba, 1994).

Second, adolescents' respect for parental authority may influence their willingness to disagree with their parents' wishes. The existence of a firm parent–child hierarchy may result in adolescents possessing less of an inclination to openly disagree and argue with their parents. In addition, maintaining family harmony is a traditional norm in many groups that deemphasize individualism. Observers have suggested that in many Asian families, including those with Chinese and Filipino backgrounds, differences and disagreements between members should be downplayed in favor of family harmony (Shon & Ja, 1982). Although an emphasis on harmony has not been as commonly used to describe Mexican families, the importance placed on the family hierarchy may result in adolescents being less willing to openly contradict their parents (Chilman, 1993; Harrison et al., 1990).

Finally, the relative importance of individual autonomy and parental authority within families should influence the ages at which adolescents are allowed to engage in autonomous behaviors. At the ages that these behaviors are perceived to be appropriate, adolescents and their parents engage in a negotiation of these new freedoms that can sometimes lead to contentious interactions (Steinberg, 1990). In a culture that stresses family obligation over individual freedom, behavioral autonomy may not be granted until quite late. Feldman and colleagues (Feldman & Quatman, 1988; Feldman & Rosenthal, 1990, 1991) found that Chinese adolescents in both Hong Kong and the United States expected to be able to engage in a variety of behaviors such as attending parties at night and choosing their own friends at a later age compared with European American adolescents. It remains to be seen whether the autonomy expectations of adolescents in Mexican and Filipino families are also later than those of their European American peers.

Together, the beliefs and norms that tend to be associated with the value of individual autonomy may influence the nature of parent–adolescent relationships. An endorsement of parental authority and a reticence to openly disagree with parents, along with later expected ages for behavioral autonomy, may lead to less parent–child conflict and distancing. Yet it is uncertain whether this would indeed be the case. The links between beliefs and actions are not always strong (Eagly & Chaiken, 1993), and it is possible that cultural ideas regarding parental authority and individual autonomy have only a modest connection to the amount of conflict and cohesion between adolescents and their parents.

The role of beliefs regarding authority and autonomy in parent–adolescent relationships may depend on the extent to which they are supported by the social settings of the larger society. Some investigators have suggested that the most significant way societies and cultures can influence development is through the settings in which children are placed (Whiting & Edwards, 1988). In the United States, family members often spend substantial amounts of time apart from one another, with the parents and children either working or attending school outside of the home (Csikszentmihalyi & Larson, 1984; Larson, 1983). Adolescents also find many opportunities to socialize with friends and engage in other activities beyond the purview of parents and other adults (Fuligni & Stevenson, 1995). These social settings may leave adolescents and their parents unable to maintain relationships that would be consistent with their traditional norms of authority and autonomy. For example, the existence of an independent peer culture in the United States may result in lower levels of closeness between family members than would be expected from the importance that they place on family cohesion and togetherness. Adolescents' desire to pursue activities with their peers may end up creating conflict with their mothers and fathers even if adolescents believe it is generally inappropriate to openly disagree with their parents.

The dissonance between traditional cultural values and American society can be particularly salient for the children of immigrant families (Portes & Rumbaut, 1996). These children are often more immersed within American culture than their parents through their exposure to peers and their experiences in school (Gibson, 1991). Children and adolescents are often asked by their parents to help the parents negotiate American society, seemingly disrupting the traditional hierarchies within these families (Suarez-Orozco & Suarez-Orozco, 1995; Sung, 1987). As a result, cultural norms may change, and adolescents' beliefs and expectations about autonomy and authority may vary according to their families' exposure to American society. For example, foreign-born adolescents may emphasize parental authority over individual autonomy more than those who were born in the United States. Similarly, among the native born, those whose parents were immigrants may hold traditional values more strongly than those whose parents were born and raised in the United States. The extent to which these differences in beliefs are associated with generational variations in parent–adolescent relationships remains to be seen.

This study was designed to examine whether American adolescents with varying cultural traditions regarding authority and autonomy evidence different developmental changes in their relationships with their parents. With the use of both cross-sectional and longitudinal data, the beliefs about parental authority and parent–child disagreement, as well as the expectations for behavioral autonomy among adolescents from immigrant and native-born families with Mexican, Chinese, Filipino, and European backgrounds, were examined. The developmental progressions of perceived conflict and cohesion with parents were also examined to determine if they varied across the different ethnic and generational groups, and whether they were associated with adolescents' beliefs and expectations regarding authority and autonomy.

METHOD

SAMPLE

Cross-Sectional Sample Participating students attended the 10th grade of two high schools, and the 6th and 8th grades of two middle schools that fed into these high schools in an ethnically diverse California school district. Approximately 84% of the

TABLE 1 SAMPLE ACCORDING TO ETHNIC BACKGROUND, GRADE, AND GENDER

| Ethnic background | Grade | | | | | | |
| | 6th | | 8th | | 10th | | |
	M	F	M	F	M	F	Total
Mexican	24	16	20	18	36	54	168
Chinese	18	23	24	26	23	34	148
Filipino	66	54	59	73	74	77	403
European	39	41	39	38	59	63	279
Total	147	134	142	155	192	228	998

Note. M = males; F = females.

enrolled students participated in the study, yielding a total sample of 1,341 adolescents; 10% of the students were absent on the day of the study, 4% declined to participate or did not have parental permission, and 2% were excluded because of learning or language difficulties.

Students completed self-reported questionnaires that were administered during social studies classes near the end of the school year. In addition to answering questions regarding their beliefs about parental authority and their relationships with their parents, adolescents were asked to indicate their ethnic background. The present study included the 998 students with Mexican, Chinese, Filipino, and European backgrounds. As shown in Table 1, the sample was fairly evenly divided according to adolescents' gender (male = 48%; female = 52%) and was reasonably distributed across the three grade levels (Grade 6, n = 281; Grade 8, n = 297; Grade 10, n = 420). The mean years of age of the students at each grade level were 12.1 (Grade 6), 14.2 (Grade 8), and 16.2 (Grade 10).

Adolescents were also asked to indicate whether they and their parents were born in the United States. With this information, students were classified as being first generation (neither the students nor their parents were born in this country), second generation (the students were born in the United States, but one of their parents was not), or third generation or greater (the students and both of their parents were born in this country). As shown in Table 2, the entire sample included a good distribution of the three generations of students. Not surprisingly, this distribution varied according to adolescents' ethnic background. The majority of the Mexican, Chinese, and Filipino students had immigrant parents, whereas few students of European backgrounds indicated being of these two generations. First-generation adolescents

TABLE 2 SAMPLE ACCORDING TO ETHNIC BACKGROUND AND GENERATION

Ethnic background	Generation			Total
	First	Second	≥ Third	
Mexican	23	70	64	157
Chinese	35	72	37	144
Filipino	152	213	27	392
European	15	39	210	264
Total	225	394	338	957

Note. Forty-one students did not provide adequate information to establish their generational status.

came to the United States at a variety of ages, with the average being 7.1 years.

Consistent with both national and local figures, greater percentages of the Chinese and Filipino students than Mexican and European students had mothers who worked outside the home (84% and 91% vs. 79% and 78%, respectively). In addition, Filipino mothers worked in the highest status occupations, whereas Mexican mothers held the lowest status jobs (e.g., 49% vs. 17%, respectively, in semiprofessional and professional occupations). Among the Chinese students, 43% of mothers held these occupations compared with 33% of the students with European backgrounds. Although the fathers of all of the adolescents were employed at equal rates, the fathers of the Mexican students worked in lower level occupations than the fathers of the students with Chinese, Filipino, and European backgrounds (22% vs. 43%, 38%, and 33%, respectively, in semiprofessional and professional occupations).

Adolescents from the four ethnic groups also varied in terms of the marital status of their parents. The biological parents of Chinese and Filipino students were more likely to be married than the parents of students with Mexican and European backgrounds (82% and 74% vs. 58% and 65%, respectively).

Longitudinal Subsample Within the large cross-sectional sample described above, a subsample of 353 students in the 8th and 10th grades completed identical questionnaires 2 years previously when they were in the 6th and 8th grades, respectively. Adolescents from all four ethnic backgrounds were represented in this subsample, though this group contained a smaller proportion of Mexican students (9% vs. 21%) and greater proportions of Chinese and Filipino students (20% vs. 12% and 47% vs. 37%, respectively) than the rest of the larger, cross-sectional sample. In addition, adolescents in the longitudinal subsample were more likely to have parents in semiprofessional

and professional occupations (e.g., mothers, 46% vs. 35%). The availability of panel data for this subsample allowed for the comparison of the cross-sectional results regarding grade differences in beliefs and relationships with longitudinal estimates of true developmental change. Because of the small size of this subsample, reliable estimates of change could be obtained only according to the four different ethnic groups. The greater power of larger cross-sectional sample was relied on to make estimates of developmental patterns for more specific subgroups of students (e.g., according to gender and generation within each ethnic group).

MEASURES

Beliefs and Expectations about Authority and Autonomy

Acceptability of disagreement with parents. A new measure was created for this study to assess adolescents' beliefs about the appropriateness of openly disagreeing with parents. Using a scale ranging from *almost never* (1) to *almost always* (5), students responded separately for mothers and fathers to three questions: "I should argue with my mother [father] when I disagree with her [him]," "It is OK for me to talk back to my mother [father]," and "If I am mad at my mother [father], I should tell her [him] so." The measure possessed acceptable internal consistencies for both the father and mother versions (αs: father = .77, mother = .67). It was also of similar reliability for the adolescents from all four ethnic groups (ranges: father = .75 – .80, mother = .62 – .69).

Endorsement of parental authority. Adolescents' beliefs about the legitimacy of parental authority were tapped using a measure from Smetana's (1988) studies of adolescents' reasoning about parent – child relationships. Students were presented with a list of 11 topics, such as dating, curfew, and choosing friends, and they were asked whether it was "OK" or "not OK" for their parents to make a rule about it. The number of items to which students indicated "OK" was then summed to yield a total score. The measure possessed marginal, but acceptable internal consistency for all four ethnic groups of students (αs: overall = .68, range = .63 – .77). The 11 topics were also divided into three domains according to Smetana's classification. The first domain, personal, included the topics of sleeping late on weekends, talking on the phone, and watching television. The conventional domain included doing chores, keeping parents informed of activities, calling them by their first names, and cleaning up after a party. The third domain, multifaceted, encompassed the topics of how to dress, going out with friends instead of the family, which friends with whom to socialize, and cleaning one's room.

Expectations for behavioral autonomy. Adolescents' expectations for when they would be allowed to engage in various autonomous behaviors were measured in this study by the same scale used by Feldman and her associates in their studies of Chinese adolescents in Hong Kong and the United States (Feldman & Quatman, 1988; Feldman & Rosenthal, 1990). Students were presented with a list of 14 behaviors, such as "watch as much TV as you want," "go to parties at night," and "do things with your friends rather than with your family." Adolescents then indicated the age at which they expected to be allowed to do each thing using a 5-point scale indicating particular ages, such as 1 (*before 14 years old*), 3 (*16–17 years old*), and 5 (*never be allowed to*). If adolescents were already engaging in any behavior, they indicated the age at which they were first allowed to engage in it. The measure possessed high internal consistency for all four ethnic groups (αs: overall = .85, range = .85–.86).

Perceived Conflict and Cohesion with Parents

Conflict. Adolescents' perception of conflict with their parents was measured using the Issues Checklist (IC), developed by Prinz, Foster, Kent, and O'Leary (1979) and Robin and Foster (1984). This measure was selected so that the results could be compared with those obtained by Steinberg (1987, 1988) in previous research on the impact of puberty and the transition to early adolescence on parent–child relationships. Students indicated whether any of 12 specific topics (e.g., spending money, chores, and cursing) were discussed with their mother and father in the last 2 weeks. For each topic that was discussed, the intensity of the discussion was rated from *very calm* (1) to *very angry* (5). For consistency with previous research (i.e., Steinberg, 1987), a measure of the incidence of parent–adolescent conflict was computed by summing the number of discussions rated as containing anger (2 or greater). Students completed two versions of the checklist, one in reference to each parent. This scale possessed good internal consistencies (αs: father = .82, mother = .77) and similar reliability for the adolescents from all four ethnic groups (ranges: father = .72–.85, mother = .67–.80).

Other researchers using this measure have scored the IC by computing the mean response across the different items (where 0 = *no discussion* and 5 = *very angry discussion*) to better reflect the level of intensity in the discussions (e.g., Galambos & Almeida, 1992). In the present study, scores obtained with this method of scoring were so similar to those resulting from the incidence scoring described above (rs = .91 and .92) that analyses were not repeated with this intensity method of scoring.

Cohesion. Students completed the cohesion subscale of the Family Adaptation and Cohesion Evaluation Scales II inventory separately for each parent (Olson, Sprenkle, & Russell, 1979). Using a scale ranging from *almost never* (1) to *almost always* (5), students responded to 10 questions such as "My mother [father] and I feel very close to each other," "My mother [father] and I are supportive of each other during difficult times," and "My mother [father] and I avoid each other at home" (reverse-scored). This scale has also been used in previous research on the changes in parent–child relationships during adolescence (Steinberg, 1987, 1988). This scale possessed good overall internal consistencies (αs: father = .85, mother = .83) and was equally reliable for the adolescents from all four ethnic backgrounds (ranges: father = .83–.88, mother = .82–.86).

RESULTS

ANALYSIS PLAN

The size of the cross-sectional sample allowed for a series of multifactor analyses of variance (ANOVAs) to examine (a) ethnic, grade, and gender differences in adolescents' beliefs and relationships (Ethnicity × Grade × Gender); (b) differences according to adolescents' generational status and whether these differences varied by grade and gender (Generation × Grade × Gender); and (c) whether generational differences could account for any observed ethnic differences and whether generational differences varied according to adolescents' ethnic background (Ethnicity × Grade × Gender, with the addition of generation and Generation × Ethnicity). For the analyses listed in (c), generation was dummy-coded and treated as a covariate because its high correlation with ethnicity prohibited treating it as a categorical main effect in the ANOVAs. Because of the skewed nature of adolescents' reports of conflict with their parents, analyses were conducted on the log of those variables. Within-subject ANOVAs were also conducted, when appropriate, to compare reported beliefs and relationships regarding mothers with those regarding fathers. Because of the large sample size and the number of analyses that were conducted, results were considered significant at the $p < .01$ level.

The cross-sectional analyses were followed by Ethnicity × Time × Cohort (6th–8th-grade cohort vs. 8th–10th-grade cohort) repeated measures ANOVAs of the longitudinal subsample to determine whether the cross-sectional findings regarding grade differences were supported by longitudinal findings of true developmental change. Because of the smaller size of this subsample, reliable estimates of change could only be obtained at the level of students' ethnic background, and the significance criterion was set at $p < .05$.

Adolescents' socioeconomic background, which was the mean of their parents' educational and occupational levels, was unassociated with students' beliefs and their reports of their relationships with their parents. Those whose biological parents were separated, divorced, or remarried indicated a greater willingness to disagree with their fathers and reported greater conflict and less cohesion with their fathers than those whose parents were married. Nevertheless, controlling for marital status did not change the observed results; neither did marital status interact with ethnicity in any analyses. Therefore, the results reported in this article are from analyses conducted without controlling for the demographic differences between the four groups of students.

For the sake of clarity, the results within each section are presented according to the predictor of interest (e.g., ethnic background) rather than according to the individual dependent variables. All results, however, are based on the multivariate analyses described above.

BELIEFS AND EXPECTATIONS ABOUT AUTHORITY AND AUTONOMY

Ethnic, Gender, and Grade Differences Adolescents from Mexican, Chinese, and Filipino backgrounds held beliefs and expectations consistent with a greater respect for parental authority and a lower emphasis on autonomy than their European American peers. As shown in Table 3, Filipino students were less willing to openly disagree with their mothers, and both Filipino and Mexican students were less willing to disagree with their fathers compared with European American students. Chinese adolescents possessed significantly later expectations for autonomy

than did their counterparts with European backgrounds. In terms of parental authority, however, adolescents from all four ethnic groups indicated a similar acceptance of the right of parents to make rules about various aspects of their lives. This ethnic similarity was evident for all three subdomains of parental authority. Within-subject analyses indicated that adolescents among all four ethnic groups endorsed parental authority over conventional topics more than over multifaceted topics, and they endorsed both of these domains more strongly than the personal domain, $F(2, 1812) = 343.86$, $p < .001$; Bonferroni contrasts, $ps < .001$. In addition, all adolescents were more willing to openly disagree with their mothers than with their fathers, $F(1, 902) = 10.07$, $p < .01$.

Girls of all ethnic backgrounds reported later expectations for autonomy than did boys (girls, $M = 2.53$; boys, $M = 2.36$), $F(1, 951) = 15.88$, $p < .001$. There were no other gender differences in adolescents' beliefs, and in no case did gender differences vary by students' ethnic background, $F(1, 906) = 0.15$ to $F(3, 959) = 4.72$, $ps > .01$.

Despite the overall ethnic variations in beliefs and expectations, the grade differences in these ideas were quite similar for the four groups of adolescents. As shown in Figures 1a and 1b, older adolescents reported a greater endorsement of disagreeing with both parents than did younger adolescents, $Fs(2, 906) = 12.52$, and $F(2, 951) = 17.85$, $ps < .001$. Bonferroni contrasts indicated that 10th-grade students reported a greater willingness to disagree with their mothers than did 6th and 8th-grade students, and a greater willingness to disagree with their fathers than did 6th-grade students ($ps < .001$). The figures suggest that the grade differences varied somewhat for Mexican students, but these variations were not great enough to attain significance, $F(6, 906) = 2.36$ to $F(6, 951) = 2.38$, $p > .01$.

TABLE 3 ADOLESCENTS' BELIEFS AND EXPECTATIONS ABOUT PARENTAL AUTHORITY AND INDIVIDUAL AUTONOMY

	Mexican (M)		Chinese (C)		Filipino (F)		European (E)		$F(3, 906)$ to $F(3, 951)$	Bonferroni contrasts
Belief	**M**	**SD**	**M**	**SD**	**M**	**SD**	**M**	**SD**		
Disagreement with mother	2.37	1.01	2.40	1.00	2.20	0.94	2.67	1.04	10.52**	E > F**
Disagreement with father	2.14	1.04	2.35	1.13	2.13	1.05	2.51	1.18	5.18*	E > M*, E > F**
Parental authority	5.17	2.43	5.58	2.61	5.23	2.18	5.39	2.18	1.21	
Behavioral autonomy	2.36	0.69	2.58	0.69	2.49	0.68	2.35	0.64	7.05**	C > E*

Note. Ns = 930–975. All were 5-point scales, except parental authority, which was 11-point.
*$p < .01$. **$p < .001$.

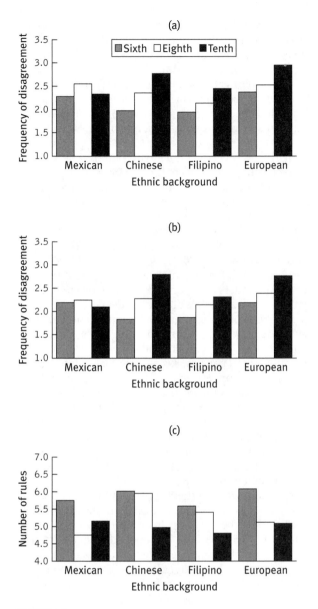

FIGURE 1

Adolescents' willingness to openly disagree with (a) mothers and (b) fathers, and (c) their endorsement of parental authority, according to grade and ethnicity.

Within each ethnic group, older adolescents were less likely than younger adolescents to accept parental authority over their lives, $F(2, 906) = 10.59$, $p < .001$. As shown in Figure 1c, 10th-grade students indicated a significantly lower endorsement than 6th-grade students (Bonferroni contrast, $p < .001$). Analyses of the different topical domains, however, revealed that this grade difference was evident for the personal and multifaceted domains, $F(2, 929) = 13.23$ and $F(2, 959) = 21.72$, $ps < .001$, and not the conventional domain, $F(2, 939) = 1.95$, $p > .01$. These domain variations in

grade trends were also observed in the within-subject analyses comparing adolescents' endorsement of the different areas of parental authority. There was an interaction between domain and grade level such that tendency for adolescents to endorse parental authority over conventional topics more than other topics was greater at the 8th and 10th grades than at the 6th grade, $F(4, 1812) = 15.37$, $p < .001$. No grade differences emerged for adolescents' expectations for behavioral autonomy, $F(2, 951) = 4.29$, $p > .01$.

Longitudinal analyses generally supported the cross-sectional findings of developmental differences in adolescents' beliefs and expectations. All adolescents became more willing to disagree with their parents over time, $F(1, 310) = 17.63$ and $F(1, 332) = 11.20$, $ps < .001$. Unlike the cross-sectional results, however, adolescents' overall acceptance of parental authority did not change over time, $F(1, 321) = 0.63$, $p > .05$. This was due to the fact that adolescents' endorsement of authority over multifaceted issues did not change, $F(1, 315) = 1.55$, $p > .05$, whereas this domain demonstrated grade differences in the cross-sectional analyses. Longitudinal analyses concurred with the cross-sectional findings and showed that adolescents withdrew their endorsement of parental authority over personal topics as they became older, $F(1, 331) = 17.68$, $p < .001$. In addition, no change was observed in adolescents' endorsement of authority over conventional issues or in their expectations for autonomy, $F(1, 316) = 3.64$ and $F(1, 338) = 1.29$, $ps > .05$. None of these longitudinal patterns varied according to adolescents' ethnic background, $F(3, 315) = 0.08$ to $F(3, 310) = 1.91$, $ps < .01$.

Generation Differences   Adolescents of different generations varied on the same beliefs and expectations for which ethnic differences were observed. Students of later generations tended to be more willing to openly disagree with their parents and had earlier expectations for autonomy than did those of earlier generations, $F(2, 875) = 8.83$ and $F(2, 915) = 21.62$, $ps < .001$. Specifically, members of the third generation were more willing to disagree with their mothers ($M = 2.64$) than members of the second generation ($M = 2.36$), and both groups reported greater willingness than first-generation adolescents ($M = 2.05$); Bonferroni contrasts, $ps < .001$. Third-generation adolescents were more willing to disagree with their fathers ($M = 2.48$) than were members of the earlier generations (Ms: first = 2.03; second = 2.22), $ps < .01–.001$. Finally, foreign-born adolescents expected later behavioral autonomy ($M = 2.69$) compared with members of the second ($M = 2.41$) and third ($M = 2.31$) generations ($p < .001$). Adolescents' endorsement of parental authority did not vary according to generation, nor did any of the observed generational differences vary according to gender or grade level, $F(2, 844) = 0.13$ and $F(4, 923) = 3.96$, $ps > .01$. The relations between adolescents' generation and their beliefs and expectations also did not vary across the four ethnic groups, $F(3, 880) = 0.13$ to $F(3, 901) = 2.64$, $ps > .01$.

Controlling for generational status reduced the previously observed ethnic variations in adolescents' willingness to disagree with parents and expectations for autonomy so that they became no longer significant, $F(3, 867) = 1.98$ and $F(3, 907) = 2.74$, $ps > .01$. These reductions ranged from a 59% to a 78% change in the variance accounted for by adolescents' ethnic background (e.g., partial eta^2 = .007 vs. .032). Among first-generation adolescents, the age at which they emigrated to the United States was related only to their expectations for autonomy. After controlling for grade level, those who had arrived in this country early in life expected behavioral autonomy at earlier ages ($r = .27$, $p < .001$).

PERCEIVED CONFLICT AND COHESION WITH PARENTS

Ethnic, Gender, and Grade Differences   Unlike the findings regarding adolescents' beliefs and expectations, results indicated no significant variations in reported conflict and cohesion according to students' ethnic background. As shown in Table 4, adolescents of all four ethnic groups reported similar amounts of conflict and cohesion with both mothers and fathers. Adolescents perceived generally low levels of conflict with both parents, though they indicated greater conflict with their mothers than their fathers, $F(1, 874) = 262.00$, $p < .001$.

Girls reported significantly less conflict ($Ms = 1.54$ vs. 2.19) and cohesion ($Ms = 2.81$ vs. 3.12) with their fathers and greater cohesion with their mothers ($Ms = 3.28$ vs. 3.14) than did boys, $F(1, 889) = 18.97$, $p < .001$ to $F(1, 963) = 12.32$, $p < .001$. Girls also reported greater cohesion with their mothers than with their fathers, whereas boys indicated a similar amount

for both parents: Adolescent Gender × Parent Gender Interaction, $F(1, 922) = 38.68$, $p < .001$. Gender differences in reported conflict and cohesion did not vary according to students' ethnic background.

Consistent with the ethnic similarity in the overall levels of conflict and cohesion, adolescents from all four ethnic backgrounds showed the same developmental patterns across the different age groups. All students, regardless of their grade level, reported a similarly low level of conflict with both mothers and fathers, $F(2, 889) = 0.83$ and $F(2, 935) = 0.65$, $ps > .01$ (see Figures 2a and 2b). Grade differences did emerge, however, in adolescents' feelings of cohesion with their parents. As shown in Figures 3a and 3b, older students of all ethnic backgrounds reported less cohesion with their mothers and fathers than did younger students, $F(2, 924) = 24.01$, $p < .001$ and $F(2, 963) = 10.67$, $p < .001$. Bonferroni contrasts indicated that 8th and 10th graders reported significantly lower cohesion with both parents than did 6th graders ($ps < .001$).

Analyses of the longitudinal sample generally replicated the cross-sectional findings regarding the developmental trends in conflict and cohesion. No change in conflict with parents was evident for adolescents of any ethnic group, $F(1, 307) = 1.15$, $p > .05$ and $F(1, 331) = 0.88$, $p > .05$. Furthermore, declines in cohesion with both parents were reported by all four groups of adolescents. There was a significant drop in feelings of closeness with father for both cohorts of longitudinal adolescents: time, $F(1, 318) = 20.13$, $p < .001$. Similar to the cross-sectional findings, the decline tended to be steeper between the 6th and 8th grades than between the 8th and 10th grades: Cohort × Time, $F(1, 318) = 4.94$, $p < .05$. In terms of cohesion with mother, there was again an overall decline: time, $F(1, 336) = 5.32$, $p < .05$. The only difference from the cross-sectional findings reported above was that the longitudinal analyses suggested a slight variation in the timing of the decline in feelings of cohesion with

---

TABLE 4   ADOLESCENTS' REPORTS OF CONFLICT AND COHESION WITH PARENTS

| Relationship dimension | Ethnic background | | | | | | | | $F(3, 889)$ to $F(3, 963)$ |
| | Mexican | | Chinese | | Filipino | | European | | |
	M	**SD**	**M**	**SD**	**M**	**SD**	**M**	**SD**	
Conflict with mother	3.09	2.40	2.78	2.42	3.15	2.50	2.70	2.07	1.81
Conflict with father	1.93	2.31	1.62	2.15	2.07	2.41	1.56	1.83	3.00
Cohesion with mother	3.22	0.81	3.13	0.75	3.18	0.73	3.31	0.84	2.32
Cohesion with father	2.93	0.88	2.99	0.82	2.92	0.84	3.02	0.98	1.16

Note. Ns = 913–987. Conflict with mother and father were 13-point (0-12) scales, whereas cohesion with mother and father were 5-point. Means and standard deviations for conflict are untransformed.

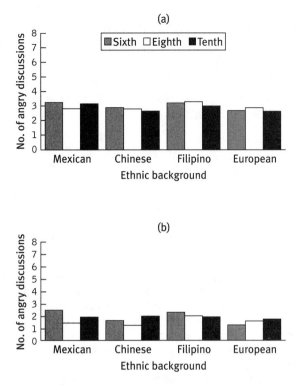

FIGURE 2

Adolescents' reports of conflict with (a) mothers and (b) fathers according to grade and ethnicity. No. = number.

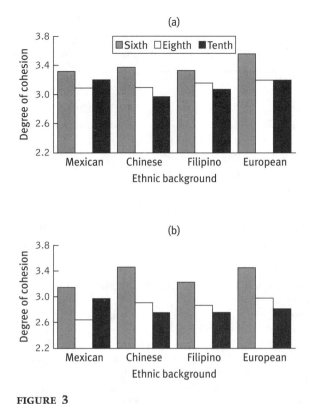

FIGURE 3

Adolescents' reports of cohesion with (a) mothers and (b) fathers according to grade and ethnicity.

mother between the ethnic groups: Ethnicity × Cohort × Time, $F(3, 336) = 2.75$, $p < .05$. A decline in feelings of closeness was evident between the 6th and 8th grades among Mexican, Filipino, and European students, whereas the drop only occurred between the 8th and 10th grades among Chinese students.

Generation Differences Along with the lack of ethnic differences, no significant effects of adolescents' generational status on their reported conflict and cohesion with parents emerged from the analyses, $F(2, 899) = 0.05$ to $F(2, 926) = 4.10$, $ps > .01$. Neither did the associations between generation and adolescents' relationships with their parents vary by ethnicity, grade, or gender, $F(2, 890) = 0.15$ to $F(3, 844) = 2.26$, $ps > .01$. Among first-generation students, their age of immigration was unrelated to their perceptions of conflict and cohesion with their parents.

ASSOCIATIONS AMONG BELIEFS, EXPECTATIONS, AND PERCEIVED RELATIONSHIPS

Cross-Sectional Relations Partial correlations of beliefs and expectations with perceived relationships, after controlling for grade level, are presented in

Table 5. Not surprisingly, adolescents who were more willing to disagree with their mothers and who were less likely to endorse parental authority indicated greater conflict with their mothers. None of the adolescents' beliefs and expectations were associated with their low level of conflict with their fathers. All of the beliefs and expectations were related to adolescents' feelings of cohesion with their mothers, and all but the adolescents' expectations for autonomy were associated with closeness with fathers. Those adolescents indicating less willingness to disagree with their parents, greater endorsement of parental authority, and later expectations for autonomy reported greater cohesion with their parents. Analyses of covariance revealed that these relatively modest associations did not vary according to adolescents' ethnic background, $F(3, 811) = 0.18$ to $F(3, 848) = 1.57$, $ps > .01$.

Longitudinal Relations Analyses were conducted with the longitudinal subsample to determine whether the changes in adolescents' beliefs and perceived relationships were associated with one another. Change scores were computed for each by regressing Time 2 measures on Time 1 measures and saving the residual scores as indicators of change. Results indicated significant associations only for

TABLE 5   PARTIAL CORRELATIONS OF BELIEFS AND EXPECTATIONS WITH PERCEIVED RELATIONSHIPS, CONTROLLING FOR GRADE LEVEL

	Relationship dimension			
Belief	Conflict with mother	Conflict with father	Cohesion with mother	Cohesion with father
Disagreement with mother	.10*		− .18*	
Disagreement with father		− .01		− .14*
Parental authority	− .13*	− .06	.23*	.18*
Behavioral autonomy	− .01	.05	.17*	.08

Note. Ns = 855–974.
*$p < .01$, significant with Bonferroni familywise error rate, set for each relationship dimension.

changes in adolescents' feelings of cohesion with their parents. As adolescents' willingness to disagree with their mothers increased and their endorsement of parental authority decreased, their feelings of cohesion with their mothers declined (rs = − .14 and .23, respectively; Bonferroni familywise ps < .05). Similarly, their closeness with their fathers decreased as their endorsement of parental authority dropped (r = .18; Bonferroni familywise p < .05).

DISCUSSION

Despite holding different beliefs about individual autonomy and parental authority, American adolescents from the various ethnic and generational backgrounds reported strikingly similar relationships with their parents. Teenagers from non-European and immigrant families tended to be the least willing to openly contradict their parents and possessed the latest expectations for autonomy. Yet these youths also indicated overall levels and developmental patterns of conflict and cohesion that mirrored those of their peers from European and native-born families. These findings suggest that within a single society, cultural variations in beliefs about autonomy and authority may play only a modest role in parent–adolescent relationships. If particular beliefs are not supported by the social settings within a society, then they may have little effect on relationships and will gradually change to more closely approximate the norms of the dominant group.

As suggested by many observers, adolescents with non-European backgrounds held some beliefs and expectations consistent with a greater respect for parental authority and less of an emphasis on individual autonomy than their European American peers. Students with Filipino backgrounds indicated less

willingness to argue and talk back to their mothers, and they and students with Mexican backgrounds believed it was less acceptable to openly contradict their fathers than did their peers with European backgrounds. Chinese adolescents believed that they would be allowed to engage in autonomous activities such as going to parties and dating at a later age than did European American adolescents, as previously observed by Feldman & Quatman (1988). Generational variations also emerged in these beliefs and expectations regardless of adolescents' ethnic backgrounds. Adolescents with foreign-born parents tended to be the least willing to argue and talk back to their mothers and fathers. Teenagers who immigrated to the United States with their parents expected to be allowed to go to parties and out on dates at later ages than their native-born peers.

The patterns of ethnic and generational differences in adolescents' beliefs and expectations highlight the need for greater specificity in characterizations of Asian and Mexican families. The results suggest that although Filipino and Mexican adolescents believe it is inappropriate to argue with their parents, they still expect to receive behavioral autonomy at a fairly early age. The opposite appears to be the case for youths with Chinese backgrounds. These ethnic differences became nonsignificant after controlling for generational variations in beliefs and expectations, indicating that the ethnic differences may actually have been due to the large proportion of youths from immigrant families among the non-European groups. These findings suggest that descriptions of ethnic groups that rely on traditional aspects of their cultures may only apply to those families whose members actually originated in their home countries. Later generations who were born and raised within a different country may be more likely to hold beliefs and values that are consistent with the norms of the host society (Portes &

Rumbaut, 1996). In this case, the traditional norms of respecting parental authority and downplaying individual autonomy apply to only those Chinese, Filipino, and Mexican adolescents who come from immigrant families. Adolescents from native-born families are more likely to share the beliefs and expectations of their European American peers.

Although they differed from one another overall, members of the various ethnic and generational groups evidenced similar developmental trends in their ideas about authority and autonomy. As they became older, adolescents indicated a greater willingness to openly disagree with their parents and a lower endorsement of parental authority over aspects of their personal lives. These findings are consistent with theories and previous research on changes in children's conceptions of parent–child relationships during adolescence (e.g., Smetana, 1988; Youniss & Smollar, 1985). They suggest that even within groups that traditionally emphasize parental authority over individual autonomy, children become more desirous of limiting the purview of parental authority as they progress through the adolescent years.

Given the ethnic and generational differences in adolescents' beliefs and expectations, the similarity in the students' reports of conflict and cohesion with their parents was surprising. Adolescents of all backgrounds and ages reported a generally small amount of conflict with mothers and fathers. Regardless of their ethnicity and generation, older adolescents indicated less cohesion with their parents compared with younger adolescents. These consistencies across ethnic and generational groups were observed even with the statistical power provided by the large sample. The developmental patterns of cohesion have been observed in previous studies of adolescents from European backgrounds (e.g., Steinberg, 1987, 1988). Although the lack of change in conflict seems to contradict the prevailing view that parent–child conflict increases during early adolescence, evidence for an increase in the actual frequency of conflict has actually not been consistent in large-scale, nonintrusive studies (Galambos & Almeida, 1992; Laursen & Collins, 1994). The lack of an increase in this and similar studies may be due to the fact that children simply spend less time with parents during adolescence (Csikszentmihalyi & Larson, 1984; Larson, 1983). Therefore, even if adolescents become increasingly willing to disagree with their parents, they have fewer opportunities for conflictual interactions.

At the individual level, teenagers' beliefs about authority and autonomy were generally related to their reports of conflict and cohesion with their parents among all ethnic groups. For example, those more willing to disagree with their parents and less likely to endorse parental authority reported more conflict with their mothers and less cohesion with both parents than their peers. Adolescents' feelings of cohesion with their mothers declined as their willingness to disagree with their mothers increased, and their closeness with both parents dropped as their endorsement of parental authority declined. Yet, the modest magnitude of these associations suggests that beliefs about authority and autonomy alone do not explain adolescents' relationships with their parents during adolescence. In addition, the ethnic similarity in adolescents' reports of conflict and cohesion with their parents suggests that other factors may be of greater importance in determining the nature of parent–child relationships during adolescence.

Given the social settings of American society, it can be difficult for adolescents and their families to act in accordance with their traditional norms of parental authority and individual autonomy. American children begin to spend less time with their families and more time with their peers when they enter adolescence (Csikszentmihalyi & Larson, 1984). Teenage employment, despite some ethnic variations, is a common experience (Fine, Mortimer, & Roberts, 1990). These and other activities outside of the home may provide sufficient enjoyment, support, and resources to pull adolescents somewhat away from their parents. Activities during adolescence, particularly those involving peers, may also create situations that bring about disagreement and conflict between children and their parents. In contrast to the demands of these social settings, adolescents' beliefs regarding authority and autonomy may be simply statements of cultural ideals or individual desires that have only a minor association with their actual relationships with their parents.

The difficulty of maintaining traditional cultural norms is suggested by the generational differences observed in adolescents' beliefs and expectations. Within every non-European group, adolescents' beliefs and expectations changed so that they were similar to those of the European American majority by the third generation. It is unclear from this study what precisely brought about these generational changes. One possibility, suggested by the generational similarity in conflict and cohesion, is that the settings in American society have an immediate impact on the relationships within immigrant families and make it difficult for members to interact in a traditional manner. Family members' views regarding authority and autonomy may then change through the generations to be consistent with the reality of their relationships with one another and with the norms of the larger society. Additional research should explore the details of this acculturative process further by taking into account other important factors such as adolescents' day-to-day activities, the ethnic composition of their peer groups, and their feelings of cultural dissonance (Suarez-Orozco & Suarez-Orozco, 1995).

The lack of cultural differences in conflict and cohesion in this study suggests other directions for future research. First, the specific scales used in this study should be complemented by additional measures. For example, the Issues Checklist may not encompass the range of topics that create conflict in families of diverse cultural backgrounds. In addition, using the amount of anger in a discussion as the criteria for conflict may not be appropriate for all families. Nevertheless, a recent study in which adolescents were asked to simply report how often they argued with their parents about a broader range of issues also indicated similar amounts of conflict during early adolescence among Chinese American and European American families (Greenberger & Chen, 1996). It remains to be seen whether such a measure would also yield similarity among families with Filipino and Latino backgrounds.

Second, combining the results from the self-report measures used in this study with those obtained by naturalistic observations of behavior would enhance one's understanding of the interactions in families with different cultural backgrounds. Adolescents' reports of conflict and cohesion were used in this investigation so that within-group variations (e.g., according to grade and generation) could be examined in a large sample of culturally diverse adolescents. Though difficult to use with large samples, observations of selected families could provide additional insights into the specific manifestations of conflict and cohesion between adolescents and their parents.

Finally, there may be other beliefs, expectations, and dimensions of parent–adolescent relationships that show important variations across families with different cultural backgrounds. For example, the cohesion measured in this study had much to do with emotional closeness between adolescents and their parents. There are other culturally specific aspects of family cohesion that could be important for adolescents' relationships with their parents, such as obligations to instrumentally and economically assist and support other family members (Harrison et al., 1990).

The role of culture in family relationships can be complex and difficult to elucidate. The results of this study suggest that cultural beliefs regarding autonomy and authority may play only a minor role in parent–adolescent relationships when those values are not supported by the larger society. As a result, members of immigrant groups may have difficulty maintaining their traditional norms of interaction between parents and adolescents when they move to a new society. Whether this is true of other aspects of family functioning remains to be seen, but the findings suggest that the influence of cultural beliefs on family relationships may depend on the social settings of everyday life.

REFERENCES

Chilman, C. S. (1993). Hispanic families in the United States: Research perspectives. In H. P. McAdoo (Ed.), *Family ethnicity: Strength in diversity* (pp. 141–163). Newbury Park, CA: Sage.

Collins, W. A. (1990). Parent–child relationships in the transition to adolescence: Continuity and change in interaction, affect, and cognition. In R. Montemayor, G. R. Adams, & T. G. Gullota (Eds.), *From childhood to adolescence: A transitional period?* (pp. 85–106). Newbury Park, CA: Sage.

Collins, W. A., & Russell, G. (1991). Mother–child and father–child relationships in middle-childhood and adolescence: A developmental analysis. *Developmental Review, 11,* 99–136.

Cooper, C. R. (1988). The role of conflict in adolescent–parent relationships. In M. R. Gunnar & W. A. Collins (Eds.), *Minnesota symposia on child psychology* (Vol. 21, pp. 181–187). Hillsdale, NJ: Erlbaum.

Csikszentmihalyi, M., & Larson, R. (1984). *Being adolescent: Conflict and growth in the teenage years.* New York: Basic Books.

Douvan, E., & Adelson, J. (1966). *The adolescent experience.* New York: Wiley.

Eagly, A. H., & Chaiken, A. (1993). *The psychology of attitudes.* New York: Harcourt Brace Jovanovich.

Feldman, S. S., & Quatman, T. (1988). Factors influencing age expectations for adolescent autonomy: A study of early adolescents and parents. *Journal of Early Adolescence, 8,* 325–343.

Feldman, S. S., & Rosenthal, D. A. (1990). The acculturation of autonomy expectations in Chinese high-schoolers residing in two Western nations. *International Journal of Psychology, 25,* 259–281.

Feldman, S. S., & Rosenthal, D. A. (1991). Age expectations of behavioral autonomy in Hong Kong, Australian and American youth: The influence of family variables and adolescents' values. *International Journal of Psychology, 26,* 1–23.

Fine, G., Mortimer, J., & Roberts, D. (1990). Leisure, work, and the mass media. In S. S. Feldman & G. R. Elliot (Eds.), *At the threshold: The developing adolescent* (pp. 225–252). Cambridge, MA: Harvard University Press.

Fuligni, A. J., & Stevenson, H. W. (1995). Time-use and mathematics achievement among Chinese, Japanese, and American high school students. *Child Development, 66,* 830–842.

Galambos, N. L., & Almeida, D. M. (1992). Does parent–adolescent conflict increase in early adolescence? *Journal of Marriage and the Family, 54,* 737–747.

Gibson, M. A. (1991). Ethnicity, gender, and social class: The school adaptation patterns of West Indian youths. In M. A. Gibson & J. U. Ogbu (Eds.), *Minority status and schooling: A comparative study of immigrant and involuntary minorities* (pp. 169–204). New York: Garland.

Greenberger, E., & Chen, C. (1996). Perceived family relationships and depressed mood in early and late adolescence: A comparison of European and Asian Americans. *Developmental Psychology, 32,* 707–716.

Grotevant, H., & Cooper, C. (1986). Individuation in family relationships. *Human Development, 29*, 82–100.

Harrison, A. O., Wilson, M. N., Pine, C. J., Chan, S. Q., & Buriel, R. (1990). Family ecologies of ethnic minority children. *Child Development, 61*, 347–362.

Hill, J. P., & Holmbeck, G. N. (1986). Attachment and autonomy during adolescence. *Annals of Child Development, 3*, 145–189.

Ho, D. Y. F. (1981). Traditional patterns of socialization in Chinese society. *Acta Psychologica Taiwanica, 23*, 81–95.

Larson, R. W. (1983). Adolescents' daily experience with family and friends: Contrasting opportunity systems. *Journal of Marriage and the Family, 45*, 739–750.

Laursen, B., & Collins, W. A. (1994). Interpersonal conflict during adolescence. *Psychological Bulletin, 115*, 197–209.

Olson, D. H., Sprenkle, D. H., & Russell, C. S. (1979). Circumplex model of marital and family systems: I. Cohesion and adaptability dimensions, family types, and clinical applications. *Family Process, 18*, 3–28.

Paikoff, R., & Brooks-Gunn, J. (1991). Do parent–child relationships change during puberty? *Psychological Bulletin, 110*, 47–66.

Portes, A., & Rumbaut, R. G. (1996). *Immigrant America: A portrait* (2nd ed.). Berkeley: University of California Press.

Prinz, R. J., Foster, S. L., Kent, R. N., & O'Leary, K. D. (1979). Multivariate assessment of conflict in distressed and nondistressed mother–adolescent dyads. *Journal of Applied Behavioral Analysis, 12*, 691–700.

Robin, A. L., & Foster, S. C. (1984). Problem-solving communication training: A behavioral-family systems approach to parent–adolescent conflict. *Advances in Child Behavior Analysis and Therapy, 3*, 195–240.

Ryan, R., & Lynch, J. H. (1989). Emotional autonomy versus detachment: Revisiting the vicissitudes of adolescence and young adulthood. *Child Development, 60*, 340–356.

Shon, S. P., & Ja, D. Y. (1982). Asian families. In M. McGoldrick, J. K. Pearce, & J. Giordano (Eds.), *Ethnicity and family therapy* (pp. 208–228). New York: Guilford Press.

Smetana, J. (1988). Adolescents' and parents' conceptions of parental authority. *Child Development, 59*, 321–335.

Steinberg, L. (1987). The impact of puberty on family relations: Effects of pubertal status and pubertal timing. *Developmental Psychology, 23*, 451–460.

Steinberg, L. (1988). Reciprocal relation between parent–child distance and pubertal maturation. *Developmental Psychology, 24*, 122–128.

Steinberg, L. (1990). Autonomy, conflict, and harmony in the family relationship. In S. S. Feldman & G. R. Elliot (Eds.), *At the threshold: The developing adolescent* (pp. 255–276). Cambridge, MA: Harvard University Press.

Steinberg, L., & Silverberg, S. (1986). The vicissitudes of autonomy in early adolescence. *Child Development, 57*, 841–851.

Suarez-Orozco, C., & Suarez-Orozco, M. M. (1995). *Transformations: Immigration, family life, and achievement motivation among Latino adolescents*. Stanford, CA: Stanford University Press.

Sung, B. L. (1987). *The adjustment experience of Chinese immigrant children in New York City*. New York: Center for Migration Studies.

Uba, L. (1994). *Asian Americans: Personality patterns, identity, and mental health*. New York: Guilford Press.

Whiting, B. B., & Edwards, C. P. (1988). *Children of different worlds: The formation of social behavior*. Cambridge, MA: Harvard University Press.

Youniss, J., & Smollar, J. (1985). *Adolescents' relations with mothers, fathers, and friends*. Chicago: University of Chicago Press.

QUESTIONS

1. What are some of the changes that occur in adolescence that relate to increased adolescent–parent conflict?
2. Do developmental psychologists consider adolescent–parent conflict a good or bad thing? Why?
3. What was the conceptual rationale used by Fuligni to select the cultures he studied for this research?
4. How is independence experienced by adolescents in these four cultural groups?
5. How did the age of the adolescent affect the patterns observed?
6. Fuligni found that first-generation adolescents who arrived in the United States early in life expected autonomy at an early age relative to other adolescents in their ethnic group. Why do you think this is the case?

32 A Developmental Perspective on Antisocial Behavior

GERALD R. PATTERSON · BARBARA DeBARYSHE · ELIZABETH RAMSEY

Violence toward other people and willful destruction of property are disturbing crimes that shatter our trust in one another, regardless of the age of the perpetrators. However, when such acts are committed by youth, they strike an especially deep chord. What are the explanations for and origins of these behaviors? Developmental psychologists have examined these questions from many perspectives, including the roles of peer relations, academic experience, and poverty in the development of antisocial behavior. But by far the largest portion of research on this topic has focused on the family as a determining factor in the development of conduct disorders and antisocial behaviors in children.

The research by Gerald R. Patterson and colleagues that is described in the following article offers a framework for understanding how parent–child interaction may influence the organization and development of delinquency. This perspective has been instrumental in reframing the psychological view of antisocial behavior. The research has shown that the developmental course of delinquency is a long one, often beginning in childhood. It has also shown that it is interactional in origin, via a process of problem interactions in the family.

These insights have led to intervention techniques that emphasize the interactional patterns of the youth and his or her parents. They are among the best presently available for helping antisocial adolescents get out and stay out of trouble.

A developmental model of antisocial behavior is outlined. Recent findings are reviewed that concern the etiology and course of antisocial behavior from early childhood through adolescence. Evidence is presented in support of the hypothesis that the route to chronic delinquency is marked by a reliable developmental sequence of experiences. As a first step, ineffective parenting practices are viewed as determinants for childhood conduct disorders. The general model also takes into account the contextual variables that influence the family interaction process. As a second step, the conduct-disordered behaviors lead to academic failure and peer rejection. These dual failures lead, in turn, to increased risk for depressed mood and involvement in a deviant peer group. This third step usually occurs during later childhood and early adolescence. It is assumed that children following this developmental sequence are at high risk for engaging in chronic delinquent behavior. Finally, implications for prevention and intervention are discussed.

In 1986, more than 1.4 million juveniles were arrested for nonindex crimes (e.g., vandalism, drug abuse, or running away) and almost 900,000 for index crimes (e.g., larceny-theft, robbery, or forcible rape; Federal Bureau of Investigation, 1987). The United States spends more than $1 billion per year to maintain our juvenile justice system. The yearly cost of school vandalism alone is estimated to be one-half billion dollars (Feldman, Caplinger, & Wodarski, 1981). These statistics are based on official records and may represent only a fraction of the true offense rate. Data on self-reported delinquent acts indicate that police records account for as little as 2% of the actual juvenile law violations (Dunford & Elliott, 1982).

Reprinted by permission of the authors and the American Psychological Association from *American Psychologist*, 44 (1989), pp. 329–335. Copyright © 1989 by the American Psychological Association.

We gratefully acknowledge the support of National Institute of Mental Health Grants 2 RO1 MH 37940 and 5 T32 MH 17126 in the preparation of this article.

Of course, not all costs can be counted in dollars and cents. Antisocial children are likely to experience major adjustment problems in the areas of academic achievement and peer social relations (Kazdin, 1987; Walker, Shinn, O'Neill, & Ramsey, 1987; Wilson & Herrnstein, 1985). Follow-up studies of antisocial children show that as adults they ultimately contribute disproportionately to the incidence of alcoholism, accidents, chronic unemployment, divorce, physical and psychiatric illness, and the demand on welfare services (Caspi, Elder, & Bem, 1987; Farrington, 1983; Robins, 1966; Robins & Ratcliff, 1979).

Antisocial behavior appears to be a developmental trait that begins early in life and often continues into adolescence and adulthood. For many children, stable manifestations of antisocial behavior begin as early as the elementary school grades (see Farrington, Ohlin, & Wilson, 1986; Loeber, 1982; and Olweus, 1979, for reviews). As Olweus noted, stability coefficients for childhood aggression rival the figures derived for the stability of IQ. Findings that early behaviors such as temper tantrums and grade school troublesomeness significantly predict adolescent and adult offenses suggest the existence of a single underlying continuum. If early forms of antisocial behavior are indeed the forerunners of later antisocial acts, then the task for developmental psychologists is to determine which mechanisms explain the stability of antisocial behavior and which control changes over time.

From a policy standpoint, a serious social problem that is predictable and understandable is a viable target for prevention. The purpose of this article is to present an ontogenic perspective on the etiology and developmental course of antisocial behavior from early childhood through adolescence. Evidence is presented in support of the notion that the path to chronic delinquency unfolds in a series of predictable steps. This model is presented in detail by Patterson, Reid, and Dishion (in press). In this model, child behaviors at one stage lead to predictable reactions from the child's social environment in the following step. This leads to yet further reactions from the child and further changes in the reactions from the social environment. Each step in this action-reaction sequence puts the antisocial child more at risk for long-term social maladjustment and criminal behavior.

A DEVELOPMENTAL PROGRESSION FOR ANTISOCIAL BEHAVIOR

BASIC TRAINING IN THE HOME

There is a long history of empirical studies that have identified family variables as consistent covariates for early forms of antisocial behavior and for later delinquency. Families of antisocial children are characterized by harsh and inconsistent discipline, little positive parental involvement with the child, and poor monitoring and supervision of the child's activities (Loeber & Dishion, 1983; McCord, McCord, & Howard, 1963).

Two general interpretations have been imposed on these findings. Control theory, widely accepted in sociology (Hirschi, 1969), views harsh discipline and lack of supervision as evidence for disrupted parent–child bonding. Poor bonding implies a failure to identify with parental and societal values regarding conformity and work. These omissions leave the child lacking in internal control. Several large-scale surveys provide correlational data consistent with this hypothesis. The correlations show that youths who have negative attitudes toward school, work, and authority tend to be more antisocial (Elliott, Huizinga, & Ageton, 1985; Hirschi, 1969). The magnitude of these correlations tends to be very small. Because the dependent and independent variables are often provided by the same agent, it is difficult to untangle the contribution of method variance to these relations.

In contrast, the social–interactional perspective takes the view that family members directly train the child to perform antisocial behaviors (Forehand, King, Peed, & Yoder, 1975; Patterson, 1982; Snyder, 1977; Wahler & Dumas, 1984). The parents tend to be noncontingent in their use of both positive reinforcers for prosocial and effective punishment for deviant behaviors. The effect of the inept parenting practices is to permit dozens of daily interactions with family members in which coercive child behaviors are reinforced. The coercive behaviors are directly reinforced by family members (Patterson, 1982; Snyder, 1977; Snyder & Patterson, 1986). While some of the reinforcement is positive (attend, laugh, or approve), the most important set of contingencies for coercive behavior consists of escape-conditioning contingencies. In the latter, the child uses aversive behaviors to terminate aversive intrusions by other family members. In these families, coercive behaviors are functional. They make it possible to survive in a highly aversive social system.

As the training continues, the child and other family members gradually escalate the intensity of their coercive behaviors, often leading to high-amplitude behaviors such as hitting and physical attacks. In this training, the child eventually learns to control other family members through coercive means. The training for deviant behaviors is paralleled by a lack of training for many prosocial skills. Observations in the homes of distressed families suggest that children's prosocial acts are often ignored or responded to inappropriately (Patterson, 1982; Patterson, Reid, & Dishion, in press; Snyder, 1977). It seems that some families produce children characterized by not one, but two problems. They have antisocial symptoms and they are socially unskilled.

A series of structural equation modeling studies by Patterson and his colleagues support the theory that disrupted parent practices are causally related to child antisocial behavior. They used multiple indicators to define parental discipline and monitoring practices, child coercive behavior in the home, and a cross-situational measure of the child antisocial trait. In four different samples, involving several hundred grade school boys, the parenting practices and family interaction constructs accounted for 30–40% of the variance in general antisocial behavior (Baldwin & Skinner, 1988; Patterson, 1986; Patterson, Dishion, & Bank, 1984; Patterson et al., in press). Forgatch (1988) used a quasi-experimental design based on data from families referred for treatment of antisocial boys. She showed that changes in parental discipline and monitoring were accompanied by significant reductions in child antisocial behavior. There were no changes in antisocial child behavior for those families who showed no changes in these parenting skills.

Social Rejection and School Failure

It is hypothesized that coercive child behaviors are likely to produce two sets of reactions from the social environment. One outcome is rejection by members of the normal peer group, and the other is academic failure.

It is consistently found that antisocial children show poor academic achievement (Hawkins & Lishner, 1987; Wilson & Herrnstein, 1985). One explanation for this is that the child's noncompliant and undercontrolled behavior directly impedes learning. Classroom observations of antisocial children show they spend less time on task than their nondeviant peers (Shinn, Ramsey, Walker, O'Neill, & Steiber, 1987; Walker et al., 1987). Earlier classroom observation studies showed that they were also deficient in academic survival skills (e.g., attending, remaining in

seat, answering questions) necessary for effective learning (Cobb, 1972; Cobb & Hops, 1973; Hops & Cobb, 1974). Two studies showed a significant covariation between antisocial behavior and failure to complete homework assignments (Dishion, Loeber, Stouthamer-Loeber, & Patterson, 1983; Fehrmann, Keith, & Reimers, 1987).

The association between antisocial behavior and rejection by the normal peer group is well documented (Cantrell & Prinz, 1985; Dodge, Coie, & Brakke, 1982; Roff & Wirt, 1984). Experimental studies of group formation show that aggressive behavior leads to rejection, not the reverse (Coie & Kupersmidt, 1983; Dodge, 1983). Rejected children are also deficient in a number of social–cognitive skills, including peer group entry, perception of peer group norms, response to provocation, and interpretation of prosocial interactions (Asarnow & Calan, 1985; Dodge, 1986; Putallaz, 1983).

It is often suggested that academic failure and peer rejection are causes rather than consequences of antisocial behavior. However, a stronger case may be made that antisocial behavior contributes to these negative outcomes. For example, some investigators have predicted that successful academic remediation will lead to a reduction in antisocial behavior (e.g., Cohen & Filipczak, 1971). However, it has been repeatedly demonstrated that programs improving the academic skills of antisocial youths have not achieved reductions in other antisocial symptoms (Wilson & Herrnstein, 1985); similar findings have been obtained for social skills training (Kazdin, 1987).

Deviant Peer Group Membership

Antisocial behavior and peer group rejection are important preludes to deviant peer group membership (Dishion, Patterson, & Skinner, 1988; Snyder, Dishion, & Patterson, 1986). These analyses also suggest that

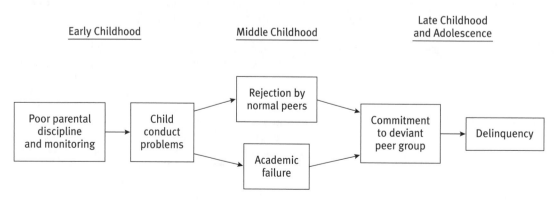

FIGURE 1

A developmental progression for antisocial behavior.

lax parental supervision also accounts for unique variance to the prediction of deviant peer affiliation.

A large number of studies point to the peer group as the major training ground for delinquent acts and substance use (Elliott et al., 1985; Hirschi, 1969; Huba & Bentler, 1983; Kandel, 1973). Peers are thought to supply the adolescent with the attitudes, motivations, and rationalizations to support antisocial behavior as well as providing opportunities to engage in specific delinquent acts. There are, however, only a small number of studies designed to investigate the hypothesized training process. One study in an institutional setting showed that delinquent peers provided considerable positive reinforcement for deviant behavior and punishment for socially conforming acts (Buehler, Patterson, & Furniss, 1966).

It seems, then, that the disrupted family processes producing antisocial behavior may indirectly contribute to later involvement with a deviant peer group. This particular product may function as an additional determinant for future antisocial behavior. In effect, the deviant peer group variable may be thought of as a positive feedback variable that contributes significantly to maintenance in the process. Common adult outcomes for highly antisocial youths include school dropout, uneven employment histories, substance abuse, marital difficulties, multiple offenses, incarceration, and institutionalization (Caspi et al., 1987; Huesmann, Eron, Lefkowitz, & Walder, 1984; Robins & Ratcliff, 1979).

Figure 1 depicts the relation among the concepts discussed up to this point.

SOME IMPLICATIONS OF THE DEVELOPMENT PERSPECTIVE

EARLY VERSUS LATE STARTERS

Boys starting their criminal career in late childhood or early adolescence are at the greatest risk of becoming chronic offenders (Farrington, 1983; Loeber, 1982). Studies of prison populations have shown that recidivists are generally first arrested by age 14 or 15, whereas one-time offenders are first arrested at a later age (Gendreau, Madden, & Leipciger, 1979). Farrington found that boys first arrested between 10 and 12 years of age average twice as many convictions as later starters (Farrington, Gallagher, Morley, St. Ledger, & West, 1986); this comparison holds into early adulthood.

One implication of the aforementioned developmental perspective is that early forms of age-prototypic antisocial behavior may be linked to the early onset of official juvenile offenses. Following this logic, the child who receives antisocial training from the family during the preschool and elementary school years is likely to be denied access to positive socialization forces in the peer group and school.

On the other hand, the late starter would be someone committing his or her first offense in middle to late adolescence. This individual lacks the early training for antisocial behaviors. This implies that he or she has not experienced the dual failure of rejection by normal peers and academic failure.

Only about half the antisocial children become adolescent delinquents, and roughly half to three quarters of the adolescent delinquents become adult offenders (Blumstein, Cohen, & Farrington, 1988; Farrington, 1987; Robins & Ratcliff, 1979). At some point in late adolescence, the incidence of delinquent acts as a function of age group begins to drop; the drop continues into the late 20s. One interpretation of these data is that many of the delinquent offenders drop out of the process. We assume that many of these dropouts are late starters, but more research is clearly needed to specify what factors determine the probability of an individual's dropping out of the antisocial training process. A proper developmental theory of antisocial behavior must delineate not only the variables that lead a child into the process but those that cause some of them to drop out of it.

CONTEXTUAL VARIABLES FOR FAMILY DISRUPTION

Because parent–child interaction is a central variable in the etiology of antisocial behavior, it is important to determine why a minority of parents engage in highly maladaptive family management practices. A number of variables, which shall be referred to as disruptors, have negative effects on parenting skill. These variables also correlate with the probability of children's antisocial behavior. Thus, the effect of disruptors on children's adjustment is indirect, being mediated through perturbations in parenting. Potential disruptors include a history of antisocial behavior in other family members, demographic variables representing disadvantaged socioeconomic status, and stressors—such as marital conflict and divorce—that hamper family functioning.

ANTISOCIAL PARENTS AND GRANDPARENTS

There is a high degree of intergenerational similarity for antisocial behavior (Farrington, 1987; Robins & Ratcliff, 1979). As a predictor of adult antisocial personality, having an antisocial parent places the child at significant risk for antisocial behavior; having two antisocial parents puts the child at even higher risk (Robins & Earls, 1985). Concordance across three generations has also been documented (Elder, Caspi, & Downy, 1983; Huesmann et al., 1984; Robins, West, & Herjanic, 1975).

There is considerable evidence that parental discipline practices may be an important mediating mechanism in this transmission. Our set of findings shows that antisocial parents are at significant risk for ineffective discipline practices. Ineffective discipline is significantly related to risk of having an antisocial child. For example, Elder et al. (1983) found a significant relation between retrospective accounts of grandparental explosive discipline and paternal irritability. Irritable fathers tended to use explosive discipline practices with their own children who tended to exhibit antisocial behavior. Patterson and Dishion (1988) also found a significant correlation between retrospective reports of grandparental explosive reactions in the home and parental antisocial traits. Furthermore, the effect of the parents' antisocial trait on the grandchildren's antisocial behavior was mediated by parental discipline practices.

FAMILY DEMOGRAPHICS

Demographic variables such as race, neighborhood, parental education, income, and occupation are related to the incidence of antisocial behavior, particularly in its more severe forms (Elliott et al., 1985; Rutter & Giller, 1983; Wilson & Herrnstein, 1985). We presume that the effect of social class on child adjustment is mediated by family management practices.

The empirical findings linking social class to parenting practices are not consistent. But, in general, middle-class parents seem more likely to use reasoning and psychological methods of discipline, allow their children more freedom of choice and self-direction, show egalitarian parenting styles, express positive affect toward their children, verbalize, and support cognitive and academic growth (Gecas, 1979; Hess, 1970). Lower class parents are more likely to use physical discipline, be controlling of their child's behavior, exhibit authoritarian parenting styles, and engage in less frequent verbal and cognitive stimulation.

The findings from the at-risk sample at the Oregon Social Learning Center are in keeping with the trends in the literature (Patterson et al., in press). Uneducated parents working in unskilled occupations were found to be significantly less effective in discipline, monitoring, problem solving, positive reinforcement, and involvement.

FAMILY STRESSORS

Stressors impinging on the family such as unemployment, family violence, marital discord, and divorce are associated with both delinquency (Farrington, 1987) and child adjustment problems in general (Garmezy & Rutter, 1983; Hetherington, Cox, & Cox, 1982; Rutter,

1979). Although stressors may well have direct and independent effects on child behavior, we assume that the major impact of stress on child adjustment is mediated by family management practices. If the stressors disrupt parenting practices, then the child is placed at risk for adjustment problems. For example, in the case of divorce, postseparation behavior problems occur with diminished parental responsiveness, affection, and involvement, and increased parental punitiveness and irritability (Hetherington et al., 1982; Wallerstein & Kelley, 1981). Structural equation modeling using data from a large sample of recently separated families provided strong support for the relation among stress, disrupted discipline, and antisocial behavior for boys (Forgatch, Patterson, & Skinner, in press).

We assume that antisocial parents and parents with marginal child-rearing skills are perhaps most susceptible to the disrupting effects of stressors and socioeconomic disadvantage. Elder, Caspi, and Nguyen (in press) described this interaction as an *amplifying effect*. External events are most disabling to those individuals who already exhibit negative personality traits or weak personal resources because stressors amplify such problems in adjustment. The interaction between the aforementioned disruptors and parental susceptibility is presented in Figure 2.

When antisocial parents or parents with minimal family management skills are faced with acute or prolonged stress, nontrivial disruptions in family management practices are likely to occur. It is these disruptions that are thought to place the child at risk for adjustment problems. A recent study by Snyder (1988) provided strong support for the mediational hypothesis. Roughly 20 hours of observation collected in the homes of three mother–child dyads showed significant covariation across days between stress and both disrupted maternal discipline and maternal irritability. Dyads characterized by high stress prior to the observation showed higher rates of disrupted behavior for the mother and increased child problem behaviors. A similar covariation was shown in the study by Wahler and Dumas (1984).

IS PREVENTION A POSSIBILITY?

Reviews of the literature summarizing efforts to intervene with antisocial adolescents invariably lead to negative conclusions (Kazdin, 1987; Wilson & Herrnstein, 1985). At best, such interventions produce short-term effects that are lost within a year or two of treatment termination. For example, efforts to apply behavior modification procedures in a halfway house setting (Achievement Place) showed no treatment effects after youths returned to their homes and communities (Jones, Weinrott, & Howard, 1981). Similarly, systematic parent training for families of delinquent adolescents produced reductions in offenses, but this

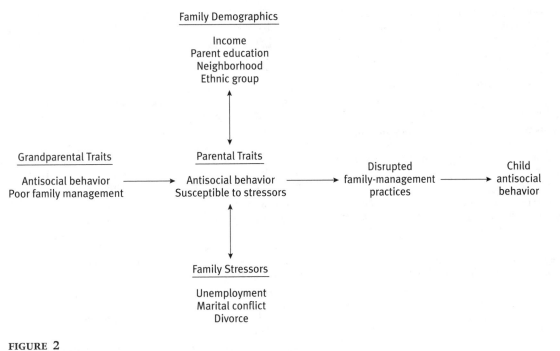

FIGURE 2
Disruptors of effective parenting.

effect did not persist over time (Marlowe, Reid, Patterson, Weinrott, & Bank, 1988).

Successful intervention appears to be possible for preadolescents, with parent–training interventions showing the most favorable outcomes (Kazdin, 1987). Parent training refers to procedures in which parents are given specific instructions in ways to improve family management practices (e.g., Forehand, Wells, & Griest, 1980; Patterson, Reid, Jones, & Conger, 1975). As shown in the review by Kazdin (1987), the parent-training programs have been evaluated in a number of random assignment evaluation studies including follow-up designs (six-month to four-year intervals). In general, the findings support the hypothesis that parent training is effective when applied to younger antisocial children. That several major studies failed to show a treatment effect led most investigators to conclude that parent training techniques *and* soft clinical skills are necessary for effective treatment. Current intervention studies have expanded their scope to include teaching academic and social-relational skills in addition to parent training. In order to alter both the problem child's lack of social skills and his or her antisocial symptoms, it seems necessary to design these more complex interventions.

We believe that prevention studies are now feasible. It seems reasonable to identify children in the elementary grades who are both antisocial and unskilled. Successful programs would probably include three components: parent training, child social-skills training, and academic remediation.

REFERENCES

Asarnow, J. R., & Calan, J. R. (1985). Boys with peer adjustment problems: Social cognitive processes. *Journal of Consulting and Clinical Psychology, 53,* 80–87.

Baldwin, D. V., & Skinner, M. L. (1988). *A structural model for antisocial behavior: Generalization to single-mother families.* Manuscript submitted for publication.

Blumstein, A., Cohen, J., & Farrington, D. P. (1988). Criminal career research: Its value for criminology. *Criminology, 26,* 1–35.

Buehler, R. E., Patterson, G. R., & Furniss, J. M. (1966). The reinforcement of behavior in institutional settings. *Behavior Research and Therapy, 4,* 157–167.

Cantrell, V. L., & Prinz, R. J. (1985). Multiple predictors of rejected, neglected, and accepted children: Relation between sociometric status and behavioral characteristics. *Journal of Consulting and Clinical Psychology, 53,* 884–889.

Caspi, A., Elder, G. H., & Bem, D. J. (1987). Moving against the world: Life course patterns of explosive children. *Developmental Psychology, 23,* 308–313.

Cobb, J. A. (1972). The relationship of discrete classroom behavior to fourth grade academic achievement. *Journal of Educational Psychology, 63,* 74–80.

Cobb, J. A., & Hops, H. (1973). Effects of academic skill training on low achieving first graders. *Journal of Educational Research, 63,* 74–80.

Cohen, H. L., & Filipczak, J. (1971). *A new learning environment.* San Francisco: Jossey Bass.

Coie, J. D., & Kupersmidt, J. B. (1983). A behavioral analysis of emerging social status in boys' groups. *Child Development, 54,* 1400–1416.

Dishion, T. J., Loeber, R., Stouthamer-Loeber, M., & Patterson, G. R. (1983). Social skills deficits and male adolescent delinquency. *Journal of Abnormal Child Psychology, 12,* 37–54.

Dishion, T. J., Patterson, G. R., & Skinner, M. L. (1988). *Peer group selection processes from middle childhood to early adolescence.* Manuscript in preparation.

Dodge, K. A. (1983). Behavioral antecedents of peer social status. *Child Development, 54,* 1386–1399.

Dodge, K. A. (1986). A social information processing model of social competence in children. In M. Perlmutter (Ed.), *Minnesota symposium on child psychology* (Vol. 18, pp. 77–125). Hillsdale, NJ: Erlbaum.

Dodge, K. A., Coie, J. D., & Brakke, N. P. (1982). Behavior patterns of socially rejected and neglected preadolescents: The roles of social approach and aggression. *Journal of Abnormal Child Psychology, 10,* 389–410.

Dunford, F. W., & Elliott, D. S. (1982). *Identifying career offenders with self-reported data* (Grant No. MH27552). Washington, DC: National Institute of Mental Health.

Elder, G. H., Jr., Caspi, A., & Downey, G. (1983). Problem behavior in family relationships: A multigenerational analysis. In A. Sorensen, F. Weinert, & L. Sherrod (Eds.), *Human development: Interdisciplinary perspective* (pp. 93–118). Hillsdale, NJ: Erlbaum.

Elder, G. H., Jr., Caspi, A., & Nguyen, T. V. (in press). Resourceful and vulnerable children: Family influences in stressful times. In R. K. Silbereisen & K. Eyferth (Eds.), *Development in context: Integrative perspectives on youth development.* New York: Springer.

Elliott, D. S., Huizinga, D., & Ageton, S. S. (1985). *Explaining delinquency and drug use.* Beverly Hills, CA: Sage.

Farrington, D. P. (1983). Offending from 10 to 25 years of age. In K. T. Van Dusen & S. A. Mednick (Eds.), *Prospective studies of crime and delinquency* (pp. 17–37). Boston: Kluwer-Nijhoff.

Farrington, D. P. (1987). Early precursors of frequent offending. In J. Q. Wilson & G. C. Loury (Eds.), *From children to citizens: Vol. III. Families, schools, and delinquency prevention* (pp. 27–51). New York: Springer-Verlag.

Farrington, D. P., Gallagher, B., Morley, L., St. Ledger, R. J., & West, D. J. (1986). *Cambridge study in delinquent development: Long term follow-up.* Unpublished annual report, Cambridge University Institute of Criminology, Cambridge, England.

Farrington, D. P., Ohlin, L. E., & Wilson, J. Q. (1986). *Understanding and controlling crime: Toward a new research strategy.* New York: Springer-Verlag.

Federal Bureau of Investigation. (1987). *Crime in the United States: Uniform crime reports, 1986,* Washington, DC: Government Printing Office.

Fehrmann, P. G., Keith, T. Z., & Reimers, T. M. (1987). Home influences on school learning: Direct and indirect effects of parental involvement in high school grades. *Journal of Educational Research, 80,* 330–337.

Feldman, R. A., Caplinger, T. E., & Wodarski, S. S. (1981). *The St. Louis conundrum: Prosocial and antisocial boys together.* Unpublished manuscript.

Forehand, R., King, H. E., Peed, S., & Yoder, P. (1975). Mother-child interactions: Comparison of a non-compliant clinic group and a nonclinic group. *Behaviour Research and Therapy, 13,* 79–85.

Forehand, R., Wells, K., & Griest, D. (1980). An examination of the social validity of a parent training program. *Behavior Therapy, 11,* 488–502.

Forgatch, M. S. (1988, June). *The relation between child behaviors, client resistance, and parenting practices.* Paper presented at the Earlscourt Symposium on Childhood Aggression, Toronto.

Forgatch, M. S., Patterson, G. R., & Skinner, M. (in press). A mediational model for the effect of divorce on antisocial behavior in boys. In E. M. Hetherington (Ed.), *The impact of divorce and step-parenting on children.* Hillsdale, NJ: Erlbaum.

Garmezy, N., & Rutter, M. (Eds,). (1983). *Stress, coping, and development in children.* New York: McGraw Hill.

Gecas, V. (1979). The influence of social class on socialization. In W. R. Burr, R. Hill, F. I. Nye, & I. L. Reiss (Eds.), *Contemporary theories about the family* (Vol. 1, pp. 365–404). New York: Free Press.

Gendreau, P., Madden, P., & Leipeiger, M. (1979). Norms and recidivism rates for social history and institutional experience for first incarcerates: Implications for programming. *Canadian Journal of Criminology, 21,* 1–26.

Hawkins, J. D., & Lishner, D. M. (1987). Schooling and delinquency. In E. H. Johnson (Ed.), *Handbook on crime and delinquency prevention* (pp. 179–221). New York: Greenwood Press.

Hetherington, E. M., Cox, M., & Cox, R. (1982). Effects of divorce on parents and children. In M. Lamb (Ed.), *Nontraditional families* (pp. 233–288). Hillsdale, NJ: Erlbaum.

Hess, R. D. (1970). Social class and ethnic influences on socialization. In P. H. Mussen (Ed.), *Charmichael's manual of child psychology* (Vol. 2, pp. 457–558). New York: Wiley.

Hirschi, T. (1969). *Causes of delinquency.* Berkeley, CA: University of California Press.

Hops, H., & Cobb, J. A. (1974). Initial investigations into academic survival-skill training, direct instruction, and first-grade achievement. *Journal of Educational Psychology, 66,* 548–553.

Huba, G. J., & Bentler, P. M. (1983). Causal models of the development of law abidance and its relationship to psychosocial factors and drug use. In W. S. Laufer & J. M. Day (Eds.), *Personality theory, moral development and criminal behavior* (pp. 165–215). Lexington, MA: Lexington Books.

Huesmann, L. R., Eron, L. D., Lefkowitz, M. M., & Walder, L. O. (1984). Stability of aggression over time and generations. *Developmental Psychology, 20,* 1120–1134.

Jones, R. R., Weinrott, M. R., & Howard, J. R. (1981). *The national evaluation of the Teaching Family Model.* Unpublished manuscript, Evaluation Research Group, Eugene, OR.

Kandel, D. B. (1973). Adolescent marijuana use: Role of parents and peers. *Science, 181,* 1067–1081.

Kazdin, A. E. (1987). Treatment of antisocial behavior in children: Current status and future directions. *Psychological Bulletin, 102,* 187–203.

Loeber, R. (1982). The stability of antisocial and delinquent child behavior: A review. *Child Development, 53,* 1431–1446.

Loeber, R., & Dishion, T. J. (1983). Early predictors of male delinquency: A review. *Psychological Bulletin, 94,* 68–99.

Marlowe, H. J., Reid, J. B., Patterson, G. R., Weinrott, M. R., & Bank, L. (1988). Treating adolescent multiple offenders: A comparison and follow up of parent training for families of chronic delinquents. Manuscript submitted for publication.

McCord, W., McCord, J., & Howard, A. (1963). Familial correlates of aggression in nondelinquent male children. *Journal of Abnormal and Social Psychology, 62,* 79–93.

Olweus, D. (1979). Stability of aggressive reaction patterns in males: A review. *Psychological Bulletin, 86,* 852–875.

Patterson, G. R. (1982). *A social learning approach: 3. Coercive family process.* Eugene, OR: Castalia.

Patterson, G. R. (1986). Performance models for antisocial boys. *American Psychologist, 41,* 432–444.

Patterson, G. R., & Dishion, T. J. (1988). Multilevel family process models: Traits, interactions, and relationships. In R. Hinde & J. Stevenson-Hinde (Eds.), *Relationships within families: Mutual influences* (pp. 283–310). Oxford: Clarendon Press.

Patterson, G. R., Dishion, T. J., & Bank, L. (1984). Family interaction: A process model of deviancy training. *Aggressive Behavior, 10,* 253–267.

Patterson, G. R., Reid, J. B., & Dishion, T. J. (in press). *Antisocial boys.* Eugene, OR: Castalia.

Patterson, G. R., Reid, J. B., Jones, R. R., & Conger, R. E. (1975). *A social learning approach to family intervention: Vol 1. Families with aggressive children.* Eugene, OR: Castalia.

Putallaz, M. (1983). Predicting children's sociometric status from their behavior. *Child Development, 54,* 1417–1426.

Robins, L. N. (1966). *Deviant children grown up: A sociological and psychiatric study of sociopathic personality.* Baltimore: Williams & Wilkins.

Robins, L. N., & Earls F. (1985). A program for preventing antisocial behavior for high-risk infants and preschoolers: A research prospectus. In R. L. Hough, P. A. Gongla, V. B. Brown, & S. E. Goldston (Eds.), *Psychiatric epidemiology and prevention: The possibilities* (pp. 73–84). Los Angeles: Neuropsychiatric Institute.

Robins, L. N., & Ratcliff, K. S. (1979). Risk factors in the continuation of childhood antisocial behavior into adulthood. *International Journal of Mental Health, 7*(3–4), 96–116.

Robins, L. N., West, P. A., & Herjanic, B. L. (1975). Arrests and delinquency in two generations: A study of black urban families and their children. *Journal of Child Psychology and Psychiatry, 16,* 125–140.

Roff, J. D., & Wirt, R. D. (1984). Childhood aggression and social adjustment as antecedents of delinquency. *Journal of Abnormal Child Psychology, 12,* 111–116.

Rutter, M. (1979). Protective factors in children's responses to stress and disadvantage. In M. W. Kent & J. E. Rolfe (Eds.), *Primary prevention of psychopathology: 3. Social competence in children.* Hanover, NH: University Press of New England.

Rutter, M., & Giller, H. (1983). *Juvenile delinquency: Trends and perspectives.* New York: Penguin Books.

Shinn, M. R., Ramsey, E., Walker, H. M., O'Neill, R. E., & Steiber, S. (1987). Antisocial behavior in school settings: Initial differences in an at-risk and normal population. *Journal of Special Education, 21,* 69–84.

Synder, J. J. (1977). Reinforcement analysis of interaction in problem and nonproblem families. *Journal of Abnormal Psychology, 86,* 528–535.

Snyder, J. J. (1988). *An intradyad analysis of the effects of daily variations in maternal stress on maternal discipline and irritability: Its effects on child deviant behaviors.* Manuscript in preparation.

Snyder, J. J., Dishion, T. J., & Patterson, G. R. (1986). Determinants and consequences of associating with deviant peers during preadolescence and adolescence. *Journal of Early Adolescence, 6*(1), 20–43.

Snyder, J. J., & Patterson, G. R. (1986). The effects of consequences on patterns of social interaction: A quasi-experimental approach to reinforcement in natural interaction. *Child Development, 57,* 1257–1268.

Wahler, R. G., & Dumas, J. E. (1984). Family factors in childhood psychopathology: Toward a coercion neglect model. In T. Jacob (Ed.), *Family interaction and psychopathology.* New York: Plenum Press.

Walker, H. M., Shinn, M. R., O'Neill, R. E., & Ramsey, E. (1987). Longitudinal assessment and long-term follow-up of antisocial behavior in fourth-grade boys: Rationale, methodology, measures, and results. *Remedial and Special Education, 8,* 7–16.

Wallerstein, J. S., & Kelley, J. B. (1981). *Surviving the breakup: How children and parents cope with divorce.* New York: Basic Books.

Wilson, J. Q., & Herrnstein, R. J. (1985). *Crime and human nature.* New York: Simon & Schuster.

QUESTIONS

1. What is the long-term prognosis for antisocial youth if they do not have effective treatment during the adolescent years?
2. What discipline practices are characteristic in families of antisocial children?
3. What are coercive behaviors and how do they contribute to the development of antisocial behavior?
4. How does experience in the peer group relate to the development of antisocial behavior?
5. How does stress affect parents' ability to manage children's behavior problems?
6. Why is it important that parents be involved in any intervention program designed to help antisocial youth?